PROBLEMS AND SOLUTIONS

FOR

BASIC FEDERAL INCOME TAXATION

By

Larry D. Ward
Orville L. and Ermina D. Dykstra Professor of Federal Tax Law
University of Iowa

THOMSON

WEST

Mat #40565668

© 2007 Thomson/West
     610 Opperman Drive
     St. Paul, MN 55123
     1–800–328–9352

Printed in the United States of America

ISBN: 978–0–314–17950–0

 *TEXT IS PRINTED ON 10% POST CONSUMER RECYCLED PAPER*

For Mary

*

Preface

The most effective way to study (and teach) federal income taxation is through the use of problems that illuminate the language of the Internal Revenue Code and bring it to life. The purpose of this book is to provide students of the tax law with hundreds of problems and model answers for use in honing their analytical skills.

The book, which is designed to accompany any basic-tax casebook, is divided into two major parts. Part One contains problems devoted to virtually every topic covered in the basic course. Problem sets begin with an "assignment" that directs the student to the relevant provisions of the Code and regulations, as well as some of the major cases that can be found in most casebooks used in the basic course. Part Two of the text repeats the statement of each problem and provides a detailed solution, often accompanied by commentary to assist students in their understanding.

A separate chapter is devoted to each of the most important items of gross income and deduction, though in some instances the income and deduction aspects of payments are treated together: e.g., the treatment of interest income and deductions in Chapter 38 and alimony, property settlements and other divorce-related issues in Chapter 39. Separate sections of the book are devoted to assignments of income, dealings in property, non-recognition, capital gains and losses, installment sales, tax accounting and congressional efforts to combat tax shelters. Chapter 48 contains some comprehensive examination-type questions for review.

Competent lawyers (and not just tax lawyers) need an understanding of the time value of money, and Chapter 47 is devoted to the concepts of present and future value. Appendix A contains tables for use in working those problems.

Appendix B provides a set of tax-rate tables for use in working problems. The tables depict what the rates would be through 2010 if inflation adjustments are ignored. Indeed, the effect of inflation adjustments on fixed dollar amounts (e.g., the personal exemption and standard deduction) is disregarded throughout the text.

Throughout, the focus is on statutory analysis—one of the most important skills that any lawyer can have.

The work is current through April, 2007.

My administrative assistant, Diana DeWalle, went way beyond the call of duty in her tireless work on this project. Thank you, Diana. And thanks always to Mary, who makes it all possible.

LARRY D. WARD

May, 2007

Table of Contents

Table of Cases

Table of Internal Revenue Code Sections

Table of Treasury Regulations and Rulings

PROBLEMS AND SOLUTIONS

FOR

BASIC
FEDERAL INCOME
TAXATION

Part One

PROBLEMS

Section A

INTRODUCTION

Chapter 1

ORIENTATION

A. SOME POLICY ASPECTS

1. Explain the following terms:

(a) Progressive tax;

(b) Proportional tax;

(c) Regressive tax.

2. P and W both live in a state that imposes a 5–percent general sales tax. P has income of $30,000, all of which is spent on consumption items subject to the tax. W has income of $500,000, of which $250,000 is spent on consumption items subject to the tax.

(a) Does P or W pay more sales tax?

(b) Is the tax progressive, regressive or proportional with respect to income?

3. Suppose that a 6.2–percent tax is imposed on the first $100,000 of an employee's salary. Salary in excess of $100,000 is not subject to the tax. Is the tax progressive, proportional or regressive?

4. What is the Haig-Simons (or Schantz-Haig-Simons) definition of income?

5. How might one impose a progressive tax on consumption?

6. What is the primary purpose of imposing heavy taxes on cigarettes and liquor?

7. Explain the difference between the legal and economic incidence of a tax.

B. AN INTRODUCTION TO FEDERAL TAX PROCEDURE

Code: §§ 6501(a) & (b)(1); 6511(a); 6513(a); 6212(a); 6213(a). Note 7805(a).

1. Describe the role in the federal tax system of:

(a) The Sixteenth Amendment;

(b) The Internal Revenue Code of 1986;

(c) The Income Tax Regulations;

(d) Revenue Rulings;

(e) Letter Rulings.

2. Explain the following terms:

(a) Audit;

(b) 90–day letter.

3. The Internal Revenue Service has issued a notice of deficiency to your client, who wishes to litigate the issue in dispute. What forums are available for the litigation?

4. Explain the following terms:

(a) Non-acquiescence;

(b) *Golsen* rule.

5. T, who uses the calendar year as her taxable year, filed her 2007 federal income-tax return on March 1, 2008. Although acting in good faith, T made an error on her return, which caused her to understate her tax liability for the year. What is the latest date on which the Internal Revenue Service can issue a notice of deficiency (90–day letter)?

6. Suppose instead that T (in 5) overpaid her tax for 2007. What is the latest date on which she can file a claim for refund?

Chapter 2

TAX COMPUTATIONS

Code: §§ 1(a)–(d) (in Appendix B); 61(a); 62(a); 63; 151(a), (b), (c), (d)(1) & (2). Note § 213(a).

1. W and H are married. They file a joint return (i.e., they combine their income and deductions on a single return) and compute their tax liability under Code § 1(a). They have taxable income of $150,000. Use the appropriate tax-rate schedule in Appendix B to answer the following questions:

(a) What is their tax liability (before credits)?

(b) What is their marginal tax rate?

(c) What "tax bracket" are they in?

(d) What is their average tax rate?

(e) Suppose you are the couple's tax advisor. Are you more interested in their marginal rate or their average rate?

2. What is the legal significance of:

(a) Gross income?

(b) Adjusted gross income (AGI)?

(c) Taxable income?

3. Explain the following terms:

(a) Exclusion;

(b) Deduction;

(c) Credit.

4. What are the principal purposes of the "inclusionary rules" (§§ 71–90) and the "exclusionary rules" (§§ 101–139A)?

5. Explain the terms:

(a) "Above-the-line" deduction;

(b) Itemized deduction;

(c) Standard deduction;

(d) Personal and dependency exemptions.

6. Determine which of the following deductions are allowable to an individual in computing AGI and which are allowable only as itemized deductions:

(a) Salaries paid by a sole proprietor to the employees of the business (allowable under § 162(a));

(b) Medical expenses (allowable under 213(a));

(c) Interest expense incurred in business (allowable under § 163(a));

(d) Interest on a home mortgage (allowable under § 163(a));

(e) Charitable contributions (allowable under § 170(a)).

7. H (age 67) and W (age 63) are a married couple who file a joint return. They have gross income of $50,000, and they are entitled to deductions for $6,000 of expenses on a rental building (allowable under § 212), $5,000 of charitable contributions (allowable under § 170), and $1,200 of state property tax on their personal residence (allowable under § 164(a)). Determine their adjusted gross and taxable incomes.

8. M and F (both age 35) are married and file a joint return. They have gross income of $90,000, and they are entitled to deductions for a $10,000 loss on the sale of business property (allowable by § 165(a) and (c)(1)), $3,000 of state income taxes (allowable by § 164(a)), and $2,000 of charitable contributions (allowable by § 170(a)). They have two dependent children for whom they are entitled to the child tax credit of § 24. They also paid $7,200 of unreimbursed medical expenses for themselves and their children (see § 213). Determine their:

(a) AGI;

(b) Taxable income;

(c) Tax liability.

9. A married couple with adjusted gross income of $174,000 files a joint return. Before the application of §§ 68 and 151(d)(3), they are entitled to $6,000 of personal and dependency exemptions and $25,000 of itemized deductions that are potentially subject to disallowance under § 68. Determine their taxable income if the year is:

(a) 2008;

(b) 2010.

Section B

GROSS INCOME

Chapter 3

ACCESSIONS TO WEALTH

A. IN GENERAL

Code: § 61(a).

Regulations: §§ 1.61–1(a); 1.61–14(a).

Cases: Commissioner v. Glenshaw Glass Co., 348 U.S. 426 (1955);
Cesarini v. United States, 296 F. Supp. 3 (N.D. Ohio 1969), aff'd per curiam, 428 F.2d 812 (6th Cir. 1970);
James v. United States, 366 U.S. 213 (1961).

1. T purchased a used sofa for $15. While cleaning the sofa, T found inside an envelope containing $5,000 cash. Must T include the $5,000 in gross income?

2. Would your answer in 1 differ if T had instead found a piece of jewelry (valued at $5,000) in the sofa?

3. T borrows $5,000 from a bank for use in purchasing a new car. Must T include the $5,000 in gross income?

4. E embezzled $5,000 from a bank. Must E include the $5,000 in gross income?

5. At an auction, T purchased for $50,000 a portrait thought to have been painted by an artist known as Vegas. After carefully examining the painting, T discovered that it was instead painted by Degas and was worth $5,000,000. Must T include anything in gross income on account of these events?

6. Several years ago, F purchased a farm in Iowa for $3,000 per acre. There were no known mineral deposits in the area. In the current year, F accepted the offer of a wildcatter to drill a test oil well on the property. Much to the astonishment of the entire community, the well was a gusher, and F's property immediately rose in value to $10,000 per acre. Must F include the increased value in gross income?

7. M owns the home in which she resides. If M rented a comparable residence, the rent would be $24,000 a year. Must M include the rental value of her home in gross income?

B. GROSS INCOME FROM SALES OF PROPERTY

Code: §§ 61(a)(3); 1001(a), (b) & (c); 1012; 1011(a).

Regulations: §§ 1.61–6(a); 1.1001–1(a).

1. In March, year 1, T, a calendar-year taxpayer, purchases a share of Y Corporation stock for $40. By December 31, the stock has appreciated in value to $100. Does T have gross income on account of these events?

2. In April, year 2, T sells the share for $120. What result to T?

3. In August, year 1, T purchases a share of Z Corporation stock for $100. By December 31, it has declined in value to $40. What result to T?

4. In July of year 2, T sells the Z Corporation share for $30. What result to T?

5. What justification, if any, do you see for the realization requirement?

Chapter 4

COMPENSATION FOR SERVICES

A. IN GENERAL

Code: § 61(a)(1). Note §§ 446(c); 451(a); 461(a).

Regulations: §§ 1.61–14(a); 1.61–2(a)(1). On accounting methods, see §§ 1.451–1(a); 1.461–1(a)(1) & (2); 1.446–1(c)(1)(i) & (ii)(A).

Case: Old Colony Trust Co. v. Commissioner, 279 U.S. 716 (1929).

1. E works for an annual salary of $100,000. E's checks for the past year totaled $70,000 after E's employer withheld amounts for federal and state income taxes and Social Security and Medicare taxes. How much salary income should E include in gross income?

2. What result to E in 1 if the Social Security and Medicare taxes were not withheld from E's salary but were paid by the employer on E's behalf?

3. The employment contracts of some corporate executives require the corporation to pay any state or federal income taxes imposed on the executive's taxable fringe benefits. Assume that in the current year an executive who receives $1,000,000 in taxable fringe benefits faces a combined state and federal income-tax rate of 40 percent. If the executive's contract requires the firm to pay all resulting taxes on the fringe benefits (so as allow the executive to receive the $1,000,000 of fringe benefits free of tax), how much tax will the company have to pay?

4. A's employer pays A's $10,000 monthly salary on the fifteenth of each month. (Both A and the employer use a calendar year as their tax year.) On January 15, year 2, A received a check covering the pay period running from December 16, year 1, through January 15, year 2. Both A and the employer use the cash method. In which year should A include the income and the employer, who can deduct the salary as a business expense, deduct the expense?

5. Same as 4, except that both A and the employer use the accrual method.

11

B. TRANSFERS OF PROPERTY AS COMPENSATION FOR SERVICES

Code: §§ 61(a)(1); 83(a), (b), (c) & (h); 1012.

Regulations: §§ 1.83–1(a) & (f), Ex. (1); 1.83–3(b); 1.83–4(b)(1); 1.83–6(a)(1). Note § 1.61–2(d)(1), (2)(i) & (6).

1. Upon going to work for an automobile company, E, a cash-method taxpayer, was given a new car as a "signing bonus." The car was E's to keep even if E quit the job. The value of the car was $25,000.

(a) Must the value of the car be included in E's gross income?

(b) What is E's unadjusted basis for the car? (Or, put differently, how much gain *should* E realize if E immediately sells the car for its value of $25,000? Explain.)

2. In year 1, Y Corp. sells its executive, E, one share of Y Corp.'s stock (publicly traded at $90) for $30. Under the terms of E's employment contract, E must surrender the share if she does not continue to work for Y through November of year 4. The restriction is prominently stated on the stock certificate. E makes no § 83(b) election and in year 4 fulfills her obligation to work for Y. At that time, the share is worth $150. E sells the stock in year 6 for $200. What tax results to E and X?

3. Same as 2, except that the restriction is not stated on the stock certificate.

4. Same as 2, except that E makes a § 83(b) election.

5. Same as 2, except that E makes a § 83(b) election but quits in year 2 and surrenders the share to Y. When E surrenders the share, the corporation returns the $30 that she paid for it.

6. Same as 2, except that in year 2 E sold the stock to an unrelated party in an arm's length transaction for $65. (The public trading price for Y shares at that time was $100.)

7. Same as 2, except that in year 2 E sold the stock to her son, S, in a non-arm's length transaction for $35. (The public trading price for Y shares at that time was $100.)

C. THE GRANTING AND EXERCISING OF STOCK OPTIONS

Code: §§ 83(e)(1), (3) & (4); 421(a) & (b); 422(a) & (b). Review § 83(a) & (h).

Regulations: §§ 1.83–4(b)(1); 1.83–7(a).

Case: Commissioner v. LoBue, 351 U.S. 243 (1956).

1. In year 1, Z Corp. grants its executive, P, a stock option (exercisable at any time in the next ten years) to purchase one share of Z common stock at $40. At that time, Z's (publicly traded) common stock was trading at $30 per share. P exercises the option just before it expires in year 10, when the stock is trading at $200. (There are no restrictions on the share when it is acquired by P.) P sells the share in year 12 for $250. What tax results to P and Z if the option is a non-statutory option (NSO) without an ascertainable value at the time of grant?

2. Same as 1, except that the option is a NSO with a readily ascertainable value of $5 at the time of grant. (Assume that the option was substantially vested in year 1.)

3. Same as 1, except that the option is an incentive stock option (ISO) described in § 422.

4. Same as 1, except that the option is an ISO and P instead sold the share in year 11 (just 10 months after exercising the option).

Chapter 5

EMPLOYEE FRINGE BENEFITS

A. MEALS AND LODGING UNDER § 119

Code: §§ 61(a)(1); 119. Note § 107.

Regulations: Skim § 1.119–1.

Case: Adams v. United States, 585 F.2d 1060 (Ct. Cl. 1978).

1. M is the manager of a large hotel owned by Hotel Corp. M is expected to be on call 24 hours a day. Hotel Corp. furnishes M and M's family living quarters in the hotel and allows them to eat for free in the hotel dining room. Must M include the value of the meals and lodging in gross income?

2. Would your answer in 1 differ if Hotel lodged the family in a residence owned by it and located two short blocks from the hotel?

3. Private University is located in a major city. Housing prices in the area surrounding the campus are very high—so high that many professors cannot afford to live in the area. To ameliorate this problem, the University purchased several residences in the area and leases them to faculty members at a discounted rent. P, a professor who participates in the University's housing program, pays rent of $24,000 annually on a residence that has an appraised value of $600,000. Although the University seldom leases property to non-employees, a residence comparable to P's would be leased to a non-employee at $36,000 per year. P's residence is located two blocks from campus. Must P treat any portion of the "subsidized" rent as compensation?

4. Would your answer in 3 differ if P was the president of the University and was required to reside (free of charge) in the residence as a condition of employment? P used the residence for entertaining people affiliated with the University, including students, faculty, alumni and major donors. Although P's principal campus office was in the University Administration Building, P maintained an office in the residence, which she used for work at night and on weekends and for taking telephone calls on University business.

15

5. A restaurant provides meals for its wait staff just before the restaurant opens for lunch each day. Is the value of the meals includable in a staff member's gross income if the restaurant furnishes the meals:

(a) free of charge?

(b) at a charge of $10 per day and the charge is deducted from the server's wages regardless of whether the server actually eats the meal? (The restaurant would charge its customers $25 for a meal comparable to those served the wait staff.)

(c) in the manner described in (b), except that the restaurant charges the servers only for the meals they actually eat?

6. B is the business manager of the restaurant. She regularly works from 8:00 a.m. until 5 p.m., but is allowed one hour for lunch. The restaurant also furnishes B's lunch free of charge. B eats lunch at the restaurant about twice a week on average; on other days B goes out for lunch. The restaurant management does not care whether B eats lunch on the premises. Must B include the value of the lunches furnished her by the restaurant?

7. The Iman of the local mosque is paid a rental allowance, which he uses to furnish a rental residence for him and his family. The residence is located a short distance away from the mosque. The allowance does not exceed the fair rental value of the residence. Does the Iman have income on account of the residence?

B. EMPLOYEE FRINGE BENEFITS UNDER § 132

Code: §§ 132(a), (b), (c), (d), (e), (f)(1), (2) & (3), (g), (h) & (j)(1); 217(a), (b) & (c); 82.

Regulations: §§ 1.132–1(b)(1) & (4); 1.132–2(a)(1), (2), (5), (c); 1.132–3(e); 1.132–5(a)(1)(vi); 1.132–6(a), (b), (c), (d)(2)(i) & (e).

E serves as store manager for D Corporation, which operates a chain of upscale department stores. D provides its employees with a number of fringe benefits. On which of the following fringe benefits will E be taxed?

1. All employees are allowed to purchase store merchandise at a discount of 20 percent from the regular price.

2. The store that E manages includes a salon. All store employees are given a discount of 20 percent on salon services.

3. The store operates a public restaurant on the store premises. All store employees pay only half price when they eat during their assigned lunch hour.

4. E uses the office copying machine to copy her personal income-tax return.

5. D pays up to $175 per month of the parking charges incurred by store employees on their workdays at a public ramp close to the store. Employees can choose between receiving this benefit or $175 per month of additional cash compensation.

6. Before assuming her present position as store manager in New City, E served as assistant manager of another store operated by D in Old City, which is 750 miles away from New City. When E was promoted to her present position earlier this year, D reimbursed E for the costs of moving E, her husband and their two children (ages 14 and 16) from Old City to New City. D's reimbursement included the cost of transporting the family's household furnishings and personal effects, the standard mileage allowance for their two cars, which they drove from Old City to New City, and the cost of the family's meals and one night of lodging in making the trip to New City.

7. E attended an interior-decorating program sponsored by the store. E usually does not attend such programs, but because she was supervising the decoration of the family's new home, she decided to attend this time. The store charges members of the public $100 to attend the program, but permits store employees to attend free of charge on a space available basis.

8. D paid $3,500 for E's (substantiated) travel, meals, lodging and tuition costs for a program covering new accounting rules for retail establishments. D did not require E to attend the program but granted her request to attend at the firm's expense.

9. The store invites all of its employees and their spouses to attend a free annual employee-recognition dinner at New City's most exclusive restaurant. E and her husband attended this year's dinner, which cost D $200 per person.

C. OTHER FRINGE BENEFITS

Code: Note §§ 79(a), (d)(1)(A), (2), (4), (5) & (6); 105(a), (b), (e); 106(a); 125(a), (d)(1) & (f).

Regulations: Treas. Reg. §§ 1.106–1; 1.79–4T, Q & A (9).

1. A is employed by X. X pays the cost of a health-insurance policy covering all of its employees, their spouses and dependent children. Must A include her share of the policy premium in gross income?

2. A (in 1) receives a $1,000 reimbursement from the insurer covering the cost of medical treatment received earlier this year by A's 14-year-old child. The child resides with A and is A's dependent under § 152. Must the reimbursement be included in A's gross income?

3. A's employer provides all of its full-time employees coverage under a group-term life insurance policy. The coverage is equal to the employee's annual compensation, up to $50,000. Must A include her share of the policy premiums in gross income?

4. The policy (in 3) also provides $2,000 of coverage on the lives of each employee's spouse and dependent children. Must A include in income the portion of the premium paid on behalf of her spouse and dependent child?

5. B's employer maintains a non-discriminatory cafeteria plan, under which employees can designate a portion of their salaries for contribution to the plan and then obtain reimbursement from the plan for medical or dependent-care expenses. B elects to have his employer reduce his salary by $2,000 and have the money contributed to the plan. Must B include the $2,000 in gross income?

Chapter 6

DEFERRING COMPENSATION— INDIVIDUAL RETIREMENT ACCOUNTS

Code: §§ 219(a), (b)(1) & (5)(A), (d)(1), (e), (f)(1), (g)(1), (3) & (5); 408(a), (d)(1) & (2), (e)(1), (*o*)(1) & (2); 408A(a), (b), (c)(1), (2), (3)(A), (4), & (5), (d)(1), (2) & (5). Note § 62(a)(7).

1. Describe the salient features of:

(a) A traditional (deductible) IRA;

(b) A Roth IRA;

(c) A traditional (non-deductible) IRA.

2. On her 45th birthday, T contributes $5,000 to a retirement-savings program to provide funds for her retirement at age 65. T plans to withdraw the entire account balance on her 65th birthday (i.e., after 20 years). T anticipates that she can earn a pre-tax return of 10 percent on her investment in the account. Assume that the maximum allowable contribution to an IRA is $5,000 and that T expects to be in the 40 percent (combined federal and state) income-tax bracket at all times. How much will T have available to consume at age 65 if she invests in:

(a) A taxable savings account?

(b) A traditional (deductible) IRA?

(c) A Roth IRA?

(d) A traditional, non-deductible IRA (non-deductible because she is covered by her employer's plan and has too much adjusted gross income to make a deductible contribution).

(e) Under which plan does T come out best?

3. S is willing to reduce her consumption by $3,000 so that she can make a contribution to an IRA account, which she will not distribute for 20 years. S can earn a pre-tax return of 10 percent on her investments and expects to be in the 40–percent (combined state and federal) tax bracket at all times. Should she invest in a traditional (deductible) IRA or a Roth IRA? Explain.

4. R, age 40 and single, has adjusted gross income (as specially defined in § 219(g)(3)(A)) of $54,000, including salary of $50,000. R is an active participant in his employer's qualified pension plan ("a plan described in section 401(a)"). To what extent can R make a contribution (and to what extent would the contribution be deductible) if the contribution is to:

(a) A traditional IRA?

(b) A Roth IRA?

Chapter 7

ANNUITIES

Code: §§ 61(a)(9); 72(a), (b) & (c). Note § 67(b)(10).

Regulations: §§ 1.72–4; 1.72–5; 1.72–9 (Tables V and VI).

1. Last year T paid $750,000 for a single-premium annuity contract under which T is to receive an annual payment of $100,000 for ten years. T received the first payment in the current year. How much of the $100,000 should T include in gross income?

2. In the current year, P (age 60) began receiving annual payments of $10,000 under a single-premium annuity contract purchased ten years before at a cost of $121,000. The annuity payments were to continue until P's death.

(a) How much of the $10,000 received in the first year should P include in gross income?

(b) If P lives to receive the 25th annual payment, how much of the payment should P include in gross income?

(c) Now suppose that P had died after receiving just four annual payments. What tax result to P?

3. Ten years ago, H and W purchased a joint-and-survivor annuity for $201,600. The $10,000 annual annuity payments were to commence at H's age 60 (when W would be 53) and continue until the death of the survivor of H and W.

(a) H attained age 60 in the current year, and the couple received their first $10,000 payment. How much of the payment should they include in gross income on their joint return?

(b) H died at age 65, survived by W, who subsequently died after receiving (either jointly with H or as surviving annuitant) thirty annual payments. What tax result to W?

Chapter 8

CANCELLATION OF INDEBTEDNESS
(DEBT-DISCHARGE INCOME)

Code: §§ 61(a)(12); 108(a), (b), (d)(1), (2) & (3), (e)(1), (2), (4) & (5), (f)(1), (2) & (3).

Regulation: § 1.61–12(a).

Cases: United States v. Kirby Lumber Co., 284 U.S. 1 (1931);
  Commissioner v. Rail Joint Co., 61 F.2d 751 (2d Cir. 1932).

Ruling: Rev. Rul. 84–176, 1984–2 C.B. 34.

1. In year 1, A, a cash-method taxpayer, borrows $100 from a bank. A is personally liable on the note, which is unsecured. The loan proceeds are used in A's business. Because of A's deteriorating financial condition, the bank agrees in year 2 to accept $70 in complete discharge of A's liability. How much must A include in gross income in each of the following cases?

(a) Immediately before the discharge, the value of A's assets exceeds the amount of A's liabilities by $20.

(b) Immediately before the discharge, the amount of A's liabilities exceeds the value of A's assets by $20?

(c) Immediately before the discharge, the amount of A's liabilities exceeds the value of A's assets by $35.

(d) Same as (a), except that the bank also discharges A from liability for $10 of accrued interest that A owed on the note.

(e) Same as (a), except that the bank also discharges A from liability for $10 of interest that had accrued in year 1, and A uses the accrual method of tax accounting.

2. It has been said that the § 108(a)(1)(B) exclusion reduces tax liability today, but at the cost of higher taxes tomorrow—i.e., it is a deferral provision rather than a true exclusion. Do you agree? Explain.

3. D owned raw land (held as an investment) with a value of $100. D borrowed $60 from a bank on a non-recourse note (i.e., a note on which D was not personally liable) secured by the land and devoted the loan proceeds to purposes unrelated to the land. Because of a subsequent recession in the housing market, D encounters problems selling the land, which D had hoped to sell to developers. In order to avoid the delay and expense of a foreclosure proceeding, the bank agreed to accept $55 in full settlement of the note and, upon payment of that amount by D, released its lien on the land. D was solvent both before and after the cancellation. Does D have debt-discharge income on account of the transaction?

4. C made an unsecured loan of $10,000 to D. D used the loan proceeds in his painting business. The business did not prosper, and D became hopelessly insolvent. At that point, C offered to forgive the $10,000 loan principal if D would paint her house, which D did. Must D include the $10,000 in gross income?

5. M lent her adult daughter, D, $25,000 to use in purchasing a new car. A year later, when the amount of the principal balance of the loan was $20,000, C married. At the wedding reception, M tore up C's note. What result to C?

6. P wins a $100,000 judgment against D for a personal injury caused by D's negligence. D appealed the judgment to the court of appeals. While the appeal was pending, P agreed to accept $75,000 in full settlement of the case. D is solvent at all times. Does the settlement result in debt-discharge income to D?

7. P purchased a business machine from S at a price of $100,000. P paid S $10,000 cash and agreed to pay the $90,000 balance in nine equal annual installments beginning in the following year. The deferred payments were secured by a security interest in the machine. Two years later, P had reduced the principal balance of the debt to $70,000, but the machine had fallen in value to $50,000. At that point, S agreed to accept $50,000 in full satisfaction of the debt principal. What result to P if:

(a) P was insolvent immediately after S reduced the debt?

(b) P was solvent at all times?

8. T, a modestly wealthy person, offered $100,000 to the first graduate of the local high school to attain an undergraduate degree from an Ivy League university. Six years later, S qualified for the payment by graduating from Harvard. In the meantime, however, T had encountered substantial financial difficulties. Although T was solvent, it became clear to S that collecting the full amount to which she was entitled would be difficult. S therefore accepted T's payment of $60,000 in full satisfaction of T's obligation. Does T have income from the discharge of the debt?

9. F owed a bank $100,000 on a loan taken out for personal purposes several years before. Though solvent, F had struggled with financial and health issues. In the current year, F's son, S, purchases the loan from the bank for $60,000. What result to F?

Chapter 9

DAMAGES AND INSURANCE RECOVERIES

A. PROPERTY AND CONTRACT RIGHTS

Code: § 61(a). Review § 1001(a).

Regulation: § 1.61–14(a).

Cases: Commissioner v. Glenshaw Glass Co., 348 U.S. 426 (1955); Raytheon Production Corp. v. Commissioner, 144 F.2d 110 (1st Cir. 1944); Sager Glove Corp. v. Commissioner, 36 T.C. 1173, aff'd, 311 F.2d 210 (7th Cir. 1962).

Ruling: Rev. Rul. 85–97, 1985–2 C.B.

1. E was fired from her job in violation of her employment contract. She recovered $100,000 in damages. Must the $100,000 be included in E's income?

2. F's barn was completely destroyed in a fire set by vandals. The miscreants were caught and forced to pay F the $50,000 value of the barn. His adjusted basis in the barn was $20,000. F did not replace the barn. Must F include the damage recovery in income?

3. R, a chemist, developed a liquid compound in which one could store a razor when not in use and quadruple the number of shaves the user could get from a blade. Through word of mouth and internet advertising, the product became very profitable. However, through the use of predatory trade practices, a large firm was able to destroy R's business. R brought suit against the predator and recovered $500,000 in compensatory damages and $200,000 of punitive damages. How should R treat the recovery if the compensatory damages are for:

(a) Lost profits?

(b) The destruction of R's goodwill?

B. PERSONAL INJURIES

Code: § 104(a). Note § 213(a), (d)(1).

Regulations: § 1.104–1(a), (c), (d).

Case: Amos v. Commissioner, 86 T.C.M. 663 (2003).

Ruling: Rev. Rul. 85–97, 1985–2 C.B. 50.

1. P suffered serious injuries when she was struck by a bus. She recovered the following damages from the bus company: $50,000 for past and future medical expenses (none of which P had deducted), $100,000 for pain and suffering, $30,000 for lost wages, and $250,000 of punitive damages. To what extent is the recovery includable in P's gross income?

2. Would your answer in 1 differ if in the preceding year P had deducted $20,000 of medical expenses incurred because of the accident?

3. P brought an action against S for intentional infliction of mental distress, which caused P to suffer insomnia, headaches and stomach disorders. P recovered and obtained a verdict for $100,000, of which $20,000 was attributable to lost wages, $30,000 was for mental suffering, and $50,000 was in reimbursement for the cost of psychiatric care necessitated by S's actions. Must P include any portion of the $100,000 recovery in gross income?

4. Through the negligence of another, D was killed in an automobile accident. D's spouse, S, recovered $500,000 from the negligent party under the state wrongful-death statute. S also recovered $250,000 for loss of consortium. Can S exclude these amounts from gross income?

5. C, a congressman, physically injured his mistress during a fight. The woman threatened to sue, but C settled the case to avoid the unfavorable publicity of a trial. The settlement agreement required C to pay the woman $400,000 but provided that she would have to return the money if she publicized the case or pressed charges against C. In the agreement, C admitted to no wrongdoing. Is the $400,000 includable in the recipient's income?

6. E was injured in an industrial accident and received workman's-compensation payments of $20,000. Must the $20,000 be included in E's gross income?

C. INSURANCE RECOVERIES

Code: §§ 104(a)(3); 105(a), (b) & (e). Note § 213(a).

Regulations: Treas. Reg. § 1.104–1(d).

1. Earlier this year, T incurred and paid $17,500 of expenses for the medical care of her dependent son. She has now received reimbursement of the $17,500 from her insurer. Must the reimbursement be included in T's gross income if she paid the premiums on the policy?

2. Would your answer in 1 differ if T's employer had paid the premiums on the policy?

3. In year 1, S paid $17,500 for medical care for himself. On his tax return for year 1, S deducted $10,000 as medical expense under § 213. (Only $10,000 was deductible because § 213 limits the deduction to the amount by which the taxpayer's medical expenses exceed 7.5 percent of adjusted gross income.) In year 2, S's insurer reimbursed him for the $17,500. The policy had been purchased by S from his own funds. S had total itemized deductions of $20,000. To what extent must the reimbursement be included in S's gross income for year 2?

4. Would your answer in 3 differ if S's employer had purchased the policy of health insurance?

Chapter 10

===

GIFTS, BEQUESTS AND RELATED ISSUES

———

A. GIFTS, BEQUESTS AND LIFE INSURANCE PROCEEDS

Code: §§ 102; 101(a); 1014(a) & (b)(1); 1015(a).

Regulation: Prop. Treas. Reg. § 1.102–1(f)(2).

Case: Commissioner v. Duberstein, 363 U.S. 278 (1960).

1. D died in the current year and left a will which contained the following provisions:

> I. I leave my residence, Purpleacre, to my niece, N.

> II. I leave my Ultrasoft stock to my nephew, M.

> III. I direct my testamentary trustee to pay the annual income from my prized farm, Blueacre, to my daughter, L, for life, remainder at's L's death to my grandchild, R.

> IV. During the administration of my estate, I direct my executor to pay $5,000 annually from the income of my estate to my brother, B.

> V. I leave my vacation home, Greenacre, to my beloved spouse, S.

> VI. In lieu of an executor's fee, I leave my executor, E, $50,000.

> VII. I leave the remainder of my estate to my child, C.

At the time of D's death, N was employed as D's secretary. D had purchased the Ultrasoft stock several years ago for $20,000. Its value on the date of D's death was $300,000. The usual executor's fee for an estate of comparable size and complexity is $40,000. S brought suit to contest the will; the suit was settled by the estate's paying S $750,000 cash.

D had paid a $10,000 premium on a policy of term insurance covering his life. D had designated R as beneficiary of the policy, and the insurer paid R the $100,000 death benefit.

D had also taken out a $150,000 whole-life policy on his life. After he had paid $25,000 in premiums, he sold the policy to M for $30,000. M paid an additional $20,000 in premiums on the policy before D's death, at which point M received the $150,000 death benefit.

Questions:

(a) Can N exclude the $400,000 value of Purpleacre from gross income?

(b) Can M exclude any dividends received on the Ultrasoft stock?

(c) What is M's basis for the Ultrasoft stock?

(d) Can L exclude the annual income received from Blueacre?

(e) Can R exclude the value of the remainder interest in Blueacre?

(f) Can S exclude the $750,000 received in settlement of the will contest?

(g) Can E exclude the $50,000?

(h) Can R exclude the $100,000 of insurance proceeds?

(i) Can M exclude the $150,000 of insurance proceeds?

2. T, a prosperous attorney, had lived most of his life in the same small town. In gratitude to the town, and because he treasured his undergraduate education at an Ivy League school, he promised to pay $100,000 to each of the graduates of the local high school who attained an undergraduate degree from an Ivy League university. After her recent graduation from Princeton, S became the first student to qualify for the $100,000 payment. T was delighted, as S had worked as a "gofer" for T's law office during her summer vacations. T's promise was enforceable under state law. Can S exclude the payment from gross income? Explain.

3. M gave her son, S, 100 shares of Megacorporation stock as a birthday gift. M had purchased the stock several years ago for $5 per share. At the time of the gift, the stock was worth $40 per share. No gift tax was payable on the transfer by M. What is S's adjusted basis for the stock?

4. C has breakfast at the Café Z nearly every weekday morning. S is his ususal server. Last week, C told S that he was going to leave her a "real" tip. To S's astonishment, C left a tip of $10,000 cash. S offered to return the money but

C insisted that she keep it. S and C never see each other apart from their encounters at the café. Must S include the tip in gross income?

B. PRIZES AND SCHOLARSHIPS

Code: §§ 117; 74.

Regulation: Prop. Treas. Reg. § 1.117–6(b), (c) & (d).

Case: Turner v. Commissioner, 13 T.C.M. 462 (1954).

1. S receives a $30,000 scholarship to Private University, where she is a full-time student. S incurs $40,000 of expenses for the year, consisting of:

Tuition	$24,000
Required books	1,500
Recommended books	1,000
Laboratory fees	500
Room and board	10,000
Travel	2,000
Computer (recommended)	1,000

How much of the grant must S include in gross income?

2. T is a graduate student at State University. T receives a $20,000 scholarship from the University. As a condition to receiving the scholarship, T performs teaching services for the University. Similar teaching is required of all graduate-degree candidates in T's department. Non-students who have educational backgrounds similar to T's and who perform similar services for the University are paid $7,500. How much can T exclude from gross income?

3. The University Law School offers grants of $30,000 to its students who are willing to commit to working full-time for a public-service or non-profit organization for at least 5 years after graduation. The selection of a position and its geographical location are left to the recipient to determine, except that the position must be within the state in which the Law School is located. A penalty is imposed if the recipient breaches the agreement. The annual tuition at the Law School exceeds $30,000. Must a recipient of a grant include it in income?

4. Would your answer in 3 differ if the grants were made to law students who agreed to accept post-graduation employment with public-sector or non–profit firms but the graduates were not required to accept positions in the state?

5. N wins a Nobel Prize in chemistry. Must N include the $1,400,000 award in gross income?

6. Since charitable contributions are deductible under § 170, what purpose is served by § 74(b)(3)?

7. W won an all-expense-paid trip for two to Cabo San Lucas on a radio quiz show. The prize was non-transferable. Similar trip packages sell for $3,000. Must W include $3,000 in gross income on account of the prize?

Section C

BUSINESS AND INVESTMENT EXPENSES

Chapter 11

DEPRECIATION AND RELATED ISSUES

Code: §§ 167(a), (b) & (c); 168(a), (b), (c), (d), (e), (g)(1), (2) & (7), (i)(1), (8)(A) & (12); 179(a), (b)(1), (2) & (3), (d)(1); 1011(a); 1016(a)(2).

Regulation: § 1.179–1(f)(1).

Case: Simon v. Commissioner, 68 F.3d 41 (2d Cir. 1995) (Non- acq.).

Ruling: Rev. Proc. 87–57, 1987–2 C.B. 674.

In each of the following problems, assume (unless otherwise indicated) that (1) the property purchased was the taxpayer's only capital expenditure for the year; (2) the dollar limitation of § 179(b)(1) is $100,000; and (3) the phaseout of the limitation in § 179(b)(2) begins at $400,000. Ignore inflation adjustments.

1. On June 26, year 1, T placed in service a piece of equipment (5–year property) to be used in her manufacturing business. She purchased the property for $175,000. Because she has very substantial amounts of income from the business, she wishes to maximize her tax deductions in years 1 and 2. What is the maximum amount she can deduct with respect to the equipment in year 1? In year 2? Explain.

2. On September 1 of year 1, F places in service on his farm a newly erected barn. The barn cost $200,000. He wishes to maximize his depreciation deduction. How much depreciation is allowable in each of years 1 and 2? (The barn has a class life of 25 years.)

3. Lawyer L purchases a Picasso sketch to hang on her office wall. Over what period can she depreciate the sketch?

4. In July, year 1, P pays $420,000 for 7–year property (class life of 10 years) to be used in her active manufacturing business. P makes no § 179 election with respect to the equipment. What is P's adjusted basis for the equipment at the end of year 2?

5. Same as 4, except that in year 1 P deducts the maximum amount permitted under § 179.

6. Same as 4, except that P makes an election under § 168(b)(3)(D) and (b)(5).

7. Same as 4, except that P makes an election under § 168(g)(1)(E) and (g)(7).

8. R placed in service two pieces of equipment (5–year property), each of which cost $210,000. The first was placed in service in July, year 1, and the second in October, year 1. R makes no § 179 election with respect to either piece of equipment. What is R's allowable depreciation for year 1? Year 2?

9. Would your answer in 8 differ if R had also purchased an apartment building for $1 million in January of year 1?

10. Suppose that in January, year 3, R (in problem (8)) sold the equipment placed in service in July of year 1. At the end of year 2, R's adjusted basis for the July equipment was $107,100. How much depreciation is allowable to R in year 3?

11. Several years ago S purchased a depreciable business asset for $100,000. Although the total amount of depreciation allowable with respect to the asset is $80,000, S mistakenly deducted only $60,000 of depreciation. S is preparing to sell the asset. What is S's adjusted basis for the property?

12. On January 1, year 1, L leased land to T for 36 years. In January, year 2, (when the lease had 35 years to run), T finished erecting a new office building on the property at a cost of $780,000. What is T's depreciation deduction for year 2?

13. Is the depreciation (cost-recovery) deduction of § 168 a tax expenditure? Explain your answer.

Chapter 12

BUSINESS AND INVESTMENT EXPENSES

A. IN GENERAL

Code: §§ 162(a), (c)(1) & (2), (f), (*l*); 212; 67; 262; 7701(a)(25). Review § 62(a).

Regulations: §§ 1.162–1(a); 1.162–4; 1.162–6; 1.62–1T(a), (b), (d) & (e)(1); 1.67–1T; 1.263(a)–4(f)(1).

Cases: United States v. Gilmore, 372 U.S. 39 (1963);
Wild v. Commissioner, 42 T.C. 706 (1964) (Acq.);
Pevsner v. Commissioner, 628 F.2d (5th Cir. 1980), rehearing en banc denied, 636 F.2d 1106 (1981);
Welch v. Helvering, 290 U.S. 111 (1933).

1. Is § 162(a) a tax-expenditure provision? Explain.

2. T is a self-employed lawyer—a solo practitioner—who uses the cash method of accounting. Which of the following (alternative) expenditures made by T qualify for deduction under § 162? In each case, specify which section allows (or disallows) the deduction and whether any allowable deduction is taken in computing AGI. Also indicate whether any deductible item is a miscellaneous itemized deduction subject to the limits of § 67.

(a) Rent on T's law office;

(b) Principal payment on liability incurred when law office was purchased by T; the liability was secured by a mortgage on the premises;

(c) Cost of a new desk-top computer for T's office;

(d) Cost of painting the interior of the office (this is done approximately every three years);

(e) Cost of dues for T's membership in the Tax Section of the American Bar Association;

(f) Cost of a health-insurance policy covering T, her spouse and children;

(g) Self-employment tax on the income from T's law practice;

(h) Amounts advanced to T's litigation clients for payment of court costs, depositions, expert witnesses, etc.;

(i) Premium payment for two year's coverage under a policy providing casualty insurance on T's business office;

(j) $25,000 annual salary paid to T's sixteen-year old son, who spends about ten hours per week running errands for the firm;

(k) Cost of transportation from T's home to her office;

(l) Cost of transportation from T's home to the courthouse for an all-day trial (T returned directly home from the courthouse at the end of the day);

(m) Investment-advisory fee in connection with the management of T's stock-market portfolio;

(n) Commissions on purchase and sale of securities;

(o) $500 gratuity to the clerk of court, who agreed to move one of T's cases up on the court's docket;

(p) Attorney's fee paid for representation in a civil inquiry by the State Judicial Ethics Committee into the payment of the gratuity in (o);

(q) Fine imposed by the Committee in (p) after its investigation found T guilty of bribing the clerk;

(r) Payment (in December) for $3,000 worth of office supplies; T keeps no inventory of the supplies and does not record their use, but T does not expect to have to replenish the supplies until late in the following year;

(s) Cost of "professional" looking clothing for office wear; the clothing cost $3,000 more than T would have spent if she were not working, as her personal lifestyle is quite casual;

(t) $5,000 paid to a public relations firm to lobby against a proposal in the state legislature that would subject payments for legal services to state sales tax;

(u) $1,000 of travel expense incurred by T to personally lobby state legislators to vote against the proposal described in (t);

(v) $5,000 expended in lobbying members of the city council to prevent the re-zoning of the land adjacent to T's law office;

(w) $1,000 to the State Supreme Court to obtain a license to practice law in the state. The license is valid indefinitely, providing L adheres to the rules governing the practice of law in the state.

3. A, a 30–year old single person with no dependents, is employed as an associate in a law firm. A has the following receipts and disbursements for the current year.

	Receipts	Disbursements
Salary	$100,000	
Rent	6,000	
Mineral royalties	5,000	
Travel expenses*		5,000
Professional dues*		1,000
Professional books		1,000
Investment-advisory fee		2,500
Rental expenses		5,000
Charitable contributions		5,000
State income tax		4,000
Severance tax on royalty income		1,000
Deductible IRA contribution		5,000

* Denotes expenditures reimbursed by T's firm.

The investment-advisory fee was paid for stock-market investment advice. Determine A's gross, adjusted gross and taxable income.

4. Consider a typical divorce that involves issues of child custody, child support, alimony, property division and (of course!) tax advice.

(a) To what extent are the legal fees attributable to those issues deductible?

(b) What can the divorce attorney do to bolster the client's chances of getting the maximum tax benefit from the expenditure?

5. R, a well-known rock musician, founded a firm that developed a chain of fast food outlets that bore R's name. At first the firm prospered, and R encouraged his musical associates (his agent, producer, band members, etc.) to invest in the firm. After three years, however, the firm failed, and R and his associates lost considerable sums. With a view to preserving his reputation as a musician, R undertook to reimburse his associates for their losses. Can R deduct the payments as business expenses?

B. TRAVEL AND ENTERTAINMENT EXPENSES

Code: §§ 162(a); 274(a), (d), (e)(1), (2) & (3), (m)(3) & (n).

Regulations: §§ 1.162–2; 1.274–2(a), (b), (c) & (d); 1.274–5T(f)(2)(i).

Cases: Hantzis v. Commissioner, 638 F.2d 248 (1st Cir. 1981);
         Robertson v. Commissioner, 190 F.3d 392 (5th Cir. 1999).

1. L practices law in University City (which is about 200 miles from Chicago). Last Thursday she attended a conference on tax law in Chicago. Early Thursday morning L left her University City residence and drove to Regional Airport, a distance of 20 miles. She flew by commercial airline to Chicago, took a cab from the airport to her conference, ate lunch (alone) in Chicago, attended the afternoon session of the conference, returned by cab to the airport, flew back to Regional Airport, and drove home. L's University City office is 5 miles from her residence. The cost of the conference is a business expense under Treas. Reg. § 1.162–5(a). Can L deduct the cost of:

(a) The roundtrip to Regional Airport?

(b) The airfare to Chicago?

(c) Lunch in Chicago?

(d) Round-trip cab fare from the Chicago airport?

2. A, an attorney, works in Capital City but chooses to live in University City, which is 120 miles from Capital City.

(a) Is A allowed a deduction for the cost of the daily roundtrip from University City to Capital City?

(b) Suppose instead that A drives to Capital City on Monday morning, stays in a hotel from Monday night through Friday morning and then returns to University City on Friday evening. Is A allowed a deduction for the cost of meals and the hotel room in Capital City?

(c) Suppose that A also taught a Saturday morning course at the University Law School in University City. Would that make any of A's costs deductible?

3. S is a second-year student at Midwestern State University School of Law. S has accepted a position as a summer associate with a large New York City law firm. In connection with her employment, S expects to incur expenses for roundtrip airfare to New York, apartment rent and meals. She plans to retain her apartment near the Midwestern State campus while she is in New York. She has been working as a clerk for a local law firm during the academic year and expects

to return to her clerkship position upon her return from New York. Will S be allowed a deduction for any of the employment costs?

4. E is employed in City X, where he resides with his family. E's employer asked him to accept an eight-month assignment at the employer's location in City Y, which is in a neighboring state, and E accepted the assignment. While in City Y, E stayed at a residential hotel, which also furnished his meals. In the eighth month of the assignment, the employer asked E if he would be willing to accept another six-month assignment in City Y beginning at the conclusion of the eighth month, and E again accepted. E continued to stay at the residential hotel throughout the sixth-month period of the second assignment. To what extent can E deduct his costs of meals and lodging in City Y?

5. C is a partner in an Indianapolis law firm. Accompanied by her husband, H, C went to New York City to attend a conference on the Sarbanes-Oxley Act. C and H flew into New York on Tuesday evening. The conference began on Wednesday morning and ran through Friday afternoon. C attended all sessions of the conference; H spent those days sightseeing and shopping. C and H both spent Saturday sightseeing and flew home on Sunday. To what extent are the couple's airfare, meals and lodging deductible?

6. A is an attorney (a solo practitioner). A is considering various ways to promote his practice and seeks your advice as to the tax deductibility of the various options. What do you advise as to the following?

(a) A is an accomplished amateur chef. Once a month, A and his wife, W, could invite three clients (and their spouses) to their home for a gourmet dinner. A thinks each meal (including wine) would cost about $100 per person.

(b) Each month A and W would invite two clients (and their spouses) to be their guests at a local comedy club. A estimates that that would also cost (including drinks) about $100 per person.

(c) A could invite three clients to play golf at the exclusive country club of which A is a member. A thinks that green fees, food and beverages would run about $200 per person.

(d) A could send a client (and spouse) two tickets to the local ballet theater. A and W would not attend, however, as A detests ballet.

(e) Whenever A has a late-morning appointment with a client, A will invite the client (and the client's spouse) to join him for lunch at A's club. A estimates the average cost of lunch at the club is $50 per person.

C. EDUCATION EXPENSE

Code: § 162(a). Note §§ 195; 25A; 222.

Regulations: §§ 1.212–1(f); 1.262–1(b)(9); 1.162–5.

Cases: Sharon v. Commissioner, 66 T.C. 515, aff'd, 591 F.2d 1273 (9th Cir. 1978), cert. denied, 442 U.S. 941 (1979);
Allemeier v. Commissioner, 90 T.C.M. 197 (2005).

1. L, a solo-practitioner in a midwestern city, is required by state law to obtain fifteen hours of continuing legal education each year to maintain his law license. This year he satisfied the requirement by attending a tax program in a city 120 miles from his home. He spent a total of $750 for travel, meals, lodging and tuition to attend the program. Are the expenses deductible by L?

2. L, (in 1) has already satisfied his state-imposed continuing education requirement for the year. In December, however, he travels to Honolulu for a program on recent developments in federal taxation. He incurs costs for airfare, meals, lodging and program tuition. Are these costs deductible by L?

3. In May, G graduates with a J.D. degree from State University Law School. From June through August S works as a summer associate for a local law firm. In September, G begins a full-time LL.M. program at Private University. G incurs costs for travel, meals, lodging, tuition and books at Private University. Can G deduct her costs as business expenses?

4. Same as 3, except that G obtained her J.D. two years ago and has been working as an associate for the local law firm since graduation. She takes a nine-month leave of absence from the firm to pursue an LL.M. at Private University. Any deduction?

5. H holds a B.S. from State University and is also a C.P.A. H practices with a C.P.A. firm. He wishes to take a tax course at the local law school. Is H's tuition for the law-school course deductible as a business expense?

6. L and M both hold undergraduate degrees in business and both hold managerial positions in a bank. L will attend law school next year; M will attend a graduate college of business to obtain an M.B.A. After they attain their degrees, they both plan to return to banking. Can they deduct as business expenses the costs of obtaining their advanced degrees?

D. THE "CARRYING ON" REQUIREMENT

Code: §§ 162(a); 217(a), (b), (c) & (d); 62(a)(15); 195(a), (b) & (c).

Regulation: § 1.212–1(f).

1.   L has been practicing law in Chicago for several years. She has long thought that she would like to live in the Pacific Northwest. This year, L hired a placement agency at a cost of $10,000 to assist her in finding a position in Seattle. The agency found L a position with a Seattle law firm, which L accepted. Is the $10,000 fee deductible by L?

2.   S, a third-year law student at Midwestern State University, is seeking a position with a law firm in Seattle. At her own expense, S flies to Seattle, incurs costs for meals, lodging and resume preparation. As a result of her efforts, S is offered and accepts a position with a Seattle law firm.   Are S's expenses deductible?

3. Suppose instead that a Seattle law firm offered S (in 2) a flyback. The firm paid S's airfare, hotel and meal costs. Do these events result in income to S?

4. S (in 2) has now graduated and is moving to Seattle. Her moving costs include:

Moving household goods and personal effects	$4,000
Cost of driving S's automobile to Seattle	1,000
Lodging expense while on the road to Seattle	1,000
Meal expense while on the road to Seattle	300

S also incurs $1,000 of temporary lodging costs in Seattle while awaiting the arrival of her household goods.

(a) S pays the above expenses herself. To what extent, if any, are they deductible?

(b) Suppose the law firm reimburses her for the expenses. Must S include the reimbursement in income?

(c) Would your answer in (a) change if she worked for the Seattle firm for six months and then accepted a position with a firm in Chicago?

(d) Same as (c), except that after six months S had been laid off by the Seattle firm?

5. R is going to open a T-shirt shop in leased space in a local mall. R obtains possession of the leased premises on April 1. The next month is spent hiring

employees, ordering and stocking merchandise, re-painting the interior walls and preparing an advertising campaign. On May 15, the shop opens for business.

(a) Can R deduct the rent, utilities, employee salaries, property taxes, payroll taxes and painting costs incurred before the shop opens?

(b) Would your answer in (a) differ if R already owned T-shirt shops in several other local malls?

Chapter 13

BUSINESS AND INVESTMENT EXPENSES— STATUTORY LIMITS ON DEDUCTIONS

A. HOBBY LOSSES

Code: § 183.

Regulation: § 1.183–1(b)(1).

1. C's cat-breeding business has had profit (i.e., an excess of gross income over deductions allocable to the activity) or loss (an excess of deductions over gross income) as follows:

Year	Profit	Loss
1		$3,000
2		1,500
3	$500	
4	250	
5	50	

(a) In year 5, would C or the Commissioner have the burden of proving the activity was not engaged in for profit?

(b) Would your answer in (a) differ if in year 5 the activity had shown a loss rather than a profit?

2. D's dog-breeding activity is determined not to be engaged in for profit. D's expenses for the year are:

State property taxes	$1,500
Food, veterinary costs, etc.	4,000
Depreciation	3,000

How much of the expenses can D deduct if his gross income from the activity is:

(a) $1,000?

(b) $6,000? (Which deductions are allowable in this case?)

3. H retired just over three years ago. He has investment income of approximately $200,000 a year. For all of his adult life, H's hobby has been big-game hunting, and before retiring he had made several safaris to Africa. After retirement H decided to make game-hunting films and to present lectures on the films. To this end he made several trips to Africa to hunt and film big game. He sent out many letters and brochures soliciting lecture engagements and stating the amount of his lecture fees. In the past three years, H has generated the following amounts of gross income and expenses from the activity:

Year	Income	Expenses
1	$900	$12,000
2	2,500	9,000
3	2,800	14,500

H has kept careful records of his income and expenses from this venture. Assess the likelihood that H will be permitted to deduct the excess of the expenses over the gross income.

B. LISTED PROPERTY

Code: § 280F(a), (b) & (d). Review §§ 168 and 179.

Regulations: §§ 1.280F–3T(a), (c)(1) & (2), (d)(1) & (2); 1.280F–6(a), (d)(2)(i), (d)(3)(i), (d)(5), Exs. (1) & (2), (e)(3); 1.179–1(d)(1) & (2), Ex., (e)(1).

1. In January, year 1, T, a solo-practitioner lawyer, purchases for $3,000 a computer for home use on evenings and weekends. T uses the computer 40 percent for her law business, 30 percent in managing her stock-market portfolio, and 30 percent for personal matters. The computer has a recovery period of 5 years for both the regular and alternative depreciation systems; § 168(i)(2)(A)(i), (e)(3)(B)(iv) & (g)(3)(C).

(a) What method of depreciation, recovery period and convention must T use for year 1?

(b) In year 2, T uses the computer 60 percent for business, 30 percent for investment management and 10 for personal use. What method of depreciation, recovery period and convention must C use for year 2?

(c) In year 1, could T elect to expense the cost of the computer under § 179?

2. Suppose instead that T (in 1) had in year 1 used the computer 60 percent for business, 30 percent for investment management and 10 percent for personal matters.

(a) Is the cost of the computer eligible for expensing under § 179?

(b) Assume that T made an election under § 179 to expense the property in year 1. In year 2, T uses the computer 40 percent for her law business, 30 percent in managing her investments, and 30 percent for personal matters. Explain in general terms (i.e., without computations) the result to T in year 2?

3. P, a law professor, has an office on campus that includes a state-of-the-art computer furnished by P's employer. Nevertheless, P purchases a computer for use at home on nights and weekends. P uses the computer exclusively for his law school work. Can P deduct depreciation with respect to the computer?

4. In January of year 1, C, a business consultant, purchases a new automobile for $30,000. The automobile is used exclusively in C's business. C makes no § 179 election. How much depreciation can C deduct in year 1? In subsequent years? (As always, ignore inflation adjustments.)

C. HOME OFFICES AND VACATION HOMES

Code:　§ 280A(a), (b), (c)(1), (3) & (5), (d)(1), (2) & (4), (e), (f)(1) & (3), (g).

Regulation:　Prop. Treas. Reg. 1.280A–2(c), (g), (h), (i)(5) & (7).

Case:　Bolton v. Commissioner, 694 F.2d 556 (9th Cir. 1982).

1. V owns a vacation home that is usable only 180 days of the year. V occupies the home for 45 of those days and rents it (at fair rental value) for the other 135 days. In the current year, V's expenses with respect to the property are:

Property taxes	$1,000
Mortgage interest	3,000
Insurance and maintenance	3,000
Advertising expense	1,000

In addition, if the property had been rented all year, depreciation would have been $3,000.

Assume that the mortgage interest qualifies as "qualified residence interest" and hence is deductible under § 163(a). At the beginning of the year V's adjusted basis in the house was $30,000. Determine (1) how much of the expenses V can deduct and (2) V's adjusted basis at the end of the year if the rental income from the property is:

(a) $7,000.

(b) $4,000.

2. How would your answers in 1 differ if V rented the home out for only 10 days (and received $600 rent).

3. How would your answers in 1 differ if V used the home for personal purposes for only 10 days?

4. P, a partner in a law firm, has an office in her firm's building downtown, where she spends most working days, but also maintains an office in her home for use on nights and weekends. She uses the home office exclusively for her law business, frequently takes phone calls there from clients and colleagues, and occasionally meets clients there. Can P depreciate the portion of her house devoted to the home office?

5. G is a professor at State University in University City. He takes an unpaid leave of absence from the school to accept a visiting appointment for the academic year at Private University, which is located several hundred miles away from University City. G leases his University City home during the period of his absence (from September, year 1 through June, year 2). After the visit ends, G intends to return to live in his University City home. To what extent can G deduct the expenses attributable to the rental of the property? Do you have any recommendations to improve G's tax situation?

Section D

WHOSE INCOME IS IT?

Chapter 14

ASSIGNMENTS OF INCOME

Code: § 61(a).

Regulation: § 1.102–1(e).

Cases: Lucas v. Earl, 281 U.S. 111 (1930);
Poe v. Seaborn, 282 U.S. 101 (1930);
Blair v. Commissioner, 300 U.S. 5 (1937);
Helvering v. Horst, 311 U.S. 112 (1940).

1. R, a cash-method taxpayer, is a commission sales representative for X Corporation. R is not an employee but an independent contractor. R directs X to pay his December commission check to R's adult child, C, and X does so. What result to R and C?

2. Instead, R directs X to pay the December commissions to R's superb administrative assistant, A. A is an employee of X whose duties consist chiefly of providing administrative support for R. A had been grumbling that she was underpaid and hinted to R that she might look for another position. R hoped that paying the commissions to A would encourage her to continue in her present position. X paid the commissions to A.

3. Same as 1, except that R directed X to pay the December commissions to a charitable organization specified in § 170(c), and X did so.

4. A owns land that is leased for a period of 30 years. A and A's adult child, C, both use the cash method of accounting.

(a) What result to A and C if A, intending to make a gift, directs the lessee to pay the current year's rent to C and the lessee does so?

(b) What result if A gratuitously assigns the remaining term of the lease to C, who thereafter collects the rental payments from the lessee?

(c) What result if A gratuitously conveyed the fee interest, subject to the lease, to C, who thereafter collected the rent?

(d) What result if the land was held in trust to pay the income to A for 30 years, remainder to B, and A irrevocably and gratuitously assigned the income interest to C?

5. What is meant by the term "marriage penalty"?

6. C and D are deciding whether to marry. Each has adjusted gross income of $120,000 and taxable income of $115,000. (They compute their tax liability under § 1(c).) If they marry and file a joint return, they will have AGI of $240,000 and taxable income of $230,000. By how much will their aggregate tax liabilities increase if they marry. (Ignore the effect of all marriage penalties other than that reflected in the tax-rate schedules of § 1 (as set forth in Appendix B).)

7. Same as 6, except that before marriage each has taxable income of $22,100 and after marriage their joint taxable income would be $44,200.

8. E has adjusted gross income of $120,000 and taxable income of $115,000. F has adjusted gross income of $5,000 and taxable income of zero. If they marry, their AGI will be $125,000 and their taxable income $115,000. What is their aggregate tax bill if:

(a) they are single (and compute their tax under § 1(c))?

(b) marry and file a joint return?

9. On January 1 of this year, a community property state adopted a Registered Domestic Partners Act. Under the Act, domestic partners are "two adults who have chosen to share one another's lives in an intimate and committed relationship of mutual caring" and who register as such with the state. They may be members of the same sex. The Act extends to registered partners the same rights as spouses have under state law, except that, for state income-tax purposes, "earned income may not be treated as community property." Consider the tax treatment of A and B, same-sex partners who registered their union at the beginning of the year.

(a) A earned $100,000 of salary for the year; B earned $20,000 in part-time work.

(b) A saved $50,000 of the salary and purchased some land, which was held for rent. The lessee paid $10,000 of rent in the current year.

Chapter 15

TAXATION OF THE INCOME
OF MINOR CHILDREN

Code: §§ 1(g); 63(c)(5); 151(d)(2); 73.

Regulations: §§ 1.1(i)–1T; 1.73–1(a).

1. C, age 14, earns $2,000 delivering newspapers. Under state law, a child's parents are entitled to the earnings of a child under age 16. Who must include the $2,000 in gross income?

2. B (age 14) and S (age 19) each receive interest income from bonds purchased by their parents and held by their mother as custodian under the Uniform Transfers to Minors Act. Both children are dependents of their parents. Apart from any effect of § 1(g), the parents have taxable income of $140,000 on their joint return. Ignore inflation adjustments to amounts fixed by statute, and use the tax tables in Appendix B to determine the tax liability of B and S if they each receive interest of:

   (a) $300;

   (b) $800;

   (c) $2,400;

   (d) $2,400 and earned income of $400;

   (e) $2,400 and earned income of $3,400.

Section E

INCOME FROM DEALINGS IN PROPERTY

Chapter 16

COMPUTATION OF REALIZED GAIN OR LOSS

Code: §§ 1001(a), (b) & (c); 1011(a); 1012; 1016(a)(2).

Regulation: § 1.263(a)–2(e).

Cases: International Freighting Corp. v. Commissioner, 135 F.2d 310 (2d Cir. 1943);
Philadelphia Park Amusement Co. v. United States, 126 F. Supp. 184 (Ct. Cl. 1954);
Inaja Land Co. v. Commissioner, 9 T.C. 727 (1947).

In the following problems, assume, unless otherwise indicated, that all parties are cash-method, calendar-year taxpayers.

1. S purchased a share of stock for $20. S later sold the stock for $80. What is S's realized gain?

2. Same as 1, except that S paid a $5 brokerage commission on the sale.

3. N owned a vacation home (held for personal use) in upstate New York. N had an adjusted basis of $200,000 for the property. S transferred the property to F in exchange for a Florida condominium, which N also held for personal use. The Florida property was worth $250,000, and F also paid N $30,000 to equalize the exchange.

(a) What is N's realized gain on the exchange?

(b) What is N's basis for the Florida property?

4. W owned a vacation home (held for personal use) in Wisconsin. The home had an adjusted basis of $250,000 in W's hands. W transferred the property to C in exchange for a California condominium, which W also held for personal use. The California condominium was worth $500,000, and W paid C $100,000 to equalize the exchange.

(a) What is W's realized gain on the exchange?

(b) What is W's basis for the California property?

5. In year 1, C became indebted in the amount of $10,000 to her attorney, A, for representing C in a personal legal matter. Because C was short of cash, C offered in year 2 to transfer to A some stock with a value of $10,000. C's adjusted basis for the stock was $2,000. A accepted the stock in full payment.

(a) What result to C?

(b) To A?

6. What result in 5 if the stock was worth only $8,000 when C transferred it to A in year 2, but A nevertheless accepted the stock in full satisfaction of the indebtedness because of concern about C's continuing financial difficulties?

7. Would your answer in 6 change if A used the accrual method? Explain.

8. Under the terms of D's will, B was entitled to a legacy of $50,000. The estate transferred stock with a basis of $35,000 (and a value of $50,000) to B in satisfaction of the legacy.

(a) What result to the estate?

(b) And to B?

9. In year 1, D made a legally enforceable pledge of $50,000 to a qualifying charity described in § 170(c). D satisfied the pledge by transferring to the charity stock with an adjusted basis of $35,000. What result to D?

10. B paid $100,000 for business equipment, properly deducted $60,000 of depreciation, and then sold the equipment for $75,000. How much gain or loss does B realize on the sale? Why?

11. P was injured in an automobile accident caused by the negligence of D. P brought an action against D seeking $1,000,000 damages. Before trial, D settled the suit by transferring to P securities with an adjusted basis of $250,000 and a value of $400,000.

(a) What is the amount, if any, of D's realized gain on the transfer?

(b) What tax results to P?

12. T purchased as an investment a large tract of undeveloped land for $1,000,000. T later sold one-quarter of the land for $400,000. What is the amount of T's realized gain or loss on the sale.

13. O owned undeveloped land that he had purchased for $200,000. After a neighbor accidently polluted the land, the neighbor paid O $150,000 for the damage and for an easement to continue polluting. Does O have income on account of the payment?

14. O owned a tract of land with a basis of $100,000 and a value of $400,000. On July 1, year 1, O granted P an option to acquire the land for $450,000. P paid O $20,000 for the option, which was exercisable at any time through June 30, year 3.

(a) At the end of year 1, P has not exercised the option. How should the parties treat the transaction for year 1?

(b) Will P exercise the option if on June 30, year 3, the land is worth:

(i) $500,000?

(ii) $440,000?

(iii) $460,000?

Explain your answers.

(c) Suppose that P exercises the option on June 30, year 3, when the land is worth $500,000. What tax result to the parties in year 3?

(d) Suppose that the land is worth only $400,000 on June 30, year 3, and P does not exercise the option, which lapses. What result to the parties in year 3?

Chapter 17

TRANSACTIONS INVOLVING MORTGAGED PROPERTY

Code: §§ 1001(b); 1011(a); 1012; 167(c). Note § 7701(g). Review§ 108.

Regulations: § 1.1001–2(a), (b) & (c), Exs. (1), (2), (7) & (8).

Cases: Crane v. Commissioner, 334 U.S. 1 (1947);
Parker v. Delaney, 186 F.2d 455 (1st Cir. 1950);
Commissioner v. Tufts, 461 U.S. 300 (1983).

Ruling:　Rev. Rul. 90–16, 1990–1 C.B. 12.

1. T purchased a building for $500 (000 omitted throughout). T paid $100 cash down and gave a non-recourse note (secured by a mortgage on the property) for the $400 balance. T held the property as an investment. In answering the following questions, ignore the land, as if only the building were purchased and sold.

(a) What is T's basis for depreciation?

(b) Over the next several years, T properly deducts $300 of depreciation, pays $100 on the mortgage principal, and makes all required interest payments. T then sells the building to P, who takes the property subject to the remaining $300 mortgage and pays T $250 cash. What is the amount of T's realized gain or loss?

(c) Suppose instead that after T had properly deducted the $300 of depreciation and reduced the mortgage principal to $300, the building declined in value to $275, at which point T surrendered the property to the mortgagee. What result to T?

(d) Same as (c), except that the building was worth only $150 when it was surrendered to the mortgagee.

(e) How would your answers in (c) and (d) differ if T had been personally liable on the indebtedness, but the mortgagee had accepted the property in full satisfaction of the indebtedness? Would your answer change if T was insolvent immediately after surrendering the building to the lender?

2. A purchased property for $100 cash and properly deducted $60 of depreciation thereon. A then borrowed $50 from a bank on a non-recourse note secured by the property and devoted the loan proceeds to purposes unconnected to the property. After properly deducting another $30 of depreciation and paying off $20 of the mortgage principal (and all accrued interest), A sold the property to P, who paid A $20 cash and took subject to the remaining $30 of indebtedness.

(a) Does A have income at the time of borrowing against the security of the property?

(b) What is the amount of A's realized gain or loss on the sale to P?

(c) What is P's basis for the property immediately after the purchase?

Chapter 18

THE BASIS OF PROPERTY
ACQUIRED BY GIFT

Code: §§ 1015(a), (d)(1) & (6); 1223(2); 167(c)(1). Review § 102(a). Note §§ 1245(b)(1); 2503(a) & (b).

Regulations: §§ 1.1015–1(a); 1.1015–5(c); 1.1015–4; 1.1001–1(e).

Cases: Farid–Es–Sultaneh v. Commissioner, 160 F.2d 812 (2d Cir. 1947); Dietrich v. Commissioner, 457 U.S. 191 (1982).

1. Several years ago, P purchased a share of stock for $100. On December 31 of last year, when the share was worth $150, P gave the stock to her adult child, C. C sells the stock on July 1 of the current year for $180.

 (a) What tax result to P?

 (b) What tax result to C?

2. How would your answer in (1) differ if the value of the stock on December 31 of last year had been $80, and C had sold the stock for:

 (a) $180?

 (b) $60?

 (c) $90?

3. On January 15, M gave a piece of depreciable equipment to her son, S, for use in his business. M had purchased the equipment for $500,000 and had properly deducted $180,000 of depreciation thereon. The equipment was worth $400,000 at the time of the gift. No gift tax was payable by M.

 (a) What is S's depreciable basis for the property?

(b) Explain in general terms how S should compute depreciation on the equipment.

(c) How would your answer in (a) differ if the value of the equipment at the time of the gift was $300,000?

4. In the current year (when the gift-tax annual exclusion is $12,000), M made a taxable gift (for gift-tax purposes) of $100,000 ($112,000 value of the property transferred less $12,000 annual exclusion) to her daughter, D. M paid a gift tax of $40,000 on the transfer, which was M's only gift for the year. M's adjusted basis in the property transferred was $52,000.

(a) What is D's adjusted basis for the property?

(b) Would your answer differ if M's adjusted basis for the property given to D was $120,000?

5. A had held some securities as an investment for several years. Intending to make a partial gift, A transferred the securities to her domestic partner, B, for $60. At that time, the securities had a value of $100, and A's adjusted basis was $20. No gift tax was payable on the transfer.

(a) What result to A?

(b) What result to B if seven months after the transfer she sells the securities for $85?

(c) What result in (a) and (b), above, if A's adjusted basis in the securities had been $150?

(d) Can you devise a more-satisfactory scheme for computing A's and B's realized gain or loss in the above transactions?

6. For several years, A has owned unimproved land with an adjusted basis of $50 and a value of $150. The land was subject to a non-recourse mortgage of $60. In the current year, A, intending to make a gift, transfers the land gratuitously (but subject to the mortgage).

(a) What result to A and the transferee if the transferee is A's daughter, D?

(b) What result if the transferee is a charitable organization specified in § 170?

7. Pursuant to the terms of their divorce decree, W transferred to her former husband, H, some securities with a value of $100,000 and an adjusted basis in her hands of $120,000.

(a) What tax result to W?

(b) What tax result to H when he sells the securities six months later for $90,000?

8. Under the terms of a valid premarital agreement, C transferred securities to her future husband, D. C had a basis of $100 in the securities, which had a value of $500 when the agreement was entered into. In the agreement D waived his marital rights to C's property in the case of divorce or C's death. The parties subsequently divorced, and D wishes to sell the securities. What is D's basis in the securities?

Chapter 19

THE BASIS OF PROPERTY
ACQUIRED BY BEQUEST OR INHERITANCE

A. IN GENERAL—§ 1014

Code: §§ 1014(a), (b) & (e); 1223(9). Note § 2032.

Regulations: §§ 1.1014–1(a); –2(a) & (b); –3(a); –4(a)(3).

Case: Kenan v. Commissioner, 114 F.2d 217 (2d Cir. 1940).

1. D died on August 31, year 1, owning a share of X Corporation stock that D had purchased for $40 earlier in year 1. At the date of D's death, the share was worth $50. D bequeathed the share to B. D's executor distributed the share to B on January 31, year 2, when the share was worth $60. By February 28, year 2, the share was worth $70. B sold the share on April 15, year 2 for $80. D's Estate makes no alternate-valuation-date election under § 2032. What are the tax results to:

(a) D?

(b) D's Estate?

(c) B?

2. Same as 1, except that the share was worth only $30 at the date of D's death (and all other values are as given in 1).

3. Same as 1, except that D's executor made a valid alternate-valuation-date (AVD) election under § 2032.

4. Would your answer in 3 differ if the Estate had distributed the share to B on March 15, year 2?

5. D also left a legacy of $100 to C. On March 31, year 2, the executor distributed to C a share of Y Corporation stock (then worth $100) in satisfaction of the legacy. The Y share had a value of $60 at the date of D's death, which is the applicable estate-tax valuation date. C sold the share for $120 on April 15, year 2. What tax results to:

(a) D's Estate?

(b) C?

6. P was suffering from a fatal illness. P's child, C, gave P a share of stock with an adjusted basis of $40 and a value of $100. At P's death six months later, P bequeathed the stock to C. At the date of P's death, the stock was worth $120.

(a) What is C's basis for the stock?

(b) Suppose instead that P bequeathed the stock to P's child, GC. What is GC's basis for the stock?

B. INCOME IN RESPECT OF A DECEDENT

Code: §§ 1014(c); 691(a)(1) & (3), (b).

Regulations: §§ 1.691(a)–1; –2; –3.

Ruling: Rev. Rul. 78–32, 1978–1 C.B. 198.

1. Define: "income in respect of a decedent."

2. What is the primary purpose of § 691?

3. D died on November 30, year 1. Both D and D's Estate use the cash method of accounting and the calendar year. Explain the tax treatment of the following items.

(a) D's salary ($10,000) covering the month of October, year 1. The salary was collected by D's executor in December, year 1.

(b) $250,000 proceeds from the sale of land, in which D had a basis of $100,000. D had entered into a contract to sell the land to B on October 15, year 1, with closing scheduled for December 1. All substantial prerequisites to the sale had been completed before D's death. D's executor closed the sale on December 1.

(c) At death D possessed a non-statutory stock option (NSO) that entitled D to purchase a share of her employer's stock for $20. The value of the stock at D's death was $80. The option was exercised by D's executor in January, year 2, at which time the value of the stock was $100.

(d) $1,000 dividend on J corporation stock held by D. The dividend, declared on November 15, was payable on December 15 to shareholders of record on December 1.

(e) $2,000 of interest, which had been credited by the bank on D's passbook savings account but which had not been withdrawn by D before death. D's executor withdrew the funds from the account on December 15.

(f) The $100,000 balance in D's IRA account at the date of death. At D's death, the account passed to her son, S. Assume, alternatively, that:

   (i) The account was a traditional IRA and D had deducted the $30,000 contributed;

   (ii) The account was a traditional IRA and D had not deducted any of the $30,000 contributed;

   (iii) The account was a Roth IRA.

4. D, who used the cash method, died in November, year 1, owing the following amounts, all of which were paid by D's executor after D's death. Both D and D's Estate use the cash method. Which are allowable as deductions on the estate's income-tax return for the year of payment?

(a) $10,000 of business expenses of D's sole proprietorship;

(b) $2,000 of interest on acquisition indebtedness on D's personal residence;

(c) $5,000 of alimony covering the period immediately before D's death;

(d) $3,500 of state income tax for D's final taxable year;

(e) $12,000 of medical expenses incurred during D's final illness.

Section F

NON-RECOGNITION TRANSACTIONS AND (DIS)ALLOWANCE OF LOSSES

Chapter 20

LIKE-KIND EXCHANGES

Code: §§ 1031(a), (b), (c), (d), (e) & (h)(1); 1223(1). Note §§ 1001(c); 7701(a)(45).

Regulations: §§ 1.1031(a)–1; 1.1031(b)–1; 1.1031(d)–1; 1.1031(d)–2.

Cases: Leslie Co. v. Commissioner, 64 T.C. 247 (1975) (Non-acq.), aff'd, 539 F.2d 943 (3d Cir. 1976);
Jordan Marsh Co. v. Commissioner, 269 F.2d 453 (2d Cir. 1959).

Ruling: Rev. Rul. 77–297, 1977–2 C.B. 304.

1. A transferred a building (the "old" building) to B in exchange for another building (the "new" building) and, in some of the following cases, other consideration. Unless otherwise indicated, the old building had an adjusted basis of $40 (000 omitted throughout) and had been held by A for two years at the time of the exchange. Both buildings were used by A in business. In each of the following cases, determine the amount of A's (1) realized gain or loss; (2) recognized gain or loss; (3) adjusted basis (immediately after the exchange) for all property acquired; and (4) holding period for all property acquired.

(a) Both the old and new buildings had a value of $100.

(b) Same as (a), except that A held the new building as an investment.

(c) The old building was worth $100, but the new building was worth only $80, and B paid A $20 cash to equalize the exchange.

(d) The old building was worth $100, but the new building was worth only $70, and B transferred to A an automobile (worth $30) to equalize the exchange.

(e) The old building was worth $70 and the new building was worth $100. In order to equalize the exchange, A paid B $30 cash.

(f) The old building was worth $70. In order to equalize the exchange, A also transferred to B shares of X Corp. stock with a value of $30 and an adjusted basis of $50.

(g) The old building, which had an unencumbered value of $100, was subject to a non-recourse mortgage of $20. The new building was worth $80.

(h) The old building was worth $100. The new building was worth $120 but was subject to a non-recourse mortgage of $20.

(i) Same as (a), except that A's adjusted basis for the old building was $125.

(j) Same as (a), except that A's adjusted basis for the old building was $125, the value of the new building was $80, and B paid A $20 cash to equalize the exchange.

2. In each of the following problems, determine whether the exchange would qualify as "like kind" under § 1031. Unless otherwise indicated, assume that all properties are to be held for use in business or investment.

(a) An apartment building in Chicago for unimproved farm land in Idaho.

(b) A condominium in Naples, Florida (held for rental) for a condominium in Naples, Italy (also to be held for rental).

(c) A mare for a stallion.

3. T owns a business building with an adjusted basis of $500 (000 omitted throughout) and a value of $300. T plans to sell the building to P for $300 cash. P will then lease the building back to T for thirty years (which is a period shorter than the building's remaining economic life) at a fair market rental for a lease of that term. Will T be permitted to deduct the loss on the sale?

4. T, a calendar-year taxpayer, owned a business building (the T building) with an adjusted basis of $200 (000 omitted throughout) and value of $500. P wished to acquire the building, either for cash or in exchange for another building. Under a written agreement between T and P, P placed $500 in escrow on March 31 to cover payment for the T building, but T was given one year to find a suitable business building for P to purchase and exchange for the T building. If T did not locate suitable replacement property within the one-year period, the deal was to be cancelled and the escrowed funds returned to P. Nine months later, T located a suitable replacement building, which P purchased for the $500 held in escrow and promptly exchanged for the T building. Must T recognize the $300 of realized gain?

5. Same as 4, except that on March 31 T transferred the T building to P, who agreed to acquire replacement property suitable to T and placed $500 in escrow to pay for the replacement property. If no replacement property had been identified by December 31, T could require that P pay the escrowed funds to T in lieu of acquiring replacement property for exchange with T. T located replacement property on September 30. P used the escrowed funds to purchase the property and transferred the replacement property to T on October 31. Must T recognize the realized gain?

Chapter 21

INVOLUNTARY CONVERSIONS

Code: §§ 1033(a), (b) & (g); 1223(1).

Regulations: §§ 1.1033(a)–2(c)(11); 1.1033(b)–1(b).

Ruling: Rev. Rul. 64–237, 1964–2 C.B. 319.

In each of the following problems, determine the amount of the taxpayer's (1) realized gain or loss; (2) recognized gain or loss; and (3) adjusted basis (immediately after the acquisition) of any replacement property acquired. Also explain how you would go about determining the holding period of the replacement property.

1. T, a calendar-year taxpayer, owned a building (the "old building") with an adjusted basis of $60 (000 omitted throughout) and a value of $100. The old building, which was situated on leased land, was used in T's restaurant business. On June 30, year 1, the old building was completely destroyed by fire, and T received $100 in insurance proceeds. On December 31, year 3, T purchased a replacement building (also situated on leased land) in which he opened a new restaurant. T paid $110 for the replacement building. T elects non-recognition under § 1033. (How should T report the transaction on T's year–1 tax return?)

2. Same as 1, except that T invested only $85 in the replacement building.

3. Same as 1, except that T received only $80 of insurance proceeds and invested $80 in the replacement building.

4. Same as 1, except that the destroyed building had been subject to a $40 non-recourse mortgage. Under the "mortgagee clause" in T's insurance policy, the insurance company paid $40 directly to the mortgagee, paid the $60 balance to T, and T purchased the replacement building for $60 cash.

5. Same as 1, except that T's adjusted basis in the old building was $120.

6. Same as 1, except that, instead of a restaurant, the replacement building was an apartment building.

7. Same as 1, except that T is a real-estate investor, who leased the old building to another for use as a restaurant. When the old building was destroyed, T replaced it with an apartment building.

8. Same as 1, except that the old property was a beach house (T's vacation home), and T replaced the property with a mountain ski lodge (also to be used by T as a vacation home).

9. Same as 1, except that, instead of the replacement building, T purchased all of the stock in a corporation that owned as its only asset the replacement building.

10. In year 1, the state condemned 20 acres of a 100–acre parcel of unimproved farm land owned by F. F's adjusted basis in the condemned land was $40, and F received $100 as compensation for the taking. F made a timely reinvestment of the $100 condemnation proceeds by erecting an apartment building on a portion of the remaining land.

11. Same as 10, except that the apartment building was not built until year 4.

Chapter 22

SALE OF A PRINCIPAL RESIDENCE UNDER SECTION 121

Code: § 121. Review § 1033.

Regulations: §§ 1.121–2; 121–3; 121–4(a) &(b). Note § 1.263(a)–2(e).

1. T, a single person, has owned and resided in her home (Home A) for the past 30 months. T's adjusted basis is $100,000. T sells the home for $600,000 and pays a brokerage commission of $30,000 on the sale. T has not used the § 121 exclusion in the two years preceding the sale. How much of the gain must T include in gross income?

2. Same as 1, except that T is married and T's spouse also resided in Home A for the past 30 months. T and her spouse file a joint return.

3. Same as 1, except that T had used the § 121 exclusion on the sale of another residence (Home B) exactly one year before the sale of Home A. Assume, alternatively, that:

(a) T sold Home A because T thought that housing prices might collapse. T moved into an apartment.

(b) T sold Home A, which was located 15 miles from her place of employment, because she was being transferred by her employer to a new place of employment located 45 miles from Home A.

(c) T sold Home A because she had just obtained a divorce.

(d) T sold Home A (a three-story house) because T had just been diagnosed as having a serious heart condition and her doctor advised her to move to one-story house so that she would not have to climb stairs.

4. Same as 2, except that T and T's spouse, S, were married just before the sale of Home A. S never resided with T in the home, as T moved into S's home. T and S file a joint return.

5. R and R's spouse, S, owned (as joint tenants with right of survivorship) and resided in their home for many years. S died earlier this year. R has just sold the home for a gain of $650,000. What is the maximum amount that R can exclude from income on the couple's joint return?

6. Would your answer in 5 differ if R was unable to sell the home until the year following S's death?

7. P and Q (husband and wife) had resided for several years in a home owned by P. They were divorced last week, and the divorce property settlement awarded ownership of the home to Q. Q, who is now single, sells the home today at a gain of $300,000. How much of the gain can Q exclude from income?

8. L and M were divorced five years ago. Under the terms of their property settlement, M was permitted to continue to occupy the couple's residence for five years, after which time the property was to be sold and the sales proceeds divided equally between L and M. (L and M owned the property as tenants-in-common.) The property was sold in the current year at a gain of $600,000. How much, if any, of the gain can L, who is single, exclude from income?

9. Would your answer in 8 differ if L had remarried and filed a joint return with L's spouse?

10. K owned a home (K's principal residence for many years) that was completely destroyed in a hurricane. K's adjusted basis in the home was $150,000 and K received $600,000 in insurance proceeds for the destruction of the home. K purchased a replacement home for $300,000. K wants to avoid recognition of gain to the extent possible. How much gain must K, who is single, recognize? (Ignore the land, as if only the building was destroyed and replaced.) What is K's adjusted basis for the replacement home?

11. H purchased a home for $100,000 and resided there for five years as her principal residence. At the end of the fifth year, H's friend, J, moved in with her, and H sold J a half-interest (as tenant-in-common) in the home for $250,000. H and J continued to reside in the home as their principal residence for 5 more years, after which they sold it for $600,000 ($300,000 each). Both H and J are single. How much gain must H include in income in the fifth year? How much gain must each include in income in the tenth year?

12. B, a single person, has owned a home since 1998. B resided in the home as his principal residence through December 31, 2003. On January 1, 2004, B, who was no longer physically capable of self-care, moved to a state-licensed, long-term-

care facility, where he still resides. B's home was sold on December 31, 2007, at a gain of $150,000. Can B exclude the gain from income?

13. Would your answer in 12 differ if B had moved to the home of his sister, S, in 2004, and S had cared for B in the interim?

Chapter 23

WASH SALES UNDER § 1091

Code: §§ 1091(a), (b), (c) & (d); 1223(4).

Regulation: § 1.1091–2(a).

1. In January, year 1, T purchased a share of the common stock of publicly traded X Corp. for $100. The stock fell in value and on December 10, year 1, T sold the stock for $40. Because T thought the firm's long-term prospects were promising, T repurchased a share at $30 on December 20. On June 30, year 2, T sold the share for $70. What results to T?

2. Same as 1, except that T purchased the X share at $50 on December 20.

3. S purchased one share of Y Corp. common stock in January of year 1 at $55. On June 1, year 1, S purchased another share at $35. On June 5, year 1, S sold the share purchased in January for $40. What result to S?

4. P purchased one share of Z stock in January at $35. On June 1, P sold the share for $40. On June 5, P purchased another share of Z for $35. What result to P?

5. R purchased a share of Z Corp. for $60. Two weeks later, R sold the share for $50. What result to R?

6. T purchased one share of P Corp. on January 15 at $50 and another on January 20 at $55. T sold both shares on June 15 at $30 per share, but on July 1 T repurchased one share of P for $35. What result to T?

Chapter 24

CONVERSION OF PROPERTY FROM PERSONAL TO PROFIT-SEEKING USE

Code: §§162(a); 212(1) & (2); 165(a), (c)(1) & (2), 167(c), 262. Note §§ 161, 261.

Regulations: §§ 1.168(i)–4(b); 1.165–9; 1.262–1(b)(3) & (4); 1.212–1(b) & (h).

Cases: McAuley v. Commissioner, 35 T.C.M. 1236 (1976);
Horrman v. Commissioner, 17 T.C. 903 (1951);
Lowry v. United States, 384 F. Supp. 257 (D.N.H. 1974).

1. T purchased a home for $100,000, of which $20,000 was allocable to the lot and $80,000 to the house. T resided in the home for several years. When the home had a value of $175,000, of which $150,000 was allocable to the house, T moved out and rented the property to a tenant. What is T's basis for depreciation of the house?

2. What result if several years later, and after properly deducting $25,000 of depreciation, T sells the property for an amount realized of $200,000, of which $175,000 is allocable to the house?

3. Assume that T purchased the home for $100,000, of which $20,000 was allocable to the lot and $80,000 to the house, T resided in the home for several years, and then rented it when the house was worth $60,000 and the lot $20,000. What is T's basis for depreciation?

4. What result in 3 if several years later, and after properly deducting $30,000 of depreciation, T sells the property for:

(a) $95,000, of which $25,000 is allocable to the lot?

(b) $45,000, of which $25,000 is allocable to the lot?

(c) $55,000, of which $25,000 is allocable to the lot?

5. Several years ago, L purchased a home for $100,000 (of which $20,000 was allocable to the land) and used it as his principal residence. Last December, L moved out, and on January 1 of the current year L put the property up for sale. L received no offers, however, and on July 1 L offered the property for either sale or rent. On November 1, L sold the property for $75,000, of which $20,000 was attributable to the land. On January 1 and July 1, the property was worth $80,000, of which $20,000 was allocable to the lot. For simplicity, assume that depreciation, if allowable, would be $250 per month (i.e., ignore § 168).

(a) As of what date can L begin deducting the maintenance expenses with respect to the property?

(b) As of what date can L begin deducting depreciation on the house?

(c) Can L deduct the loss on the sale?

(d) Can you reconcile your answers in (b) and (c)?

6. T, a solo practitioner, purchases an automobile for $20,000 and uses the vehicle 75 percent for business and 25 percent for personal use. She properly deducts $8,000 of depreciation and then sells the car for $8,000. What result to T?

Chapter 25

LOSSES ON TRANSACTIONS BETWEEN RELATED PARTIES

Code: § 267(a)(1), (b), (c), (d) & (g).

Regulations: §§ 1.267(a)–1(c); 1.267(c)–1(a); 1.267(d)–1(a) & (c).

Case: McWilliams v. Commissioner, 331 U.S. 694 (1947).

1. Suppose S sells investment property at a loss in a bona fide sale at fair market value. Would S's loss be allowed if, alternatively, the purchaser was:

(a) S's daughter?

(b) S's adopted daughter?

(c) S's niece?

(d) S's father-in-law?

(e) S's registered domestic partner?

(f) A corporation in which each of the following persons owns 200 shares: S's spouse, S's daughter, S's aunt, S's son-in-law, and a trust of which S and S's daughter are each fifty-percent beneficiaries?

(g) A trust for the benefit of S's niece? S was grantor of the trust.

(h) A trust for the benefit of S's daughter? S's spouse was grantor of the trust.

(i) S's mother and step-father as tenants-in-common?

2. On June 1, year 1, P sells investment property to her adult child, C, for $100 (the property's value). P had an adjusted basis of $150 for the property. The sale is bona fide. What result to P?

3. What result to C (in problem 2) if C also holds the property for investment and on March 31, year 2, sells it to an unrelated party for:

(a) $75?

(b) $130?

(c) $180?

4. Suppose instead that the property purchased from P had been land held by P (and then C) as an investment. In year 5, C exchanges the land for other land (worth $200) to be held for investment. In year 7, C sells the land acquired in the exchange for $250. What result to C?

5. Suppose instead that on March 31, year 2, C gives the property (then worth $120) to her adult child, GC.

(a) What result if GC sells the property in year 4 for $180.

(b) What result if instead C had transferred the property to her former spouse, X, in accordance with the parties' divorce decree, and X later sells the property for $180?

6. For several years, R has owned a share of X Corp. common stock, which he had purchased for $100. On April 1 of the current year, he sold the share for $40. That same day, he purchased for $40 a share of X Corp. common as custodian for his minor child, S, under the Uniform Transfers to Minors Act. Both transactions were effected by R's broker through the New York Stock Exchange.

(a) What result to R?

(b) What result to S if, after attaining age 21, S sells the share for $90?

(c) What result to R if he had purchased the share for the custodial account on May 5 of the current year?

7. Why does section 267 disallow losses even on bona fide sales to a related party when the sale is made at FMV?

Section G

CAPITAL GAINS AND LOSSES

Chapter 26

THE SIGNIFICANCE OF
CHARACTERIZATION

Code: §§ 1221(a); 1222; 1211(b); 1212(b); 61(a)(3); 62(a)(3). Note §§ 1231; 64; 65; 408(m); 1(h)(1)–(7) & (11).

1. S is in the 35–percent tax bracket for ordinary income and had no capital losses for the year. What tax rate would apply to the capital gains recognized by S on each of the following transactions?

(a) Sale of New York Stock Exchange listed securities held for 6 months.

(b) Sale of New York Stock Exchange securities held for 18 months.

(c) Sale of a building (held by S as an investment for several years) for $500,000. S had purchased the building for $400,000 and had properly deducted $250,000 of straight-line depreciation thereon. (Ignore the land, as if only the building were bought and sold.).

(d) Sale of S's coin collection (all the coins had been held for more than a year).

(e) Sale of S's yacht (used by S for recreation for the past 3 years).

2. On their joint return, H and W have taxable income of $150,000, which includes $15,000 of long-term capital gain, $3,000 of long-term capital loss, and $2,000 of short-term capital loss. They have no dividend income, and the capital gain and losses are from New York Stock Exchange securities transactions. Using the tax-bracket figures set forth in Appendix B, determine their tax liability before credits.

3. T, an individual, has ordinary gross income of $120,000 and has capital gains and losses in the amounts specified below. In each alternative case, determine (i) T's gross and adjusted gross income; and (ii) the amount and character of any capital-loss carryover to the next year.

| (a) | long-term capital gain | $10,000 |
| | long-term capital loss | $12,000 |

| (b) | long-term capital loss | $8,000 |
| | short-term capital loss | $5,000 |

(c)	long-term capital gain	$10,000
	long-term capital loss	$ 5,000
	short-term capital gain	$ 4,000
	short-term capital loss	$14,000

(d)	long-term capital gain	$6,000
	long-term capital loss	$4,000
	short-term capital gain	$2,000
	short-term capital loss	$5,000

4. Where both short-term and long-term capital loss is available to offset ordinary income, Congress determined that the short-term loss should be so applied before the long-term loss. Suppose instead that Congress wanted long-term loss to be applied before short-term loss. Could that be accomplished by changing a single word in the statute? Explain.

5. Evaluate each of the following policy justifications for taxing capital gains at a lower rate than ordinary income:

(a) The lower rate of tax on capital gains is necessary in order to limit the tax resulting from the "bunching" in a single year of gains accruing over many years.

(b) Because of inflation, capital gains often contain an element of illusory gain. The lower rate of tax on capital gains mitigates the effect of taxing people on these illusory gains.

(c) The lower rate of tax encourages people to realize or "unlock" their capital gains.

(d) A lower rate of tax on capital gains encourages taxpayers to save and invest.

Chapter 27

THE SALE OR EXCHANGE OF
CAPITAL ASSETS

A. THE CAPITAL-ASSET DEFINITION

Code: § 1221(a). Note §§ 197(c), (d)(1)(A) & (f)(7); 1235(a) & (b)(1).

In each of the following problems, the taxpayer owns the asset described. Determine whether the asset is a capital asset.

1. The residence in which the taxpayer resides.

2. 100 shares of Microsoft stock held by a full-time practicing lawyer.

3. Land held for use in business.

4. Automobiles held for sale by a Chevrolet dealer.

5. An automobile used exclusively in business.

6. A painting, held by the artist who painted it.

7. A painting, held by the adult child of the artist who painted it. The child received it by gift from her parent, the artist.

8. Same as 7, except the child received the painting by bequest when her parent, the artist, died.

9. A patent held by the professional inventor who developed it.

10. A single residential rental property held by a full-time practicing lawyer.

11. A lawyer's accounts receivable arising from the lawyer's performance of legal services; the lawyer uses the cash method of accounting.

12. Office supplies owned by the lawyer in 11.

13. The self-created goodwill of a business.

14. The purchased goodwill of a business.

15. Ten building lots held for sale through real-estate brokers. The lots were part of a 100–acre parcel of farm land that the taxpayer, a full-time practicing lawyer, had inherited from her father 6 years ago. When she first acquired the land, which is located just outside the limits of University City, the taxpayer had rented it out for use as a farm. Two years ago, the taxpayer subdivided 20 acres, installed streets, drainage, water, sewage and electricity, and sold the land (through brokers) to 20 different purchasers for use as building lots. After making similar improvements to another 10 acres last year, the taxpayer subdivided that subparcel into another 10 lots, all of which were sold through brokers to different buyers. Earlier this year, she made similar improvements to another 10 acres, which she subdivided into the 10 lots now being offered for sale.

B. THE SALE-OR-EXCHANGE REQUIREMENT

Code: §§ 1271(a); 331(a); 165(g)(1) & (2); 166(d); 1241; 1235(a) & (b). Note § 1234A.

1. In the absence of a special statutory rule treating the disposition as a sale or exchange, which of the following recognized gains result from a sale or exchange?

(a) M owned a building with an adjusted basis of $40 (000 omitted throughout) and a value of $100. The building was completely destroyed by fire. The building was fully insured, and the insurer paid M $100 for the loss.

(b) M's building (in (a)) was condemned by the state under its power of eminent domain. The state paid M $100 as compensation for the taking.

(c) C owned a $100 promissory note of which D was the maker. C's adjusted basis in the note was $40. D pays C $100 cash, and C marks the note "paid in full."

(d) D satisfied the note (in (c)) by transferring to C corporate stock with an adjusted basis of $50 and a value of $100.

(e) O owned property (adjusted basis of $50) subject to a non-recourse debt of $100. The property had fallen in value to $80, and O conveyed the property to the mortgagee.

2. T owned a non-depreciable capital asset (held for investment for several years) with an adjusted basis of $40. Determine whether each of the following alternative dispositions of the asset results in capital gain or capital loss.

(a) The property is land. T exchanged the property for another parcel of land to be held for investment. The property received has a value of $90, and T also received $10 cash to equalize the exchange.

(b) The property is a corporate bond. The issuer retired the bond by paying T the $100 face amount of the bond.

(c) The property is stock in X Corporation. X is liquidated and T receives $100 in the liquidating distribution.

(d) The property is stock in Y Corporation. Y goes into bankruptcy, and the stock becomes worthless.

(e) The property is a note of which T's son-in-law, S, is the maker. T, who is not in the business of lending money, received the note when he lent S $40 to start a business. The business failed, and S, who is hopelessly insolvent, is unable to repay.

(f) The property is a claim for breach of contract, fraud and misrepresentation, which T purchased from a third party. T receives $100 in full settlement of the claim.

3.   T receives $100 from her landlord in consideration of cancelling T's apartment lease. How should T treat the payment?

4. P, a professional inventor, transfers all substantial rights to a patent to L. L will pay P an annual royalty based upon L's sales of the product covered by the patent. How should P treat the royalty payments?

Chapter 28

QUASI-CAPITAL GAINS AND LOSSES— SECTION 1231

Code: §§ 1221(a)(2); 1231; 1222(1)–(4). Note § 1033(a)(2).

In each of the following problems, determine the character of the recognized gain or allowable loss. In each case, these are all of T's *realized* gains and losses for the year. No asset is held for sale to customers in the ordinary course of business nor subject to depreciation recapture. Unless otherwise indicated, assume that T had held each asset for more than one year and that § 1033 does not apply to any involuntary conversion.

1. $10,000 gain on sale of land used in business.

2. $10,000 loss on sale of equipment used in business.

3. $10,000 gain on condemnation of land used in business. How would your answer differ if T had held the land for only 8 months?

4. $10,000 loss on condemnation of land used in business. How would your answer differ if T had held the land for only 8 months?

5. $10,000 gain on condemnation of land held for investment. How would your answer differ if T had held the land for only 8 months?

6. $10,000 loss on condemnation of land held for investment. How would your answer differ if T had held the land for only 8 months?

7. $10,000 gain on condemnation of T's vacation home.

8. $10,000 loss on condemnation of T's vacation home.

9. $10,000 gain on the destruction by fire of T's business building. How would your answer differ if T had held the building for only eight months?

10. $10,000 loss on the destruction by fire of T's business equipment.

11. $10,000 gain on sale of land held for use in business and $5,000 loss on sale of equipment used in business.

12. $10,000 loss on sale of equipment used in business and $5,000 gain on condemnation of land held for investment, and T:

(a) made a timely reinvestment of the entire condemnation proceeds under § 1033;

(b) did not make a timely reinvestment under § 1033.

13. $10,000 gain on sale of land used in business and $5,000 loss on destruction by fire of business equipment.

14. $10,000 loss on sale of land used in business and $15,000 gain on destruction by fire of business equipment.

15. $10,000 gain on sale of a business building, $10,000 gain on destruction by fire of a business building and $5,000 loss on hurricane damage to business equipment.

16. $10,000 gain on sale of a business building, $5,000 gain on destruction by fire of a business building, and $10,000 loss on hurricane damage to business equipment.

17. $10,000 loss on sale of a business building, $25,000 gain on destruction by fire of a business building, and $10,000 loss on hurricane damage to business equipment.

18. $5,000 loss on sale of a business building, $6,000 gain on the condemnation of a building held for investment, and $10,000 loss on hurricane damage to business equipment.

In the following problems, characterize the recognized gains and allowable losses. In each case assume that (1) these are the taxpayer's only recognized gains and losses for the year, (2) each asset had a long-term holding period, (3) the taxpayer engaged in no § 1231 transactions before year 1, and (4) no asset is subject to depreciation recapture under § 1245 or § 1250.

19. In year 1, T recognized a $100,000 loss on the sale of land used in business and a $50,000 gain on the destruction of a building held for investment. In year 2, T recognized a $20,000 gain on the sale of a business building. In year 3, T recognized a $40,000 gain on the sale of a business building.

20. In year 1, S recognized a $100,000 gain on the sale of land used in business and a $50,000 loss on the condemnation of an investment asset. In year 2, T recognized a $100,000 loss on the sale of a business building.

Chapter 29

DEPRECIATION RECAPTURE AND RELATED ISSUES

A. SECTION 1245

Code: § 1245. Review §§ 179(a); 1001(a), (b) & (c); 1012; 1011(a); 1231; 1015(a); 1014(a) & (b); 1031(a), (b), (c) & (d).

Regulations: §§ 1.179–1(f)(1); 1.1245–1(b) & (d); 1.1245–2(c)(1)(i) & (iv); 1.1245–2(c)(4).

General facts for problems 1–7: In year 1, T purchased for $150 (000 omitted throughout) moveable equipment for use in her business and properly deducted $90 of depreciation before disposing of the equipment in year 3. Unless otherwise indicated, T made no election under § 179 when the equipment was acquired. Assume that when a party disposes of the equipment, the disposition is the party's only disposition of property for that year. Determine the amount and character of the various parties' recognized gain or allowable loss.

1. T sells the equipment in year 3 for $200.

2. T sells the equipment in year 3 for $45.

3. In year 3, T gives the equipment (then worth $75) to her daughter, D, who uses the equipment for personal use and then sells it in year 5 for:

   (a) $100.

   (b) $50.

4. In year 3, T gives the equipment (then worth $75) to her daughter, D, who uses the equipment in her business, properly deducts another $15 of depreciation, and then sells the equipment in year 5 for:

   (a) $65.

(b) $25.

5. In year 3, T dies and the equipment passes to her estate. At the time of T's death, the equipment is worth $65. T's estate continues T's business and properly deducts $20 of additional depreciation before selling the equipment in year 5 for $75.

6. In year 3, T exchanged the equipment (then worth $80) for equipment of like kind to be used in T's business. The new equipment had a value of $70 and T received $10 of cash to equalize the exchange.

7. Same as 1, except that T had properly elected under § 179 to deduct $100 of the cost of the equipment in the year of purchase. At the time of the sale, T had also been allowed depreciation of $30.

B. SECTION 1250

Code: §§ 1250(a)(1)(A) & (B)(v), (b)(1) & (3), (c), (d)(1), (2) & (4). Note §§ 1(h)(6) & (h)(1)(D).

1. In year 1, F spent $200,000 to build a barn for use in his farming business. Assume that F properly deducted $80,000 of depreciation under the 150% declining balance method, which is applicable to farm buildings. F sold the barn in year 8 for $220,000. (Ignore the land, as if only the barn had been sold.) Straight-line depreciation over the period the barn was held by F would have been $35,000. The barn sale was F's only property disposition for the year. F's tax rate on ordinary income is 35 percent. Determine F's recognized gain and the tax rate applicable to each component of the gain.

C. SECTION 1239

Code: §§ 1239(a), (b) & (c); 267(c)(2), (4) & (5).

Regulation: § 1.1245–6(f).

In each of the following problems, determine (1) the seller's recognized gain, (2) the character of the gain, and (3) the tax rate applicable to each component of the gain. Assume in each case that the seller is in the 35% bracket for ordinary income and that the sale is the seller's only property disposition for the year.

1. Several years ago, M paid $300,000 for an office building for use in her business, properly deducted $100,000 of straight-line depreciation, and sold it in the current year for $550,000. The purchaser plans to use the building in business. (Ignore the land as if only the building were purchased and sold.). Alternatively, the purchaser is:

(a) X Corporation, of which M is the sole shareholder;

(b) Y Corporation, of which M's son, S, is sole shareholder;

(c) D, who is M's daughter;

(d) F, who is M's spouse.

2. S purchased depreciable business equipment for $100,000, properly deducted $60,000 of depreciation, and sold it for $120,000 (its value) to a trust of which S's wife, W, was entitled to the income for life. The trust used the equipment in its business.

3. Several years ago D paid $400,000 for a large tract of land and held it as an investment. In the current year, D sells the land for $1,000,000 to L Corporation, which plans to divide the parcel and sell it for building lots (i.e., the land will be held for sale in the ordinary course of L's business). All of L's stock is owned by D.

Chapter 30

OTHER CHARACTERIZATION ISSUES

A. THE ARROWSMITH DOCTRINE

Case: Arrowsmith v. Commissioner, 344 U.S. 6 (1952).

1. In year 1, T sold all of the stock in a closely held corporation to B for $500,000 cash. T's adjusted basis for the stock, which he had held for several years, was $200,000. In year 3, B sued T for making fraudulent representations in connection with the stock sale. T settled the matter by paying B $100,000 cash. How should T treat the $100,000 payment?

2. What results in 1 if, instead of stock, the asset sold was a § 1231 asset that was not subject to depreciation recapture? For simplicity, assume that T has not engaged in any other § 1231 transaction (in any year).

3. In year 1, C, the chief executive officer of publicly held P Corporation, purchased and sold P stock within a six-month period. Under § 16(b) of the Securities Exchange Act of 1934, C was required to pay to P his profit on the transaction. C made the payment in year 2. What tax result to C?

B. BAD DEBTS AND WORTHLESS SECURITIES

Code: §§ 165(a), (b), (c) & (g); 166(a), (b), (d) & (e), 1244(a), (b) (c)(1) & (3), (d)(3). Review §§ 1222(2) & (4); 1271(a).

Regulations: §§ 166–1(c) & (e); 1.166–2(a), (b) & (c); 1.166–5(a) & (b); 1.166–9(a), (b), (d), (e)(1) & (2).

Cases: Putnam v. Commissioner, 352 U.S. 82 (1956); United States v. Generes, 405 U.S. 93 (1972).

1. Two years ago, S, a cash-method taxpayer, was persuaded by a friend to make a $50,000 unsecured loan at market-rate interest to closely held X Corporation. (S is not in the business of lending money and is not a shareholder

of X.) X did not prosper, and, though it kept interest payments current, it was never able to pay any principal on the note.

(a) Last week S sold the X note for $20,000. What is the character of S's loss?

(b) What result if S agreed to accept $20,000 from X in full satisfaction of the note, and X paid S the $20,000?

(c) What result to S if X went into bankruptcy, was unable to pay its unsecured creditors, and was discharged from liability?

(d) What result to S if S's claim for $5,000 of unpaid interest for prior years was also discharged in the bankruptcy proceeding?

(e) What result in (d) if S had been an accrual-method taxpayer?

2. T lent $10,000 to his brother-in-law, B, to assist him in starting a new business. The business failed, the debt was discharged in B's bankruptcy, and T was therefore unable to collect the principal due on the loan.

(a) Is T allowed a deduction for the loss?

(b) What if a bank had lent B the money and T had served (without consideration) as guarantor on the loan. When B took bankruptcy, T was required to pay the bank the $10,000 of principal. Is T allowed a deduction?

3. R purchased for $150,000 stock in Z Corporation from another shareholder. Three years later, Z goes into bankruptcy and the stock becomes worthless.

(a) Describe the tax consequences to R.

(b) Suppose instead that R, a single person, was one of five shareholders who organized Z. Each contributed $150,000 cash in exchange for stock when the corporation was organized. Z derived all of its gross receipts from its active business. Although Z later tried to raise more equity capital, it was never able to do so. Z went into bankruptcy, and R's stock became worthless. What tax result to R?

(c) Suppose that P, another shareholder of Z Corporation, was employed by the corporation. When the firm began experiencing financial difficulties, P lent Z $25,000 at market-rate interest. P thought the money (along with other funds being lent by other employees) might keep Z in business and preserve P's $75,000 a year job with the firm. When the firm failed, it also owed P $5,000 of back wages. Z was unable to repay either amount. P, a cash-method taxpayer, originally had paid $150,000 for his Z stock. What result to P?

C. SALE OF A GOING BUSINESS

Code: §§ 1060(a) & (c); 197(a), (b), (c), (d)(1), (f)(1), (3) & (7).

Regulations: §§ 1.263(a)–4(c)(4), Ex. 5; 1.263(a)–5(g); 1.1060–1(a)(1), (b)(1), (2)(ii) & (7), (c), (d), Ex. 2.

1. S, an individual, owned a sole proprietorship consisting of the assets listed below. The value figures shown below have been determined by an appropriate allocation of the total purchase price (all figures are in $ with 000 omitted throughout):

	Adjusted Basis	Value	Notes
Accounts receivable	0	$100	1
Supplies	0	40	2
Business equipment	40	100	3
Building	100	200	4
Land	120	140	
Goodwill	0	120	
	260	700	

Notes:

1. S uses the cash method of accounting.

2. S deducted the $50 cost of the supplies in the preceding year.

3. S purchased the equipment for $85 and has properly deducted $45 of depreciation thereon.

4. S purchased the building (exclusive of the land) for $160 and has properly deducted $60 of straight-line depreciation thereon.

All of the capital and § 1231 assets have a long-term holding period.

(a) S sold the business to P, an individual, for $700. This is S's only transaction for the year. What is the amount and character of S's income or loss?

(b) What is P's basis for the assets acquired?

(c) Would your answers in (a) and (b) be affected if S and P had entered into an agreement as to the allocation of the total consideration among the various assets?

(d) How would your answer differ if S's business had been incorporated, S, the sole shareholder, had a basis of $260 and long-term holding period for the stock, and P, an individual, purchased S's stock for $700?

2. In connection with the transaction in 1(a), P paid S $150,000 for S's agreement not to compete with P for five years in the same line of business in the area in which the business was located.

(a) What result to P?

(b) To S?

3. Five years have elapsed since the transaction in 2. P wants to know if she can write off as a loss her remaining adjusted basis in the non-compete covenant since it has no further economic value. What say you?

4. P and S both incurred attorney's fees in connection with the sale and purchase of the business. How should the attorney's fees be treated for tax purposes?

D. SALE OF RIGHTS TO INCOME

Code: §§ 1234A; 1241; 273; 1001(e).

Regulations: §§ 1.263(a)–4(d)(7); § 1.167(a)–3(b)(1)(iii); 1.1014–4(a); 1.1015–1(b).

Cases: Hort v. Commissioner, 313 U.S. 28 (1941);
McAllister v. Commissioner, 157 F.2d 235 (2d. Cir. 1946);
Lattera v. Commissioner, 477 F.3d 399 (3d Cir. 2006);
Estate of Stranahan v. Commissioner, 472 F.2d 867 (6th Cir. 1973).

1. T, a tenant of a business building owned by L, paid L $100,000 as consideration for cancellation of a lease on the building. The lease had a remaining term of 20 years.

(a) What result to L?

(b) To T?

(c) What result to L if T paid the $100,000 as consideration for L's releasing T from a requirement that the premises be restored upon termination of the lease?

2. Suppose in 1 that L paid T $100,000 as consideration for cancellation of the lease with a remaining term of 20 years?

(a) What result to T?

(b) To L?

3. L won the state lottery, which entitles her payments of $100,000 a year for 25 years. After receiving the first payment, L sold her right to the remaining payments for $1,000,000 cash. What result to L?

4. D dies and bequeaths farm land to A for life, remainder to B. At D's death, the land was worth $1,000,000. (D's estate was valued at the date of death for the purpose of the federal estate tax.)

(a) At D's death, the actuarial present value of A's interest is $600,000. Can A amortize that amount over A's remaining life expectancy of 30 years?

(b) Suppose that, immediately after D's death, A sold her interest to an unrelated party, P, for $600,000. What result to A? To P?

(c) What result if A and B simultaneously sold their interests to P, who paid A $600,000 and B $400,000?

5. F has a large net operating loss that is going to expire this year. He does not have sufficient income to fully utilize the loss. To increase his income for the year, he offers to sell to his son, S, his right to the next two years' dividends on 100,000 shares of a publicly traded stock owned by F. The expected dividend for the two-year period is $400,000 ($200,000 per year). S purchases the right to the dividends for $360,000. What result to F?

Section H

DEFERRED PAYMENT-SALES

Chapter 31

INSTALLMENT SALES UNDER § 453

A. IN GENERAL

Code: §§ 453(a), (b), (c), (d)(1), (f), (i), (j), (k) & (*l*)(1). Note §§ 1239; 1(h)(6)(A)(i). Review § 1031(a) & (b).

Regulations: Temp. Treas. Reg. § 15a.453–1(a), (b), (c)(1) & (3). Note §§ 1.1001–1(g); 1.453–12(a); Prop. Treas. Reg. § 1.453–1(f).

1. In year 1, S sells to P some land that S had held for investment for several years. S's adjusted basis in the land was $100 (000 omitted throughout). S sells the property to P for $400, payable $100 down and $100 per year in each of years 2 through 4. The contract of sale provides for market-rate interest on the deferred payments, S and P are not related, and S makes no election under § 453(d). P makes all required payments on time. Determine the amount, timing and character of S's recognized gain.

2. Same as 1, except that S makes an election under § 453(d)(1).

3. Same as 1, except that S pays a brokerage fee of $20 on the sale.

4. Same as 1, except that the land had been held by S for use in business.

5. Same as 1, except that the land had been held by S for sale to customers in the ordinary course of business.

6. Same as 1, except that the property sold was moveable equipment that S had used in business. S had purchased the equipment for $300 and had properly deducted $200 of depreciation up to the time of the sale.

7. Same as 1, except that P's note was guaranteed by P's brother, B.

8. Same as 1, except that P's note was secured by an irrevocable standby letter of credit issued by P's bank.

9. Same as 1, except that the property sold was stock in a publicly traded corporation.

10. Same as (1), except that S's basis in the land was $600.

11. O purchased for $400 a building (and the land on which it was located) to be used in O's business. The $400 purchase price was allocable $300 to the building and $100 to the land. Over the next few years, O properly deducted $150 of straight-line depreciation on the building, and then sold the property for $600, of which $150 was allocable to the land. The $600 was payable $120 down in the year of sale (year 1) and $120 for each of the following four years (years 2–5), with market-rate interest on the deferred balance. All amounts of principal and interest were paid when due. This was O's only property transaction for years 1–5. Determine the amount and character of O's gain for each year and the tax rate applicable to each component of the gain.

12. A transferred a building used in business (the "old" building) to B in exchange for a building (also to be used in A's business) with a value of $350 and $150 cash, payable $15 down and $15 per year for each of the following nine years. A's adjusted basis for the old building was $200.

(a) Determine (i) the amount, timing and character of A's recognized gain and (ii) A's basis for the new building.

(b) Same as (a), except that A's adjusted basis for the old building was $400.

B. TRANSACTIONS WITH RELATED PERSONS

Code: §453(e) & (g). Review § 1239(a), (b) & (c).

1. On March 31, year 1, M sells land (a capital asset held for several years) to her daughter, D, for $500, payable $100 down and $100 per year (plus market rate interest) on March 31 of years 2–5. In January, year 2, and before making the year–2 payment, D sells the land to an unrelated party for $550 cash. D continues to make all principal and interest payments when due. M's adjusted basis in the land was $200. What result to M and D?

2. Would your answer in 1 differ if D re-sold the property in April, year 3 (after having made timely payment of the amounts due in years 2 and 3)?

3. Would your answer in 1 differ if M had died in December, year 1?

4. S owned a business building with an adjusted basis of $200 and a value of $500. S sold the building to P Corporation for $500, payable $100 down and $100 per year (plus market-rate interest) for each of the next 4 years. S owns 60 percent of P's stock. (Ignore the land, as if only the building were purchased and sold.) What result to S?

5. Would your answer in 4 differ if S had instead sold P unimproved land (held for investment for several years), which P planned to subdivide and sell to customers in the ordinary course of business?

C. PROPERTY SUBJECT TO LIABILITY

Code: Review § 453(a), (b) & (c).

Regulation: Temp. Treas. Reg. § 15a.453–1(b)(2), (3) & (5), Exs. (2) & (3).

1. S owns a non-depreciable capital asset (held for several years) with a basis of $260 and a value of $500, but which is subject to a $200 mortgage incurred by S in purchasing the property. In year 1, S sells the property to P, who takes subject to the mortgage, and agrees to pay S $100 cash down and $100 (plus market-rate interest) in each of years 2 and 3. What is the amount and timing of S's gain recognized?

2. Would your answer in 1 differ if S's basis for the asset had been $100?

3. Would your answer in 1 differ if S had incurred the $200 mortgage liability in anticipation of the sale to P, and S had used the loan proceeds for a purpose unrelated to the property?

Chapter 32

DISPOSITION OF INSTALLMENT OBLIGATIONS

Code: §§ 453B(a), (b), (c), (f) & (g); 453A(d)(1), (2) & (3). Review §§ 1015(a); 1014(a), (b) & (c); 691(a); 1041(a); 1223(2); 1271(a).

Regulations: §§ 1.102–1(e); 1.691(a)–5(a).

Ruling: Rev. Rul. 79–371, 1979–2 C.B. 294.

General Facts: In year 1, S, a ccash-method taxpayer, sold property (a non-depreciable capital asset with an adjusted basis of $200) to P for $1,000, payable $500 down and $100 per year (plus market-rate interest) payable at the end of each of years 2 through 6. P makes all principal and interest payments on time. S properly reported the gain under the installment method of § 453.

1. What is S's basis in the $500 installment obligation immediately following the sale?

2. What is the amount and character of S's recognized gain if later in year 1 S sells the obligation for:

(a) $530?

(b) $480?

3. In each of the following cases, S transfers the note in year 1 when its value is $480. Describe the results of the transfer by S. How should the transferee treat the payments received on the note?

(a) S gave the installment obligation to S's child, C.

(b) S gave the installment obligation to S's child, P, the purchaser of the property.

(c) S dies and bequeaths the obligation to C.

(d) S dies and bequeaths the obligation to P, the purchaser of the property.

(e) S transferred the note to S's former spouse, F, as part of a divorce property settlement?

4. What result (in 1) if, immediately after the sale, S borrowed $600 from a bank and pledged the installment note as security for the loan? What result as S receives payments on the note?

Section I

PERSONAL DEDUCTIONS AND CREDITS

Chapter 33

MEDICAL EXPENSES

Code: § 213. Note §§ 104(a)(3); 2053(a)(3).

Regulation: § 1.213-1.

Case: Ferris v. Commissioner, 582 F.2d 1112 (7th Cir. 1978);

Rulings: Rev. Rul. 2003–57, 2003–1 C.B. 959;
Rev. Rul. 2003–58, 2003–1 C.B. 959.

1. T, a cash-method taxpayer, has gross income as follows:

Salary	$90,000
Dividends	10,000

T also paid the following expenses:

Charitable contributions	5,000
Medical expenses	12,000

Before the end of the year T received an insurance reimbursement for $2,000 of the medical expense. T pays the premiums on the policy. All of the medical expenses were incurred for T's medical care.

(a) To what extent are T's medical expenses deductible if T itemizes deductions?

(b) How would your answer change if T used the accrual method and, in addition to the $12,000 of medical expenses that were incurred and paid in the current year, T had also incurred an additional $5,000 of medical expenses (but had not paid the additional $5,000 before the end of the year)?

(c) How would your answer to (a) change if a subsequent audit of T's return resulted in a $10,000 increase in T's gross and adjusted gross income?

2. A pays some qualifying medical expenses incurred by others. Subject to the § 213(b) floor, can A deduct the amounts paid in the current year on behalf of:

(a) A's mother, M? A provides over half of M's support because M's only source of income is a (taxable) annual pension of $24,000.

(b) A's late husband, D, who died last year? A remarried in the current year.

(c) A's 12-year old son, S? A is divorced, and S is a dependent of A's former husband, X, with whom S resides and from whom S receives a majority of his support.

3. Do expenditures for the following items qualify for deduction under § 213?

(a) Contact lenses.

(b) Non-prescription nicotine gum or patches designed to help the taxpayer stop smoking.

(c) A wig for a taxpayer whose hair loss was caused by treatment for disease.

(d) A weight-loss program.

(e) Aspirin (taken on the recommendation of a physician).

(f) Non-prescription insulin and blood-sugar-test kits.

(g) Teeth whitening.

(h) The cost of a prescribed drug that was ordered by the taxpayer from a Canadian on-line pharmacy.

(i) A one-month stay at an alcoholism rehabilitation center.

(m) A face lift.

(n) Breast-reconstruction surgery following a mastectomy.

(j) Birth-control pills.

(k) Installing railings and support bars in the bathroom of a wheelchair-bound person.

(l) Transportation to a tertiary-care hospital located 250 miles from the taxpayer's home.

(m) Meals and lodging while receiving out-patient treatment at the tertiary-care center.

(n) Meals and lodging paid on behalf of a family member who accompanies the taxpayer to the tertiary-care center.

(o) Medical insurance.

(p) Long-term care insurance.

(q) Treatment by a chiropractor.

(r) The 1.45–percent Medicare tax on an employee's salary.

(s) Medicare Part D insurance (covering prescription-drug benefits).

4. T has a serious heart condition. Upon the recommendation of his physician, T installed an elevator in his home so that he would not have to climb stairs. Installation of the elevator cost $15,000. The value of T's home immediately before the installation was $200,000. Immediately after the installation, the value of the home was $205,000.

(a) To what extent, if any, does the cost of the elevator qualify as a medical expense?

(b) T's adjusted gross income for the year is $100,000. How much of the $15,000 cost should T include in his adjusted basis for the home? (For simplicity, assume that T paid no other medical expenses for the year.)

5. In year 1, S paid $10,000 of medical expenses. S's adjusted gross income for the year was $100,000 and her itemized deductions other than medical expenses totaled $15,000. In year 2, S received partial reimbursement for the expenses from her insurer. S pays the premiums on the medical-insurance policy from her after-tax income. How much should S include in gross income in year 2 if the amount of the reimbursement was:

(a) $2,000?

(b) $6,000?

6. D died in December of last year. In the month preceding his death, D incurred unreimbursed medical expense of $25,000. D's executor paid the expense from D's estate early this year. Can the estate deduct the medical expense under § 213? Explain.

Chapter 34

CHARITABLE CONTRIBUTIONS

Code: § 170(a), (b), (c), (d)(1), (e)(1), (f)(2), (3), (6) & (8), (i), (j) & (*l*). Note § 1011(b). Review §§ 1221(a)(3); 1231(b)(1)(C); 1245(a) & (b)(1).

Regulations: §§ 1.170A–1(a), (b), (c)(1), (g), (h)(1), (2) & (3); 1.170A–4(b)(3); 1.170A–13(f)(8)(i).

1. In the current year, T, an individual, made the following cash payments. How much of each payment is deductible as a charitable contribution? (Ignore the percentage limits of § 170(b). Assume that T can substantiate the contributions in the manner required by the Code and regulations.)

(a) $15,000 paid to Y University as tuition for T's niece, N. N comes from an impecunious, single-parent home, and her immediate family is not able to assist her financially.

(b) $5,000 to T's church for the saying of masses for T's late mother and father.

(c) $1,000 to the American Red Cross to be used for tsunami relief in Indonesia.

(d) $500 to the Unity Party, which, in the next presidential election, expects to nominate a ticket consisting of a member of one of the major political parties for president and a member of the other major party for vice president.

(e) $1,000 to the Veterans of Foreign Wars.

(f) $20,000 to State University. Donors of $5,000 or more are entitled to priority seating at the school's home football games, nearly all of which sell out. (The actual cost of tickets is extra.)

(g) $2,500,000 to University Law School to endow the "T Family Chair in Federal Tax Law."

(h) $500 for a ticket to the University Medical School "Have A Heart" Gala, which raises money for the school's heart-research program. The gala includes a dinner and dance, the reasonable cost of which would be $100 per ticket.

(i) $100 to the local public-radio station. In return for the contribution, T received a coffee mug emblazoned with the station's logo and call letters.

2. D, an individual, has today made the following gifts to an organization qualifying under § 170(c) and described in § 170(b)(1)(A). In each of the following cases, determine the amount deductible by D. Ignore the effect of the percentage limits of § 170(b). D can substantiate the amount of each contribution.

(a) Shares of X Corporation stock, which D had purchased two years ago for $40,000. The stock was worth $100,000 at the time of the gift.

(b) Same as (a), except that D purchased the stock eight months ago.

(c) Same as (a), except that the stock was worth only $30,000 on the date of the gift.

(d) A business computer that D had purchased several years ago for $5,000 and on which D had properly deducted $3,000 of depreciation. The equipment was worth $10,000 at the time of the gift. The donee, a university, planned to install the computer in a faculty office.

(e) Same as (d), except that the university planned to sell the computer to raise money for student scholarships.

(f) A portrait, painted by D. (D therefore had a zero basis.) The painting had a value of $100,000.

(g) A portrait, painted by D's mother, M. M, whose basis in the painting was zero, had given the painting to D several years ago when it was worth $20,000. D gave the painting to the charity when it was worth $100,000.

(h) Same as (g), except that D had acquired the painting (then worth $20,000) by bequest at M's death.

(i) A portrait painted by A. A had sold the painting in a bona fide sale for $1,000. Twenty years later, A saw the painting in a collection and repurchased it for $20,000. After the painting had appreciated in value to $30,000, A gave it to the § 170 organization.

(j) One day of D's professional services, for which a client would have paid D $1,000.

(k) $1,000 cash, which D earned in one day performing services for professional clients.

(l) Same as (j), except that D also incurred $200 of out-of-pocket expenses in performing the services.

(m) $1,000 worth of books received free of charge from publishers, who hoped that D, a professional book reviewer, would publish reviews of the books. D had not included the value of the books in income when received.

(n) A remainder interest in a trust created by D to pay the income to D's child, C, for life, remainder to the charitable organization. The trust corpus consisted of a well-diversified portfolio of publicly traded securities. A bank served as trustee. Based upon C's life expectancy, the actuarial present value of the remainder interest in the trust was $40,000.

(o) Same as (n), except that the trust corpus consisted of D's vacation home.

(p) Same as (n), except that D gave C a legal life estate in D's vacation home, with remainder to a qualifying charity.

(q) A check for $1,000, mailed by D on December 31, year 1. The check was received and cashed by the charity on January 4 of the following year.

(r) D's promissory note in the amount of $10,000, payable in two years and bearing annual market-rate interest. The note was delivered to the charity on December 31 of the current year.

(s) Same as (a), except that the stock was delivered in satisfaction of D's legally enforceable pledge of $100,000. D made the pledge last year. (Would your answer differ if D were an accrual-method taxpayer?)

3. S transferred corporate stock (valued at $100,000) to a charity described in § 170(b)(1)(A) for $50,000. S's adjusted basis in the stock was $40,000. What result to S?

4. In the current year, D has adjusted gross income of $100,000. How much can D deduct in the current year in each of the following alternative cases? What happens to any amount not deductible in the current year? Assume in each case that the contribution is D's only contribution for the year.

(a) $60,000 cash to Private University.

(b) $60,000 worth of stock to Private University. D purchased the stock several years ago for $10,000.

(c) Same as (b), except that D purchased the stock several years ago for $59,000.

(d) Same as (a), except that D donated the money to the D Family Foundation, a non-operating private foundation. (Generally speaking, a private foundation is an exempt organization that is privately rather than publicly supported. A non-operating private foundation is one that uses its income for the making of grants rather than the active conduct of charitable activities, such as, e.g., operating a museum. Non-operating foundations are organizations described in § 170(c), but deductions to such organizations are limited by § 170(b)(1)(B) & (D).)

(e) Same as (b), except that D donated the stock to the D Family Foundation, a non-operating private foundation.

Chapter 35

STATE AND LOCAL TAXES

Code: §§ 164(a), (b)(1), (2), (5)(A), (B), (C) & (H), (c), (d) & (f); 275(a)(1). Review §§ 62(a); 162(a); 212.

Regulations: §§ 1.164–1(a); 1.164–3(c); 1.164–4(a); 1.62–1T(d).

1. T, a cash-method taxpayer, paid the following taxes this year. Determine which of the tax payments are deductible and whether they are deductible in computing adjusted gross income or as itemized deductions.

(a) State income tax;

(b) State and local property tax on T's home;

(c) State and local property tax on T's business building;

(d) State general sales tax;

(e) State general sales tax that covers all retail sales other than groceries and prescription medicines;

(f) Local-option sales tax (imposed in addition to the state general sales tax);

(g) Employee's share of Social Security and Medicare taxes;

(h) Employer's share of Social Security and Medicare taxes;

(i) Federal self-employment tax;

(j) Sales tax on business automobile;

(k) State severance taxes imposed upon oil production in which T has a royalty interest;

(l) Automobile registration fee based upon value of personal automobile;

(m) Automobile registration fee based upon a combination of the value and weight of the automobile;

(n) Special real-property-tax assessment to pay for the installation of sidewalks adjacent to T's home.

(o) Special real-property-tax assessment to pay for the repair of sidewalks adjacent to T's home.

(p) Estimated property taxes paid in escrow to T's mortgagee, so that the account would contain sufficient cash to pay the taxes when they came due.

2. S sells his home to P on October 9, 2008. The state's 2008 real-property tax year runs from July 1, 2008 through June 30, 2009. One-half of the taxes for the 2008 tax year are payable on September 30, 2009 and one-half on March 31, 2010. S and P are both calendar-year, cash-method taxpayers. P pays the 2008 taxes ($3,650) when due. To what extent are the taxes deductible by S? By P?

Chapter 36

CASUALTY LOSSES TO
PERSONAL-USE PROPERTY

Code: § 165(a), (b), (c)(3), (e) & (h). Review §§ 1222(4); 1231(a)(4)(C); 1033(a)(2).

Regulations: §§ 1.165–7; 1.165–8.

Cases: White v. Commissioner, 48 T. C. 430 (1967);
Chamales v. Commissioner, 79 T.C.M. 1428 (2000).

1. Which of the following calamities constitutes a casualty loss?

(a) H accidentally slammed a car door on his wife's (W's) hand. W's diamond wedding ring absorbed the full impact of the blow, which broke the flanges holding the diamond in place. The excruciating pain caused W to shake her hand vigorously, and, as a result of the shaking, the diamond setting flew out of her wedding ring and was lost in the crushed-gravel driveway.

(b) C and D are husband and wife. D was suffering from arthritis. To relief the arthritic pain, she took off her wedding ring, wrapped it in a tissue, and put it on a stand beside her bed. C, not realizing that the tissue contained the ring, flushed the tissue down the toilet. Despite the taxpayers' diligent efforts, the ring was never recovered.

(c) N's neighbor, S, a well-known celebrity, committed a notorious murder in his house, which is located next door to N's. After the murder and ensuing trial, thousands of sightseers regularly descended upon N's neighborhood to catch a glimpse of the murder scene. Tour buses even began making the neighborhood a regular part of their rounds. Although N's property suffered no physical damage, N's realtor estimates that the notoriety of the neighborhood and the invasive crowds have caused a large drop in the value of N's home.

(d) While on vacation, T was involved in an automobile accident that was caused by his negligence. T, who had no insurance, paid to have the other party's car repaired and also paid to have his own car repaired.

(e) Same as (d), except that T had both liability and collision insurance but declined to make a claim on his insurer because he thought it would drastically increase his insurance premiums.

2. In each of the following alternative cases, determine the amount and character of T's casualty loss or gain. Ignore the effect of the $100 and 10–percent floors of § 165(h)(1) & (2).

(a) T's oriental rug (held several years for personal use) was completely destroyed by fire. The rug had an adjusted basis of $2,000 and a value of $5,000. T received no insurance proceeds.

(b) Same as (a), except that T received $5,000 of insurance proceeds.

(c) Same as (a), except that the rug had an adjusted basis of $5,000 and a value of $2,000.

(d) Same as (c), except that instead of a rug, the destroyed asset (which T had held for several years) was a depreciable asset used in T's business.

(e) T's (uninsured) vacation home was damaged by a hurricane. Immediately before the casualty, the home was worth $600,000; immediately after it was worth $200,000. T's basis for the home is $300,000.

(f) Same as (e), except that, immediately after the hurricane, the home was worth $400,000.

3. V suffered a $50,000 loss when her vacation home (adjusted basis $150,000) was damaged by a hurricane. She also received $10,000 of insurance proceeds when her diamond bracelet (adjusted basis $5,000) was stolen. V did not replace the bracelet. Apart from these transactions, V's gross and adjusted gross income is $100,000. What tax result to V?

4. How would your answer in 3 differ if V's gain on the theft of the bracelet was $50,000 and her loss on the vacation home was $5,000?

5. R's personal bookkeeper embezzled $750,000 from R's bank account last year. R just discovered the theft this year. In which year should R take the deduction?

Chapter 37

EDUCATION DEDUCTIONS AND CREDITS

Code: §§ 25A(a), (b), (c), (d), (f)(1) & (g)(3); 222.

Regulations: §§ 1.25A–2(a) & (d); 1.25A–4(b) & (c); 1.25A–5(a), (b)(1) & (3), (c)(1), (3) & (4), Exs. 1 & 2.

In working the problems, use the dollar figures set forth in the Code and ignore the effect of inflation adjustments.

1. Compare the Hope Scholarship Credit with the Lifetime Learning Credit:

(a) Ignoring inflation adjustments, what is the maximum allowable Hope Credit? The Lifetime Learning Credit?

(b) For how many years can one use the Hope Credit? The Lifetime Learning Credit?

(c) Must the student be seeking a degree to use the Hope Credit? The Lifetime Learning Credit?

(d) Must the student be a full-time student to use the Hope Credit? The Lifetime Learning Credit?

(e) May a graduate student (who has never before claimed an education credit) use the Hope Credit? The Lifetime Learning Credit?

(f) Is one who has been convicted of a felony drug conviction eligible for the Hope Credit? The Lifetime Learning Credit?

2. Which of the following constitute "qualified tuition and related expenses" that are eligible for the credits?

(a) Tuition paid by the student to the educational institution;

(b) Laboratory fees required for enrollment in the basic chemistry course;

(c) Required books for courses in which the student is enrolled;

(d) Mandatory student- activity fee, which the school uses to defray the costs of student-run organizations;

(e) Room and board;

(f) Mandatory student health fee.

3. Q pays her tuition with a Pell Grant, R pays her tuition with the proceeds of a loan, S pays his tuition with a scholarship, and T's grandparents pay his tuition directly to the school. (T is not a claimed dependent for the year.)

(a) Do the sums paid from those sources count toward the student's qualified tuition and related expenses?

(b) Would your answer differ if S instead used the scholarship money to pay room and board and paid the tuition from his own funds?

4. A is a freshman at State College, where he pays $6,000 of tuition from earnings from part-time and summer work.

(a) Is A better off claiming the Hope Scholarship or Lifetime Learning Credit?

(b) Would your answer differ if A paid tuition of $10,000?

5. B is a dependent of her parents, who pay $20,000 of college tuition for her in the current year. (Ignore the phaseout rules of § 25A(d).)

(a) What is the maximum educational credit allowable on account of the tuition payment?

(b) Who is entitled to the credit?

(c) Same as (b), except that $5,000 of the tuition had been paid by B.

(d) What result in (a) if the tuition had been paid by B's grandmother?

6. What is the maximum deduction under § 222 for qualified tuition and related expenses?

7. S, a dependent of his parents, is a freshman in college. S's parents pay for his tuition at the college. S is a full-time student. S's parents file a joint return. Should the parents claim the Hope Scholarship Credit, the Lifetime Learning Credit or the educational expense deduction of § 222 if the parents' modified AGI (under both §§ 25A(d)(3) and 222(b)(2)(C)) is $80,000, and they pay tuition of:

(a) $3,000?

(b) $10,000?

8. Would your answers in 8 differ if the parents' MAGI is:

(a) $90,000?

(b) $100,000?

Chapter 38

INTEREST INCOME AND DEDUCTIONS

A. DEDUCTIBLE AND NON-DEDUCTIBLE INTEREST

Code: §§ 61(a)(4); 103(a) & (c); 163(a), (d) & (h); 221; 161; 261; 265(a)(2). Review §§ 62; 67; 71; 215; 280A(d)(1) & (2); 469; 104(a)(2).

Regulations: §§ 1.163–8T; 1.163–9T; 1.163–10T(b).

1. T, an individual, borrows money (an unsecured loan) that is allocable to the following (alternative) expenditures. Determine in each case whether (and to what extent) the interest is deductible.

(a) A personal automobile.

(b) An addition to T's principal residence.

(c) New York Stock Exchange securities.

(d) State of Iowa bonds.

(e) A business (sole proprietorship) in which T materially participates.

(f) A limited partnership interest.

(g) Law school tuition.

(h) A vacation home.

(i) A federal income tax deficiency attributable to T's underreported business income.

2. How would your answers in 1 change if the loan is secured by a mortgage on T's (previously unencumbered) principal residence?

3. Five years ago, S purchased a personal residence for $400,000. To finance the purchase, she used the proceeds of a five-year, interest-only loan (a loan that requires the borrower to pay only interest rather than retiring any of the principal before the loan matures) in the amount of $250,000. The loan was secured by the residence. At the beginning of this year (when the principal of the loan remained $250,000), S refinanced the loan (still secured by the residence) and increased the principal to $450,000. (The value of the residence had increased to $600,000.) S spent $25,000 of the additional borrowing on improvements to the home and spent the balance on personal consumption. S paid $45,000 in interest on the refinanced loan this year. To what extent is the interest deductible by S?

4. Is § 265(a)(2) consistent with the purpose of § 103(a)?

5. B borrows $20,000 for the purchase of a automobile (to be used for personal use) and pledges corporate stock as collateral for the loan. B has ample investment income. Is the interest deductible?

6. R borrowed $100,000 on margin from his stockbroker and invested the loan proceeds in publicly traded stocks and bonds. In the current year, T received dividends of $4,000 and interest income of $2,500. He paid a $5,000 fee for stock-market investment advice and spent $1,200 on commissions on approximately 30 stock trades. He had no net recognized capital gains or losses for the year. R paid margin interest for the year of $10,000. R's adjusted gross income is $200,000. Except for the items mentioned above, R's only itemized deductions (totaling $40,000) were for qualified residence interest, charitable contributions and state income and property taxes.

(a) How much of the margin interest can R deduct in the current year?

(b) What happens to any interest not deductible in the current year?

(c) How would your answer in (a) change if R's adjusted gross income was $100,000?

7. H and W were divorced last year. The divorce decree requires that, for the next five years (that is, until their daughter, D, attains age 18), H make the mortgage payments on a residence owned by W and H as tenants-in-common and in which W and D reside. H's obligation is to terminate in the event of W's death. When D attains age 18, the property is to be sold and the proceeds divided equally between H and W. H and W are jointly liable on the mortgage liability, which was incurred when H and W purchased the residence. In the current year H pays $5,000 on the indebtedness ($2,000 of interest and $3,000 of principal). To what extent can H deduct the $5,000?

8. P suffered serious physical injuries in an automobile accident. In compensation, the tortfeasor agreed to pay P $200,000 at the rate of $10,000 a year for twenty years, plus 10% (market-rate) interest on the unpaid principal balance.

(a) Must P include the annual interest in gross income?

(b) If you were P's attorney, how would you recommend that the settlement be structured?

9. B has a balance of $5,000 in her checking account. She borrows (without security) $15,000 from the bank and places the loan proceeds in her checking account. B intends to pay both personal and business expenses from the account. Which expenses will be treated as paid with the borrowed funds?

10. Suppose (in 9) that $10,000 of the borrowed funds is properly allocable to business and $5,000 to personal expenditures. B repays $7,500 of the loan. What portion of the $7,500 balance is allocable to business?

B. INTEREST-FREE LOANS

Code: § 7872.

1. P has $100,000 earning interest in the bank. At the midpoint of year 1, P directs the bank to begin paying the interest on the account to her adult child, C, and the bank does so. P reserves the right to revoke the assignment at any time, and she revokes it at the midpoint of year 2. Before P revokes the assignment, the bank pays C $5,500 of interest in each of years 1 and 2. What result to P and C?

2. At the midpoint of year 1, P lends her adult child, C, $100,000. The loan does not bear interest. C delivers to P her promissory note, which is payable on demand. C invests the money and earns interest of $5,500 in each of years 1 and 2. C repays the loan at the midpoint of year 2. The applicable federal rate is 10 percent. What results to P and C?

3. Same as 2, except that C earned interest of $4,000 in each year.

4. Same as 2, except that the loan was a one-year term loan.

5. Same as 2, except that P is a corporation (with a large amount of accumulated earnings) and C is a shareholder of the corporation.

Chapter 39

ALIMONY, PROPERTY SETTLEMENTS
AND RELATED ISSUES

Code: §§ 71(a)–(f); 215; 62(a)(10); 1041; 152(e) 1223(2); 1245(b)(1); 453B(g).

Regulations: §§ 1.71–1T; 1.1.1041–1T.

Cases: Okerson v. Commissioner, 123 T.C. 258 (2004);
Kean v. Commissioner, 407 F.3d 186 (3d Cir. 2005);
Young v. Commissioner, 240 F.3d 369 (4th Cir. 2001).

Ruling: Rev. Rul. 2002–22, 2002–1 C.B. 849.

1. H recently moved out of the family home that he shared with his wife, W, and their 13–year old child, C. H and W are considering divorce, though neither has commenced legal action nor even consulted with an attorney about the matter. At the beginning of each month, H transfers $5,000 to W, just as he did when the parties lived together. W uses the money to pay the costs of maintaining the household and providing for C and herself. If H and W file separate returns, how should they treat the monthly payments?

2. A and B have obtained a divorce. The decree requires A to pay B $3,000 monthly for 10 years. If B dies within the ten-year period, A is to pay $2,000 a month to their adult child, C, for the remainder of the ten-year period. The decree specifically provides that all payments be deductible by A and includable in B's income. How should A and B treat the payments on their tax returns?

3. A dissolution decree requires C to pay the following amounts to C's former husband, D. Which of the payments are deductible by C and includable in D's gross income?

(a) Spousal support of $10,000 a month (terminable at D's death);

(b) Child support of $5,000 a month for the couple's two children.

4. Would your answer to 3 differ if the child support was "bundled" into a $15,000 "family-support allowance" (terminable at D's death)?

5. Suppose the following tax rates apply to unmarried taxpayers:

If taxable income is:	The tax is:
Not over $30,000	10 percent of taxable income.
Over $30,000 but not over $60,000	$3,000 plus 20 percent of the excess.
Over $60,000	$9,000 plus 30 percent of the excess.

(a) A and B are negotiating a divorce settlement. Apart from the effect of any alimony payments, A has annual income of $100,000 and B has annual income of $20,000. Suppose that the parties agree that A will pay $30,000 annually, and the payment is not alimony. How much will each party have left after tax?

(b) Same as (a), except that A will pay B $40,000, and the payment is alimony.

(c) Which arrangement is preferable?

6. A divorce decree requires I to pay the premiums on a term life-insurance policy on her life. The policy is owned by her ex-husband, J. I's obligation terminates at J's death. Are the premium payments deductible by I?

7. As part of a divorce property settlement, M transferred to M's former spouse, N, the items of property listed below. In each case, determine the consequences of the transfer to M and N.

(a) Greenacre, which had a value of $100,000 and in which M had an adjusted basis of $20,000.

(b) Blueacre, which had a value of $20,000 and in which M had an adjusted basis of $100,000.

(c) A claim for $5,000 of unpaid rent due from the lessee of Greenacre.

(d) An installment obligation arising from M's sale of a capital asset. M had been reporting the gain under the installment method of § 453. M's adjusted basis in the obligation was $40,000. It had a value (and face amount) of $200,000.

(e) Business equipment (§ 1245 property) with an adjusted basis of $20,000 and a value of $50,000. M had originally purchased the equipment for $100,000 and had properly deducted $80,000 of depreciation with respect thereto.

(f) M's $100,000 promissory note, which was payable (without interest) in 4 years.

8. M (in 7) failed to pay the $100,000 due on the promissory note that was due after 4 years. N sued M and obtained a judgment for the $100,000. M satisfied the judgment in the fifth year after the decree by transferring to N Purpleacre, which had a value of $100,000 and in which M had an adjusted basis of $30,000. What result to the parties?

9. Re-Examine problem 4 in Chapter 12.

10. Re-examine problems 7 and 8 in Chapter 18.

11. Re-examine problems 7, 8 and 9 in Chapter 22.

10. Examine problems 5, 6 and 7 in Chapter 40.

Chapter 40

PERSONAL AND DEPENDENCY
EXEMPTIONS AND FILING STATUS

A. PERSONAL AND DEPENDENCY EXEMPTIONS

Code: §§ 151(a), (b), (c) & (d); 152.   Note §§ 24(c)(1); 213(d)(5); 21(e)(5); 32(c)(3)(A).

Regulations: §§ 1.151–1(b); 1.152–1(a) & (b); 1.152–3; 1.152–4(b); Temp Treas. Reg. § 1.152–4T.

1. T furnishes over half the support of the following persons. For whom is T entitled to a dependency exemption? (Ignore the effect of inflation adjustments.)

(a) T's son, A, who is 23 years old and attends medical school at State University in University City. For the past two years, A has resided alone in University City, approximately 120 miles from T's home. A's gross income for the year is $4,500.

(b) T's 19–year-old step-daughter, B, who resides with T. B attends a local college half time. B has gross income of $4,500.

(c) T's 15–year-old adopted daughter, C, who resides with her father (T's former spouse). The parties' divorce decree is silent as to the allocation of the dependency exemption for C. C had gross income of $1,500.

(d) D, age 13, who resides with T as a foster child.

(e) T's domestic partner J, who has resided with T for several years. J's only income ($1,500) was from a part-time job.

(f) K, age 16, who is the child of T's domestic partner, J (in (e)), and who resides with T and J. K has no gross income.

2. N, age 20, resides with his aunt, A, and her husband, U, while N attends college as a full-time student. U furnishes over 50 percent of N's support. N's only income is $4,500 earned from a part-time job. He pays no rent, though he contributes to the household by helping with laundry, cooking, yard work, and minor repairs. S and U file a joint return. Does B qualify as their dependent?

3. R's 90–year-old grandmother, G, resides with R's sister, S. R contributes 40, S 40, and G 20 percent of G's support. All of G's contribution comes from her savings. G's only income is interest of $1,800 on her bank savings account.

4. D (age 12) and her single mother, M, share a home with M's parents, GM and GF. Although M contributes to the cost of the household from her $25,000 per year salary, GM and GF, who file a joint return, pay most of the family's living expenses. Who is entitled to the dependency exemption for D?

5. M has physical custody of her 13-year-old son, S, who resides with her. M has waived her right to the dependency exemption for S so that it can be claimed by S's father (S's former husband), F (see § 152(e)(1) & (2)). Under these circumstances, determine whether M or F is entitled to:

(a) The child tax credit of § 24;

(b) The medical-expense deduction of § 213 for medical expenses paid on behalf of S;

(c) The dependent-care credit of § 21 for child-care expenses paid by M so that she could work;

(d) Count S as a qualifying child for the purpose of the earned income credit of § 32.

6. In November of year 1, H moved out of the house that he had occupied with his wife, W, and their two young children, ages 3 and 6, and moved into an apartment. The children continued to reside in the house with W. In December, W filed for divorce, but the parties were still married at the end of year 1. H and W are filing separate returns for year 1, even though H's income is considerably higher than W's. Who is entitled to the dependency exemptions for the two children for year 1?

7. Would your answer in 6 differ if H had moved out of the home in January, year 2 (after residing there with W and the children throughout year 1)?

8. K, age 17, resides with her parents, who furnish all of her support. She earns $4,500 at a part-time job. Is K entitled to a personal exemption on her return?

9. L, a single person (not a surviving spouse or head of household), has adjusted gross income of $140,000. L is entitled to three personal and dependency exemptions. How much can L deduct for the exemptions if the year is 2009? 2010?

B. FILING STATUS AND RELATED ISSUES

Code: §§ 6012(a)(1) & (b)(1); 6013(a), (c) & (d); 2. Note §§ 1(a), (b) & (c) (Appendix B); 7701(a)(38); 7703(a)(1).

In working these problems, ignore the effect of inflation adjustments.

1. T has taxable income of $100,000. Use the tax-rate schedules in Appendix B to determine T's tax before credits if T's filing status is:

(a) Married filing jointly with T's spouse. (The $100,000 of taxable income is their combined income.)

(b) Surviving spouse (defined in § 2(a)).

(c) Head of household (defined in § 2(b)).

(d) Single (not a head of household or surviving spouse).

2. Does the taxpayer's filing status determine the treatment of items other than the computation of tax liability?

3. Each of the following taxpayers has gross income of $7,000. Determine which of them must file a federal income-tax return:

(a) S, a 25–year-old single person (not a surviving spouse or head of household);

(b) H, a 25–year-old head of household (within the meaning of § 2(b));

(c) P, a 60–year-old surviving spouse (within the meaning of § 2(a));

(d) W, a 70–year old widow who is a head of household (because she maintains a household in which she resides with (only) her 12–year old grandchild).

4. H and W have been married for ten years and have a child, age 6. Last December H moved out of the family home and filed for divorce, though, of course, no decree had been entered by the end of the year. What is the parties' filing status for last year?

5. What result in 4 if the parties had entered into a written separation agreement that required H to make payments to W for her support?

6. On June 30 of the current year, a decree of divorce was entered (in 4). W was awarded custody of the child. W waived her right to the dependency exemption for the child. What is the filing status of H? Of W?

7. W died on August 15, 2007, survived by her husband, H, and a 10–year old son, S. Can H file a joint return on behalf of the couple for 2007?

8. What is H's filing status for 2008 if H and S continue to reside in a household furnished by H?

9. What is H's filing status for 2010 if H and S continue to reside in a household furnished by H?

Chapter 41

PERSONAL TAX CREDITS

A. THE CHILD TAX CREDIT

Code: §§ 24(a), (b) & (c); 152(c).

1. S, an unmarried, single parent, has two children, A and B, who reside with her. A is age 14. B is age 19 and a full-time college student. Both are dependents of S. What is the amount of S's child tax credit if S's modified adjusted gross income (as defined in § 24(b)(1)) is:

(a) $50,000?

(b) $80,000?

(c) $100,000?

2. Would your answers in 1 differ if S was divorced and had waived her right to the dependency exemption for A so that the exemption can be claimed by A's father under § 152(e)?

B. THE CREDIT FOR HOUSEHOLD AND DEPENDENT CARE SERVICES

Code: § 21(a), (b), (c), (d) & (e). Note § 129.

Regulations: Prop. Treas. Reg §§ 1.21–1; 1.21–2; 1.21–4.

1. M, a single parent, is employed full time. M makes the following alternative expenditures for the care of her child, C, while M works. Which of the expenditures qualify as "employment-related expenses" under § 21?

(a) C is 3 years old. M sends C to nursery school. The nursery school provides meals and some educational services.

(b) C is 9 years old. Instead of taking C to day care, M sends her for a week to a summer day camp specializing in soccer.

(c) Would your answer in (b) differ if the soccer camp were an overnight camp?

(d) C is 9 years old. M pays her mother $5,000 a year to keep C after school and during days when school is not in session.

(e) Same as (d), except that M's 18–year-old daughter, D, keeps C. D is not M's dependent.

(f) Same as (d), except C is age 13.

(g) Same as (a). M is divorced and her former husband is entitled to the dependency exemption for C because M waived her right to the exemption under § 152(e)(2).

2. N, who works full time, employs a nanny to care for her two children, ages 3 and 14. The nanny cooks meals and cleans the apartment in which N and the children reside. Do the amounts paid the nanny qualify as employment-related expenses?

3. A and B, husband and wife, provide a home for A's aged father, F, who is incapable of self-care. They pay a housekeeper to watch over F while they are at work. F is not their dependent because his income exceeds the limit of § 152(d)(1)(B). Do amounts paid the housekeeper qualify as employment-related expenses?

4. Same as 3, except that instead of caring for F in their home, A and B contribute to the cost of F's care at a nursing home for the last three months of the year. The rest of the year F resided with A and B. Do the amounts paid the nursing home qualify?

5. M and F, husband and wife, file a joint return. They have two children, ages 3 and 6. In each of the following cases, determine the amount of their dependent-care credit.

(a) M is employed full time at a salary of $30,000 a year. F is self-employed and his income for the current year is $4,000. They paid a dependent-care center (which complies with all applicable laws) $5,000 to care for the children to enable them to work. The AGI on their joint return (see § 21(e)(2)) is $34,000.

(b) Same as (a), except that M was reimbursed for $3,000 of the child-care expense through her employer's cafeteria plan.

(c) Same as (a), except that H earned $10,000 (and the couple's AGI was $40,000), and they paid the dependent-care center $7,000.

(d) M is employed full time at a salary of $30,000 a year. F is a full-time student throughout the year and has no earned income. The couple's AGI is $30,000. They pay the dependent-care center $5,000 to care for the children while M works and F attends school.

(e) Same as (d), except that both M and F are full-time students. Although they have investment income (and AGI) of $15,000, they have no actual earned income.

C. THE EARNED-INCOME CREDIT

Code: § 32(a), (b), (c)(1) & (3) & (i). Note §§ 32(k); 152(c) & (e).

Ignore the effect of inflation adjustments in working the following problems.

1. A is the single parent of her 15–year old child who resides with her. (The child does not furnish over half her own support.) What is the amount of A's earned-income credit for 2007 if she has earned income of:

(a) $10,000?

(b) $20,000?

2. A (in 1) has earned income of $10,000 in 2007. She marries B, who has earned income of $10,000 and has a 12–year-old child who resides with him. How does their marriage affect the amount of their aggregate earned-income credits?

3. What result in problem 1(b) if A also received $2,500 of dividend income during the year?

4. What result in problem (1)(b) if the Service had disallowed A's earned income credit for 2005 and had determined that her claim of the credit was due to reckless disregard of the rules (but not due to fraud)?

5. S is a single law student with no children. S's earned income for 2007 is $10,000. Is S eligible for the earned-income credit if he is:

(a) Age 23?

(b) Age 26?

D. EDUCATION CREDITS

See Chapter 37.

Section J

TIMING OF INCOME AND DEDUCTIONS

Chapter 42

"ANNUAL" vs. "TRANSACTIONAL" ACCOUNTING

A. NET OPERATING LOSSES

Code: § 172(a), (b)(1)(A), (2) & (3), (c), (d)(1), (2), (3) & (4).

1. Explain the rationale for the net operating loss (NOL) deduction.

2. Explain the difference between the NOL and the NOL deduction.

3. L Corp. has a net operating loss (NOL) of $250,000 in year 3. Apart from the effect of the NOL deduction, it has taxable income of $100,000 for year 1, 50,000 for year 2, and $120,000 for year 4. How does the year–3 NOL affect L's taxable income for years 1, 2 and 4?

4. M, an individual sole proprietor, has $100,000 of business gross income, $40,000 of non-business gross income, $150,000 of business deductions, $30,000 of non-business deductions (other than her personal exemption), and a $2,000 personal exemption. Determine M's NOL for the year.

5. Same as 4, except that M had $30,000 of non-business gross income and $40,000 of non-business deductions (other than the personal exemption).

6. Late in the current year, J, an individual who uses the cash method, seeks your advice. J anticipates that her business expenses will considerably exceed her business gross income for the year. J expects to have $20,000 of non-business ordinary income (from dividends and interest) and has paid $30,000 of non-business expenses. J could pay another $10,000 of non-business expenses before the end of the year. Would you advise J to do so, or should she wait until next year to pay the remaining non-business expenses?

7. Individual A, a self-employed person, has gross income and deductions as follows:

Gross income	
Ordinary business income	$200,000
Dividends	5,000
Alimony	10,000
Capital gain on sale of investment property	10,000
Deductions	
Business deductions	$250,000
Capital loss on sale of investment property	30,000
State income taxes	15,000
Interest	20,000
Personal exemption	2,000

Both the capital gain and the capital loss are long-term. The interest was paid on indebtedness incurred by A to purchase her principal residence. A's standard deduction would be $3,000.

Determine A's taxable income and NOL for the year.

B. THE TAX-BENEFIT RULE

Code: § 111.

Regulation: § 1.111–1(a).

Cases: Continental Illinois Nat'l Bank and Trust Co. v. Commissioner, 69 T.C. 357 (1977) (Acq.);
Hillsboro Nat'l Bank v. Commissioner, 460 U.S. 370 (1983).

1. In year 1, T, a single person, would have been entitled to a $3,000 standard deduction, but because T had $15,000 of itemized deductions T elected to itemize. Included in the $15,000 of itemized deductions was $5,000 of state income tax that had been withheld from T's salary. In year 2, T filed a state income-tax return for year 1 and received a $2,000 refund. T's year–1 taxable income was $50,000. Must T include the $2,000 refund in gross income?

2. Same as 1, except that in year 1 T had total itemized deductions of only $4,000, of which $3,000 was state income tax withheld from T's salary. Must the $2,000 refund for year 1 be included in T's year–2 gross income?

3. In year 1, D donated a building with a value of $100,000 to University City for use as a government building and properly deducted the $100,000 as a charitable contribution under § 170. In year 2, the City decided that it could not afford to maintain the building and, though it had no legal obligation to do so, re-

conveyed the building, then valued at $90,000, to D. D had ample income to offset the $100,000 deduction. Must D include some amount in gross income in year 2? If so, how much?

4. How would your answer in (3) change if, because of the § 170(b) limits on the charitable-contribution deduction, D had been able to deduct only $30,000 of the contribution in year 1 (and carried over the balance to year 2)?

5. In year 1, L lent $100,000 to B, who was not related to L. In year 2, before repaying any of the principal of the indebtedness, B obtained a discharge in bankruptcy, and L treated the $100,000 as a worthless non-business bad debt (i.e., as a short-term capital loss under § 166(d)). (This was L's only capital-gain or capital-loss transaction in year 2.) In year 3, B inherited some money and, though B had no legal obligation to do so, repaid $40,000 of the indebtedness. Must L include the $40,000 in gross income if, because of the limits on the deductibility of capital losses imposed by § 1211(b), L had been able to deduct only $3,000 of the loss (in year 2) by the time the repayment occurred? (L had positive taxable income in year 2.)

6. In year 1, L lent $100,000 to B Corp. In year 2, before repaying any of the principal of the indebtedness, B Corp. filed a petition under Chapter 11 of the Bankruptcy Act. In the bankruptcy proceeding, L received 1,000 shares of B Corp. stock in satisfaction of the indebtedness. The stock had a value of $1,000, and L deducted $99,000 as a loss with full tax benefit. Several years later, the B Corp. stock had appreciated in value to $120,000, at which point L gave the shares to State University and properly claimed a $120,000 charitable deduction for the gift. Does L have gross income in the year of the gift as a result of these events?

7. P purchased a building (held for investment) for $100,000, properly deducted $30,000 of straight-line depreciation, and then sold the building for $120,000. P did not have sufficient income to absorb the $30,000 of depreciation deductions and therefore got no tax benefit from the deductions. What result to P on the sale?

8. Would your answer in 7 differ if P had mistakenly deducted $40,000 of depreciation instead of the $30,000 that was properly allowable?

9. In year 1, T was injured in an automobile accident caused by the negligence of N. T paid $15,000 of medical expenses in year 1, of which only $10,000 was deductible (because of the 7.5–percent floor of § 213(a)). In year 2, T received a settlement from N that included reimbursement for the $15,000 of year–1 medical expenses. T had positive taxable income in year 1. Must T include the $15,000 reimbursement in gross income for year 2?

10. Would your answer in 9 differ if, because of very large itemized deductions, T had not had sufficient year–1 income to absorb the $10,000 medical-expense deduction?

C. SECTION 1341

Code: § 1341(a).

Regulation: § 1.1341–1(b)(2), (c), (d)(2)(iii), (d)(4)(ii), (h).

Case: Van Cleave v. United States, 718 F.2d 193 (6th Cir. 1983).

1. In year 1, B, a beneficiary of a trust, received a cash distribution of $50,000 from the trust and included that amount in gross income. In year 2, the trustee discovered a miscalculation in the amount to which B was entitled in year 1 and commenced an action to recover the $20,000 excess distribution. B restored the $20,000 to the trust in year 3. Is B entitled to use § 1341 in the calculation of her year–3 tax liability?

2. In year 1, E embezzled $750,000 from his employer. E's defalcation was discovered in year 3, he promptly filed an amended return for year 1, including the $750,000 in gross income, and he repaid $100,000 to the employer later that year. Can E invoke § 1341 in calculating his year–3 tax liability?

3. In year 1, S sold some stock in a closely held corporation and reported a long-term capital gain of $100,000 on the sale (S's only capital-gain or -loss transaction for year 1). In year 3, P, the purchaser of the stock, brought an action against S for negligent misrepresentation in the sale. Although continuing to deny any wrongdoing, S settled the suit in year 4 by refunding to P $40,000 of the purchase price. Under Arrowsmith v. Commissioner, 344 U.S. 6 (1952), the $40,000 payment must be treated as a capital loss in year 4. S has no capital gains in year 4.

(a) May S use § 1341 to compute his year–4 tax liability?

(b) Assume that at all times the tax rate is 15 percent for capital gains and 40 percent for ordinary income. How much tax does S save in year 4 by using § 1341?

(c) Suppose that S also paid $10,000 in legal fees in resisting P's claim. Does § 1341 apply to that payment?

4. E, an executive of X, has an employment contract that requires E to repay to X any amounts of compensation that the Commissioner determines to be "unreasonable" and hence non-deductible by X under § 162(a). In year 3, E is required under this provision to repay to X $40,000 of the compensation received in year 1. Apart from any effect of the repayment, E's taxable income is $120,000 for year 1 and $90,000 for year 3. The (hypothetical) tax rates applicable to both

years provide that the tax is 20% on the first $100,000 of taxable income and 30% on income exceeding $100,000. What result to E under § 1341?

Chapter 43

AN INTRODUCTION TO
TAX ACCOUNTING

A. INTRODUCTION

Code: §§ 446(a), (b), (c) & (d). Note § 6001.

Regulation: §1.446–1(a), (b), (c)(1)(i) & (ii)(A).

Case: Thor Power Tool Co. v. Commissioner, 439 U.S. 522 (1979).

1. What is a method of accounting?

2. What is *your* method of accounting?

3. Describe in general terms when income is includable and deductions allowable under the cash method.

4. Describe in general terms when income is includable and deductions allowable under an accrual method.

5. Can a taxpayer use the cash method for one business and an accrual method for another?

6. Explain generally when use of the accrual method is required.

7. For tax purposes, T Corporation uses a method of accounting that is acceptable in the preparation of its financial statements under generally accepted accounting principles. Does it follow that the method is acceptable for tax purposes?

B. THE CASH METHOD OF ACCOUNTING

Code: §§ 451(a); 461(a) & (g); 409A.

Regulations: §§ 1.446–1(c)(1)(i); 1.451–1(a); 1.451–2; 1.461–1(a); 1.83–3(e); 1.263(a)–4(d)(3) & (f)(1).

1. In year 1, L performed legal services for C and billed C for $1,000, which will be deductible as a business expense by C. Both C and L are calendar-year, cash-method taxpayers. In each of the following cases, determine when C is entitled to a deduction and when L has gross income.

(a) C pays L in cash in year 2.

(b) C gives L a check for the $1,000 on December 31, year 1. L deposits the check on January 4, year 2. The check clears C's bank in due course.

(c) Same as (b), except that C died on January 1, year 2. (Although C's estate could have challenged the bank's payment of the check, it did not.)

(d) Same as (b), except that C asked L to hold the check until January because C was short of funds, and L agreed. In January, L deposited the check and it cleared C's bank in due course.

(e) C mails the check to L on December 31; L receives it on January 4. L promptly deposits the check and it clears in due course.

(f) In year 2 C gives L a $1,000 promissory note, payable (with market rate interest) $500 in year 3 and $500 in year 4. Soon after receiving the note, L sells ("discounts") it to a bank for $950, plus accrued interest. C makes the required note payments (to the bank) as scheduled.

(g) Late in year 1, C charges the payment to L on a VISA credit card. C pays the charge in year 2, and L collects payment from L's processing bank in year 2.

(h) L performs the services without charge in exchange for the free use of C's vacation condominium for a week in year 2. The fair rental value of a week's stay at the condominium is $1,000.

2. F, a farmer, offers to sell grain to D, with delivery to be made in December but payment to be deferred until the following January. Although D tells F that he would be willing to make payment in December, the parties enter into a sales agreement calling for December delivery and January payment. Is F in constructive receipt of the sales price in December?

3. C, a cash-method taxpayer, makes the following payments of business expenses on December 31, year 1. Determine in each case whether the payment is deductible in year 1.

(a) Interest (covering the period from January 1, year 2 through December 31, year 2).

(b) Rent on the business premises covering the same period as in (a).

4. T is an employee of corporation X. In addition to salary, T is entitled to additional compensation from X for each year. The amount of the additional compensation is credited to a bookkeeping reserve on X's books. It is to be paid upon the earlier of (1) the termination of T's employment or (2) T's becoming totally incapacitated. If T dies before receiving payment, the balance in the account is to be paid to T's estate. Must T, a cash-method taxpayer, include the deferred compensation in gross income as earned?

5. Same as 4, except that T can elect on or before December 31 to have the following year's additional compensation paid to him or deferred until the earlier of his retirement, disability or death.

6. Same as 4, except that each year X transferred the deferred compensation earned in that year to a trust located in the United States. T will be entitled to the trust assets at the earlier of his retirement, disability or death (in which case, the trust assets become the property of his estate). Until the occurrence of one of those "triggering" events, the trust assets remain subject to the claims of X's general creditors.

7. Same as 6, except that the plan provides that the trust assets will become restricted to the provision of benefits to T if X's financial health deteriorates in specified ways.

8. Same as 6, except that the trust was located in the Bahamas. (T's services for X are performed in the United States.)

C. THE ACCRUAL METHOD OF ACCOUNTING

Code: §§ 451(a); 461(a), (f) & (h); 267(a)(2), (b)(2), (c)(2) & (4)

Regulations: §§ 1.446–1(c)(1)(ii); 1.451–1(a); 1.461–1(a)(2); 1.461–2(a)(3) & (4), Ex. (2); 1.461–2(c)(1); 1461–4(d) & (e); 1.263(a)–4(d)(3), (f)(1), (6) & (8), Ex. 10.

Cases: Schlude v. Commissioner, 372 U.S. 128 (1963);
North American Oil Consol. v. Burnet, 286 U.S. 417 (1932).

Rulings: Rev. Proc. 2004–34, 2004–1 C.B. 991;
Rev. Rul. 96–51, 1996–2 C.B. 36.

1. Describe the all-events test.

2. L practices law as a solo practitioner. In year 1, L performs $1,000 of legal services for C, who can deduct the cost of the services as a business expense. L bills C in year 1, and C pays L in year 2. Both L and C use the accrual method. What results to L and C?

3. L (in 2) leases her law office from R at a rental of $4,000 a month. The lease term runs from October 1, year 1, through September 30, year 2. On October 1, year 1, L pays the rent for the entire lease year. What results to L and R, who also uses the accrual method?

4. L (in 2) also paid $12,000 of interest on a business loan. The interest was paid on November 1, year 1, and covered the 12–month period ending on October 31, year 2. What result to L?

5. In June, year 1, L (in 2) also paid a $1,000 fee to the State Supreme Court to renew her license to practice for the period July 1, year 1, through June 30, year 2. When is the payment allowable?

6. S is in the business of offering dancing lessons in a studio that she owns. A customer can purchase lessons at the lowest cost per lesson by paying in advance for a 2–year contract under which the customer pays $1,000 for 100 hours of instruction over the 2–year period beginning on the date the contract is signed. The customer can schedule the lessons at any time during the contract term, but the payment is not refundable. On October 1, year 1, C enters into a 2–year contract and pays S the $1,000 fee. In the financial statements that S furnishes to her bank lender, she recognizes as income $125 in year 1, $500 in year 2, and $375 in year 3. For income-tax purposes, S wishes to defer the income to the extent permitted. For what years (and in what amounts) must S include the $1,000 in gross income?

7. In January, year 1, P commenced an action against D to determine title to a tract of land of which both P and D claimed ownership. While the litigation was pending, D, who was in possession of the land, continued to collect the rent from the lessee of the land. In January, year 2, the court entered judgment for P and ordered D to pay P money damages in the amount of the year–1 rents collected by D. D paid the amount of the judgment in year 3. Both P and D use the accrual method. Who is taxable on the year–1 rents?

8. T contests $20,000 of a $100,000 bill received from C, who provided services to T's business in year 1. (The cost of the services would be deductible by T as a business expense.) In year 2, T pays C the undisputed portion of the bill ($80,000). The dispute is settled in year 3 by T's paying C $5,000 of the claimed $20,000 balance. T uses the accrual method of accounting.

(a) What results to T?

(b) Suppose instead that T had paid the disputed $20,000 into escrow in year 2 under an agreement between T, C and the escrow agent that the funds would be held until the dispute was resolved and then disbursed in accordance with the settlement. The dispute was settled in year 3, and the escrowee disbursed $5,000 to C and the remaining $15,000 to T.

9. A and B, husband and wife, respectively own 40 percent and 20 percent of the stock of X Corporation. B has also lent money to the corporation. For year 1, interest of $20,000 accrued on the loan, but X did not pay the interest until year 2. X uses the accrual method and B the cash method. What results to X and B?

D. INVENTORIES

Code: § 471(a).

Regulations: §§ 1.61–3(a); 1.471–1.

1. A started a retail widget business in year 1. In year 1, A purchased 3 widgets at $1 and sold 2 for $3 each. In year 2, she purchased 4 units at $2 and sold 3 at $4. Assume (contrary to fact) that A can deduct the purchase of widgets as a business expense. Determine A's income from the sale of widgets for :

(a) Year 1.

(b) Year 2.

2. Same as 1, except that A uses the first-in-first-out (FIFO) method of inventory accounting.

3. Same as 1, except that A uses the last-in-first-out (LIFO) method of inventory accounting.

4. Why does LIFO result in lower gross income when prices are rising?

5. What is the "LIFO conformity requirement"?

6. What is the policy justification for permitting the use of LIFO for tax purposes?

7. Why must a taxpayer who maintains inventories account for purchases and sales under the accrual method?

Section K

CONGRESSIONAL EFFORTS TO COMBAT TAX SHELTERS

Chapter 44

THE AT-RISK RULES

Code: §§ 465(a)(1) & (2); (b)(1), (2), (5) & (6); (c)(1) & (3)(A), (d), (e); 49(a)(1)(D)(iv) & (v).

Regulation: Prop. Treas. Reg. §§ 1.465–12(a) & (b); 1.465–39(b).

1. In year 1, T, an individual, purchases equipment for use in an activity to which the at-risk rules apply. T pays $200,000 cash and finances the $800,000 balance of the purchase price with a non-recourse bank loan secured by the equipment.

(a) What is T's basis for the equipment immediately after the purchase?

(b) To what extent is T at risk immediately after the purchase?

(c) In year 1, T's gross income from the activity is $100,000. Apart from the effect of § 465, T could deduct depreciation of $200,000 and interest of $80,000. How much can T deduct after applying § 465? Ignore § 469.

(d) How do these events affect T's amount at risk?

(e) In year 2, gross income is again $100,000, depreciation is $320,000, interest is $80,000, and T pays $100,000 on the loan principal. How much can T deduct for year 2?

(f) In year 3, T sells the property. The purchaser pays T $100,000 cash and takes the property subject to the remaining $700,000 of indebtedness. Before the sale, the activity generated operating gross income of $100,000, depreciation of $100,000 and interest expense of $70,000.

(i) What is T's realized gain or loss on the sale?

(ii) How much can T deduct under § 465 in year 3?

2. In year 1, S, an individual, purchases for $40,000 cash equipment for use in an activity to which the at-risk rules apply. The purchase was made from S's personal funds. For years 1–6, S's cash income from the property equals her cash expenses with respect to the property, and she properly deducts a total of $40,000 of depreciation. In year 7, S's cash gross income from the property again equals her cash expenses, but S borrows $10,000 on a non-recourse note (secured by the equipment) and withdraws the $10,000 from the activity. What result to S?

3. P, an individual, purchases a building for $1,000,000, paying $100,000 cash down from his personal funds and executing a non-recourse note (secured by the building) to the seller for the $900,000 balance of the purchase price.

(a) To what extent is P at risk immediately after the purchase?

(b) Would your answer in (a) differ if the $900,000 non-recourse loan had been made by a bank?

Chapter 45

THE PASSIVE-LOSS RULES

Code: §§ 469(a), (b), (c)(1), (2), (4) & (7), (d)(1), (e)(1) & (3), (g)(1) & (2), (h)(1), (2), (3) & (5), (i)(1), (2), (3) & (6), (j)(8), (*l*)(3).

Regulations: § 1.469–2(f)(6); 1.469–1T(f)(2)(A); 1.469–2T(6)(i); 1.469–5T.

1. Which of the following are passive activities with respect to the taxpayer?

(a) A is a limited partner in a limited partnership that is producing a movie.

(b) B is a member of a limited-liability company that is engaged in the restaurant business; B is strictly an investor and plays no role in the management or operation of the restaurant.

(c) C owns an apartment building. Although C practices law nearly full time, he actively manages the apartment building.

2. Trailerhouse Records, Inc., is an S corporation engaged in the business of recording and producing music for local artists. Several shareholders participate in the firm's business, though all of them earn most of their income from other activities. In each of the following *alternative* cases, determine whether the shareholder is a material participant in the firm?

(a) A devotes 600 hours per year to the business.

(b) B devotes 250 hours per year to the business; no shareholder or employee devotes more time to the business.

(c) C devotes 90 hours per year to the business; the business has no employees, and no other shareholder participates in the business.

(d) D devotes 400 hours per year to the business; D's spouse, S, devoted 200 hours a year to the business.

(e) E devoted 600 hours per year to the business until her retirement 3 years ago.

(f) Same as (e), except E retired 6 years go.

3. In year 1, T, a full-time lawyer, had $40 (000 omitted throughout) of loss passed through to him from a limited partnership in which T is a limited partner; $20 of dividend income; $12 of income passed through from an S corporation that is engaged in a business in which T does not materially participate; and $20 of loss from an apartment building that T owns. All of the losses would be deductible but for the application of § 469.

(a) What result to T in year 1?

(b) In year 2 (before taking account of the deductions from § 469(b)), T had $20 of loss passed through from the limited partnership, $30 of dividend income, $18 of income from the S corporation, and $10 of loss from the apartment building. What result?

4. T owns an asset used in an activity to which § 465 applies. The activity produces a loss of $250 for the year. At the end of the year, T was at risk with respect to the activity only to the extent of $100. The activity is also a passive activity. T has no passive income. To what extent is the loss deductible?

5. B owned an apartment building that produced a passive loss of $100 for the year. B also owned an office building that he leased to his wholly owned C corporation, in which B was employed full-time. That rental produced income of $60 for the year. To what extent is the $100 loss deductible?

6. P purchased an apartment building for $500, properly deducted $200 of depreciation, and then sold it. At the time of the sale, P had $100 of suspended passive losses attributable to the property. (P just broke even in the year of the sale.) The rental of the apartment building is P's only passive activity. What result to P if she sells the property for:

(a) $350?

(b) $250?

7. D owned an apartment building with an adjusted basis of $300. D died when the building was worth $360. At the time of D's death, D had $100 of suspended passive losses with respect to the property. (The transferee of property acquired from a decedent generally obtains a basis equal to the fair market value of the property at the date of the decedent's death—see 1014(a).) What result to D?

8. B spends 1500 hours a year working as partner in a real-estate brokerage firm. That is more than half the time B devotes to performing personal services. B also owns an apartment building which produced a $100,000 loss in the current year. All of the loss would be deductible but for the application of § 469. B materially participates in the operation of the apartment building. Can B use the loss to offset her considerable income from her brokerage and investment activities?

9. A, a single person who practices law nearly full-time, owns and manages an apartment building. A handles all leasing, hires contractors to make necessary repairs and does the bookkeeping for the project. In the current year, A has a loss of $45,000 from the rental of the building, all of which would be allowable but for § 469. A's adjusted gross income is $110,000. A has no other passive deductions or passive income. How much of the loss can A deduct?

Chapter 46

THE ALTERNATIVE MINIMUM TAX

Code: §§ 55(a), (b)(1)(A) & (2), (c)(1), (d)(1); 56(a)(1)(A) & (6), (b)(1) & (3), (e)(1) & (2); 57(a)(5).

1. On their joint return, H and W report taxable income of $75,000, computed as follows:

Salaries		$120,000
Less: Alimony paid		(20,000)
Adjusted gross income		$100,000
Less:		
State and local taxes	$5,000	
Charitable contribution	3,000	
Medical expenses	5,000	
Mortgage interest	4,000	
Miscellaneous itemized deductions	2,000	
Personal exemptions	6,000	
Total deductions		25,000
Taxable income		$75,000

They also received $10,000 interest on "specified private-activity bonds" (defined in § 57(a)(5)(C)). Upon exercise of an incentive stock option, W paid $10,000 for stock of her employer that had a value of $50,000. The mortgage interest was paid on a home-equity loan the proceeds of which were used to make a down payment on an airplane for recreational use. The charitable contribution represents a gift of stock with an adjusted basis of $1,000 and a value of $3,000. The total amount of medical expenses was $12,500. They are entitled to no credits against tax.

Determine the couple's alternative minimum taxable income (AMTI).

2. A, a single person (not a surviving spouse), owes $16,000 of regular tax. Assume that the exemption amount for singles is $45,000. Compute A's alternative minimum tax (AMT) if her AMTI is:

(a) $112,500;

(b) $212,500.

3. What is A's marginal tax rate in problem 2(b)?

4. In January, C paid $100,000 for a business machine (5–year property) for use in business (a sole proprietorship). For regular-tax purposes, her depreciation deduction for the equipment is $20,000, leaving her with an adjusted basis of $80,000 at the end of the year.

(a) How much deprecation is allowable in computing AMTI?

(b) At the end of the year, what is C's adjusted basis for the machine for purposes of the AMT?

5. R received a state income-tax refund that was fully includable in gross income for regular-tax purposes. How should the refund be treated in computing AMTI?

6. The AMT was originally conceived as a tax on a few hundred wealthy taxpayers who used tax preferences extensively. In 2005, the President's Advisory Panel on Federal Tax Reform estimated that, unless Congress provides relief, 52 million taxpayers may be liable for the AMT by 2015. What features of the AMT (or the regular tax) are turning the AMT into a mass tax?

Section L

OTHER TOPICS

Chapter 47

PRESENT AND FUTURE VALUE

In working the problems in this chapter, use the tables in Appendix A and ignore the effect of taxes (!).

A. FUTURE VALUE

1. R invests $10,000 today at a rate of return of 9 percent. How much should R expect to have after ten years?

2. I plans to invest $1,000 in a 6–year certificate of deposit. What will the investment cumulate to if I invests with:

(a) Bank A, which offers interest of 12 percent annually on such CDs?

(b) Bank B, which offers 12 percent compounded semi-annually?

(c) Bank C, which offers 12 percent compounded quarterly?

3. What is the effective annual interest rate offered by each bank in 2? (Use the first year's interest to determine the effective annual rate.)

4. T anticipates that on account of a certain transaction he will owe approximately $15,000 in taxes after ten years. If T can earn an after-tax rate of return of 10% annually, how much should T set aside today in order to have $15,000 for the tax payment after ten years?

5. At what approximate rate of (after-tax) return must B invest her money if she wishes to double her investment in ten years?

6. J has $10,000 of cash to invest today. If J wants to increase that amount to $15,000 over six years, what approximate rate of return must J earn on the investment?

7. G is going to invest $10,000 at an after-tax rate of return of 6 percent. For approximately how long must the fund be invested to cumulate to $19,000?

B. FUTURE VALUE OF AN ANNUITY

1. A is going to set aside $10,000 at the end of each of the next 20 years. A can earn an after-tax return of 8 percent. What will be the balance in the fund after 20 years?

2. B will invest $5,000 on January 1, year 1, and a like sum on each subsequent January 1 through January 1, year 10. After B's last contribution, the fund will remain invested through January 1, year 15. If B earns an after-tax return of 8 percent at all times, what will be the balance in the fund on January 1, year 15?

3. D is planning to start a savings fund for her child, C, who turns 11 years old today. Beginning on C's 12th birthday, D will invest $1,000 a year in the fund, which earns a return of 12 percent at all times. D will make the final contribution when C attains age 21. What will be the balance in the fund when C attains 21?

4. Suppose instead that D made the first contribution on C's 11th birthday and the tenth (and final) contribution on C's 20th birthday. What would be the balance in the fund on C's 21st birthday?

5. The terms of E's $100,000 student loan require repayment in a single payment due ten years after E's graduation. E graduates on June 1, year 1. In addition to paying the interest each year, E plans to invest a fixed amount on the anniversary of her graduation for each of the next ten years, which sum will then be used to pay the student loan when it matures on June 1, year 11. E thinks she can earn a 10 percent after-tax return on her investments. How much must E invest on each anniversary of her graduation in order to repay the loan in timely fashion?

6. Same as 5, except that E will make the first contribution to the fund on her graduation day and the final contribution on June 1, year 10 (one year before the principal is due). Determine the amount of E's annual contribution.

7. F would like to be able to purchase a new car in three years. F estimates that the car will cost $25,000. How much must F set aside at the end of each month in order to accumulate sufficient funds for the purchase after three years? F thinks he can earn 12% interest (compounded monthly) on the investment.

C. PRESENT VALUE

1. If A can earn 7 percent annual interest on a comparably risky investment, how much should A be willing to pay for a $1,000 zero-coupon bond due in ten years? (The purchaser of a zero-coupon bond does not receive periodic interest payments but instead receives a single payment at maturity. The bond is purchased at a discount from its face amount (i.e., the amount payable at maturity) for an amount equal to the present value of the future payment.)

2. B sells property for $500,000, payable (without interest) after five years. What is the equivalent cash selling price for the property if B can earn 8 percent on comparably risky investments?

3.   Same as 2, except that the expected return on comparably risky investments is 8% compounded quarterly.

4. Explain why your answer in 3 is less than in 2.

5. A seller of property offers it at $100,000, payable immediately, or $130,000 payable (without interest) after 5 years. C wishes to purchase the property. If C can earn a return of 5 percent on comparable investments, which payment method would she prefer?

D. PRESENT VALUE OF AN ANNUITY

1. In settlement of a suit for personal injury, P is entitled to receive $100,000 at the end of each of the next 20 years. If the appropriate discount rate is 9 percent, what is the present value of P's right?

2. R intends to make a partial gift to a charitable organization specified in § 170(c)(2). R transfers $100,000 cash to the charity in exchange for an annuity of $8,137.27 payable at the end of each of the next ten years. To what extent has R made a charitable contribution? Assume that the annuity is valued using a discount rate of 10 percent.

3. On January 1, year 1, S sold a farm for $600,000, payable $100,000 down and $100,000 on January 1 of each of the following 5 years. The contract made no provision for interest on the deferred payments. Comparably risky credits earn interest at the rate of 6%. What is the equivalent cash selling price of the farm on January 1, year 1?

4. T is to receive property rentals of $1,000 a month for a 12–month lease. Each month's rent is due at the beginning of the month, and the appropriate discount rate is 12% compounded monthly. What is the present value of the lease payments at the inception of the lease?

5. A $1,000 bond (the "old bond") with a remaining term of 6 years bears interest at 6% payable semiannually. If a new bond of comparable riskiness yields 8% compounded semi-annually, at what price will the old bond sell?

6. U, who can earn 10% annually on his investments at all times, expects to accumulate $998,474 in his Roth IRA by the time of his 65th birthday. He wants to withdraw the balance in the account in 25 equal annual installments beginning when he attains age 65. How much can U withdraw in each year?

7. On January 1, year 1, H borrows $120,000 from a bank at 10–percent annual interest for the purpose of purchasing a home. The loan must be amortized (repaid) in equal annual installments at the end of each of the next twenty years. Each payment will be credited first to interest and then to principal.

(a) What is the amount of each annual payment?

(b) How is the first payment apportioned between interest and principal?

8. The tiny island country of Bikinia is offering a new issue of its bonds that will pay $240 a year annual interest in perpetuity but with no return of principal (ever). I, an investor, thinks that she can earn 12 percent annually on comparably risky securities. What price should I be willing to pay for one of the Bikinia bonds?

Chapter 48

PRACTICE EXAMINATION QUESTIONS

---

1. 1. (2 hours) *Basic Facts*: Theresa (T) (who is in the 35% tax bracket) owns a building (ignore the land) that she purchased several years ago at a price of $500 (000 omitted throughout). She has properly deducted $100 of straight-line depreciation (through the date of disposition of the property in the current year) and her adjusted basis is $400. During her ownership of the property, T has not sustained any loss with respect to the property (i.e., the gross income from the property has been sufficient to cover her out-of-pocket and depreciation expenses). Assume that, except where otherwise stated, (1) the property was worth $600 when it was disposed of by T; (2) the disposition of the building is T's only disposition of property for the year; (3) all parties are unrelated; and (4) all sales are bona fide.

Explain fully the tax consequences to T (and only T), including the tax rate applicable to any recognized gain, in each of the following *alternative* transactions.

(a) The building is in downtown University City and is held for use in T's business. T sells the building for $600 cash and pays a brokerage commission of $40 on the sale.

(b) The building (held for investment) is located in University City and held for rent. T receives $600 cash for the property when the City, through exercise of its power of eminent domain, condemns the building to build a parking ramp. T promptly reinvests $550 of the condemnation proceeds in an oceanside condominium (also to be held as investment rental property). The condominium is located in Puerto Vallarta, Mexico.

(c) T exchanges the building (held for investment) for an apartment building (to be used in business). The apartment building is worth $450, and T also receives a vintage Mercedes worth $150 to equalize the exchange. (The automobile had a basis of $60 in the hands of the other party to the exchange.)

(d) T transferred the building (held for investment) to Y Corp. in exchange for $500 cash and $100 worth of Microsoft stock. Half of the stock of Y Corp. is owned by T's son-in-law, (S) and half by her daughter, D.

179

(e) The building was held for use in business. When T purchased the building, she paid $100 cash down and borrowed the $400 balance of the purchase price from a bank on a non-recourse note secured by the building. Although T made all interest payments on time, T paid only $20 on the note principal. This year, when the value of the building was $350 and its adjusted basis $400, T surrendered the property to the lender. T was hopelessly insolvent at that time.

(f) The building, which T held for investment, had an adjusted basis of $400 and was encumbered with a $500 mortgage that secured a loan on which T was personally liable. (The liability was incurred when T borrowed part of the purchase price for the building.) When the value of the building was $380, T surrendered it to the lender. Although T was not insolvent, the lender discharged T from further liability.

2. (1 hour, 20 minutes) Discuss the income-tax results to P of the following transactions. (Ignore the effect of inflation adjustments and §§ 68 and 151(d)(3). Computation of the tax is not required.)

P holds a half-time appointment as a professor on the faculty of State University, where he serves on the botany faculty. He is also employed as chief research scientist by Superplant, Inc., a firm that attempts to develop exotic hybrid plants.

P's salary from the University is $120,000 ($10,000 a month). P is very concerned that R, his principal post-doctoral research assistant at the University, may leave her post because the University has skimped on her salary. He has therefore requested the University to pay his salary for the month of December to R, and the University has agreed to do so.

Superplant pays P a salary of $250,000 for the current year. It also has a non-statutory stock-option plan. Five years ago, when Superplant stock was selling at $10,000 a share, the firm granted P a non-statutory option to purchase one of its shares for $20,000. P exercised the option today, when the share has a value of $50,000. There are no restrictions on the share.

Because some of P's work at Superplant exposes him to hazardous chemicals, P must wear protective clothing in the Superplant lab. He spent $6,000 on such clothing during the current year. P also spent $1,000 commuting between his office at the University and his laboratory at Superplant (a distance of 15 miles).

This year P began receiving annual payments of $10,000 under a single-premium annuity contract that his father had purchased for him ten years ago at a cost of $121,000. The annuity payments were to commence when P attained age 60, which he did this year, and continue until P's death.

P owns his home (Greenacre), which is valued at $400,000. Although P long ago retired the mortgage on Greenacre, he re-mortgaged it this year for $250,000 and applied the loan proceeds toward the purchase of a vacation home in Florida. During the year, he paid $25,000 of interest on the loan. He also paid $4,000 of property taxes on Greenacre and $6,000 of property taxes on the Florida vacation home.

P is divorced and pays alimony to his former wife, W, in the amount of $50,000 a year for the duration of W's life. In addition, if W survives P, the payments to W continue and must be made from P's estate. The divorce decree also requires that P pay the property taxes on the home in which W resides (the former marital home of P and W, which is now owned by W). P paid $5,000 of such taxes in the current year.

P also made two gifts to charities qualifying under § 170(c)(2): $10,000 worth of X stock that he purchased six months ago for $8,000, and $20,000 worth of Y stock that he inherited from his father five years ago when its value was $5,000.

3. (1 hour) Renowned sketch artist Avare Artiste (A) resides in New York City, where his studio is located. In November of this year, he spent a week in University City (for which he received a handsome stipend), where he gave a series of lectures and demonstrations of his technique in State University's Department of Art.

On the last night of his visit, he and his wife dined at University City's most-prominent local eatery, the Bistro Café Restaurant, where they ran up a $200 bill. The restaurant is owned by Betty Bistro (B), who also serves as the principal chef. At the conclusion of the couple's meal, B approached their table, introduced herself, gushed that she had long admired A's work, and requested his autograph. In response, A sketched B's portrait on the back of a napkin and signed it: "For Betty Bistro, with thanks for your superb cuisine and warm hospitality. Avare Artiste 11/25/XX." B thanked A profusely and tore up the unpaid dinner check.

The next day B learned that similar sketches signed by A typically sell for $300.

(a) Describe fully the tax results of these events to A and B.

(b) What further tax consequences to B if B had the sketch covered with glass, framed, and hung in a prominent place in the restaurant for her customers to admire?

(c) What are the tax consequences to B if she donated the sketch (then worth $400) to the State University Museum of Art?

Part Two

PROBLEMS AND SOLUTIONS

Section A

INTRODUCTION

Chapter 1

ORIENTATION

A. SOME POLICY ASPECTS

1. Explain the following terms:

(a) Progressive tax;

A tax is progressive with respect to income if it takes a greater *percentage* of the income of a high-income person than of a low-income person. In other words, the tax, stated as a percentage of the taxpayer's income, rises as the taxpayer's income rises. It is wrong to say that a tax is progressive just because a higher-income person pays more tax than a lower-income person. That can also be true of proportional and regressive taxes.

(b) Proportional tax;

A tax is proportional with respect to income if the tax, stated as a percentage of a person's income, remains constant as income increases.

(c) Regressive tax.

A tax is regressive with respect to income if the tax, stated as a percentage of a person's income, decreases as income increases.

2. P and W both live in a state that imposes a 5–percent general sales tax. P has income of $30,000, all of which is spent on consumption items subject to the tax. W has income of $500,000, of which $250,000 is spent on consumption items subject to the tax.

(a) Does P or W pay more sales tax?

W pays more ($12,500) than P ($1,500).

(b) Is the tax progressive, regressive or proportional with respect to income?

It is regressive. As a percentage of income, W pays at a 2.5–percent rate ($12,500/$500,000), while P pays at a 5–percent rate ($1,500/$30,000). Sales taxes are regressive because lower-income people consume a much greater proportion of their incomes than do high-income people. Lower-income folks therefore pay a higher proportion of their income in sales tax than do those with higher incomes. Some states exempt food and medicine from their sales taxes in an effort to mitigate the regressivity of the tax.

3. Suppose that a 6.2–percent tax is imposed on the first $100,000 of an employee's salary. Salary in excess of $100,000 is not subject to the tax. Is the tax progressive, proportional or regressive?

The tax is proportional over the first $100,000 of salary or wages and regressive above that amount. To see why, notice that someone with $1,000,000 of salary pays the same amount of tax as someone with a salary of $100,000. The tax rate is .62 percent for the high-income earner and 6.2 percent for the lower-income person.

The tax in the problem roughly approximates the Social Security tax, which is imposed at a rate of 6.2 percent on an amount of wages or salary up to the Social Security wage base ($97,500 for 2007 but adjusted annually). A matching tax is imposed upon the employer. Self-employed persons must pay both the employee's and employer's share of the tax (12.40 percent). The federal government also imposes a Medicare tax of 1.45 percent upon both the employee and employer (2.9 percent for the self-employed). The Medicare tax applies to all earned income without limitation. For income-tax purposes, the self-employed can deduct half of their tax payments under § 164(f).

4. What is the Haig-Simons (or Schantz-Haig-Simons) definition of income?

Simons, Personal Income Taxation 50 (1938) defines income as:

* * * the algebraic sum of (1) the market value of rights exercised in consumption and (2) the change in the value of the store of property rights between the beginning and end of the period in question. In other words, it is merely the result obtained by adding consumption during the period to "wealth" at the end of the period and then subtracting "wealth" at the beginning.

Put differently, income is the sum of consumption and saving $(I = C + S)$. This definition of income is often used as a starting point in discussing tax-policy issues.

5. How might one impose a progressive tax on consumption?

Some students of tax policy favor taxing consumption rather than income. Taxing consumption under, e.g., a sales tax is regressive, as discussed above. But one can use the Haig-Simons definition of income to discern how an income tax could be turned into a progressive consumption tax. If we subtract savings (S) from both sides of the above equation, we get: $I - S = C + S - S$, which implies that $C = I - S$. In other words, we could convert our present income tax into a consumption tax by allowing an unlimited deduction for savings and subjecting the resulting tax base to a progressive rate schedule. There is a large literature on the progressive consumption tax. The seminal article is Andrews, A Consumption-type or Cash Flow Personal Income Tax, 87 Harv. L. Rev. 1113 (1974).

6. What is the primary purpose of imposing heavy taxes on cigarettes and liquor?

The primary purpose of taxing cigarettes and liquor is to raise their price to better reflect the costs of the externalities that users of these products impose on society. In the absence of a tax, these products would tend to be priced at their (private) costs of production. But the marginal cost of these products to society are much greater than their costs of production. For example, those who overindulge in alcohol sometimes cause accidents, often have serious health problems, etc., which impose real costs on society that are not reflected in the production costs of liquor. By imposing tax on the purchase of these products, government raises their price to more clearly reflect the true cost of the products to society.

7. Explain the difference between the legal and economic incidence of a tax.

The legal incidence of a tax falls upon the one who is responsible under the law for paying the tax; the economic incidence falls upon the one who bears the economic burden of the tax, regardless of whether that person actually writes a check to the government. The tax may be "shifted" from those who bear the legal incidence of the tax as people adjust their economic behavior in response to the tax. For example, the legal incidence of the Social Security tax is one-half on the employee and one-half on the employer. Few economists think that the economic burden of the tax is one-half on each. The existence of the payroll tax causes employers to hire fewer employees at the margin and probably causes some employees to accept a lower wage than they would in the absence of the tax. These adjustments shift some of the employer's tax burden to the employee, who winds up bearing more than half of the economic burden of the tax.

As another example, consider the corporate income tax. The tax is imposed upon the corporation. But a corporation is a legal fiction. Who are the real humans who bear the tax burden? The Congress that first enacted the corporate income tax probably assumed that the shareholders would bear the burden of the tax. Although the precise economic incidence of the tax is uncertain, it is probably borne partly by shareholders and other owners of capital and partly by consumers of the firm's products, its employees, and perhaps others.

B. AN INTRODUCTION TO FEDERAL TAX PROCEDURE

Code: §§ 6501(a) & (b)(1); 6511(a); 6513(a); 6212(a); 6213(a). Note 7805(a).

1. Describe the role in the federal tax system of:

(a) The Sixteenth Amendment;

Congress's power to tax income stems from its general taxing power under Article I, § 8 of the Constitution, which authorizes Congress "To lay and collect Taxes, Duties, Imposts, and Excises * * *." However, Article I, §§ 2 and 9 require that "direct taxes" be apportioned among the states on the basis of their relative populations. That is, if State X has 2 percent of the nation's population, its citizens must provide 2 percent of the revenue from a direct tax. Unfortunately, however, the term "direct tax" does not have a clear meaning. Most authorities agree that a "capitation" or "head tax" is a direct tax and that taxes on imports, exports and consumption are indirect. What of a tax on income? The Union enacted an income tax during the Civil War, and the tax was held to be indirect in Springer v. United States, 102 U.S. (12 Otto) 586 (1880). The Civil War income tax was repealed after the war emergency ended, but Congress enacted another income tax in 1894. That tax was struck down by the Supreme Court. The Court reasoned that (1) a tax on real or personal property would be a direct tax; (2) therefore, a tax on the income from such property was direct; and (3) the tax was invalid as a direct tax that did not provide for apportionment on the basis of population; Pollock v. Farmers' Loan and Trust Co., 157 U.S. 429 (1895).

In 1913, the Sixteenth Amendment was ratified. It supersedes *Pollock* by empowering Congress to "lay and collect taxes on incomes, from whatever source derived, without apportionment among the several States, and without regard to any census or enumeration." By eliminating the apportionment requirement, the Sixteenth Amendment made possible the enactment of the modern federal income tax.

(b) The Internal Revenue Code of 1986;

The first modern federal income tax was enacted shortly after ratification of the Sixteenth Amendment in 1913. For the first 26 years of its existence, the tax law consisted of "revenue acts," which were usually enacted every two years. In 1939, the tax law was codified into a permanent body of law (the Internal Revenue Code of 1939). After an extensive revision of the Code in 1954, it was re-named the Internal Revenue Code of 1954. And, after yet another major overhaul in 1986, the Code was re-christened the Internal Revenue Code of 1986. The 1986 Code, as amended to date, is *the* law. It is found in Title 26 of the United States Code.

(c) The Income Tax Regulations;

Section 7805(a) empowers the Treasury to issue regulations interpreting the Code ("interpretive regulations"). Regulations are the law, unless they are invalid. An interpretive regulation may be invalidated by a court if the regulation conflicts with the Code. But such regulations are usually upheld, especially if they reflect a consistent, long-standing interpretation. A second type of regulation is a "legislative regulation," which is issued under legislation authorizing the Treasury to make rules on a particular subject. For example, § 1502 delegates to the Treasury the task of promulgating rules under which affiliated corporations may file consolidated tax returns. Legislative regulations are generally thought to be entitled to more deference from the courts than interpretive regulations.

(d) Revenue Rulings;

Issued by the Internal Revenue Service, a revenue ruling poses a legal issue concerning the interpretation of the Code, describes the facts that give rise to the issue, analyzes the relevant authorities that bear on resolution of the issue, and states a conclusion. They are published in the Service's weekly Internal Revenue Bulletin, which are then cumulated into bound volumes (called Cumulative Bulletins). Revenue rulings rank below regulations in the precedential hierarchy, but they often provide helpful authority.

(e) Letter Rulings.

The Service issues a letter ruling in response to a taxpayer request for guidance on (usually) the tax consequences of a contemplated transaction. Letter rulings are made public (after redaction of information that might identify the taxpayer seeking the ruling), but they are not intended to have precedential value; indeed, they cannot even be cited as precedent; § 6110(k)(3).

2. Explain the following terms:

(a) Audit;

Audit is the process by which the Service investigates a return's accuracy. The taxpayer may be asked to meet with a revenue agent and furnish additional information concerning the taxpayer's income and deductions. At the conclusion of the audit, the agent makes a report reflecting any recommended adjustments to the taxpayer's tax liability. If the taxpayer agrees with the agent's report, the adjustments stand. A taxpayer who disagrees with the proposed changes has 30 days to file an appeal within the Service. If the taxpayer does not appeal within 30 days, or if agreement is not reached on appeal, the taxpayer will be sent a "90–day letter." See below.

(b) 90–day letter.

When the Service asserts that the taxpayer owes additional tax and the matter is not resolved within the administrative processes described above, the Service sends the taxpayer a 90–day letter ("notice of deficiency"). The taxpayer then has 90 days to pay the tax or to challenge the alleged deficiency by filing a petition with the Tax Court. (The 90–day letter is sometimes described as the taxpayer's "ticket" to the Tax Court.) If the taxpayer does neither, the Service will assess the tax and demand payment by a specified date; if the taxpayer still does not pay, the Service will commence the collection process.

3. The Internal Revenue Service has issued a notice of deficiency to your client, who wishes to litigate the issue in dispute. What forums are available for the litigation?

As explained above, the taxpayer can litigate a deficiency (i.e., a case where the Service claims the taxpayer owes additional tax) in the United States Tax Court. This may be advantageous for the taxpayer, as the taxpayer does not have to pay the tax until the case is concluded. Most cases are decided by a single judge, and jury trial is not available. A small-case procedure is available for cases involving an alleged deficiency of less than $50,000. The taxpayer is always the petitioner and the Commissioner the respondent in Tax Court cases.

An appeal from a decision of the Tax Court lies to the United States Court of Appeals for the circuit in which the taxpayer resided when the Tax Court petition was filed. No appeal is available from decisions rendered in the small-case procedure.

The taxpayer can also pay the tax, file a claim for refund, and, if the refund claim is denied or not acted upon for six months, file a suit for refund in either the United States District Court or the Court of Federal Claims. In the district court, jury trial is available on factual issues. Appeal lies to the United States Court of Appeals for the circuit in which the district court sits.

In the Court of Federal Claims, there is no jury trial. Appeals lie to the United States Court of Appeals for the Federal Circuit.

Weighing the precedential value of tax decisions can be challenging because the decisions of courts other than the Supreme Court are not always binding on other courts. A district court must follow the decisions of the court of appeals for its circuit, the Court of Federal Claims must follow the decisions of the Court of Appeals for the Federal Circuit, and the Tax Court, under the *Golsen* doctrine, discussed below, follows the decisions of the court of appeals to which an appeal would lie. Apart from these instances, however, a decision of another court is persuasive, but not mandatory, authority.

4. **Explain the following terms:**

(a) **Non-acquiescence;**

Suppose the government loses a tax case, but does not appeal. What should the Service's agents and tax practitioners infer from that? Does the failure to appeal signify that the government has changed its view on the issue? Or only that, for some reason other than the merits, the government did not think the case should be appealed? The Service often signals its intentions in such a case by publishing an "acquiescence" or "non-acquiescence" in the case. An acquiescence indicates that the government accepts the holding of the unappealed decision; a non-acquiescence says to the tax world that the government is adhering to its position and will continue the litigate the issue as appropriate cases arise.

(b) *Golsen* **rule.**

As discussed above, the Tax Court is bound to follow decisions of only the Supreme Court. But suppose that a court of appeals has previously reversed a Tax Court decision on a particular issue, and the issue arises in another Tax Court case that is appealable to the same court of appeals. Even though the Tax Court adheres to the validity of its original view and need not follow the decision of the appeals court, it will in fact follow the decision of that court of appeals. This rule is referred to as the *Golsen* rule, after Golsen v. Commissioner, 54 T.C. 742 (1970), the decision announcing the rule.

5. **T, who uses the calendar year as her taxable year, filed her 2007 federal income-tax return on March 1, 2008. Although acting in good faith, T made an error on her return, which caused her to understate her tax liability for the year. What is the latest date on which the Internal Revenue Service can issue a notice of deficiency (90–day letter)?**

The tax generally must be assessed within three years of the due date or the actual filing date of the return, whichever is later; § 6501(a) & (b)(1). In this case, the due date is the later (April 15, 2008), and so the Service would have until April 15, 2011, to issue a notice of deficiency. If T omitted an item of gross income that exceeds 25 percent of the gross income shown on the return, the statute of limitations is extended to six years and would not run until April 15, 2014.

6. **Suppose instead that T (in 5) overpaid her tax for 2007. What is the latest date on which she can file a claim for refund?**

A refund claim must be filed by the latest of: (1) three years from the actual filing date of the return; (2) three years from the due date of the return; and (3) two years from the date on which the tax was paid; §§ 6511(a); 6513(a). If we assume that T paid the tax not later than the date on which she filed her return, T will have until April 15, 2011 to file a refund claim.

Chapter 2

TAX COMPUTATIONS

Code: §§ 1(a)–(d) (in Appendix B); 61(a); 62(a); 63; 151(a), (b), (c), (d)(1) & (2). Note § 213(a).

    1. **W and H are married. They file a joint return (i.e., they combine their income and deductions on a single return) and compute their tax liability under Code § 1(a). They have taxable income of $150,000. Use the appropriate tax-rate schedule in Appendix B to answer the following questions:**

    (a) What is their tax liability (before credits)?

$34,705.50 ($31,405.50 + $3,300).

Where does the $31,405.50 figure come from? That's the tax on the first $140,000 of taxable income (i.e., the sum of the tax on the first $14,000 of taxable income at 10%, the next $30,200 at 15%, the next $44,950 at 25%, and the next $50,850 at 28%, for a total of $31,405.50).

    (b) What is their marginal tax rate?

33 percent. The marginal rate is the rate applicable to the last dollar of taxable income.

    (c) What "tax bracket" are they in?

They are in the 33–percent bracket; this is just another way of expressing their marginal rate.

    (d) What is their average tax rate?

23.14 percent ($34,705.50 tax/$150,000 income).

(e) Suppose you are the couple's tax advisor. Are you more interested in their marginal rate or their average rate?

The couple's tax advisor will be more interested in their marginal rate. In tax planning, the marginal rate is important because it helps us to understand the tax cost of earning additional income or the tax benefit of an additional deduction. For example, suppose that the couple is considering the effect of making a charitable contribution before the end of the year. If they expect to be in the 33–percent bracket and the contribution is fully deductible, a $1,000 gift to charity costs them only $670 after tax. They write a check to the charity for $1,000, but the additional deduction reduces their taxable income by $1,000 and, at their 33–percent marginal rate, reduces their taxes by $330. So, the couple's net cost of making the contribution is $670 ($1,000 contribution less $330 tax savings).

If they had been in the 15–percent bracket, the net cost of the contribution would have been $850 ($1,000 contribution less $150 tax saving).

2. What is the legal significance of:

(a) Gross income?

The computation of taxable income, which is the tax base to which the tax rates of § 1 apply, involves three major steps: (1) determine gross income; (2) subtract from gross income the deductions specified in § 62 to arrive at adjusted gross income (AGI); and (3) subtract from AGI any other deductions to which the taxpayer is entitled to arrive at taxable income.

Although gross income, defined in § 61(a), is the starting point in computing one's taxable income, the legal significance of the gross-income figure is limited. Indeed, the individual income-tax return (form 1040) does not even have a line for total gross income. Nevertheless, the gross-income figure may be significant in determining: (1) whether the taxpayer is required to file a return (§ 6012(a)); (2) whether one can be claimed as a dependent by another (§ 152(a) & (d)(1)(B)); and (3) the applicable statute of limitations (§ 6501(e)(1)(A)).

(b) Adjusted gross income (AGI)?

The term adjusted gross income (defined in § 62) means gross income less the deductions specified in § 62. To be deducted, an item must be *allowable* under some provision of the Code. Section 62 itself does not allow any deductions—it just tells us whether to subtract the deduction from gross income in computing AGI or whether to subtract it from AGI in computing taxable income. So, we must first determine whether the item is allowable as a deduction under some provision other than § 62. For example, § 162(a) allows a deduction for business expenses and § 170(a) for charitable contributions. Then we turn to § 62 to determine whether to take the deduction into account in computing AGI or only in moving from AGI to taxable income.

AGI is legally significant because that figure (or some percentage of it) sometimes serves as a ceiling or floor on certain other deductions. For example, § 170 generally allows a deduction for charitable contributions, but the deduction for any year cannot exceed a specified percentage of AGI (20, 30 or 50 percent, depending upon the type of gift and the nature of the donee organization). In that case, AGI serves as a ceiling on the amount deductible. In other cases, only deductions in excess of the AGI figure are allowable. For example, § 213 allows a deduction for medical expenses, but only to the extent that the expenses exceed 7.5 percent of the taxpayer's AGI. The notion underlying § 213 is that people with extraordinarily large medical expenses have less ability to pay than otherwise similarly situated people who do not incur such costs. But how are we to judge the level at which medical expenses become sufficiently burdensome to warrant tax relief? After all, the effect of (say) $3,000 in medical costs bears much more heavily on a taxpayer whose AGI is $20,000 than on one whose AGI is $200,000. The congressional solution is to allow a deduction only to those whose medical expenses exceed 7.5 percent of their AGI.

In recent years, Congress has created a number of deductions and credits that are designed to benefit lower- and middle-income taxpayers but not those at the higher end of the income scale. To ensure that the tax benefits are not captured by higher-income taxpayers, those provisions often include a "phaseout" that reduces (or eliminates) the amount of the deduction or credit as the taxpayer's AGI increases. Sometimes the phaseout is based upon the taxpayer's "modified" AGI, which is AGI with some minor modification. One cannot generalize about the definition of modified AGI, as each provision that uses modified AGI contains its own definition. For the overwhelming majority of taxpayers, the modifications do not apply, and modified AGI does not differ from "regular" AGI under § 62.

(c) Taxable income?

Taxable income is defined as gross income less all of the allowable deductions to which the taxpayer is entitled. As the tax base for our federal income tax, taxable income is the figure to which the tax rates of § 1 are applied to compute the amount of tax imposed for the year. (As discussed below, however, the actual amount of tax owed is reduced by the amount of any credits against tax to which the taxpayer is entitled.)

3. Explain the following terms:

(a) Exclusion;

An exclusion prevents an item of income (or potential income) from being included in the computation of gross income. For example, § 102(a) excludes from gross income the value of any property acquired by gift or bequest. So, a taxpayer who receives $100,000 of salary and also receives a $2,000 birthday gift from her parents has gross income of only $100,000. Since the excluded items never enter into gross income, they are not included in the taxable-income base and not subject to income tax.

(b) Deduction;

A deduction is subtracted from gross income or AGI in computing taxable income. Although one must understand the distinction between exclusions and deductions to be able to speak the language of the tax law, it would be wrong to overemphasize the importance of the distinction. Both are just means to the determination of the tax base (taxable income).

(c) Credit.

A credit is a reduction of the amount of tax owed. For example, § 24 allows the parent of a qualifying child a $1,000 credit against the parent's tax liability. Thus, if P's § 1 tax before credits is $1,600, and P is entitled to a $1,000 child tax credit, P's tax for the year is only $600. The distinction between deductions and credits is an important one. Deductions reduce taxable income (the tax base). How much money the deduction saves the taxpayer depends upon the taxpayer's marginal tax rate. Thus, a $1,000 deduction reduces taxable income by $1,000; the deduction saves $280 for a taxpayer in the 28–percent bracket and saves $330 for one in the 33–percent bracket. A credit of $1,000 saves each $1,000 (assuming that each would otherwise owe at least $1,000 of tax).

4. What are the principal purposes of the "inclusionary rules" (§§ 71–90) and the "exclusionary rules" (§§ 101–139A)?

Section 61 says that, "except as otherwise provided," gross income includes all "income," including the items specified in § 61(a)(1)–(15). Among the most important of those "otherwise-providing" provisions are the "inclusionary rules" of §§ 71–90 and the "exclusionary rules" of §§ 101–139A. The inclusionary rules usually begin "Gross income includes * * *," while the exclusionary rules say "Gross income does not include * * *."

The various inclusionary and exclusionary rules serve one of two purposes: (1) Some clarify the treatment of an item where there might be doubt as to whether the item constitutes "income" and hence should be included in gross income under § 61; (2) Others provide preferential tax treatment for an item even where there is no doubt that the item constitutes "income." As an example of the former, consider the appropriate treatment of the value of property received by bequest: Should the value of the bequest be characterized as "income"? Reasonable people could disagree about that. On the one hand, the bequest does increase the recipient's ability to save or consume. But most people probably do not think of bequests as "income." They liken a bequest to a transfer payment rather than to a new round of earning and consuming or saving. To resolve any ambiguity, Congress has provided guidance in § 102(a): Gross income does not include the value of property acquired by bequest.

In other cases, an inclusionary or exclusionary rule may provide special tax relief for items that all would agree were "income" in a normative sense. For example, § 103(a) excludes from income interest received on state and local government bonds. No one could argue with a straight face that interest is not "income." But the exclusion of the interest from the investor's income reduces the borrowing costs of state governments by allowing them to issue their bonds at a lower rate of interest than they would have to pay if the interest were taxable. In other words, § 103 is an example of using the tax law to achieve a "non-tax" goal, in this case aiding state and local governments.

Section 103 is a "tax expenditure"—a special tax provision (e.g., a deduction, exclusion or credit) that exists to further some *non-tax* goal rather than to measure income in a normative sense.

5. Explain the terms:

(a) "Above-the-line" deduction;

An above-the-line deduction is one that is subtracted from gross income in computing AGI. It is a deduction allowed by some Code provision (other than § 62, which is a definition of AGI and does not purport to "allow" any deductions) and included among those deductible in computing AGI by § 62. The above-the-line deductions must be distinguished from the itemized deductions (discussed below), which are subtracted from AGI in computing taxable income.

(b) Itemized deduction;

Itemized deductions are those other than (1) the above-the-line deductions, (2) the personal and dependency exemptions, and (3) (by implication) the standard deduction; § 63(d).

After computing AGI, the taxpayer must choose whether to itemize deductions or take the standard deduction. A taxpayer who itemizes subtracts the itemized deductions and the personal and dependency exemptions to determine taxable income. A taxpayer who chooses to take the standard deduction subtracts the standard deduction and the personal and dependency exemptions to arrive at taxable income. Taxpayers choose to itemize their deductions whenever the itemized deductions exceed the standard deduction.

(c) Standard deduction;

Before turning to the standard deduction, a word about filing status: The taxpayer's filing status is important in determining which of the tax-rate schedules in § 1(a)–(d) must be used in computing the tax liability. For example, a married couple may combine their income and deductions on a joint return, in which case they compute their tax under § 1(a), or they can file separate returns and compute their tax under § 1(d). A single person must use the rates of § 1(c), unless she is a head of household under § 2(b) or a surviving spouse under § 2(a). (Don't worry about the details of these classifications right now; we'll examine them more thoroughly in Chapter 40.)

In addition to determining what tax-rate schedule the taxpayer must use, the taxpayer's filing status sometimes affects the amount of a credit or deduction, and the standard deduction is one of those.

The standard deduction (§ 63(c)) is a statutorily prescribed amount that depends upon the taxpayer's filing status, age and eyesight(!). It is made up of the sum of the basic standard deduction and the additional standard deduction for the aged and blind.

The basic standard deduction for a single person (who is not a surviving spouse or a head of household) is $3,000 (before inflation adjustments); § 63(c)(2)(C). For a married couple filing a joint return, the basic standard deduction is "200 percent" of the amount allowable for a single person under § 63(c)(2)(C); § 63(c)(2)(A). So, ignoring inflation adjustments, the basic standard deduction for a married couple filing a joint return is $6,000 (200% of $3,000).

To determine the additional standard deduction (defined in § 63(c)), we turn to § 63(f), which provides additional allowances for taxpayers over age 65 and those who are blind.

Keep in mind that in this text we always ignore inflation adjustments to fixed-dollar amounts such as the standard deduction. So, in working the problems, use the statutory amounts before adjustment for inflation.

(d) Personal and dependency exemptions.

Except where the taxpayer is the dependent of another, she is allowed a personal-exemption deduction for herself. If a husband and wife file a joint return, both are taxpayers and both are entitled to an exemption. In addition, taxpayers are allowed exemptions for their "dependents," a term defined in § 152, which we will examine in more detail later. For present purposes, note that the most-common dependents are (1) the taxpayer's children who share the taxpayer's place of abode and (2) the taxpayer's parents and other relatives who receive more half of their support from the taxpayer.

Don't be confused by the use of the term "exemption" instead of "deduction." Exemption is just another word for deduction. The exemption amount (before inflation adjustment) is $2,000; § 151(d)(1). The personal- and dependency-exemption deductions are reduced (phased out) for higher-income taxpayers; see § 151(d)(3). The phaseout is itself being phased out and will terminate in 2010; § 151(d)(3)(E).

6. Determine which of the following deductions are allowable to an individual in computing AGI and which are allowable only as itemized deductions:

(a) Salaries paid by a sole proprietor to the employees of the business (allowable under § 162(a));

This would be an above-the-line deduction under § 62(a)(1). Notice that all of the deductions in this problem are allowed by some provision other than § 62, as that provision is a definition of AGI and does not itself allow any deductions; it just tells us at what point in our computations to take otherwise allowable deductions into account.

(b) Medical expenses (allowable under 213(a));

An itemized deduction because not specified in § 62.

(c) Interest expense incurred in business (allowable under § 163(a));

Above the line; § 62(a)(1).

(d) Interest on a home mortgage (allowable under § 163(a));

Itemized.

(e) Charitable contributions (allowable under § 170(a)).

Itemized.

7. H (age 67) and W (age 63) are a married couple who file a joint return. They have gross income of $50,000, and they are entitled to deductions for $6,000 of expenses on a rental building (allowable under § 212), $5,000 of charitable contributions (allowable under § 170), and $1,200 of state property tax on their personal residence (allowable under § 164(a)). Determine their adjusted gross and taxable incomes.

Since the couple's only above-the-line deduction is the $6,000 rental expense (see § 62(a)(4)), their AGI is $44,000 ($50,000 gross income less $6,000 rental expense). H and W will itemize deductions or take the standard deduction, whichever results in the greater deduction. They have itemized deductions of $6,200 (the charitable contributions and the state property tax, as neither are specified as above-the-line deductions). Their basic standard deduction is $6,000; § 63(c)((2)(A). Their additional standard deduction is $600 (because H has attained age 65); § 63(f)(1)(A). Their standard deduction is $6,600 (the sum of the basic and additional standard deduction); § 63(c)(1). H and W will therefore take the standard deduction. Each is also entitled to a $2,000 personal exemption.

Their taxable income is $33,400 ($44,000 AGI less $6,600 standard deduction and $4,000 personal exemptions).

8. M and F (both age 35) are married and file a joint return. They have gross income of $90,000, and they are entitled to deductions for a $10,000 loss on the sale of business property (allowable by § 165(a) and (c)(1)), $3,000 of state income taxes (allowable by § 164(a)), and $2,000 of charitable contributions (allowable by § 170(a)). They have two dependent children for whom they are entitled to the child tax credit of § 24. They also paid $7,200 of unreimbursed medical expenses for themselves and their children (see § 213). Determine their:

(a) AGI;

M and F have only one above-the-line deduction—for the $10,000 loss on the sale of business property; see § 62(a)(1) & (3). Their AGI is $80,000 ($90,000 of gross income less $10,000 business loss).

(b) Taxable income;

The medical expenses are allowable under § 213(a) only to the extent that they exceed 7.5 percent of AGI. In this case, 7.5 percent of AGI is $6,000 (7.5% of $80,000), and the medical expenses are therefore deductible to the extent of $1,200. Itemized deductions total $6,200 ($3,000 of state income taxes, $2,000 of charitable contributions and $1,200 of medical expenses). The standard deduction is only $6,000 (§ 63(c)(1) & (2)), so the taxpayers will itemize deductions. Their taxable income is $65,800 ($80,000 AGI less $6,200 itemized deductions and $8,000 personal exemptions).

(c) Tax liability.

The couple's tax liability (before credits) is determined under § 1(a) (Appendix B) to be $11,330 ($5,930 plus $5,400). After subtracting the two tax credits for the children, we see that their tax is $9,330 ($11,330 less $2,000).

9. A married couple with adjusted gross income of $174,000 files a joint return. Before the application of §§ 68 and 151(d)(3), they are entitled to $6,000 of personal and dependency exemptions and $25,000 of itemized deductions that are potentially subject to disallowance under § 68. Determine their taxable income if the year is:

(a) 2008;

These problems involve the phaseout of the personal exemptions and itemized deductions for higher-income taxpayers. As this problem illustrates, these phaseouts are themselves being phased out and will disappear entirely in 2010. Therefore, your instructor may choose not to cover this material.

Section 151(d)(3) reduces the deductions for personal and dependency exemptions by 2 percent for each $2,500 increment (or fraction thereof) by which the taxpayers' AGI exceeds the "threshold amount." For a married couple filing a joint return, the threshold amount is $150,000; § 151(d)(3)(C)(i). Here the couple's AGI exceeds the threshold amount by $24,000 ($174,000 AGI less $150,000 threshold amount). When we divide the $24,000 excess by $2,500, we see that there are 9.6 $2,500 increments in the excess. The couple must reduce their exemption deductions by 2 percent for each increment ("or fraction thereof"); § 151(d)(3)(B). In this case, there are ten increments (including the fractional increment). The reduction would therefore be 20 percent of $6,000, or $1,200, but in 2008 the reduction itself is limited to one-third of this amount or $400. Therefore, the couple's exemption deductions are limited to $5,600 ($6,000 less $400).

Section 68 generally reduces the itemized deductions by 3 percent of the amount by which the taxpayer's AGI exceeds the "applicable amount." For a married couple filing a joint return, the applicable amount is $100,000, the couple's AGI exceeds the applicable amount by $74,000, and the tentative disallowance of itemized deductions is 3 percent of that excess, or $2,220. Because the year is 2008, however, the reduction is only one-third of that amount, or $740, and the couple can deduct itemized deductions of $24,260 ($25,000 less $740).

The couple's taxable income is $144,140 ($174,000 less $24,260 of itemized deductions and $5,600 of exemptions).

(b) 2010.

Sections 151(d)(3) and 68 do not apply to tax years beginning after 2009; see §§ 151(d)(3)(F); 68(f)(1). So, if the year is 2010, the full amount of the itemized deductions and personal exemptions are allowable, and taxable income would be $143,000 ($174,000 AGI less $6,000 of personal exemptions and $25,000 of itemized deductions.

Section B

GROSS INCOME

Chapter 3

ACCESSIONS TO WEALTH

A. IN GENERAL

Code: § 61(a).

Regulations: §§ 1.61–1(a); 1.61–14(a).

Cases: Commissioner v. Glenshaw Glass Co., 348 U.S. 426 (1955);
Cesarini v. United States, 296 F. Supp. 3 (N.D. Ohio 1969), aff'd per curiam, 428 F.2d 812 (6th Cir. 1970);
James v. United States, 366 U.S. 213 (1961).

1. T purchased a used sofa for $15. While cleaning the sofa, T found inside an envelope containing $5,000 cash. Must T include the $5,000 in gross income?

Gross income includes all "income" from whatever source derived; § 61(a). So, the question is whether the found money is income. It is, and it must be included in gross income in the year found and reduced to T's undisputed possession; see Cesarini v. United States, 296 F. Supp. 3 (N.D. Ohio 1969), aff'd per curiam, 428 F.2d 812 (6th Cir. 1970) (taxpayers found cash in used piano purchased seven years before; held, includable in gross income in year discovered); Treas. Reg. § 1.61–14(a) (treasure trove includable in gross income in year in which it is reduced to undisputed possession). *Cesarini* relied upon Commissioner v. Glenshaw Glass Co., 348 U.S. 426 (1955), which held punitive damages includable in gross income. The *Glenshaw Glass* Court said that Congress intended "to tax all gains except those specifically exempted." Rather than trying to define income, it observed that the punitive damages represented "accessions to wealth, clearly realized, over which the taxpayers have complete dominion."

2. Would your answer in 1 differ if T had instead found a piece of jewelry (valued at $5,000) in the sofa?

The regulations suggest that the value of the jewelry would be includable when reduced to undisputed possession; Treas. Reg. § 1.61–14(a) (treasure trove).

However, no case has ever applied the regulation to include found property (other than cash) in income when found, and commercial fishermen, miners and professional treasure hunters are not taxed until they turn their "receipts" into cash by selling them; see McMahon & Zelenak, Baseballs and Other Found Property, 84 Tax Notes 1299 (1999) (trenchantly criticizing the regulation and urging the Treasury to revise it).

3. T borrows $5,000 from a bank for use in purchasing a new car. Must T include the $5,000 in gross income?

No. The borrowing does not represent an accession to wealth. T has more money than before the borrowing, but T also has an offsetting obligation to repay. Income is "gain," and T has no gain from the transaction.

4. E embezzled $5,000 from a bank. Must E include the $5,000 in gross income?

Yes; Treas. Reg. § 1.61–14(a); James v. United States, 366 U.S. 213 (1961). We have just seen that a borrower does not have income because of the offsetting obligation to repay the borrowed funds, and, under state law, an embezzler also has an obligation to repay the victim. Why then does the embezzler have income when the borrower does not? In the embezzlement case there is no *consensual* recognition of the obligation to repay at the time the embezzler takes the money. Moreover, the borrower is much more likely to repay than is the embezzler.

5. At an auction, T purchased for $50,000 a portrait thought to have been painted by an artist known as Vegas. After carefully examining the painting, T discovered that it was instead painted by Degas and was worth $5,000,000. Must T include anything in gross income on account of these events?

No. Although T has had an accession to wealth on account of the transaction, the Supreme Court has said in dictum that the bargain element in a bargain purchase is not taxable in the year of purchase; Commissioner v. LoBue, 351 U.S. 243, 248 (1956). T will be taxed on the gain when realized by a sale of the painting. The decision not to tax bargain purchases rests on administrative concerns. It is much easier to detect and measure gain or loss when the taxpayer closes out the transaction by selling the property. Nevertheless, the bargain element *is* taxed when the bargain purchase is just the medium through which another transaction is carried out, as, e.g., when an employer sells property to an employee at a bargain price as a means of compensating the employee. For more on this, see Chapter 4B.

6. Several years ago, F purchased a farm in Iowa for $3,000 per acre. There were no known mineral deposits in the area. In the current year, F accepted the offer of a wildcatter to drill a test oil well on the property. Much to the astonishment of the entire community, the well was a gusher, and F's property immediately rose in value to $10,000 per acre. Must F include the increased value in gross income?

No. Although F has an accession to wealth on account of the discovery, the appreciation in value will not be taxed until T makes a taxable *disposition* of the property. Here again, the accession to wealth has not been "clearly realized."

7. M owns the home in which she resides. If M rented a comparable residence, the rent would be $24,000 a year. Must M include the rental value of her home in gross income?

No, this is an example of imputed income, and the statute does not tax imputed income. Imputed income arises when one performs services for oneself or uses one's capital to purchase property for one's personal use, as in this case, rather than investing it for a monetary return.

Our failure to tax imputed income causes some taxpayers to make different choices than they would make in a tax-free world. Suppose, for example, that, apart from tax considerations, M is indifferent between owning her own home or renting. If instead of buying a home M uses the funds to purchase corporate bonds that pay $24,000 a year in interest, the interest would be taxable, and, if she used the money to pay rent on a comparable residence, the rent would be a non-deductible personal-living expense. If she buys the residence, the (imputed) $24,000 return on her invest will not be taxed. So, by buying rather than renting, M saves the tax on $24,000 a year. That is an important reason why people purchase a home rather than renting.

B. GROSS INCOME FROM SALES OF PROPERTY

Code: §§ 61(a)(3); 1001(a), (b) & (c); 1012; 1011(a).

Regulations: §§ 1.61–6(a); 1.1001–1(a).

1. In March, year 1, T, a calendar-year taxpayer, purchases a share of Y Corporation stock for $40. By December 31, the stock has appreciated in value to $100. Does T have gross income on account of these events?

No. Although there has been an accession to the taxpayer's wealth, the accession is not taxed until the gain is realized by a sale or other taxable disposition of the share. The $60 represents "mere" unrealized appreciation at year's end.

2. In April, year 2, T sells the share for $120. What result to T?

T realizes gain to the extent the "amount realized" on the sale exceeds T's "adjusted basis" for the share; § 1001(a). The adjusted basis is the "basis" as adjusted to the date of sale; § 1011(a). In this case, the basis is the $40 cost of the share to T; see § 1012. Assuming that there are no adjustments to the basis, the adjusted basis is also $40. The amount realized is the amount of money received, plus the fair market value of any property received; § 1001(b). T's realized gain is therefore $80 ($120 amount realized less $40 adjusted basis).

T has invested $40 in the share and sold it for $120. Even though T received $120 cash, T's wealth has not increased by $120. She is better off by only $80 on account of the purchase and sale of the share. That is her profit on the transaction, and that is what T must include in gross income under § 61(a)(3).

Basis is the tax law's way of tracking the taxpayer's previously taxed investment in the property. Here T may have earned a salary, paid the tax on that salary, and invested $40 of the money left after taxes in the stock. When she sells the share, T should be able to recover that $40 without additional tax because she has already paid tax on that $40.

Taxpayers often hold property for long periods of time, and the basis must be "adjusted" whenever T increases or decreases the previously taxed investment in the property. For example, suppose T purchased a building for $200,000 and built a new wing on the building for $100,000. T's original (unadjusted) basis is the $200,000 cost of the building. But she then increased her investment in the building by $100,000 when she built the addition. Her basis must be adjusted upward to $300,000 because she has increased her previously taxed investment in the building.

In practice, lawyers sometimes carelessly use the term basis when they really mean adjusted basis. To avoid confusion, we will often use the non-statutory term "unadjusted basis" to refer to the basis of property before taking account of adjustments.

A final point: Even though a gain (or loss) is realized, it is not included in gross income (nor allowed as a deduction) unless it is also "recognized." Code § 1001(c) provides generally for the recognition of gains (and losses), but we will see later that there are also numerous "non-recognition" rules in the Code. These non-recognition rules cover cases in which a gain or loss has been realized, but in circumstances where Congress didn't think the transaction was an appropriate occasion for imposing tax or permitting deduction of a loss. (We will examine non-recognition in detail later in the text.) In our problem case, T's gain would be recognized under § 1001(c) and includable in T's gross income.

The terminology (basis, adjusted basis, amount realized, realized gain, recognized gain) is important, and you should master it as soon as possible because it comes up throughout this text.

3. In August, year 1, T purchases a share of Z Corporation stock for $100. By December 31, it has declined in value to $40. What result to T?

As in 1, T cannot take the loss into account until it is realized, and it has not been realized in year 1.

4. In July of year 2, T sells the Z Corporation share for $30. What result to T?

The sale is a realization event on which T realizes loss of $70. The unadjusted basis is the $100 cost; § 1012. If we assume that there are no adjustments to basis, the adjusted basis is also $100; § 1011(a). The amount realized is $30; § 1001(b). The realized loss is $70 ($100 adjusted basis less $30 amount realized). The loss is recognized; § 1001(c).

5. What justification, if any, do you see for the realization requirement?

There are three principal justifications for the realization requirement: (1) without realization, taxpayers might not have the cash to pay the tax; (2) measurement of gain or loss in the absence of market transactions would pose formidable valuation difficulties in many cases; (3) "psychologically," unrealized appreciation ("paper gain") does not seem to most people to be income.

Chapter 4

COMPENSATION FOR SERVICES

A. IN GENERAL

Code: § 61(a)(1). Note §§ 446(c); 451(a); 461(a).

Regulations: §§ 1.61–14(a); 1.61–2(a)(1). On accounting methods, see §§ 1.451–1(a); 1.461–1(a)(1) & (2); 1.446–1(c)(1)(i) & (ii)(A).

Case: Old Colony Trust Co. v. Commissioner, 279 U.S. 716 (1929).

1. E works for an annual salary of $100,000. E's checks for the past year totaled $70,000 after E's employer withheld amounts for federal and state income taxes and Social Security and Medicare taxes. How much salary income should E include in gross income?

$100,000. The federal and state income taxes and E's share of the Social Security and Medicare taxes are imposed upon E; they are E's liability even though the employer is required to withhold the taxes from E's salary and pay the amounts withheld to the governments on E's behalf. E will get credit for the amount of income tax withheld when E files her federal and state tax returns.

2. What result to E in 1 if the Social Security and Medicare taxes were not withheld from E's salary but were paid by the employer on E's behalf?

Under the principle of Old Colony Trust Co. v. Commissioner, 279 U.S. 716 (1929), the payment by the employer of E's share of the payroll taxes would constitute additional income to E. The employer's payment of E's legal obligation is treated as though the employer paid the money to E and E paid the taxes.

3. The employment contracts of some corporate executives require the corporation to pay any state or federal income taxes imposed on the executive's taxable fringe benefits. Assume that in the current year an executive who receives $1,000,000 in taxable fringe benefits faces a combined state and federal income-tax rate of 40 percent. If the executive's contract requires the firm to pay all resulting taxes on the fringe benefits (so as allow the executive to receive the $1,000,000 of fringe benefits free of tax), how much tax will the company have to pay?

Under *Old Colony*, the firm's payment of the executive's taxes results in additional income to the executive. At a 40–percent rate, the tax on the $1,000,000 is $400,000, and that sum is income to the executive. But under the agreement the firm is obligated to pay the taxes on the $400,000 of additional income, which results in additional tax of $160,000, which, in turn, leads to more income and more tax, etc. In *Old Colony*, the government did not insist upon collecting the tax on the additional tax ("full-pyramiding"), but it does so today; see Safe Harbor Water Power Corp. v. United States, 303 F.2d 928 (Ct. Cl. 1962).

If the executive is to receive the $1,000,000 in fringe benefits free of tax, the gross amount of compensation (i.e, the fringe benefit and the tax) is some amount (X), where X minus the tax on X (40% of X) equals $1,000,000:

$X - .40X = \$1,000,000$, which implies that,

$.6X = \$1,000,000$, and that,

$X = \$1,000,000/.6 = \$1,666,667.$

To confirm the computation, notice that the tax on income of $1,666,667 is $666,667 (40% of $1,666,667). That is the amount of tax the corporation will have to pay ensure that the executive enjoys the $1,000,000 fringe benefit free of tax.

4. A's employer pays A's $10,000 monthly salary on the fifteenth of each month. (Both A and the employer use a calendar year as their tax year.) On January 15, year 2, A received a check covering the pay period running from December 16, year 1, through January 15, year 2. Both A and the employer use the cash method. In which year should A include the income and the employer, who can deduct the salary as a business expense, deduct the expense?

The timing of income and deductions depends upon the taxpayer's method of tax accounting; §§ 451(a); 461(a). The permissible methods of tax accounting are set forth in § 446(c). In the basic course, we focus principally on the cash and accrual methods.

Under the cash method, a taxpayer usually includes items in income when actually received in the form of cash or property; Treas. Reg. § 1.451–1(a). A cash-method taxpayer generally deducts expenses when paid; Treas. Reg. §§ 1.446–1(c)(1); 1.461–1(a)(1).

A includes the $10,000 salary in income when received in year 2. The employer deducts the salary as a business expense in year 2 when it is paid.

5. Same as 4, except that both A and the employer use the accrual method of accounting.

Under the accrual method, a taxpayer generally takes income into account when all of the events have occurred that fix the taxpayer's right to the income and when the amount of the income can be ascertained with reasonable accuracy (the "all-events" test); Treas. Reg. §§ 1.446–1(c)(1)(ii); 1.451–1(a). An accrual-method taxpayer generally takes deductions when all of the events have occurred that fix the fact of liability and when the amount of the liability can be ascertained with reasonable accuracy; Treas. Reg. §§ 1.446–1(c)(1)(ii)(A); 1.461–1(a)(2). (We will refine our discussion of the all-events test in Chapter 43.)

By the end of year 1, all of the events (namely, A's performance of services from December 16–31) have occurred that fix A's right to (eventual) payment for that period, and the amount of the income can be ascertained with reasonable accuracy—here the amount appears to be $5,000. Therefore, A must include $5,000 of gross income for year 1; the $5,000 balance is income when earned in year 2. Likewise, by the end of year 1, all of the events have occurred that fix the employer's obligation to pay for work performed by A through December 31, and the amount of the employer's liability ($5,000) can be ascertained with reasonable accuracy. The employer would deduct $5,000 in year 1 and the remaining $5,000 in year 2.

B. TRANSFERS OF PROPERTY AS COMPENSATION FOR SERVICES

Code: §§ 61(a)(1); 83(a), (b), (c) & (h); 1012.

Regulations: §§ 1.83–1(a) & (f), Ex. (1); 1.83–3(b); 1.83–4(b)(1); 1.83–6(a)(1). Note § 1.61–2(d)(1), (2)(i) & (6).

1. Upon going to work for an automobile company, E, a cash method taxpayer, was given a new car as a "signing bonus." The car was E's to keep even if E quit the job. The value of the car was $25,000.

(a) Must the value of the car be included in E's gross income?

This exercise is pedagogically useful, though somewhat unrealistic. (Would the company really allow E to keep the car if he quit his job the first day?)

Of course, E has $25,000 of income; the fact that E received a car instead of cash does not prevent the receipt from being income, even to a cash-method taxpayer; see § 83(a). This case is equivalent to one in which E received $25,000 of cash compensation and used the money to purchase the car.

(b) What is E's unadjusted basis for the car? (Or, put differently, how much gain *should* E realize if E immediately sells the car for its value of $25,000? Explain.)

Upon selling the car, E's amount realized would be $25,000 (the amount of money received); § 1001(b). But what is E's unadjusted basis? Code § 1012 says that the (unadjusted) basis is the "cost" of the car. However, E has not paid any money for the car. Does it follow that E's unadjusted basis is zero? After the sale, we can say that E has been compensated and wound up with $25,000 cash, so E's total income must be $25,000. Since E had $25,000 of income upon receipt of the car, E's gain on selling the car must be zero. But if E's amount realized on the sale is $25,000 and her gain is zero, E's unadjusted basis must be $25,000. So, E's realized gain on the sale would be zero ($25,000 amount realized less $25,000 adjusted basis). (We will assume throughout this chapter that there are no adjustments to the basis of any property.)

We use the term "tax-cost basis" to refer to the unadjusted basis of property whose value was included in gross income (or amount realized in the case of property received in a taxable exchange). The amount included in gross income (or amount realized) thereafter represents previously taxed income, which the taxpayer should be able to recover without realizing gain when the property is disposed of. Think of it as if the company paid E $25,000 in cash compensation (includable in E's gross income) and then E used the money to purchase the car. For further examples of tax-cost basis, see Treas. Reg. §§ 1.61–2(d)(2)(i); 1.83–4(b)(1).

Keep in mind that E's $25,000 basis does not arise because E "invested" $25,000 of labor in earning the property. The cost basis of § 1012 does not include the value of E's services, which economists refer to as "opportunity cost." If E got basis credit of $25,000 for the value of her services, the value of the car would not have been income to her (because offset by E's basis in the services). If taxpayers got basis credit for their opportunity costs, little personal-service income would be taxable.

2. In year 1, Y Corp. sells its executive, E, one share of Y Corp.'s stock (publicly traded at $90) for $30. Under the terms of E's employment contract, E must surrender the share if she does not continue to work for Y through November of year 4. The restriction is prominently stated on the stock certificate. E makes no § 83(b) election and in year 4 fulfills her obligation to work for Y. At that time, the share is worth $150. E sells the stock in year 6 for $200. What tax results to E and X?

In year 1, the share is subject to a substantial risk of forfeiture since E can keep the share only if she performs substantial future services; § 83(c)(1). It is also nontransferable, since the share certificate bears a legend that reflects the restriction; a transferee would therefore take the share subject to the restriction and would have to forfeit the share if E left her employment before the end of November, year 4; see § 83(c)(2). The regulations describe property as "substantially nonvested" when it is subject to a substantial risk of forfeiture and is nontransferable and as "substantially vested" when it is either transferable or not subject to a substantial risk of forfeiture; Treas. Reg. § 1.83–3(b). Using this terminology, we can say that § 83(a) makes E taxable only when the share becomes substantially vested, and that does not occur until E fulfills her employment obligation in year 4.

So, there are no tax consequences to the parties in years 1, 2 or 3. In year 4, however, E must include $120 in gross income (the excess of the $150 value of the share over the $30 paid by E); § 83(a). E obtains an unadjusted basis of $150; Treas. Reg. § 1.83–4(b)(1). This $150 basis is the sum of E's actual cost of $30 and her tax cost of $120.

When E sells the share in year 6 for $200, E would realize gain of $50 ($200 amount realized less $150 adjusted basis).

Notice that E invests $30 of cash and winds up (after the sale in year 6) with $200 cash, for a total accession to wealth of $170. E is taxed on $120 of compensation income in year 4 and $50 of gain in year 6, so the entire $170 gets taxed. The compensation gets taxed at the applicable tax rate in § 1(a)–(d). The gain, however, is a capital gain that is subject to tax at a maximum rate of 15 percent.

Section 83(h) conforms the amount and timing of Y's compensation-expense deduction to the amount and timing of E's compensation-income inclusion. So, Y can deduct $120 in year 4.

3. Same as 2, except that the restriction is not stated on the stock certificate.

If the restriction is not stated on the stock certificate, a bona fide purchaser for value would take the share free of the restriction that it be forfeited if E does not fulfill her employment obligation. That would make the share transferable under § 83(c)(2), and hence substantially vested, when received in year 1. E would have to include $60 ($90 value of the share less $30 cost) in year 1's gross income. (For this purpose, the share is valued without regard to the restriction; § 83(a)(1).) E's unadjusted basis would be $90 ($30 actual cost plus $60 tax cost). Y would deduct the $60 as a business expense in year 1; § 83(h).

There would be no further tax consequences to E or Y when the restriction expires in year 4.

When E sells the share for $200 in year 6, E would realize gain of $110 ($200 amount realized less $90 adjusted basis). These events result in E's realizing an accession to her wealth in the amount of $170 ($200 cash received in year 6 less $30,000 paid for the stock). E must include $170 in gross income—$60 as compensation income in year 1 and $110 as capital gain in year 6.

4. Same as 2, except that E makes a § 83(b) election.

Under § 83(b), E can elect to include in gross income in year 1 (the year of transfer) the excess of the value of the share over its cost. In valuing the share for this purpose, the restriction related to E's employment obligation is disregarded; § see 83(b)(1)(A).

E will thus include $60 in gross income in year 1 and obtain an unadjusted basis of $90 ($30 actual cost plus $60 tax cost) for the share. Y gets a $60 deduction in year 1. There are no further tax consequences to the parties when the restriction expires in year 4.

When E sells the share for $200 in year 6, E would realize gain of $110 ($200 amount realized less $90 adjusted basis).

5. Same as 2, except that E makes a § 83(b) election but quits in year 2 and surrenders the share to Y. When E surrenders the share, the corporation returns the $30 that she paid for it.

As in the preceding problem, E includes $60 in gross income and Y gets a $60 deduction in year 1. When E forfeits the share in year 2, she cannot deduct the amount previously included in income; § 83(b) (second sentence). E received no economic benefit from the stock grant, but was taxed on $60 without any offsetting deduction when the stock was forfeited—odd result.

Y must restore its year–1 deduction of $60 to income in year 2; Treas. Reg. § 1.83–6(c).

6. Same as 2, except that in year 2 E sold the stock to an unrelated party in an arm's length transaction for $65. (The public trading price for Y shares at that time was $100.)

The share can be transferred, even though it is not *transferable* in the statutory sense because the purchaser would have to forfeit the share if E leaves her employment before the end of November, year 4. Notice also that the sale can be at arm's length even though the selling price is less than the public trading price for Y shares; the arm's length purchaser discounts the price to reflect the risk that E might quit, which would cause the purchaser to forfeit the stock.

The stock is substantially nonvested when received, and E therefore has no gross income in year 1. In year 2, E realizes *compensation* income of $35 on the sale ($65 amount realized less $30 cost of the share); Treas. Reg. § 1.83–1(b)(1). Y gets a $35 deduction in year 2; Treas. Reg. § 1.83–6(a)(1). Because the last sentence of § 83(a) makes that subsection inapplicable when the share substantially vests, there are no further tax consequences to the parties when the restriction expires in year 4; Treas. Reg. 1.83–1(b)(1).

The purchaser obtains a $65 cost basis for the share; § 1012; Treas. Reg. § 1.83–4(b)(2).

7. Same as 2, except that in year 2 E sold the stock to her son, S, in a non-arm's length transaction for $35. (The public trading price for Y shares at that time was $100.)

Again, A has no income in year 1 because the share is substantially non-vested. When nonvested property is sold in a non-arm's length transaction, the employee usually must include the entire amount realized (without any offset for the property's basis) as *compensation* income. This general rule applies here, so E has $35 of compensation income in year 2; Treas. Reg. § 1.83–1(c). In addition, § 83(a) applies when vesting occurs in year 4. (This can be inferred from the last sentence of § 83(a), which says that the first sentence of § 83(a) does not apply after the sale of the property in an *arm's length* transaction; the first sentence of § 83(a) *does* continue to apply when the disposition was *not* at arm's length.)

In year 4, E (not S, as E was the person who performed the services) must include an additional amount in gross income; Treas. Reg. § 1.83–1(c). To figure out the amount includable in year 4, E treats the $35 included in income in year 2 as an additional amount paid for the share, so that amount won't be taxed a second time; id. That brings the total paid for the share to $65 ($30 actual cost plus $35 tax cost). The amount includable in income in year 4 is $85 (the excess of the $150 value of the share at vesting over the $65 paid for the share). When the dust settles, E has included a total of $120 of compensation income, just as she would have if she had continued to hold the stock until it vested.

Under § 83(h), Y can deduct $35 in year 2 and $85 in year 4.

S obtains a basis of $150. That includes the $30 paid by E for the property and the $120 of compensation income that E had to recognize in years 2 and 4; Treas. Reg. § 1.83-4(b)(1)).

In the absence of these special rules for non-arm's length transfers, E could deflect income to family members by selling the nonvested property to them at an artificially low price. These rules also prevent the conversion of compensation income into capital gain, which is taxable at a lower rate than compensation income.

C. THE GRANTING AND EXERCISING OF STOCK OPTIONS

Code: §§ 83(e)(1), (3) & (4); 421(a) & (b); 422(a) & (b). Review § 83(a) & (h).

Regulations: §§ 1.83–4(b)(1); 1.83–7(a).

Case: Commissioner v. LoBue, 351 U.S. 243 (1956).

1. In year 1, Z Corp. grants its executive, P, a stock option (exercisable at any time in the next ten years) to purchase one share of Z common stock at $40. At that time, Z's (publicly traded) common stock was trading at $30 per share. P exercises the option just before it expires in year 10, when the stock is trading at $200. (There are no restrictions on the share when it is acquired by P.) P sells the share in year 12 for $250. What tax results to P and Z if the option is a non-statutory option (NSO) without an ascertainable value at the time of grant?

Note on terminology: The term "non-statutory option" (NSO) refers to any compensatory stock option other than an incentive stock option (ISO) described in § 422(b). NSOs are also called "non-qualified options." ISOs are sometimes referred to as "statutory options" or "qualified options."

Although the option is "property" transferred to P "in connection with the performance of services," § 83 does not apply to the transfer of an option without a readily ascertainable fair market value; § 83(e)(3). P therefore has no income when the option is granted in year 1.

When P exercises the option in year 10, § 83(a) applies, and P has compensation income of $160 ($200 value of share less $40 cost). P's unadjusted basis for the share is $200 ($40 actual cost plus $160 tax cost).

When P sells the share for $250 in year 12, P realizes gain of $50 ($250 amount realized less $200 adjusted basis).

Z gets a $160 deduction for compensation expense in year 10; § 83(h).

2. Same as 1, except that the option is a NSO with a readily ascertainable value of $5 at the time of grant. (Assume that the option was substantially vested in year 1.)

Section 83(a) applies to the grant of a NSO that has a readily ascertainable value at the time of grant. This is the implication of § 83(e)(3), which makes § 83 inapplicable to the grant of an option that *does not* have a readily ascertainable value, and § 83(e)(4), which says that § 83 does not apply to the transfer of property pursuant to the exercise of an option that *did* have a readily ascertainable value at the time of the grant. This means that, when the option has a readily ascertainable value, it is the *grant* of the option (and not its exercise) that is the taxable event. When the option does not have a readily ascertainable value, it is the *exercise* of the option (and not its grant) that is the taxable event.

Since in this case the option has a readily ascertainable value of $5, P must include $5 ($5 value less zero cost) in gross income when the option is granted in year 1; § 83(a). P also obtains a tax-cost basis of $5 for the option; Treas. Reg. 1.83–4(b)(1). Under § 83(e)(4), however, E recognizes no additional income when the option is exercised in year 10. P obtains a basis for the stock of $45 ($40 cost plus $5 basis for the option).

On the sale of the share in year 12, P realizes gain of $205 ($250 amount realized less $45 adjusted basis). If we consider the transaction from beginning to end, P reports compensation income of $5 (in year 1) and gain of $205 (in year 12), for total income of $210. That makes sense, in that P invests $40 of cash and winds up with $250, for an accession to wealth of $210.

Z gets a $5 deduction for compensation expense in year 1; § 83(h).

3. Same as 1, except that the option is an incentive stock option (ISO) described in § 422.

Section 83 does not apply to the grant of an ISO even if it has a readily ascertainable value; Treas. Reg. § 1.83–7(a). Nor does it apply to the exercise of an ISO, as § 83(e)(1) makes § 83 inapplicable to "a transaction to which § 421 applies," and § 422(a) tells us that § 421 generally applies to the transfer of a share of stock pursuant to the employee's exercise of an ISO. Section 421(a)(1) says P has no income upon exercise of the option in year 10. P obtains a $40 cost basis for the stock; § 1012. When the stock is sold for $250 in year 12, P has a realized gain of $210 ($250 amount realized less $40 basis). Z gets no deduction—ever; § 421(a)(2).

Notice that, as in problem 1, P has total income of $210 over the 12 years. But in problem 1, $160 was compensation income and only $50 capital gain. Here, in contrast, all of the $210 is capital gain. (Remember that capital gain is usually taxed at a lower rate than ordinary compensation income.) Why does any firm ever grant options that are not ISOs? Because the employer gets no compensation-expense deduction upon the exercise of an ISO; § 421(a)(2).

4. Same as 1, except that the option is an ISO and P instead sold the share in year 11 (just 10 months after exercising the option).

Section 422(a) says that the no-income-upon-exercise rule of § 421 applies only if the employee makes no disposition of the share within one year after the exercise of the option. In this case, P held the share for only 10 months, and so § 421(a) does not apply. If § 421 does not apply, § 83(a) does, and the latter requires P to include compensation income when the share vests (here in year 10). Does it follow that P must file an amended return for year 10? No. Section 421(b) says that, where the employee has made a disqualifying disposition of the share, the compensation income is includable for the year in which the disposition occurred—here year 11. So, P must include $160 of compensation income for year 11. P obtains a basis for the share of $200 ($40 actual cost plus $160 tax cost). P realizes gain of $50 ($250 amount realized less $200 adjusted basis) on the sale.

Z gets its $160 compensation-expense deduction (determined under § 83(h)) in year 11; § 421(b).

Chapter 5

EMPLOYEE FRINGE BENEFITS

A. MEALS AND LODGING UNDER § 119

Code: §§ 61(a)(1); 119. Note § 107.

Regulations: Skim § 1.119–1.

Case: Adams v. United States, 585 F.2d 1060 (Ct. Cl. 1978).

1. M is the manager of a large hotel owned by Hotel Corp. M is expected to be on call 24 hours a day. Hotel Corp. furnishes M and M's family living quarters in the hotel and allows them to eat for free in the hotel dining room. Must M include the value of the meals and lodging in gross income?

No. Section 119 excludes from gross income the value of meals or lodging when furnished on the business premises for the convenience of the employer. In the case of lodging, the employee must also be required to accept the lodging as a condition of the employment.

In this case, both the meals and lodging are furnished on the business premises of the hotel. As to the meals, the convenience-of-the-employer test is satisfied whenever the meals are furnished for a substantial non-compensatory business reason—in this case, to have M available for emergency call during the meal period; see Treas. Reg. § 1.119–1(a)(2)(i). The value of the lodging also qualifies for exclusion. The convenience-of-the-employer test is satisfied because M is required to be available for duty at all times. The condition-of-employment requirement means that the employee be required to accept the employment in order to properly perform his employment duties. That seems to be the case here because M is required to be available for duty at all times; Treas. Reg. § 1.119–1(b). Notice that there does not appear to be "any substantial difference between the * * * 'convenience of the employer' test and the 'required as a condition of his employment' test"; United States Junior Chamber of Commerce v. United States, 334 F.2d 660, 664 (Ct. Cl. 1964).

Section 119 also excludes the value of meals and lodging furnished to M's spouse and dependents; see § 119(a).

2. Would your answer in 1 differ if Hotel lodged the family in a residence owned by it and located two short blocks from the hotel?

The value of the meals and lodging are probably includable. The meals and lodging are probably not furnished on the business premises, which means the place of employment of the employee; Treas. Reg. § 1.119–1(c). Although the Tax Court once allowed the exclusion where a motel manager lived "two short blocks" from the motel, the Sixth Circuit reversed, noting:

> To make "two short blocks" or nearness to other business property of the employer the test is to disregard the word "on" as contained in the phrase "on the business premises of the employer", thereby rendering uncertain that which is certain and requiring litigation in each case to determine what may be sufficiently near under the circumstances of the particular case. Had Congress so intended, it would appear that it could readily have used the words "in the vicinity of" or "nearby" or "close to" or "contiguous to" or similar language, rather than say "on" the business premises.

Commissioner v. Anderson, 371 F.2d 59, 67 (6th Cir. 1966).

See also Dole v. Commissioner, 43 T.C. 697, 707, aff'd, 351 F.2d 308 (1st Cir. 1965) (houses located a mile from the employer's mill not on the business premises; the houses were neither "an integral part of the business property" nor "premises on which the company carries on some of its business activities").

3. Private University is located in a major city. Housing prices in the area surrounding the campus are very high—so high that many professors cannot afford to live in the area. To ameliorate this problem, the University purchased several residences in the area and leases them to faculty members at a discounted rent. P, a professor who participates in the University's housing program, pays rent of $24,000 annually on a residence that has an appraised value of $600,000. Although the University seldom leases property to non-employees, a residence comparable to P's would be leased to a non-employee at $36,000 per year. P's residence is located two blocks from campus. Must P treat any portion of the "subsidized" rent as compensation?

As an employee of an educational institution, P can exclude from income a portion of the rental value of "qualified campus lodging" under § 119(d). To determine the amount includable, P compares 5 percent of the appraised value of the residence ($30,000) with the average amount of rent charged by the University on comparable property leased to non-employees ($36,000). The amount includable is the excess of the lesser of these two figures ($30,000) over the rent paid by P ($24,000). So, P must include $6,000 in income on account of the bargain rental.

In the case of qualified campus lodging, the residence must be located on, or in the proximity of, the campus; § 119(d)(3). Therefore, P qualifies for the exclusion even though the residence is two blocks from campus.

4. Would your answer in 3 differ if P is the president of the University and is required to reside (free of charge) in the residence as a condition of employment? P uses the residence for entertaining people affiliated with the University, including students, faculty, alumni and major donors. Although P's principal campus office is in the University Administration Building, P maintains an office in the residence, which she uses for work at night and on weekends and for taking telephone calls on University business.

P can exclude the entire value of the lodging from income if P meets the requirements of § 119(a). (Note that § 119(d)(3) says qualified campus lodging is "lodging to which subsection (a) does not apply * * *.") The university requires the president to live in the residence, but the condition -of-employment test is satisfied only if P is required to accept the lodging in order to enable her to properly perform her presidential duties. Perhaps P could have used the residence for greeting guests without residing there, and the home office, although convenient, seems only tangential to P's performing her duties as president.

On the other hand, Adams v. United States, 585 F.2d 1060 (Ct. Cl. 1978), permitted the president of a Japanese subsidiary of an American oil company to exclude the rental value of a Tokyo residence furnished him by the company. The court said that the condition-of-employment test was satisfied because the employer wanted to ensure that the taxpayer's residence was "sufficiently dignified" to support his effectiveness in the Japanese business community, he did business entertaining in the residence, and he had a den which was used for work and business phone calls. The *Adams* court also found that the residence was located on the employer's business premises because the business-premises requirement implies a "functional rather than a spatial unity." P could also find support in Rev. Rul. 75–540, 1975–2 C.B. 53 (excluding rental value of governor's official residence furnished by state; business-premises test met because the residence enabled the governor to carry out efficiently the administrative, ceremonial and social duties required by his office). So, P has a decent argument for excluding the entire rental value of the residence.

5. A restaurant provides meals for its wait staff just before the restaurant opens for lunch each day. Is the value of the meals includable in a staff member's gross income if the restaurant furnishes the meals:

(a) free of charge?

The value is excludable; meals furnished to a restaurant employee for each meal period during which the employee works is furnished for a substantial noncompensatory business reason of the employer; the exclusion applies whether the meal is furnished during, immediately before, or immediately after the employee's working hours; Treas. Reg. § 1.119–1(d).

(b) at a charge of $10 per day and the charge is deducted from the server's wages regardless of whether the server actually eats the meal? (The restaurant would charge its customers $25 for a meal comparable to those served the wait staff.)

In determining whether the meals are furnished for the convenience of the employer, the fact that a charge is made for the meals or that the employee may accept or decline the meals is not taken into account; § 119(b)(2). Where, as here, the employer makes a mandatory fixed charge for the meal, the server can exclude the value of the meals he eats and also the $10 per day charge; § 119(b)(3)(A) & (B).

(c) in the manner described in (b), except that the restaurant charges the servers only for the meals they actually eat?

The value of the meals is excludable, but not the $10 charge; § 119(b)(3)(A) does not apply here because of § 119(b)(3)(B)(ii) (server here is not required to pay for meals not eaten).

6. B is the business manager of the restaurant. She regularly works from 8:00 a.m. until 5 p.m., but is allowed one hour for lunch. The restaurant also furnishes B's lunch free of charge. B eats lunch at the restaurant about twice a week on average; on other days B goes out for lunch. The restaurant management does not care whether B eats lunch on the premises. Must B include the value of the lunches furnished her by the restaurant?

B can exclude the value of the meals if more than half of the employees to whom meals are furnished by the restaurant are furnished the meals for the restaurant's convenience. Since lunches furnished to the serving and food-preparation staffs are furnished for the restaurant's convenience, and since those employees are likely to constitute more than half the employees to whom meals are furnished, B can probably exclude the value of the meals.

7. The Iman of the local mosque is paid a rental allowance, which he uses to furnish a rental residence for him and his family. The residence is located a short distance away from the mosque. The allowance does not exceed the fair rental value of the residence. Does the Iman have income on account of the residence?

In this case, § 119 probably does not apply because (1) the allowance is paid in cash (and § 119 excludes only meals and lodging furnished in kind), (2) the residence is not on the business premises and (3) it is (arguably) not furnished to enable the Iman to carry out his duties properly. Can the value of the lodging be excluded under § 107? The Iman is not "a minister of the gospel," but the exclusion surely applies, as Congress cannot discriminate between religions in parceling out exclusions. Indeed, some think § 107 is constitutionally invalid as an impermissible subsidy to religion, though it is difficult to get standing to challenge the provision.

B. EMPLOYEE FRINGE BENEFITS UNDER § 132

Code: §§ 132(a), (b), (c), (d), (e), (f)(1), (2) & (3), (g), (h) & (j)(1); 217(a), (b) & (c); 82.

Regulations: §§ 1.132–1(b)(1) & (4); 1.132–2(a)(1), (2) & (5), (c); 1.132–3(e); 1.132–5(a)(1)(vi); 1.132–6(a), (b), (c), (d)(2)(i) & (e).

E serves as store manager for D Corporation, which operates a chain of upscale department stores. D provides its employees with a number of fringe benefits. On which of the following fringe benefits will E be taxed?

1. All employees are allowed to purchase store merchandise at a discount of 20 percent from the regular price.

The discount can be excluded as a qualified employee discount if it does not exceed D's usual mark up on property that is being offered to D's non-employee customers; § 132(a)(2) & (c). Any excess discount would be includable in income; Treas. Reg. § 1.132–3(e). If E is highly compensated, the discount is excludable only if D offers the discount to its employees on a non-discriminatory basis, which it does here; § 132(j)(1).

2. The store that E manages includes a salon. All store employees are given a discount of 20 percent on salon services.

The discount is excludable as a qualified employee discount since it does not exceed 20 percent; § 132(c)(1)(B).

3. The store operates a public restaurant on the store premises. All store employees pay only half price when they eat during their assigned lunch hour.

The value of meals provided to employees by the restaurant on the store's business premises may qualify as a de minimis fringe benefit if revenue derived from the restaurant normally is at least equal to the restaurant's direct operating costs; § 132(e)(1). Direct operating costs include the costs of food and beverages and the costs of cooks, servers and others employed on the restaurant premises; Treas. Reg. § 1.132–7(b)(1). Because D charges its employees less than non-employees, D must apply the direct-operating-cost test by disregarding the costs and revenues of meals attributable to the non-employees; Treas. Reg. § 1.132–7(a)(ii). Although a non-discrimination rule (§ 132(e)(2)) applies to eating facilities, that poses no problem here since the same privileges are extended to all store employees. Assuming that the direct-operating-cost test is met here, the discount on the meals can be excluded.

4. E uses the office copying machine to copy her personal income-tax return.

Excludable as a de minimis fringe (§ 132(e)(1)), at least if D exercises sufficient control and imposes significant restrictions on the personal use of the machine so that at least 85 percent of the machine's use is for business purposes; Treas. Reg. § 132–6(e)(1). A de minimis fringe is one with a value "so small as to make accounting for it unreasonable or administratively impracticable"; § 132(e)(1). That seems to cover occasional use of the copying machine.

5. D pays up to $175 per month of the parking charges incurred by store employees on their workdays at a public ramp close to the store. Employees can choose between receiving this benefit or $175 per month of additional cash compensation.

The payment appears to be for "qualified parking"—i.e., parking provided to an employee on or near the employer's business premises; § 132(f)(5)(C)—and hence a "qualified transportation fringe"; § 132(f)(1). Even though employees who do not use the parking can receive cash, those who take the parking are not taxed; § 132(f)(3). (Of course, those who take the cash are taxed.) Although the exclusion is limited to $175 per month (§ 132(f)(2)), the limit is not exceeded here. (The limit is adjusted annually for inflation; § 132(f)(6); as usual, we ignore inflation adjustments in working the problems.)

6. Before assuming her present position as store manager in New City, E served as assistant manager of another store operated by D in Old City, which is 750 miles away from New City. When E was promoted to her present position earlier this year, D reimbursed E for the costs of moving E, her husband and their two children (ages 14 and 16) from Old City to New City. D's reimbursement included the cost of transporting

the family's household furnishings and personal effects, the standard mileage allowance for their two cars, which they drove from Old City to New City, and the cost of the family's meals and one night of lodging in making the trip to New City.

The reimbursement may be excludable in part as a "qualified moving expense reimbursement" to the extent that the reimbursed expenses would have been deductible by E as moving expenses under § 217 if not reimbursed; § 132(g). We must therefore turn to § 217 to determine which of E's expenses qualify as moving expenses.

Under § 217(b)(1), the costs of moving household goods and personal effects and of traveling (including lodging) to the New City residence qualify; the meal costs do not. Costs attributable to E's husband and children qualify if, as appears to be the case here, their principal place of abode is with E at both the new and old residences; § 217(b)(2). So, the reimbursement is excludable, except to the extent of the reimbursed meal costs, which must be included in gross income under § 82.

7. E attended an interior-decorating program sponsored by the store. E usually does not attend such programs, but because she was supervising the decoration of the family's new home, she decided to attend this time. The store charges members of the public $100 to attend the program, but permits store employees to attend free of charge on a space available basis.

The value of attendance at the program should be excludable as a "no-additional-cost service"; § 132(a)(1) & (b). The program is offered for sale to customers in the ordinary course of the business in which E is engaged as manager, and D incurs no substantial additional cost (including forgone revenue) in allowing E to attend, as E could attend only on a space-available basis. A non-discrimination rule applies (§ 132(j)), but that's not a problem here, as the store extends the same privilege all employees.

8. D paid $3,500 for E's (substantiated) travel, meals, lodging and tuition costs for a program covering new accounting rules for retail establishments. D did not require E to attend the program but granted her request to attend at the firm's expense.

Excludable as a working-condition fringe; § 132(a)(3) & (d). If E had paid the costs of attending this program, it would have been deductible by her as an employee business expense under § 162(a). The deduction would be allowed only as an itemized deduction, and it might be limited in its deductibility by §§ 67 and 68. Section 132(d), however, requires only that the amount be allowable as a deduction under *§ 162* if it had been paid by E. Amounts *disallowed* under §§ 67 and 68 are nevertheless allowable under § 162, so the reimbursement should be excludable; see Treas. Reg. § 1.132–5(a)(1)(vi).

9. The store invites all of its employees and their spouses to attend a free annual employee-recognition dinner at New City's most exclusive restaurant. E and her husband attended this year's dinner, which cost D $200 per person.

Although it is debatable whether $200 per person is an amount "so small as to make accounting for it unreasonable or administratively impracticable," (§ 132(e)(1)), the meal cost is probably excludable as a de minimis fringe benefit; § 132(a)(4) & (e). The employee-recognition dinner occurs annually, and the value of "occasional" group meals is excludable; Treas. Reg. § 1.132–6(e)(1).

C. OTHER FRINGE BENEFITS

Code: Note §§ 79(a), (d)(1)(A), (2), (4), (5) & (6); 105(a), (b), (e); 106(a); 125(a), (d)(1) & (f).

Regulations: Treas. Reg. §§ 1.106–1; 1.79–4T, Q & A (9).

1. A is employed by X. X pays the cost of a health-insurance policy covering all of its employees, their spouses and dependent children. Must A include her share of the policy premium in gross income?

No. Section 106(a) generally excludes employer-provided coverage under an accident or health plan, including a plan under which the employer pays the premium on a policy of accident or health insurance; Treas. Reg. § 1.106–1.

2. A (in 1) receives a $1,000 reimbursement from the insurer covering the cost of medical treatment received earlier this year by A's 14-year-old child. The child resides with A and is A's dependent under § 152. Must the reimbursement be included in A's gross income?

No, but the statutory analysis is complicated. Although § 104(a)(3) generally provides an exclusion for amounts received through health insurance on account of personal injuries or sickness, the exclusion does not apply to amounts attributable to employer-paid premiums that were not includable in the employee's income under § 106(a). Section 105(a) provides generally for *inclusion* of amounts received under health insurance acquired through employer-paid premiums. Under § 105(b), however, an employee can *exclude* amounts received in reimbursement of medical expense incurred for the medical care of the taxpayer, the taxpayer's spouse or dependents. Here the child is A's dependent, and the reimbursement is excludable.

3. A's employer provides all of its full-time employees coverage under a group-term life insurance policy. The coverage is equal to the employee's annual compensation, up to $50,000. Must A include her share of the policy premiums in gross income?

No, the premiums are excludable under § 79(a). Only the cost of $50,000 of coverage is excludable, but that is all the employer is providing in this case. Section 79(d)(1) prevents "key employees" from excluding the premiums if the plan discriminates in favor of key employees as to eligibility to participate or if the benefits discriminate in favor of key employees; § 79(d)(2). (Key employees are generally those whose annual earnings exceed $130,000 per year (before inflation adjustments); § 416(i)(1).) We don't know whether A is a key employee, but, in any event, the plan is not discriminatory. Here all employees are covered, so the plan does not discriminate in favor of key employees as to eligibility. And § 79(d)(5) says that the plan does not discriminate in benefits if, as here, the plan provides coverage bearing a uniform relationship to compensation. (Although the ratio of coverage to compensation is uniform over the first $50,000 of compensation, the ratio diminishes as compensation exceeds $50,000. In that respect the coverage is not truly "uniform," but the temporary regulations make clear that the coverage is not discriminatory as long as the ratio does not *increase* for the key employees; Treas. Reg. § 1.79–4T, Q & A (9).)

4. The policy (in 3) also provides $2,000 of coverage on the lives of each employee's spouse and dependent children. Must A include in income the portion of the premium paid on behalf of her spouse and dependent child?

No, the premium is excludable as a de minimis fringe benefit; § 132(a)(4) & (e). Although Treas. Reg. § 1.132–6(e)(2) says that the cost of covering the employee's spouse and dependents is not excludable, Notice 89–110, 1989–2 C.B. 447, postponed indefinitely the effective date of that regulation and allows the exclusion for $2,000 of coverage on a spouse and each dependent.

5. B's employer maintains a non-discriminatory cafeteria plan, under which employees can designate a portion of their salaries for contribution to the plan and then obtain reimbursement from the plan for medical or dependent-care expenses. B elects to have his employer reduce his salary by $2,000 and have the money contributed to the plan. Must B include the $2,000 in gross income?

No. The cafeteria plan permits employees to choose between receiving cash and "qualified benefits" without being taxed on amounts diverted to the plan; see § 125(a), (d)(1) & (f). The reimbursements for the medical expenses can be excluded from income under § 105(b) and those for dependent care can be excluded under § 129. In effect, the cafeteria plan allows those expenses to be paid from pre-tax dollars.

Chapter 6

DEFERRING COMPENSATION—
INDIVIDUAL RETIREMENT ACCOUNTS

Code: §§ 219(a), (b)(1) & (5)(A), (d)(1), (e), (f)(1), (g)(1), (3) & (5); 408(a), (d)(1) & (2), (e)(1), (*o*)(1) & (2); 408A(a), (b), (c)(1), (2), (3)(A), (4), & (5), (d)(1), (2) & (5). Note § 62(a)(7).

1. Describe the salient features of:

(a) A traditional (deductible) IRA;

The traditional "individual retirement account" (IRA), defined in § 408(a), is a device for encouraging people to save for retirement. An individual who has compensation income generally can deduct up to $5,000 per year (in 2008 and following) for contributions to an IRA; § 219(a), (b)(1) & (5)(A). (The maximum allowable deduction is adjusted for inflation after 2008; as usual, we ignore inflation adjustments here.) People over age 50 can deduct an additional $1,000 per year; § 219(b)(5)(B). However, the total amount contributed cannot exceed the taxpayer's compensation income for the year; § 219(b)(1). Higher-income taxpayers who are active participants in any of the tax-favored retirement plans described in 219(g)(5) cannot make deductible contributions to an IRA; § 219(g)(1)–(3). No deduction is allowed for contributions made after the account owner attains age 70½; 219(d)(1).

The IRA is tax-exempt; § 408(e)(1). This means that the income from the funds invested in the IRA (dividends, interest, capital gains, etc.) can be compounded free of tax.

Distributions from traditional (deductible) IRAs are fully taxable because the taxpayer has a zero basis in the account—i.e., the taxpayer deducted all of the contributions and so does not have any previously taxed investment in the account. (To discern this result in the Code requires very careful reading of §§ 408(d)(1) & (2) and 72(e)(1) & (2); we won't go into the details here.) Distributions made before the taxpayer attains age 59½ are subject to an additional 10–percent penalty tax; § 72(t)(1) & (2)(A). The early-distribution penalty does not apply to certain distributions made for the purpose of paying for medical care or higher education or buying a first home; § 72(t)(2)(B), (E) & (F). IRAs are intended for use in accumulating retirement savings (not for accumulating an estate), and so distributions must begin when the account owner attains age 70½; § 408(a)(6). The details of the regulations implementing the mandatory-distribution requirement are beyond our scope.

(b) A Roth IRA;

The Roth IRA, defined in § 408A(b), is another means of savings for retirement. The maximum contribution is the same as for a traditional IRA (generally, the lesser of $5,000 or the taxpayer's compensation income), but the amount must be reduced by any amount contributed to another (traditional) IRA; § 408A(c)(2). Higher-income people are not allowed to make contributions to a Roth IRA even if they are not participants in another retirement plan; § 408A(c)(3). Contributions to a Roth are not deductible, but the IRA itself is tax-exempt (so earnings compound tax-free), and "qualified distributions" are excluded from the recipient's income; § 408A(a), (c)(1) & (d)(1). Qualified distributions are generally those made after the recipient attains age 59½, dies or is disabled, or distributions for a first-time home buyer; § 408A(d)(2) & (5). No qualified distribution can be made within the five-year period beginning with the first year for which the person made a contribution to a Roth IRA. The recipient of a non-qualified distribution is taxable on amounts received in excess of the amounts contributed to the account (i.e., amounts received in excess of the taxpayer's basis); § 408A(d)(4). Again, the details are beyond our scope. A 10–percent tax applies to the taxable portion of non-qualified distributions made before age 59½, unless the distribution is for the cost of medical care or higher education; § 72(t)(1), (2)(A), (B) & (E). Mandatory distributions are not required before the taxpayer's death; § 408A(c)(5).

(c) A traditional (non-deductible) IRA.

As mentioned above, § 219(g) prohibits higher-income taxpayers who are active participants in one of the retirement plans specified in § 219(g)(5) from making *deductible* contributions to a traditional IRA. However, § 408(o)(1) allows the making of non-deductible contributions to the extent of the amount that could have been deducted if the income limit of § 219(g) did not apply. Even though the taxpayer gets no deduction, the amount contributed gets the benefit of tax-free compounding; § 408(e)(1). The non-deductible contribution gives the taxpayer a basis in the account that can be offset against the amounts received as a distribution.

2. On her 45th birthday, T contributes $5,000 to a retirement-savings program to provide funds for her retirement at age 65. T plans to withdraw the entire account balance on her 65th birthday (i.e., after 20 years). T anticipates that she can earn a pre-tax return of 10 percent on her investment in the account. Assume that the maximum allowable contribution to an IRA is $5,000 and that T expects to be in the 40-percent

(combined federal and state) income-tax bracket at all times. How much will T have available to consume at age 65 if she invests in:

(a) A taxable savings account?

These problems involve the calculation of the future value of the $5,000 after 20 years. Their purpose is to help you understand the differences between the savings vehicles. (Future-value calculations are discussed in Chapter 47.)

Since the income from the investment in the account will be subject to tax each year as earned, the after-tax rate of return will be only 6 percent. That is, after one year T will have earned $500 of income, but will have to pay tax of $200 (40% of $500), leaving her with only $300 of after-tax income from the account; T's after-tax rate of return is 6 percent ($300/$5,000).

Using Table I in Appendix A, we see that the future-value factor ($r = 6\%$, $n = 20$) is 3.20714. After 20 years, the $5,000 will cumulate to $16,035.70 ($5,000 x 3.20714).

When T withdraws the account balance, she incurs no additional liability because the account earnings have already been taxed. She has $16,035.70 to spend.

(b) A traditional (deductible) IRA?

Since the IRA is exempt from tax under § 408(e)(1), T can earn a 10–percent return on the investment. The future-value factor ($r = 10\%$, $n = 20$) is 6.72750, and the $5,000 cumulates to $33,637.50 ($5,000 x 6.72750). Unfortunately, however, T has a zero basis in the account (because she deducted each contribution as made and so has no previously taxed investment in the account). She is therefore liable for tax of $13,455 (40% of $33,637.50) on the distribution. After tax, she is left with $20,182.50.

As noted, however, T can deduct the $5,000 invested in the traditional IRA. The deduction saves her tax of $2,000, which sum can also be invested in a taxable savings account. After 20 years, the $2,000 cumulates to $6,414.28 ($2,000 x 3.20714) (the future-value factor is for ($r = 6\%$, $n = 20$)).

In total, T has $26,596.78 so spend at age 65.

(c) A Roth IRA?

T's $5,000 non-deductible contribution to the Roth IRA cumulates to $33,637.50 ($5,000 x 6.72750). The distribution is a qualified distribution and is excluded from income; § 408A(d)(1) & (2). T has $33,637.50 to spend.

(d) A traditional, non-deductible IRA (non-deductible because she is covered by her employer's plan and has too much adjusted gross income to make a deductible contribution).

By T's age 65, the $5,000 cumulates to $33,637.50 ($5,000 x 6.72750). T includes $28,637.50 in gross income ($33,637.50 distribution less $5,000 basis in the account). She must pay tax of $11,455 (40% of $28,637.50) on the distribution, leaving her with $22,182.50 ($33,637.50 distribution less $11,455 tax) to spend.

(e) Under which plan does T come out best?

The Roth IRA produces the best result.

3. S is willing to reduce her consumption by $3,000 so that she can make a contribution to an IRA account, which she will not distribute for 20 years. S can earn a pre-tax return of 10 percent on her investments and expects to be in the 40–percent (combined state and federal) tax bracket at all times. Should she invest in a traditional (deductible) IRA or a Roth IRA? Explain.

If S diverts $3,000 of consumption to a Roth IRA for 20 years, the $3,000 will cumulate to $20,182.50 ($3,000 x 6.72750), which will be excluded from S's income when distributed, leaving her $20,182.50 to spend.

Consider how much S can contribute to the traditional IRA. Since S can deduct the contribution, a $3,000 contribution would save S $1,200 (40% of $3,000) in taxes. If S spent the $1,200 tax savings on consumption, she would be reducing her consumption by only $1,800 instead of $3,000. S can therefore contribute more than $3,000 to the traditional IRA if she is willing to forgo $3,000 of consumption.

To calculate how much she can contribute, let X equal the amount of the contribution. We know that S is willing to give up $3,000 of consumption, so X less the tax saved by deducting X must equal $3,000: $X - .40X = \$3,000$, which implies that $.60X = \$3,000$ and $X = \$3,000/.60 = \$5,000$. To verify the computation, notice that if S deducts the $5,000 contributed to the IRA, her tax bill goes down by $2,000 (40% of $5,000). S contributes $5,000 to the IRA but gets $2,000 back through a reduced tax bill, so she gives up only $3,000 of consumption.

The $5,000 cumulates to $33,637.50 ($5,000 x 6.72750) after 20 years. When the account balance is distributed, T pays tax of $13,455 (40% of $33,637.50) and is left with $20,182.50 to spend—exactly what she has to spend if she invests in the Roth IRA!

On these facts, S would be indifferent between making a deductible contribution to a traditional IRA and a non-deductible contribution to a Roth IRA. Why, then, do tax advisors advise eligible taxpayers to contribute to a Roth IRA? For one thing, a taxpayer can divert more consumption to a Roth than to a traditional IRA. Although the dollar limits on contributions are the same for both, the Roth limit is an after-tax limit, while the traditional IRA limit is a pre-tax limit.

To illustrate, suppose that in 2008 a 40–percent bracket taxpayer has compensation income of $8,333.33 and wishes to make the largest possible contribution to an IRA. She can pay tax of $3,333.33 (40% of $8,333.33) on the income and contribute the $5,000 balance to a Roth IRA, leaving none of the compensation left for current consumption. After 20 years, the fund would cumulate to $33,637.50 ($5,000 x 6.72750), and the taxpayer could receive that amount tax-free.

If instead the taxpayer wanted to invest in a traditional IRA, she could contribute (and deduct) $5,000 but the deduction would save $2,000 in taxes, leaving her that $2,000 to spend on consumption. Of course, instead of consuming the $2,000, she could invest it in a taxable account, but the earnings would be taxed as earned, and, therefore, she would still come out worse than if she had invested in the Roth; see problem 2(b), above. She would have $20,182.50 ($33,637.50 distribution less taxes of $13,455) left after taxes in 2028. In effect, the maximum-contribution limit for the Roth is higher than for the traditional IRA in the sense that one can divert more consumption to saving in a Roth than in a traditional IRA.

Young people may prefer the Roth IRA for another reason: They may expect to be in a lower tax bracket in the year of the contribution than in the year of distribution. Forgoing the tax deduction may be relatively painless for people with low current income but good prospects (say, law students). At retirement, they will likely be in a higher tax bracket, which makes even more valuable the exclusion from income of distributions from a Roth.

A final thought. This problem demonstrates the equivalence between allowing an immediate deduction for the cost of an asset (the traditional IRA) and disallowing a deduction for the asset's cost but exempting the income from the asset from tax. The taxpayer comes out the same in our problem regardless of whether she deducts the contribution but is taxed on the distribution or whether she gets no deduction but the earnings are tax-exempt.

4. R, age 40 and single, has adjusted gross income (as specially defined in § 219(g)(3)(A)) of $54,000, including salary of $50,000. R is an active participant in his employer's qualified pension plan ("a plan described in section 401(a)"). To what extent can R make a contribution (and to what extent would the contribution be deductible) if the contribution is to:

(a) A traditional IRA?

Because R is an active participant in his employer's plan, R is an "active participant" within the meaning of 219(g)(5)(A)(i). Therefore, the maximum deduction allowable to R may be reduced; § 219(g)(1). Since R's AGI exceeds the applicable dollar amount by $4,000 ($54,000 AGI less $50,000 applicable amount), § 219(g)(2)(A) tells us that the amount of the reduction (X) is given by:

$$X/\$5,000 = \$4,000/\$10,000,$$

which implies that:

$$X = \$5,000 \times (\$4,000/\$10,000) = \$2,000.$$

The maximum deductible contribution is $3,000 ($5,000 less $2,000); § 219(b)(1). R can also make a $2,000 non-deductible contribution under § 408(o)(1) & (2).

Notice that the deduction is fully phased out for active participants under age 50 at $60,000 of AGI because at that level the reduction (X) is $5,000:

$$X/\$5,000 = (\$60,000 - \$50,000)/\$10,000, \text{ which implies that:}$$

$$X = \$5,000 \times (\$10,000/\$10,000) = \$5,000.$$

After the $5,000 reduction, the limit on deductible contributions is zero.

(b) A Roth IRA?

R can make a full contribution to the Roth IRA. The phasing out of contributions begins at an AGI of $95,000 for a single person; § 408A(c)(3). The phaseout is complete at AGI of $110,000 for one under age 50.

Chapter 7

ANNUITIES

Code: §§ 61(a)(9); 72(a), (b), (c). Note § 67(b)(10).

Regulations: §§ 1.72–4; 1.72–5; 1.72–9 (Tables V and VI).

1. Last year T paid $750,000 for a single-premium annuity contract under which T is to receive an annual payment of $100,000 for ten years. T received the first payment in the current year. How much of the $100,000 should T include in gross income?

Sections 61(a)(9) and 72(a) say that amounts received as an annuity must be included in gross income. However, those general provisions are trumped by § 72(b), which excludes from gross income some amount (E) that bears the same ratio to the annuity payment (A) as the investment in the contract (I) bears to the expected return (R). That is, E/A = I/R. If we multiply both sides of this equation by A, we see that E = A x I/R. So, we exclude from gross income that portion of each annuity payment determined by multiplying the payment by the ratio of I/R, which is known as the exclusion ratio; Treas. Reg. § 1.72–4(a)(1)(i).

The investment in the contract usually means the aggregate amount of consideration or other premiums paid for the contract (§ 72(c)(1)), which in this case is $750,000. The expected return is the aggregate of the amounts receivable as an annuity under the contract, or $1,000,000 (ten payments of $100,000 each); see § 72(c)(3)(B). The exclusion ratio is thus 75% ($750,000/$1,000,000), and $75,000 of each payment can be excluded from income; the remaining $25,000 must be included. So, T must include $25,000 in gross income for each of the ten years during which the annuity payments are received.

2. In the current year, P (age 60) began receiving annual payments of $10,000 under a single-premium annuity contract purchased ten years before at a cost of $121,000. The annuity payments were to continue until P's death.

(a) How much of the $10,000 received in the first year should P include in gross income?

Unlike in the preceding problem, where the annuity was to continue for a term of years, the payments in this case continue for P's life. Section 72(c)(3)(A) tells us that where the expected return under the annuity contract depends upon the life expectancy of one or more individuals, we are to determine the expected return under actuarial tables prescribed by the government. Since this an annuity for a single life (P's), we use Treas. Reg. § 1.72–9, Table V (because P's investment in the contract was made after June, 1986). Since P is age 60 on the annuity starting date, the "multiple" is 24.2. Therefore, the expected return is $242,000 (24.2 x $10,000). The exclusion ratio is 50% ($121,000 investment in the contract divided by $242,000 expected return). Of the $10,000 received in the current year, P excludes $5,000 and includes $5,000 in gross income.

(b) If P lives to receive the 25th annual payment, how much of the payment should P include in gross income?

Section 72(b)(2) says that the portion of any payment excluded cannot exceed the taxpayer's "unrecovered investment in the contract" immediately before receipt of the payment. The unrecovered investment in the contract is the investment in the contract less the amount excluded from income in preceding periods. Just before the twenty-fifth annual payment was received in this case, P had received twenty-four $10,000 payments and excluded one-half of each payment from income. Thus, P had excluded a total of $120,000 (24 x $5,000). Since P's investment in the contract is $121,000, the unrecovered investment in the contract is $1,000 ($121,000 less $120,000).

Upon receipt of the twenty-fifth annual payment of $10,000, P can exclude an amount equal to the remaining $1,000 of unrecovered investment and must include the $9,000 balance. P must include all subsequent payments received in gross income.

(c) Now suppose that P had died after receiving just four annual payments. What tax result to P?

By the terms of the contract, the annuity payments cease at P's death. P invested $121,000 in the contract and received $40,000 in pre-death payments, of which $20,000 was excluded from income. At the time of P's death, therefore, the unrecovered investment in the contract was $101,000 ($121,000 investment less $20,000 excluded from income before death). Section 73(b)(3)(A) allows P a deduction for this amount in the year of death.

Of course, P may not have sufficient gross income in her final year (which ends on the date of P's death) to absorb a deduction of this size. We will see later, however, that when a taxpayer has deductions in excess of gross income, the excess may result in a net operating loss that can be carried back to offset income in the taxpayer's two preceding years. (A net operating loss generally can also be carried forward for as many as 20 years to offset income in those years. However, the loss cannot be carried over from a decedent to the decedent's estate, so it is only the carryback that is of interest here.) In determining the taxpayer's net operating loss, deductions that are not attributable to the taxpayer's business can be taken into account only to the extent of the taxpayer's non-business income. The loss on the annuity is not attributable to business, and, in the absence of a special rule, it could not contribute to a net operating loss if the deduction exceeded the amount of P's non-business income. To obviate this problem, § 72(b)(3)(C) treats the loss as if it were attributable to business, which may enable P to carry the loss back as part of a net operating loss if P does not have sufficient income in her last taxable year to absorb the loss.

The § 72(b)(3) deduction is an itemized deduction, though not a miscellaneous itemized deduction; see § 67(b)(10).

3. Ten years ago, H and W purchased a joint-and-survivor annuity for $201,600. The $10,000 annual annuity payments were to commence at H's age 60 (when W would be 53) and continue until the death of the survivor of H and W.

(a) H attained age 60 in the current year, and the couple received their first $10,000 payment. How much of the payment should they include in gross income on their joint return?

This problem requires us to determine the expected return when the annuity is to continue for the longer of two lives, here those of H and W. Treas. Reg. § 1.72–5(b) refers us to Table VI in Treas. Reg. § 1.72–9 for the expected-return multiple. At the intersection of the row for age 60 and the column for age 53, we see that the multiple is 33.6, which means that the expected return under the contract is $336,000 (33.6 x $10,000). Therefore, the exclusion ratio is 60% ($201,600/$336,000), and the parties can exclude $6,000 of the first payment from gross income and must include $4,000.

(b) H died at age 65, survived by W, who subsequently died after receiving (either jointly with H or as surviving annuitant) thirty annual payments. What tax result to W?

By the time of W's death, the parties had excluded $180,000 of the annuity payments from gross income (i.e., $6,000/year x 30 years). The unrecovered investment in the contact at W's death was $21,600 ($201,600 less $180,000 excluded from income). W is entitled to deduct that amount on her final return;

§ 72(b)(3)(A). As noted above, the deduction could give rise to a net operating loss, which could be carried back to the two years preceding the year of W's death.

Chapter 8

CANCELLATION OF INDEBTEDNESS (DEBT-DISCHARGE INCOME)

Code: §§ 61(a)(12); 108(a), (b), (d)(1), (2) & (3), (e)(1), (2), (4) & (5), (f)(1), (2) & (3).

Regulation: § 1.61–12(a).

Cases: United States v. Kirby Lumber Co., 284 U.S. 1 (1931);
Commissioner v. Rail Joint Co., 61 F.2d 751 (2d Cir. 1932).

Ruling: Rev. Rul. 84–176, 1984–2 C.B. 34.

1. **In year 1, A, a cash-method taxpayer, borrows $100 from a bank. A is personally liable on the note, which is unsecured. The loan proceeds are used in A's business. Because of A's deteriorating financial condition, the bank agrees in year 2 to accept $70 in complete discharge of A's liability. How much must A include in gross income in each of the following cases?**

(a) Immediately before the discharge, the value of A's assets exceeds the amount of A's liabilities by $20.

A must include $30 in gross income; § 61(a)(12). One can say that the discharge "freed" $30 of A's assets from the claims of creditors; this is the freeing-of-assets rationale applied by Justice Holmes in United States v. Kirby Lumber Co., 284 U.S. 1 (1931). Alternatively, one could say that (1) A received $100 cash when he borrowed the money; (2) A did not include the loan proceeds in income (because the loan did not result in an accession to A's wealth, as he was expected to repay the loan); (3) as a result of the discharge, A will never have to repay the $30; and (4) therefore, A should now be taxed on that cash that he spent or saved but won't have to repay. This alternative approach is usually thought of as the deferred-tax-on-the-loan-proceeds rationale of Commissioner v. Rail Joint Co., 61 F.2d 751 (2d Cir. 1932). In this problem, both rationales lead us to the same result—A is taxable on $30 of debt-discharge income. In other cases, the outcome may differ depending upon which rationale applies.

(b) Immediately before the discharge, the amount of A's liabilities exceeds the value of A's assets by $20?

At first glance, A appears again to have $30 of income under § 61(a)(12), *Kirby Lumber* and *Rail Joint*. In this case, however, A's liabilities exceeded the value of his assets by $20 immediately before the discharge occurred, so A was insolvent before the discharge; § 108(d)(3). Section 108(a)(1)(B) excludes debt-discharge income if the discharge occurs when the taxpayer is insolvent. But § 108(a)(3) limits the exclusion to the amount by which the taxpayer was insolvent. So, only $20 can be excluded under the insolvency exception, and A must include the $10 balance of the discharge in gross income.

(c) Immediately before the discharge, the amount of A's liabilities exceeds the value of A's assets by $35.

In this case, A was insolvent by $35 immediately before the discharge occurred. A remains insolvent by $5 after the discharge, and the full $30 of debt-discharge income is excluded; § 108(a)(1)(B).

(d) Same as (a), except that the bank also discharges A from liability for $10 of accrued interest that A owed on the note.

The $10 of debt-discharge income attributable to the accrued interest can be excluded from gross income under § 108(e)(2) because *payment* of the business interest by A, who uses the cash method, would have entitled A to a deduction under § 163(a). If A had received $10 of cash income and paid the interest, the $10 interest deduction would have offset the $10 of income. Here the income was in the form of a discharge of indebtedness, which is excluded from income, but A gets no interest deduction because the interest was not paid. A is left in the same tax and economic positions as if he had included the income and deducted the interest.

(e) Same as (a), except that the bank also discharges A from liability for $10 of interest that had accrued in year 1, and A uses the accrual method of tax accounting.

Now § 108(e)(2) does not apply because A would not have been entitled to a deduction if he had *paid* the interest. As an accrual-method taxpayer, A was allowed a deduction for the business interest when it accrued in year 1; A would not have been allowed a deduction at the time of payment. In effect, the inclusion of the debt-discharge income here just "makes up" for the deduction that A got when the interest accrued.

2. It has been said that the § 108(a)(1)(B) exclusion reduces tax liability today, but at the cost of higher taxes tomorrow—i.e., it is a deferral provision rather than a true exclusion. Do you agree? Explain.

Yes. In problem 1(b), above, A excluded $20 under § 108(a)(1)(B) because he was insolvent by that amount immediately before the discharge occurred. A must apply the amount excluded to reduce his "tax attributes"; § 108(b)(1). The tax attributes, and the order in which they must be reduced, are set forth in § 108(b)(2). At this early stage, you might not understand what some (or all) of these tax attributes are. It is sufficient at this point to understand that the effect of reducing one of these attributes will be to increase the amount of the taxpayer's taxable income (or reduce the credits against tax) in the future. In other words, § 108(a)(1)(B) does not permanently eliminate the tax on the excluded income, but just defers it until a future year. From a policy standpoint, that makes sense because a taxpayer just emerging from insolvency is usually not in a very good position to pay tax.

3. D owned raw land (held as an investment) with a value of $100. D borrowed $60 from a bank on a non-recourse note (i.e., a note on which D was not personally liable) secured by the land and devoted the loan proceeds to purposes unrelated to the land. Because of a subsequent recession in the housing market, D encounters problems selling the land, which D had hoped to sell to developers. In order to avoid the delay and expense of a foreclosure proceeding, the bank agreed to accept $55 in full settlement of the note and, upon payment of that amount by D, released its lien on the land. D was solvent both before and after the cancellation. Does D have debt-discharge income on account of the transaction?

The issue here is whether D can have income from the discharge of a debt on which he was never personally liable. In principle, the answer is yes. Under the freeing-of-assets approach, we can say that $5 of A's assets have been freed from the claims of creditors. Or, under the delayed-tax-on-the-loan-proceeds approach, we can say that he received that $5 of cash tax-free when he borrowed it and must account for it now when it turns out that he is not going to repay. It is therefore not surprising that § 108(d)(1) treats as "indebtedness of the taxpayer" any indebtedness on which the taxpayer was personally liable or subject to which the taxpayer held property. D must include $5 in gross income.

4. C made an unsecured loan of $10,000 to D. D used the loan proceeds in his painting business. The business did not prosper, and D became hopelessly insolvent. At that point, C offered to forgive the $10,000 loan principal if D would paint her house, which D did. Must D include the $10,000 in gross income?

Yes, as compensation income. It is as if C paid D $10,000 to paint the house and then D used the money to pay the debt. In this case, the debt discharge is "simply the medium for payment of some other form of income," and therefore

§ 108 does not apply; see Rev. Rul. 84–176, 1984–2 C.B. 34, 35. Compensation income is taxable to D even though he is insolvent.

5. M lent her adult daughter, D, $25,000 to use in purchasing a new car. A year later, when the amount of the principal balance of the loan was $20,000, C married. At the wedding reception, M tore up C's note. What result to C?

Here again the debt discharge is the medium through which another transaction is being carried out. In this case, M appears to making a wedding gift to C. Gifts are excludable from income under § 102(a), so no income to C.

6. P wins a $100,000 judgment against D for a personal injury caused by D's negligence. D appealed the judgment to the court of appeals. While the appeal was pending, P agreed to accept $75,000 in full settlement of the case. D is solvent at all times. Does the settlement result in debt-discharge income to D?

No. Since the case was apparently still being contested, the question of whether D owed $100,000 was still in dispute. The compromise of a disputed liability does not give rise to debt-discharge income.

7. P purchased a business machine from S at a price of $100,000. P paid S $10,000 cash and agreed to pay the $90,000 balance in nine equal annual installments beginning in the following year. The deferred payments were secured by a security interest in the machine. Two years later, P had reduced the principal balance of the debt to $70,000, but the machine had fallen in value to $50,000. At that point, S agreed to accept $50,000 in full satisfaction of the debt principal. What result to P if:

(a) P was insolvent immediately after S reduced the debt?

Since P was insolvent, the $20,000 of debt-discharge income is excludable under § 108(a)(1)(B). P will have to reduce his tax attributes by $20,000 under 108(b).

(b) P was solvent at all times?

Now § 108(a)(1)(B)'s exclusion does not apply, but § 108(e)(5) treats the discharge as an adjustment of the purchase price of the machine. P does not include the $20,000 in gross income but must reduce his adjusted basis by $20,000 (since the machine's unadjusted basis was the original $100,000 cost). P does not adjust the depreciation for periods before the discharge occurs; the adjustment to basis is prospective only. If the amount of debt discharged exceeds P's adjusted basis immediately before the discharge, P must include the excess in income.

8.   T, a modestly wealthy person, offered $100,000 to the first graduate of the local high school to attain an undergraduate degree from an Ivy League university. Six years later, S qualified for the payment by graduating from Harvard. In the meantime, however, T had encountered substantial financial difficulties. Although T was solvent, it became clear to S that collecting the full amount to which she was entitled would be difficult. S therefore accepted T's payment of $60,000 in full satisfaction of T's obligation. Does T have income from the discharge of the debt?

If we apply the freeing-of-assets approach of *Kirby Lumber*, we would be tempted to say that T has realized debt-discharge income. After all, $40,000 of T's assets have been freed from the obligations owed creditors. However, under the delayed-tax-on-the loan-proceeds approach of *Rail Joint*, the cancellation does not appear to result in income to T. In *Rail Joint*, the corporate taxpayer issued a dividend to its shareholders payable in its own bonds. (The firm gets no deduction for the payment of a dividend, as the dividend is not a business expense but a distribution of profits.)   The bonds subsequently declined in value, and the taxpayer repurchased some of the bonds for less than their face amount. The Second Circuit held that the debt discharge did not result in gross income because the bonds had been issued gratuitously rather than for monetary consideration. That is also true in this case. When the obligation was incurred, T received no cash, property or services that could be consumed or saved. So, T should not be treated as having debt-discharge income on account of the transaction.

9.   F owed a bank $100,000 on a loan taken out for personal purposes several years before. Though solvent, F had struggled with financial and health issues. In the current year, F's son, S, purchases the loan from the bank for $60,000. What result to F?

Under the authority of § 108(e)(4), the Commissioner has issued regulations treating the acquisition of a debt by a party related to the debtor as an acquisition by the debtor; Treas. Reg. § 1.108–2. Because S is a member of F's family (§§ 108(e)(4)(B); 267(c)(4)), they are related parties (§ 267(b)(1)), and S's acquisition of the indebtedness is treated as if F acquired the $100,000 note for $60,000. F therefore has $40,000 of debt-discharge income.

Chapter 9

DAMAGES AND INSURANCE RECOVERIES

A. PROPERTY AND CONTRACT RIGHTS

Code: §§ 61(a). Review § 1001(a).

Regulation: § 1.61–14(a).

Cases: Commissioner v. Glenshaw Glass Co., 348 U.S. 426 (1955);
Raytheon Production Corp. v. Commissioner, 144 F.2d 110 (1st Cir. 1944);
Sager Glove Corp. v. Commissioner, 36 T.C. 1173, aff'd, 311 F.2d 210 (7th Cir. 1962).

Ruling: Rev. Rul. 85–97, 1985–2 C.B.

1. E was fired from her job in violation of her employment contract. She recovered $100,000 in damages. Must the $100,000 be included in E's income?

In Raytheon Production Corp. v. Commissioner, 144 F.2d 110 (1st Cir. 1944), the taxpayer recovered $450,000 for anti-trust violations that had destroyed a segment of its business. In considering the taxability of the recovery, the court said "the question to be asked is 'In lieu of what were the damages awarded?'"; 144 F.2d at 113. The in-lieu-of test has become the method for determining the taxability of business damages.

In this case, the $100,000 is received in lieu of salary, and salary would be includable in gross income. So, yes, E must include the recovery.

2. F's barn was completely destroyed in a fire set by vandals. The miscreants were caught and forced to pay F the $50,000 value of the barn. His adjusted basis in the barn was $20,000. F did not replace the barn. Must F include the damage recovery in income?

In this case, the $50,000 was received as compensation for the destruction of the barn—i.e., F has $50,000 "in lieu of" the barn. Of course, the fire and damage recovery did not enrich F. But the conversion of the barn into cash is a realization of gain to the extent that the amount realized on the conversion exceeds F's adjusted basis for the barn. Therefore, F has a realized gain of $30,000 ($50,000 amount realized less $20,000 adjusted basis); § 1001(a).

3. R, a chemist, developed a liquid compound in which one could store a razor when not in use and quadruple the number of shaves the user could get from a blade. Through word of mouth and internet advertising, the product became very profitable. However, through the use of predatory trade practices, a large firm was able to destroy R's business. R brought suit against the predator and recovered $500,000 in compensatory damages and $200,000 of punitive damages. How should R treat the recovery if the compensatory damages are for:

(a) Lost profits?

Under the in-lieu-of test of *Raytheon*, an amount received as compensation for lost profits is includable in income, just as the profits would have been income. So, R must include the $500,000 in gross income. The punitive damages must be included in gross income; Commissioner v. Glenshaw Glass Co., 348 U.S. 426 (1955); Treas. Reg. § 1.61–14(a).

(b) The destruction of R's goodwill?

Goodwill is the excess of the value of a business over the aggregate value of the identifiable tangible and intangible assets of the business. For example, suppose that X, a sole proprietor, owns property, plant, equipment, vehicles and other business assets with an aggregate value of $4,500,000. If, however, a purchaser were to purchase for $4,500,000 assets substantially identical to those held by X, the purchaser would not necessarily have a firm as valuable as X's. That is because X's business may have another intangible asset—goodwill. Goodwill may arise from X's having a favorable business reputation, an established customer base, good relationships with its employees, suppliers and host community, etc. Goodwill makes X's sole proprietorship, as a firm, worth more than the sum of the values of its identifiable assets. A purchaser might have to pay, say, $5,000,000 to purchase the firm. If the identifiable assets were worth only $4,500,000, we would say that the purchaser paid $500,000 for the goodwill.

Turning now to the problem, it is similar to 2, above, except that R's goodwill rather than his barn has been destroyed. And, as in the barn case, the conversion of the goodwill to cash is a realization of gain to the extent that the amount realized exceeds R's basis in the goodwill. R's goodwill is self-developed, and R would have deducted as business expenses the costs incurred in developing the goodwill—e.g., the costs of advertising, promotions, employee salaries, etc. For that reason, self-developed goodwill has a zero basis. R must therefore include the $500,000 in income.

If R had purchased the business (including goodwill) and had an adjusted basis of $200,000 in the goodwill when it was destroyed, R would include only $300,000 in gross income ($500,000 amount realized less $200,000 adjusted basis); § 1001(a).

Again, of course, the punitive damages must be included in gross income under *Glenshaw Glass* and Treas. Reg. § 1.61–14(a).

B. PERSONAL INJURIES

Code: § 104(a). Note § 213(a), (d)(1).

Regulations: § 1.104–1(a), (c), (d).

Case: Amos v. Commissioner, 86 T.C.M. 663 (2003).

Ruling: Rev. Rul. 85–97, 1985–2 C.B. 50.

1. P suffered serious injuries when she was struck by a bus. She recovered the following damages from the bus company: $50,000 for past and future medical expenses (none of which P had deducted), $100,000 for pain and suffering, $30,000 for lost wages, and $250,000 of punitive damages. To what extent is the recovery includable in P's gross income?

Section 104(a)(2) excludes from gross income damages (other than punitive damages) received on account of personal physical injuries. P can therefore exclude the recovery except for the punitive damages. Rev. Rul. 85–97, 1985–2 C.B. 50, makes clear that even the lost wages can be excluded under § 104(a)(2). Although the exclusion for lost wages is somewhat surprising, juries usually do not "itemize" their verdicts, and perhaps the drafters of § 104 thought that it would be difficult to administer a rule that required allocating part of a general damage award to lost wages.

2. Would your answer in 1 differ if in the preceding year P had deducted $20,000 of medical expenses incurred because of the accident?

Yes, the $20,000 attributable to the medical expenses deducted in the preceding year would have to be included in gross income. Section 104 excludes the compensatory damages except for "amounts attributable to * * * deductions allowed under section 213" in a prior year.

P deducted the medical expenses in the prior year, but then was reimbursed for those expenses. As it turned out, P got a deduction for costs that were not borne by her. Rather than requiring P to disgorge the deduction by filing an amended return for the prior year, the statute includes the recovery in P's income to "make up" for the "excess" deduction she got in the earlier year.

3. P brought an action against S for intentional infliction of mental distress, which caused P to suffer insomnia, headaches and stomach disorders. P recovered and obtained a verdict for $100,000, of which $20,000 was attributable to lost wages, $30,000 was for mental suffering, and $50,000 was in reimbursement for the cost of psychiatric care necessitated by S's actions. Must P include any portion of the $100,000 recovery in gross income?

Until its amendment in 1996, § 104(a)(2) would have excluded the entire recovery from P's gross income. The amendment, however, limits the exclusion to damages received on account of personal *physical* injuries or *physical* sickness. The amendment also added the next-to-last sentence of § 104(a), which says that "emotional distress shall not be treated as a physical injury or physical sickness." Although P suffered insomnia, headaches and stomach disorders, the conference committee report on the 1996 amendments says that "emotional distress includes physical symptoms (e.g., insomnia, headaches, stomach disorders) which may result from such emotional distress"; Joint Explanatory Statement of the Committee of Conference on H.R. 3448 at p. 143 (the Conference Report). Moreover, the damages were not received "on account of" the physical disorders but rather on account of the mental suffering. Even if the balance of the recovery is taxable, P can exclude the $50,000 reimbursement for the psychiatric care because of the last sentence of § 104(a), which treats emotional distress as a physical injury to the extent of amounts paid for medical care attributable to the emotional distress.

One can argue that repealing the exclusion does not automatically make recoveries for non-physical injuries taxable. The Conference Report (p. 142) says that "the exclusion from gross income only applies to damages received on account of a personal physical injury or physical sickness," and that might suggest that Congress intended to tax recoveries for non-physical injuries. Section 61(a), however, defines gross income as "income," and a receipt that is not *income* within the meaning of § 61 is not includable in gross income, even if it is not excluded by a specific statutory provision.

Under the in-lieu-of test of *Raytheon* and Sager Glove Corp. v. Commissioner, 114 F.2d 110 (1st Cir. 1944), a damage recovery is not considered "income," except to the extent that it takes the place of a taxable receipt. Under that test, the $20,000 attributable to the lost wages would still be includable. But if we think of the $30,000 as being received for P's loss of mental health, perhaps the recovery should be excludable because we don't impute income to people who are mentally healthy. On the other hand, some might counter that S has $30,000 of income as a result of receiving money for the damage to her (zero-basis) mental health, just as *Raytheon* had income when it received money for its zero-basis goodwill. Income denotes an accession to wealth—gain—and P has a *financial* or monetary gain, even if the money just compensates her for her lost emotional well-being; see Roemer v. Commissioner, 716 F.2d 693, 696, n.2 (9th Cir. 1983) ("Since there is no tax basis in a person's health and other personal interests, money received as compensation for an injury to those interests might be considered a realized accession to wealth.") So, even under the in-lieu-of test, the damages for the mental suffering may still be taxable.

To make matters even more complicated, a recent court of appeals decision held § 104(a)(2) unconstitutional to the extent that it permitted taxation of an award for mental distress and injury to professional reputation; Murphy v. Internal Revenue Service, 460 F.3d 79 (D.C. Cir. 2006). Although the judgment has since been vacated and set for rehearing, 2006 WL 4005276 (D.C. Cir.), it is worthy of a brief discussion. The court applied the in-lieu-of test, determined that the recovery just restored the taxpayer to her pre-injury position, and concluded that the recovery was not "income." It went on to say that any receipt that was not income under the statute could not be income within the Sixteenth Amendment, that Congress's constitutional power to tax income stems from that amendment, and therefore that Congress had no power under the Constitution to tax damages received on account of non-physical injuries.

Apart from its application of the in-lieu-of test on these facts (see the preceding discussion), the court's constitutional analysis is flawed. Congress's power to tax income does not stem from the Sixteenth Amendment but from its general taxing power under Article I, § 8, cl. 1, which authorizes Congress "To lay and collect Taxes, Duties, Imposts, and Excises * * *." Article I, §§ 2 and 9 require that *direct* taxes be apportioned among the states on the basis of population, and Pollock v. Farmers' Loan & Trust Co., 158 U.S. 601 (1895), held that the 1894 income tax was a direct tax as applied to income from real and personal property. The ratification of the Sixteenth Amendment did not authorize Congress to levy an income tax; it just removed the apportionment requirement. As applied in *Murphy*, the tax would be unconstitutional only if the imposition of a tax on the receipt of damages is considered to be a direct tax that required apportionment, which seems unlikely. We shall see.

4. Through the negligence of another, D was killed in an automobile accident. D's spouse, S, recovered $500,000 from the negligent party under the state wrongful-death statute. S also recovered $250,000 for loss of consortium. Can S exclude these amounts from gross income?

Yes. The damages resulted from a personal physical injury and so are excludable under § 104(a)(2) even though S was not the injured party.

5. **C, a congressman, physically injured his mistress during a fight. The woman threatened to sue, but C settled the case to avoid the unfavorable publicity of a trial. The settlement agreement required C to pay the woman $400,000 but provided that she would have to return the money if she publicized the case or pressed charges against C. In the agreement, C admitted to no wrongdoing. Is the $400,000 includable in the recipient's income?**

This problem is loosely based on Amos v. Commissioner, 86 T.C.M. 663 (2003). In *Amos*, the professional-basketball player Dennis Rodman deliberately kicked a photographer in the groin during a game. The photographer threatened suit, but the parties settled the case six days after the injury under an agreement that required Rodman to pay the photographer $200,000 and forbade the photographer from pressing charges or publicizing the case. If he violated the agreement, the photographer had to return the $200,000 as "liquidated damages." The Tax Court determined that $120,000 of the recovery was received on account of the physical injury and the balance was taxable because received on account of the hush-money provisions.

As *Amos* shows, only the portion of the recovery attributable to the personal physical injury is excludable. It is a question of fact as to how the recovery should be apportioned between the personal injury and the hush money. The court says that, unless the agreement makes an allocation of the recovery, a court must attempt to infer the intention of the payor in making the payment. In *Amos*, the taxpayer predictably asserted that all of the recovery was for the personal injury; the Government retorted that only $1 was for the personal injury and the balance was taxable. One might have thought that the liquidated-damages clause was a "smoking gun" that would require most of the recovery to be attributed to the hush-money provision, but the Tax Court did not find that fact persuasive.

Since the allocation of the award is a question of fact, we cannot answer the problem definitively, but some observations are in order. First, why should a court give any deference to an allocation made by the parties in the agreement? Unless they have adverse interests in making the allocation, it is hard to see why their allocation should be given weight. The recipient of the settlement wants to allocate a large proportion of the settlement to the personal injury; the payor doesn't seem to have much at stake in the allocation. On facts such as these, it seems unlikely that any portion of the payment would be deductible by the payor. If the payment is deductible, the payor might want a larger allocation to the personal-injury portion because of a fear that the deduction for the hush-money portion of the payment might be disallowed on public-policy grounds. So, the parties do not have adversarial interests in making the allocation.

Second, many settlement agreements contain confidentiality provisions. Must there always be an allocation to the confidentiality provision? Or are such provisions worthy of an allocation only where the "embarrassment" factor is especially significant to the payor? Could it be argued that the entire recovery should be excludable because received on account of the injury, in the sense that there would be no need for confidentiality if no injury had occurred? (I'm indebted to Professor Peter van Zante for the latter suggestion.)

6. E was injured in an industrial accident and received workman's-compensation payments of $20,000. Must the $20,000 be included in E's gross income?

Amounts received as workman's compensation are generally excludable under § 104(a)(1). However, any portion of the payments that reimburse E for medical expenses deducted in a prior year must be included.

C. INSURANCE RECOVERIES

Code: §§ 104(a)(3); 105(a), (b) & (e). Note § 213(a).

Regulations: Treas. Reg. § 1.104–1(d).

1. Earlier this year, T incurred and paid $17,500 of expenses for the medical care of her dependent son. She has now received reimbursement of the $17,500 from her insurer. Must the reimbursement be included in T's gross income if she paid the premiums on the policy?

No. Amounts received through health insurance for personal injuries or sickness are generally excludable from income; § 104(a)(3); Treas. Reg. § 1.104–1(d). However, she cannot deduct the expenses under § 213 to the extent that they were reimbursed.

2. Would your answer in 1 differ if T's employer had paid the premiums on the policy?

T can exclude from income the premiums paid by the employer under § 106(a). In that case, however, the exclusion of § 104(a)(3) does not apply to insurance reimbursements received under the policy. Section 105(a) provides generally that health-insurance reimbursements received by an employee must be included in income to the extent that they are attributable to contributions by the employer that were not includable in the employee's gross income. That is the case here. But § 105(b) provides an exception to the general rule and excludes reimbursements attributable to employer contributions whenever they reimburse the employee for medical expenses of the employee or her spouse or dependents. Here T was reimbursed for the expenses of medical care provided to her dependent son, so T can exclude the $17,500 from income.

3. **In year 1, S paid $17,500 for medical care for himself. On his tax return for year 1, S deducted $10,000 as medical expense under § 213. (Only $10,000 was deductible because § 213 limits the deduction to the amount by which the taxpayer's medical expenses exceed 7.5 percent of adjusted gross income.) In year 2, S's insurer reimbursed him for the $17,500. The policy had been purchased by S from his own funds. S had total itemized deductions of $20,000.   To what extent must the reimbursement be included in S's gross income for year 2?**

S must include $10,000.   Section 104(a)(3) generally excludes health-insurance reimbursements from income, but the first phrase of § 104(a) makes the reimbursement includable to the extent that the reimbursed expenses were allowed as a deduction in a prior year. If the reimbursement had been received in year 1, S would not have been allowed to deduct the expenses in year 1, as only expenses "not compensated for by insurance" are deductible under § 213(a). But in that case, the reimbursement would have been excluded from S's income by § 104(a)(3). Here, S took the year–1 deduction because the reimbursement had not been received by the end of year 1. Rather than making S file an amended return for year 1 and disgorge the deduction, section 104(a) requires that S include the reimbursement in year–2 income to counterbalance the earlier deduction. This approach avoids the necessity of amending the earlier return because of events that occurred after the close of the year.

4. **Would your answer in 3 differ if S's employer had purchased the policy of health insurance?**

S would still have to include $10,000 in gross income for year 2. Like § 104(a), § 105(b), which applies to reimbursements received under employer-provided policies, requires inclusion of amounts deducted in a prior year.

Chapter 10

GIFTS, BEQUESTS AND RELATED ISSUES

A. GIFTS, BEQUESTS AND LIFE INSURANCE PROCEEDS

Code: §§ 102; 101(a); 1014(a) & (b)(1); 1015(a).

Regulation: Prop. Treas. Reg. § 1.102–1(f)(2).

Case: Commissioner v. Duberstein, 363 U.S. 278 (1960).

1. D died in the current year and left a will which contained the following provisions:

I. I leave my residence, Purpleacre, to my niece, N.

II. I leave my Ultrasoft stock to my nephew, M.

III. I direct my testamentary trustee to pay the annual income from my prized farm, Blueacre, to my daughter, L, for life, remainder at's L's death to my grandchild, R.

IV. During the administration of my estate, I direct my executor to pay $5,000 annually from the income of my estate to my brother, B.

V. I leave my vacation home, Greenacre, to my beloved spouse, S.

VI. In lieu of an executor's fee, I leave my executor, E, $50,000.

VII. I leave the remainder of my estate to my child, C.

At the time of D's death, N was employed as D's secretary. D had purchased the Ultrasoft stock several years ago for $20,000. Its value on the date of D's death was $300,000. The usual executor's fee for an estate of comparable size and complexity is $40,000. S brought suit to contest the will; the suit was settled by the estate's paying S $750,000 cash.

D had paid a $10,000 premium on a policy of term insurance covering his life. D had designated R as beneficiary of the policy, and the insurer paid R the $100,000 death benefit.

D had also taken out a $150,000 whole-life policy on his life. After he had paid $25,000 in premiums, he sold the policy to M for $30,000. M paid an additional $20,000 in premiums on the policy before D's death, at which point M received the $150,000 death benefit.

Questions:

(a) Can N exclude the $400,000 value of Purpleacre from gross income?

Probably. Although the bequest of property appears to be excluded from income under § 102(a), N was D's employee, and § 102(c) says the exclusion does not apply to an amount transferred to an employee. However, Prop. Treas. Reg. § 1.102–1(f)(2) may permit the exclusion here, as $400,000 is a lot to leave an employee, *qua* employee. The size of the bequest suggests that D transferred the property to N for personal reasons rather than in recognition of her employment.

(b) Can M exclude any dividends received on the Ultrasoft stock?

No. Although in a sense both the stock and the dividends have been received by bequest, § 102(b) makes the exclusion of subsection (a) inapplicable to income from property acquired by bequest.

(c) What is M's basis for the Ultrasoft stock?

In M's hands, the Ultrasoft stock is property acquired from a decedent under § 1014(b)(1) ("property acquired by bequest"). The basis of property acquired from a decedent is (generally) its fair market value on the date of the decedent's death; § 1014(a). (We'll consider § 1014 in detail in Chapter 19.)

(d) Can L exclude the annual income received from Blueacre?

No. The exclusion does not apply where the bequest is of income from property; § 102(b)(2).

(e) Can R exclude the value of the remainder interest in Blueacre?

Yes; § 102(a).

(f) Can S exclude the $750,000 received in settlement of the will contest?

Yes. This is an application of the in-lieu-of test for damages discussed in Chapter 9A; damages received in settlement of a will contest are not taxed because bequests are not taxed; see Lyeth v. Hoey, 305 U.S. 188 (1938).

(g) Can E exclude the $50,000?

This appears not to be a bona fide bequest but rather a method of compensating the executor. Under Commissioner v. Duberstein, 363 U.S. 278 (1960), the determination of whether this is a bequest or compensation is a question of fact that must be resolved by determining the decedent's dominant reason for making the transfer. Although this is a bequest under state law, the state-law characterization of the transaction does not bind the Commissioner or the federal courts in a tax controversy. If E is not a natural object of D's bounty, the $50,000 is likely to treated as compensation; see Wolder v. Commissioner, 493 F.2d 608 (2d Cir. 1974). A transfer to an unrelated executor was not likely to have been motivated by affection, respect, admiration, charity or like impulses or made out of disinterested generosity. Indeed, compensation treatment seems appropriate here even if E is related to D. Even the $10,000 excess of the bequest over the usual fee may have been intended as compensation, as D probably could not know the precise amount of the fee when preparing his will. Here the bequest is not grossly disproportionate to the amount of the fee, and compensation treatment seems likely.

(h) Can R exclude the $100,000 of insurance proceeds?

Yes. Section 101(a)(1) excludes amounts received under a life-insurance contract if paid by reason of the death of the insured.

(i) Can M exclude the $150,000 of insurance proceeds?

Under the transferee-for-value rule of § 101(a)(2), M can exclude only an amount equal to the sum of the consideration paid by him ($30,000) and the premiums paid by him after he acquired the policy ($20,000). So, M excludes $50,000 and includes $100,000.

2. T, a prosperous attorney, had lived most of his life in the same small town. In gratitude to the town, and because he treasured his undergraduate education at an Ivy League school, he promised to pay $100,000 to each of the graduates of the local high school who attained an undergraduate degree from an Ivy League university. After her recent graduation from Princeton, S became the first student to qualify for the $100,000 payment. T was delighted, as S had worked as a "gofer" for T's law office during her summer vacations. T's promise was enforceable under state law. Can S exclude the payment from gross income? Explain.

Although T was legally obligated to make the payment, and thus it was not a common-law gift, that fact should not be decisive in determining whether the transfer was a gift. T seems to be acting out of disinterested generosity or a charitable impulse rather than in anticipation of future economic benefit. So, gift treatment should be possible, though under *Duberstein* the issue is one of fact.

A second issue is whether § 102(c) prevents S from excluding the $100,000 because S worked for T during summer vacations. Of course, maybe S no longer works for T since she has graduated. (Does § 102(c) cover a *former* employee? For how long?) Because the $100,000 is greatly disproportionate to the value of the "gofer" services performed by S, it does not appear that the payment represents disguised compensation. Prop. Treas. Reg. § 1.102–1(f)(2) would be helpful to S if she were a natural object of T's bounty, though that designation seems to be aimed more at family members. Maybe all the high-school students in town are potentially natural objects of T's bounty in a case such as this. The $100,000 should be excludable, as the transfer surely was not occasioned by the circumstances of S's employment.

3. M gave her son, S, 100 shares of Megacorporation stock as a birthday gift. M had purchased the stock several years ago for $5 per share. At the time of the gift, the stock was worth $40 per share. No gift tax was payable on the transfer by M. What is S's adjusted basis for the stock?

The donee of property acquired by gift generally assumes the donor's adjusted basis; § 1015(a). M's basis would be her cost of $5 (§ 1012), and, assuming no adjustments to basis, that is also S's adjusted basis. We will examine § 1015 in more detail in Chapter 18.

4. C has breakfast at the Café Z nearly every weekday morning. S is his ususal server. Last week, C told S that he was going to leave her a "real" tip. To S's astonishment, C left a tip of $10,000 cash. S offered to return the money but C insisted that she keep it. S and C never see each other apart from their encounters at the café. Must S include the tip in gross income?

Tips are includable in gross income as compensation. The question here is whether the $10,000 payment is a tip or a gift, and, under *Duberstein*, that depends upon the transferor's intention, as objectively inferred. The Commissioner would argue that S has performed a service for C, and C was compensating her for that service. Moreover, we usually associate "gifts" with transfers to family members or close friends, and the parties here do not have a "personal" relationship outside of the business setting. Since C is presumably continuing as a regular customer, the $10,000 may be viewed as being paid, in part, for future services by S.

One factor militating in favor of gift treatment is that $10,000 seems grossly disproportionate to the value of the service rendered by S, and that suggests that C did not intend the payment (or at least not all of it) as compensation. Maybe a factfinder would determine that the most-extravagant "true" tip in this setting would be $100, in which case, maybe $9,900 would be characterized as a gift. The problem with that argument is that (1) courts generally have not been willing to bifurcate a single transfer between gift and compensation (Should some portion of the value of Duberstein's Cadillac have been a gift on the theory that his services were not worth *that* much?); and (2) maybe $10,000 is not so extravagant when we consider both past and future services (Even if Duberstein's suggestions for new customers were not worth the value of the automobile, Berman might have expected that the "gift" of the car would induce Duberstein to provide similar information in the future.)

The absence of a personal relationship is not fatal to characterizing the payment as a gift. *Stanton*, the companion case to *Duberstein*, shows that a gift can occur in a "business" setting. Although *Stanton* has been overturned by the enactment of § 102(c), the case shows that the parties to a gift transfer need not have anything other than a business relationship in a situation not covered by § 102(c). (Whether § 102(c) applies here is discussed below.) In any event, if C has been S's customer for years, perhaps they have established a sufficiently "personal" relationship.

Of course, we need additional information to determine C's intention. Suppose, for example, that C says, "S is always cheerful and attentive and just gives splendid service every time, and I wanted to show her how much I admire her wonderful attitude and work ethic." Or, suppose that C says, "I know that S is a single mother of two and a part-time college student, and I just wanted to help her out." The likelihood of characterizing the transfer as a gift seems higher in the latter case than in the former.

Does § 102(c) preclude treating any part of the payment as a gift? S is not C's employee, of course, but the employee of the café. Suppose that the café has a policy that all tips must be turned over to it for distribution among the entire wait staff. (Some restaurants do this on the theory that it is not just the server but also the bus person, host/hostess, bartender, etc., who provide service to the customer and they should share in the tips.) In that case, the payment may be seen as going from C to the café, and then from the café to its employees, and § 102(c) may apply. But that presupposes that all of the payment was a tip rather than, at least in part, a gift to S.

B. PRIZES AND SCHOLARSHIPS

Code: §§ 117; 74.

Regulation: Prop. Treas. Reg. § 1.117–6(b), (c) & (d).

Case: Turner v. Commissioner, 13 T.C.M. 462 (1954).

1. S receives a $30,000 scholarship to Private University, where she is a full-time student. S incurs $40,000 of expenses for the year, consisting of:

Tuition	$24,000
Required books	1,500
Recommended books	1,000
Laboratory fees	500
Room and board	10,000
Travel	2,000
Computer (recommended)	1,000

How much of the grant must S include in gross income?

S must include $4,000 in gross income. A "qualified scholarship" can be excluded from income to the extent that it is used to pay "qualified tuition and related expenses"; § 117(a) & (b)(1). Qualified tuition and related expenses include tuition and, to the extent required for courses, the amounts paid for fees, books, supplies and equipment; § 117(b)(2). In this case, qualified tuition and related expenses total $26,000 ($24,000 tuition, $1,500 of required books and $500 of laboratory fees). The recommended books and computer do not qualify. Neither do the costs of travel and room and board.

2. T is a graduate student at State University. T receives a $20,000 scholarship from the University. As a condition to receiving the scholarship, T performs teaching services for the University. Similar teaching is required of all graduate-degree candidates in T's department. Non-students who have educational backgrounds similar to T's and who perform similar services for the University are paid $7,500. How much can T exclude from gross income?

T can exclude $12,500 as a qualified scholarship under § 117(a). The major issue is whether the payment represents compensation for T's teaching services, which would disqualify T for the exclusion because of § 117(c)(1). But if non-student teaching assistants with educational backgrounds similar to T's are paid $7,500 for similar work, then the University could reasonably take the position that only $7,500 of T's grant represents compensation; see Prop. Treas. Reg. § 1.117-6(d)(3). That is, § 117(b) trumps the exclusion only to the extent of "that portion of any amount received which represents payment for teaching * * * services * * *." So, if the institution allocates only the $7,500 to compensation and treats the balance as a scholarship, T need include only $7,500 in income; see id.

3. The University Law School offers grants of $30,000 to its students who are willing to commit to working full-time for a public-service or non-profit organization for at least 5 years after graduation. The selection of a position and its geographical location are left to the recipient to determine, except that the position must be within the state in which the Law School is located. A penalty is imposed if the recipient breaches the agreement. The annual tuition at the Law School exceeds $30,000. Must a recipient of a grant include it in income?

Although § 117(c)(1) says that a student generally cannot exclude any amount received "as payment" for teaching, research or "other services," there is a factual issue here as to whether the grant is received as payment for services. The Service apparently takes the position that the grant is compensation in a case such as this. In Rev. Rul. 77–44, 1977–1 C.B. 355, a private foundation made grants to college students who promised to teach in the public schools *of a particular state* after graduation. The ruling holds that the grants did not qualify as scholarships because they furthered the foundation's objective of attracting qualified teachers to the state's public schools. Perhaps in our case the Law School does not have the objective of keeping more of its graduates in the state, but then why else would it make such grants? So, the grant recipients probably would be taxable here under Rev. Rul. 77–44.

4. Would your answer in 3 differ if the grants were made to law students who agreed to accept post-graduation employment with public-sector or non–profit firms but the graduates were not required to accept positions in the state?

Yes, here the grant would apparently be a qualified scholarship under § 117(b); PLR 9526020. The ruling characterized similar grants as "designed to accomplish public rather than private or proprietary purposes" and noted that any benefit inuring to the University "appears remote, insubstantial, and inconsequential." The letter ruling distinguished Rev. Rul. 77–44, discussed in the preceding solution, because in the latter the grant recipients were expected to perform services in the state specified by the grantor. The distinction is tenuous at best.

5. N wins a Nobel Prize in chemistry. Must N include the $1,400,000 award in gross income?

Yes; § 74(a). Section 74(b) creates an exception for awards made primarily in recognition of religious, charitable, scientific, educational, artistic, literary or civic achievement, but only if three conditions are satisfied. First, the recipient must be selected without any action on his part to enter the proceeding. The Nobel prizewinners are nominated by others, so this condition appears to be satisfied (though that's not to say that people don't actively compete to win Nobel Prizes). Second, the recipient must not be required to render substantial future services as a condition to receiving the award. Though it is customary for Nobel Prize winners to make an acceptance speech, that alone would not constitute substantial future services. Third, the award must be transferred to a governmental unit or charitable organization described in § 170(c)(1) or (2). Here there is no such transfer, and the award will be includable in N's income.

6. Since charitable contributions are deductible under § 170, what purpose is served by § 74(b)(3)?

At first glance, one might think that § 74(b)(3) is superfluous because, even if the award is included in the winner's gross income, it will be offset by the charitable deduction if the prize is given to charity. However, § 170 imposes several limits on the amount that can be deducted as charitable contributions. For example, deductions for cash contributions are limited to 50 percent or 30 percent of the taxpayer's adjusted gross income, depending upon the type of charity to which the contribution is made; see § 170(b)(1)(A) & (B). When the limits on the charitable deduction apply, the inclusion of the award in gross income may not be completely offset by the charitable deduction. To illustrate, suppose that, after taking into account the $1,400,000 award, N had AGI of $1,600,000. If N gave the prize money to a public charity, only $800,000 would be deductible in the current year because of the 50–percent limit of § 170(b)(1)(A). Even if the $800,000 were fully deductible (and ignoring other deductions), N would have taxable income of $800,000. The other $600,000 of the charitable contribution could be carried forward to the next year, where it would again be subject to the 50–percent limit, and so on for up to 5 years; § 170(d)(1)(A). But because of the limits on the charitable deduction, N would have to pay a hefty amount of tax in the year in which the prize was taxable. Under § 74(b), however, N could designate the charity as the transferee of the award, exclude the prize from income, and have only $200,000 of AGI. In effect, § 74(b) permits N to circumvent the limits on the charitable deduction.

Recall also that the itemized deductions of higher-income taxpayers are sometimes reduced under § 68. That's another reason why § 74(b) produces a more-favorable result than would including the prize in gross income and deducting it as a charitable contribution.

7. W won an all-expense-paid trip for two to Cabo San Lucas on a radio quiz show. The prize was non-transferable. Similar trip packages sell for $3,000. Must W include $3,000 in gross income on account of the prize?

The prize is includable under § 74(a), but at what value? In Turner v. Commissioner, 13 T.C.M. 462 (1954), the Commissioner sought to value at retail some non-transferable tickets that Turner had won as a prize. The Tax Court, however, held that their value to the Turners was not equal to their retail cost.

The court pointed out that, even if Turner could have sold the tickets, he probably could not have sold them for as much as their retail cost. The court therefore valued the tickets at about 63 percent of their retail value. So, W has a good argument for valuing the tickets at less than $3,000.

Treas. Reg. § 1.61-21(b)(2) deals with the valuation of non-cash fringe benefits furnished by an employer to its employees. It says that fringe benefits must be valued at fair market value (usually the amount the employee "would have to pay * * * in an arm's-length transaction") and that "an employee's subjective perception of the value of a fringe benefit is not relevant to the determination of a fringe benefit's fair market value." But that regulation should not apply in a case like *Turner*. Unlike Turner, employees can bargain with their employers to avoid receiving items whose retail value exceeds their worth to the employees. So the regulation's approach should not be used in a case like *Turner*.

Section C

BUSINESS AND INVESTMENT EXPENSES

Chapter 11

DEPRECIATION AND RELATED ISSUES

Code: §§ 167(a), (b) & (c); 168(a), (b), (c), (d), (e), (g)(1), (2) & (7), (i)(1), (8)(A) & (12); 179(a), (b)(1), (2) & (3), (d)(1); 1011(a); 1016(a)(2).

Regulation: § 1.179–1(f)(1).

Case: Simon v. Commissioner, 68 F.3d 41 (2d Cir. 1995) (Non- acq.).

Ruling: Rev. Proc. 87–57, 1987–2 C.B. 674.

In each of the following problems, assume (unless otherwise indicated) that (1) the property purchased was the taxpayer's only capital expenditure for the year; (2) the dollar limitation of § 179(b)(1) is $100,000; and (3) the phaseout of the limitation in § 179(b)(2) begins at $400,000. Ignore inflation adjustments.

1. On June 26, year 1, T placed in service a piece of equipment (5–year property) to be used in her manufacturing business. She purchased the property for $175,000. Because she has very substantial amounts of income from the business, she wishes to maximize her tax deductions in years 1 and 2. What is the maximum amount she can deduct with respect to the equipment in year 1? In year 2? Explain.

Since T wishes to maximize her deductions in years 1 and 2, she should elect to expense $100,000 of the asset's cost under § 179. The remaining cost can then be depreciated under § 168.

The property satisfies the definition of "section 179 property"; see § 179(d)(1). She can therefore elect to deduct as an expense up to $100,000 of the cost of the property ($100,000 being the maximum amount she can expense under § 179(b)(1)). Her unadjusted basis must be reduced by the amount charged to expense; Treas. Reg. § 1.179–1(f)(1). Thus, her unadjusted basis is $75,000.

Next, we compute her depreciation deduction for year 1. The equipment is 5–year property, so the applicable depreciation method is the 200% declining-balance method with an eventual switch to the straight-line method (§ 168(b)(1)); the applicable recovery period is 5 years (§ 168(c)); and the applicable convention is the half-year convention (§ 168(d)(1)). We ignore salvage value because of § 168(b)(4).

Since the property is 5–year property, the straight-line depreciation rate is 20 percent (i.e., 1/5) per year. The 200% declining-balance rate is therefore 40 percent (200% of 20%). To calculate year–1 depreciation, we multiply the adjusted basis at the beginning of year 1 by 40 percent, which gives us a figure of $30,000 ($75,000 x 40%). But the half-year convention dictates that T gets only a half-year's deduction for year 1; the year–1 deduction is therefore $15,000 (1/2 of $30,000). The adjusted basis at the end of year 1 is $60,000 ($75,000 unadjusted basis less $15,000 depreciation); §§ 1016(a)(2); 1011(a).

For year 2, the depreciation deduction is $24,000 (40% of the $60,000 adjusted basis of the equipment at the beginning of year 2). Notice that we are applying a constant percentage to the asset's adjusted basis at the beginning of each year. (This is a different approach than that of the tables from Rev. Proc. 87–57 (discussed below), which require us to apply differing percentages to the (constant) unadjusted basis of the property.

T's adjusted basis at the end of year 2 is $36,000 ($60,000 adjusted basis at the beginning of year 2 less $24,000 of depreciation for year 2).

Alternatively we could compute the depreciation by using Table 1 from Rev. Proc. 87–57, 1987–2 C.B. 674 (which is reproduced in the Appendix to *Selected Federal Taxation–Statutes and Regulations* published by Thomson/West). Under that approach, we calculate the depreciation for year 1 at $15,000 (20% of the unadjusted basis of $75,000). (The half-year convention is incorporated into the Table's percentage for year 1, so we don't have to account for that separately.) As above, T's adjusted basis at the end of year 1 is $60,000 ($75,000 unadjusted basis less $15,000 depreciation for year 1).

Referring again to Table 1, we see that T's depreciation deduction for year 2 is $24,000 (32% of the unadjusted basis of $75,000). (Remember that in applying Table 1, we multiply the *unadjusted basis* by the percentage prescribed for the year by the Table.) Her adjusted basis at the end of the second year is $36,000 ($60,000 adjusted basis at the beginning of the year less $24,000 depreciation for year 2).

2. On September 1 of year 1, F places in service on his farm a newly erected barn. The barn cost $200,000. He wishes to maximize his depreciation deduction. How much depreciation is allowable in each of years 1 and 2? (The barn has a class life of 25 years.)

We begin by classifying the barn under § 168(e). Your first impulse might be to classify the barn as "nonresidential real property" under § 168(e)(2)(B) because it is "section 1250 property" (i.e., depreciable real property—see § 1250(c)) and it is not "residential rental property." But § 168(e)(2)(B)(ii) excludes from nonresidential real property any "property with a class life of less than 27.5 years." The barn has a class life of only 25 years, so it cannot be nonresidential real property. Instead it is classified as 20–year property under § 168(e)(1) because it has a class life of "25 years or more."

The applicable depreciation method is the 150% declining-balance method (with a later switch to straight-line) both because it is 20–year property and because it is used in farming; § 168(b)(2)(A) & (B). The applicable recovery period is 20 years; § 168(c); the applicable convention is the half-year convention; 168(d)(1). Notice that the mid-month convention, which usually applies to depreciable real property, does not apply in this case; see § 168(d)(2).

The straight-line depreciation rate for 20–year property is 5 percent (1/20). The 150% declining balance rate is therefore 7.5 percent (150% of 5%). A full year's depreciation would be $15,000 (7.5% of $200,000), and so a half-year's depreciation would be $7,500 (1/2 of $15,000). At the end of the year, the adjusted basis would be $192,500 ($200,000 unadjusted basis less $7,500 of year–1 depreciation).

The depreciation for year 2 would be $14,437.50 (7.5% of $192,500), and the adjusted basis at the end of year 2 would be $178,062.50 ($192,500 adjusted basis at the beginning of year 2 less year–2 depreciation of $14,437.50).

3. Lawyer L purchases a Picasso sketch to hang on her office wall. Over what period can she depreciate the sketch?

The sketch is not depreciable because it does not suffer wear and tear, according to Simon v. Commissioner, 68 F.3d 41 (2d Cir. 1995) (Non- acq.). Nor does the sketch have a limited and ascertainable useful life, though *Simon* says that, at least under the version of § 168 in effect for the years involved in that case, property can be depreciable even if it does not have a limited and ascertainable useful life.

4. In July, year 1, P pays $420,000 for 7–year property (class life of 10 years) to be used in her active manufacturing business. P makes no § 179 election with respect to the equipment. What is P's adjusted basis for the equipment at the end of year 2?

The applicable depreciation method is the 200% declining-balance method; § 168(b)(1). The applicable recovery period is 7 years; § 168(c). The applicable convention is the half-year convention; § 168(d)(1).

For 7-year property, the straight-line rate would be 14.29 percent (1/7), and the 200% declining-balance rate is 28.57percent (200% x 14.29%). For year 1, a full year's depreciation would be $120,000 (28.57% of the unadjusted basis of

$420,000). Under the half-year convention, however, the year–1 deduction is limited to $60,000 (50% of $120,000). The adjusted basis at the end of year 1 is $360,000 ($420,000 cost less $60,000 depreciation).

For year 2, the deduction is $102,852 (28.57% of $360,000), and the adjusted basis at the end of the second year is $257,148 ($360,000 adjusted basis at the beginning of year 2 less year–2 depreciation of $102,852).

5. Same as 4, except that in year 1 P deducts the maximum amount permitted under § 179.

The property is § 179 property because it is tangible § 1245 property (see § 1245(a)(3)) that was acquired by purchase for use in the active conduct of business; § 179(d)(1). The § 179 deduction can in no event exceed $100,000 (§ 179(b)(1)), but here the $100,000 limit is reduced under § 179(b)(2). Because the cost of the § 179 property placed in service by P in year 1 exceeds $400,000, the $100,000 limit must be reduced by the amount by which the $420,000 cost of the § 179 property placed in service exceeds $400,000. That excess is $20,000 ($420,000 less $400,000). P's maximum § 179 deduction is therefore $80,000 ($100,000 less $20,000), which reduces P's unadjusted basis to $340,000 ($420,000 cost less $80,000 § 179 deduction); Treas. Reg. § 1.179–1(f)(1).

Remember that the § 179 deduction is in addition to, not in lieu of, the regular depreciation deduction. As discussed in the solution to (4), the 200% declining-balance rate for 7–year property is 28.57%. So, P's year–1 depreciation deduction is $48,569 (28.57% x $340,000 x ½), and the adjusted basis of the property at the end of year 1 is $291,431 ($340,000 unadjusted basis less year–1 depreciation of $48,569).

The year–2 depreciation deduction is $83,262 (28.57% of the $291,431 adjusted basis at the beginning of year 2). The adjusted basis at the end of year 2 is $208,169 ($291,431 adjusted basis at beginning of year 2 less year–2 depreciation of $83,262).

6. Same as 4, except that P makes an election under § 168(b)(3)(D) and (b)(5).

Here P has elected under § 168(b)(3)(D) to use straight-line depreciation. The recovery period remains 7 years and the half-year convention still applies. A full year's straight-line depreciation would be $60,000 ($420,000/7). So, under the half-year convention, P's depreciation for year 1 is $30,000 (½ of $60,000). The year–2 deduction would be $60,000, leaving P with an adjusted basis of $330,000 at the end of the second year ($420,000 unadjusted basis less depreciation of $90,000 for years 1 and 2).

7. Same as 4, except that P makes an election under § 168(g)(1)(E) and (g)(7).

In this case, P has elected to use the "alternative depreciation system" of § 168(g)(2). Under that system, P uses straight-line depreciation over the class life of the property (here 10 years); § 168(g)(2)(A) &(C). The usual convention applies (here the half-year convention); § 168(g)(2)(B).

A full year's depreciation would be $42,000 ($420,000/10), so the year–1 deduction is $21,000 because of the half-year convention. The year–2 deduction is $42,000, and the adjusted basis after the second year is $357,000 ($420,000 unadjusted basis less $63,000 of depreciation for years 1 and 2).

8. R placed in service two pieces of equipment (5–year property), each of which cost $210,000. The first was placed in service in July, year 1, and the second in October, year 1. R makes no § 179 election with respect to either piece of equipment. What is R's allowable depreciation for year 1? Year 2?

Again we use the 200% declining-balance method with a recovery period of 5 years. In this case, however, we must apply the special rule of § 168(d)(3) in determining the applicable convention. The aggregate basis of property placed in service in the last three months of the year ($210,000) exceeds 40 percent of the aggregate bases of all properties placed in service during the year ($168,000, which is 40% of $420,000). Therefore, R must use the mid-quarter convention under which the property is deemed to have been placed in service at the mid-point of the quarter; § 168(d)(3)(A) & (d)(4)(C).

A full year's deprecation on each piece of equipment would be $84,000 (40% of $210,000). The equipment placed in service in July (the third quarter) would qualify for 3/8 of a year's depreciation (i.e., it is deemed to have been in service for half the third quarter and all of the fourth quarter). The equipment placed in service in October (the fourth quarter) qualifies for only 1/8 of a year's depreciation (i.e., half a quarter's depreciation).

R's year–1 deduction for the July equipment is $31,500 (3/8 of a full year's depreciation of $84,000) and for the October equipment is $10,500 (1/8 of $84,000). At the end of year 1, R's adjusted basis for the July equipment is $178,500 ($210,000 cost less $31,500 depreciation), and her adjusted basis for the October equipment is $199,500 ($210,000 cost less $10,500 depreciation).

For year 2, the depreciation deduction for the July equipment is $71,400 (40% of $178,500 adjusted basis at the beginning of year 2) and for the October equipment is $79,800 (40% of its $199,500 adjusted basis at the beginning of year 2). These adjustments reduce R's adjusted basis for the July equipment to $107,100 ($178,500 adjusted basis at beginning of year 2 less $71,400 of year–2 depreciation). R's adjusted basis for the October equipment is reduced to $119,700

($199,500 adjusted basis at the beginning of the year less $79,800 of year–2 depreciation).

9. Would your answer in 8 differ if R had also purchased an apartment building for $1 million in January of year 1?

No. Although far less than 40 percent of the total bases of property placed in service in year 1 were placed in service in the last three months of the year, § 168(d)(3)(B) tells us to disregard nonresidential real property, residential rental property and certain other properties in applying the 40–percent test § 168(d)(3)(A).

10. Suppose that in January, year 3, R (in problem (8)) sold the equipment placed in service in July of year 1. At the end of year 2, R's adjusted basis for the July equipment was $107,100. How much depreciation is allowable to R in year 3?

A full year's depreciation would be $42,840 (40% of the $107,100 adjusted basis at the beginning of year 3). However, the applicable convention applies not only to the year in which property is placed in service, but also to the year of disposition; § 168(d)(4). Since the property was sold in January, R gets only 1/8 (i.e., one-half of one quarter) of a full year's depreciation in year 3. So, the deduction is limited to $5,355 (1/8 of $42,840), and R's adjusted basis at the time of sale is $101,745 ($107,100 adjusted basis at the beginning of year 3 less $5,355 of year–3 depreciation).

11. Several years ago S purchased a depreciable business asset for $100,000. Although the total amount of depreciation allowable with respect to the asset is $80,000, S mistakenly deducted only $60,000 of depreciation. S is preparing to sell the asset. What is S's adjusted basis for the property?

Section 1016(a)(2) requires that adjusted basis be reduced by the amount of depreciation allowed, "but not less than the amount allowable." So, even though only $60,000 of depreciation has been *allowed*, S must reduce his adjusted basis by the $80,000 that was *allowable*. S's adjusted basis is therefore $20,000. S should file amended returns for any open years and claim the correct amount of depreciation.

12. On January 1, year 1, L leased land to T for 36 years. In January, year 2, (when the lease had 35 years to run), T finished erecting a new office building on the property at a cost of $780,000. What is T's depreciation deduction for year 2?

The building is classified as nonresidential real property under § 168(e)(2)(B). The applicable depreciation method is the straight-line method; § 168(b)(3)(A). The applicable convention for nonresidential real property is the mid-month convention, under which the property is deemed to have been placed in service at the mid-point of the month in which it was placed in service; § 168(d)(2)(A) & (d)(4)(B). The recovery period is 39 years; § 168(c).

Notice that T's lease only had 35 years to run when the building was placed in service. Does it follow that T should be allowed to use a recovery period co-extensive with the lease term instead of the longer period prescribed by the statute? Before the Tax Reform Act of 1986, taxpayers were permitted to depreciate buildings on leased ground over the remaining term of the lease whenever that was shorter than the building's usual recovery period. Today, however, § 168(i)(8) requires that buildings on leased property (and improvements made to leased property) be depreciated over the recovery periods prescribed by § 168(c).

A full year's depreciation on the building would be $20,000 ($780,000/39). The property is treated as having been placed in service at the mid-point of the month of January, so T is entitled to 11.5 months of depreciation. The deduction is therefore $19,166.67 (11.5/12 x $20,000).

You can also compute the year's depreciation by using the Instructions for Form 4562, which are reproduced in the Appendix to *Selected Federal Taxation–Statutes and Regulations* (Thomson/West). From Table E, which applies to nonresidential real property, we see that for property placed in service in the first month of the year the deduction for the first year is 2.461% of the property's basis. So, the deduction is $19,195.80. (The difference between this amount and the computation above is due to rounding.)

13. Is the depreciation (cost-recovery) deduction of § 168 a tax expenditure? Explain your answer.

A tax expenditure is a special tax provision that exists to further some non-tax goal rather than to measure "income" in some normative sense. A depreciation deduction is required in a normative income tax, for if we are to tax only "net" income we must allow a deduction for the "using up" of depreciable property. But while depreciation deductions are necessary in order to measure taxpayers' net incomes, § 168 allows deductions at a more rapid rate than the property declines in value (i.e., it allows deductions in excess of "economic depreciation" in the early years of an asset's life). Thus, to some extent § 168 is a tax expenditure that subsidizes investment in depreciable assets, with the predictable effect that it creates a bias in favor of investing in depreciable as opposed to non-depreciable assets. As in the case of most other tax expenditures, the subsidy is "upside down" in the sense that the excess deductions benefit those in high tax brackets more than those in lower brackets.

Chapter 12

BUSINESS AND INVESTMENT EXPENSES

A. IN GENERAL

Code: §§ 162(a), (c)(1) & (2), (f), (*l*); 212; 67; 262; 7701(a)(25). Review § 62(a).

Regulations: §§ 1.162–1(a); 1.162–4; 1.162–6; 1.62–1T(a), (b), (d) & (e)(1); 1.67–1T; 1.263(a)–4(f)(1).

Cases: United States v. Gilmore, 372 U.S. 39 (1963);
Wild v. Commissioner, 42 T.C. 706 (1964) (Acq.);
Pevsner v. Commissioner, 628 F.2d (5th Cir. 1980), rehearing en banc denied, 636 F.2d 1106 (1981);
Welch v. Helvering, 290 U.S. 111 (1933).

1. Is § 162(a) a tax-expenditure provision? Explain.

A tax expenditure is a special tax provision (e.g., a deduction, exclusion or credit) that exists to further some *non-tax* goal rather than to measure "income" in some normative sense. A deduction for business expenses is required in a normative income tax, for if we are to tax only "net" income we must allow a deduction for the costs of earning income. If business expenses were not deductible, we would be taxing people in business on more than their net incomes.

2. T is a self-employed lawyer—a solo practitioner—who uses the cash method of accounting. Which of the following (alternative) expenditures made by T qualify for deduction under § 162? In each case, specify which section allows (or disallows) the deduction and whether any allowable deduction is taken in computing AGI. Also indicate whether any deductible item is a miscellaneous itemized deduction subject to the limits of § 67.

(a) Rent on T's law office;

Deductible; § 162(a)(3); Treas. Reg. § 1.162–1(a). The deduction is taken in computing AGI; § 62(a)(1).

(b) Principal payment on liability incurred when law office was purchased by T; the liability was secured by a mortgage on the premises;

Not deductible. The liability incurred when the property was purchased is reflected in the property's adjusted basis. Since we give T advance basis credit for the amounts she has promised to pay in the future, she can neither deduct, nor increase her basis for, principal payments on the mortgage note. As T makes principal payments on the mortgage, she increases her equity investment in the property but decreases her "debt" investment, so the unadjusted basis of the property remains the same. As the owner of the property, T can depreciate it under § 167(a)(1).

(c) Cost of a new desk-top computer for T's office;

The cost of an asset with a life extending substantially beyond the close of the taxable year is a capital expenditure rather than an "expense" under § 162(a); Treas. Reg. § 1.446–1(a)(4)(ii); 1.461–1(a)(1). However, the cost of the computer may qualify for the expensing election of § 179, which is discussed in Chapter 11. Any amount that is not charged to expense under § 179 is depreciable under § 167(a)(1). The depreciation (and any amount deducted as expense under § 179) are allowable as above-the-line deductions; § 62(a)(1).

(d) Cost of painting the interior of the office (this is done approximately every three years);

This is a repair expense, even though it is required to be done only every third year; it "neither materially add[s] to the value of the property nor appreciably prolong[s] its life, but keep[s] it in an ordinarily efficient operating condition * * *"; Treas. Reg. § 1.162–4. It's an above-the-line deduction; § 62(a)(1).

(e) Cost of dues for T's membership in the Tax Section of the American Bar Association;

Deductible; Treas. Reg. § 1.162–6 ("dues to professional societies"). T takes the deduction above the line; § 62(a)(1)

(f) Cost of a health-insurance policy covering T, her spouse and children;

Although this appears to be T's personal expense, one must keep in mind that an employee whose employer pays medical-insurance premiums on the employee's behalf can exclude the amount of the premiums from income under § 106. And the employer deducts the payment as a business expense under § 162(a). In the absence of a special rule, a self-employed taxpayer could deduct the premiums only to the extent that they (when combined with the person's other medical expenses) exceeded 7.5 percent of AGI. To prevent this inequality, Congress enacted § 162(*l*)(1)(A), which allows a deduction for the cost of medical insurance on the taxpayer, spouse and dependents. The deduction cannot exceed the taxpayer's earned income from the business; § 162(*l*)(2)(B). Any amount deducted under § 162(*l*) cannot be taken into account in computing the medical-expense deduction under § 213. The deduction is an above-the-line deduction; § 62(a).

(g) Self-employment tax on the income from T's law practice;

An employer can deduct its one-half of the Social Security and Medicare taxes as a business expense. A self-employed person must, in effect, pay both the employer's and the employee's share of these taxes. To put the self-employed person in roughly the same position as an employer, § 164(f)(1) allows a deduction for one-half the self-employment taxes ("taxes imposed by section 1401"). The deduction is treated as attributable to business (and not the business of being an employee), so as to make the deduction allowable above the line; see §§ 164(f)(2); 62(a)(1).

(h) Amounts advanced to T's litigation clients for payment of court costs, depositions, expert witnesses, etc.;

Such advances should be treated as loans to the client rather than business expenses. So, no deduction.

(i) Premium payment for two year's coverage under a policy providing casualty insurance on T's business;

In general, the cost of business insurance is deductible under § 162; Treas. Reg. § 1.162–1(a). However, prepaid expenses generally must be capitalized; Treas. Reg. § 1.263(a)–4(d)(3). Although capitalization is generally not required for expenditures whose benefit does not extend more than twelve months (see Treas. Reg. § 1.263(a)–4(f)(1)), here the premium provides coverage for two years and will therefore have to be capitalized and amortized over the 24–month period of the subscription.

(j) $25,000 annual salary paid to T's sixteen-year old son, who spends about ten hours per week running errands for the firm;

Section 162(a)(1) limits the deduction for compensation expense to a "reasonable allowance * * * for personal services actually rendered." Here the son's hourly compensation works out to about $50 per hour, which seems too high for a 16–year old "gofer." The deduction should be limited to the amount earned by similarly situated employees who are not the boss's son. If that amount is , say, $10 per hour, then T's deduction should be limited to $5,000. The other $20,000 is a non-deductible gift to the son, which might also be a gift-taxable transaction. The allowable portion is deductible above the line; § 62(a)(1).

(k) Cost of transportation from T's home to her office;

This is commuting and its cost is not deductible; Treas. Reg. § 1.162–2(e).

(l) Cost of transportation from T's home to the courthouse for an all-day trial (T returned directly home from the courthouse at the end of the day);

This is deductible. The courthouse is a temporary work location in the same law business that T conducts through her office, which is her regular work location. T can therefore deduct the cost of transportation from her residence to the temporary work location, regardless of distance; Rev. Rul. 99–7, 1999–1 C.B. 361 (Holding (2)). The deduction is above the line; § 62(a)(1).

(m) Investment-advisory fee in connection with the management of T's stock-market portfolio;

The fee is deductible as an expense for the production or collection of income under § 212(1). It is an itemized deduction (because not listed in § 62(a)), and a miscellaneous itemized deduction (because not listed in § 67(b)). T can deduct miscellaneous itemized deductions only to the extent that their sum exceeds 2 percent of AGI; § 67(a).

(n) Commissions on purchase and sale of securities;

Commissions paid in purchasing securities are capital expenditures that must be added to the basis of the securities; commissions paid on the sale of securities is an offset against the sales price in computing the amount realized on the sale; Treas. Reg. § 1.263(a)–2(e). So, no deduction.

(o) $500 gratuity to the clerk of court, who agreed to move one of T's cases up on the court's docket;

This appears to be an illegal bribe, as state law generally prohibits state employees from accepting anything of value with the understanding that the gratuity will influence the act of the employee. Although the payment may otherwise be an ordinary and necessary business expense, § 162(c)(1)) disallows a deduction for an illegal bribe paid to a government employee. Therefore, no deduction.

(p) Attorney's fee paid for representation in a civil inquiry by the State Judicial Ethics Committee into the payment of the gratuity in (o);

The attorney's fee is allowable as a business expense because the proceeding arose out of T's business activities; see Tellier v. Commissioner, 383 U.S. 687 (1966) (rejecting Commissioner's argument that deduction should be denied on "public policy" grounds). The deduction is an above-the-line deduction; § 62(a)(1).

(q) Fine imposed by the Committee in (p) after its investigation found T guilty of bribing the clerk;

Fines (whether civil or criminal) are not deductible as business expenses; § 162(f); Treas. Reg. § 1.162–21(b)(1).

(r) Payment (in December) for $3,000 worth of office supplies; T keeps no inventory of the supplies and does not record their use, but T does not expect to have to replenish the supplies until late in the following year;

Taxpayers generally may deduct the cost of supplies only as they are actually used; Treas. Reg. § 1.162–3. But where a taxpayer purchases supplies for which no record of consumption (or physical inventories) are kept, the cost of the supplies can be deducted when purchased, provided that the method clearly reflects taxable income; id. Therefore, unless the deduction would seriously distort taxable income, T can probably deduct the $3,000 cost of the supplies in the year purchased.

(s) Cost of "professional" looking clothing for office wear; the clothing cost $3,000 more than T would have spent if she were not working, as her personal lifestyle is quite casual;

No deduction because the cost of the clothing is a personal expense; see § 262; Pevsner v. Commissioner, 628 F.2d (5th Cir. 1980), rehearing en banc denied, 636 F.2d 1106 (1981); Kosmal v. Commissioner, 39 T.C.M. 651 (1979), aff'd mem., 670 F.2d 842 (9th Cir. 1982) (lawyer could not deduct cost of suits).

(t) $5,000 paid to a public relations firm to lobby against a proposal in the state legislature that would subject payments for legal services to state sales tax;

Section 162(e)(1) generally denies a deduction for any amount paid in influencing legislation. That includes an attempt to influence legislation through communication with any member of a legislative body; § 162(e)(4)(A). "In-house" expenditures not exceeding $2,000 can be deducted, but payments to a lobbyist do not come within the de minimis exception; § 162(e)(5)(B). So, no deduction.

(u) $1,000 of travel expense incurred by T to personally lobby state legislators to vote against the proposal described in (t);

This falls within the de minimis exception for in-house expenditures; § 162(e)(5)(B). It is deductible in computing AGI; § 62(a)(1).

(v) $5,000 expended in lobbying members of the city council to prevent re-zoning of the land adjacent to T's law office.

These costs fall within the "local legislation" exception of § 162(e)(2) and should be deductible above the line.

(w) $1,000 to the State Supreme Court to obtain a license to practice law in the state. The license is valid indefinitely, providing L adheres to the rules governing the practice of law in the state.

The amount paid for a governmental license of indefinite duration must be capitalized; Treas. Reg. § 1.263(a)–4(d)(5)(ii), Ex. 2. In Sharon v. Commissioner, 66 T.C. 515, aff'd, 591 F.2d 1273 (9th Cir. 1978), the Commissioner conceded that such an expenditure could be amortized over the taxpayer's expected working life (i.e., until the taxpayer's expected retirement age of 65). Today Treas. Reg. § 1.167(a)–3(b) permits an intangible asset to be amortized over fifteen years unless its useful life can be estimated with reasonable accuracy. So, perhaps 15–year amortization would now be permitted in a case such as this. It's an above-the-line deduction; § 62(a)(1).

3. A, a 30–year old single person with no dependents, is employed as an associate in a law firm. A has the following receipts and disbursements for the current year.

	Receipts	Disbursements
Salary	$100,000	
Rent	6,000	
Mineral royalties	5,000	
Travel expenses*		5,000
Professional dues*		1,000
Professional books		1,000
Investment-advisory fee		2,500
Rental expenses		5,000
Charitable contributions		5,000
State income tax		4,000
Severance tax on royalty income		1,000
Deductible IRA contribution		5,000

* Denotes expenditures reimbursed by T's firm.

The investment-advisory fee was paid for stock-market investment advice. Determine A's gross, adjusted gross and taxable income.

A's gross income is $117,000 ($100,000 salary, plus $6,000 rent, plus $5,000 royalty income, plus $6,000 reimbursed expense); § 61(a). (The reimbursed expenses of $6,000 may either be included in gross income and then deducted as reimbursed employee-business expenses under § 62(a)(2), or omitted from gross income and not deducted.)

As an employee, A can deduct his business expenses under § 162(a). Except for those expenses that are reimbursed, however, the employee-business expenses are itemized deductions; see § 62(a)(1) & (2). So, the $6,000 of reimbursed expenses are deductible above the line; Treas. Reg. § 1.62–1T(e)(1).

The $5,000 rental expense is allowable under either § 162(a) (business expense) or § 212 (investment expense). It is an above-the-line deduction under § 62(a)(4). The $1,000 severance tax is also deductible under 212; it is deductible in computing AGI, though any state income tax on the royalty income is not; see Treas. Reg. § 1.62–1T(d). The $5,000 IRA contribution is allowable under § 219 and deductible in computing AGI by § 62(a)(7). None of the other deductions is allowable in computing AGI. Thus, A has deductions in computing AGI of $17,000:

Reimbursed expenses	$ 6,000
Rental expenses	5,000
Severance tax	1,000
IRA contribution	5,000
	$17,000

AGI is $100,000 ($117,000 gross income less $17,000 above-the-line deductions).

Next we compute A's miscellaneous itemized deductions (MID) under § 67. A's MID include only the costs of the professional books and the investment-advisory fee, neither of which is excepted from MID by § 67(b). The other itemized deductions are excepted: the charitable deduction by § 67(b)(4) and the state income tax by § 67(b)(2). So, A's MID total $3,500 ($1,000 for books and $2,500 for investment advice). The deductions are allowable only to the extent that they exceed 2 percent of AGI, or $2,000 (2% of $100,000). A's deduction for MID is therefore limited to $1,500 ($3,500 MID less $2,000 AGI percentage floor); § 67(a).

A's total allowable itemized deductions comes to $10,500 ($5,000 charitable contribution, plus $4,000 state income tax, plus $1,500 MID). That figure exceeds A's $3,000 standard deduction (§ 63(c)), so A will itemize deductions. A's taxable income is $87,500 ($100,000 AGI less $10,500 itemized deductions and $2,000 personal exemption).

4. Consider a typical divorce that involves issues of child custody, child support, alimony, property division and (of course!) tax advice.

(a) To what extent are the legal fees attributable to those issues deductible?

The costs of the basic divorce and resolution of any child-custody and child-support issues are not deductible; Treas. Reg. § 1.262–1(b)(7). Under the origin-of-the-claim test of United States v. Gilmore, 372 U.S. 39 (1963) ("*Gilmore No. 1*"), the cost of defending against a divorcing spouse's property claims is not deductible as a cost of preserving income-producing property (§ 212(2)) because the origin of the dispute is in the parties' personal lives. However, Gilmore later sold some of the property that he was defending in the divorce action, and, in a subsequent tax case, he was permitted to add the attorney's fees incurred in defending the property to his basis in computing his realized gain from the sale; Gilmore v. United States, 245 F. Supp. 383 (N.D. Cal. 1965) ("*Gilmore No. 2*"). *Gilmore No.*

2 seems inconsistent with *Gilmore No. 1*, which was grounded in the personal nature of the expenditure rather than that it was a capital expenditure, but in Spector v. Commissioner, 71 T.C. 1017 (1979), the Commissioner conceded the capitalization of legal fees attributable to property received in a divorce settlement.

Wild v. Commissioner, 42 T.C. 706 (1964) (Acq.), allowed a deduction for legal fees incurred in obtaining an alimony award. (Note also Treas. Reg. § 1.262–1(b)(7) (attorney's fees and other costs attributable to production or collection of amounts includable in gross income under § 71 deductible by the recipient of alimony).) Although *Wild*, too, seems inconsistent with the origin-of-the-claim test of *Gilmore No. 1*, the Commissioner has acquiesced in the case, and one can therefore rely upon it in planning. (The cost of resisting an alimony claim has been held non-deductible.)

Section 212(3) allows a deduction for expenses incurred "in connection with the determination, collection, or refund of any tax." That provision has been interpreted as covering the costs of tax planning.

So, the recipient of alimony can deduct the cost of obtaining the alimony award. One who incurs legal costs in obtaining (or resisting) a property award can add those costs to the basis of the contested property (other than cash). And the cost of tax advice in connection with the divorce is deductible.

The § 212 deductions for the cost of obtaining an alimony award and for tax advice are miscellaneous itemized deductions, which are allowable only to the extent that they exceed 2 percent of AGI; see § 67.

(b) What can the divorce attorney do to bolster the client's chances of getting the maximum tax benefit from the expenditure?

Sometimes the settlement can be shaped to increase the tax benefits to the parties. For example, instead of the higher-bracket spouse paying the lower-bracket spouse's attorney fee, the higher-bracket spouse might increase the amount of deductible alimony and allow the lower-bracket spouse to pay his own attorney fee. The higher-bracket spouse would get a deduction for alimony paid, and, while the lower-bracket spouse would have additional income, that income could be offset at least in part by the § 212 deduction. (Unless it qualifies as alimony under § 71(b), a payment by one spouse of the other's fee is not deductible by the payor and may not be deductible by the other spouse; see Jernigan v. Commissioner, 34 T.C.M. 615 (1975).)

It is clear from the above discussion that the attorney's fee must be allocated among several items. The Service will usually accept an allocation of legal fees made by the attorney to the different aspects of the case. So, it is incumbent upon the attorney to present the client with an itemized statement that shows the allocation of the fee to the different facets of the divorce.

5. R, a well-known rock musician, founded a firm that developed a chain of fast food outlets that bore R's name. At first the firm prospered, and R encouraged his musical associates (his agent, producer, band members, etc.) to invest in the firm. After three years, however, the firm failed, and R and his associates lost considerable sums. With a view to preserving his reputation as a musician, R undertook to reimburse his associates for their losses. Can R deduct the payments as business expenses?

This problem is based loosely upon the facts of Jenkins v. Commissioner, 47 T.C.M. 238 (1983) (Non-acq.). Jenkins was a musician who used the stage name Conway Twitty. He had 43 number one hits from his recordings and the largest fan club of any country music entertainer. Although most of his income was dereived from the music business, he formed a corporation that franchised fast-food outlets to operate under the name Twitty Burger Fast Food Restaurants, and several of his friends and business associates lent money to the firm. Within three years the business failed, and Twitty thereupon undertook personally to repay the investors. He claimed business-expense deductions for the payments under § 162, but the Commissioner challenged the deductions on the grounds that, because there was not a sufficient nexus between the payments and Twitty's musical career, the payments were not ordinary and necessary. The Tax Court, however, allowed the deduction. It found as a fact that Twitty acted primarily to protect his personal business reputation, as the adverse publicity emanating from Twitty's namesake corporation's failing to pay would have damaged his career as a country-music artist. The court even offered an "Ode to Conway Twitty," 47 T.C.M. at 247, n. 14:

> 'Twitty Burger went belly up
> But Conway remained true
> He repaid his investors, one and all
> It was the moral thing to do.
> His fans would not have liked it
> It could have hurt his fame
> Had any investors sued him
> Like Merle Haggard or Sonny James.
> When it was time to file taxes
> Conway thought what he would do
> Was deduct those payments as a business expense
> Under section one-sixty-two.
> In order to allow these deductions
> Goes the argument of the Commissioner
> The payments must be ordinary and necessary
> To a business of the petitioner.
> Had Conway not repaid the investors
> His career would have been under cloud,
> Under the unique facts of this case
> Held: The deductions are allowed.

The Commissioner issued a non-acquiescence in the case (AOD 1984–22, 1984 WL 270668) with the following retort:

> Harold Jenkins and Conway Twitty
> They are both the same
> But one was born
> The other achieved fame.
> The man is talented
> And has many a friend
> They opened a restaurant
> His name he did lend.
> They are two different things
> Making burgers and song
> The business went sour
> It didn't take long.
> He repaid his friends
> Why did he act
> Was it business or friendship
> Which is fact?
> Business the court held
> It's deductible they feel
> We disagree with the answer
> But let's not appeal.

The seminal case is, of course, Welch v. Helvering, 290 U.S. 111 (1933), in which the former officer of a bankrupt grain firm (which bore Welch's name) entered a new business as a commission purchaser of grain for Kelloggs. In order to restore himself to the good graces of the farmers wth whom he had dealt, he began to repay their losses from the bankruptcy though he had no legal obligation to do so. In a protean opinion, Justice Cardozo disallowed a business-expense deduction for the payments seemingly on the ground that the payments were capital expenditures. *Welch* may be distinguishable from *Jenkins* in that Welch was starting a new business while Twitty was trying to preserve the goodwill of his (pre-existing) music business. That is, Twitty's payments might be thought of as involving "repairs" to his old business reputation, but Welch was "buying" goodwill of a new business.

Our problem case will come down to a question of a fact. Is R motivated primarily by his personal sense of morality or his interest in protecting his personal business reputation? Twitty persuaded the Tax Court, though not the Commissioner, that he was motivated chiefly by the latter.

B. TRAVEL AND ENTERTAINMENT EXPENSES

Code: §§ 162(a); 274(a), (d), (e)(1), (2) & (3), (m)(3) & (n).

Regulations: §§ 1.162–2; 1.274–2(a), (b), (c) & (d); 1.274–5T(f)(2)(i).

Cases: Hantzis v. Commissioner, 638 F.2d 248 (1st Cir. 1981);
Robertson v. Commissioner, 190 F.3d 392 (5th Cir. 1999).

1. **L practices law in University City (which is about 200 miles from Chicago). Last Thursday she attended a conference on tax law in Chicago. Early Thursday morning L left her University City residence and drove to Regional Airport, a distance of 20 miles. She flew by commercial airline to Chicago, took a cab from the airport to her conference, ate lunch (alone) in Chicago, attended the afternoon session of the conference, returned by cab to the airport, flew back to Regional Airport, and drove home. L's University City office is 5 miles from her residence. The cost of the conference is a business expense under Treas. Reg. § 1.162–5(a). Can L deduct the cost of:**

(a) The roundtrip to Regional Airport?

Yes, this is transportation expense. It makes no difference that L went directly from her home to the airport; see Rev. Rul. 99–7, 1999–1 C.B. 361 (Holding (1)).

(b) The airfare to Chicago?

Yes, even tough L is not "away rom home" (see (c) below), the airfare is deductible as transportation expense. (If L is away from home, then meals and lodging ("traveling expenses") become deductible.)

(c) Lunch in Chicago?

No deduction because L is not away from home—i.e., not away *overnight*; see United States v. Correll, 389 U.S. 299 (1967).

(d) Round-trip cab fare from the Chicago airport?

Deductible for the reason given in (b).

2.   A, an attorney, works in Capital City but chooses to live in University City, which is 120 miles from Capital City.

(a) Is A allowed a deduction for the cost of the daily roundtrip from University City to Capital City?

No; this is non-deductible (and long-distance) commuting; Treas. Reg. § 1.162–2(e).

(b) Suppose instead that A drives to Capital City on Monday morning, stays in a hotel from Monday night through Friday morning and then returns to University City on Friday evening. Is A allowed a deduction for the cost of meals and the hotel room in Capital City?

No; these facts are very similar to Commissioner v. Flowers, 326 U.S. 465 (1946) (lawyer who worked in Jackson, Mississippi, could not deduct the cost of traveling to work in Mobile, Alabama). No *professional* interest was served by Flowers' keeping his home in Jackson.

(c) Suppose that A also taught a Saturday morning course at the University Law School in University City. Would that make any of A's costs deductible?

A's principal post of duty is Capital City, so A cannot deduct the costs of his meals and lodging there; Robertson v. Commissioner, 190 F.3d 392 (5th Cir. 1999). But if A's tax home is in Capital City, is he "away from home" when he is in University City? University City is his "real" home, and deductions are generally denied to those who are not away from *both* their tax home and their real home. So, A probably gets no deduction, even though that result seems a little unfair, as A does duplicate some expenses because he had jobs in two different places.

3. S is a second-year student at Midwestern State University School of Law. S has accepted a position as a summer associate with a large New York City law firm. In connection with her employment, S expects to incur expenses for roundtrip airfare to New York, apartment rent and meals. She plans to retain her apartment near the Midwestern State campus while she is in New York. She has been working as a clerk for a local law firm during the academic year and expects to return to her clerkship position upon her return from New York. Will S be allowed a deduction for any of the employment costs?

This is based upon Hantzis v. Commissioner, 638 F.2d 248 (1st Cir. 1981), in which a student at Harvard Law School incurred travel, meals and lodging while working as a summer associate for a New York firm. The First Circuit sustained the Commissioner's disallowance of a deduction for those costs because the taxpayer was not away from home. New York City was her home for the summer because no *professional* interest was served by keeping her home in Boston. (Her husband was living in the couple's Boston home while the taxpayer was in New York.) In other words, she could not deduct her expenses unless she had *business* ties in both Boston and New York. Judge Keeton, concurring, declined to say that the taxpayer was not away from home when she was in New York, but would have disallowed the expenses because the taxpayer kept her Boston home for personal, rather than business reasons. He thus avoided placing a strained interpretation on the word "home."

Our problem contains a wrinkle not present in *Hantzis*: Here S is clerking for a local firm during the academic year, so, in a sense, S has business ties both to New York and her college town. Still, S's tie to the college town is *primarily* personal—i.e., for educational reasons, and the deduction for the New York expenses will be denied.

4. E is employed in City X, where he resides with his family. E's employer asked him to accept an eight-month assignment at the employer's location in City Y, which is in a neighboring state, and E accepted the assignment. While in City Y, E stayed at a residential hotel, which also furnished his meals. In the eighth month of the assignment, the employer asked E if he would be willing to accept another six-month assignment in City Y beginning at the conclusion of the eighth month, and E again accepted. E continued to stay at the residential hotel throughout the sixth-month period of the second assignment. To what extent can E deduct his costs of meals and lodging in City Y?

Section 162(a) provides that "the taxpayer shall not be treated as being temporarily away from home during any period of employment if such period exceeds 1 year." Rev. Rul. 93–86, 1993–2 C.B. 71, applies the one-year rule by asking whether the employment is realistically expected to last, and does last, for no more than a year. In this case, E should be permitted to deduct the cost of the meals (but only to the extent of 50%—274(n)) and lodging up to the point in the eighth month when he accepted the additional assignment.

5. C is a partner in an Indianapolis law firm. Accompanied by her husband, H, C went to New York City to attend a conference on the Sarbanes-Oxley Act. C and H flew into New York on Tuesday evening. The conference began on Wednesday morning and ran through Friday afternoon. C attended all sessions of the conference; H spent those days sightseeing and shopping. C and H both spent Saturday sightseeing and flew home on Sunday. To what extent are the couple's airfare, meals and lodging deductible?

H's expenses are not deductible because his presence in New York serves no business purpose; § 274(m)(3). As to C, Tuesday and Sunday are travel days, Wednesday, Thursday and Friday are "business" days, and Saturday is a non-business day. So, 5 days are spent on business or travel and only 1 day on recreation. Because C spends more time on the business than she does on recreation, the trip appears to relate "primarily" to business; see Treas. Reg. § 1.162–1 (in determining primary purpose of trip, time spent on each kind of activity "is an important factor"). If the trip is primarily business-related, C can deduct her airfare in full. C can deduct her meals and lodging for each day except Saturday. Only one-half the meal costs are deductible; § 274(n)(1).

6. A is an attorney (a solo practitioner). A is considering various ways to promote his practice and seeks your advice as to the tax deductibility of the various options. What do you advise as to the following?

(a) A is an accomplished amateur chef. Once a month, A and his wife, W, could invite three clients (and their spouses) to their home for a gourmet dinner. A thinks each meal (including wine) would cost about $100 per person.

Even though the cost of furnishing meals to clients might be allowable as a business expense under § 162(a), § 274 disallows deductions for "entertainment" expenses unless the requirements of that provision are satisfied. The term "entertainment" includes the furnishing of food and beverages; Treas. Reg. § 1.274–2(b)(1)(i). Entertainment expenditures are generally not deductible unless the taxpayer establishes either that (1) the expenditure was directly related to the active conduct of the taxpayer's business; or (2) the expenditure directly preceded or followed a substantial and bona fide business discussion and the expenditure was associated with the active conduct of the taxpayer's business; Treas. Reg. § 1.274–2(a)(1).

In this case, it seems unlikely that the dinner party would directly precede or follow a substantial and bona fide business discussion, so A probably can deduct the cost of the meal only if the expenditure was directly related to the active conduct of the taxpayer's business. For the entertainment to be directly related, the parties would have to actively engage in business discussion during the evening; (2) the principal aspect of the entertainment would have to be the active conduct of A's business; (3) A would have to include his and his clients' spouses in the business discussions; and (4) the entertainment would have to occur in a clear business setting, which A's home presumably is not; see Treas. Reg. § 1.274–2(c). So, it seems unlikely that the cost of the meals would be deductible.

(b) Each month A and W would invite two clients (and their spouses) to be their guests at a local comedy club. A estimates that that would also cost (including drinks) about $100 per person.

The cost of the comedy club would not qualify as "directly related" entertainment under Treas. Reg. § 1.274–2(c) because (1) it seems unlikely that A would actively engage in business discussion during the visit to the comedy club; (2) the principal aspect of the visit to the club probably would not be the active conduct of A's business; (3) the expenditure would also cover the spouses of A and the clients, and A probably would not be engaged in active business with the spouses during the entertainment; and (4) the entertainment would not occur in a clear business setting. Assuming that the entertainment would not directly precede or follow a substantial and bona fide business discussion, the cost would not be deductible.

(c) A could invite three clients to play golf at the exclusive country club of which A is a member. A thinks that green fees, food and beverages would run about $200 per person.

The expenditure is for entertainment; Treas. Reg. § 1.274–2(b)(1). Assuming that the golf game does not directly precede or follow a substantial and bona fide business discussion, A can deduct the expense only if it is "directly related" entertainment.   That appears to be unlikely here, unless (1) during the entertainment period A actively engages in business discussion for the purpose of deriving income; and (2) the principal aspect of the combined business and entertainment is the active conduct of business.

A cannot deduct any portion of the club dues; § 274(a)(3).

(d) A could send a client (and spouse) two tickets to the local ballet theater. A and W would not attend, however, as A detests ballet.

If A does not accompany the client to the performance, the cost of the tickets would be considered a gift, unless A treats the cost as attributable to entertainment; Treas. Reg. § 1.274–2(b)(2). Business gifts are deductible only to the extent of $25 per donee per year. Query whether the gift to the spouse would qualify for deduction at all (i.e., under § 162). Although the regulation permits A to treat the expenditure as entertainment, he should not do so because no deduction would be allowed, unless the performance happened to directly precede or follow a substantial and bona fide business discussion between A and the client.

(e) Whenever A has a late-morning appointment with a client, A will invite the client (and the client's spouse) to join him for lunch at A's club. A estimates the average cost of lunch at the club is $50 per person.

The expenditure could qualify as "associated" entertainment because the lunch apparently would follow a substantial and bona fide business discussion with the client, and A would have a clear business purpose of continuing the existing business relationship. The portion of the expenditure allocable to the spouse would also considered to be "associated" with the active conduct of A's business even if the spouse was not involved in the business discussion; Treas. Reg. § 1.274–2(d)(2). A's portion of the meal would also be deductible. Remember, however, only half the cost of the meals is allowable under § 274(n)(1).

A cannot deduct any portion of the club dues; § 274(a)(3).

C. EDUCATION EXPENSE

Code: § 162(a). Note §§ 195; 25A; 222.

Regulations: §§ 1.212–1(f); 1.262–1(b)(9); 1.162–5.

Cases: Sharon v. Commissioner, 66 T.C. 515, aff'd, 591 F.2d 1273 (9th Cir. 1978),
cert. denied, 442 U.S. 941 (1979);
Allemeier v. Commissioner, 90 T.C.M. 197 (2005).

1. L, a solo-practitioner in a midwestern city, is required by state law to obtain fifteen hours of continuing legal education each year to maintain his law license. This year he satisfied the requirement by attending a tax program in a city 120 miles from his home. He spent a total of $750 for travel, meals, lodging and tuition to attend the program. Are the expenses deductible by L?

Treas. Reg. § 1.262–1(b)(9) provides that educational expenditures are generally considered personal expenses, which are not deductible except as provided in Treas. Reg. § 1.162–5. The latter permits a taxpayer who is in business to deduct expenses of education that (1) maintains or improves skills required by the taxpayer in the taxpayer's employment or other business or (2) meets the express requirements of the taxpayer's employer, or applicable law, imposed as a condition to the retention by the taxpayer of an established employment relationship, status or rate of compensation; Treas. Reg. § 1.162–5(a). Even though one of the above conditions is satisfied, however, the expenditure is not deductible if (1) the education is necessary to meet the minimum educational requirements for qualification in a business or (2) the education is part of a "program of study" that will lead to qualifying the taxpayer in a new business; Treas. Reg. § 1.162–5(b)(2) & (3).

In this case, L is in the business of being a lawyer, so the cost of the mandatory continuing education should be deductible as the education meets the requirements of state law imposed as a condition to retaining his law license. The travel, lodging and tuition costs are fully deductible; Treas. Reg. § 1.162–5(e)(1); one-half of the meal costs are deductible; § 274(n)(1).

2.   L (in 1) has already satisfied his state-imposed continuing education requirement for the year. In December, however, he travels to Honolulu for a program on recent developments in federal taxation. He incurs costs for airfare, meals, lodging and program tuition. Are these costs deductible by L?

The expenses should qualify for deduction as the education maintains or improves L's present skills. It makes no difference that the program is in Hawaii in December. Again, however, only one-half the meal costs are deductible because of § 274(n)(1).

   3. In May, G graduates with a J.D. degree from State University Law School. From June through August S works as a summer associate for a local law firm. In September, G begins a full-time LL.M. program at Private University. G incurs costs for travel, meals, lodging, tuition and books at Private University. Can G deduct her costs as business expenses?

   Where the taxpayer is already in business, the cost of education that leads to specialization in some aspect of the business can be deductible as a business expense; see Treas. Reg. § 1.162–5(b)(3)(ii), Ex. (4) (psychiatrist training in psychoanalysis). So it has been held that the obtaining of an LL.M. (in taxation) does not lead to qualification for a new business; Ruehmann v. Commissioner, 30 T.C.M. 675 (1971).

   The main issue here is whether the expense is incurred in "carrying on" business. Does G's summer employment sufficiently establish her in business to make the expenses deductible? Link v. Commissioner, 90 T.C. 460 (1988), denied a deduction for the costs of an M.B.A. program where the taxpayer got an undergraduate business degree from Cornell, took a summer job with Xerox, and then entered graduate school at Chicago. The court found as a fact that the taxpayer had not become "established" in his profession before starting the graduate program. But Ruehmann v. Commissioner, 30 T.C.M. 675 (1971), allowed a deduction for the costs of attending an LL.M. program in the case of a lawyer who graduated from law school in June, was admitted to practice, worked for a firm until September, and then took an unpaid leave of absence from the firm to pursue an LL.M. degree.

   Here there is no indication that G took a leave of absence from the firm; indeed her position as a "summer associate" implies that the firm has not committed to take her back. So, G may not get the deduction under § 162.

   It could be argued, however, that the education expenses here are "start-up expenditures" under § 195—i.e., an amount paid in connection with creating an active business; § 195(c)(1)(A)(ii). The educational expenses would be deductible if paid by a lawyer who was already in business, as required by § 195(c)(1)(B). If this argument prevails, the first $5,000 of expenses (other than half the cost of the meals) generally would be deductible in the year G begins practice and the balance would be amortized over the 180 months beginning with the month in which her practice begins. If G obtains a position as an employee, the expenses would be itemized deductions (because of § 62(a)(1)) and miscellaneous itemized deductions (defined in § 67(b)), which can be deducted only to the extent that such deductions exceed 2 percent of AGI; § 67(a).

   As to the tuition and fees, G may be able to deduct up to $4,000 a year under § 222 or obtain a Lifetime Learning Credit of up to $2,000 under § 25A(c). But those provisions do not allow a deduction or credit for travel, meals and lodging expenses paid in obtaining the graduate degree. Those items (though just half the meal costs) could be deducted if G meets the requirements of § 162, which is why she would want to qualify the expenses as business expenses.

4. Same as 3, except that G obtained her J.D. two years ago and has been working as an associate for the local law firm since graduation. She takes a nine-month leave of absence from the firm to pursue an LL.M. at Private University. Any deduction?

Yes. Now G is carrying on business and her expenses of obtaining the LL.M. (other than half the meal costs) should be deductible under § 162(a). Since G is an employee, the deduction is a miscellaneous itemized deduction and subject to the 2–percent-of-AGI floor.

5. H holds a B.S. from State University and is also a C.P.A. H practices with a C.P.A. firm. He wishes to take a tax course at the local law school. Is H's tuition for the law-school course deductible as a business expense?

It should be. Taking a single course does not seem to be a "program of study" that will lead to qualifying H in a new business (law).

6. L and M both hold undergraduate degrees in business and both hold managerial positions in a bank. L will attend law school next year; M will attend a graduate college of business to obtain an M.B.A. After they attain their degrees, they both plan to return to banking. Can they deduct as business expenses the costs of obtaining their advanced degrees?

Even though L does not intend to practice law, he cannot deduct the costs of attending law school because that is a "program of study" that will lead to qualifying L for a new business (law); Treas. Reg. § 1.162–5(b)(3), Ex. (1).

In Sharon v. Commissioner, 66 T.C. 515, aff'd, 591 F.2d 1273 (9th Cir. 1978), cert. denied, 442 U.S. 941 (1979), the taxpayer contended that he should be permitted to amortize his license to practice law. He included in his basis for the license the costs of his undergraduate and law degrees. The court concluded that the educational costs were personal and non-deductible.

M's case is harder because, unlike the J.D., which is necessary in order to qualify for professional certification as a lawyer, the MBA does not qualify one for professional certification or licensure. In Allemeier v. Commissioner, 90 T.C.M. 197 (2005), the Tax Court allowed a deduction for the costs incurred in obtaining an MBA where the degree provided the taxpayer "with a general background to perform tasks and activities that he had performed previously" for his employer. So, M has a good chance of qualifying for the deduction.

D. THE "CARRYING ON" REQUIREMENT

Code: §§ 162(a); 217(a), (b), (c) & (d); 62(a)(15); 195(a), (b) & (c).

Regulation: § 1.212–1(f).

1. **L has been practicing law in Chicago for several years. She has long thought that she would like to live in the Pacific Northwest. This year, L hired a placement agency at a cost of $10,000 to assist her in finding a position in Seattle. The agency found L a position with a Seattle law firm, which L accepted. Is the $10,000 fee deductible by L?**

The costs of seeking employment in the same business are deductible; the costs of seeking employment in a new business are not deductible even if the attempt succeeds; Rev. Rul. 75–120, 1975–1 C.B. 55. The courts have held that the practice of law in one state is a different "trade or business" than practice in another state; e.g., Sharon v. Commissioner, 66 T.C. 515, aff'd, 591 F.2d 1273 (9th Cir. 1978), cert. denied, 442 U.S. 941 (1979). Here L's placement-agency fee is probably not deductible under § 162 because it was incurred in finding a position in a new business.

If she were already practicing in the State of Washington and hired an agency to assist her in finding another position in that state, she could deduct the fee. That suggests the possibility of treating the agency fee as a start-up cost under § 195, in which case L could deduct $5,000 upon commencing employment with the Seattle firm and amortize the remaining $5,000 over the following 180 months.

2. **S, a third-year law student at Midwestern State University, is seeking a position with a law firm in Seattle. At her own expense, S flies to Seattle, incurs costs for meals, lodging and resume preparation. As a result of her efforts, S is offered and accepts a position with a Seattle law firm. Are S's expenses deductible?**

No, because S was not yet carrying on business when the expenses were incurred. Perhaps S can treat the expenses as start-up expenditures under § 195 on the theory that, if she were already in the business of being a lawyer, the job-search expenses would be deductible.

3. **Suppose instead that a Seattle law firm offered S (in 2) a flyback. The firm paid S's airfare, hotel and meal costs. Do these events result in income to S?**

The reimbursement is not income, except to the extent that it exceeds S's actual expenses; Rev. Rul. 75–120, 1975–1 C.B. 55.

4. S (in 2) has now graduated and is moving to Seattle. Her moving costs include:

Moving household goods and personal effects	$4,000
Cost of driving S's automobile to Seattle	1,000
Lodging expense while on the road to Seattle	1,000
Meal expense while on the road to Seattle	300

S also incurs $1,000 of temporary lodging costs in Seattle while awaiting the arrival of her household goods.

(a) S pays the above expenses herself. To what extent, if any, are they deductible?

Section 217(a) allows a deduction for moving expenses paid in connection with the taxpayer's commencement of work at a new principal place of work. Moving expenses include only the costs of (1) moving household goods and personal effects from the former residence to the new residence and (2) travel (including lodging but not meals) from the former residence to the new place of residence; § 217(b)(1).

To qualify for the deduction, S must meet the distance and employment tests. As applicable here, the distance test requires that her new workplace be at least 50 miles from her former residence—which seems to be the case here; see § 217(c)(1). The employment test requires that S be employed for 39 weeks during the first 12 months after her arrival in the general location of her new principal place of work (or satisfy the alternative test of § 217(c)(2)(B)); § 217(c)(2)(A). Although S may not have satisfied the 39–week employment requirement by the time for filing her tax return for the year, she can take the deduction but, if it becomes impossible to satisfy the employment requirement, she must include the amount deducted in gross income for the first subsequent year in which it becomes impossible to fulfill the employment requirement; § 217(d)(3).

S can deduct the moving expenses even though she was not employed before the move; it is sufficient that she is commencing work at a new principal place of work; Treas. Reg. § 1.217–2(a)(3)(i).

S can deduct all of her expenses except for the meals and the temporary lodging. So, her deduction is $6,000. It's an above-the-line deduction; § 62(a)(15).

(b) Suppose the law firm reimburses her for the expenses. Must S include the reimbursement in income?

Only to the extent of the reimbursements for the costs of meals and temporary lodging. The moving-expense reimbursement is an excludable fringe benefit under § 132(g) and (a)(6), but only to the extent that the items reimbursed would be deductible by S under § 217; hence she cannot exclude the portion of the reimbursement allocable to the meals and the temporary lodging. (This assumes, of course, that S had not already deducted the expenses; if she had, the reimbursement would be includable in her gross income; § 82.)

(c) Would your answer in (a) change if she worked for the Seattle firm for six months and then accepted a position with a firm in Chicago?

Yes, because she would not satisfy the 39–week employment test of § 217(c)(2). If she had already claimed the deduction, she would have to include the amount of the deduction in gross income for the year in which it becomes impossible to satisfy the employment test; § 217(d)(3).

(d) Same as (c), except that after six months S had been laid off by the Seattle firm?

If S could reasonably have been expected to satisfy the employment test, she does not lose the deduction if the failure to satisfy the test resulted from being laid off, unless she was laid because of willful misconduct; § 217(d)(1)(B).

5. R is going to open a T-shirt shop in leased space in a local mall. R obtains possession of the leased premises on April 1. The next month is spent hiring employees, ordering and stocking merchandise, repainting the interior walls and preparing an advertising campaign. On May 15, the shop opens for business.

(a) Can R deduct the rent, utilities, employee salaries, property taxes, payroll taxes and painting costs incurred before the shop opens?

These expenditures are not deductible as business expenses because R is not yet carrying on business when they are incurred. Most of these costs are typical start-up expenditures—i.e., (1) amounts paid in connection with creating an active business; and (2) which, if paid in connection with the operation of an existing business in the same field, would have been deductible when paid; § 195(c)(1). The property taxes, however, are deductible when paid under § 164 and do not qualify as start-up expenditures (nor would any interest paid); id (last sentence).

If the start-up expenditures are less than $50,000, R can elect to deduct $5,000 in the year in which the business commences (i.e., when the shop opens its doors to its customers) and the balance can be amortized over the following 180 months. If the expenditures exceed $50,000, the $5,000 initial deduction must be reduced dollar-for-dollar by the amount in excess of $50,000, and the balance of the expenditures can be amortized over 180 months; § 195(b).

As noted, § 195 is an elective provision; if the taxpayer does not elect amortization, no deduction is allowed for the expenditures; § 195(a).

(b) Would your answer in (a) differ if R already owned T-shirt shops in several other local malls?

The expenses of expanding an existing business are currently deductible. The opening of additional shops in the same line of business probably constitutes the expansion of an existing business, and the expenses would be currently deductible, as § 195 does not apply to expenditures made in connection with the operation of an existing business.

Chapter 13

BUSINESS AND INVESTMENT EXPENSES— STATUTORY LIMITS ON DEDUCTIONS

A. HOBBY LOSSES

Code: § 183.

Regulation: § 1.183–1(b)(1).

1. C's cat-breeding business has had profit (i.e., an excess of gross income over deductions allocable to the activity) or loss (an excess of deductions over gross income) as follows:

Year	Profit	Loss
1		$3,000
2		1,500
3	$500	
4	250	
5	50	

(a) In year 5, would C or the Commissioner have the burden of proving the activity was not engaged in for profit?

If the activity has been profitable for at least 3 of the 5 years, it is presumed to be engaged in for profit, and the Commissioner would be bear the burden of showing the contrary; § 183(d).

(b) Would your answer in (a) differ if in year 5 the activity had shown a loss rather than a profit?

Yes, because then C would not have the benefit of the § 183(d) presumption that the business was operated for profit and C would bear the burden of persuading the factfinder that she had a profit motive in operating the business.

2. D's dog-breeding activity is determined not to be engaged in for profit. D's expenses for the year are:

State property taxes	$1,500
Food, veterinary costs, etc.	4,000
Depreciation	3,000

How much of the expenses can D deduct if his gross income from the activity is:

(a) $1,000?

D can deduct $1,500. Section 183(b) allows a deduction for items that would be allowable regardless of whether the activity is engaged in for profit, even though such amounts exceed the gross income from the activity. Here the $1,500 of state property taxes would be allowable under § 164(a) regardless of whether the breeding business was engaged in for profit, and so D can deduct that amount.

(b) $6,000? (Which deductions are allowable in this case?)

Now D can deduct $6,000 of the expenses. D first takes into account the property taxes because they are allowable without regard to whether the activity is engaged in for profit. Then D can also deduct the other expenses up to the amount of gross income from the activity reduced by the deductions allowable regardless of whether the breeding operation is a for-profit activity. The limit on the other expenses here is $4,500 ($6,000 gross income less $1,500 property taxes). The $4,500 is deemed to come first from those costs that do not result in an adjustment to the basis of property; see Treas. Reg. § 1.183–1(b)(1). Thus, in addition to the $1,500 of property taxes, D deducts $4,000 of the food and veterinary costs, etc., and $500 of depreciation.

3. H retired just over three years ago. He has investment income of approximately $200,000 a year. For all of his adult life, H's hobby has been big-game hunting, and before retiring he had made several safaris to Africa. After retirement H decided to make game-hunting films and to present lectures on the films. To this end he made several trips to Africa to hunt and film big game. He sent out many letters and brochures soliciting lecture engagements and stating the amount of his lecture fees. In the past three years, H has generated the following amounts of gross income and expenses from the activity:

Year	Income	Expenses
1	$900	$12,000
2	2,500	9,000
3	2,800	14,500

H has kept careful records of his income and expenses from this venture. Assess the likelihood that H will be permitted to deduct the excess of the expenses over the gross income.

The issue is whether H's film and lecture business is an "activity * * * not engaged in for profit" under § 183(a). If the activity is not engaged in for profit, then no deductions are allowable except to the extent provided by § 183(b). An activity not engaged in for profit is an activity other than one for which deductions are allowable under § 162 or § 212; § 183(c).

In determining whether H is carrying on business so that his expenses are deductible under § 162, the question is whether H has a good faith belief that profit can be made, regardless of the reasonableness of that belief; Treas. Reg. § 1.183–2(a). This is a question of fact. Of course, H's subjective testimony that he had a profit motive is not determinative; see id. ("greater weight is given to objective facts than to the taxpayer's mere statement of his intent"). Among the factors that the factfinder might weigh are (1) whether H attempted to survey the market to see if there was profit potential for his films and lectures; (2) whether he employed a booking agent; (3) the amount of time devoted to the activity; and (4) the amount of his expenses in relation to his gross income from the activity. Here he appears to have "attempted to transform a longstanding hobby into a business venture"; McGowan v. Commissioner, 23 T.C.M. 1439, 1443 (1964), aff'd, 347 F.2d 728 (7th Cir. 1965). Also, H's substantial investment income ($200,000 per year) may indicate that the film and lecture business is not engaged in for profit, especially since there are personal or recreational elements involved; see Treas. Reg. § 1.183–2(b)(8). In other words, H may just be trying to deduct the cost of his hobby to offset his investment income. Although H kept careful records of his income and expense, that, by itself, does not establish a profit motive; see Golanty v. Commissioner, 72 T.C. 411, 430, aff'd, 647 F.2d 170 (9th Cir. 1981) ("the keeping of books and records may represent nothing more than a conscious attention to detail"). Although it is a question of fact whether H had a profit motive, it seems unlikely that he can prevail on these facts.

B. LISTED PROPERTY

Code:　§ 280F(a), (b) & (d). Review §§ 168 and 179.

Regulations:　§§ 1.280F–3T(a), (c)(1) & (2), (d)(1) & (2); 1.280F–6(a), (d)(2)(i), (d)(3)(i), (d)(5), Exs. (1) & (2), (e)(3); 1.179–1(d)(1) & (2), Ex., (e)(1).

1. In January, year 1, T, a solo-practitioner lawyer, purchases for $3,000 a computer for home use on evenings and weekends. T uses the computer 40 percent for her law business, 30 percent in managing her stock-market portfolio, and 30 percent for personal matters. The computer has a recovery period of 5 years for both the regular and alternative depreciation systems; § 168(i)(2)(A)(i), (e)(3)(B)(iv) & (g)(3)(C).

(a) What method of depreciation, recovery period and convention must T use for year 1?

The computer is "listed property"; § 280F(d)(4)(A)(iv). If listed property is not "predominantly used" in a "qualified business use," the deduction for depreciation must be calculated under the alternative depreciation system of § 168(g). Qualified business use means any use in a trade or business of the taxpayer; § 280F(d)(6)(B). Property is predominantly used in business in any year in which the "business use percentage" exceeds 50 percent. The business use percentage means the percentage of the use of the listed property which is qualified business use. In this case, the business use percentage is only 40 percent. (Use in investment activity does not qualify as business use; Temp. Treas. Reg. §§ 1.280F–3T(a); 1.280F–6(d)(2)(i).) Therefore, T must depreciate the computer using the alternative deprecation method of § 168(g).

Section 168(g) generally requires the use of straight-line depreciation over the property's class life; § 168(g)(2)(A) & (C). In the case of computers ("qualified technological equipment"), however, the § 168(g) recovery period is 5 years; § 168(g)(3)(C). The half-year convention applies; see § 168(g)(2)(B).

If T had used the property 100 percent for "business/investment use" (defined in Treas. Reg. § 1.280F–6(d)(3)(i)), the straight-line depreciation deduction for year 1 (using the half-year convention) would be $300 ($3,000/5 x 1/2). Since T uses the computer 70 percent for business/investment use, T's depreciation deduction for year 1 would be $210 (70 percent of $300). The $120 (40% of $300) of depreciation attributable to T's business use would be an above-the-line deduction; § 62(a)(1). The $90 (30% of $300) of depreciation attributable to the investment use of the property would be a miscellaneous itemized deduction and subject to the 2–percent-of-AGI floor on deductibility.

Incidentally, one determines the business use percentage of a computer by dividing the number of hours the computer is used for business during the year by the total number of hours the computer is used; Treas. Reg. § 1.280F–6(e)(3).

(b) In year 2, T uses the computer 60 percent for business, 30 percent for investment management and 10 for personal use. What method of depreciation, recovery period and convention must C use for year 2?

Although T uses the computer predominantly for business in year 2, T must continue using the alternative depreciation system. The alternative system applies for year 1 and "any subsequent taxable year"; § 280F(b)(1).

If the property were used solely for business/investment use, year–2 depreciation would be $600 ($3,000/5). Depreciation attributable to business use is $360 (60% of $600) and to investment use $180 (30% of $600).

(c) In year 1, could T elect to expense the cost of the computer under § 179?

No. For the purpose of § 280F, any deduction allowable under § 179 is treated as a depreciation deduction allowable under § 168, and depreciation can be deducted only under the alternative depreciation system of § 168(g). This precludes an expense deduction under § 179; see Temp. Treas. Reg. § 1.280F–3T(c)(1).

2. Suppose instead that T (in 1) had in year 1 used the computer 60 percent for business, 30 percent for investment management and 10 percent for personal matters.

(a) Is the cost of the computer eligible for expensing under § 179?

Yes, in part. The computer is predominantly used for business in year 1, so the § 179 election can be made. But since the property is used only 60 percent for business, only 60 percent of the cost qualifies for deduction; see Treas. Reg. § 1.179–1(d)(1) & (2), Ex. (Only the "business" portion of the computer qualifies for expensing; the "investment" portion does not; see § 179(d)(1)(C) (property must be used in "active conduct of trade or business"). So, $1,800 (60% of $3,000) of the cost qualifies for expensing.

Since the machine is used predominantly for business purposes, the portion of the cost attributable to investment use can be depreciated under § 168 using the 200–percent declining balance method, 5–year recovery period and the half-year convention. Thus, year–1 depreciation for investment purposes is $180 ($3,000 x 30% investment use x 20% depreciation rate).

If T had not elected to expense the business portion of the machine under § 179, both the business and investment portions of the machine could have been depreciated under § 168 using the 200–percent declining-balance method, half-year convention and 5–year recovery period. Business depreciation would have been $360 ($3,000 x 60% business use x 20% deprecation rate) and investment depreciation would have been $180 (as above).

(b) Assume that T made an election under § 179 to expense the property in year 1. In year 2, T uses the computer 40 percent for her law business, 30 percent in managing her investments, and 30 percent for personal matters. Explain in general terms (i.e., without computations) the result to T in year 2?

Here the computer was used predominantly in business for year 1, but not in year 2 when the business use fell to 40 percent. As a result, any "excess depreciation" must be included in gross income as ordinary income for year 2, and the depreciation deduction for year 2 and all subsequent years must be computed under the alternative depreciation system of § 168(g); § 280F(b)(2).

In this case, excess depreciation means the excess of the depreciation (including the § 179 deduction) for year 1 over the amount that would have been allowable if the computer had not been used predominantly in business in year 1 (i.e., if the computer had been depreciated under the alternative depreciation system of § 168(g) with no § 179 deduction); see Treas. Reg. § 1.179–1(e)(1).

3. P, a law professor, has an office on campus that includes a state-of-the-art computer furnished by P's employer. Nevertheless, P purchases a computer for use at home on nights and weekends. P uses the computer exclusively for his law school work. Can P deduct depreciation with respect to the computer?

No. The computer is listed property; § 280F(d)(4)(A)(iv). An employee's use of listed property is not treated as use in trade or business unless such use is for the "convenience of the employer" and required as a "condition of employment"; § 280F(d)(3)(A). The terms convenience of the employer and condition of employment have the same meaning as they do under § 119 (relating to the exclusion for meals and lodging furnished for the convenience of the employer); Treas. Reg. § 1.280F–6(a)(2). P's use of the computer satisfies the condition-of-employment test only if its use is required to enable P to perform the duties of his employment properly; id. Since P has a computer at his campus office, he is working at home for his own convenience and thus the use of the home computer is not required as a condition of his employment; see Treas. Reg. § 1.280F–6(a)(4), Ex. (5). Therefore, P's use is not considered to be business use for the purpose of determining the depreciation deduction allowable to the employee; § 280F(d)(3)(A). Since the computer is treated as not used in business, no deduction is allowable under § 167(a).

4. In January of year 1, C, a business consultant, purchases a new automobile for $30,000. The automobile is used exclusively in C's business. C makes no § 179 election. How much depreciation can C deduct in year 1? In subsequent years? (As always, ignore inflation adjustments.)

An automobile is 5–year property (§ 168(e)(3)(B)(i)), and, in the absence of a special rule, C would compute depreciation on the automobile using 200–percent declining balance deprecation over a 5–year recovery period using the half-year convention. Using Rev. Proc. 87–57, 1987–2 C.B. 687, discussed in Chapter 11, we see that the depreciation deductions would be:

Year	Depreciation
1	$6,000
2	9,600
3	5,760
4	3,456
5	3,456
6	1,728
	$30,000

Under § 280F(a)(1), however, the annual depreciation deductions are limited to specified dollar amounts. Since the specified amounts are not large enough to permit recovery of the automobile's cost over the usual recovery period, the unrecovered basis is treated as an expense of up to $1,475 per year for years following the recovery period until the basis has been fully recovered. In this case, the depreciation would be as follows:

Year	Depreciation
1	$2,560
2	4,100
3	2,450
4	1,475
5	1,475
6	1,475
7	1,475, etc., until the basis is completely recovered in year 18.

Few people drive a business automobile for a sufficiently long period to recover the entire basis. The reduced depreciation deductions result in the taxpayer's having a larger loss (or smaller gain) when the car is disposed of.

C. HOME OFFICES AND VACATION HOMES

Code: § 280A(a), (b), (c)(1), (3) & (5), (d)(1), (2) & (4), (e), (f)(1) & (3), (g).

Regulation: Prop. Treas. Reg. 1.280A–2(c), (g), (h), (i)(5) & (7).

Case: Bolton v. Commissioner, 694 F.2d 556 (9th Cir. 1982).

1. V owns a vacation home that is usable only 180 days of the year. V occupies the home for 45 of those days and rents it (at fair rental value) for the other 135 days. In the current year, V's expenses with respect to the property are:

Property taxes	**$1,000**
Mortgage interest	**3,000**
Insurance and maintenance	**3,000**
Advertising expense	**1,000**

In addition, if the property had been rented all year, depreciation would have been $3,000.

Assume that the mortgage interest qualifies as "qualified residence interest" and hence is deductible under § 163(a). At the beginning of the year V's adjusted basis in the house was $30,000. Determine (1) how much of the expenses V can deduct and (2) V's adjusted basis at the end of the year if the rental income from the property is:

(a) $7,000.

Although § 162 or § 212 might allow a deduction for the expenses attributable to the rental of the property, the deductibility of the expenses in this case must be determined under § 280A. Section 280A applies whenever the taxpayer claims a deduction "with respect to a dwelling unit which is used by the taxpayer during the taxable year as a residence"; § 280A(a). The vacation home is a dwelling unit; see § 280A(f)(1) (dwelling unit includes a house). V used the house as a "residence" because he used it for "personal purposes" for more than 14 days; § 280A(d)(1). (V's occupancy of the home constituted use of the property for personal purposes; § 280A(d)(2).) So, § 280A(a) applies.

There are two exceptions to the disallowance rule that apply here. First, V can deduct any item that is deductible without regard to whether the item is connected to business or investment activity (e.g., mortgage interest and property taxes); § 280A(b). Second, other items that are attributable to the rental of the dwelling unit are allowable to the extent that the gross income from the property exceeds (1) the deductions attributable to the rental use that are allowable regardless of whether the property was used by the taxpayer as a residence (again, that is the mortgage interest and taxes) and (2) deductions (such as advertising expense) that are allocable to the rental activity but not allocable to the rental use of the home itself; § 280A(e)(5).

Here the gross income from the property is $7,000. We must also allocate the various expenses to the rental period. The items that are not allowable except to the extent allocable to the period of profit-seeking use (i.e., maintenance, insurance and depreciation) are allocated in the ratio of the number of days the property was *rented* at fair value to the number of days the property was *used*. Here that ratio is 75 percent (135 days of rental use/180 days of total use). Thus, $2,250 (75% of $3,000) of the insurance and maintenance costs and $2,250 of depreciation (75% of $3,000) must be considered for deduction. However, the deduction for those items cannot exceed the excess of gross income over (1) the portion of the interest and property taxes allocable to the rental period and (2) the advertising expense; see § 280A(e)(5).

In allocating the taxes and interest to the rental use of the property, Prop. Treas. Reg. § 1.280A–3(d) uses the allocation ratio that is used to allocate the maintenance, insurance and deprecation—namely, the ratio of rental days to total days of use. However, Bolton v. Commissioner, 694 F.2d 556 (9th Cir. 1982), refused to follow the proposed regulation. It pointed out that § 280A(e)(2) makes subsection (e), including the allocation formula of (e)(1), inapplicable to items such as taxes and interest that would be deductible regardless of whether they were incurred in profit-seeking activity. Instead, the court permitted those items to be allocated according to the ratio of rental days to total days in the year—12 percent (45/365) in our problem.

The *Bolton* formula results in larger deductions for the maintenance, etc., expenses:

	Proposed Regulation	Bolton
Gross Rents	$7,000	$7,000
Less: Allocation of taxes and interest	3,000*	480**
Advertising expense	1,000	1,000
Balance	$3,000	$5,520
Less: Maintenance and insurance	2,250	2,250
Balance	$750	$3,270
Depreciation	750	2,250

* 75% of $4,000.
** 12% of $4,000.

Under the proposed regulation, $6,000 of expenses are allocable to the profit-seeking use of the property ($3,000 of taxes and interest, plus $2,250 of maintenance and insurance, plus $750 of deprecation). In addition, $1,000 ($4,000 total taxes and interest less $3,000 allocable to profit-seeking) of additional taxes and interest are allowable even though attributable to non-profit-seeking use of the property. Also, the $1,000 of advertising expense is allowable under § 162 or § 212. V's deductions total $8,000. Under the *Bolton* formula, the profit-seeking expenses are $4,980 ($480 of taxes and insurance, plus $2,250 of maintenance and insurance, plus $2,250 of depreciation). In addition, $3,520 ($4,000 total taxes and interest less $480 allocable to profit-seeking) of additional taxes and interest and $1,000 of advertising expense are allowable, for total deductions of $9,500. So, V comes out far better under the *Bolton* approach.

Prop. Treas. Reg. § 1.280A–2(i)(5) requires that the deductions with respect to the profit-seeking use of the property be taken in the following order: (1) taxes and interest; (2) maintenance and insurance expenses (i.e., the deductions that do not result in an adjustment to the basis of property); and (3) depreciation. Under the allocation method prescribed by the Prop. Treas. Reg. § 1.280A–3(d), only $750 of depreciation would be allowable, and the year-end adjusted basis of the house would be $29,250 ($30,000 adjusted basis at the beginning of the year less $750 depreciation). Under the *Bolton* approach, the year-end adjusted basis would be $27,750 ($30,000 adjusted basis at beginning of the year less $2,250 depreciation).

(b) $4,000.

Under the regulation, the $4,000 of gross income would first be reduced by the $3,000 of taxes and interest and $1,000 advertising expense, leaving none of the maintenance and insurance expenses deductible. Total deductions would be $5,000 ($4,000 of taxes and interest, plus $1,000 of advertising expense). Under *Bolton*, however, the $4,000 of gross income would be reduced by only $480 of taxes and interest and $1,000 of advertising expense, leaving all of the $2,250 maintenance and insurance expenses and $270 of the depreciation deductible, for total deductions of $7,520 ($4,000 of taxes and interest, plus $1,000 advertising expense, plus $2,250 of maintenance and insurance, plus $270 of depreciation).

V's year-end adjusted basis for the house would remain $30,000 under the regulations' approach because no depreciation was allowable. Under *Bolton*, the adjusted basis would be reduced to $29,730 ($30,000 less $270).

2. How would your answers in 1 differ if V rented the home out for only 10 days (and received $600 rent).

Since the home was rented out for less than 15 days, no deduction attributable to the rental use of the property is allowable, but V need not include the rent in gross income; § 280A(g). The taxes and interest remain deductible because they are allowable even if the property is not used for business.

3. How would your answers in 1 differ if V used the home for personal purposes for only 10 days?

Since V used the property for personal purposes for fewer than 14 days, she is not considered to have used the home as a residence during the year. In that case, § 280A does not apply, and V can deduct the maintenance and insurance costs regardless of the amount of gross income received on account of the property. The taxes and interest remain fully deductible.

4. P, a partner in a law firm, has an office in her firm's building downtown, where she spends most working days, but also maintains an office in her home for use on nights and weekends. She uses the home office exclusively for her law business, frequently takes phone calls there from clients and colleagues, and occasionally meets clients there. Can P depreciate the portion of her house devoted to the home office?

No, § 280A(a) applies to deny a depreciation deduction. Although § 280A(c)(1) provides some exceptions to the disallowance rule, neither of the exceptions that might apply here provide relief: The office is neither her principal place of business nor "a place of business which is used by * * * clients * * * in meeting or dealing with the taxpayer in the normal course of * * * business"; § 280A(c)(1)(A) & (B). To qualify as a place for meeting clients in the normal course of business, the use by clients must be "substantial and integral to the conduct of the taxpayer's

business. Occasional meetings are insufficient to make this exception applicable.";
Prop. Treas. Reg. § 1.280A–2(c). Telephone conversations do not constitute the use
of the premises by clients; id. So, P gets no depreciation deduction.

5. **G is a professor at State University in University City. He takes
an unpaid leave of absence from the school to accept a visiting
appointment for the academic year at Private University, which is located
several hundred miles away from University City. G leases his University
City home during the period of his absence (from September, year 1
through June, year 2). After the visit ends, G intends to return to live in
his University City home. To what extent can G deduct the expenses
attributable to the rental of the property? Do you have any
recommendations to improve G's tax situation?**

Unfortunately for G, his use of the home as a residence in both years 1 and
2 invokes the disallowance rule of § 280A, and he can deduct his rental expenses
only in the manner discussed in problem 1, above. G might improve his situation
by leasing the home at fair rental for at least 12 months (a "qualified rental
period"), for then he would not be treated as using the home for personal purposes
(and hence as a residence) before or after the rental period. In that case, all of the
deductions attributable to the rental use of the property would be allowable. One
caveat: If G leases the property for at least 12 months, any loss from the rental
activity might not be deductible because of the passive-loss rules, which are
discussed in Chapter 45.

Section D

WHOSE INCOME IS IT?

Chapter 14

ASSIGNMENTS OF INCOME

Code: § 61(a).

Regulation: § 1.102–1(e).

Cases: Lucas v. Earl, 281 U.S. 111 (1930);
Poe v. Seaborn, 282 U.S. 101 (1930);
Blair v. Commissioner, 300 U.S. 5 (1937);
Helvering v. Horst, 311 U.S. 112 (1940).

1. **R, a cash-method taxpayer, is a commission sales representative for X Corporation. R is not an employee but an independent contractor. R directs X to pay his December commission check to R's adult child, C, and X does so. What result to R and C?**

R is taxed on the income because he is the person who earned it; Lucas v. Earl, 281 U.S. 111 (1930). C, who receives the money is not taxed; Treas. Reg. § 1.102–1(e) (donee not taxed on income that is taxed to assignor).

2. **Instead, R directs X to pay the December commissions to R's superb administrative assistant, A. A is an employee of X whose duties consist chiefly of providing administrative support for R. A had been grumbling that she was underpaid and hinted to R that she might look for another position. R hoped that paying the commissions to A would encourage her to continue in her present position. X paid the commissions to A.**

Here also the income would be taxed to the earner, R. Could R get an offsetting deduction? He should. Although § 162(a) requires that a cash-method taxpayer gets the deduction only when *paid*, R should be treated if the money were paid to him and he paid A. Since R is not an employee, the deduction would be taken above the line; § 62(a)(1).

3. Same as 1, except that R directed X to pay the December commissions to a charitable organization specified in § 170(c), and X did so.

Here again the income is taxable to R. The transaction should be treated as if R received the money and paid it over to the charity. If R itemizes deductions, he would be entitled to a charitable-contribution deduction under § 170, but the deduction might not offset the full amount included in gross income. Section 170(b) imposes limits (based upon the taxpayer's adjusted gross income) on the amount that can be deducted for the year. If R's gifts to charity exceed those limits, the excess is carried forward to the following year, and so forth, for up to five years; see § 170(d). Another reason why the offset might not be exact is that R's AGI may be high enough to trigger the phasing out of itemized deductions under § 68.

4. A owns land that is leased for a period of 30 years. A and A's adult child, C, both use the cash method of accounting.

(a) What result to A and C if A, intending to make a gift, directs the lessee to pay the current year's rent to C and the lessee does so?

The rent is includable in A's income. This is Helvering v. Horst, 311 U.S. 112 (1940) (father transferred bond-interest coupon to son, who collected it; father retained ownership of the bond; *held*: interest was taxed to the father because he retained ownership of the bond). Here A is taxable because he owns the asset (the land) that produced the income. C is not taxed; Treas. Reg. § 1.102–1(e) (donee not taxed on income that is taxed to assignor). It is as if A collected the year's rent and gave the money to C.

(b) What result if A gratuitously assigns the remaining term of the lease to C, who thereafter collects the rental payments from the lessee?

A is still taxable on each year's rental payment at the time it is received by C. Although now the assignment is for a longer term (30 years), A retains ownership of the land, which is the asset that produces the income; *Horst*. As noted above, C is not taxable on the amounts received.

(c) What result if A gratuitously conveyed the fee interest, subject to the lease, to C, who thereafter collected the rent?

C is taxable on the rents; Blair v. Commissioner, 300 U.S. 5 (1937) (father gave daughter an undivided portion of his entire interest in property; *held*: post-transfer income taxable to daughter). C would be taxable only on income accruing after the date of the conveyance; any income accrued at that date would be taxable to A when collected by C; see First Nat'l Bank v. United States, 194 F.2d 389 (7th Cir. 1952) (bank transferred mineral interests to its shareholders as dividend;

bank was taxable on royalty income attributable to production up to the date of transfer).

(d) What result if the land was held in trust to pay the income to A for 30 years, remainder to B, and A irrevocably and gratuitously assigned the income interest to C?

This is based upon *Blair*, which makes C taxable because A transferred his entire interest in the property. (It makes no difference that A's interest was an *income* interest; so was Blair's.)

5. What is meant by the term "marriage penalty"?

A marriage penalty occurs whenever a married couple pays more tax than the two of them would pay if they were not married (and everything else was unchanged). Common sources of marriage penalties are dollar limits on expense deductions, the amount of adjusted gross income at which a tax benefit is phased out, and the tax-rate schedules of § 1. For example, suppose that A and B each have AGI of $75,000, and each has a qualifying child under § 24(c). If they are single, each is entitled to a $1,000 child tax credit. If they marry, their AGI is $150,000 and they get no child tax credits because of the limits of § 24(b). Because of the loss of the credits, the couple will be $2,000 worse off if they marry than if they remain single. (This example is from Alan Gunn and Larry D. Ward, *Cases, Text and Problems on Federal Income Taxation* (6th ed. 2006) at p. 470.)

Here is an example where the couple's tax bill could be higher in the future because of a marriage penalty: A and B each have AGI of $95,000. If they are single, they can each contribute $5,000 to a Roth IRA (in 2008). If they marry, they cannot contribute to a Roth because of the limit of § 408A(c)(3). (Remember that earnings on amounts invested in a Roth IRA compound tax-free and qualified distributions are tax-free.)

6. C and D are deciding whether to marry. Each has adjusted gross income of $120,000 and taxable income of $115,000. (They compute their tax liability under § 1(c).) If they marry and file a joint return, they will have AGI of $240,000 and taxable income of $230,000. By how much will their aggregate tax liabilities increase if they marry. (Ignore the effect of all marriage penalties other than that reflected in the tax-rate schedules of § 1 (as set forth in Appendix B).)

Before they marry, each has tax liability of $28,035 (§ 1(c)) for an aggregate liability of $56,070. If they marry and file a joint return, their tax liability will be $61,105 ($31,405.50 plus 33% of $90,000). They would suffer a marriage penalty of $5,035 ($61,105 less $56,070).

7. **Same as 6, except that before marriage each has taxable income of $22,100 and after marriage their joint taxable income would be $44,200.**

As singles, each would have a tax liability of $2,965; § 1(c). Their total tax would be $5,930. If they marry, their joint-return liability would be $5,930; 1(a). There is no marriage penalty because Congress has made the size of the 10– and 15–percent brackets for married filing jointly double that for single filers under § 1(c). Making similar adjustments for higher brackets was deemed too costly.

8. **E has adjusted gross income of $120,000 and taxable income of $115,000. F has adjusted gross income of $5,000 and taxable income of zero. If they marry, their AGI will be $125,000 and their taxable income $115,000. What is their aggregate tax bill if:**

(a) **they are single (and compute their tax under § 1(c))?**

E's tax liability is $28,035; § 1(c). F's is zero. The total is $28,035.

(b) **marry and file a joint return?**

Their joint liability is $24,405.50; § 1(a). E and F are the beneficiaries of a "marriage bonus"—their tax bill is lower if they are married.

9. **On January 1 of this year, a community property state adopted a Registered Domestic Partners Act. Under the Act, domestic partners are "two adults who have chosen to share one another's lives in an intimate and committed relationship of mutual caring" and who register as such with the state. They may be members of the same sex. The Act extends to registered partners the same rights as spouses have under state law, except that, for state income-tax purposes, "earned income may not be treated as community property." Consider the tax treatment of A and B, same-sex partners who registered their union at the beginning of the year.**

(a) **A earned $100,000 of salary for the year; B earned $20,000 in part-time work.**

This problem is patterned on the California Domestic Partner Rights and Responsibilities Act (codified at California Family Code § 207.5), which became effective on January 1, 2005.

The California Family Code provides that all property "acquired by a married person during the marriage * * * is community property"; § 760. It also provides that the interests of the husband and wife are "present, existing and equal interests"; § 751. Section 207.5(a) extends to registered domestic partners the same rights, duties and benefits "as are granted to and imposed upon spouses."

Poe v. Seaborn, 282 U.S. 101 (1930), held that one-half of the salary earned by a spouse (or, perhaps more accurately, by the marital community) in a community property state belonged to the non-earner spouse. As a result, if spouses who reside in community property states file separate returns, each reports one-half of the compensation earnings of the community regardless of which spouse performed the services. However, in CCA 200608038, 2006 WL 469500, the Service ruled that *Seaborn* applied only to a husband and wife and, therefore, California domestic partners could not split their compensation income. ("CCA" stands for Chief Counsel Advisory; it is prepared in the office of the Chief Counsel of the IRS and provides legal guidance to other Service personnel.)

The CCA is not persuasive. Even though they are not married, California registered domestic partners have the same rights in community income that married people do. *Seaborn* said that "the wife has * * * a vested property right in the community property, equal with that of her husband; and in the income of the community, including salaries or wages of either husband or wife, or both." *Seaborn* was thus based upon the theory that both spouses had an equal ownership in the property and income—not that they were husband and wife.

The CCA does not mention the Defense of Marriage Act, 1 U.S.C § 7, which limits "'marriage" to "a legal union between one man and one woman" and "spouse" to "a person of the opposite sex who is a husband or wife." DOMA does not apply here, as the California law just defines the parties' property rights—it doesn't purport to make them spouses.

As in our problem, California Family Code § 297.5(g) prevents domestic partners from treating their earned income as community property for *state* income-tax purposes. However, that should not affect the federal tax treatment of the income.

A and B will have to file as unmarried taxpayers. Although the CCA would require A to include $100,000 and B $20,000 in gross income, litigation on the income-splitting issue is inevitable.

(b) A saved $50,000 of the salary and purchased some land, which was held for rent. The lessee paid $10,000 of rent in the current year.

If A and B were husband and wife, the money that A received as salary would be community property, as would any property purchased with such funds. California law extends that treatment to registered domestic partners. Therefore, it seems that the land belongs one-half to each of A and B, and the rent is reportable one-half by each. The CCA discussed above deals only with compensation income, but its tone suggests that the Service would tax all of the rent to A.

Chapter 15

TAXATION OF THE INCOME
OF MINOR CHILDREN

Code: §§ 1(g); 63(c)(5); 151(d)(2); 73.

Regulations: §§ 1.1(i)–1T; 1.73–1(a).

1. **C, age 14, earns $2,000 delivering newspapers. Under state law, a child's parents are entitled to the earnings of a child under age 16. Who must include the $2,000 in gross income?**

C must include the $2,000 in gross income; § 73(a). It is C's income "regardless of the provisions of State law relating to who is entitled to the earnings of the child"; Treas. Reg. § 1.73–1(a). In other words, § 73 follows the rule of Lucas v. Earl rather than Poe v. Seaborn.

2. **B (age 14) and S (age 19) each receive interest income from bonds purchased by their parents and held by their mother as custodian under the Uniform Transfers to Minors Act. Both children are dependents of their parents. Apart from any effect of § 1(g), the parents have taxable income of $140,000 on their joint return. Ignore inflation adjustments to amounts fixed by statute, and use the tax tables in Appendix B to determine the tax liability of B and S if they each receive interest of:**

(a) $300;

Although B is a child to whom § 1(g) applies (because B has not attained age 18, his parents are alive, and he does not file a joint return—§ 1(g)(2)), B has no "net unearned income" under § 1(g)(4). Section 1(g) does not apply to S because she has attained age 18.

Neither B nor S has any taxable income. The standard deduction for a taxpayer who is the dependent of another person is limited to $500 (or, if greater, the taxpayer's earned income plus $250); § 63(c)(5). Since in this case the children have no earned income, their standard deductions are limited to $500. But that amount is sufficient to offset each child's gross income.

(b) $800;

Each child has taxable income of $300 ($800 gross income less $500 standard deduction). Again B is a child to whom § 1(g) applies, but B has no "net unearned income" because net unearned income is (generally) the excess of unearned income ($800) over twice the standard deduction ($1000); § 1(g)(4)(A). Neither child is entitled to a personal exemption because their parents can claim dependency exemptions for them; § 151(d)(2). Each child therefore has tax liability of $30 (10% of $300); § 1(c).

(c) $2,400;

Each child has taxable income of $1,900 ($2,400 gross income less $500 standard deduction).

Since S has attained age 18, she is taxed at her own rates (rather than at her parents' rate under § 1(g)). Her tax is therefore $190 (10% of $1,900); § 1(c).

As noted above, B is covered by the special rule of § 1(g). See § 1(g)(2). In computing B's "net unearned income," we first determine the sum of the amounts specified in § 1(g)(4)(A)(ii)(I) and (II). That is, the sum of (I) the standard deduction under § 63(c)(5)(A) ($500) and (II) the $500 amount described in (I) (because B does not itemize deductions). The total for § 1(g)(4)(A)(ii) is thus $1,000, and that figure is subtracted from B's unearned income to arrive at B's *net* unearned income, which is taxable at his parents' marginal rate. B's net unearned income is $1,400 ($2,400 of unearned income less $1,000); § 1(g)(4)(A). Since his parents are in the 33–percent bracket, his share of the allocable parental tax is $462 (the excess of the parents' § 1(a) tax on $141,400 over their tax on $140,000); § 1(g)(3). The tax on the remaining $500 of taxable income is $50 (10% of $500); § 1(c). B's total tax liability is therefore $512 ($462 plus $50), since this is more than his tax liability computed without regard to § 1(g) ($190); § 1(g)(1).

(d) $2,400 and earned income of $400;

Each child has gross and adjusted gross income of $2,800. Each is entitled to a standard deduction of $650 (the sum of $250 and the $400 of earned income); § 63(c)(5)(B). Each has taxable income of $2,150.

S computes her tax at the rates of § 1(c), which produces a tax of $215 (10% of $2,150).

As in (c), B is subject to § 1(g), and his net unearned income is $1,400, on which his share of the allocable parental tax is $462, as in (c). The tax on the remaining $750 of taxable income is $75 (10% of $750); § 1(c). B's total tax is $537 ($462 plus $75)

(e) $2,400 and earned income of $3,400.

Now each child has gross and adjusted gross income of $5,800. Each is entitled to a standard deduction of $3000; § 63(c)(2)(C). Although the sum of $250 and the $3,400 of earned income totals $3,650, § 63(c)(5)(B) is a limit on the standard deduction; it does not increase the standard deduction to an amount exceeding $3,000 for a single person. Taxable income is $2,800 ($5,800 AGI less $3,000 standard deduction).

S's tax is $280 (10% of $2,800); § 1(c).

B's share of the allocable parental tax is $462, as in (c) and (d), above. B's tax on the remaining $1,400 of taxable income is $140 (10% of $1,400); § 1(c). B's total tax is $602 ($462 plus $140).

Section E

INCOME FROM DEALINGS IN PROPERTY

Chapter 16

COMPUTATION OF REALIZED GAIN OR LOSS

_____

Code: §§ 1001(a), (b) & (c); 1011(a); 1012; 1016(a)(2).

Regulation: § 1.263(a)–2(e).

Cases: International Freighting Corp. v. Commissioner, 135 F.2d 310 (2d Cir. 1943);
Philadelphia Park Amusement Co. v. United States, 126 F. Supp. 184 (Ct. Cl. 1954);
Inaja Land Co. v. Commissioner, 9 T.C. 727 (1947).

In the following problems, assume, unless otherwise indicated, that all parties are cash-method, calendar-year taxpayers.

1. S purchased a share of stock for $20. S later sold the stock for $80. What is S's realized gain?

S's amount realized on the sale is $80 (the amount of cash received); § 1001(b). S's basis is $20 (cost); § 1012. There are no adjustments to the basis, so S's adjusted basis is also $20; § 1011(a). S's realized gain is $60 ($80 amount realized less $20 adjusted basis); § 1001(a).

2. Same as 1, except that S paid a $5 brokerage commission on the sale.

The brokerage commission paid on the sale is an offset to the sale price and thus reduces the amount realized; Treas. Reg. § 1.263(a)–2(e). Therefore, the amount realized is $75, and the realized gain is $55.

3. N owned a vacation home (held for personal use) in upstate New York. N had an adjusted basis of $200,000 for the property. S transferred the property to F in exchange for a Florida condominium, which N also held for personal use. The Florida property was worth $250,000, and F also paid N $30,000 to equalize the exchange.

(a) What is N's realized gain on the exchange?

N's amount realized is $280,000 (the $250,000 value of the Florida property, plus the $30,000 cash); § 1001(b). N's realized gain is $80,000 ($280,000 amount realized less $200,000 adjusted basis); § 1001(a).

(b) What is N's basis for the Florida property?

N's basis for the Florida property is $250,000 (the amount at which it was includable in N's amount realized); this is an example of tax-cost basis under § 1012.

4. W owned a vacation home (held for personal use) in Wisconsin. The home had an adjusted basis of $250,000 in W's hands. W transferred the property to C in exchange for a California condominium, which W also held for personal use. The California condominium was worth $500,000, and W paid C $100,000 to equalize the exchange.

(a) What is W's realized gain on the exchange?

As to W, this is a hybrid transaction—in part a purchase and in part an exchange. We are interested in the amount of gain realized on the exchange part of the transaction, which in turn depends upon the amount realized on the *exchange*. In this arm's length exchange, we can presume that the value of the consideration given by W was equal to the value of the consideration received; see Philadelphia Park Amusement Co. v. United States, 126 F. Supp. 184 (Ct. Cl. 1954). We can therefore infer that the total value of the consideration received by W ($500,000) is equal to the sum of the value of the Wisconsin property and the $100,000 cash paid by W. This analysis suggests that the value of the Wisconsin property was $400,000 ($500,000 of consideration received by W less $100,000 cash paid by W). In effect, W has traded the Wisconsin property for an undivided 80% interest in the California property and purchased an undivided 20% interest in the California property for $100,000 cash. The amount realized by W on the exchange is the $400,000 value of the undivided 80% interest in the California property acquired by exchange, and W's realized gain on the exchange is $150,000 ($400,000 amount realized less $250,000 adjusted basis).

There is a simpler way to analyze the transaction: We could just pretend that W sold the Wisconsin property for cash at its $400,000 value, which would produce a realized gain of $150,000. Then W uses the $400,000 sales proceeds plus another $100,000 cash to purchase the California property for $$500,000.

(b) What is W's basis for the California property?

W's basis for the California property is $500,000, comprising an actual cost ($100,000) and a tax-cost basis equal to the amount at which the California property was includable in W's amount realized on the exchange ($400,000). Or, using the fictional-sale approach in the preceding paragraph, W gets a cost basis of $500,000 for the California property.

5. In year 1, C became indebted in the amount of $10,000 to her attorney, A, for representing C in a personal legal matter. Because C was short of cash, C offered in year 2 to transfer to A some stock with a value of $10,000. C's adjusted basis for the stock was $2,000. A accepted the stock in full payment.

(a) What result to C?

C realizes gain when she transfers the stock to A in year 2. The transaction is analyzed as though C sold the stock for $10,000 cash and paid the cash to A in satisfaction of her debt; International Freighting Corp. v. Commissioner, 135 F.2d 310 (2d Cir. 1943). C's realized gain is $8,000 ($10,000 value of stock less $2,000 adjusted basis). C is apparently not entitled to a deduction for the legal expense since it pertained to a "personal" matter.

(b) To A?

As a cash-method taxpayer, A has gross income of $10,000 upon receipt of the stock in year 2; § 83(a). A obtains a tax-cost basis of $10,000 for the stock, as if A collected $10,000 cash from C and used the cash to purchase the stock.

6. What result in 5 if the stock was worth only $8,000 when C transferred it to A in year 2, but A nevertheless accepted the stock in full satisfaction of the indebtedness because of concern about C's continuing financial difficulties?

If the stock is worth only $8,000 when C transfers it to A, C realizes gain of $6,000 ($8,000 amount realized less $2,000 adjusted basis) on the disposition of the stock. C also has $2,000 of debt-discharge income on the transaction if C was not insolvent when A forgave the balance of the debt.

A would have gross income of $8,000 upon receipt of the stock; § 83(a). A would obtain a tax-cost basis for the stock equal to its $8,000 value when received. A has a $2,000 economic loss, but cannot deduct the loss because, as a cash-method taxpayer, A has a zero basis in the account receivable due from C.

7. Would your answer in 6 change if A used the accrual method? Explain.

If A used the accrual method, A would have to include $10,000 in gross income in year 1, when the all-events test for accrual was satisfied. A would obtain a $10,000 tax cost basis in the account receivable due from C. When C transferred stock worth $8,000 in satisfaction of the debt, A would have realized a loss of $2,000. A's adjusted basis for the stock would be its $8,000 value at the time acquired by A.

8. Under the terms of D's will, B was entitled to a legacy of $50,000. The estate transferred stock with a basis of $35,000 (and a value of $50,000) to B in satisfaction of the legacy.

(a) What result to the estate?

The estate realizes gain of $15,000 when it satisfies the $50,000 fixed-dollar legacy by the transfer of appreciated property with an adjusted basis of $35,000; Treas. Reg. § 1.1014–4(a)(3). The transaction is analyzed as if the estate sold the securities for cash and distributed the sales proceeds to the beneficiary in satisfaction of the legacy.

(b) And to B?

B excludes the $50,000 from gross income under § 102(a); B's basis for the securities is $50,000 (fair market value); Treas. Reg. § 1.1014–4(a)(3). It is as if B received $50,000 cash from the estate and used the money to purchase the securities at their $50,000 value.

9. In year 1, D made a legally enforceable pledge of $50,000 to a qualifying charity d escribed in § 170(c). D satisfied the pledge by transferring to the charity stock with an adjusted basis of $35,000. What result to D?

Your first impulse might be to think that D's transfer of property in satisfaction of a legally enforceable charitable pledge would be a realization event. In fact, however, the Treasury has ruled that no gain is realized when property is transferred to charity in satisfaction of a binding pledge; Rev. Rul. 55–410, 1955–1 C.B. 297. The ruling notes that § 170 allows a deduction for charitable gifts only when "payment" is made and concludes that it would be inconsistent to treat the same event as both a gift and the satisfaction of a debt. Professors Bittker and Lokken offer a more persuasive justification:

> [A] contrary rule would be merely a trap for taxpayers who impulsively fill out a charitable pledge card with a specific dollar amount rather than follow the more prudent course of promising to give specified property in kind.

2 B. Bittker & L. Lokken, Federal Taxation of Income, Estates and Gifts ¶ 40.4.3, p. 40-18 (3d ed. 2000).

Unless the limits of § 170(b) or (e)(1)(A) apply, D can deduct $50,000 (the value of the stock) as a charitable contribution.

10.   B paid $100,000 for business equipment, properly deducted $60,000 of depreciation, and then sold the equipment for $75,000. How much gain or loss does B realize on the sale? Why?

B's (unadjusted) basis is $100,000. The adjusted basis is $40,000 ($100,000 unadjusted basis less $60,000 depreciation); § 1016(a)(2). When the property is sold, B's gain is $35,000 ($75,000 amount realized less $40,000 adjusted basis); § 1011(a).

Why does B have a *gain* when he buys property for $100,000 and sells for $75,000? To the unpracticed eye, that looks very much like a *loss* rather than a gain. But to the student of the tax law, the result is perfectly comprehensible. B purchased the property for $100,000 and sold it for $75,000; in effect, B "used up" $25,000 of the property's value in producing income. B (properly) deducted depreciation of $60,000 over the years. The $60,000 of deductions was used to offset gross income and prevent that amount of gross income from being taxed. In effect, the tax system treated B as if $60,000 of the property would be consumed in producing income. When it turns out that only $25,000 of value was consumed, we could, in principle, either (1) require B to file amended returns for the years during which the property was in service and reduce the depreciation to the amount that actually occurred, or (2) treat B as having realized a gain in the year of disposition that "makes up" for the over-depreciation of the property. This latter approach is the one followed by the Code. So, the $35,000 gain in the year of disposition is a "make-up" gain that arises because, in allowing depreciation the statute anticipated that $60,000 worth of property would be consumed in producing income, while in reality only $25,000 of value was so consumed. B must make up for the $35,000 of "excess" deductions by including $35,000 in gross income as realized gain in the year of sale.

11.   P was injured in an automobile accident caused by the negligence of D. P brought an action against D seeking $1,000,000 damages. Before trial, D settled the suit by transferring to P securities with an adjusted basis of $250,000 and a value of $400,000.

(a) What is the amount, if any, of D's realized gain on the transfer?

D's transfer of the securities to P in satisfaction of P's claim is a realization event to D. Although we do not know the value of the claim that P relinquished, we can assume in this arm's-length exchange that it is equal in value to the property given up by D ($400,000). (The amount of damages which P claimed in the suit would not be reliable evidence of the value of P's claim; plaintiffs frequently overstate their claims in their pleadings. Hence the amount realized by D would not be $1,000,000. For the same reason, the difference between the $1,000,000 claim and the $400,000 value of the property is not discharge-of-indebtedness income to D.)   D's realized gain is $150,000 ($400,000 amount realized less $250,000 adjusted basis).

(b) What tax results to P?

P can exclude the value of the securities from her gross income because they was received in settlement of a claim for "personal physical injuries"; § 104(a). P's basis is $400,000 (that is, the transaction should be viewed as if D received $400,000 cash in settlement of her claim and used the cash to purchase the securities, thus giving her a cost basis under § 1012).

12. T purchased as an investment a large tract of undeveloped land for $1,000,000. T later sold one-quarter of the land for $400,000. What is the amount of T's realized gain or loss on the sale.

Even though T has sold only part of the property, T must determine the amount of realized gain or loss on the portion sold; T cannot defer the tax reckoning until the entire property has been disposed of. In computing the realized gain or loss on the sale, T must equitably apportion the cost of the entire tract between the portion sold and that retained; Treas. Reg. § 1.61–6(a). The apportionment of the basis should be based upon the relative values of the various parcels in the tract at the time acquired by T. For example, if the portion that has now been sold represented 50 percent of the total value of the tract at the time of acquisition, T should allocate 50 percent of the cost to that parcel. Assuming that the tract was of uniform value, T should allocate 25 percent of the total cost to the parcel sold. Therefore, T's realized gain is $150,000 ($400,000 amount realized less $250,000 adjusted basis).

13. O owned undeveloped land that he had purchased for $200,000. After a neighbor accidentally polluted the land, the neighbor paid O $150,000 for the damage and for an easement to continue polluting. Does O have income on account of the payment?

This problem is based upon Inaja Land Co. v. Commissioner, 9 T.C. 727 (1947), where the court agreed with the taxpayer that allocation of part of the property's basis to the easement would be "impracticable or impossible" and treated the amount received as a return of basis. Under this approach, O would have no gain upon receipt of the $150,000 and would reduce the property's basis to $50,000.

14. O owned a tract of land with a basis of $100,000 and a value of $400,000. On July 1, year 1, O granted P an option to acquire the land for $450,000. P paid O $20,000 for the option, which was exercisable at any time through June 30, year 3.

(a) At the end of year 1, P has not exercised the option. How should the parties treat the transaction for year 1?

The transaction has no tax effect until the option either lapses or is exercised. The parties must "wait and see" what happens in a future year.

(b) Will P exercise the option if on June 30, year 3, the land is worth:

(i) $500,000?

(ii) $440,000?

(iii) $460,000?

Explain your answers.

(i) If the land is worth $500,000, P will exercise the option, thus obtaining $500,000 worth of property for only $450,000. Of course, if the option is assignable, P could always sell the option rather than exercising it.

(ii) P will not exercise the option in this case. If P exercised the option, P would have to pay $450,000 for land that is worth only $440,000.

(iii) P will exercise the option to obtain land valued at $460,000 for only $450,000. Some students find this confusing, since, upon exercise, P will have invested $470,000 in the land, which is worth only $460,000. But keep in mind that the $20,000 P invested in the option is a "sunk" cost when P is deciding whether to exercise the option. P cannot get that $20,000 back, so P must decide whether to pay another $450,000 and get the $460,000 worth of land. As the option approaches expiration, its value approaches $10,000 (the excess of the value of the land over the exercise price). Assuming that sale of the option is not a possibility, P should exercise it as a way of limiting his loss to $10,000. (That is, P will have invested a total of $470,000 to obtain land worth $460,000.) If P allows the option to lapse, P loses the $20,000 cost of the option.

(c) Suppose that P exercises the option on June 30, year 3, when the land is worth $500,000. What tax result to the parties in year 3?

At the time of exercise in year 3, the option, in which P has a cost basis of $20,000, is worth $50,000 (the excess of the $500,000 value of the land over the $450,000 exercise price of the option). However, P is not taxed on the $30,000 of unrealized appreciation in the option at the time of exercise. Instead, P adds the

$20,000 basis for the option to the $450,000 exercise price to arrive at a $470,000 basis for the property. If P were then to sell the land for its $500,000 value, P would realize gain of $30,000, which represents the appreciation in the value of the option that went untaxed when the option was exercised.

When P exercises the option, O can close the transaction that has been held open since year 1. O's amount realized on the sale of the land includes the $20,000 received upon granting the option and the $450,000 received upon its exercise, for a total of $470,000. O's realized gain is $370,000 ($470,000 amount realized less $100,000 adjusted basis).

(d) Suppose that the land is worth only $400,000 on June 30, year 3, and P does not exercise the option, which lapses. What result to the parties in year 3?

If the option lapses, O must close out the transaction by including the $20,000 option premium in gross income for year 3. P can deduct the $20,000 cost of the option as a loss in year 3 if the option was obtained for business or investment purposes.

Chapter 17

TRANSACTIONS INVOLVING
MORTGAGED PROPERTY

Code: §§ 1001(b); 1011(a); 1012; 167(c). Note § 7701(g). Review§ 108.

Regulations: § 1.1001–2(a), (b) & (c), Exs. (1), (2), (7) & (8).

Cases: Crane v. Commissioner, 334 U.S. 1 (1947);
            Parker v. Delaney, 186 F.2d 455 (1st Cir. 1950);
            Commissioner v. Tufts, 461 U.S. 300 (1983).

Ruling: Rev. Rul. 90–16, 1990–1 C.B. 12.

1. **T purchased a building for $500 (000 omitted throughout). T paid $100 cash down and gave a non-recourse note (secured by a mortgage on the property) for the $400 balance. T held the property as an investment. In answering the following questions, ignore the land, as if only the building were purchased and sold.**

(a) **What is T's basis for depreciation?**

Under Crane v. Commissioner, 334 U.S. 1 (1947), and its progeny, T's basis is $500 ($100 cash investment, plus the $400 borrowed on the non-recourse note). The *Crane* Court reasoned that, even though the taxpayer did not have a legal obligation to make the required payments on the note (because it was non-recourse), she would have an economic compulsion to make the payments, so as to avoid foreclosure. We therefore give T advance basis credit for the payments that we expect her to make on the mortgage, just as we would if the indebtedness were with recourse to T.

(b) Over the next several years, T properly deducts $300 of depreciation, pays $100 on the mortgage principal, and makes all required interest payments. T then sells the building to P, who takes the property subject to the remaining $300 mortgage and pays T $250 cash. What is the amount of T's realized gain or loss?

T's amount realized is $550 ($250 cash, plus the $300 liability encumbering the property at the time of disposition); Parker v. Delaney, 186 F.2d 455 (1st Cir. 1950). T's adjusted basis is $200 ($500 unadjusted basis less $300 depreciation). T's realized gain is $350 ($550 amount realized less $200 adjusted basis).

To see why T has a gain of $350, consider that T invested $200 cash in the property and received $250 cash from the sale, for an economic gain of $50. In addition, T deducted $300 of depreciation, even though the property did not decline in value while held by T. T must disgorge the $300 of "excess" depreciation as a "make-up" gain. So, T's total gain (economic and make-up) is $350.

(c) Suppose instead that after T had properly deducted the $300 of depreciation and reduced the mortgage principal to $300, the building declined in value to $275, at which point T surrendered the property to the mortgagee. What result to T?

The surrender of the property to the lender is a realization event. Because T has no personal liability on the mortgage note, T's amount realized is $300 (the amount of the liability encumbering the property when it is disposed of); Treas. Reg. § 1.1001–2(c), Ex. (7). The amount realized is not limited to the property's value. This was the holding in Commissioner v. Tufts, 461 U.S. 300 (1983), which properly rejected the contrary implication of footnote 37 in Crane v. Commissioner, 334 U.S. 1 (1947). T therefore realizes a gain of $100 ($300 amount realized less $200 adjusted basis).

To see why T should realize gain of $100 upon surrender of the building, recall that T deducted depreciation of $300, even though T is out-of-pocket only $200 cash (the $100 down payment, plus $100 of principal paid on the mortgage note). The gain is the $100 excess of the $300 of depreciation deductions over the $200 out-of-pocket loss.

(d) Same as (c), except that the building was worth only $150 when it was surrendered to the mortgagee.

The result would be the same as in (c), as T's amount realized is the amount of the liability encumbering the property rather than the value of the building; Tufts v. Commissioner, 461 U.S. 300 (1983).

(e) How would your answers in (c) and (d) differ if T had been personally liable on the indebtedness, but the mortgagee had accepted the property in full satisfaction of the indebtedness? Would your answer change if T was insolvent immediately after surrendering the building to the lender?

When the owner is personally liable on the mortgage, the surrender is bifurcated and treated as (1) a sale of the property for its fair market value and (2) a discharge of indebtedness to the extent of the difference between the liability and the value of the property. In (c), therefore, T realizes a gain of $75 on the disposition of the building ($275 value of building less $200 adjusted basis). T also has $25 of debt-discharge income, as T has been discharged from $300 of liability in consideration of T's transferring $275 worth of property to the lender; Rev. Rul. 90–16, 1990–1 C.B. 12. If T is insolvent after the discharge, the $25 can be excluded from gross income under § 108(a)(1)(B). The $75 gain, however, cannot be excluded from gross income even if T is insolvent.

On surrender of the building in (d), T realizes a loss of $50 ($200 adjusted basis less $150 value of the property). T also has debt-discharge income of $150 ($300 liability less $150 value of building). Again, however, T can exclude the $150 from income if T was insolvent immediately after the transfer.

2. A purchased property for $100 cash and properly deducted $60 of depreciation thereon. A then borrowed $50 from a bank on a non-recourse note secured by the property and devoted the loan proceeds to purposes unconnected to the property. After properly deducting another $30 of depreciation and paying off $20 of the mortgage principal (and all accrued interest), A sold the property to P, who paid A $20 cash and took subject to the remaining $30 of indebtedness.

(a) Does A have income at the time of borrowing against the security of the property?

Even though A has borrowed an amount in excess of the property's adjusted basis and has no personal liability for repayment, no gain is realized at the time of the borrowing; Woodsam Assocs., Inc. v. Commissioner, 198 F.2d 357 (2d Cir. 1952). Although A has no personal obligation to repay the loan, he has an economic compulsion to repay (so as to avoid losing the property in foreclosure) as long as the value of the property exceeds the amount of indebtedness.

(b) What is the amount of A's realized gain or loss on the sale to P?

A's amount realized on the sale is $50 (the sum of the $20 cash and the $30 of indebtedness to which the property is subject). A's adjusted basis is $10 ($100 unadjusted basis less $90 of depreciation). The realized gain is $40 ($50 amount realized less $10 adjusted basis).

(c) What is P's basis for the property immediately after the purchase?

P's basis is $50, the sum of the $20 cash paid and the $30 liability to which the property was subject when acquired by P.

Chapter 18

THE BASIS OF PROPERTY
ACQUIRED BY GIFT

Code: §§ 1015(a), (d)(1) & (6); 1223(2); 167(c)(1). Review § 102(a). Note §§ 1245(b)(1); 2503(a) & (b).

Regulations: §§ 1.1015–1(a); 1.1015–5(c); 1.1015–4; 1.1001–1(e).

Cases: Farid–Es–Sultaneh v. Commissioner, 160 F.2d 812 (2d Cir. 1947); Dietrich v. Commissioner, 457 U.S. 191 (1982).

1. **Several years ago, P purchased a share of stock for $100. On December 31 of last year, when the share was worth $150, P gave the stock to her adult child, C. C sells the stock on July 1 of the current year for $180.**

(a) What tax result to P?

P recognizes no gain upon the transfer of the stock by gift.

(b) What tax result to C?

C excludes the value of the stock from income (§ 102(a)) and assumes P's $100 basis for the stock under § 1015(a). When C sells the stock for $180, C realizes a gain of $80 ($180 amount realized less $100 basis).

In a later chapter, we will see that C's gain is a capital gain and that long-term capital gains are taxed at lower tax rates than ordinary income. The gain qualifies as "long-term" gain if the taxpayer held the property sold for more than one year. In this case, C's actual holding period is only six months. But because C's basis for the stock is the same as P's, C can include the period during which P held the stock in determining whether her holding period exceeds one year; see § 1223(2). P had held the stock for several years, so when P's holding period is added ("tacked"), C's gain is characterized as long-term. (The holding-period issue is raised at this point because holding period generally follows basis: When basis is transferred from one person to another or from one item of property to another, the holding period of the other person or the other property usually can be tacked on.)

2. How would your answer in (1) differ if the value of the stock on December 31 of last year had been $80, and C had sold the stock for:

(a) $180?

C has a realized gain of $80 ($180 amount realized less $100 adjusted basis). Although P's adjusted basis of $100 exceeded the $80 value of the share on the date of the gift, the split-basis (or lower-of-basis-or-value) rule does not apply here because the property was sold at a gain, as measured by the donor's basis.

(b) $60?

Now the split-basis rule comes into play. Using P's $100 basis, C computes a loss of $40 ($100 basis less $60 amount realized). So, § 1015(a) says that C must recompute the loss by using as her adjusted basis for loss the $80 value of the share at the date of the gift (because that value was less than the donor's basis of $100). C therefore realizes a loss of $20 ($80 adjusted basis for loss less $60 amount realized).

Since C's adjusted basis for loss is based upon the value of the stock (rather than the donor's basis), C does not tack on P's holding period, and the loss is short-term; see Rev. Rul. 59–416, 1959–2 C.B. 159.

(c) $90?

C first compares the $90 amount realized with the $100 basis transferred from P. This results in a realized loss of $10. C must therefore recompute the loss using as the adjusted basis for loss the $80 value of the property at the date of gift. But this computation produces a realized gain of $10. Since C determines a realized loss when using the adjusted basis for gain and a realized gain when using the adjusted basis for loss, C has neither a realized gain nor a realized loss; Treas. Reg. § 1.1015–1(a)(2), Ex.

3. On January 15, M gave a piece of depreciable equipment to her son, S, for use in his business. M had purchased the equipment for $500,000 and had properly deducted $180,000 of depreciation thereon. The equipment was worth $400,000 at the time of the gift. No gift tax was payable by M.

(a) What is S's depreciable basis for the property?

Section 167(c) says that the basis for depreciation is the taxpayer's basis for computing gain. In this case, S would use the $320,000 adjusted basis transferred from M.

(b) Explain in general terms how S should compute depreciation on the equipment.

Where the property was depreciable in the hands of the donor and will also be depreciable in the hands of the donee, the donor's transfer apparently is not treated as a disposition that would invoke the applicable convention in determining the donor's depreciation deduction in the year of disposition. Regulations promulgated under the original Accelerated Cost Recovery System (ACRS) said that the term "disposition" does not include a transfer of property by gift, and there is no reason to think that the result would be different under today's Modified Accelerated Cost Recovery System (MACRS). This suggests that the depreciation deduction for the year of the gift is apportioned between the donor and donee based upon the number of months in the year that each held the property. The donee then presumably continues depreciating the property using the same method and convention used over the donor's remaining recovery period.

(c) How would your answer in (a) differ if the value of the equipment at the time of the gift was $300,000?

If the equipment was worth only $300,000, its value at the date of the gift would be less than M's adjusted basis ($320,000). If S were to sell the property, the split-basis rule of § 1015(a) would force S to use the $300,000 value of the property in computing loss. One might logically expect that the basis for depreciation would also be limited to $300,000. In fact, however, § 167(c) specifies that for depreciation purposes S is to use the adjusted basis that would be used in computing "gain" on a sale of the property. So, S computes depreciation by using the $320,000 adjusted basis for gain, even though that exceeds the value of the equipment at the time of the gift.

4. In the current year (when the gift-tax annual exclusion is $12,000), M made a taxable gift (for gift-tax purposes) of $100,000 ($112,000 value of the property transferred less $12,000 annual exclusion) to her daughter, D. M paid a gift tax of $40,000 on the transfer, which was M's only gift for the year. M's adjusted basis in the property transferred was $52,000.

(a) What is D's adjusted basis for the property?

D assumes M's $52,000 adjusted basis and can increase that basis by that proportion of the $40,000 gift tax paid which the net appreciation in value of the gift property bears to the amount of the gift; § 1015(d)(1) & (6)(A). Here, the net appreciation is $60,000 (the amount by which the $112,000 value of the property exceeds the donor's $52,000 adjusted basis immediately before the gift);

§ 1015(d)(6)(B). The amount of the gift is $100,000 ($112,000 value of the property transferred less $12,000 gift-tax exclusion); Treas. Reg. § 1.1015–5(c)(2). The gift-tax adjustment is therefore $24,000 ($60,000/$100,000 x $40,000 gift tax), and D's adjusted basis for the property is $76,000.

(b) Would your answer differ if M's adjusted basis for the property given to D was $120,000?

Yes, because there would be no net appreciation in the value of the gift property (M's basis exceeded the value of the property); and, in any event, the gift-tax adjustment cannot increase the basis to an amount in excess of the property's value; § 1015(d)(1)(A).

5. A had held some securities as an investment for several years. Intending to make a partial gift, A transferred the securities to her domestic partner, B, for $60. At that time, the securities had a value of $100, and A's adjusted basis was $20. No gift tax was payable on the transfer.

(a) What result to A?

This is a part-gift, part-sale transaction. Under Treas. Reg. § 1.1001–1(e), A is not required to apportion her basis between the gift and sale elements of the transaction but can apply her entire basis in offsetting the amount realized on the sale. A therefore realizes gain of $40 ($60 amount realized less $20 adjusted basis).

(b) What result to B if seven months after the transfer she sells the securities for $85?

B obtains a basis equal to the greater of: (1) the amount paid by B; or (2) A's adjusted basis for the property at the time of transfer; Treas. Reg. 1.1015–4(a). In this case, the amount paid by B ($60) exceeds A's adjusted basis ($20), and B's basis is therefore $60. When B sells the securities for $85, B realizes gain of $25. The Service takes the view that the gain is short-term because B's basis is the property's cost rather than a transferred basis from A.

(c) What result in (a) and (b), above, if A's adjusted basis in the securities had been $150?

According to the regulations, a transferor never sustains a loss on a part-gift, part-sale transaction; Treas. Reg. § 1.1001–1(e)(1). So, no deduction for A.

For the purpose of computing gain, B's basis in the securities is the same as A's, $150 (because that is more than the amount paid by B); Treas. Reg. § 1.1015–4(a). For the purpose of computing loss, however, B's basis is the value of the securities on the date of gift where, as here, that value is less than the transferor's basis. So, B obtains a $150 basis for determining gain and a $100 basis for determining loss.

When B sells for $85, she first compares her $150 adjusted basis for gain with the $85 amount realized. Since that results in a loss, B must recompute the loss using as her adjusted basis for loss the $100 value of the property at the time of the gift, which results in a loss of $15.

(d) Can you devise a more-satisfactory scheme for computing A's and B's realized gain or loss in the above transactions?

A taxpayer who sells a partial interest in property usually apportions the basis between the portion sold and the portion retained. For example, if A had sold an undivided 60–percent interest in the property to B and retained the other 40–percent interest, A could offset against the amount realized only the 60 percent of her basis allocable to the property sold. So, where the entire property was worth $100, A's adjusted basis was $20, and A sold an undivided 60–percent interest to B for $60, A would apply $12 of basis (60% of $20) against the $60 amount realized on the sale, which would result in a gain of $48. B would obtain a $60 cost basis in the interest. If A later gave the remaining undivided 40–percent interest to B, A would recognize no gain and B would assume A's remaining basis of $8, giving B total basis of $68 for the securities. It is difficult to see any justification for allowing A to offset her entire basis against the amount realized on the partial sale to B just because A gave the remaining interest to B as part of the same transaction when A would not be permitted to do so when the sale and gift were separate transactions. Requiring the transferor to apportion the basis between the interests transferred by sale and by gift would better comport with general tax principles.

6. For several years, A has owned unimproved land with an adjusted basis of $50 and a value of $150. The land was subject to a non-recourse mortgage of $60. In the current year, A, intending to make a gift, transfers the land gratuitously (but subject to the mortgage).

(a) What result to A and the transferee if the transferee is A's daughter, D?

Under Crane v. Commissioner, 334 U.S. 1 (1947), and Dietrich v. Commissioner, 457 U.S. 191 (1982), the amount of the liability encumbering the property at the time of the transfer to D is included in A's amount realized; see Treas. Reg. § 1.1001–2(a)(1) & (4)(iii). That means that the transaction is a part-gift, part-sale transaction. A realizes a gain of $10 ($60 amount realized less $50 adjusted basis); Treas. Reg. §1.1001–1(e)(1). N obtains a cost basis of $60 for the property; Treas. Reg. § 1.1015–4(a).

(b) What result if the transferee is a charitable organization specified in § 170?

Subject to the various limits of § 170(b) & (e), A is entitled to a charitable deduction for the $90 excess of the land's value over the amount of the encumbrance. In this case, however, § 1011(b) requires that A apportion the property's basis between the gift and sale parts of the transaction. The $60 amount realized represents 40 percent of the $150 value of the property, and so A apportions 40 percent of the $50 basis, or $20, to the sale portion of the transaction. A therefore has a realized gain of $40 ($60 amount realized less $20 adjusted basis).

7. Pursuant to the terms of their divorce decree, W transferred to her former husband, H, some securities with a value of $100,000 and an adjusted basis in her hands of $120,000.

(a) What tax result to W?

W recognizes no gain on the transfer to her former husband on this transfer incident to their divorce; § 1041(a).

(b) What tax result to H when he sells the securities six months later for $90,000?

H is treated as having received the securities by gift and therefore does not include the value of the securities in gross income; §§ 1041(b); 102(a). H's basis is not determined by § 1015, however, but by § 1041(b), under which H assumes W's $120,000 adjusted basis. Unlike § 1015(a), § 1041(b) contains no lower-of-basis-or-value rule. H therefore realizes a loss of $30,000 ($120,000 basis less $90,000 amount realized) on the sale of the securities. H tacks on W's holding period in determining whether the loss is short-term or long-term; § 1223(2).

8. Under the terms of a valid premarital agreement, C transferred securities to her future husband, D. C had a basis of $100 in the securities, which had a value of $500 when the agreement was entered into. In the agreement D waived his marital rights to C's property in the case of divorce or C's death. The parties subsequently divorced, and D wishes to sell the securities. What is D's basis in the securities?

D probably assumes C's $100 basis for the securities. Farid–Es–Sultaneh v. Commissioner, 160 F.2d 812 (2d Cir. 1947), held that a taxpayer who had acquired stock under a prenuptial agreement had given consideration for the transfer and therefore obtained a cost basis for the stock under § 1012. Today, however, premarital agreements usually take effect only upon marriage; see e.g., Uniform Premarital Agreement Act § 4, 9B U.L.A. 369 (1987). Even though C appears to have transferred the securities to D before their marriage, the transfer would be conditional on the marriage, and D would probably be required to return the securities if the marriage did not occur. Since C and D were wife and husband when the transfer became final, § 1041(b) gives D a transferred basis of $100 in the securities.

Chapter 19

THE BASIS OF PROPERTY ACQUIRED BY BEQUEST OR INHERITANCE

A. IN GENERAL—§ 1014

Code: §§ 1014(a), (b) & (e); 1223(9). Note § 2032.

Regulations: §§ 1.1014–1(a); –2(a) & (b); –3(a); –4(a)(3).

Case: Kenan v. Commissioner, 114 F.2d 217 (2d Cir. 1940).

1. D died on August 31, year 1, owning a share of X Corporation stock that D had purchased for $40 earlier in year 1. At the date of D's death, the share was worth $50. D bequeathed the share to B. D's executor distributed the share to B on January 31, year 2, when the share was worth $60. By February 28, year 2, the share was worth $70. B sold the share on April 15, year 2 for $80. D's Estate makes no alternate-valuation-date election under § 2032. What are the tax results to:

(a) D?

D recognizes no gain on the transfer of property at death; Rev. Rul. 73–183, 1973–1 C.B. 364. Since D's Estate generally obtains a basis equal to the value of the property at the date of death, any pre-death appreciation (or depreciation) in the value of the property disappears from the system. This is the step-up (or step-down) in basis at death.

(b) D's Estate?

The share is "property acquired from the decedent" within the meaning of § 1014(b)(1) ("property acquired * * * by the decedent's estate from the decedent"), and, therefore, the Estate gets a basis equal to the stock's $50 value on the date of death; § 1014(a). Since the share was specifically bequeathed to B, the Estate does not recognize gain upon the distribution of the share (then worth $60) to B. It is B, rather than the Estate, who benefits from the post-death appreciation, and there is no reason to tax that appreciation to the Estate when it distributes the property to B.

(c) B?

B excludes the receipt of the share from gross income under § 102(a)(property acquired by bequest). In B's hands, the property is property acquired from the decedent because it is property acquired by bequest; § 1014(b)(1). Thus, B obtains a basis of $50 (value of the share at D's death). When B sells the stock on April 15, B realizes gain of $30 ($80 amount realized less $50 basis). Although B does not have an actual long-term holding period for the stock (B's holding period begins the day following D's death), § 1223(9) gives B a long-term holding period for the share because (1) it is property acquired from a decedent under § 1014(b), (2) B has a § 1014 basis, and (3) B sold the property within one year after D's death. So, assuming, as seems likely, that the stock is a capital asset in B's hands, B's gain is a long-term capital gain.

2. Same as 1, except that the share was worth only $30 at the date of D's death (and all other values are as given in 1).

D is not allowed to deduct a loss on the transfer of depreciated property at death, and D's Estate obtains a basis of $30 (the share's value at the date of death) under § 1014(a). As above, the Estate recognizes no gain upon the distribution of the share to B, and B excludes the value of the share from gross income under § 102(a). When B sells the share for $80, B's realized gain is $50 ($80 amount realized less $30 basis). As in 1, the gain is a long-term capital gain.

3. Same as 1, except that D's executor made a valid alternate-valuation-date (AVD) election under § 2032.

If D's Estate made a valid AVD election under § 2032, then all of the assets included in D's gross estate for federal estate-tax purposes must be valued on the AVD for federal estate-tax purposes, and the alternate value of the property (rather than the date-of-death value) serves as the income-tax basis; § 1014(a)(2).

In that case, the Estate distributed the property to B on January 31, year 2, which was five months after the date of death. Where, as here, the property is distributed (or sold, exchanged, or otherwise disposed of) within six months of the date of death, the AVD is the date of distribution (or sale, exchange or other disposition). Therefore, the alternate value of the share is $60, its value on the date of distribution, and § 1014(a)(2) makes that figure the property's basis. On the subsequent sale by B, the realized gain is $20 ($80 amount realized less $60 basis). Again, § 1223(9) gives B an automatic long-term holding period, which makes the gain a long-term capital gain.

Notice that the executor's making of the AVD election gave B a higher basis than B would have gotten if the gross estate had been valued on the date of death.

Keep in mind, however, that the executor cannot make an AVD election unless the election decreases both (1) the *overall* value of the gross estate and (2) (generally) the amount of estate tax imposed. But while the overall value of the gross estate must be less on the AVD than on the date of death, some assets may be worth more on the AVD. That appears to be the case here, as we are told that the AVD election was valid; to be valid it must have reduced the overall value of the gross estate.

4. Would your answer in 3 differ if the Estate had distributed the share to B on March 15, year 2?

Yes. For property not disposed of within the six months after the decedent's death, the AVD is the sixth-month anniversary of the date of death. Here the date of death was August 31, and there is no date corresponding to the 31st in the sixth month following the date of death (February, which has only 28 or 29 days). In that case, the AVD is the last day of the sixth month; Rev. Rul. 74–260, 1974–1 C.B. 275. So, B's basis for the share is $70, its value on February 28, year 2. B's realized gain on the sale is $10 ($80 amount realized less $70 basis). Section 1223(9) makes the gain long-term.

5. D also left a legacy of $100 to C. On March 31, year 2, the executor distributed to C a share of Y Corporation stock (then worth $100) in satisfaction of the legacy. The Y share had a value of $60 at the date of D's death, which is the applicable estate-tax valuation date. C sold the share for $120 on April 15, year 2. What tax results to:

(a) D's Estate?

D's Estate must recognize gain or loss on the transfer of property in satisfaction of a fixed-dollar legacy such as this; Kenan v. Commissioner, 114 F.2d 217 (2d Cir. 1940); Treas. Reg. § 1.1014–4(a)(3). The Estate realizes and recognizes gain of $40 (the excess of the $100 value of the stock over its $60 basis). The gain is a long-term capital gain (because § 1223(9) supplies the long-term holding period). The Estate is treated as if it sold the share for its $100 value and transferred the sale proceeds to C.

(b) C?

C excludes the $100 from gross income under § 102(a), and obtains a $100 cost basis for the share under § 1012. (It is as if the Estate sold the share for $100, distributed the $100 sale proceeds to C, and C purchased the share for $100.) This result makes sense because C did not benefit from the appreciation in the value of the share from $60 (on the date of death) to $100 (on the date of distribution). C would have been entitled to $100 even if the Y share had declined in value. It is the Estate, as surrogate for the remainder beneficiaries, which is enriched by the post-death appreciation in the Y share. That's why the Estate, rather than C, is taxed on that appreciation.

When C sells the share, C realizes a gain of $20 ($120 amount realized less $100 basis). Assuming that the share is a capital asset in C's hands, the gain is a short-term capital gain because C's holding period does not exceed one year. In this case, § 1223(9) provides no relief, as the *stock* was acquired by *purchase* rather than from a decedent and C's basis is determined under § 1012 rather than § 1014.

6. P was suffering from a fatal illness. P's child, C, gave P a share of stock with an adjusted basis of $40 and a value of $100. At P's death six months later, P bequeathed the stock to C. At the date of P's death, the stock was worth $120.

(a) What is C's basis for the stock?

The stock was "appreciated property" when transferred to P because its value exceeded its adjusted basis; § 1014(e)(2). Since the appreciated property was (1) acquired by P within the year preceding P's death and (2) bequeathed by P to C (the donor), C must assume P's adjusted basis for the property; 1014(e)(1). P's adjusted basis would be that of C under § 1015(a), and, assuming no adjustments to basis while the share was held by P, C would get the share with a basis of $40.

(b) Suppose instead that P bequeathed the stock to P's child, GC. What is GC's basis for the stock?

GC would get a § 1014(a) basis of $100. Section 1014(e) does not apply because P did not bequeath the stock to the donor or the donor's spouse.

B. INCOME IN RESPECT OF A DECEDENT

Code: §§ 1014(c); 691(a)(1) & (3), (b).

Regulations: §§ 1.691(a)–1; –2; –3.

Ruling: Rev. Rul. 78–32, 1978–1 C.B. 198.

1. Define: "income in respect of a decedent."

The term "income in respect of a decedent" (IRD) is not defined in the Code. However, Treas. Reg. § 1.691(a)–1(b) says that IRD refers to:

> those amounts to which a decedent was entitled as gross income but which were not properly includible in computing his taxable income for the taxable year ending with the date of his death or for a previous taxable year under the method of accounting employed by the decedent.

2. What is the primary purpose of § 691?

The primary purpose of § 691 is to provide parity of treatment between cash-method and accrual-method taxpayers. Consider two lawyers: A uses the accrual method of tax accounting and C uses the cash method. Both perform $1,000 of legal services in their last taxable year, bill the client for the work performed and then die before collecting payment. Each estate values the claim at $1,000 for estate-tax purposes. A must accrue the $1,000 of gross income on her final return because, before A died, all of the events had occurred to fix A's right to payment and the amount of the income was determinable with reasonable accuracy. A's Estate obtains a $1,000 basis for the claim under § 1014(a) and has no further income when the executor collects the claim. C's final return does not include the $1,000 of earned but uncollected fees because cash-method taxpayers generally report income only as it is received. In the absence of a special rule, C's Estate would also obtain a $1,000 basis for the claim under § 1014(a), and C's executor would have no income when the receivable was collected after C's death. Thus, absent a special rule, the income would be taxable to the accrual-method taxpayer but would not be taxable to the cash-method taxpayer (or that person's estate).

Congress addressed this inequity by denying a step-up in basis for an item of IRD (§ 1014(c)) and requiring that IRD be included in the gross income of the decedent's successor-in-interest who collects the money. The recipient must treat the receipt as income in the same amount and of the same character (i.e., as compensation, interest, capital gain, etc.) as the decedent would have if the decedent had lived to collect the money.

An analogous problem arises in the treatment of deductions, which in most cases are allowable to an accrual-method taxpayer when the taxpayer becomes liable under the all-events test while the cash-method taxpayer's deduction is postponed until payment. For example, if the lawyers A and C, described above, died owing $500 of business expenses, A's would be deductible on her final return because the expenses had accrued before A's death, while C's would not be deductible because not paid before death. In both cases, the estate will pay the expenses after death, but, in the absence of a special rule, neither estate would get an income-tax deduction for the payment because the expenses were not incurred in "carrying on" the estate's business. That's no problem for A's Estate, as A got the deduction before she died. But it means neither C nor C's Estate will ever get an income-tax deduction for those costs of earning income. Section 691(b) ameliorates this harsh treatment of the cash-method taxpayer by allowing (generally) the estate a deduction in respect of a decedent for some expenses incurred before the taxpayer's death but paid by the estate. Notice, however, that § 691(b) allows only specified deductions; it does not cover all items that one might think would be deductions in respect of a decedent.

3. D died on November 30, year 1. Both D and D's Estate use the cash method of accounting and the calendar year. Explain the tax treatment of the following items.

(a) D's salary ($10,000) covering the month of October, year 1. The salary was collected by D's executor in December, year 1.

This is the prototype of IRD. D earned the salary before death, but it was not includable on D's final return under the cash method of accounting. Section 1014(c) denies D's Estate a stepped-up basis; § 691(a)(1) requires the Estate to include the $10,000 in its gross income when it collects the money.

(b) $250,000 proceeds from the sale of land, in which D had a basis of $100,000. D had entered into a contract to sell the land to B on October 15, year 1, with closing scheduled for December 1. All substantial prerequisites to the sale had been completed before D's death. D's executor closed the sale on December 1.

Here everything of importance was done before death to effect the sale; it remained for the executor to perform only the ministerial acts of closing the transaction and collecting the purchase price. D's Estate gets no stepped-up basis for the land and must report a gain of $150,000 ($250,000 amount realized less $100,000 basis); see Rev. Rul. 78–32, 1978–1 C.B. 198. The character of the gain (e.g., capital gain or § 1231 gain) would be the same as it would have been if D had lived to close the sale; § 691(a)(3).

(c) At death D possessed a non-statutory stock option (NSO) that entitled D to purchase a share of her employer's stock for $20. The value of the stock at D's death was $80. The option was exercised by D's executor in January, year 2, at which time the value of the stock was $100.

If D had lived to exercise the option in year 2, D would have had compensation income of $80 ($100 stock value less $20 paid); § 83(a). (This, of course, assumes that D had not made an election under § 83(b).) When the executor exercises the option, D's Estate has $80 of compensation income; § 691(a)(1) & (3).

(d) $1,000 dividend on J corporation stock held by D. The dividend, declared on November 15, was payable on December 15 to shareholders of record on December 1.

The $1,000 is includable in the income of D's Estate under § 61(a)(7). It is not an item of IRD because D did not survive until the record date. Since a dividend collected by an estate is generally going to be taxable to the estate, either as IRD or as ordinary gross income, you might ask what difference the classification makes. It makes a difference where the estate pays federal estate tax because § 691(c) allows the recipient of an item of IRD an income-tax deduction for the amount of estate tax attributable to the inclusion of the IRD item in the gross estate. The details are beyond the scope of the basic tax course.

(e) $2,000 of interest, which had been credited by the bank on D's passbook savings account but which had not been withdrawn by D before death. D's executor withdrew the funds from the account on December 15.

The $2,000 of interest would includable in gross income before D's death because D was in constructive receipt of the money; the funds had been credited to D's account, and D could have withdrawn the funds without any substantial restriction; Treas. Reg. § 1.451–2(a). The interest would be includable in whichever year D was in constructive receipt.

(f) The $100,000 balance in D's IRA account at the date of death. At D's death, the account passed to her son, S. Assume, alternatively, that:

(i) The account was a traditional IRA and D had deducted the $30,000 contributed;

Since D had deducted all of the contributions to the account, D's basis in the account was zero. If D had collected the balance in the account at the date of death, the entire balance would have been taxable to her. The date-of-death balance in the account is an item of IRD, which S must include in gross income when he withdraws the funds. Any income earned after D's death is not IRD but is ordinary income to S.

This is an example of a case in which someone other than the decedent's estate is taxable on the IRD. Here, it is S "who, by reason of the death of the decedent acquires the right to receive the amount" of IRD; § 691(a)(1)(B).

(ii) The account was a traditional IRA and D had not deducted any of the $30,000 contributed;

In this case, D had a $30,000 basis in the account. D's basis carries over to S, and S must include $70,000 in gross income as IRD when the date-of-death balance is withdrawn; § 691(a)(1).

(iii) The account was a Roth IRA.

Qualified distributions from a Roth IRA are excluded from income; 408A(d)(1). Qualified distributions include those made to a beneficiary after the account holder's death; § 408A(d)(2). So, no gross income to S.

4. D, who used the cash method, died in November, year 1, owing the following amounts, all of which were paid by D's executor after D's death. Both D and D's Estate use the cash method. Which are allowable as deductions on the estate's income-tax return for the year of payment?

(a) $10,000 of business expenses of D's sole proprietorship;

The $10,000 would be allowable to D's Estate as a deduction in respect of a decedent (DRD), as it was an amount accrued at D's death but not allowable to D because not paid before D's death. It is an expense specified in § 162 and therefore is allowable to D's Estate when paid by it; § 691(b)(1).

(b) $2,000 of interest on acquisition indebtedness on D's personal residence;

This deduction would have been allowable to D under § 163(a) (and not disallowed under § 163(h)) if paid by D before death. It is allowed as a DRD to D's Estate.

(c) $5,000 of alimony covering the period immediately before D's death;

Section 215 would have allowed a deduction to D if D had lived to pay the alimony, but § 215 is not included among the sections that can give rise to DRD; see § 691(b). D's Estate cannot deduct the alimony arrearage under § 691(b), but it may get some tax benefit by treating the payment as a distribution to the spouse as a beneficiary. The details, prescribed by § 682, are beyond the scope of the basic course.

(d) $3,500 of state income tax for D's final taxable year;

This qualifies as a DRD by D's Estate, as it is a deduction specified by § 164; see § 691(b).

(e) $12,000 of medical expenses incurred during D's final illness.

The medical-expense deduction of § 213 is not specified in § 691(b), and D's Estate cannot deduct the $12,000 as a DRD. Under § 213(c), however, expenses paid by a decedent's estate within the year following the decedent's death can, at the estate's election, be treated as having been paid by the decedent at the time incurred. If D's executor makes this election, D may be able to deduct the expenses on the return covering the period in which the expenses were incurred. The expenses would be subject to the 7.5–percent AGI floor on the deduction imposed by § 213(a).

In order to make this election, the Estate must waive its right to an estate-tax deduction for the expenses as a claim against the estate under § 2053. The election should always be made when the estate will not owe estate tax. It should not be made if foregoing the estate-tax deduction would increase the amount of estate tax due, as the estate-tax rate for a taxable estate is 45 percent, which is higher than the top income-tax rate of 35%.

Section F

NON-RECOGNITION TRANSACTIONS AND (DIS)ALLOWANCE OF LOSSES

Chapter 20

LIKE-KIND EXCHANGES

Code: §§ 1031(a), (b), (c), (d), (e) & (h)(1); 1223(1). Note §§ 1001(c); 7701(a)(45).

Regulations: §§ 1.1031(a)–1; 1.1031(b)–1; 1.1031(d)–1; 1.1031(d)–2.

Cases: Leslie Co. v. Commissioner, 64 T.C. 247 (1975) (Non-acq.), aff'd, 539 F.2d
943 (3d Cir. 1976);
Jordan Marsh Co. v. Commissioner, 269 F.2d 453 (2d Cir. 1959).

Ruling: Rev. Rul. 77–297, 1977–2 C.B. 304.

1. A transferred a building (the "old" building) to B in exchange for
another building (the "new" building) and, in some of the following cases,
other consideration. Unless otherwise indicated, the old building had an
adjusted basis of $40 (000 omitted throughout) and had been held by A for
two years at the time of the exchange. Both buildings were used by A in
business. In each of the following cases, determine the amount of A's (1)
realized gain or loss; (2) recognized gain or loss; (3) adjusted basis
(immediately after the exchange) for all property acquired; and (4)
holding period for all property acquired.

(a) Both the old and new buildings had a value of $100.

Introduction: This is the first non-recognition provision that we have
examined in detail, so let's consider briefly this idea of non-recognition. We have
noted that § 1001(a) prescribes the method of computing realized gain and loss.
But realized gains are not includable in gross income (nor are realized losses
deductible), unless they are also *recognized*. Section 1001(c) tells us that all
realized gains and losses are also recognized, *except where otherwise provided*.
These otherwise-providing provisions are known as non-recognition rules, of which
§ 1031 is a prime example.

Why might Congress have concluded that an exchange of property such as that in our problem was not an appropriate occasion for tax reckoning? If A does not engage in the exchange, there is no realization event, and A is not taxed on the gain potential in the old building. Is the exchange a sufficiently salient event that we can justify taxing A when we don't tax one who does not trade properties? To be sure, the exchange is a realization event, but, from an economic standpoint, one can argue that nothing very interesting has occurred. Both before and after the exchange A's capital is tied up in a business building—i.e., A's investment continues without interruption, albeit in slightly different form. The transaction does not generate any cash with which to pay tax. And valuing the new building for the purpose of determining A's amount realized and realized gain may be difficult. Recall that illiquidity and valuation difficulties are two important reasons why we have the realization requirement. Taxing a like-kind exchange would engender some of the same problems that we would encounter in attempting to tax unrealized gains. Congress therefore concluded that the like-kind exchange is not an appropriate occasion for reckoning tax gains and losses.

Even though Congress agreed that the exchange should not trigger tax on A's gain, it did not intend to exempt that gain from tax forever. It acquiesced only in postponing the tax until a more-appropriate taxing opportunity arose. That is, non-recognition entails *deferral* of the gain—not tax exemption. The mechanism for achieving deferral is the transfer of the basis from the old property to the new. Notice in the discussion below how the basis transfer preserves the unrecognized gain for future recognition when the new property is sold.

As to the particulars of the problem, A's amount realized is $100 (the value of the new building), the adjusted basis of the old building was $40, and, therefore, A has a realized gain on the exchange of $60. The old and new buildings are properties of like kind (both held for use in business), and the exchange qualifies for non-recognition under § 1031(a). Thus, A's recognized gain is zero. A's adjusted basis for the new building is $40, the same as the basis for the old; § 1031(d).

Notice that if A were to sell the new building for its value of $100, A would realize and recognize a gain of $60. That $60 represents the gain that was realized but unrecognized on the like-kind exchange. You can see from this example how non-recognition entails deferral—not exemption of the gain.

The building is a § 1231 asset (discussed in Chapter 28), and so A's holding period (for capital-gain purposes) includes the period during which A held the old building; § 1223(1).

A depreciates the new building over the remaining recovery period for the old building using the same convention and depreciation method that was used for the old building; Treas. Reg. § 1.168(i)–6.

(b) Same as (a), except that A held the new building as an investment.

Same result as (a); property used in business can be exchanged for property to be used for investment and vice versa; Treas. Reg. § 1.1031(a)–1(a)(1).

(c) The old building was worth $100, but the new building was worth only $80, and B paid A $20 cash to equalize the exchange.

A's amount realized is $100 ($80 value of new building, plus $20 cash), and A's realized gain is $60, as before. Section 1031(a) does not apply because the old building was not exchanged "solely" for property of like kind but for like-kind property and cash. (Cash or property other than like-kind property is referred to as "boot.") In a pattern that we will see recur in the non-recognition provisions, § 1031(b) requires that, where the taxpayer receives boot in an exchange, the taxpayer's realized gain is recognized to the extent of the boot received. Here, therefore, § 1031(b) requires that A recognize gain of $20.

A's basis for the new building is $40 ($40 adjusted basis of old building, less $20 cash received, plus $20 gain recognized); § 1031(d). Think about the reasons for these adjustments. In non-recognition, we first transfer the basis from the old property to the new in order to preserve for future reckoning the unrecognized gain or loss from the old property. The receipt of cash represents disinvestment from the old property, which means the basis of the old property should be reduced by that amount. (Think of that $20 of basis as being reassigned from the old property to the cash, which always attracts basis equal to its face amount.) To the extent that the taxpayer recognizes gain on the exchange, the basis of the new property should be increased so that same gain is not recognized a second time when the new property is sold. (This is another example of tax-cost basis.)

To satisfy ourselves that the basis computation is correct, let us suppose that immediately after the exchange (and before taking further depreciation) A sells the new building for its value of $80. A's realized and recognized gain would be $40 ($80 amount realized less $40 adjusted basis). In effect, A would have converted the old building (adjusted basis $40) into $100 of cash in two steps—first exchanging the old building for the new plus $20 cash and then selling the new for $80 cash. The total gain recognized on the two transactions is $60 ($20 on the exchange, plus $40 on the sale of the new building). That is the same amount that would have been recognized if A had sold the old building for cash. Our basis analysis thus produces the correct result.

As in (a), A can "tack on" the holding period of the old building to that of the new, as the properties are treated as having the same basis "in part" whenever the basis of the new property is determined by reference to the basis of the old, even though there are adjustments made (in this case, for cash received and gain recognized) to the basis of the old in arriving at the basis of the new.

(d) The old building was worth $100, but the new building was worth only $70, and B transferred to A an automobile (worth $30) to equalize the exchange.

A's amount realized is $100 ($70 value of he building, plus $30 value of the automobile), and the realized gain is $60 ($100 amount realized less $40 adjusted basis). Section 1031(b) requires that the realized gain be recognized to the extent of the boot received. Here the automobile is boot, and its receipt triggers the recognition of $30 of gain on the exchange.

A's basis for *all* of the property received is $70 ($40 adjusted basis of the old building, plus the $30 of gain recognized on the exchange); § 1031(d). A must allocate this basis between the new building and the automobile by apportioning to the automobile an amount equal to its value. So, $30 of basis is allocated to the automobile, leaving basis of $40 for the new building.

A's holding period for the new building includes the period during which A held the old building. A's holding period for the automobile begins the day following the day of the exchange. (Holding periods are computed by excluding the day of acquisition and including the day of disposition; Rev. Rul. 66–97, 1966–1 C.B. 190.)

(e) The old building was worth $70 and the new building was worth $100. In order to equalize the exchange, A paid B $30 cash.

Now A is the payor of boot. A receives an interest in the new building in exchange for the old building, so the exchange is within § 1031(a)—i.e., A *receives* no boot on the exchange. A receives a $70 portion of the new building in exchange for the old and therefore realizes a gain of $30 ($70 amount realized less $40 adjusted basis). The gain is not recognized. A's basis for the new building is $70 ($40 adjusted basis of the old building, plus $30 of additional cash invested); §§ 1031(d); 1012; Treas. Reg. § 1.1031(d)–1(a). A's holding period for the new building includes the holding period of the old; § 1223(1).

(f) The old building was worth $70. In order to equalize the exchange, A also transferred to B shares of X Corp. stock with a value of $30 and an adjusted basis of $50.

Again A is the payor of boot, but now A can recognize the loss on the transfer of the stock because an exchange of stock for a building is not an exchange of like kind. In determining the amount of loss realized on the transfer of the stock, A is deemed to have received a $30 portion of the building in exchange; Treas. Reg. § 1.1031(d)–1(e). Thus, A realizes loss of $20 ($50 adjusted basis less $30 amount realized) on the stock-for-building exchange, and the loss must be recognized under the general rule of recognition; § 1001(c). A's adjusted basis for the new building is $70 ($90 total adjusted bases of the old building and the stock, less $20 of loss recognized); § 1031(d); Treas. Reg. § 1.1031(d)–1(e). A can tack the holding period of the old building to that of the new; § 1223(1).

(g) The old building, which had an unencumbered value of $100, was subject to a non-recourse mortgage of $20. The new building was worth $80.

The last sentence of § 1031(d) treats the transferee's taking subject to the mortgage as a payment of cash to A, so the answers are the same as in problem (c).

(h) The old building was worth $100. The new building was worth $120 but was subject to a non-recourse mortgage of $20.

Now A is, in effect, paying boot by acquiring the new building subject to the mortgage. A's realized gain on the exchange is not recognized under § 1031(a). A's basis for the new building is $60 ($40 of basis transferred from the old building under § 1031(d), plus $20 of cost basis under § 1012 and *Crane*). A's holding period for the new building includes the holding period for the old under § 1223(1).

(i) Same as (a), except that A's adjusted basis for the old building was $125.

A realizes a loss of $25 ($125 adjusted basis less $100 amount realized), but § 1031(a) provides for non-recognition of the loss. A's adjusted basis for the new building is $125, the same as for the old building; § 1031(d). A can tack on the holding period of the old building to that of the new; § 1223(1).

(j) Same as (a), except that A's adjusted basis for the old building was $125, the value of the new building was $80, and B paid A $20 cash to equalize the exchange.

A's amount realized on the transfer of the old building is $100 ($80 value of the new building, plus $20 cash); § 1001(b). A's realized loss is $25 ($125 adjusted basis less $100 amount realized); § 1001(a). No loss is recognized on the like-kind exchange even though A receives boot on the exchange; § 1031(c). A's adjusted basis for the new building is $105 ($125 adjusted basis of the old less $20 cash received); § 1031(d). (Notice how the basis result preserves the $25 unrecognized loss for future recognition when the new building is sold for its value of $80.) A can again tack on the holding period of the old building to that of the new; § 1223(1).

2. **In each of the following problems, determine whether the exchange would qualify as "like kind" under § 1031. Unless otherwise indicated, assume that all properties are to be held for use in business or investment.**

(a) An apartment building in Chicago for unimproved farm land in Idaho.

Yes, these are like-kind properties, even though the investment characteristics of the properties differ markedly. Real estate is considered to be a single, broad class of property for purposes of the like-kind requirement; see Treas. Reg. § 1.1031(a)–1(b) & (c). A fee interest in one parcel of real estate is therefore considered to be of like kind with another; e.g., Treas. Reg. § 1.1031(a)–1(c) (exchange of city real estate for a farm or ranch qualifies as like kind, as does an exchange of improved for unimproved real estate); Hamilton v. Commissioner, 30 B.T.A. 160 (1934) (improved city real estate exchanged for ranch land was like-kind exchange). Parcels of real estate are of like kind even though they are located in different geographic areas. For example, Rev. Rul. 68–363, 1968–2 C.B. 336, which was issued before the enactment of § 1031(h), held that a ranch located in the United States was like kind with a ranch located in a foreign country.

(b) A condominium in Naples, Florida (held for rental) for a condominium in Naples, Italy (also to be held for rental).

These are not of like kind because of § 1031(h), which says that real property located within the United States is not of like kind with property located outside the United States.

(c) A female calf for a male calf.

Not of like kind; § 1031(e). The idea seems to be that male calves, which are usually sold in the ordinary course of business, should not be exchanged tax-free for female calves in order to build up a breeding herd. Section 1031(e) just clarifies prior law, as property held for sale in the ordinary course of business could never be exchanged without the recognition of gain or loss (see § 1031(a)(2)(A)), but some tax-shelter promoters advertised to the contrary, and Congress responded with the enactment of § 1031(e).

3. **T owns a business building with an adjusted basis of $500 (000 omitted throughout) and a value of $300. T plans to sell the building to P for $300 cash. P will then lease the building back to T for thirty years (which is a period shorter than the building's remaining economic life) at a fair market rental for a lease of that term. Will T be permitted to deduct the loss on the sale?**

Probably. The Commissioner has had limited success in attacking these sale-leaseback transactions where the property is leased back to the former owner at fair rental value. The regulations say that real property and a 30–year leasehold of real property are properties of like kind; Treas. Reg. §1.1031(a)–1(c)(1). The Commissioner's argument is that the transaction is a like-kind exchange of the fee for the leasehold, with the transferee also paying cash boot (the purchase price). Under this analysis, T cannot recognize loss even though boot is received; § 1031(c). T acquires the leasehold with a basis of $200 ($500 basis of property exchanged less $300 cash received). The basis could be amortized over the 30–year term of the lease; Treas. Reg. 1.167(a)–3(b)(1).

When the lease is at fair rental value, however, it is difficult to detect any "exchange," as the transferee of the building is paying full value for the fee; see, e.g., Leslie Co. v. Commissioner, 64 T.C. 247 (1975) (Non-acq.), aff'd, 539 F.2d 943 (3d Cir. 1976) (holding for taxpayer); Jordan Marsh Co. v. Commissioner, 269 F.2d 453 (2d Cir. 1959) (holding for taxpayer and distinguishing Century Electric Co. v. Commissioner, 192 F.2d 155 (8th Cir. 1951), which held for the Commissioner, as involving an exchange for a below-market lease that had a capital value and cash boot). So, on these facts, § 1031(c) probably does not apply, and T's loss will be recognized.

The Commissioner might also argue that the arrangement is equivalent to T's giving a 30-year mortgage on the property, though this argument seems unlikely to succeed here where the economic life of the building exceeds the lease term, and the property does not revert to T at the end of the 30 years.

4. **T, a calendar-year taxpayer, owned a business building (the T building) with an adjusted basis of $200 (000 omitted throughout) and value of $500. P wished to acquire the building, either for cash or in exchange for another building. Under a written agreement between T and P, P placed $500 in escrow on March 31 to cover payment for the T building, but T was given one year to find a suitable business building for P to purchase and exchange for the T building. If T did not locate suitable replacement property within the one-year period, the deal was to be cancelled and the escrowed funds returned to P. Nine months later, T located a suitable replacement building, which P purchased for the $500 held in escrow and promptly exchanged for the T building. Must T recognize the $300 of realized gain?**

No. T has exchanged the T building for the replacement building; Rev. Rul. 77–297, 1977–2 C.B. 304. The deferred-exchange rules of § 1031(a)(3) do not come into play here, as T made no conveyance of the T building until P had acquired the replacement property.

5. **Same as 4, except that on March 31 T transferred the T building to P, who agreed to acquire replacement property suitable to T and placed $500 in escrow to pay for the replacement property. If no replacement property had been identified by December 31, T could require that P pay the escrowed funds to T in lieu of acquiring replacement property for exchange with T. T located replacement property on September 30. P used the escrowed funds to purchase the property and transferred the replacement property to T on October 31. Must T recognize the realized gain?**

Yes, T must recognize the $300 gain because the deferred-exchange rules of § 1031(a)(3) were not complied with. The replacement property was not identified to the contract until September 30, which is more than 45 days after T transferred the T property; this violates the identification-period requirement of § 1031(a)(3)(A). And the exchange-period requirement of § 1031(a)(3)(B) was also violated because the replacement property was not conveyed to T within 180 days of T's transfer of the T building. As a result, § 1031(a)(3) treats the replacement property as property of other than like kind with the T building.

If the replacement property had been identified to the contract by May 15 (i.e., within 45 days after March 31), and the property conveyed to T by September 27 (i.e., within 180 days after March 31), then the replacement property would have qualified as property of like kind with the T building under § 1031(a)(3).

Chapter 21

INVOLUNTARY CONVERSIONS

Code: §§ 1033(a), (b) & (g); 1223(1).

Regulations: §§ 1.1033(a)–2(c)(11); 1.1033(b)–1(b).

Ruling: Rev. Rul. 64–237, 1964–2 C.B. 319.

In each of the following problems, determine the amount of the taxpayer's (1) realized gain or loss; (2) recognized gain or loss; and (3) adjusted basis (immediately after the acquisition) of any replacement property acquired. Also explain how you would go about determining the holding period of the replacement property.

1. T, a calendar-year taxpayer, owned a building (the "old building") with an adjusted basis of $60 (000 omitted throughout) and a value of $100. The old building, which was situated on leased land, was used in T's restaurant business. On June 30, year 1, the old building was completely destroyed by fire, and T received $100 in insurance proceeds. On December 31, year 3, T purchased a replacement building (also situated on leased land) in which he opened a new restaurant. T paid $110 for the replacement building. T elects non-recognition under § 1033. (How should T report the transaction on T's year–1 tax return?)

T realizes gain of $40 ($100 amount realized less $60 adjusted basis); § 1001(a). This is an involuntary conversion of the building into money, and T elected to avoid recognition of gain as permitted under § 1033(a)(2)(A). T was required to replace the property within two years following the close of the year in which the gain was realized; § 1033(a)(3). The last day for acquiring replacement property was December 31, year 3, and T's replacement was timely because made on that day. The replacement property—another restaurant building—is similar "in service or use" to the property involuntarily converted, as required by § 1033(a)(2)(A).

Since T made a timely reinvestment in qualifying replacement property, T recognizes the realized gain only to the extent that the amount realized on the involuntary conversion exceeds the cost of the replacement property. Here the amount realized was $100 and T reinvested $110—more than the amount realized—and therefore T recognizes no gain.

T's adjusted basis for the replacement property is its cost less the amount of realized but unrecognized gain on the involuntary conversion; § 1033(b)(2). Here the unrecognized gain was $40, and the adjusted basis of the replacement property is $70 ($110 replacement cost less $40 of unrecognized gain on involuntary conversion). Consider what would happen if T were to sell the replacement property for its value of $110. T would realize and recognize a gain of $40, which represents the gain that was deferred at the time of the involuntary conversion. (Remember: Non-recognition entails deferral—not exemption.)

We will see later that the old building was a § 1231 asset (depreciable real property used in business), and, therefore, the holding period of the replacement building includes the period during which T held the old building; § 1223(1). Notice how § 1223(1)(A) treats the involuntary conversion as an "exchange" so as to fit the transaction into the requirement that the new property be "received in an exchange." A question may also arise as to whether the replacement property has the same basis "in whole or in part" as the old building since our starting point in determining the basis of the replacement building was its cost rather than the basis of the old building. Yet, § 1223(1)(A) suggests that Congress intended to permit tacking of holding periods in § 1033 involuntary conversions, and Rev. Rul. 72–451, 1972–2 C.B. 480, confirms that tacking is indeed permitted.

Since the replacement property has not been acquired by the time to file her year–1 tax return, what is T to report on that return concerning the involuntary conversion? According to the regulations, T should report the details of the involuntary conversion on her year–1 return but signify her election not to recognize the gain by excluding the gain from gross income; Treas. Reg. § 1.1033(a)–2(c)(2). T should also report the details of acquiring the replacement property on her return for the year in which the replacement occurs—year 3 in this case. If T does not make a timely replacement of the old building, T must file an amended return for year 1 and recognize the gain realized on the involuntary conversion; id. The statute of limitations on assessing a deficiency attributable to the gain is extended until three years after the taxpayer notifies the Commissioner of the replacement of the converted property or of an intention not to replace it; § 1033(a)(2)(C).

The rationale for non-recognition under § 1033 is that the position of one who suffers an involuntary conversion, receives insurance compensation, and reinvests the insurance proceeds in similar property differs little from one who suffered no conversion of her property. Of course, if T had voluntarily sold the property and reinvested the sales proceeds, T would be taxed on any realized gain. But non-recognition is thought justified in the involuntary-conversion case because (1) the disposition is non-volitional and (2) business exigencies often require the taxpayer to promptly replace the converted property.

2. Same as 1, except that T invested only $85 in the replacement building.

Now T must recognize the $40 realized gain to the extent of $15 (the excess of the $100 amount realized on the involuntary conversion over the $85 replacement cost); § 1033(a)(2). T has pocketed the $15 of cash insurance proceeds and is taxed on the realized gain to that extent. This leaves $25 of gain unrecognized ($40 gain realized less $15 gain recognized). T's adjusted basis for the replacement property is $60 ($85 replacement cost less $25 unrecognized gain); § 1033(b)(2). T can continue to tack the holding period of the old building to that of the replacement property; § 1223(1).

3. Same as 1, except that T received only $80 of insurance proceeds and invested $80 in the replacement building.

Now T's realized gain is $20 ($80 amount realized less $60 adjusted basis). T reinvested the full amount realized, so no gain is recognized. T's adjusted basis for the replacement building is $60 ($80 replacement cost less $20 unrecognized gain). T's holding period for the replacement includes the holding period for the old building. The $20 economic loss ($100 value of building less $80 insurance proceeds) is not deductible.

4. Same as 1, except that the destroyed building had been subject to a $40 non-recourse mortgage. Under the "mortgagee clause" in T's insurance policy, the insurance company paid $40 directly to the mortgagee, paid the $60 balance to T, and T purchased the replacement building for $60 cash.

Under Crane v. Commissioner, 334 U.S. 1 (1947), and its progeny, T's amount realized includes the amount paid by the insurer to the mortgagee; see Treas. Reg. § 1.1033(a)–2(c)(11). Therefore, T's amount realized is $100, the realized gain is $40 ($100 amount realized less $60 adjusted basis), and the recognized gain is $40 ($100 amount realized less $60 replacement cost). T's adjusted basis for the replacement building is $60 ($60 cost less zero unrecognized gain). T's holding period for the replacement includes the holding period for the old building.

5. Same as 1, except that T's adjusted basis in the old building was $120.

Now T realizes a loss of $20 ($120 adjusted basis less $100 amount realized). The loss is recognized, as § 1033(a)(2) provides non-recognition only for gains. T's unadjusted basis for the replacement property is its cost of $110; § 1012. T's holding period begins on January 1, year 4 (the day after the property is acquired); Rev. Rul. 66–97, 1966–1 C.B. 190.

6. Same as 1, except that, instead of a restaurant, the replacement building was an apartment building.

Here the replacement building does not meet the similar-use test of § 1033(a)(2)(A). The Commissioner generally interprets the similar-use test as requiring the converted and replacement properties to have a close functional similarity; Rev. Rul. 64–237, 1964–2 C.B. 319. Use as an apartment building is not similar to use as a restaurant, and T's realized gain of $40 must therefore be recognized. T gets a $110 cost basis in the replacement building and starts afresh on the holding period.

7. Same as 1, except that T is a real-estate investor, who leased the old building to another for use as a restaurant. When the old building was destroyed, T replaced it with an apartment building.

In this case, the replacement property probably satisfies the similar-use test. Where the taxpayer is an investor, the test is applied by considering the similarity in the uses to which the converted and replacement properties have been put by the taxpayer. If the taxpayer is a lessor, as here, the test focuses on "whether the properties are of similar service to the taxpayer, the nature of the business risks connected with the properties, and what such properties demand in the way of management services and relations to * * * tenants." Rev. Rul. 64–237, 1964–2 C.B. 319, 320. This is sometimes referred to as the taxpayer-use test, as it focuses on the way in which the taxpayer uses the property. Here both buildings have been rented to tenants. Assuming that the level of services that T provided the tenants was similar and that the nature of T's business risks in the two properties were similar, the properties should satisfy the similar-use test, and the results are the same as in 1.

8. Same as 1, except that the old property was a beach house (T's vacation home), and T replaced the property with a mountain ski lodge (also to be used by T as a vacation home).

Same as 1. The point of this problem is that, unlike the non-recognition rule of § 1031, § 1033 applies to personal-use property. The only question is whether the ski lodge and the beach house meet the similar-use test. They should. T uses them in a similar way—as a vacation home. The fact that one is located on a beach and the other in the mountains should not be sufficient reason to deny non-recognition.

9. Same as 1, except that, instead of the replacement building, T purchased all of the stock in a corporation that owned as its only asset the replacement building.

Same as 1. Section 1033(a)(2)(A) permits the taxpayer to avoid recognition by purchasing a controlling interest in the stock of a corporation that owns qualifying replacement property. ("Control" refers to ownership of at least 80 percent of the total combined voting power of all classes of voting stock and at least 80 percent of the total number of shares of all other classes of stock; § 1033(a)(2)(E)(i).) T recognizes no gain and obtains a basis in the stock of $70 ($110 cost less $40 unrecognized gain). The holding period of the stock includes the holding period of the old building.

10. In year 1, the state condemned 20 acres of a 100–acre parcel of unimproved farm land owned by F. F's adjusted basis in the condemned land was $40, and F received $100 as compensation for the taking. F made a timely reinvestment of the $100 condemnation proceeds by erecting an apartment building on a portion of the remaining land.

The apartment building does not appear to be similar in use to the farm land that was condemned. But § 1033(g)(1) says that, where business or investment property is condemned, replacement property of like kind with the condemned property is considered to be property of similar use. Therefore, the replacement may qualify if the farm land is property of like kind with the apartment building. Although it is well established under the like-kind-exchange rules of § 1031 that a fee interest in real property, including any buildings located thereon, is like kind with unimproved real property, the Commissioner asserts that improvements alone are not like kind with a fee interest in land. The Service contends that, although the term "real estate" is often used to embrace both land and improvements, land is not of the same nature or character as a building even though one term is used to describe both; e.g., Rev. Rul. 76-391, 1976-2 C.B. 243 (commercial building erected on land already owned by taxpayer not like kind with unimproved farm land that had been condemned); Rev. Rul. 71-41, 1971-1 C.B. 223 (gas station erected on land already owned by the taxpayer not like kind with condemned warehouse and land on which it was situated).

The Commissioner's position is inconsistent with the regulations and cases that treat improved land as property of like kind with unimproved land. If unimproved land is exchanged for improved land, there is necessarily an exchange of some portion of the interest in the unimproved land for the improvements on the improved land. In the only decided case on the issue, a United States District Court rejected the Commissioner's position that improvements are not like kind with real property; Davis v. United States, 411 F. Supp. 964 (D. Hawaii 1976), aff'd on other grounds, 589 F.2d 446 (1979) (rural agricultural land was like kind with storm drains, water systems and roads constructed on land already owned by taxpayer for use as industrial park). So, F may not be required to recognize the gain but may have to litigate the issue.

11. Same as 10, except that the apartment building was not built until year 4.

Although the replacement property generally must be acquired not later than two years after the close of the first taxable year in which the gain was realized, § 1033(g)(4) extends the replacement period by one year when business or investment property is condemned. Therefore, F's acquisition of the replacement property was timely. As discussed in the preceding answer, however, the difficult question is whether F can persuade the Service (or a court) that the farm land and apartment building are properties of like kind.

Chapter 22

SALE OF A PRINCIPAL RESIDENCE UNDER SECTION 121

Code: § 121. Review § 1033.

Regulations: §§ 1.121–2; 121–3; 121–4(a) &(b). Note § 1.263(a)–2(e).

1. T, a single person, has owned and resided in her home (Home A) for the past 30 months. T's adjusted basis is $100,000. T sells the home for $600,000 and pays a brokerage commission of $30,000 on the sale. T has not used the § 121 exclusion in the two years preceding the sale. How much of the gain must T include in gross income?

T's amount realized on the sale is $570,000 ($600,000 selling price less $30,000 brokerage commission); cf. Treas. Reg. § 1.263(a)–2(e) (commission paid on sale of securities reduces amount realized). Her realized gain is $470,000 ($570,000 amount realized less $100,000 adjusted basis). T can exclude a portion of the gain from gross income if she meets the requirements of § 121. In order to qualify for the exclusion, T must satisfy the "ownership" and "use" requirements of § 121(a). For two out of the five years preceding the sale, T must have *owned* the property and must have *used* it as her principal residence. Having owned and resided in the residence for the 30 months preceding the sale, T satisfies those requirements. The exclusion is limited to $250,000 for a single person; § 121(b)(1). T must include the remaining $220,000 of gain in gross income.

Section 121 provides an exclusion from gross income rather than non-recognition. Be clear about the difference: The gain excluded by § 121 will never be subject to tax; a true non-recognition rule (e.g., § 1031 or § 1033) entails deferral—the unrecognized gain or loss is deferred until the taxpayer makes a taxable disposition of the property.

Why, you might ask, is § 121 discussed in this section of the book (dealing with non-recognition) rather than in the material on exclusions? It's tradition. Section 121 was enacted in response to problems with former § 1034, which used to provide non-recognition when taxpayers sold one home and purchased another.

2. Same as 1, except that T is married and T's spouse also resided in Home A for the past 30 months. T and her spouse file a joint return.

Since both spouses meet the use requirement and T satisfies the ownership requirement, they can exclude up to $500,000 on their joint return; § 121(b)(2)(A). (This assumes that T's spouse has not used the § 121 exclusion in the preceding two years.) They can therefore exclude the entire $470,000 gain from income.

3. Same as 1, except that T had used the § 121 exclusion on the sale of another residence (Home B) exactly one year before the sale of Home A. Assume, alternatively, that:

(a) T sold Home A because T thought that housing prices might collapse. T moved into an apartment.

Notice at the outset that when Home B was sold one year ago, T could have satisfied the two-out-of-five-year-ownership and -use requirements with respect to that residence even though T has resided in Home A for the past 30 months. So, we can safely assume that the earlier sale qualified for the § 121 exclusion.

A taxpayer generally cannot use the § 121 exclusion if it was used on another sale that occurred within the preceding two years, as T did here; § 121(b)(3). T does not qualify for any of the exceptions in § 121(c), so the entire $470,000 gain must be included in gross income.

What if the earlier sale had produced a much smaller gain than the current sale? Suppose, e.g., that T's earlier sale had resulted in a gain of only $10,000, all of which was excluded from income under § 121. Section 121(f) permits T to elect not to have the provision apply to the earlier sale. T can elect not to apply § 121 by filing an amended return for the year in which the earlier sale occurred and including the $10,000 in gross income; Treas. Reg. § 1.121–4(g). Then T could exclude $250,000 of the gain on the current sale.

(b) T sold Home A, which was located 15 miles from her place of employment, because she was being transferred by her employer to a new place of employment located 45 miles from Home A.

In this case, T may qualify for an exception to the once-every-two-years rule because the sale of Home A was occasioned by a change in the place of T's employment; § 121(c)(2). The regulations create a "safe harbor" under which a taxpayer is deemed to have sold the property because of a change in employment if (1) the change in place of employment occurs while the taxpayer owned and was using the residence as her principal residence, and (2) her new place of employment is at least 50 miles farther from the residence sold than was the former place of employment; Treas. Reg. § 1.121–3(c)(2). T satisfies the first condition, but not the second, as the new place of employment is only 45 miles farther from Home A than was her old place of employment.

Even though T does not qualify under the safe harbor, she can still qualify for the change-of-employment exception if she can establish, based upon all of the facts and circumstances, that the primary reason for the sale of Home A was her change in place of employment. T has a strong argument for qualifying here because (1) the sale was close in time to the change in employment; (2) T was using the property as her principal residence while she owned it; (3) the employment change was presumably not reasonably foreseeable when T purchased Home A 30 months earlier; and (4) the changed circumstances occurred while T was occupying the property as her principal residence; see Treas. Reg. § 1.121–3(b) & (c)(4), Exs. 3 & 4.

Assuming that T qualifies for the change-of-employment exception, she can use the exclusion, but the maximum amount excludable is reduced; § 121(c)(1). Since the prior sale occurred one year before the current sale, T gets a maximum exclusion of $125,000 (one-half of $250,000); § 121(c)(1)(A). T excludes $125,000 of gain and includes $345,000.

(c) T sold Home A because she had just obtained a divorce.

T qualifies for the "unforeseen circumstances" exception of § 121(c)(2)(B). Divorce is a specific-event safe harbor, which means that the sale is deemed to be by reason of an unforeseen circumstance; Treas. Reg. § 1.121–3(e)(2)(iii)(D). So, as in (b), T excludes $125,000 of gain and includes $345,000.

(d) T sold Home A (a three-story house) because T had just been diagnosed as having a serious heart condition and her doctor advised her to move to a one-story house so that she would not have to climb stairs.

This case falls within the health exception to the once-every-two-years rule. Where the sale is recommended by a physician for reasons of health, it falls within the physician's-recommendation safe harbor; Treas. Reg. § 1.121–3(d)(2).

Again, T excludes $125,000 of gain and includes $345,000.

4. Same as 2, except that T and T's spouse, S, were married just before the sale of Home A. S never resided with T in the home, as T moved into S's home. T and S file a joint return.

The sale by T obviously qualifies for the exclusion. The issue is whether the ceiling on the exclusion is $250,000 or $500,000. Although the parties file a joint return, S does not meet the use requirement of § 121(a), and therefore the special rule for joint returns does not apply; see § 121(b)(2)(A)(ii).

The parties exclude $250,000 of gain and include $220,000.

5. R and R's spouse, S, owned (as joint tenants with right of survivorship) and resided in their home for many years. S died earlier this year. R has just sold the home for a gain of $650,000. What is the maximum amount that R can exclude from income on the couple's joint return?

The ownership and use requirements are satisfied. Both R and S satisfy the two-out-of-five-year-use requirement. R satisfies the ownership requirement only as to an undivided half interest, but in the case of a joint return the ownership and use requirements are met if either spouse meets them (§ 121(d)(1)), and S meets the ownership requirement for the other half interest. They can exclude $500,000 (and include $150,000) on their joint return.

6. **Would your answer in 5 differ if R was unable to sell the home until the year following S's death?**

As noted above, R easily satisfies the use requirement of § 121(a), but what about the ownership requirement? R owned only an undivided half-interest in the property until S's death. That's not a problem, however, as S's ownership is attributed to R by § 121(d)(2). R cannot file a joint return with S in the year following S's death, and the exclusion is therefore limited to $250,000. The remaining $400,000 of gain is includable in R's gross income.

7. **P and Q (husband and wife) had resided for several years in a home owned by P. They were divorced last week, and the divorce property settlement awarded ownership of the home to Q. Q, who is now single, sells the home today at a gain of $300,000. How much of the gain can Q exclude from income?**

The value of property acquired from a former spouse incident to the divorce is excluded from gross income, and the transferee spouse assumes the transferor's basis for the property; § 1041(b). Q meets the use requirement of § 121, but she has owned the residence for only a week. Relief is provided by § 121(d)(3)(A), which attributes P's ownership to Q where Q acquired the property in a transfer covered by § 1041. Q thus qualifies for the exclusion to the extent of $250,000. The other $50,000 of gain must included in Q's gross income.

8. **L and M were divorced five years ago. Under the terms of their property settlement, M was permitted to continue to occupy the couple's residence for five years, after which time the property was to be sold and the sales proceeds divided equally between L and M. (L and M owned the property as tenants-in-common.) The property was sold in the current year at a gain of $600,000. How much, if any, of the gain can L, who is single, exclude from income?**

L does not appear to meet the use test since L has not resided in the residence for five years. Again, § 121(d) provides relief by attributing M's use to L where the "divorce instrument" (which includes a written instrument incident to a divorce decree—§ 71(b)(2)(A)) granted M the use of the property; see § 121(d)(3)(B). L's share of the gain is $300,000, of which $250,000 can be excluded from gross income.

9. Would your answer in 8 differ if L had remarried and filed a joint return with L's spouse?

No, because the spouse would not satisfy the use test as would be required in order for the parties to get the benefit of the $500,000 exclusion on a joint return; § 121(b)(2)(A)(ii).

10. K owned a home (K's principal residence for many years) that was completely destroyed in a hurricane. K's adjusted basis in the home was $150,000 and K received $600,000 in insurance proceeds for the destruction of the home. K purchased a replacement home for $300,000. K wants to avoid recognition of gain to the extent possible. How much gain must K, who is single, recognize? (Ignore the land, as if only the building was destroyed and replaced.) What is K's adjusted basis for the replacement home?

This problem illustrates the relationship between §§ 121 and 1033. K has a realized gain of $450,000 ($600,000 amount realized less $150,000 adjusted basis). K excludes $250,000 of this gain from income under § 121. (Section 121(d)(5)(A) treats the destruction of the residence as a "sale," so as to bring the transaction within § 121(a).)

With respect to the remaining $200,000 of gain, K should elect non-recognition to the extent permitted under § 1033. For the purpose of § 1033, K's amount realized is $350,000—the $600,000 received from the insurance company minus the $250,000 gain excluded from income by § 121; § 121(d)(5)(B). Under § 1033, K must recognize $50,000 of gain ($350,000 amount realized less $300,000 replacement cost). K's basis for the replacement home is $150,000 ($300,000 cost less the $150,000 unrecognized gain under § 1033); § 1033(b)(2). Notice that, in determining the periods of ownership and use for the replacement property, K can include the periods of ownership and use for the converted property; § 121(d)(5)(C).

11. H purchased a home for $100,000 and resided there for five years as her principal residence. At the end of the fifth year, H's friend, J, moved in with her, and H sold J a half-interest (as tenant-in-common) in the home for $250,000. H and J continued to reside in the home as their principal residence for 5 more years, after which they sold it for $600,000 ($300,000 each). Both H and J are single. How much gain must H include in income in the fifth year? How much gain must each include in income in the tenth year?

The sale by H in year 5 qualifies for the § 121 exclusion, even though only a partial interest in the residence was sold; Treas. Reg. § 1.121–4(e)(1). In computing the realized gain, H must apportion her basis between the interest sold and that retained; Treas. Reg. § 1.61–6(a). Since a half-interest was sold, H can offset one-half the $100,000 basis (assuming no adjustments) against the $250,000 amount realized, which produces a realized gain of $200,000. Although H sold only a half-interest, H is not limited to one-half of the maximum exclusion amount in year 5; Treas. Reg. 1.121–4(e)(1)(ii)(A). The $200,000 gain in year 5 is fully covered by the exclusion.

When H sells the remaining half-interest in year 10, H's realized gain is $250,000 ($300,000 amount realized less remaining $50,000 basis). Only one maximum $250,000 exclusion amount applies to the two sales combined; id. Since H used $200,000 of the exclusion in year 5, H can exclude only $50,000 of the year–10 gain. The $200,000 remainder of the year–10 gain must included in H's income.

J has a realized gain of $50,000 ($300,000 amount realized less $250,000 basis). J meets the ownership and use requirements of § 121(a), and the entire $50,000 gain is excludable.

12. B, a single person, has owned a home since 1998. B resided in the home as his principal residence through December 31, 2003. On January 1, 2004, B, who was no longer physically capable of self-care, moved to a state-licensed, long-term-care facility, where he still resides. B's home was sold on December 31, 2007, at a gain of $150,000. Can B exclude the gain from income?

The issue here is whether B has used the property as his principal residence for two of the five years preceding the sale. Although he has spent the last four years in a long-term care facility, § 121(d)(7) credits B with use of the residence while residing in the care facility if he resided in the residence for at least one of the five years preceding the sale. In this case, B did reside in the home for at least one of the five years preceding the sale (2003). Therefore, the use requirement is met, and B can exclude the gain from income.

13. Would your answer in 12 differ if B had moved to the home of his sister, S, in 2004, and S had cared for B in the interim?

Yes. The relief of § 121(d)(7) applies only if the taxpayer resides in a facility "licensed by a State or political subdivision to care for an individual in the taxpayer's condition." Unless S is licensed to provide this service, B fails the use requirement of § 121(a), and the gain is fully taxable.

Chapter 23

WASH SALES UNDER § 1091

Code: §§ 1091(a), (b), (c) & (d); 1223(4).

Regulation: § 1.1091–2(a).

1. **In January, year 1, T purchased a share of the common stock of publicly traded X Corp. for $100. The stock fell in value and on December 10, year 1, T sold the stock for $40. Because T thought the firm's long-term prospects were promising, T repurchased a share at $30 on December 20. On June 30, year 2, T sold the share for $70. What results to T?**

T realizes a loss of $60 ($100 basis less $40 amount realized) on the December sale. The loss is not recognized because within 30 days following the sale T purchased a share of identical stock; § 1091(a).

To determine the basis of the share purchased in December, you must remember that § 1091(a) is a rollover non-recognition rule—i.e., it provides for deferral (not disallowance) of the loss, and the deferral is achieved by building the unrecognized loss into the basis of the "replacement" share. Recall that in computing the basis of replacement property under the rollover non-recognition rule of § 1033, we subtracted the unrecognized gain from the cost of the replacement property, thus building that gain into the basis for recognition when the replacement property was sold. Section 1091's basis rule operates in a similar fashion. We use as the basis of the replacement share its cost, *increased* by the loss that was unrecognized because of the purchase of the replacement share. So, the basis of the share purchased in December is $90 ($30 cost plus $60 unrecognized loss).

Section 1091(d) takes a slightly different route to the same end. It tells us that the basis of the replacement share is the same as the basis of the share sold, "increased or decreased, as the case may be, by the difference, if any, between the price at which the * * * [replacement share] was acquired and the price at which the * * * [the original share] was disposed of." In our case, the original share was sold for $40 and the replacement share was purchased for $30. In effect, T made a $10 "profit" on the sale and repurchase, and this profit reduces the amount invested in the new share. So, using the approach of § 1091(d), the basis of the replacement share is $90 ($100 basis of original share less $10 "profit" on the sale and repurchase). Most students find this approach much harder to apply than the method suggested in the preceding paragraph, so in the following problems we will use the method of the preceding paragraph.

When T sells the replacement share in June, year 2, T realizes (and recognizes) loss of $20 ($90 adjusted basis less $70 amount realized). Although T's actual holding period for the share is less than a year (from December until the following June), T can "tack on" the period during which he held the original share; § 1223(4). The holding period of the replacement share thus dates from January, year 1, and T's loss is a long-term capital loss.

Notice how the year–2 outcome makes sense: T invested a total of $130 in X Corp. stock ($100 plus $30), and received total sales proceeds of $110 ($40 plus $70). T lost $20 on the entire series of transactions, and T recognizes that $20 loss in year 2.

2.   Same as 1, except that T purchased the X share at $50 on December 20.

Again T's $60 realized loss on the December sale is unrecognized because of § 1091(a). T's basis for the replacement stock is $110 ($50 cost plus $60 unrecognized loss). When the replacement share is sold in year 2, T realizes (and recognizes) loss of $40. That is, T invested a total of $150 ($100 plus $50) and received total sales proceeds of $110 ($40 plus $70) for a loss of $40, which is recognized in year 2. The loss is a long-term capital loss; § 1223(4).

3.   S purchased one share of Y Corp. common stock in January of year 1 at $55. On June 1, year 1, S purchased another share at $35. On June 5, year 1, S sold the share purchased in January for $40. What result to S?

In this case S purchased the replacement share before selling the original share, but § 1091(a) still applies because it also covers the case of the purchase of a substantially identical security within 30 days preceding the sale. Implicit in this problem is the idea that a seller of securities can specifically identify the particular securities sold. S can therefore designate by appropriate instructions to his broker that the share sold was the one purchased in January rather than in June; see Treas. Reg. § 1.1012–1(c).

S realizes a loss of $15 ($55 basis less $40 amount realized) on the sale in June, but the loss is not recognized. The basis of the replacement share is $50 ($35 cost plus $15 unrecognized loss).

4. P purchased one share of Z stock in January at $35. On June 1, P sold the share for $40. On June 5, P purchased another share of Z for $35. What result to P?

P would have a realized and recognized (short-term) gain of $5 ($40 amount realized less $35 basis). Section 1091(a) does not apply to gains—just losses.

5. R purchased a share of Z Corp. for $60. Two weeks later, R sold the share for $50. What result to R?

R realizes and recognizes a short-term loss of $10 ($60 basis less $50 amount realized). Section 1091(a) does not apply. It applies only where the purchase is of "substantially similar" stock. Here the purchase was of the *very security sold*—not a similar one. R has closed out the investment altogether, and there is no replacement property in whose basis the deferred loss can reside.

6. T purchased one share of P Corp. on January 15 at $50 and another on January 20 at $55. T sold both shares on June 15 at $30 per share, but on July 1 T repurchased one share of P for $35. What result to T?

Here T sold two shares during the prohibited period but acquired only one. T has a realized loss of $20 on the share purchased on January 15 and a realized loss of $25 on the share purchased on January 20, but to what extent are the losses recognized? Where it cannot be determined which of the two shares disposed of were sold first (here they were sold in a single transaction), the replacement share is matched against the sale of the share that was first purchased—in this case, the share purchased on January 15; Treas. Reg. § 1.1091–1(b). So, the $20 loss is not recognized, the $25 loss is recognized, and the basis of the replacement share is $55 ($35 cost plus $20 unrecognized loss).

Chapter 24

CONVERSION OF PROPERTY FROM PERSONAL TO PROFIT-SEEKING USE

Code: §§162(a); 212(1) & (2); 165(a), (c)(1) & (2), 167(c), 262. Note §§ 161, 261.

Regulations: §§ 1.168(i)–4(b); 1.165–9; 1.262–1(b)(3) & (4); 1.212–1(b) & (h).

Cases: McAuley v. Commissioner, 35 T.C.M. 1236 (1976);
Horrman v. Commissioner, 17 T.C. 903 (1951);
Lowry v. United States, 384 F. Supp. 257 (D.N.H. 1974).

1. T purchased a home for $100,000, of which $20,000 was allocable to the lot and $80,000 to the house. T resided in the home for several years. When the home had a value of $175,000, of which $150,000 was allocable to the house, T moved out and rented the property to a tenant. What is T's basis for depreciation of the house?

$80,000; § 167(c). T cannot deduct depreciation on the appreciation in value over the original cost, and, of course, the land is not depreciable.

2. What result if several years later, and after properly deducting $25,000 of depreciation, T sells the property for an amount realized of $200,000, of which $175,000 is allocable to the house?

T's adjusted basis at the time of sale is $55,000 ($80,000 unadjusted basis less $25,000 depreciation) for the house and $20,000 for the land. (The gains on the sale of the house and the land must be computed separately because different rates of tax may apply to the two types of gain.) T realizes a gain of $120,000 ($175,000 amount realized less $55,000 adjusted basis) on the house and $5,000 ($25,000 amount realized less $20,000 basis) on the land. The gains are recognized; § 1001(c).

3. Assume that T purchased the home for $100,000, of which $20,000 was allocable to the lot and $80,000 to the house, T resided in the home for several years, and then rented it when the house was worth $60,000 and the lot $20,000. What is T's basis for depreciation?

The depreciable basis of the house is the lesser of its fair market value or its "adjusted depreciable basis" at the time of the conversion to income-producing use; Treas. Reg. § 1.168(i)–4(a). The adjusted depreciable basis is the "unadjusted depreciable basis" of the property less any adjustments for depreciation; Treas. Reg. § 1.168(b)-1T(a)(4). The unadjusted depreciable basis is the basis of the property without regard to any adjustments for depreciation; Treas. Reg. § 1.168(b)-1T(a)(3).

In this case, T's unadjusted depreciable basis is the $80,000 cost of the house. Since the house was not depreciable before its conversion to income-producing use, its adjusted depreciable basis is also $80,000. The depreciable basis is $60,000 (the value of the house) since that is less than its adjusted depreciable basis.

The depreciation is computed as if the property was placed in service on the date the conversion from personal use occurred; Treas. Reg. § 1.168(i)–4(b)(1). The house would be residential rental property (§ 168(e)(2)(A)), the recovery period would be 27.5 years (§ 168(c)), the mid-month convention would apply (§ 168(d)(2)), and straight-line would be the applicable depreciation method (§ 168(b)(3)).

4. What result in 3 if several years later, and after properly deducting $30,000 of depreciation, T sells the property for:

(a) $95,000, of which $25,000 is allocable to the lot?

At the time of the sale, T's adjusted basis is $50,000 for the house ($80,000 cost less $30,000 depreciation) and $20,000 for the land (cost). T realizes a gain on the house of $20,000 ($70,000 amount realized less $50,000 basis) and a gain on the land of $5,000 ($25,000 amount realized less $20,000 adjusted basis).

The gains must be computed separately because the gain on the sale of the house may be characterized as "unrecaptured section 1250 gain" (defined in § 1(h)(6)(A)), which is subject to tax at a maximum rate of 25 percent; see § 1(h)(1)(D). The gain on the land may qualify for a maximum tax rate of 15%; see § 1(h)(1)(C).

(b) $45,000, of which $25,000 is allocable to the lot?

A loss on the sale of personal-use property is not allowable; a loss on the sale of business or investment property is. When property has been converted from personal to profit-seeking use, we need a mechanism to ensure that any loss is not attributable to the personal use of the property. If the property has declined in value while being used as the taxpayer's residence, the resulting loss should not become deductible just because the taxpayer rents the property out for a short time before selling it.

The regulations attempt to deal with this problem by creating a special adjusted basis that is to be used in computing loss. If, at the time of conversion, the value of the property is less than its adjusted basis, the adjusted basis for loss is the value of the property at the time of conversion reduced by the post-conversion depreciation; Treas. Reg. § 1.165–9(b)(2). This approach effectively disallows a loss deduction for any decline in the property's value that occurred while the property was devoted to personal use.

Turning to our problem, we first compare the amount realized with the adjusted basis for gain. The adjusted basis for gain is the cost of the property less depreciation. If this computation produces a loss, we must recompute the loss using our adjusted basis for loss. For this purpose, the regulation treats the land and building as a single asset; see Treas. Reg. § 1.165–9(c) (examples).

Here, the unadjusted basis for gain is the $100,000 cost of the property, and the adjusted basis for gain is $70,000 ($100,000 unadjusted basis less $30,000 depreciation). Comparing this figure to the $55,000 amount realized, we see that it produces a loss of $15,000. But we must then recompute the loss using the adjusted basis for loss. Since the value of the property (land and building) at the date of conversion ($80,000) was than the property's adjusted basis at that time ($100,000), the adjusted basis for loss is determined by subtracting the post-conversion depreciation from that value. This gives us an adjusted basis for loss of $50,000 ($80,000 less $30,000).

The realized loss on the sale is $5,000 ($50,000 adjusted basis for loss less $45,000 amount realized). Too see why this is the correct result, consider that, from the time of purchase until time of sale, T has sustained an economic loss of $55,000 ($100,000 cost less $45,000 selling price). Of this $55,000, $20,000 was sustained before conversion and $30,000 was deducted as depreciation, leaving just $5,000 to be deducted as a loss at the time of sale.

(c) $55,000, of which $25,000 is allocable to the lot?

Once again, when we compare the adjusted basis for gain ($70,000) with the amount realized ($55,000), we have a loss. We therefore must compare the adjusted basis for loss ($50,000) to the amount realized ($55,000), but that produces a gain. So, using the adjusted basis for gain, we reckon a loss, and using the adjusted basis for loss, we get a gain. This is an indeterminant transaction—it results in neither gain nor loss. (Compare the similar result in the case of the sale of property acquired by gift in Treas. Reg. § 1.1015–1(a)(2), Ex.)

5. Several years ago, L purchased a home for $100,000 (of which $20,000 was allocable to the land) and used it as his principal residence. Last December, L moved out, and on January 1 of the current year L put the property up for sale. L received no offers, however, and on July 1 L offered the property for either sale or rent. On November 1, L sold the property for $75,000, of which $20,000 was attributable to the land. On January 1 and July 1, the property was worth $80,000, of which $20,000 was allocable to the lot. For simplicity, assume that depreciation, if allowable, would be $250 per month (i.e., ignore § 168).

(a) As of what date can L begin deducting the maintenance expenses with respect to the property?

Maintenance expenses are allowable as expenses for the production of income or the maintenance of income-producing property; § 212(1) & (2). The question here is whether the property has been converted to income-producing use and, if so, when. Abandonment of the residence and listing it for sale generally does not convert the property to income-producing use, unless the property is being held for post-conversion appreciation; Lowry v. United States, 384 F. Supp. 257 (D.N.H. 1974). There is no indication here that L was seeking post-conversion appreciation. But when the owner makes a good-faith offer to rent the property, the conversion occurs; e.g., Horrman v. Commissioner, 17 T.C. 903 (1951). So the maintenance expenses become deductible beginning with L's offer to rent on July 1.

(b) As of what date can L begin deducting depreciation on the house?

Section 167(a)(2) allows depreciation on property held for the production of income. This language is the same as that in § 212, and depreciation is allowed once the owner offers the property for rent; Horrman v. Commissioner, 17 T.C. 903 (1951). The property was offered for rent for four months before the sale, so L could deduct $1,000 of depreciation with respect to the property.

(c) Can L deduct the loss on the sale?

A loss is allowable under § 165(c)(2) if sustained in a "transaction entered into for profit." The difference in language between § 165(c)(2) on the one hand and §§ 212(2) and 167(a)(2) on the other has led the courts to insist upon an actual rental of the property in order to make a loss allowable; e.g., McAuley v. Commissioner, 35 T.C.M. 1236 (1976). So, the loss on the sale of the property is not allowable here.

(d) Can you reconcile your answers in (b) and (c)?

Although the language in § 165(c)(2) differs from that in §§ 212(2) and 167(a)(2), it hardly makes sense to apply different standards for determining the deductibility of losses and expenses. A loss on the sale of depreciable property signifies that the property was under-depreciated—that more of the value of the property was "used up" in trying to produce income than was allowable as depreciation under the statute. In other words, depreciation anticipates loss. Amounts spent on maintenance may keep the property from declining in value and thus reduce the loss when the property is sold. In view of the close relationship between depreciation and maintenance expenses on the one hand and a loss deduction on the other, it seems odd that the former are deductible here but the latter is not.

6. T, a solo practitioner, purchases an automobile for $20,000 and uses the vehicle 75 percent for business and 25 percent for personal use. She properly deducts $8,000 of depreciation and then sells the car for $8,000. What result to T?

When T sells the automobile, she must fragment the transaction, treating it as if two separate assets (a business asset and a personal-use asset) had been purchased and sold. The business asset has an unadjusted basis of $15,000 (75% of $20,000) and an adjusted basis of $7,000 ($15,000 unadjusted basis less $8,000 of depreciation). The personal-use asset has an unadjusted and adjusted basis of $5,000 (because no depreciation is allowable with respect to the personal-use asset). The amount realized on the sale of the business asset is $6,000 (75% of $8,000), and T's realized loss is $1,000 ($7,000 adjusted basis less $6,000 amount realized). The loss is recognized and allowable as a deduction because incurred in business. T also has a realized loss of $3,000 ($5,000 adjusted basis less $2,000 amount realized) on the personal-use asset, but that loss is disallowed by § 165(c).

Chapter 25

LOSSES ON TRANSACTIONS BETWEEN RELATED PARTIES

Code: § 267(a)(1), (b), (c), (d) & (g).

Regulations: §§ 1.267(a)–1(c); 1.267(c)–1(a); 1.267(d)–1(a) & (c).

Case: McWilliams v. Commissioner, 331 U.S. 694 (1947).

1. **Suppose S sells investment property at a loss in a bona fide sale at fair market value. Would S's loss be allowed if, alternatively, the purchaser was:**

(a) S's daughter?

No. Section 267(a)(1) disallows losses on transactions between related parties specified in § 267(b). Section 267(b)(1) treats members of a family as related parties. For this purpose, a person's family includes a lineal descendant; § 267(c)(4).

(b) S's adopted daughter?

No. In determining whether a family relationship exists, full effect is given to a legal adoption; Treas. Reg. § 1.267(c)–1(a)(4).

(c) S's niece?

Yes. S's niece is not a member of S's family under § 267(c)(4).

(d) S's father-in-law?

Yes. S's father-in-law is not a member of S's family under § 267(c)(4).

(e) S's registered domestic partner?

Yes. S's domestic partner is not a member of S's family under § 267(c)(4).

(f) A corporation in which each of the following persons owns 200 shares: S's spouse, S's daughter, S's aunt, S's son-in-law, and a trust of which S and S's daughter are each fifty-percent beneficiaries?

No.   Section 267(b)(2) includes as related parties an individual and a corporation more than 50 percent in value of the outstanding stock of which is owned, directly or indirectly, by the individual.   Although S actually owns no shares, he is treated under § 267(c) as owning the shares of those shareholders with whom he is in familial or economic solidarity, and S can therefore own constructively more than 50 percent by value of the stock; Treas. Reg. § 1.267(c)–1(a)(2).   Under § 267(c)(1), any stock owned by a trust is treated as owned proportionately by the trust beneficiaries.   The trust's shares are therefore imputed one-half to S and one-half to S's daughter.   Under § 267(c)(2), S is treated as owning any stock owned by his family, which includes S's spouse and daughter, but not S's aunt or son-in-law.   Although shares owned by S's son-in-law are imputed to S's daughter, those shares cannot be re-attributed to S because of § 267(c)(5).   However, the 100 shares constructively owned by S's daughter through the trust can be re-attributed to S under that provision.   S therefore owns, actually or constructively, 600 shares:

S's spouse	200
S's daughter	200
Trust (through the daughter)	100
Trust (by S as beneficiary)	<u>100</u>
	600

When the constructive-stock-ownership rules are taken into account, S owns 60 percent of the stock, and the loss is disallowed.

(g) A trust for the benefit of S's niece? S was grantor of the trust.

No. The grantor of a trust and the fiduciary of the trust are related parties; § 267(b)(4).

(h) A trust for the benefit of S's daughter? S's spouse was grantor of the trust.

Yes. S is not related to the trust under § 267(b).

(i) S's mother and step-father as tenants-in-common?

Yes, as to one-half of the loss. S's mother is a member of S's family under § 267(c)(4); S's step-father is not because he is not S's "ancestor." But if the step-father had adopted S, the entire loss would be disallowed; see Treas. Reg. § 1.267(c)–1(a)(4).

2. On June 1, year 1, P sells investment property to her adult child, C, for $100 (the property's value). P had an adjusted basis of $150 for the property. The sale is bona fide. What result to P?

P realizes a loss of $50 ($150 adjusted basis less $100 amount realized). The loss is recognized; § 1001(c). Although a loss on the sale of investment property would be allowable under § 165(a) and (c)(2), the loss is disallowed because the sale is to C, a member of P's family; § 267(a)(1), (b)(1) & (c)(4). Section 267 disallows the loss even though the sale is bona fide; see, e.g., Englehart v. Commissioner, 30 T.C. 1013 (1958).

3. What result to C (in problem 2) if C also holds the property for investment and on March 31, year 2, sells it to an unrelated party for:

(a) $75?

C's basis is $100; § 1012. On the sale, C realizes a loss of $25 ($100 basis less $75 amount realized). The loss is recognized under § 1001(c) and allowed by § 165(a) & (c)(2). The $50 loss disallowed to P disappears from the system—it cannot be deducted even though the property has passed outside of the family group.

(b) $130?

C has a realized gain of $30 ($130 amount realized less $100 adjusted basis). Under § 267(d), the gain is recognized only to the extent that it exceeds the loss disallowed to P when the property was sold to C. The disallowed loss was $50, so none of the $30 gain is recognized.

(c) $180?

C has a realized gain of $80 ($180 amount realized less $100 adjusted basis). Under § 267(d), the gain is recognized only to the extent that it exceeds the $50 loss disallowed to P. So, C recognizes gain of $30. The gain is a short-term gain, as C's holding period does not exceed one year and C cannot tack on P's holding period because C's basis was not determined by reference to P's; see Treas. Reg. § 1.267(d)–1(c)(3).

4. Suppose instead that the property purchased from P had been land held by P (and then C) as an investment. In year 5, C exchanges the land for other land (worth $200) to be held for investment. In year 7, C sells the land acquired in the exchange for $250. What result to C?

On the year–5 exchange, C realizes gain of $100 ($200 amount realized less $100 basis). C does not recognize the gain because this is a like-kind exchange under § 1031(a). C's basis for the new land is $100, the same as C's basis for the old; § 1031(d).

When C sells the land in year 7, C realizes a gain of $150 ($250 amount realized less $100 basis). Because C's basis for the land was determined by reference to the basis of the land that P sold to C, § 267(d) provides for non-recognition of $50 of the gain because that amount was disallowed as a loss to P on the sale to C; Treas. Reg. § 1.267(d)–1(a)(2) & (4), Ex. (4).

5. Suppose instead that on March 31, year 2, C gives the property (then worth $120) to her adult child, GC.

(a) What result if GC sells the property in year 4 for $180.

C recognizes no gain on the transfer of the property by gift. GC excludes the value of the property from income (§ 102(a)) and assumes C's adjusted basis of $100 under § 1015(a). When GC sells the property, GC realizes gain of $80 ($180 amount realized less $100 adjusted basis). The gain is fully recognized under § 1001(c). Section 267(d) does not apply because it affords non-recognition only to the "taxpayer" who acquired the property in the transaction on which loss was disallowed to the taxpayer's transferor; § 1.267(d)–1(a)(3) & (4), Ex. (3). Therefore, only C could get the benefit of non-recognition.

(b) What result if instead C had transferred the property to her former spouse, X, in accordance with the parties' divorce decree, and X later sells the property for $180?

C recognizes no gain or loss on the transfer; § 1041(a). Even if C realized a loss on the transfer to X, § 267 does not come into play. For one thing, § 267 is a disallowance rule, and we never get to the question of the allowability of an unrecognized loss. Section 267(g) makes this clear, though that provision probably is not necessary. And, in this case, C and X apparently were no longer married when the transfers occurred, so they were no longer related parties under § 267(b).

X excludes the value of the property received from C and assumes C's $100 basis; § 1041(b). When X sells the property, X realizes gain of $80 ($180 amount realized less $100 adjusted basis). The gain is recognized under § 1001(c). Section 267(d) does not apply because X is not the "taxpayer" who acquired the property in the transaction on which loss was disallowed—that was C.

6. For several years, R has owned a share of X Corp. common stock, which he had purchased for $100. On April 1 of the current year, he sold the share for $40. That same day, he purchased for $40 a share of X Corp. common as custodian for his minor child, S, under the Uniform Transfers to Minors Act. Both transactions were effected by R's broker through the New York Stock Exchange.

(a) What result to R?

This will probably be treated as an indirect sale by R to S. In McWilliams v. Commissioner, 331 U.S. 694 (1947), a husband managed the investments of his wife. He ordered his broker to sell shares from his account and simultaneously buy a like number of shares of the same stock for his wife's account. The transactions were effected on the stock exchange. The Supreme Court sustained the Commissioner's disallowance of the losses as indirect sales between the husband and wife under the predecessor of § 267.

If the transaction is treated as an indirect sale to S, R's $60 realized loss will be recognized but disallowed; § 267(a)(1), (b)(1) & (c)(4).

(b) What result to S if, after attaining age 21, S sells the share for $90?

S's basis for the share was its $40 cost; § 1012. S realizes gain of $50 ($90 amount realized less $40 basis). The gain is not recognized because it does not exceed the amount of loss disallowed to R ($60); § 267(d).

(c) What result to R if he had purchased the share for the custodial account on May 5 of the current year?

McWilliams and § 267 probably should not apply in this case because R could have repurchased the share himself on May 5 without running afoul of the wash-sale rules of § 1091. So, R's $60 loss should be allowed.

7. Why does section 267 disallow losses even on bona fide sales to a related party when the sale is made at FMV?

It would be administratively impossible to inquire into the bona fides of transactions between related parties. Congress therefore chose to disallow such losses automatically.

Section G

CAPITAL GAINS AND LOSSES

Chapter 26

THE SIGNIFICANCE OF CHARACTERIZATION

Code: §§ 1221(a); 1222; 1211(b); 1212(b); 61(a)(3); 62(a)(3). Note §§ 1231; 64; 65; 408(m); 1(h)(1)–(7) & (11).

1. S is in the 35–percent tax bracket for ordinary income and had no capital losses for the year. What tax rate would apply to the capital gains recognized by S on each of the following transactions?

(a) Sale of New York Stock Exchange listed securities held for 6 months.

35%. This short-term capital gain (STCG) is taxed at ordinary-income rates. Only the "net capital gain" (NCG) qualifies for the preferential rates of § 1(h). The NCG is the excess of the net long-term capital gain (NLTCG) over the net short-term capital loss (NSTCL); § 1222(11). The NLTCG is the excess of the long-term capital gain (LTCG) over the long-term capital loss (LTCL); § 1222(7). Since short-term capital gain does not increase the NLTCG, it cannot increase the NCG that gets the benefit of the lower capital-gains rates. The STCG is thus taxed at ordinary-income rates.

(b) Sale of New York Stock Exchange securities held for 18 months.

Since S is in the 35–percent bracket for ordinary income, S's tax rate for NCG is 15, 25 or 28 percent depending upon the nature of the asset disposed of. The NCG is the excess of NLTCG over NSTCL. The lowest rates are reserved for the portion of the NCG called the "adjusted net capital gain," which is taxed at a maximum rate of 15 percent; see § 1(h)(1)(C). The adjusted net capital gain is the net capital gain reduced by (1) the "unrecaptured section 1250 gain" (the "make-up" gain on the sale of a building), and (2) the "28–percent rate gain" (the sum of the collectibles gain and the § 1202 gain); § 1(h)(3). In this case, the gain on the securities is a long-term gain and is neither unrecaptured § 1250 gain, collectibles gain, nor § 1202 gain. The gain is therefore part of the adjusted net capital gain, taxable at 15 percent; § 1(h)(1)(C).

(c) Sale of a building (held by S as an investment for several years) for $500,000. S had purchased the building for $400,000 and had properly deducted $250,000 of straight-line depreciation thereon. (Ignore the land, as if only the building were bought and sold.)

The sale of the building involves the recognition of unrecaptured § 1250 gain. (The description of such gain here is non-technical. We will examine the technical details in Chapter 29.) On the sale of the building, S has realized and recognized gain of $350,000 ($500,000 amount realized less $150,000 adjusted basis). Of the $350,000, $250,000 just "makes up" for the $250,000 depreciation deducted by S, though the building was actually increasing in value. The other $100,000 is real economic gain—the excess of the $500,000 selling price over the $400,000 purchase price. The make-up gain (called unrecaptured § 1250 gain) is taxed at 25 percent (§ 1(h)(1)(D)); the economic gain is part of the adjusted net capital gain and taxed at 15 percent. So, $250,000 of gain is taxed at 25 percent and $100,000 at 15 percent.

(d) Sale of S's coin collection (all the coins had been held for more than a year).

The coins are collectibles under § 408(m)(2)(D), and gain on their sale is collectibles gain; § 1(h)(5)(A). Collectibles gain is taxed at a maximum rate of 28 percent; § 1(h)(1)(E). So, S's gain on the sale of the coins is taxed at 28 percent.

(e) Sale of S's yacht (used by S for recreation for the past 3 years).

The gain on the sale of the yacht, a capital asset, is part of the adjusted net capital gain, as the gain is neither unrecaptured § 1250 gain nor 28–percent rate gain. S is taxed at 15 percent on the gain.

2. On their joint return, H and W have taxable income of $150,000, which includes $15,000 of long-term capital gain, $3,000 of long-term capital loss, and $2,000 of short-term capital loss. They have no dividend income, and the capital gain and losses are from New York Stock Exchange securities transactions. Using the tax-bracket figures set forth in Appendix B, determine their tax liability before credits.

The couple has a net long-term capital gain of $12,000 ($15,000 long-term gain less $3,000 long-term loss); § 1222(7). They have a net short-term capital loss of $2,000 ($2,000 short-term loss less zero short-term gain); § 1222(6). Their net capital gain is $10,000 ($12,000 net long-term capital gain less $2,000 net short-term capital loss); § 1222(11). They have no unrecaptured § 1250 gain nor 28–percent rate gain. Their adjusted net capital gain is therefore $10,000; § 1(h)(3).

Section 1(h)(1)(A) requires the computation of two partial taxes: One on ordinary income (i.e., taxable income reduced by the net capital gain) and the other on the net capital gain. The couple's tax liability is the sum of those two partial taxes. In this case, the tax on the ordinary taxable income ($140,000) is $31,405.50; § 1(a). The tax on the adjusted net capital gain is $1,500 (15% of $10,000). The total tax is $32,905.50.

3. T, an individual, has ordinary gross income of $120,000 and has capital gains and losses in the amounts specified below. In each alternative case, determine (i) T's gross and adjusted gross income; and (ii) the amount and character of any capital-loss carryover to the next year.

    (a)   **long-term capital gain $10,000**
                long-term capital loss $12,000

Gross income is $130,000 because it includes the capital gain unreduced by the capital loss. That is, § 61(a)(3) requires the inclusion of the gains in gross income; the losses are allowable under §§ 165 and 62(a)(3) in computing adjusted gross income.

Adjusted gross income is $118,000 ($130,000 gross income less $12,000 capital-loss deduction). The capital-loss deduction is allowable only to the extent of capital gains ($10,000), plus (since the losses exceed the gains) the $2,000 excess of the losses over the gains (because that figure is less than $3,000); § 1211(b). The $2,000 is being deducted against ordinary income.

T has no "net capital loss" because her capital losses ($12,000) do not exceed the amount deducted under § 1211(b) ($12,000); see § 1222(10). All the loss having been deducted, there is none to carry over to the next year; § 1212(b)(1).

    (b)   **long-term capital loss $8,000**
                short-term capital loss $5,000

Gross income is $120,000. The capital losses are deductible to the extent of capital gains, plus up to $3,000 against ordinary income. T has no capital gains to be offset by capital losses; but T can deduct $3,000 against ordinary income (because the $3,000 is less than the $13,000 excess of capital losses over capital gains); § 1211(b)(1). The capital-loss deduction is an above-the-line deduction; § 62(a)(3). T's AGI is therefore $117,000.

The capital loss that is not allowable in the current year does not just disappear; it is carried over to the following year, where it can again be deducted to the extent of capital gains, plus a limited allowance against ordinary income, etc., indefinitely. The taxpayer has a capital-loss carryover whenever he has a "net capital loss" (NCL) for the year—i.e., whenever the capital losses exceed the amount allowed as a deduction under § 1211(b); § 1222(10). T has a NCL for the year, as capital losses ($13,000) exceed the amount allowable under § 1211(b)

($3,000). It follows that T is entitled to a capital-loss carryover to the following year.

Because (net) long-term and short-term gains are subject to different tax rates, the Code preserves the character (as short- or long-term) of the capital loss that is being carried over. So, we must make separate computations of the short-term- and long-term-loss carryovers.

The short-term-capital-loss carryover is determined under § 1212(b)(1)(A) to be the excess of the net short-term capital loss (NSTCL) over the net long-term capital gain (NLTCG). However, in determining the amount of the carryovers (short- and long-term), we treat as a (make-believe) STCG an amount equal to the amount of capital loss allowed in offsetting ordinary income under § 1211(b)(1) or (2). In this case, $3,000 was allowed against ordinary income under § 1211(b)(1). (The obvious purpose of treating the $3,000 as STCG is to reduce the amount of capital loss to be carried over by the amount that was used in offsetting ordinary income and therefore cannot be carried over to offset capital gain or ordinary income in the following year.) So, we pretend that we had a STCG of $3,000. The STCL carryover is the excess of the NSTCL over the NLTCG. We first compute the NSTCL, which is the excess of STCL over STCG; § 1222(6). The STCL is $5,000; the STCG is the sum of the *actual* STCG (none in this case) and the *make-believe* gain of $3,000, for total STCG of $3,000. The NSTCL is therefore $2,000 ($5,000 STCL less $3,000 STCG). The NTLTG is the excess of the LTCG over the LTCL. In this case, there is no such excess, as LTCL ($8,000) exceeds LTCG (zero), and the NTLTG is zero. The STCL carryover is $2,000 ($2,000 NSTCL less zero NLTCG). This makes sense, as $3,000 of the $5,000 STCL was used in offsetting ordinary income, leaving $2,000 to be used in the following year.

The long-term-capital-loss carryover is the excess of the NLTCL over the NSTCG; § 1212(b)(1)(B). The NLTCL is the excess of LTCL over LTCG; § 1222(8). T has LTCL of $8,000 and no LTCG, for a NLTCL of $8,000. The NSTCG is the excess of the STCG over the STCL. In this case, we have no actual STCG, but we have the $3,000 of make-believe STCG from § 1212(b)(2)(A), discussed above. Nevertheless, the STCG ($3,000) does not exceed the STCL ($5,000), so we have no NSTCG. The LTCL carryover is therefore $8,000 ($8,000 NLTCL less zero NSTCG). Again, this makes sense, as none of the LTCL was used in offsetting capital gain or ordinary income, and the entire $8,000 should be available in the following year.

(c)	long-term capital gain	$10,000
	long-term capital loss	$ 5,000
	short-term capital gain	$ 4,000
	short-term capital loss	$14,000

Gross income is $134,000 (including the $14,000 of capital gains). T's capital-loss deduction is $17,000 (losses to the extent of the $14,000 of gains, plus $3,000 to be applied against ordinary income); see § 1211(b). T's AGI is $117,000 ($134,000 gross income less $17,000 capital-loss deduction); § 62(a).

T has a NLTCG of $5,000 ($10,000 LTCG less $5,000 LTCL); § 1222(7). T also has a NSTCL of $10,000 ($14,000 STCL less $4,000 STCG); § 1222(6). T has no net capital gain (NCG), which enjoys the benefits of the lower tax rates of § 1(h), because the NCG is the excess of NLTCG over NSTCL, and here there is no such excess.

T has a NCL of $2,000 ($19,000 capital losses less $17,000 allowable under § 1211(b)) and therefore has a capital-loss carryover. Recall that the STCL carryover is the excess of the NSTCL over the NLTCG. In computing NSTCL for the purpose of the carryover, however, we take into account the amount of the make-believe STCG created by § 1212(b)(2)(A)—here $3,000 because that is the amount of ordinary income offset by capital loss. The STCG is therefore $7,000 ($4,000 of actual STCG, plus $3,000 of make-believe STCG), the STCL is $14,000, and the NSTCL is $7,000. The NLTCG is $5,000 ($10,000 LTCG less $5,000 LTCL); § 1222(7). The STCL carryover is $2,000 ($7,000 NSTCL less $5,000 NLTCG).

This result makes sense, as $4,000 of the STCL was used in offsetting (the real) STCG, $5,000 was used in offsetting the portion of LTCG that was not offset by LTCL, and $3,000 was used in offsetting ordinary income under § 1211(b)(1). That leaves $2,000 of STCL to carry forward to the next year.

T has no LTCL carryover, as all of the LTCL was absorbed offsetting LTCG.

(d)	long-term capital gain	$6,000
	long-term capital loss	$4,000
	short-term capital gain	$2,000
	short-term capital loss	$5,000

T's gross income is $128,000. T's capital-loss deduction is $9,000: The $9,000 of capital losses are allowable to the extent of the capital gains ($8,000), plus the excess of the $9,000 of losses over the $8,000 of gains ($1,000), which is applied to offset ordinary income. T's AGI is thus $119,000 ($128,000 gross income less $9,000 capital-loss deduction); § 62(a).

T has no NCG because the $2,000 NLTCG does not exceed the $3,000 NSTCL, so there is no amount qualifying for the preferential tax rates of § 1(h).

Nor is there any carryover of capital losses to the following year. T has no NCL because the capital losses ($9,000) do not exceed the amount allowed as a deduction for the year ($9,000).

4. Where both short-term and long-term capital loss is available to offset ordinary income, Congress determined that the short-term loss should be so applied before the long-term loss. Suppose instead that Congress wanted long-term loss to be applied before short-term loss. Could that be accomplished by changing a single word in the statute? Explain.

Yes. Simply change the word "short" to "long" in § 1212(b)(2)(A). The make-believe gain of § 1212(b)(2)(A) is a proxy for the amount of ordinary income that is offset by capital gain. By characterizing the make-believe gain as short-term gain, Congress ensured that the make-believe gain would first reduce any NSTCL (and hence any STCL carryover), as short-term transactions are first netted together in computing the amount of STCL carried over; § 1212(b)(1)(A). Only if the make-believe gain results in (or increases) a NSTCG would the LTCL carryover be reduced; see § 1212(b)(1)(B).

5. Evaluate each of the following policy justifications for taxing capital gains at a lower rate than ordinary income:

(a) The lower rate of tax on capital gains is necessary in order to limit the tax resulting from the "bunching" in a single year of gains accruing over many years.

Proponents of the "bunching" or "income averaging" rationale for a lower rate of tax on capital gains think it inappropriate to tax (at the full marginal rates) in the year of sale appreciation that occurred over many years. As the Supreme Court put it in Burnet v. Harmel, 287 U.S. 103, 106 (1932):

> Before the act of 1921, gains realized from the sale of property were taxed at the same rates as other income, with the result that capital gains, often accruing over long periods of time, were taxed in the year of realization at the high rates resulting from their inclusion in the higher surtax brackets. The provisions of the 1921 Revenue Act for taxing capital gains at a lower rate * * * were adopted to relieve the taxpayer from these excessive tax burdens on gains resulting from a conversion of capital investments, and to remove the deterrent effect of those burdens on such conversions.

One problem with the bunching rationale is that the taxpayer need hold the property only for a year and a day to obtain the relief of the lower capital-gains rates. Thus, it is not true that the gain necessarily represents appreciation that occurred over a long period of time. Moreover, many capital gains are reported by persons who are in the top tax bracket every year; in those cases, it is not as if a single asset sale propelled them temporarily into a higher bracket and they will fall back into a lower bracket in the following year when their incomes retreat to their "normal" level. The burden of taxing the gain at ordinary-income rates is ameliorated to some extent by the benefits of deferring the tax until the gain is realized. The "bunching" rationale does not justify today's regime for taxing capital gains.

For an excellent discussion of the justifications for a capital-gains preference, see the seminal article by Andrews, A Consumption-type or Cash Flow Personal Income Tax, 87 Harv. L. Rev. 1113 (1974). Many of the thoughts expressed here are derived from that article.

(b) Because of inflation, capital gains often contain an element of illusory gain. The lower rate of tax on capital gains mitigates the effect of taxing people on these illusory gains.

It is true that capital gains sometimes reflect inflation rather than real changes in economic value. But that hardly justifies today's capital-gains-tax regime. An asset held for a year and a day qualifies for the same rate of tax as one held for 30 years. The statute does not correlate the tax rate with the amount of inflation that occurred during the taxpayer's holding of the asset. Moreover, inflationary gains are not limited to appreciation in the value of property. Consider a taxpayer who earns 5–percent interest on a savings account in a year when the rate of inflation is 3 percent. The taxpayer is taxed on the full amount of "interest" received, even though a substantial part of the earnings just restores the principal to its original purchasing power. The theoretical solution to adjusting income for inflation would require comprehensive indexing of basis, income and deductions, and that would make the statute, already marred by excessive complexity, almost unworkable as a mass tax. So, inflation is a problem; but not one that can be dealt with adequately through the present capital-gains tax.

(c) The lower rate of tax encourages people to realize or "unlock" their capital gains.

The excerpt from *Harmel* (in (a)) touches on this rationale: To remove the deterrent effect of tax burdens on the taxpayer's willingness to realize gains. This "locking-in" rationale is perhaps the strongest justification for a preferential rate of tax on capital gains. The preference promotes economic efficiency by mitigating the tax disincentive to investors of making those switches in investments that they would make in the absence of an income tax. It also reduces the inequity of taxing realized but reinvested gains at ordinary-income rates while permitting unrealized gains to accumulate tax-free. The present capital-gains regime can be seen as a compromise between allowing tax-free rollover of gains and taxing realized gains at ordinary-income rates. Note also that, even with the lower rates on capital gains, older investors continue to be "locked-in" to their investments because of the prospect of the stepped-up basis at death.

(d) A lower rate of tax on capital gains encourages taxpayers to save and invest.

This justification for the capital-gains preference is sometimes referred to as the "capital-formation" rationale. Proponents of this view argue that, with lower capital-gains rates, taxpayers will be more willing to divert their consumption expenditures to investment generally and particularly to investments in risky ventures that offer the potential for large capital gains. Although a preferential rate of tax on capital gains might, at the margin, induce taxpayers to save more, it also encourages them to shift their investments from those that produce ordinary income (such as interest) to those that produce capital gains. The Code provides no relief for other receipts (such as salary or interest) that are saved rather than consumed. As to encouraging risky investment, one can say that the benefits of the present preference are not limited to investment in risky new ventures. Perhaps a sounder approach to promoting economic growth would be to tax all income at the same rate, but set the rates as low as possible, consistent with a given level of federal expenditure and deficit.

Chapter 27

THE SALE OR EXCHANGE OF CAPITAL ASSETS

A. THE CAPITAL-ASSET DEFINITION

Code: § 1221(a). Note §§ 197(c), (d)(1)(A) & (f)(7); 1235(a) & (b)(1).

In each of the following problems, the taxpayer owns the asset described. Determine whether the asset is a capital asset.

1. The residence in which the taxpayer resides.

The residence is a capital asset because it is property held by the taxpayer and not within any of the exceptions to the capital-asset definition in § 1221(a)(1)–(8). Personal-use assets are always capital assets, though most such assets are disposed of for an amount less than their basis, and, since losses on the disposition of personal-use property are not allowable, the characterization issue is unimportant when the property is disposed of at a loss. (Capital losses include recognized losses only to the extent that "the loss is taken into account in computing taxable income"—i.e., allowable; § 1222(2) & (4).)

2. 100 shares of Microsoft stock held by a full-time practicing lawyer.

Stock held by one who is not a dealer in securities is the prototypical capital asset. Stock is property and not within any of the exceptions of § 1221(a)(1)–(8). (If the taxpayer's stock-trading activity is so extensive as to make her a "trader," she can elect under § 475(f) to have stock-trading gains and losses treated as ordinary income and loss.)

3. Land held for use in business.

The land is not a capital asset because of the exclusion of § 1221(a)(2) (real property used in business). We will see later that, if the land has a holding period of more than one year, it is a § 1231 asset, and its disposition can still result in capital gain or loss.

4. Automobiles held for sale by a Chevrolet dealer.

The automobiles are held for sale to the dealer's customers in the ordinary of business and therefore excluded from the capital-asset category by § 1221(a)(1). The exclusion of § 1221(a)(1) recognizes that gains from the sale of inventory and the like are an ordinary, everyday source of business profits, and therefore capital-gain treatment would be inappropriate.

5. An automobile used exclusively in business.

The automobile is business property subject to the allowance for depreciation and, therefore, it is not a capital asset because of § 1221(a)(2).

6. A painting, held by the artist who painted it.

The painting is not a capital asset because it is an artistic composition held by the taxpayer whose personal efforts created the property; § 1221(a)(3)(A). Congress viewed the gain on the sale of a painting as compensation for the personal services of the artist and therefore denied capital-asset treatment.

7. A painting, held by the adult child of the artist who painted it. The child received it by gift from her parent, the artist.

The painting is not a capital asset in the hands of the child because the child's basis in the painting is determined by reference to its basis in the hands of the artist whose personal efforts created the property; see § 1221(a)(3)(C). (Recall that when property is acquired by gift, the donee generally assumes the donor's basis under § 1015(a).)

8. Same as 7, except the child received the painting by bequest when her parent, the artist, died.

Now the painting is a capital asset in the hands of the child because her basis is not determined by reference to her parent's basis but rather by the fair market value of the property on the date of death (or, if applicable, the alternate valuation date); see § 1014(a). So, the exception of § 1221(a)(3)(C) does not apply.

9. A patent held by the professional inventor who developed it.

One might think that a patent held by its (professional) developer would be ordinary-income property under § 1221(a)(1). That may be so, but it does not matter because § 1235(a) generally treats a transfer of all substantial rights to a patent as the sale or exchange of a capital asset. The holder of the patent obtains capital-gain treatment even though she is a professional inventor whose efforts created the property; see § 1235(b)(1). Unlike the case of the artist, it makes no difference here that the inventor is being rewarded with capital-gain treatment for the product of her personal efforts.

10. A single residential rental property held by a full-time practicing lawyer.

The residential property is depreciable and real property. The issue is whether the property is held as an investment, in which case it is a capital asset, or whether it is held in business, in which case it is excluded from the capital-asset definition by § 1221(a)(2). Here the lawyer's involvement with the property appears to be minimal, which suggests that the property was not used in his business but was held for the production of income; see, e.g., Grier v. United States, 120 F. Supp. 395 (D. Conn. 1954), aff'd per curiam, 218 F.2d 603 (2d Cir. 1955) (ownership and management of single rental residence not a business). Other courts have held the property to be business property on similar facts; see, e.g., Hazard v. Commissioner, 7 T.C. 372 (1946) (Acq.) (taxpayer rented out his former residence for several years after he moved to another city; *held*, the residence was business, rather than investment, property). There's no clear answer.

11. A lawyer's accounts receivable arising from the lawyer's performance of legal services; the lawyer uses the cash method of accounting.

The accounts receivable are not capital assets because of § 1221(a)(4). Section 1221(a)(4) serves two purposes. With respect to a cash-method taxpayer, whose receivables have a zero basis, the provision prevents the taxpayer from holding the receivables for more than a year and then selling them and claiming long-term-capital-gain treatment for receipts that represent income from the taxpayer's personal services. Second, § 1221(a)(4) prevents an inequity to accrual-method taxpayers who include the amount of their receivables in income under the all-events test and later sell the receivables at a loss. If the receivables were capital assets, the loss on their sale would be a capital loss, whose deductibility is limited by § 1211. Yet, the loss just makes up for the prior over-inclusion of ordinary income and should be an ordinary loss.

12. Office supplies owned by the lawyer in 11.

The office supplies are not capital assets because of § 1221(a)(8). The cost of incidental supplies (for which the taxpayer maintains no record of consumption) is usually deducted against ordinary income at the time the supplies are purchased; Treas. Reg. § 1.162–3. If the taxpayer deducts the cost of the supplies and then later sells the unconsumed portion, the gain should be ordinary to compensate for the ordinary deduction obtained when the supplies were purchased.

13. The self-created goodwill of a business.

Self-created goodwill is a capital asset because it is property held by the taxpayer and not within any of the exceptions of § 1221(a)(1)–(8). The only exception that could conceivably apply is § 1221(a)(2) (business property of a character subject to the allowance for deprecation). Self-developed goodwill cannot be depreciated because it has a zero basis. (The costs incurred in developing the goodwill are deducted as paid, and therefore the taxpayer never cumulates a basis greater than zero.) But property can still be "of a character subject to the allowance for depreciation" even though it has a zero basis. Nevertheless, self-developed goodwill is not of a character subject to the allowance for depreciation because it has no limited and ascertainable useful life; see Treas. Reg. § 1.167(a)–3(a).

14. The purchased goodwill of a business.

Goodwill acquired by purchase is an "amortizable section 197 intangible"; § 197(d)(1)(A) & (c)(1). It can be amortized over 15 years; § 197(a). Under § 197(f)(7), any amortizable § 197 intangible is treated as property of a character subject to the allowance for depreciation. Thus, purchased goodwill falls within § 1221(a)(2) and is not a capital asset.

15. Ten building lots held for sale through real-estate brokers. The lots were part of a 100–acre parcel of farm land that the taxpayer, a full-time practicing lawyer, had inherited from her father 6 years ago. When she first acquired the land, which is located just outside the limits of University City, the taxpayer had rented it out for use as a farm. Two years ago, the taxpayer subdivided 20 acres, installed streets, drainage, water, sewage and electricity, and sold the land (through brokers) to 20 different purchasers for use as building lots. After making similar improvements to another 10 acres last year, the taxpayer subdivided that subparcel into another 10 lots, all of which were sold through brokers to different buyers. Earlier this year, she made similar improvements to another 10 acres, which she subdivided into the 10 lots now being offered for sale.

The issue here is whether the lots are capital assets or whether they are excluded from the capital-asset category because they are being held for sale in the ordinary course of business; see § 1221(a)(1). That is, it is necessary to determine whether the property is held "primarily for sale" and whether the sales are made in the ordinary course of business. In resolving these issues, the courts examine a multitude of factors. All we can do here is to list some of the considerations that might induce the court to resolve the issue for one side or the other.

Probably the single most important criterion is the frequency and regularity of the taxpayer's sales. Ordinary-income treatment is likely whenever sales extend over a long period of time and are numerous, as opposed to a few isolated sales or a "passive or gradual liquidation" of the property; Biedenharn Realty Co., Inc. v. United States, 526 F.2d 409, 416 (5th Cir. 1976). In our problem, T has made 30 lot sales in the preceding two years and is offering ten more for sale. On these facts, a court could conclude that T's sales were not "isolated" but evinced a systematic plan to develop and sell the entire parcel. We do not know whether T is reinvesting the sales proceeds in additional property with development potential; if she is, that strengthens the case for ordinary-income treatment, for it makes the activity appear to be a side business. Even if T is not purchasing more land, however, she appears to have an adequate supply for future development. T did not purchase the land, of course, but inherited it. That may suggest T is simply attempting to liquidate an inheritance. But if T is just interested in disposing of the property, she could surely sell a 100–acre parcel in a single transaction. By subdividing the land and selling it off as building lots, she may increase her profit, but the "business-like" nature of the liquidation suggests that she has entered the development business. That is, what was once an inheritance held as an investment may turn into a business in which sales are being made in the ordinary course.

Where, as here, the taxpayer has made substantial improvements to aid in the sale of the property, the gains are more likely to be treated as ordinary; e.g., *Biedenharn*, 526 F.2d at 417. A program of solicitation and advertising also militates in favor of ordinary-income treatment. Although there is no indication that T advertised the lots directly, T's brokers presumably did. Indeed if business is good enough, maybe active promotion is not necessary.

Although T utilized brokers in selling the lots, the employment of brokers does not shield T from ordinary-income treatment; see *Beidenharn*, 526 F.2d at 419. It may be important to know what role T played in the broker's sales: Were the selling prices and credit policy determined by T or by the brokers? How much time did T devote to the development and sales activities? A court might also inquire into how the income earned from lot sales compared to T's income from law practice over the period in question, though the relevance of that question is unclear.

B. THE SALE-OR-EXCHANGE REQUIREMENT

Code: §§ 1271(a); 331(a); 165(g)(1) & (2); 166(d); 1241; 1235(a) & (b). Note § 1234A.

1. In the absence of a special statutory rule treating the disposition as a sale or exchange, which of the following recognized gains result from a sale or exchange?

(a) M owned a building with an adjusted basis of $40 (000 omitted throughout) and a value of $100. The building was completely destroyed by fire. The building was fully insured, and the insurer paid M $100 for the loss.

The destruction of property by fire or other casualty and reimbursement from insurance is not considered a sale or exchange because the property does not survive the transaction; Helvering v. William Flaccus Oak Leather Co., 313 U.S. 247 (1941). Today the statute sometimes treats such transactions as sales or exchanges; e.g., §§ 1231; 165(h), which are discussed in Chapters 28 and 36, respectively.

Keep in mind that if M made a timely purchase of qualifying replacement property, she could elect under § 1033 not to recognize the gain, in which case we would not reach the characterization issue. Only recognized gains and recognized and allowable losses are characterized, though in determining whether a loss is allowable for this purpose, the limits on the allowability of capital losses are necessarily disregarded; Treas. Reg. § 1.1222–1(a).

(b) M's building (in (a)) was condemned by the state under its power of eminent domain. The state paid M $100 as compensation for the taking.

Even in the absence of a special rule, the taking of the taxpayer's property by condemnation is considered a "sale," albeit a non-volitional one, because the property survives in the hands of the transferee; Hawaiian Gas Prods., Ltd. v. Commissioner, 126 F.2d 4 (9th Cir. 1942). Today § 1231, discussed in Chapter 28, prescribes the character of many condemnation gains and losses.

(c) C owned a $100 promissory note of which D was the maker. C's adjusted basis in the note was $40. D pays C $100 cash, and C marks the note "paid in full."

In the absence of a special rule, the collection of the balance due on a note would not be a sale or exchange because the note is extinguished by payment and therefore does not survive the transaction; see e.g., Hudson v. Commissioner, 20

T.C. 734 (1953). Today, however, § 1271(a)(1) treats an amount received in "retirement" of a debt instrument as an amount received "in exchange therefor."

(d) D satisfied the note (in (c)) by transferring to C corporate stock with an adjusted basis of $50 and a value of $100.

As noted in the preceding problem, in the absence of § 1271(a), C's collection of the note would not be a sale or exchange.

D's transfer of the stock in satisfaction of the $100 debt is considered a sale or exchange of the stock; Kenan v. Commissioner, 114 F.2d 217 (2d Cir. 1940). The transaction is viewed as if D sold the stock for cash and used the proceeds to pay the debt.

(e) O owned property (adjusted basis of $50) subject to a non-recourse debt of $100. The property had fallen in value to $80, and O conveyed the property to the mortgagee.

O realizes and recognizes gain of $50 on the transfer to the mortgagee. Early cases held that the transfer was not a sale or exchange because the mortgagor received no consideration on the transfer. Today, however, it is well-established that a conveyance of property subject to non-recourse indebtedness is a sale or exchange; see, e.g., Freeland v. Commissioner, 74 T.C. 970 (1980) (overruling contrary decisions).

2. T owned a non-depreciable capital asset (held for investment for several years) with an adjusted basis of $40. Determine whether each of the following alternative dispositions of the asset results in capital gain or capital loss.

(a) The property is land. T exchanged the property for another parcel of land to be held for investment. The property received has a value of $90, and T also received $10 cash to equalize the exchange.

T realizes a gain of $60. The transaction qualifies as a like-kind exchange under § 1031. Because T also received cash, the realized gain is recognized to the extent of the $10 boot received. Only recognized gain is characterized; § 1222(3) ("to the extent such gain is taken into account in computing gross income"). The gain is a long-term capital gain because it arose from the "exchange" of a capital asset with a long-term holding period.

(b) The property is a corporate bond. The issuer retired the bond by paying T the $100 face amount of the bond.

In the absence of a special rule, the retirement of a bond would not be a sale or exchange by T because the bond is extinguished by payment and does not survive T's disposition. However, § 1271(a) treats the amount received by the holder on retirement of any debt instrument as received "in *exchange* therefor" (emphasis added). Thus T's realized and recognized gain of $60 is treated as arising from the exchange of a capital asset and is therefore a long-term capital gain.

(c) The property is stock in X Corporation. X is liquidated and T receives $100 in the liquidating distribution.

In the absence of a special rule, the gain recognized by a shareholder on the liquidation of a corporation would be ordinary for want of a sale or exchange. (The stock is extinguished in the liquidation and does not survive the transaction.) However, § 331(a) treats amounts received by a shareholder in complete liquidation of a corporation as "payment in *exchange* for the stock) (emphasis added). That furnishes the necessary exchange to make T's $60 recognized gain a long-term capital gain.

(d) The property is stock in Y Corporation. Y goes into bankruptcy, and the stock becomes worthless.

Here's another case where, in the absence of a special rule, the loss would be ordinary for lack of a sale or exchange because the stock does not survive its becoming worthless. But again Congress has supplied the requisite exchange by statute: Section 165(g)(1) provides that if a "security" that is a capital asset becomes worthless during the year, the loss is treated as arising from the sale or exchange of a capital asset on the last day of the year. (For this purpose, the term security includes a share of stock in a corporation; § 165(g)(2).) T's $40 loss is therefore a long-term capital loss.

(e) The property is a note of which T's son-in-law, S, is the maker. T, who is not in the business of lending money, received the note when he lent S $40 to start a business. The business failed, and S, who is hopelessly insolvent, is unable to repay.

Assuming that this was a bona fide loan, T is entitled to a $40 deduction when the note becomes worthless. But as in the preceding problem, the note appears not to have been disposed of by means of a sale or exchange. However, § 166(d) treats a non-business debt such as this as a "loss from the sale or exchange * * * of a capital asset held for not more than 1 year." T's loss is therefore a short-term capital loss.

(f) The property is a claim for breach of contract, fraud and misrepresentation, which T purchased from a third party. T receives $100 in full settlement of the claim.

The claim would be a capital asset (property held by the taxpayer and not within any of the exceptions to the capital-asset definition in § 1221(a)). However, in Nahey v. Commissioner, 111 T.C. 256 (1998), aff'd, 196 F.3d 866 (7th Cir. 1999), the court held that the settlement of a claim was not a sale or exchange because the claim was extinguished in the transaction. The $60 recognized gain would therefore be ordinary income.

3. T receives $100 from her landlord in consideration of cancelling T's apartment lease. How should T treat the payment?

The apartment lease is a capital asset, but has T disposed of it by sale or exchange? In the absence of a special rule, the answer would apparently be no, as the lease does not survive its surrender to the landlord. However, § 1241 treats an amount received by a lessee in cancellation of a lease as received "in exchange for" the lease. So, the payment can be treated as a capital gain, long- or short-term, depending upon how long T had held the lease.

4. P, a professional inventor, transfers all substantial rights to a patent to L. L will pay P an annual royalty based upon L's sales of the product covered by the patent. How should P treat the royalty payments?

One might wonder whether the transfer of the patent would be considered a "sale or exchange" where the consideration for the transfer is based upon the exploitation of the patent. Moreover, it seems doubtful that a patent held by a professional inventor is a capital asset—would it not be excluded by § 1221(a)(1)? Happily for P, however, § 1235(a) answers both of these questions in the affirmative: The "holder's" transfer of all substantial rights to a patent is treated as a sale or exchange of a capital asset with a long-term holding period even though the payments to be received are contingent on the productivity or use of the patent. The term holder includes an individual whose efforts created the property; § 1235(b)(1).

Chapter 28

QUASI-CAPITAL GAINS AND LOSSES—
SECTION 1231

Code: §§ 1221(a)(2); 1231; 1222(1)–(4). Note § 1033(a)(2).

In each of the following problems, determine the character of the recognized gain or allowable loss. In each case, these are all of T's *realized* gains and losses for the year. No asset is held for sale to customers in the ordinary course of business nor subject to depreciation recapture. Unless otherwise indicated, assume that T had held each asset for more than one year and that § 1033 does not apply to any involuntary conversion.

1. $10,000 gain on sale of land used in business.

The gain is recognized; § 1001(c). The land is not a capital asset because it is real property used in business; § 1221(a)(2). The land is "property used in the trade or business" within the meaning of § 1231(b)(1) (real property used in business and held for more than one year). (We will use the term "§ 1231 property" or "§ 1231 asset" as a shorthand expression for property that qualifies as "property used in the trade or business" under § 1231(b).) The gain is a "§ 1231 gain" because it arose from the sale of § 1231 property; § 1231(a)(3)(A). T's § 1231 gain ($10,000) exceeds his § 1231 loss (zero), and therefore the gain is characterized as a long-term capital gain; § 1231(a)(1).

2. $10,000 loss on sale of equipment used in business.

The loss is recognized (§ 1001(c)) and allowable (§ 165(a) & (c)(1)). The equipment is not a capital asset because of § 1221(a)(2) (depreciable property used in business). It is § 1231 property; § 1231(b). The loss is therefore a § 1231 loss (because arising from the sale of the property); § 1231(a)(3)(B). Because T's § 1231 gain (zero) does not exceed the § 1231 loss ($10,000), the loss is characterized as an ordinary loss; § 1231(a)(2).

3. $10,000 gain on condemnation of land used in business. How would your answer differ if T had held the land for only 8 months?

As noted above, the land is § 1231 property; see § 1231(b)(1). The gain is therefore a § 1231 gain (recognized gain from the involuntary conversion of § 1231 property); § 1231(a)(3)(A)(ii). Since the § 1231 gain ($10,000) exceeds the § 1231 loss (zero), the gain is a long-term capital gain; § 1231(a)(1).

If T had held the land for only 8 months before the condemnation, the land would not be § 1231 property, as § 1231(b)(1) requires that a qualifying asset be held for more than one year. The land is not a capital asset because it is real property used in business (without regard to the length of its holding period); § 1221(a)(2). A condemnation is a sale (see Hawaiian Gas Prods. Ltd. v. Commissioner, 126 F.2d 4 (1942)), but the sale of a non-capital asset results in ordinary gain. So, T's recognized gain would be ordinary.

If § 1033 provided non-recognition, we would not reach the question of characterization. We don't characterize *unrecognized* gains.

4. $10,000 loss on condemnation of land used in business. How would your answer differ if T had held the land for only 8 months?

T's $10,000 loss is recognized (§ 1001(c)) and allowable (§ 165(a) & (c)(1)). (Section 1033 applies only to gains.) The loss is a § 1231 loss because arising from the involuntary conversion of § 1231 property; § 1231(a)(3)(B). Because T's § 1231 gain (zero) does not exceed the § 1231 loss ($10,000), the loss is ordinary; § 1231(a)(2).

If the land had been held for only 8 months, the land would not be § 1231 property, which must be held for more than one year; see § 1231(b)(1). And it would not be a capital asset because used in business; see § 1221(a)(2). Although, as noted above, condemnation has been held to constitute a "sale," loss on the sale of a non-capital asset results in ordinary loss unless some special characterization rule applies, and no such rule applies here. T has an ordinary loss of $10,000.

5. $10,000 gain on condemnation of land held for investment. How would your answer differ if T had held the land for only 8 months?

The land, which is held for investment, is a capital asset; the exclusion from capital-asset status of § 1221(a)(2) does not apply unless the property is held for use in *business*, and here the land is held for investment. The gain is nevertheless a § 1231 gain because it is a gain from the condemnation of a capital asset (1) with a long-term holding period and (2) held in connection with a transaction entered into for profit; see § 1231(a)(3)(A)(ii)(II). Since the § 1231 gain ($10,000) exceeds the § 1231 loss (zero), the gain is a long-term capital gain; § 1231(a)(1).

If T had held the land for only 8 months, the gain is not a § 1231 gain because T's holding period is not greater than a year; see § 1231(a)(3)(A)(ii)(II). The land is a capital asset (with a short-term holding period), the condemnation is a sale (under *Hawaiian Gas Prods.*, discussed above), and therefore the gain is characterized as a short-term capital gain; § 1222(1).

6. $10,000 loss on condemnation of land held for investment. How would your answer differ if T had held the land for only 8 months?

The loss is recognized (§ 1001(c)) and allowable (§ 165(a) & (c)(2)). The loss is a § 1231 loss because it arose from the condemnation of a long-term capital asset that was held for investment; § 1231(a)(3)(B). Since T's § 1231 gain (zero) does not exceed the loss ($10,000), the loss is ordinary; § 1231(a)(2).

If the land had been held for only 8 months, the loss would be a short-term capital loss, as the land is a capital asset and condemnation is regarded as a sale under *Hawaiian Gas Prods.*

7. $10,000 gain on condemnation of T's vacation home.

If the gain is recognized (i.e., § 1033 non-recognition does not apply), it is characterized under § 1222(3) as a long-term capital gain, as the vacation home is a capital asset under § 1221(a) and condemnation is a sale. So, T has made a sale of a capital asset with a long-term holding period. Section 1231 does not apply here because, even though we have the condemnation of a capital asset held for more than one year, the asset is not held in connection with business or investment, as required by § 1231(a)(3)(ii)(II).

8. $10,000 loss on condemnation of T's vacation home.

The loss is not allowed, so we don't characterize the loss.

9. $10,000 gain on the destruction by fire of T's business building. How would your answer differ if T had held the building for only eight months?

The building is § 1231 property (depreciable and real property used in business); § 1231(b)(1). The gain is a § 1231 gain (involuntary conversion of § 1231 property; § 1231(a)(3)(A)(ii)(I)). The gain is initially assigned to the "firepot" or casualty hotchpot of § 1231(a)(4)(C) because the gain arose from the destruction by fire of § 1231 property. However, the firepot loss (zero) does not exceed the firepot gain ($10,000), and so the gain is aggregated with T's other § 1231 gains and losses (T has no other gains or losses in this case). Because the § 1231 gain ($10,000) exceeds the § 1231 loss (zero), the gain is a long-term capital gain; § 1231(a)(1).

If the building had been held for only 8 months, it would not be § 1231 property (because not held for more than one year). The gain would be ordinary because the property is not a capital asset and the disposition is not by means of a "sale or exchange" as is required for short-term-capital-gain treatment under § 1222(1); see Helvering v. William Flaccus Oak Leather Co., 313 U.S. 247 (1941) (fire destroyed taxpayer's factory and taxpayer reimbursed by insurance proceeds; *held*: not a "sale or exchange").

10. $10,000 loss on the destruction by fire of T's business equipment.

The business equipment is § 1231 property (depreciable business property); § 1231(b)(1). The loss from the fire is assigned to the firepot; § 1231(a)(4)(C). Since the firepot loss ($10,000) exceeds the firepot gain (zero), § 1231 does not characterize the loss, and it must be characterized under 1222. It is ordinary because the equipment is not a capital asset and, as noted above, the disposition is not by way of sale or exchange.

11. $10,000 gain on sale of land held for use in business and $5,000 loss on sale of equipment used in business.

Both the land and the equipment are § 1231 properties, so we have a § 1231 gain of $10,000 and § 1231 loss of $5,000. Because the gains exceed the losses, the gain is a long-term capital gain and the loss is a long-term capital loss; § 1231(a)(1).

12. $10,000 loss on sale of equipment used in business and $5,000 gain on condemnation of land held for investment, and T:

(a) made a timely reinvestment of the entire condemnation proceeds under § 1033;

If T elects not to recognize the $5,000 gain, it is not characterized; see § 1231(a)(4)(A)(i) (gains included in hotchpot only to extent "taken into account in computing gross income"). The $10,000 loss on the sale of the equipment is a § 1231 loss, and because the § 1231 gains (none) do not exceed the losses ($10,000), the loss is ordinary; § 1231(a)(2).

(b) did not make a timely reinvestment under § 1033.

T must recognize the $5,000 gain, which is a § 1231 gain (condemnation of long-term capital asset held in connection with investment); § 1231(a)(3)(A)(ii)(II). The 1231 gain ($5,000) does not exceed the § 1231 loss ($10,000), so both are characterized as ordinary; § 1231(a)(2).

13. $10,000 gain on sale of land used in business and $5,000 loss on destruction by fire of business equipment.

Both assets are § 1231 assets. We begin with the firepot, to which the $5,000 loss is assigned. Since the firepot loss ($5,000) exceeds the firepot gain (zero), the loss is not characterized under § 1231 ("this subsection shall not apply"); § 1231(a)(4)(C). The loss is ordinary for lack of (1) a capital asset and (2) a sale or exchange.

The § 1231 gain ($10,000) exceeds the § 1231 loss (zero), so the gain is a long-term capital gain; § 1231(a)(1).

14. $10,000 loss on sale of land used in business and $15,000 gain on destruction by fire of business equipment.

The $15,000 gain (assuming that it is recognized) is assigned initially to the firepot. But since firepot losses (zero) do not exceed gains ($15,000), the gain is aggregated in the 1231(a)(1) hotchpot with the $10,000 loss. Since the gain exceeds the loss, the gain is a long-term capital gain and the loss is a long-term capital loss; § 1231(a)(1).

15. $10,000 gain on sale of a business building, $10,000 gain on destruction by fire of a business building and $5,000 loss on hurricane damage to business equipment.

The $10,000 gain from the fire and the $5,000 loss from hurricane damage are firepot transactions. Since the firepot loss ($5,000) does not exceed the firepot gain ($10,000), the firepot loss and gain are aggregated with the $10,000 gain on the sale of the building. The aggregate gains ($20,000) exceed the loss ($5,000), so T has long-term capital gain of $20,000 and long-term capital loss of $5,000.

16. $10,000 gain on sale of a business building, $5,000 gain on destruction by fire of a business building, and $10,000 loss on hurricane damage to business equipment.

Now the firepot loss ($10,000) exceeds the firepot gain ($5,000), so the gain and loss are not characterized under § 1231; § 1231(a)(4)(C). Both are ordinary because (1) neither asset disposed of was a capital asset (see § 1221(a)(2)) and (2) neither was disposed of in a sale or exchange; see § 1222(3) & (4).

The $10,000 gain is a § 1231 gain, and, since the § 1231 gain ($10,000) exceeds the § 1231 loss (zero), the gain is a long-term capital gain.

17. $10,000 loss on sale of a business building, $25,000 gain on destruction by fire of a business building, and $10,000 loss on hurricane damage to business equipment.

The casualty gain and loss are assigned to the firepot, but the loss ($10,000) does not exceed the gain ($25,000), so they are aggregated with the $10,000 loss from the sale under § 1231(a). The § 1231 gain ($25,000) exceeds the § 1231 losses ($20,000), so T has $25,000 of long-term capital gain and $20,000 of long-term capital loss; § 1231(a)(1).

18. $5,000 loss on sale of a business building, $6,000 gain on the condemnation of a building held for investment, and $10,000 loss on hurricane damage to business equipment.

The hurricane loss is assigned initially to the firepot. Even though the $6,000 gain resulted from an involuntary conversion, that gain is not assigned to the firepot because it did not result from "fire, storm, shipwreck, or other casualty, or from theft"; § 1231(a)(4)(C). The firepot loss ($10,000) exceeds the firepot gain (zero), so the loss is ordinary for want of (1) a capital asset and (2) a sale or exchange. The remaining gain and loss are capital because the $6,000 gain exceeds the $5,000 loss; § 1231(a)(1).

In the following problems, characterize the recognized gains and allowable losses. In each case assume that (1) these are the taxpayer's only recognized gains and losses for the year, (2) each asset had a long-term holding period, (3) the taxpayer engaged in no § 1231 transactions before year 1, and (4) no asset is subject to depreciation recapture under § 1245 or § 1250.

19. In year 1, T recognized a $100,000 loss on the sale of land used in business and a $50,000 gain on the destruction by fire of a building held for investment. In year 2, T recognized a $20,000 gain on the sale of a business building. In year 3, T recognized a $40,000 gain on the sale of a business building.

Year 1: The $50,000 gain is a § 1231 gain (involuntary conversion of capital asset held in connection with investment); § 1231(a)(3)((A)(ii)(II). It is initially assigned to the firepot (see § 1231(a)(4)(C)(ii)), but since the firepot loss (zero) does not exceed the firepot gain ($50,000), the $50,000 gain must be characterized in the § 1231(a) hotchpot. Since the § 1231 loss ($100,000) exceeds the § 1231 gain ($50,000), both the loss and the gain are ordinary; § 1231(a)(2).

Year 2: Although the $20,000 gain at first appears to be a long-term capital gain under § 1231(a)(1), § 1231(c) makes the gain ordinary. T has a "net § 1231 gain" of $20,000; § 1231(c)(3). In year 1, T had a net § 1231 loss of $50,000 ($100,000 § 1231 loss less $50,000 § 1231 gain). In year 2, T also has a "non-recaptured net § 1231 loss" of $50,000 ($50,000 net § 1231 loss for year 1, since none of the loss has been recaptured in preceding years); § 1231(c)(2). T's year–2 net § 1231 gain is therefore characterized as ordinary income since it does not exceed the amount of the non-recaptured net § 1231 loss; § 1231(c)(1).

Year 3: Again the gain would be long-term capital gain under § 1231(a)(1) but for the recapture rule of § 1231(c). T has a net non-recaptured § 1231 loss of $30,000 ($50,000 aggregate net § 1231 loss from year 1, less $20,000 recaptured in year 2); § 1231(c)(2). So, the first $30,000 of net § 1231 gain for year 3 is characterized as ordinary income; § 1231(c)(1). The $10,000 balance is long-term capital gain.

20. In year 1, S recognized a $100,000 gain on the sale of land used in business and a $50,000 loss on the condemnation of an investment asset. In year 2, T recognized a $100,000 loss on the sale of a business building.

Both of the year–1 transactions are § 1231 transactions; § 1231(a)(3)(A)(i), (a)(3)(A)(ii)(II) & (a)(3)(B). Because the § 1231 gain ($100,000) exceeds the § 1231 loss ($50,000), the gain is a long-term capital gain and the loss is a long-term capital loss; 1231(a)(1). In year 2, the loss is ordinary under § 1231(a)(2). Section 1231(c) has no application to the year–2 loss. Thus § 1231 permits the taxpayer capital-gain treatment followed by ordinary-loss treatment.

Chapter 29

DEPRECIATION RECAPTURE AND
RELATED ISSUES

A. SECTION 1245

Code: § 1245. Review §§ 179(a); 1001(a), (b) & (c); 1012; 1011(a); 1231; 1015(a); 1014(a) & (b); 1031(a), (b), (c) & (d).

Regulations: §§ 1.179–1(f)(1); 1.1245–1(b) & (d); 1.1245–2(c)(1)(i) & (iv); 1.1245–2(c)(4).

General facts for problems 1–7: In year 1, T purchased for $150 (000 omitted throughout) moveable equipment for use in her business and properly deducted $90 of depreciation before disposing of the equipment in year 3. Unless otherwise indicated, T made no election under § 179 when the equipment was acquired. Assume that when a party disposes of the equipment, the disposition is the party's only disposition of property for that year. Determine the amount and character of the various parties' recognized gain or allowable loss.

1.   T sells the equipment in year 3 for $200.

This problem introduces depreciation recapture under § 1245. Before turning to the problems, let's consider the problem that § 1245 attempts to solve. Suppose that the taxpayer purchases business equipment for $50,000, properly deducts $18,000 of depreciation and then sells the property to an unrelated party for $40,000. On the sale, the taxpayer realizes and recognizes $8,000 of gain ($40,000 amount realized less $32,000 adjusted basis). In the absence of § 1245, the gain would be a § 1231 gain, which often results in characterizing the gain as a long-term capital gain. The gain is strictly a "make-up" gain, in that it results from the taxpayer's deducting $18,000 of depreciation with respect to the property, which declined in value by only $10,000 during the taxpayer's use. On the sale, the taxpayer must make up for this "overdepreciation" by recognizing gain. The depreciation deductions, however, reduced ordinary income; if the make-up gain were long-term capital gain, the taxpayer would effectively be converting ordinary income into capital gain. Section 1245 prevents this possibility by characterizing the make-up gain as ordinary income.

At the time of disposition, T's adjusted basis is $60 ($150 cost less $90 depreciation); § 1011(a). T realizes a gain of $140 on the sale ($200 amount realized less $60 adjusted basis); § 1001(a). The gain is recognized; § 1001(c).

Although the equipment is a § 1231 asset (depreciable property used in business—§ 1231(b)(1)), it is also "§ 1245 property" because it is "property of a character subject to the allowance for depreciation" and "personal property" (in the sense of being a "moveable" rather than in the sense of being personal-use property); § 1245(a)(3). Section 1245(a)(1) treats some or all of the gain on the disposition of § 1245 property as ordinary income. To determine how much of the gain is ordinary, we compare the "recomputed basis" with the amount realized to determine which is the lesser; the excess of the lesser of those two figures over the adjusted basis is characterized as ordinary income.

Here the recomputed basis is $150 ($60 adjusted basis, plus the $90 of depreciation adjustments "reflected" in the adjusted basis). (The $90 of depreciation deductions reduced the adjusted basis and hence are "reflected" in the adjusted basis.) The amount realized is $200. The lesser of these two figures is the recomputed basis of $150. The § 1245 ordinary gain is $90 ($150 recomputed basis less $60 adjusted basis).

The total recognized gain on the sale is $140. How is the other $50 of gain to be characterized? Since the equipment is a § 1231 asset, the balance of the gain is § 1231 gain. Since this is T's only disposition for the year, the § 1231 gain ($50) exceeds the § 1231 loss (zero), and the $50 gain is a long-term capital gain; § 1231(a)(1). So, T has $90 of ordinary gain and $50 of long-term capital gain.

Section 1245 contains some strange new terminology that we have not encountered before. But reflect on how the provision works in practice. We take the smaller of recomputed basis or amount realized and then subtract the adjusted basis to arrive at the § 1245 ordinary gain. The recomputed basis is adjusted basis, plus depreciation. When recomputed basis is less than amount realized, we have RB = AB + Depreciation, and the § 1245 gain is given by RB – AB = AB + Depreciation – AB = Depreciation. When the amount realized is less than the recomputed basis, the § 1245 gain is AR – AB, which is the realized gain. In other words, § 1245 recaptures as ordinary income the lesser of the taxpayer's realized gain or the amount of depreciation taken with respect to the property.

2. T sells the equipment in year 3 for $45.

T realizes a loss of $15 ($60 adjusted basis less $45 amount realized). The loss is recognized (§ 1001(c)) and allowable (§ 165(a) & (c)(1)). The equipment is a § 1231 asset. Since the § 1231 gain (zero) does not exceed the § 1231 loss ($15), the loss is ordinary; § 1231(a)(2). Section 1245 does not apply to losses; Treas. Reg. § 1.1245–1(d).

   3. In year 3, T gives the equipment (then worth $75) to her daughter, D, who uses the equipment for personal use and then sells it in year 5 for:

   (a) $100.

   The first issue is whether is T must recognize gain on the transfer of the equipment to D. A donor who transfers property by gift usually does not recognize gain or loss on the transfer. (Section 1015, which generally transfers the donor's adjusted basis to the donee, can be seen as a sort of "implicit" non-recognition rule.) But here the property is § 1245 property, and the last sentence of § 1245(a) tells us that the § 1245 gain "shall be recognized notwithstanding any other provision of this subtitle." Here, however, § 1245(b)(1) provides an exception for the transfer of property by gift. So, T does not recognize gain on the transfer of the equipment to D.

   D assumes T's $60 adjusted basis; § 1015(a). Since D cannot depreciate property that she holds for personal use (recall § 167(a)(1) & (2)), D's adjusted basis remains the same at the time of the sale in year 5. On the sale, D realizes a gain of $40 ($100 amount realized less $60 adjusted basis); § 1001(a). The gain is recognized; § 1001(c). The equipment remains § 1245 property in D's hands (property which "has been" subject to the allowance for depreciation—as it was here when the equipment was held by T); § 1245(a)(3). D's recomputed basis is the property's adjusted basis ($60) recomputed by adding back all adjustments for depreciation allowable to D (here there are none) or "to any other person"; § 1245(a)(2)(A). The $90 of depreciation allowed to T is "reflected" in D's adjusted basis, as the adjustments were reflected in T's adjusted basis, which was assumed by D. Therefore, D's recomputed basis is $150 ($60 adjusted basis, plus $90 of depreciation taken when T held the property).

   D's amount realized ($100) is less than the recomputed basis ($150), so D's ordinary gain is $40 ($100 amount realized less $60 adjusted basis); § 1245(a)(1).

   (b) $50.

   D realizes a loss of $10. The loss is recognized but not allowed because it is not incurred in business or a transaction entered into for profit; see § 165(c)(1) & (2). The characterization issue does not arise.

4. In year 3, T gives the equipment (then worth $75) to her daughter, D, who uses the equipment in her business, properly deducts another $15 of depreciation, and then sells the equipment in year 5 for:

(a) $65.

Again § 1245(b)(1) prevents T from having to recognize gain on the gift transfer to D. At the time of the sale, D's adjusted basis is $45 ($60 adjusted basis assumed from T, less $15 of depreciation taken by D). On the sale, D realizes gain of $20 ($65 amount realized less $45 adjusted basis). D's recomputed basis is $150 ($45 of adjusted basis, plus the $90 of depreciation that T took, plus the $15 of depreciation that D took). D's amount realized ($65) is less than D's recomputed basis ($150), and D's ordinary gain is $20 ($65 amount realized less $45 adjusted basis).

(b) $25.

As in (a), D's adjusted basis at the time of sale is $45, and D realizes a loss of $20 on the sale ($65 amount realized less $45 adjusted basis). The loss is recognized (§ 1001(c)) and allowed (§ 165(a) & (c)(1)). As mentioned above, § 1245 does not apply to losses. This being D's only § 1231 transaction for the year, the loss is characterized as an ordinary loss; § 1231(a)(2).

5. In year 3, T dies and the equipment passes to her estate. At the time of T's death, the equipment is worth $65. T's estate continues T's business and properly deducts $20 of additional depreciation before selling the equipment in year 5 for $75.

The transfer of property from the decedent to her estate does not result in the recognition of gain or loss; Rev. Rul. 73–183, 1973–1 C.B. 364. But does the last sentence of § 1245(a)(1) force the recognition of gain when § 1245 property passes at death? No, because of the exception of § 1245(b)(2). So, T recognizes no gain with respect to the transfer.

The equipment is property "acquired from a decedent" (property acquired by the decedent's estate from the decedent—§ 1014(b)(1)), and so the estate acquires a basis for the equipment equal to (generally) its value on the date of the decedent's death—$65 in this case; § 1014(a).

Since the estate uses the equipment in its business, it can depreciate the property; § 167(a)(1). Its basis for depreciation is $65 (the estate's unadjusted basis, as it has not yet been depreciated by the estate); § 167(c)(1). After deducting depreciation of $20, the estate's adjusted basis is $45. On the sale, the estate realizes and recognizes gain of $30 ($75 amount realized less $45 adjusted basis).

In the estate's hands, the equipment is both a § 1231 asset and § 1245 property. (To be a § 1231 asset, it must have a long-term holding period. But even if the estate has not actually held the property for more than a year, § 1223(9) makes the holding period long-term.)

The estate's recomputed basis is $65 ($45 adjusted basis, plus $20 of depreciation allowable to the estate). Notice that the depreciation taken by T is not "reflected" in the estate's adjusted basis, as the starting point in computing the estate's basis was not T's adjusted basis but the value of the property at the time of T's death. In effect, the step-up in basis at death erases the § 1245 ordinary-income taint.

Since the estate's recomputed basis ($65) is less than its amount realized ($75), the estate's ordinary gain is $20 ($65 recomputed basis less $45 adjusted basis); § 1245(a)(1). The estate's other $10 of recognized gain is § 1231 gain. Since the estate's § 1231 gain ($10) exceeds its § 1231 loss (zero), the gain is a long-term capital gain; § 1231(a)(1). In summary, the estate has $20 of ordinary gain and $10 of long-term capital gain.

6.   In year 3, T exchanged the equipment (then worth $80) for equipment of like kind to be used in T's business. The new equipment had a value of $70 and T received $10 of cash to equalize the exchange.

On the exchange, T realizes a gain of $20 ($80 amount realized less $60 adjusted basis). The exchange is a like-kind exchange with boot received. Apart from § 1245, T would recognize the gain to the extent of the $10 boot received; § 1031(b). Does § 1245(a) require the recognition of the other $10 of gain? No. The transaction falls under the exception of § 1245(b)(4), which provides generally that the gain recognized under § 1245(a) "shall not exceed * * * the amount of gain recognized on such disposition (determined without regard to this section [1245] * * *." In this case, T would have been required to recognize only $10 of gain (under § 1031(b)) if § 1245 did not apply.

In the usual fashion, we determine the character of the $10 recognized gain by comparing T's amount realized ($80) with her recomputed basis ($150). The amount realized is the smaller figure, so the potential § 1245 gain is $20 ($80 amount realized less $60 adjusted basis). However, the § 1245 gain is limited to the amount that would be recognized under § 1031(b)—here $10.

T's adjusted basis for the equipment received is $60 ($60 adjusted basis of the old equipment, less the $10 of cash received, plus $10 gain recognized); § 1031(d). T's recomputed basis for the new equipment is $140 ($60 adjusted basis, plus $90 depreciation allowed on old equipment, less $10 of ordinary gain recaptured on the like-kind exchange); Treas. Reg. § 1.1245–2(c)(4)(including examples). Notice that the depreciation adjustments taken on the old property are "reflected" in the adjusted basis of the new because the adjusted basis of the new property is derived by reference to the adjusted basis of the old under § 1031(d). Under the parenthetical phrase in § 1245(a)(2)(A), depreciation adjustments reflected in the adjusted basis of the new equipment must be added back even if the adjustments reflect depreciation taken on the old property.

7. Same as 1, except that T had properly elected under § 179 to deduct $100 of the cost of the equipment in the year of purchase. At the time of the sale, T had also been allowed depreciation of $30.

At the time of the sale, T's adjusted basis is $20 ($150 cost, less $100 expensed and $30 depreciation); see Treas. Reg. § 1.179–1(f)(1). T's realized and recognized gain is $180 ($200 amount realized less $20 adjusted basis). The equipment is both a § 1231 asset and § 1245 property.

In determining T's recomputed basis, we treat any deduction allowable under § 179 as allowable for amortization; § 1245(a)(2)(C). So, T's recomputed basis is $150 ($20 adjusted basis, plus $30 of depreciation adjustments, plus $100 of amortization adjustments); § 1245(a)(2)(A). T's recomputed basis ($150) is less than the (amount realized), so the § 1245 ordinary gain is $130 ($150 recomputed basis less $20 adjusted basis). The other $50 of gain is § 1231 gain, and since T has no other § 1231 transactions, the gain is a long-term capital gain. In summary, T has $130 of ordinary gain and $50 of long-term capital gain.

B. SECTION 1250

Code: §§ 1250(a)(1)(A) & (B)(v), (b)(1) & (3), (c), (d)(1), (2) & (4). Note §§ 1(h)(6) & (h)(1)(D).

1. In year 1, F spent $200,000 to build a barn for use in his farming business. Assume that F properly deducted $80,000 of depreciation under the 150% declining balance method, which is applicable to farm buildings. F sold the barn in year 8 for $220,000. (Ignore the land, as if only the barn had been sold.) Straight-line depreciation over the period the barn was held by F would have been $35,000. The barn sale was F's only property disposition for the year. F's tax rate on ordinary income is 35 percent. Determine F's recognized gain and the tax rate applicable to each component of the gain.

We have seen that § 1245 trumps § 1231 to recapture depreciation on the disposition of personal property and (some) fixtures. A related provision, § 1250, recaptures depreciation on the disposition of depreciable real property (buildings). Section 1250 is more modest in scope in that it recaptures only the excess of accelerated over straight-line depreciation. Since today most buildings can be depreciated only under the straight-line method (see § 168(b)(3)(A) & (B)), the scope of § 1250 is limited. But as this problem illustrates, it can still come into play occasionally.

At the time of the sale, F's adjusted basis is $120,000 ($200,000 cost less $80,000 deprecation). F realizes and recognizes gain of $100,000 ($220,000 amount realized less $120,000 adjusted basis). The barn is a § 1231 asset (depreciable and real property used in business—§ 1231(b)(1)) and "§ 1250 property" (real property of a character subject to the allowance for depreciation—§ 1250(c)). In characterizing the gain, § 1250, like § 1245, trumps § 1231; § 1250(h).

To determine the ordinary-income portion of the gain, § 1250(a)(1) directs us to compare the "additional depreciation" with the realized gain and to select the smaller of those amounts. The additional depreciation is (generally) the excess of the deprecation taken with respect to the property over the amount that would have been allowable if depreciation had been computed under the straight-line method; § 1250(b)(1). In this case, the additional depreciation is $45,000 ($80,000 depreciation less $35,000 allowable under the straight-line method). The realized gain is $100,000. The additional depreciation ($45,000) is less than the realized gain ($100,000), and so § 1250(a)(1) recaptures as ordinary income the "applicable percentage" of the additional depreciation. In this case, the applicable percentage is 100 percent, so the $45,000 is ordinary income. The balance of the recognized gain ($55,000) is § 1231 gain, and since F had no other property dispositions during the year, the $55,000 would be characterized as long-term capital gain.

Our work is still not finished, however, because the "unrecaptured § 1250 gain," though a long-term capital gain, is subject to tax at a 25–percent rate; § 1(h)(1)(D). The unrecaptured § 1250 gain is the *additional* amount that would be treated as ordinary income if § 1250 recaptured *all* depreciation rather than just the excess of accelerated depreciation over straight-line; § 1(h)(6)(A)(i). In this case, an additional $35,000 would have been recaptured if § 1250 recaptured *all* depreciation, so that is the amount of the unrecaptured § 1250 gain, which is subject to tax at 25 percent. The remaining $20,000 of gain is part of the adjusted net capital gain and taxable at a maximum rate of 15 percent. (Notice that, at least if we ignore the effect of inflation, the $20,000 is the "economic" gain on the transaction—the excess of the $220,000 selling price over the $200,000 cost of the property.)

To summarize: F has $45,000 of ordinary income taxable at 35 percent; $35,000 of unrecaptured § 1250 gain taxable at 25 percent; and $20,000 of long-term capital gain taxable at 15 percent.

C. SECTION 1239

Code: §§ 1239(a), (b) & (c); 267(c)(2), (4) & (5).

Regulation: § 1.1245–6(f).

In each of the following problems, determine (1) the seller's recognized gain, (2) the character of the gain, and (3) the tax rate applicable to each component of the gain. Assume in each case that the seller is in the 35% bracket for ordinary income and that the sale is the seller's only property disposition for the year.

1. Several years ago, M paid $300,000 for an office building for use in her business, properly deducted $100,000 of straight-line depreciation, and sold it in the current year for $550,000. The purchaser plans to use the building in business. (Ignore the land as if only the building were purchased and sold.). Alternatively, the purchaser is:

(a) X Corporation, of which M is the sole shareholder;

At the time of sale, M's adjusted basis is $200,000 ($300,000 cost less $100,000 depreciation). M's realized and recognized gain is $350,000 ($550,000 amount realized less $200,000 adjusted basis).

Turning to characterization, we note that § 1250 does not apply because M used straight-line depreciation; see § 1250(b)(1). The building is a § 1231 asset (depreciable and real property used in business—§ 1231(b)(1)), but in this case § 1239 trumps § 1231 because M sold the building to a "related person," which includes all entities that are "controlled entities" with respect to M; see § 1239(b)(1). X Corporation, of which M is sole shareholder is a controlled entity with respect to M because M owns more than 50 percent in value of the stock; § 1239(c)(1)(A). The building is depreciable in the hands of X, and so the $350,000 gain is ordinary.

(b) Y Corporation, of which M's son, S, is sole shareholder;

Same as (a)—ordinary income of $350,000. In determining whether Y is a controlled entity with respect to M, we must take account of the constructive-stock ownership rules of § 267(c); § 1239(c)(2). S is a member of M's family (a lineal descendant—§ 267(c)(4)), M is considered as owning the stock owned by his family (§ 267(c)(2)), and Y is therefore deemed to be 100–percent owned by M.

(c) D, who is M's daughter;

Although § 1239 covers a sale to a corporation owned by D, it does not apply to a sale to D directly—an odd result. So, M's gain is a long-term capital gain by virtue of § 1231(a)(1). The first $100,000 of the gain is unrecaptured § 1250 gain, which is taxable at a 25–percent rate; the remaining $250,000 of gain is taxable at 15 percent.

(d) F, who is M's spouse.

M's gain is not recognized because the sale is to M's spouse; § 1041(a)(1). Unrecognized gains are not characterized.

2. S purchased depreciable business equipment for $100,000, properly deducted $60,000 of depreciation, and sold it for $120,000 (its value) to a trust of which S's wife, W, was entitled to the income for life. The trust used the equipment in its business.

At the time of sale, S's adjusted basis is $40,000 ($100,000 cost less $60,000 depreciation). S has a realized and recognized gain of $80,000 ($120,000 amount realized less $40,000 adjusted basis). The equipment is a § 1231 asset (depreciable business property) and also § 1245 property (depreciable personal property). Whenever it applies, § 1245 trumps all of the other characterization provisions of the Code; see § 1245(d), making § 1245 applicable notwithstanding any other provision. Since the recomputed basis ($100,000) is less than the amount realized ($120,000), the § 1245 ordinary gain is $60,000 ($100,000 recomputed basis less $40,000 adjusted basis); § 1245(a)(1).

The remainder of the gain is characterized as ordinary under § 1239 because (1) the equipment is depreciable in the hands of the trust; and (2) the trust is related to S under § 1239(b)(2) (related persons include a taxpayer and a trust in which the taxpayer *or the taxpayer's spouse* is a beneficiary). So, S has $80,000 of ordinary gain—$60,000 under § 1245 and $20,000 under § 1239.

3. Several years ago D paid $400,000 for a large tract of land and held it as an investment. In the current year, D sells the land for $1,000,000 to L Corporation, which plans to divide the parcel and sell it for building lots (i.e., the land will be held for sale in the ordinary course of L's business). All of L's stock is owned by D.

D's $600,000 of realized and recognized gain will result in a long-term capital gain under § 1222(3) because the gain arose from the sale of a capital asset (see § 1221). Section 1239 does not apply here because the land is not depreciable in the hands of L. This seems very similar to the mischief § 1239 was intended to prevent—i.e., giving the taxpayer's controlled corporation a stepped-up basis that could be used to offset ordinary income at the cost of only a capital-gains tax to the taxpayer. But § 1239 does not cover this case.

Chapter 30

OTHER CHARACTERIZATION ISSUES

A. THE ARROWSMITH DOCTRINE

Case: Arrowsmith v. Commissioner, 344 U.S. 6 (1952).

1. In year 1, T sold all of the stock in a closely held corporation to B for $500,000 cash. T's adjusted basis for the stock, which he had held for several years, was $200,000. In year 3, B sued T for making fraudulent representations in connection with the stock sale. T settled the matter by paying B $100,000 cash. How should T treat the $100,000 payment?

The sale in year 1 produced a $300,000 long-term capital gain. The issue in the problem is whether the $100,000 payment in year 3 should be treated as an ordinary or capital loss.

Arrowsmith v. Commissioner, 344 U.S. 6 (1952), suggests that the loss should be capital because it relates so closely to the earlier sale. If T had not misrepresented the facts, the purchase price presumably would have been $100,000 less, and the capital gain only $200,000. If accidents of timing are not to affect the character of income, the argument goes, T should have the same long-run capital gain as someone who sold the stock for $400,000 in year 1.

As Justice Jackson's dissent points out, however, the *Arrowsmith* approach does not necessarily put T in the same position as if the original purchase price had been $100,000 less. If the $100,000 is a capital loss in year 3, T can deduct it only to the extent of his year–3 capital gains, plus up to $3,000 against ordinary income; § 1211(b). Although any amount not allowable under § 1211(b) can be carried forward indefinitely, it may be a very long time before T can obtain the tax benefit of the deduction.

Section 1341, which is discussed in Chapter 42, may provide relief for T if the tax saved by the year–3 deduction is less than the tax on the incremental $100,000 of gain in year 1.

2. What results in 1 if, instead of stock, the asset sold was a § 1231 asset that was not subject to depreciation recapture? For simplicity, assume that T has not engaged in any other § 1231 transaction (in any year).

The question here is whether *Arrowsmith* requires us to treat the year–1 gain as a long-term capital gain, which it was after the application of § 1231, or as a § 1231 gain. If we characterize the year–1 gain as a § 1231 gain, then the year–3 payment would be a § 1231 loss, which, since it is T's only § 1231 transaction, would be an ordinary loss; see § 1231(a)(2). *Arrowsmith* seems to focus on the favorable or unfavorable treatment of the original transaction in justifying corresponding treatment of the current year's transaction, an approach that suggests the year–3 loss is a capital loss.

Again, § 1341 may provide relief for T.

3. In year 1, C, the chief executive officer of publicly held P Corporation, purchased and sold P stock within a six-month period. Under § 16(b) of the Securities Exchange Act of 1934, C was required to pay to P his profit on the transaction. C made the payment in year 2. What tax result to C?

Although the Tax Court has routinely allowed ordinary deductions in § 16(b) cases, every court of appeals to consider the issue has reversed; see, e.g., Cummings v. Commissioner, 506 F.2d 449 (2d Cir. 1974) (*Arrowsmith* requires capital-loss treatment of deductions "sufficiently related to an earlier capital-gains transaction"; "sufficient" relationship existed in § 16(b) case because contrary result would give the taxpayer a "windfall" and frustrate "the policy of § 16(b) as well"). So, according to the courts of appeal, the payment results in a capital loss. Once again, § 1341 may provide relief.

B. BAD DEBTS AND WORTHLESS SECURITIES

Code: §§ 165(a), (b), (c) & (g); 166(a), (b), (d) & (e), 1244(a), (b) (c)(1) & (3), (d)(3). Review §§ 1222(2) & (4); 1271(a).

Regulations: §§ 166–1(c) & (e); 1.166–2(a), (b) & (c); 1.166–5(a) & (b); 1.166–9(a), (b), (d), (e)(1) & (2).

Cases: Putnam v. Commissioner, 352 U.S. 82 (1956);
United States v. Generes, 405 U.S. 93 (1972).

1. Two years ago, S, a cash-method taxpayer, was persuaded by a friend to make a $50,000 unsecured loan at market-rate interest to closely held X Corporation. (S is not in the business of lending money and is not a shareholder of X.) X did not prosper, and, though it kept interest payments current, it was never able to pay any principal on the note.

(a) Last week S sold the X note for $20,000. What is the character of S's loss?

S's realized and recognized loss is $30,000 ($50,000 adjusted basis less $20,000 amount realized. The loss is allowed because it arises from a transaction entered into for profit; § 165(a) & (c)(2). The note is a capital asset with a long-term holding period, and the loss on its sale is a long-term capital loss; § 1222(4).

(b) What result if S agreed to accept $20,000 from X in full satisfaction of the note, and X paid S the $20,000?

The issue here is whether the extinguishing of the note keeps the disposition from being a sale or exchange, which is a prerequisite for capital-loss treatment under § 1222(4). Although the retirement of a note would not be a sale or exchange under the caselaw, today § 1271(a) provides that an amount received on retirement of a debt instrument is treated as received in *exchange* therefor. Therefore, S's loss is a long-term capital loss.

(c) What result to S if X went into bankruptcy, was unable to pay its unsecured creditors, and was discharged from liability?

S sustains a $50,000 loss when the note becomes worthless. Again, a question arises as to whether the note's becoming worthless is a sale or exchange. In this case, § 166(d) supplies the requisite sale or exchange: it treats the loss on a non-business debt (defined in § 166(d)(2)) as "a loss from the sale or exchange * * * of a capital asset held for not more than 1 year"; § 166(d)(1). S's loss is therefore a short-term capital loss, even though her holding period in fact exceeded one year.

Characterization of the loss as short-term is favorable to the taxpayer, as short-term capital loss is first applied against short-term capital gain, with only the excess of the short-term loss over the short-term gain being offset against the net long-term capital gain that gets the benefit of the lower tax rates of § 1(h).

(d) What result to S if S's claim for $5,000 of unpaid interest for prior years was also discharged in the bankruptcy proceeding?

S is not allowed a deduction for the lost interest because, as a cash-method taxpayer, she had a zero basis in the accrued interest—i.e., she had no actual cost and no tax cost because the interest had never been included in her gross income. Section 166(b) makes clear that the loss cannot exceed the taxpayer's basis.

(e) What result in (d) if S had been an accrual-method taxpayer?

As the interest accrued, S would have been required to include the interest in gross income and would therefore obtain a tax-cost basis of $5,000 for the interest receivable. When S's claim became worthless as a result of X's bankruptcy, S would be entitled to a $5,000 deduction. Although the loss just counterbalances the earlier year's inclusion of the interest as ordinary income, the $5,000 loss is apparently treated as a short-term capital loss from a non-business bad debt under § 166(d), unless S can obtain ordinary-loss treatment under *Arrowsmith*.

2. T lent $10,000 to his brother-in-law, B, to assist him in starting a new business. The business failed, the debt was discharged in B's bankruptcy, and T was therefore unable to collect the principal due on the loan.

(a) Is T allowed a deduction for the loss?

The issue here is whether the payment is a loan or a gift to B. Although purported loans between family members are subject to special scrutiny, a non-business-bad-debt deduction is allowable for worthless intra-family debt if the parties intended to create a true debtor-creditor relationship; see e.g., Shirar v. Commissioner, 54 T.C.M. 698 (1987) (husband and wife allowed non-business bad-debt deduction for amounts lent to his brother). The lender must show that the parties intended to create an enforceable obligation and that the lender intended to enforce collection. The lender's case for a deduction is strengthened if the debtor executes a formal note, the note bears interest, the borrower made at least some payments of interest and principal, and the lender took steps to collect the note when a default occurred, though the lender's failure to make formal collection demands or take legal action may not be fatal; see id. The "gift" versus "loan" question is one of fact. If T can establish that the transfer of the cash was a loan rather than a gift, then the loss is deductible as a non-business bad debt, which is characterized as a short-term capital loss; § 166(d)(1).

(b) What if a bank had lent B the money and T had served (without consideration) as guarantor on the loan. When B took bankruptcy, T was required to pay the bank the $10,000 of principal. Is T allowed a deduction?

Not according to the regulations. Treas. Reg. § 166–9(e)(1) denies a deduction to a guarantor who receives no compensation for guaranteeing the loan. Although no provision of the statute denies a deduction to an uncompensated guarantor, the Ways and Means Committee's report on the Tax Reform Act of 1976 says that no deduction is allowable to the guarantor unless the guaranty is entered into as part of the guarantor's business or a transaction entered for profit; H.R. Rep. No. 94–658 at 177. The Report goes on to say that "a father guaranteeing a loan for his son would ordinarily not be entitled to a deduction even if he received nominal consideration for making the guaranty"; id. The regulation seems to be based upon this "non-legislative" history rather than any provision of the statute. The validity of the regulation is debatable, as the only change made by the 1976 Act to the language of § 166 was the repeal of former § 166(f), which provided business bad-debt treatment to guarantors of certain non-corporate obligations.

As a matter of policy, it is hard to see why a deduction should be allowable for the worthlessness of a direct loan (problem (a)) but not for the worthlessness of the right of subrogation where the taxpayer was the guarantor rather than the direct lender. Perhaps no deduction should ever be allowed for a bad-debt loss that was not sustained in business or in a transaction entered into for profit.

If the taxpayer guarantees a bank loan for a corporation in which he was a major shareholder, he should be entitled to a non-business bad-debt deduction when his right to recover against the original creditor becomes worthless. Even if the taxpayer receives no direct consideration in money or property for the guarantee, one who acts in good faith to protect or enhance his investment in the stock receives "reasonable consideration" for the guarantee within the meaning of Treas. Reg. § 1.166–9(e)(1).

3. R purchased for $150,000 stock in Z Corporation from another shareholder. Three years later, Z goes into bankruptcy and the stock becomes worthless.

(a) Describe the tax consequences to R.

The Z stock is a "security" within the meaning of § 165(g)(2) ("a share of stock in a corporation"). When a security which is a capital asset becomes worthless, the loss is treated as a "loss from the sale or exchange, on the last day of the taxable year, of a capital asset"—a long-term capital loss if the taxpayer's holding period by year-end exceeds one year; see § 165(g)(1). The Z stock would be a capital asset in R's hands, and R's loss is a long-term capital loss.

Keep in mind that, in the absence of § 165(g), a loss on the worthlessness of stock would be an ordinary loss for lack of a sale or exchange. A sale of the stock for a nominal consideration would give rise to a capital loss, and the thought behind § 165(g) is that major tax stakes should not turn on whether the taxpayer sells the security for a loss just before it becomes worthless or holds it until it is worthless. Both are investment-type losses and should be treated as capital losses.

(b) Suppose instead that R, a single person, was one of five shareholders who organized Z. Each contributed $150,000 cash in exchange for stock when the corporation was organized. Z derived all of its gross receipts from its active business. Although Z later tried to raise more equity capital, it was never able to do so. Z went into bankruptcy, and R's stock became worthless. What tax result to R?

Section 165(g) suggests that the loss would be a capital loss, but § 1244(a) trumps that provision to make a loss on "section 1244 stock" ordinary, at least in part. The Z stock appears to qualify as § 1244 stock: It was issued for money (or property) by a "small business corporation" and more than 50 percent of its gross receipts were derived from active business; see § 1244(c)(1). The firm is a small business corporation because the aggregate amount received by it as equity capital

($750,000) does not exceed $1,000,000. R was the original issuee of the stock, as required by § 1244(a) ("issued to such individual"). The maximum treated as ordinary loss for any year is $50,000 ($100,000 if the taxpayer is married and filing a joint return); § 1244(b). As an unmarried person, R can deduct $50,000 of the loss as an ordinary loss under § 1244(a) and the $100,000 balance as a long-term capital loss under § 165(g)(1).

Suppose R does not have enough income to absorb the $50,000 ordinary-loss deduction. Section 1244(d)(3) says that, for the purpose of the net operating loss rules of § 172, the loss (which is really an investment loss) is treated as a business loss. A business loss may enhance a net operating loss, which can be carried back to the two preceding years (and carried forward for as many as 20 years). An unused capital loss is carried forward indefinitely but is limited in its deductibility; see §§ 1211(b); 1212(b).

Note that § 1244 ordinary-loss treatment is not available in problem (a) because R was not the original issuee of the stock, as required by § 1244(a).

(c) Suppose that P, another shareholder of Z Corporation, was employed by the corporation. When the firm began experiencing financial difficulties, P lent Z $25,000 at market-rate interest. P thought the money (along with other funds being lent by other employees) might keep Z in business and preserve P's $75,000 a year job with the firm. When the firm failed, it also owed P $5,000 of back wages. Z was unable to repay either amount. P, a cash-method taxpayer, originally had paid $150,000 for his Z stock. What result to P?

No deduction is allowable to P with respect to the unpaid wages because, as a cash-method taxpayer, P had a zero basis for the wage claim; see Treas. Reg. § 1.166–1(e). The inability to collect is reflected in P's income by never reporting the $5,000; a deduction is unnecessary.

The issue with respect to the $25,000 cash advance is whether the debt is a business or non-business bad debt. If it's a business bad debt, the loss is ordinary; if it is non-business, the loss is a short-term capital loss. P will argue that he lent the funds in order to preserve his job and, since his employment is a business, the indebtedness arose out of his business. The Commissioner will counter that the advance was made for the purpose of preserving P's investment in Z and is therefore a non-business, investment loss.

In United States v. Generes, 405 U.S. 93 (1972), the Court said that the resolution of the business versus non-business issue turned upon the shareholder-employee's "dominant" (as opposed to "significant") motivation for lending money to the corporation. In *Generes*, the taxpayer had lost $320,000 advanced (directly or through indemnification agreements) to his 44–percent owned corporation. (The remainder of the stock was owned by members of the taxpayer's family.) He contended that the advances were motivated by a desire to protect his $12,000 annual salary rather than his investment of $38,900 in the corporation's stock. Declining to remand the case for a new trial, the Court found nothing in the record of the case that "would support a jury verdict in this taxpayer's favor had the dominant-motivation standard" been used in the jury instructions.

Generes poses a significant obstacle to a business-loss deduction for P. The *Generes* ruling that the indebtedness was investment-related appears to be based upon a comparison of the $38,000 stock cost and the $12,000 salary—not much different proportionally from the $150,000 stock cost and $75,000 salary in the problem. However, the Court's analysis ignores that the present value of a stream of $12,000 salary payments (even discounted at a high rate because of the risk that the corporation would not be able to pay the salary) might be much more than $38,000. One might also want to factor in the opportunity cost to P of working for Z and the value of P's stock interest at the time the advance was made. So, despite *Generes*, one cannot give a definitive answer to the question of whether P's loss was sustained in business or investment.

With respect to the worthless stock, P suffers an ordinary loss of $50,000 (§ 1244) and a long-term capital loss of $100,000 (§ 165(g)). That assumes P was the original issuee of the stock. If he wasn't, § 1244 would not apply, and the entire loss would be a long-term capital loss.

C. SALE OF A GOING BUSINESS

Code: §§ 1060(a) & (c); 197(a), (b), (c), (d)(1), (f)(1), (3) & (7).

Regulations: §§ 1.263(a)–4(c)(4), Ex. 5; 1.263(a)–5(g); 1.1060–1(a)(1), (b)(1), (2)(ii) & (7), (c) & (d), Ex. 2.

1. **S, an individual, owned a sole proprietorship consisting of the assets listed below. The value figures shown below have been determined by an appropriate allocation of the total purchase price (all figures are in $ with 000 omitted throughout):**

	Adjusted Basis	Value	Notes
Accounts receivable	0	$100	1
Supplies	0	40	2
Business equipment	40	100	3
Building	100	200	4
Land	120	140	
Goodwill	0	120	
	260	700	

Notes:

1. S uses the cash method of accounting.

2. S deducted the $50 cost of the supplies in the preceding year.

3. S purchased the equipment for $85 and has properly deducted $45 of depreciation thereon.

4. S purchased the building (exclusive of the land) for $160 and has properly deducted $60 of straight-line depreciation thereon.

All of the capital and § 1231 assets have a long-term holding period.

(a) S sold the business to P, an individual, for $700. This is S's only transaction for the year. What is the amount and character of S's income or loss?

Under Williams v. McGowan, 152 F.2d 570 (2d Cir. 1945), a sole proprietorship is not a unitary asset; its sale involves the sale of a basket of goods. The sale must be comminuted into a sale of each item of property (accounts receivable, supplies, etc.), and the $700 amount realized must be allocated among the assets sold. The allocation governs the amount and character of S's gain or loss on the sale of each asset and also determines the basis for each asset in the hands of P; see § 1060(a); Treas. Reg. § 1.1060–1(a)(1).

The sale of a business is an "applicable asset acquisition" (defined in § 1060(c)). Section 1060(a) therefore requires that the consideration received for the assets be allocated as provided by § 338(b)(5). That provision authorizes the Treasury to promulgate regulations allocating consideration in connection with certain acquisitions. So, § 1060 piggybacks on allocation rules that were issued for a different purpose. We assume that the total $700 of consideration has been allocated among the assets in accordance with the methodology of the regulation, which is beyond our scope.

Accounts receivable: S realizes and recognizes a $100 ordinary gain on the sale of the receivables because the receivables are neither capital assets (§ 1221(a)(4)) nor § 1231 assets (§ 1231(b)(1)) (not depreciable).

Supplies: S has a realized and recognized gain of $40. (The basis of the supplies is zero because S deducted the cost of the supplies when purchased.) The gain is ordinary because the supplies are not a capital asset; § 1221(a)(8). The ordinary gain makes up for the ordinary deduction that S took when the supplies were purchased.

Business equipment: S has a recognized gain of $60 ($100 amount realized less $40 adjusted basis) on the sale of the equipment. The equipment is § 1245 property; § 1245(a)(3). S's recomputed basis is $85 ($40 adjusted basis, plus $45 deprecation). Since the recomputed basis is less than the amount realized, the § 1245 ordinary gain is $45 ($85 recomputed basis less $40 adjusted basis); § 1245(a)(1). Because the equipment is a § 1231 asset (§ 1231(b)(1)—depreciable business property), the $15 balance of the gain is a § 1231 gain (see below).

Building: S has a realized and recognized gain of $100 on the sale of the building. It is a § 1231 asset (§ 1231(b)(1)—depreciable business property), and the gain is a § 1231 gain (see below). (The building is not subject to depreciation recapture since S used straight-line depreciation.)

Land: S recognizes $20 of gain on the land, which is also a § 1231 asset (real property used in business), and the $20 gain is a § 1231 gain (see below).

Goodwill: S realizes and recognizes $120 of gain on the disposition of the goodwill. The goodwill is a capital asset (§ 1221) and the $120 gain on its sale is a long-term capital gain.

The § 1231 gains (a total of $135) exceed the § 1231 loss (zero). As a result, all the § 1231 gains are long-term capital gains; § 1231(a)(1).

S thus recognizes ordinary income of $185 ($100 on the accounts receivable, $40 on the supplies, and $45 of depreciation recapture on the equipment) and long-term capital gain of $255 ($135 from the § 1231 hotchpot and $120 on the goodwill), for total gain of $440.

(b) What is P's basis for the assets acquired?

P must allocate the $700 total consideration paid among the assets in proportion to their value in the same manner described in (a); see § 1060(a); Treas. Reg. § 1.1060–1.

P must capitalize the cost of the goodwill; see Treas. Reg. § 1.263(a)–4(c)(4), Ex. 5. The goodwill is a "§ 197 intangible"; § 197(d)(1)(A). It is an "amortizable § 197 intangible" because it is held in connection with the conduct of business; § 197(c)(1). An amortizable § 197 intangible can be amortized ratably over the 15–year period beginning with the month in which it was acquired; § 197(a).

(c) Would your answers in (a) and (b) be affected if S and P had entered into an agreement as to the allocation of the total consideration among the various assets?

An agreement as to the values of the assets generally binds the seller and purchaser; § 1060(a) (last sentence). If either wishes to challenge the allocation in the agreement, he must generally show its unenforceability because of mistake, undue influence, fraud, duress, etc.; Treas. Reg. § 1.1060–1(c)(4). The Commissioner, however, can always challenge the parties' allocation; id. In practice, the Service will usually accept an allocation reached in an arm's length negotiation where the parties have adverse tax interests in making the allocations. The parties' interests are often antagonistic, as the seller will prefer a larger allocation of the consideration to capital and § 1231 assets that are not subject to depreciation recapture and a smaller allocation to ordinary-income assets. The purchaser will prefer a larger allocation to ordinary income assets and depreciable assets that have relatively short recovery periods.

(d) How would your answer differ if S's business had been incorporated, S, the sole shareholder, had a basis of $260 and long-term holding period for the stock, and P, an individual, purchased S's stock for $700?

The $440 gain would have been a long-term capital gain because the stock is a capital asset with a long-term holding period. P would obtain a basis of $700 for the stock, but the purchase would not affect the corporation's basis for the assets. (For that reason, P probably would not be willing to pay $700 for the *stock* even if he was willing to pay that for the *assets*. An asset purchase would give P a fair-market-value basis for the assets.)

2. In connection with the transaction in 1(a), P paid S $150,000 for S's agreement not to compete with P for five years in the same line of business in the area in which the business was located.

(a) What result to P?

The covenant is treated as an asset transferred as part of the business; Treas. Reg. § 1.1060–1(b)(7). P must treat the $150,000 amount paid for the covenant as a capital expenditure; § 197(f)(3). The covenant is a "§ 197 intangible"—a covenant not to compete entered into in connection with the acquisition of a business; § 197(d)(1)(E). It is an "amortizable § 197 intangible" because it is held in connection with the conduct of business; § 197(c)(1). An amortizable § 197 intangible can be amortized ratably over the 15–year period beginning with the month in which it was acquired; § 197(a).

(b) To S?

S treats the $150,000 received for the non-compete covenant as ordinary income.

3. Five years have elapsed since the transaction in 2. P wants to know if she can write off as a loss her remaining adjusted basis in the non-compete covenant since it has no further economic value. What say you?

After 5 years, P's adjusted basis for the covenant is $100,000 ($150,000 cost less $50,000 amortization). Although P is correct that the expired covenant no longer has value, § 197(d)(1)(B) provides that the covenant cannot be treated as disposed of (or becoming worthless) before the disposition of the entire business interest in connection with which the covenant was entered into. The thought behind the provision is that there is a close relationship between a non-compete agreement and goodwill, and since goodwill must be amortized over 15 years, the covenant should be amortized over the same period. So, P must continue to amortize the covenant over the remaining 10 years. If P disposes of the entire business before the remaining amortization period elapses, any unamortized basis can be written off as a loss at that time.

4. P and S both incurred attorney's fees in connection with the sale and purchase of the business. How should the attorney's fees be treated for tax purposes?

S treats the attorney's fees as a reduction of the amount realized; P adds the fees to the basis of the acquired assets; Treas. Reg. § 1.263(a)–5(g). If a portion of the attorney's fee is attributable to transferring a specific asset (e.g., real-estate transfer costs), that portion of the fee is added to the basis of the particular asset; but fees associated with the acquisition of the business as a whole are taken into account in determining the total purchase price and must be allocated as additional consideration in the manner provided in the regulations. In many cases, this approach will result in allocating the general attorney's fees to goodwill.

D. SALE OF RIGHTS TO INCOME

Code: §§ 1234A; 1241; 273; 1001(e).

Regulations: §§ 1.263(a)–4(d)(7); § 1.167(a)–3(b)(1)(iii); 1.1014–4(a); 1.1015–1(b).

Cases: Hort v. Commissioner, 313 U.S. 28 (1941);
McAllister v. Commissioner, 157 F.2d 235 (2d. Cir. 1946);
Lattera v. Commissioner, 477 F.3d 399 (3d Cir. 2006);
Estate of Stranahan v. Commissioner, 472 F.2d 867 (6th Cir. 1973).

1. T, a tenant of a business building owned by L, paid L $100,000 as consideration for cancellation of a lease on the building. The lease had a remaining term of 20 years.

(a) What result to L?

This is Hort v. Commissioner, 313 U.S. 28 (1941), in which the Court said the receipt was ordinary because it was merely a substitute for the ordinary rental income that L would have received if the lease had not been cancelled. So, on the authority of *Hort*, L would have $100,000 of ordinary income.

There is a question, however, whether *Hort* is still good law. As amended in 1997, § 1234A treats gain attributable to "cancellation" or "other termination" of a "right or obligation * * * with respect to property which is * * * a capital asset" as gain from the sale of a capital asset. The lease entitled L to future rental payments, and the cancellation of that right would seem to come within § 1234A if the building were a capital asset. Here, however, the building (a "business" building) is not a capital asset but a § 1231 asset. By its terms, § 1234A does not apply to § 1231 assets. But interestingly, the two cases criticized in the committee reports as being cases "that will be affected by the committee bill" both involved § 1231 assets; S. Rep. No. 105–33, 105th Cong., 1st Sess. 134–35. So, the drafters may have intended that § 1234A reach the cancellation of rights with respect to § 1231 assets. If so, one would think the gain should be characterized under § 1231, though § 1234A says that the "gain shall be treated" as capital gain. In short, the answer here is unclear.

A final thought: If the 1997 amendment to § 1234A did overturn *Hort*, Congress probably did so inadvertently. Overturning a case of major importance is usually done with more fanfare than evident in the legislative history of § 1234A.

(b) To T?

T must capitalize the $100,000 paid to terminate the lease; Treas. Reg. § 1.263(a)–4(d)(7). T should be permitted to amortize the $100,000 over the remaining 20–year term of the lease; Treas. Reg. § 1.167(a)–3(b)(1)(iii).

(c) What result to L if T paid the $100,000 as consideration for L's releasing T from a requirement that the premises be restored upon termination of the lease?

Section 1234A would apply if the building was a capital asset, but if T's rental activity constitutes a business, the building is a § 1231 asset. The 1997 amendment to § 1234A was enacted in part to overturn the results in two cases that had refused capital-gain treatment for amounts received by a lessor in release of the lessee's obligation to restore the premises. Whether § 1234A applies with respect to § 1231 assets is debatable, as discussed in (a). If § 1234A does not apply, the receipt is ordinary income; see, e.g., Sirbo Holdings, Inc. v. Commissioner, 509 F.2d 1220 (2d Cir. 1975).

2. Suppose in 1 that L paid T $100,000 as consideration for cancellation of the lease with a remaining term of 20 years?

(a) What result to T?

Assume that T had a zero basis in the leasehold. The $100,000 would be treated as an amount received "in exchange for" the leasehold; § 1241. If the leasehold was a capital asset in T's hands, the $100,000 gain would be a capital gain; if the leasehold was a § 1231 asset, the gain would be a § 1231 gain and its ultimate character would depend upon the outcome of the § 1231 hotchpot.

(b) To L?

L must capitalize the $100,000 payment; Treas. Reg. § 1.263(a)–4(d)(7). L should be permitted to amortize the $100,000 over the remaining 20–year term of the lease; Treas. Reg. § 1.167(a)–3(b)(1)(iii).

3. L won the state lottery, which entitles her to payments of $100,000 a year for 25 years. After receiving the first payment, L sold her right to the remaining payments for $1,000,000 cash. What result to L?

Applying the substitute-for-ordinary-income doctrine of *Hort*, Lattera v. Commissioner, 477 F.3d 399 (3d Cir. 2006), holds that a sale of lottery proceeds does not produce capital gain. The problem with that doctrine is that the value of every asset is the present discounted value of the future (ordinary) income that it will produce over its life. A literal application of the doctrine would leave very little of the capital-gains preference. In *Lattera*, the court conceded that the taxpayer had not created a carved-out interest—e.g., by selling a 5–year term out of the taxpayer's 17–year right to lottery proceeds. It found, however, the sale of the lottery proceeds was a sale of a right to "earned" income rather than a right to "earn" income. It reasoned that the lottery winner had nothing further to do to "earn" the income, except wait to collect the payments. The court concluded that the sale of a right to earned income did not merit capital-gains treatment.

The court's reasoning is not entirely persuasive. Consider the holder of a government bond whose interest payments keep arriving due simply to ownership of the bond. Is the interest "earned" income in the sense in which the *Lattera* court used the term? There is no question that the sale of the bond (by one other than a dealer) produces capital gain or loss. Nevertheless, every court of appeals to consider the issue has agreed with *Lattera* that the sale of lottery proceeds produces ordinary gain.

4. D dies and bequeaths farm land to A for life, remainder to B. At D's death, the land was worth $1,000,000. (D's estate was valued at the date of death for the purpose of the federal estate tax.)

(a) At D's death, the actuarial present value of A's interest is $600,000. Can A amortize that amount over A's remaining life expectancy of 30 years?

When property is divided temporally, as in this case, the regulations require that the basis of the property be apportioned between the present income interest and the future remainder interest in proportion to their present values; Treas. Reg. §§ 1.1014–4(a); 1.1015–1(b). Each party's share of the "uniform basis" is adjusted with the passage of time, so that eventually (if the property is not sold) the remainderman winds up with all of the basis. Here the present value of A's life estate is $600,000, and so her share of the $1,000,000 uniform basis is $600,000. (The reference to "actuarial present value" in the problem denotes that in determining the value of A's interest, we must take into account her life expectancy, for her interest terminates at her death.)

A cannot amortize her $600,000 basis. Although A's interest is a wasting asset, § 273 forbids the amortization of a life or term interest acquired by gift, bequest or inheritance. (Some students find confusing the reference in § 273 to "amounts paid under the laws of a State." After all, the life estate is created by D's will—not a state statute, etc. The confusion goes away when one thinks of the property law as part of the "laws of the state.")

To understand the purpose of § 273, recall that the remainderman, B, eventually winds up with the *entire* uniform basis. If A were allowed to amortize her *life estate*, the parties would get to count A's portion of the basis twice.

(b) Suppose that, immediately after D's death, A sold her interest to an unrelated party, P, for $600,000. What result to A? To P?

Even if A sells her life interest, she cannot offset her basis against the amount realized unless the sale of the interest is part of a transaction in which the entire property is transferred; § 1001(e). So, A has a $600,000 gain on the sale. Section 1001(e) serves a purpose similar to that of § 273: A cannot amortize the basis if she holds the property and cannot use the basis to offset the amount realized if she anticipates the future income through a sale of the property.

McAllister v. Commissioner, 157 F.2d 235 (2d. Cir. 1946), holds that the gain on the sale of a life estate is capital gain. (The case was decided before the enactment of § 1001(e); today the life tenant would not be permitted to offset her basis against the amount realized on the sale, as McAllister was permitted to do.) *McAllister* has been criticized on the capital-gain issue; e.g., Clopton v. Commissioner, 87 T.C.M. 1217, 1219 (2004) (*McAllister* "decided before relevant Supreme Court decisions applying the substitute for ordinary income doctrine," referring to, among others, Commissioner v. P.G. Lake, Inc., 356 U.S. 260 (1958)). However, the Service acquiesced in *McAllister* 14 years after the decision in *Lake* (Rev. Rul. 72–243, 1972–1 C.B. 233), and the case can therefore be relied upon today.

Even though A sold the interest immediately after D's death, the gain would be a *long*-term capital gain because of the automatic long-term-holding-period rule of § 1223(9).

P obtains a $600,000 cost basis for the estate *per autre vie* and can amortize the basis over A's life expectancy. Section 273 does not prevent amortization because P acquired the interest by purchase rather than by gift, bequest or inheritance.

(c) What result if A and B simultaneously sold their interests to P, who paid A $600,000 and B $400,000?

Now A can use her basis to offset her amount realized because § 1001(e)(1) does not apply when the entire interest in the property is sold; § 1001(e)(3). Because the remainder is also sold, B's uniform basis ceases to matter, so it won't be increased by A's basis with the passage of time and there's no reason not to let A use her share of the basis. Neither A nor B realize gain or loss on the sale, as their respective bases just offset their amounts realized. P obtains a cost basis of $1,000,000. As a result of the purchase, P owns the fee interest, which is not amortizable.

5. F has a large net operating loss that is going to expire this year. He does not have sufficient income to fully utilize the loss. To increase his income for the year, he offers to sell to his son, S, his right to the next two years' dividends on 100,000 shares of a publicly traded stock owned by F. The expected dividend for the two-year period is $400,000 ($200,000 per year). S purchases the right to the dividends for $360,000. What result to F?

This problem is based upon Estate of Stranahan v. Commissioner, 472 F.2d 867 (6th Cir. 1973). In *Stranahan*, a father sold to his son the right to future dividend income in an attempt to accelerate the income into the year of sale where it would be offset by a large interest deduction. The taxpayer did not claim capital-gain treatment on the sale but instead recognized the gain as ordinary income. The court found that the sale was bona fide and should be recognized for tax purposes. The court distinguished Helvering v. Horst, 311 U.S. 112 (1940) (father transferred bond coupon to son, but retained ownership of the bond; *held*: father was taxable on the interest even though the son received the money), as involving a gratuitous assignment.

In *Stranahan*, the Service argued that the transaction should be viewed as a loan from the son to the father of $360,000 and that the father should be taxed on the $400,000 of dividends earned (less interest, if deductible). That approach seems to be more in consonance with assignment-of-income principles.

Section H

DEFERRED PAYMENT-SALES

Chapter 31

INSTALLMENT SALES UNDER § 453

A. IN GENERAL

Code: §§ 453(a), (b), (c), (d)(1), (f), (i), (j), (k) & (l)(1). Note §§ 1239; 1(h)(6)(A)(i). Review § 1031(a) & (b).

Regulations: Temp. Treas. Reg. § 15a.453–1(a), (b), (c)(1) & (3). Note §§ 1.1001–1(g); 1.453–12(a); Prop. Treas. Reg. § 1.453–1(f).

1. In year 1, S sells to P some land that S had held for investment for several years. S's adjusted basis in the land was $100 (000 omitted throughout). S sells the property to P for $400, payable $100 down and $100 per year in each of years 2 through 4. The contract of sale provides for market-rate interest on the deferred payments, S and P are not related, and S makes no election under § 453(d). P makes all required payments on time. Determine the amount, timing and character of S's recognized gain.

Since at least one payment is to be received after the close of the taxable year, this is an installment sale (§ 453(b)), the gain on which is recognized under the installment method; § 453(a). Under the installment method, the gain recognized for any year is that proportion of the *payments* received which the *gross profit* bears to the *total contract price*; § 453(c). The gross profit is the excess of the selling price over the adjusted basis. Where, as here, the purchaser does not assume (or take subject to) any indebtedness of the seller, the total contract price means the total amount of principal payments to be received by the taxpayer under the contract. The ratio of the gross profit to the total contract price is known as the gross-profit ratio.

In this case, the gross profit is $300 ($400 selling price less $100 adjusted basis), the total contract price is $400, and the gross-profit ratio is 75 percent ($300 gross profit/$400 contract price). The payments include amounts paid toward the purchase price (e.g., the down payment and any principal payments on the installment obligation), but not interest on the installment obligation. The term payment generally does not include the purchaser's evidence of indebtedness (i.e., the installment obligation itself); § 453(f)(3). In year 1, S receives a payment of $100 (the down payment) and must recognize $75 (75% of $100) of that amount as gain. The character is determined according to the nature of the asset sold—here a capital asset (land held for investment) held for several years. The gain is therefore a long-term capital gain; § 1222(3). The other $25 received is a return of basis.

In years 2, 3 and 4, S will also recognize a long-term capital gain of $75 (the product of the 75–percent exclusion ratio and the $100 principal payment received in each year). Over the four years, S recognizes total gain of $300 and recovers basis of $100. All interest payments received are includable in gross income as ordinary income.

2. Same as 1, except that S makes an election under § 453(d)(1).

If S elects out of installment reporting under § 453(d)(1), all of the gain is recognized in the year of sale. The amount realized is the sum of the $100 cash received and the fair market value of the installment note received. Without delving too deeply into details that are beyond the scope of the basic course, we can say that installment notes that, when issued, bear interest at the market rate generally are valued at their face amount—here $300; for details, see Treas. Reg. § 1.1001–1(g). So, S's amount realized is $400, the adjusted basis is $100, and S realizes and recognizes in year 1 a long-term capital gain of $300.

3. Same as 1, except that S pays a brokerage fee of $20 on the sale.

In computing the gross profit, we increase the property's adjusted basis by the amount of the selling commission paid by S; Temp. Treas. Reg. § 15a.453–1(b)(2)(v). So, the selling price is $400, the adjusted basis $120 ($100 adjusted basis, plus $20 commission), the gross profit $280 ($400 selling price less $120 adjusted basis), and the gross-profit ratio 70 percent ($280 gross profit/ $400 contract price). As S receives payment of the $100 each year, $70 (70% of $100) must be recognized as long-term capital gain. S recognizes total long-term capital gain of $280 at the rate of $70 per year.

4. Same as 1, except that the land had been held by S for use in business.

The answer is the same as 1 (i.e., gain of $75 recognized each year), except that the character of the gain differs. Land used in business is a § 1231 asset, so each year's gain would initially be characterized as a § 1231 gain, which would be aggregated with S's other § 1231 gains and losses for the year in which the gain is recognized. If in year 1 S has no other § 1231 gain or loss, the $75 gain is characterized as long-term capital gain under § 1231(a)(1).

5. Same as 1, except that the land had been held by S for sale to customers in the ordinary course of business.

The disposition of real property held for sale to customers in the ordinary course of the taxpayer's business is a "dealer disposition"; § 453(*l*)(1)(B). A dealer disposition does not qualify as an installment sale, so S's gain would be recognized in year 1. The gain would be ordinary because the land is not a capital asset.

6. Same as 1, except that the property sold was moveable equipment that S had used in business. S had purchased the equipment for $300 and had properly deducted $200 of depreciation up to the time of the sale.

The equipment is § 1245 property (depreciable personal property); § 1245(a)(3)(A). When § 1245 property is sold for deferred payments, the recapture income must be recognized in the year of sale; the adjusted basis of the property sold is increased by the amount of recapture income recognized in the year of sale, and any remaining gain can be recognized under the installment method; 453(i).

Consider the situation as if S had received all of the payments in the year of sale. She would have been required to recognize $200 ($300 recomputed basis less $100 adjusted basis) as ordinary income under § 1245(a)(1). Section 453(i) calls this amount "recapture income" and says that the recapture income must be recognized in the year of disposition. But S can report the remaining gain under § 453. In computing the remaining gain, S increases the adjusted basis of the equipment by the $200 of ordinary income recognized in year 1. That increases the adjusted basis of the equipment to $300 ($100 adjusted basis at time of sale, plus $200 increase attributable to ordinary gain recognized in year 1). (That is, S deducted $200 more depreciation than the asset declined in value. S's recognition of the $200 of § 1245 gain in year 1 counterbalances the excess depreciation deductions. But in computing the § 453(c) gain, S increases the adjusted basis by the $200 of § 1245 gain. The basis increase puts S in roughly the same position she would have been in if only the "proper" amount of depreciation had been allowable.)

Now we are ready to compute the § 453 gain. S's selling price is $400, the adjusted basis $300, the gross profit $100 ($400 selling price less $300 adjusted basis), and the gross-profit ratio 25 percent ($100 gross profit/$400 total contract price). So, S must recognize gain of $25 (25% of $100) in each of years 1–4. The gain is characterized as § 1231 gain in each year, with the ultimate characterization being dependent upon each year's computation under § 1231(a).

To summarize, in year 1 S recognizes $200 of ordinary income and $25 of § 1231 gain, and in each of years 2–4 S recognizes $25 of § 1231 gain.

7. Same as 1, except that P's note was guaranteed by P's brother, B.

Although deferred-payment sellers like the deferral permitted by § 453, they are always concerned about the possibility of the purchaser's defaulting. One way to lessen that concern is find someone to guarantee the purchaser's obligation. The issue in this problem is whether B's guarantee might make the obligation that of B (rather than the purchaser, P), in which case the receipt of the obligation (rather than its payment) would be the "payment" received in the year of sale. In that case, the sale would not be an installment sale because *all* of the payments would be received in the year of sale; see § 453(b). However, § 453(f)(3) makes clear that the obligation is still that of P, even though it is guaranteed by B. So, the results are the same as in (1).

8. Same as 1, except that P's note was secured by an irrevocable standby letter of credit issued by P's bank.

This is similar to problem 7, but adds the additional wrinkle that the "guarantee" is coming from a bank. A standby letter of credit (defined in Temp. Treas. Reg. § 15a.453–1(b)(3)(iii)) is treated as a third-party guarantee and the year-of-sale payment does not include P's promissory note; Temp. Treas. Reg. § 15a.453–1(b)(3)(i).

9. Same as 1, except that the property sold was stock in a publicly traded corporation.

Section 453 reporting does not apply to a sale of securities traded on an established securities market; § 453(k). All of S's gain must be reported in the year of disposition.

10. Same as (1), except that S's basis in the land was $600.

S has a realized loss of $200 ($600 adjusted basis less $400 amount realized). The loss is recognized (§ 1001(c)) and allowed in year 1 (subject to the limit on the deductibility of capital losses); § 165(a) & (c)(1). Section 453 does not apply to losses.

11. O purchased for $400 a building (and the land on which it was located) to be used in O's business. The $400 purchase price was allocable $300 to the building and $100 to the land. Over the next few years, O properly deducted $150 of straight-line depreciation on the building, and then sold the property for $600, of which $150 was allocable to the land. The $600 was payable $120 down in the year of sale (year 1) and $120 for each of the following four years (years 2–5), with market-rate interest on the deferred balance. All amounts of principal and interest were paid when due. This was O's only property transaction for years 1–5. Determine the amount and character of O's gain for each year and the tax rate applicable to each component of the gain.

The transaction must be bifurcated into two sales—one of the building and one of the land, and the consideration received must be apportioned between the building and land in proportion to their values at the time of the sale. In this case, we allocate $450 of the selling price to the building and $150 to the land. The gross profit on the sale of the building is $300 ($450 selling price less $150 adjusted basis), the contract price is $450, and the gross-profit ratio 2/3 ($300 gross profit/$450 contract price). The gross profit on the land is $50 ($150 selling price less $100 adjusted basis), the contract price is $150, and the gross-profit ratio 2/3 ($100/$150).

Each $120 payment received by O must be allocated between the building and the land in accordance with their relative selling prices—i.e., 75 percent ($450/$600) to the building and 25 percent ($150/$600) to the land. Of the $90 (75% of $120) of each payment allocable to the building, $60 (2/3 of $90) would be recognized as gain. Of the $30 (25% of $120) of each payment allocable to the land, $20 (2/3 of $30) would be recognized as gain.

Both the land and the building are § 1231 assets, and, this being O's only disposition in the years involved, each year's gain is a long-term capital gain; § 1231(a)(1). Of the total $300 gain to be recognized on the sale of the building, $150 is unrecaptured § 1250 gain (i.e., the amount of depreciation that would have been recaptured if § 1250 recaptured all depreciation instead of just the excess of accelerated depreciation over straight-line); see § 1(h)(6)(A)(i). (Unrecaptured § 1250 gain is discussed in Chapter 29.) The unrecaptured § 1250 gain is subject to tax at a maximum rate of 25 percent. The remaining $150 of gain on the building and all of the $50 gain on the land is part of the adjusted net capital gain taxable at a maximum rate of 15 percent.

How is the gain recognized each year on the building to be allocated between the unrecaptured § 1250 gain and the adjusted net capital gain? Treas. Reg. § 1.453–12(a) provides that the unrecaptured § 1250 gain is taken into account first. The $60 recognized in years 1 and 2 and $30 of the gain recognized in year

3 would be characterized as unrecaptured § 1250 gain. The remaining $30 of gain recognized in year 3, along with the $60 of gain recognized with respect to the building in years 4 and 5 would be adjusted net capital gain.

12. A transferred a building used in business (the "old" building) to B in exchange for a building (also to be used in A's business) with a value of $350 and $150 cash, payable $15 down and $15 per year for each of the following nine years. A's adjusted basis for the old building was $200.

(a) Determine (i) the amount, timing and character of A's recognized gain and (ii) A's basis for the new building.

A realizes a gain of $300 ($500 amount realized less $200 adjusted basis) on the like-kind exchange, of which $150 must be recognized because of the receipt of boot; 1031(b). However, the transaction also qualifies as an installment sale within the meaning of § 453 because it is a disposition of property in which at least one payment is to be received after the close of the year in which the disposition occurs; § 453(b)(1).

In applying § 453 to the receipt of installment boot in a like-kind exchange, we reduce the total contract price by the value of the like-kind property received and reduce the gross profit by the amount of the unrecognized gain; § 453(f)(6)(A) & (B). Thus A's total contract price is $150 ($500 less $350 value of like-kind property received, and the gross profit is $150 ($300 gross profit less $150 of gain unrecognized under § 1031). The gross-profit ratio is therefore 100 percent ($150 gross profit/$150 contract price).

In this context, the term "payment" does not include the receipt of the like-kind (non-recognition) property; § 453(f)(6)(B). The payments are the $15 cash received each year, and 100 percent of each payment is recognized as gain.

The building is a § 1231 asset (depreciable and real property used in business—§ 1231(b)(1)), and the gain is therefore a § 1231 gain (§ 1231 gain includes gain recognized on the "exchange" of a § 1231 asset—§ 1231(a)(3)(A)(i)). The ultimate characterization of each year's gain depends upon the outcome of the § 1231(a) hotchpot for that year.

A's basis for the new building is $200 ($200 adjusted basis of old building, less $150 cash (to be) received, plus $150 gain (to be) recognized); § 1031(d); Prop. Treas. Reg. § 1.453–1(f). A steps up the basis for the new building immediately even though recognition of the gain on the exchange is deferred.

(b) Same as (a), except that A's adjusted basis for the old building was $400.

Now the realized gain is $100 ($500 amount realized less $400 adjusted basis), all of which will be recognized under § 1031(b) because of the $150 boot received. The total contract price is $150 ($500 "true" contract price, less $350 value of non-recognition property received); § 453(f)(6)(A). The gross profit is $100 ($100 "true" gross profit less zero amount of gain not recognized under § 1031(b)); § 453(f)(6)(B). The gross-profit ratio is 2/3 ($100 gross profit/$150 contract price). As each $15 payment is received, A recognizes $10 (2/3 of $15) as gain. The gain is § 1231 gain; its ultimate character as ordinary or capital depends upon the outcome of each year's § 1231 hotchpot.

B. TRANSACTIONS WITH RELATED PERSONS

Code: §453(e) & (g). Review § 1239(a), (b) & (c).

1. On March 31, year 1, M sells land (a capital asset held for several years) to her daughter, D, for $500, payable $100 down and $100 per year (plus market rate interest) on March 31 of years 2–5. In January, year 2, and before making the year–2 payment, D sells the land to an unrelated party for $550 cash. D continues to make all principal and interest payments when due. M's adjusted basis in the land was $200. What result to M and D?

M's gross profit is $300 ($500 selling price less $200 adjusted basis), the total contract price is $500, and the gross-profit ratio is 60 percent ($300 gross profit/$500 contract price). When M receives the $100 down payment, she must recognize gain of $60 (60% of $100). The gain is a long-term capital gain because it arose from the sale of a capital asset with a long-term holding period; see § 1222(3).

D is a "related person" with respect to M because D is a member of M's family within the meaning of § 267(b)(1) & (c)(4); see § 453(f)(1). Since M sold property to related-person D (the first disposition), and, before M received all of the payments to which she is entitled, D disposed of the property (the second disposition), the amount realized by D on the second disposition is generally treated as received by M at the time of the second disposition; see § 453(e)(1).

From this, it appears that M will be deemed to have received $550 in January, year 2. Here, however, D's $550 amount realized exceeds M's $500 total contract price, and so the amount imputed to M from the second disposition is limited initially to $500; § 453(e)(3)(A). Moreover, that limit must be further reduced by the *actual* payments of $200 received by M before the close of year 2 when the second disposition occurred. D paid $100 down in year 1 and pays another $100 on principal in year 2. Thus, the maximum of D's amount realized that can be imputed to M is $300 ($500 contract price less $200 payments received by M before the end of year 2).

The total payments received by M in year 2 total $400 ($100 actual payment, plus $300 imputed payment). M must recognize a long-term capital gain of $240 (60% of $400) in year 2.

The payments received by M in years 3, 4 and 5 are treated as tax-paid amounts, so M recognizes no further gain from the transaction in those years; see § 453(e)(5).

2. Would your answer in 1 differ if D re-sold the property in April, year 3 (after having made timely payment of the amounts due in years 2 and 3)?

Yes, because § 453(e) generally does not apply where the second disposition is more than 2 years after the date of the first disposition; § 453(e)(2)(A). M's gain would not be accelerated in that case.

3. Would your answer in 1 differ if M had died in December, year 1?

Yes, because a disposition made after the death of the person making the first transfer is not treated as a second disposition; § 453(e)(6)(C)(i). Payments received after M's death would be analyzed as items of income in respect of a decedent under § 691.

4. S owned a business building with an adjusted basis of $200 and a value of $500. S sold the building to P Corporation for $500, payable $100 down and $100 per year (plus market-rate interest) for each of the next 4 years. S owns 60 percent of P's stock. (Ignore the land, as if only the building were purchased and sold.) What result to S?

Section 453(g)(1) generally prohibits installment reporting of gain on the sale of depreciable property to a related person. P Corporation is a "controlled entity" with respect to S because S owns more than 50 percent of the value of P's stock; see § 1239(c)(1). That makes S and P related parties under §§ 1239(b)(1) and 453(g)(3). As a result, all payments to be received by S are deemed received in the year of sale; § 453(g)(1)(A)(i).

S realizes and recognizes gain of $300 in the year of sale. The gain is an ordinary gain because of § 1239.

This assumes that the parties cannot establish to the satisfaction of the Service "that the disposition did not have as one of its principal purposes the avoidance of Federal income tax"; § 453(g)(2). If S can establish a non-tax-avoidance purpose, then the gain could be recognized under the installment method (at $60 per year), but it would still be characterized as ordinary gain because of § 1239.

The notion underlying § 453(g) is similar to that underlying § 1239. Section 1239 denies the benefit of the capital-gains tax rates to taxpayers who sell depreciable property to a related party which can then use the stepped-up cost basis to generate depreciation deductions that reduce ordinary income. In the case of § 453(g), the concern is with the related-party purchaser obtaining a stepped-up basis for depreciation before the seller recognizes the deferred gain on the sale. There is no non-tax-avoidance exception to § 1239; why should there be such an exception to § 453(g)?

5. Would your answer in 4 differ if S had instead sold P unimproved land (held for investment for several years), which P planned to subdivide and sell to customers in the ordinary course of business?

Yes, since the land is not depreciable, § 453(g) does not prohibit the recognition of the gain under the installment method. The gross profit is $300, the contract price is $500, the gross-profit ratio is 60 percent, and S recognizes gain of $60 (60% of $100) each year. The gain is long-term capital gain because arising from the sale of land held as an investment—a capital asset—for more than 1 year. (Section 1239 does not apply because the land is not depreciable in the hands of P.)

P gets a cost basis of $500 for the land. It can use the basis to offset its amount realized on the sale of the subdivided property, thus reducing its ordinary income. It is strange that neither § 1239 nor § 453(g) covers a case such as this. Notice, however, that if P realizes gain from the sale of the subdivided property within two years of the purchase of the property from S, any payments received by P may be imputed to S under § 453(e).

C. PROPERTY SUBJECT TO LIABILITY

Code: Review § 453(a), (b) & (c).

Regulation: Temp. Treas. Reg. § 15a.453–1(b)(2), (3) & (5), Exs. (2) & (3).

1. S owns a non-depreciable capital asset (held for several years) with a basis of $260 and a value of $500, but which is subject to a $200 mortgage incurred by S in purchasing the property. In year 1, S sells the property to P, who takes subject to the mortgage, and agrees to pay S $100 cash down and $100 (plus market-rate interest) in each of years 2 and 3. What is the amount and timing of S's gain recognized?

The mortgage doesn't affect the selling price, which is $500,000; see Temp. Treas. Reg. § 15a.453–1(b)(2)(ii). However, the contract price is reduced by the amount of any "qualifying indebtedness"; Id. § 15a.453–1(b)(2)(iii). Qualifying indebtedness includes a mortgage obligation undertaken when the property was acquired by S; see id. § 15a.453–1(b)(2)(iv).

So, the gross profit is $240 ($500 selling price less $260 adjusted basis), the contract price $300 ($500 selling price less $200 qualifying indebtedness), and the gross-profit ratio 80 percent ($240/$300). In determining the amount of the payments for the year of sale, we include qualifying indebtedness only to the extent that it exceeds the property's adjusted basis, which here it does not. The payments thus include only the $100 received by S in each of the 3 years. Of each payment, $80 must be recognized as gain (long-term capital gain since the gain arises from the sale of a capital asset with a long-term holding period).

2. Would your answer in 1 differ if S's basis for the asset had been $100?

Yes. The contract price is reduced by the qualifying indebtedness, but only to the extent that the qualifying indebtedness does not exceed the property's basis; Temp. Treas. Reg. § 15a.453–1(b)(2)(iii). Therefore, the contract price is $400 ($500 total contract price less $100 qualifying indebtedness to the extent of the property's basis), the gross profit is $400 ($500 selling price less $100 adjusted basis), and the gross-profit ratio is 100 percent ($400 gross profit/$400 contract price). S's year-of-sale payments include the $100 down payment and also the $100 by which the amount of qualifying indebtedness to which the property was subject ($200) exceeds the property's adjusted basis ($100). So, year-of-sale payments total $200, all of which must be recognized as gain. Likewise, all of the $100 payment received in each of the following 2 years must be recognized as gain. For the reasons given in 1, the gain is characterized as long-term capital gain.

3. Would your answer in 1 differ if S had incurred the $200 mortgage liability in anticipation of the sale to P, and S had used the loan proceeds for a purpose unrelated to the property?

Yes, because the indebtedness would no longer be considered qualifying indebtedness, and the amount of the indebtedness to which the property was subject would be considered a payment by the purchaser to the seller in the year of sale. In this case, the indebtedness is not qualifying indebtedness because the obligation is not functionally related to the acquisition, holding or operating of the property, but the loan proceeds were instead used for a purpose unrelated to the property; see Temp. Treas. Reg. § 15a.453–1(b)(2)(iv). Accordingly, the year-of-sale payments include the $100 cash down payment and also the $200 of mortgage debt to which the property was subject at the time of transfer.

The contract price is $500, the gross profit is $240 ($500 selling price less $260 adjusted basis), and the gross-profit ratio is 48 percent ($240 gross profit/$500 contract price). In the year of sale, S recognizes gain of $144 (48% of $300 payment); in each of the following two years, S recognizes gain of $48 (48% of $100 payment). The gains are classified as long-term capital gains for the reasons given in 1.

Chapter 32

DISPOSITION OF INSTALLMENT OBLIGATIONS

Code: §§ 453B(a), (b), (c), (f) & (g); 453A(d)(1), (2) & (3). Review §§ 1015(a); 1014(a), (b) & (c); 691(a); 1041(a); 1223(2); 1271(a).

Regulations: §§ 1.102–1(e); 1.691(a)–5(a).

Ruling: Rev. Rul. 79–371, 1979–2 C.B. 294.

General Facts: In year 1, S, a cash-method taxpayer, sold property (a non-depreciable capital asset with an adjusted basis of $200) to P for $1,000, payable $500 down and $100 per year (plus market-rate interest) payable at the end of each of years 2 through 6. P makes all principal and interest payments on time. S properly reported the gain under the installment method of § 453.

1. What is S's basis in the $500 installment obligation immediately following the sale?

The contract price is $1,000, the gross profit is $800 ($1,000 selling price less $200 adjusted basis of property sold), and the gross-profit ratio is 80 percent ($800 gross profit /$1,000 contract price). T would recognize $400 (80% of $500) of gain upon receipt of the down payment and recover $100 of basis.

To determine S's basis for the note, we first observe that, if the face amount of the note were collected in full, S would recognize $400 gain (80% of $500). The basis of the note is $100 ($500 face amount less the $400 that would be recognized as gain if the face amount were collected in full); § 453B(b). (Students sometimes find the language of § 453B(b) confusing. The word "returnable" means includable on the taxpayer's return, or, better yet, "recognized.")

The basis of the installment obligation can also be determined by noting that the basis of the property sold was $200 and $100 of basis was recovered when the down payment was received, leaving an adjusted basis of $100 in the note.

2. **What is the amount and character of S's recognized gain if later in year 1 S sells the obligation for:**

(a) $530?

S recognizes gain of $430 ($530 amount realized less $100 adjusted basis); § 453B(a). The gain is long-term capital gain because it is "considered as resulting from the sale or exchange of the property in respect of which the installment obligation was received," and in this case the obligation was received upon the sale of a capital asset with a long-term holding period; see § 453B(a) (last sentence).

(b) $480?

S recognizes long-term capital gain of $380 ($480 amount realized less $100 adjusted basis); § 453B(a).

3. **In each of the following cases, S transfers the note in year 1 when its value is $480. Describe the results of the transfer by S. How should the transferee treat the payments received on the note?**

(a) S gave the installment obligation to S's child, C.

In most cases, a gift of property with a value in excess of its basis does not trigger the recognition of gain to the donor. But where the donor makes a gift of an installment obligation, the donor is required to recognize gain to the extent that the value of the obligation exceeds its adjusted basis; § 453B(a)(2). (Section 453B(a)(2) codifies assignment-of-income principles: S has done everything to "earn" the gain except collect the money. At that late point, S cannot deflect the gain to her donee.)

We know from the discussion above that S has an adjusted basis in the obligation of $100. Upon making the gift, S must recognize gain to the extent of $380 ($480 value of note less $100 adjusted basis). The gain is characterized by reference to the asset that was sold in the installment sale (a non-depreciable capital asset with a long-term holding period) (§ 453B(a) (last sentence)), and so the $380 gain is long-term capital gain.

Under the assignment-of-income doctrine, S must also include in gross income any interest accrued to the date of the gift (because S was the owner of the note when the interest accrued); see Helvering v. Horst, 311 U.S. 112 (1940). S includes the interest in the year in which it is collected by C; Harrison v. Schaffner, 312 U.S. 570 (1941) (donor taxable in year income collected by donee). C is not taxable on the portion of the interest taxable to S under the assignment-of-income doctrine; see Treas. Reg. § 1.102–1(e) (income that is taxed to assignor not taxed to assignee).

C excludes the value of the installment obligation from income as a gift; § 102(a). C assumes S's adjusted basis (§ 1015(a)), as increased by the amount of gain recognized to S on the transfer (to prevent that same gain from being taxed a second time when S collects payment on the note); Rev. Rul. 79–371, 1979–2 C.B. 294. C thus obtains an adjusted basis of $480 ($100 basis of S, plus $380 gain recognized by S on transfer to C).

Although C has not made an installment sale, it seems appropriate to allow C to recognize the remaining gain by allocating her basis ratably to each payment received; see Witte v. Commissioner, 31 T.C.M. 1137, 1143 (1972), rev'd on other grounds, 513 F.2d 391 (D.C. Cir. 1975). Under that approach, 96 percent ($480 basis/$500 face amount) of each remaining principal payment would be treated as a return of basis and 4 percent as gain. S would therefore recognize $4 (4% of $100) of gain in each of years 2, 3, 4, 5 and 6. Notice how the entire $800 of gain from S's original sale has been accounted for—$780 was taxed to S and $20 to C.

What is the character of C's gain? The installment note is a capital asset in C's hands (at least if we assume that C is not a dealer in such notes) (see § 1221(a)), C's holding period for the note should include S's (because C's basis is determined by reference to S's—see § 1223(2)), and S's holding period for the note probably includes the period during which S held the asset sold, in which case C would have a long-term holding period for the note from the time she acquired it. What of the requirement of a "sale or exchange" for capital-gain treatment? Section 1271(a) provides that amounts received on "retirement" of a debt obligation are received "in exchange therefor," and that provision can easily be read as furnishing the necessary exchange to make C's gain a long-term capital gain.

(b) S gave the installment obligation to S's child, P, the purchaser of the property.

When S gives the note to P, the debtor and creditor interests merge, thus extinguishing the obligation, and the note becomes unenforceable. When an installment obligation becomes unenforceable, it is treated as if it had been disposed of other than by means of a sale or exchange; § 453B(f)(1). Furthermore, if the obligee and obligor are related persons under § 453(f)(1), the note's value is treated as not less its face amount; § 453B(f)(2). Here S and P are related persons (members of a family), so S must recognize gain of $400 ($500 face amount less $100 adjusted basis), which is characterized as a long-term capital gain for the reason given above.

P does not recognize cancellation-of-indebtedness income because the cancellation represents a gift excludable from income under § 102(a). Nor does P reduce the basis of the property from $1,000 even though P winds up paying only $500 toward the purchase price. The Code treats the transaction as if S gave P $500 and P paid off the balance due on the note.

(c) S dies and bequeaths the obligation to C.

Although the language of § 453B(a) is sufficiently broad to require the recognition of the deferred gain on an installment obligation when it passes at the death of the holder, § 453B(c) excepts from the general rule of recognition "the transmission of installment obligations at death." Thus, the passage of the installment obligation from S to her estate does not trigger the recognition of the deferred gain; see Treas. Reg. § 1.691(a)–5(a).

Neither S's estate nor C obtains a stepped-up basis for the installment obligation under section 1014(a). Instead, the obligation is treated as an item of income in respect of a decedent (IRD) to the extent provided in § 691, and the estate and beneficiary assume the decedent's basis; § 1014(c). Under § 691(a)(4), the $400 excess of the obligation's face amount ($500) over its basis in the hands of S ($100) is an item of income in respect of a decedent.

The estate does not recognize gain when the obligation is distributed to C. Under the general rule of § 691(a)(2), the "transfer" by the estate of a right to receive an item of income in respect of a decedent requires the estate to include the value of the item in its income. But the second sentence of § 691(a)(2) excludes from the definition of "transfer" for this purpose "a transfer to a person pursuant to a right of such person to receive such amount by reason of the death of the decedent or by bequest, devise or inheritance from the decedent." Therefore, S's estate has not made a "transfer" that would cause it to recognize gain.

C excludes the value of the note from income under § 102(a). As C collects each $100 principal payment on the note, C must recognize $80 (80% of $100) of gain. The gain would be characterized as capital gain—that is, gain of the same type as it would have been had S lived to collect payment; § 691(a)(3) & (a)(4)(B). (C may also be entitled to a § 691(c) deduction for the estate tax attributable to the inclusion of the IRD in S's gross estate for federal estate-tax purposes.)

If C collects some amount other than the face amount of the installment obligation, C must include in income only the excess of the amount collected over the adjusted basis of the obligation (determined under section 453B(b)); § 691(a)(2) & (a)(4)(B). Thus, if C accepted $400 in full satisfaction of the $500 installment note, C would recognize $300 of gain ($400 amount realized less $100 adjusted basis for the note); Treas. Reg. § 1.691(a)–5(a).

The statutory mechanism for achieving this result is somewhat complicated. Section 691(a)(2) generally provides that, in the case of a "transfer" of a right to an item of income in respect of a decedent, the transferor must include in gross income the fair market value of the right. Section 691(a)(2) goes on to provide expressly that the term "transfer" for this purpose includes the satisfaction of an installment obligation at other than its face amount. Section 691(a)(2), if standing alone, thus appears to treat C's receipt of $400 in full satisfaction of the installment note as a "transfer" that would require the inclusion of $400 (the fair market value of the obligation) in income. Section 691(a)(4)(B) intervenes, however, to provide that the amount includable in income under § 691(a)(2) "shall be reduced by an amount equal to the basis of the obligation in the hands of the decedent * * *." Therefore, C includes only $300 of gain ($400 value of obligation less D's $100 basis therein) in income under § 691(a)(2).

Any interest accrued to the date of S's death but collected after her death is taxable as IRD to C when C collects it.

(d) S dies and bequeaths the obligation to P, the purchaser of the property.

When the estate transfers the installment obligation to the obligor, P, the estate must recognize as IRD the $400 excess of the obligation's face amount ($500) over its adjusted basis in the hands of S immediately prior to S's death ($100).

We have already seen that the estate's transfer of an installment obligation to the beneficiary generally does not cause the estate to recognize the deferred gain. But if the obligation is transferred to a beneficiary who happens to be the obligor, the estate must recognize gain on the transfer to the extent that the value of the obligation exceeds its basis in the hands of the decedent; see § 691(a)(5)(A)(i). And where the decedent and the obligor are related persons (within the meaning of § 453(f)(1)), the value of the obligation is deemed for this purpose to be not less than its face amount; § 691(a)(5)(B).

When S's executor transfers the installment obligation to P, the estate must include in income the excess of the value of the obligation over S's $100 basis therein immediately before her death. But since S and P are related parties (see § 453(f); § 267(b)(1) & (c)(4)), the value of the installment obligation is deemed to be not less than its $500 face amount at the time of the distribution. Thus, the estate must recognize gain of $400 ($500 face amount less $100 basis) when it distributes the obligation to P. The estate's gain is characterized as capital gain, as it would have been in the hands of S if she had lived to collect the unpaid balance of the purchase price. (The estate may also be entitled to a § 691(c) deduction for the estate tax attributable to the inclusion of the installment obligation in S's gross estate for federal estate-tax purposes.)

P has no cancellation-of-indebtedness income from the transaction because the cancellation was by way of a bequest, which is excludable from income under § 102(a). P's $1,000 cost basis for the property is preserved even though P winds up paying only $500 of the purchase price. The transaction is treated as if S left P a $500 bequest, which P used to pay off the balance due on the contract.

Sometimes the contract of sale provides that no further payments be made after the seller's death (self-cancelling installment notes). Where the seller dies before all payments have been received, the gain element in the unpaid balance is treated as income in respect of a decedent to the estate; see Frane v. Commissioner, 998 F.2d 567 (8th Cir. 1993).

(e) S transferred the note to S's former spouse, F, as part of a divorce property settlement.

This transfer is covered by § 1041(a), which provides that a taxpayer does not recognize gain on a transfer of property to a former spouse if the transfer is "incident to the divorce," as this appears to be; see § 1041(c); Treas. Reg. § 1.1041–1T(b), Q & A (6) & (7). Section 453B(g) makes § 453B(a) inapplicable to transfers to which § 1041 applies, and so S recognizes no gain on the transfer of the installment obligation. F assumes S's $100 adjusted basis for the installment obligation. Although F has obviously not made an installment sale of the property, he continues recognizing the gain under § 453 in the same manner that S would if S were receiving the installment payments; § 453B(g)(2). So, F assumes S's gross-profit ratio of 80 percent and treats 80 percent of each principal payment received as long-term capital gain. Any interest that is accrued but unpaid when S transfers the note to F is taxable to F when collected by him; that is, § 1041 trumps the assignment-of-income doctrine; see Rev. Rul. 2002–22, 2002–1 C.B. 849.

4. What result (in 1) if, immediately after the sale, S borrowed $600 from a bank and pledged the installment note as security for the loan. What result as S receives payments on the note?

Generally speaking, when the taxpayer pledges an installment obligation as security for a loan, the amount of the loan proceeds received by the taxpayer is treated as a constructive payment on the installment obligation; § 453A(d)(1). As a matter of policy this makes sense, as there is little reason to continue deferral once the taxpayer has "cashed out" by borrowing against the security of the installment obligation. The amount treated as received is generally limited to the unpaid portion of the total contract price; § 453A(d)(2). In this case, S pledged the installment obligation in year 1 when the unpaid portion of the contract price was $500 (total contract price of $1,000 less $500 down payment), so only $500 is treated as a constructive payment at the time of the borrowing. The receipt of the $500 constructive payment requires S to recognize additional gain of $400 (80% of $500).

All of the gain from the sale of the asset has now been recognized ($400 when the down payment was received and $400 when the loan proceeds were received). Accordingly, the future payments received by S are treated as tax-paid amounts on which no further gain is recognized; § 453A(d)(3).

Section I

PERSONAL DEDUCTIONS AND CREDITS

Chapter 33

MEDICAL EXPENSES

Code: § 213. Note §§ 104(a)(3); 2053(a)(3).

Regulation: § 1.213-1.

Case: Ferris v. Commissioner, 582 F.2d 1112 (7th Cir. 1978).

Rulings: Rev. Rul. 2003–57, 2003–1 C.B. 959;
Rev. Rul. 2003–58, 2003–1 C.B. 959.

1. **T, a cash-method taxpayer, has gross income as follows:**

Salary	**$90,000**
Dividends	**10,000**

T also paid the following expenses:

Charitable contributions	5,000
Medical expenses	12,000

Before the end of the year T received an insurance reimbursement for $2,000 of the medical expense. T pays the premiums on the policy. All of the medical expenses were incurred for T's medical care.

(a) To what extent are T's medical expenses deductible if T itemizes deductions?

Although T paid $12,000 of medical expenses, only the $10,000 that was not reimbursed by insurance can be considered for deduction under § 213(a), and even that amount can be deducted only to the extent that it exceeds 7.5 percent of T's AGI under § 213(b). We therefore begin by computing T's AGI.

T has gross income of $100,000 (the salary and dividends), and AGI of $100,000, as T has no above-the-line deductions under § 62(a). The floor on the medical-expense deduction is $7,500 (7.5% of $100,000).

T's medical-expense deduction is therefore $2,500, the amount by which the $10,000 of unreimbursed expenses exceed $7,500.

(b) How would your answer change if T used the accrual method and, in addition to the $12,000 of medical expenses that were incurred and paid in the current year, T had also incurred an additional $5,000 of medical expenses (but had not paid the additional $5,000 before the end of the year)?

The answer would not change. Section 213(a) allows a deduction only for medical expenses actually "paid" during the year; Treas. Reg. § 1.213–1(a)(1). So, even an accrual-method taxpayer cannot deduct accrued but unpaid amounts.

Of course, subject to the 7.5%–percent floor, T can deduct the expenses when they are paid even though they were incurred in a previous year. So, T may yet get a deduction for the $5,000.

(c) How would your answer to (a) change if a subsequent audit of T's return resulted in a $10,000 increase in T's gross and adjusted gross income?

The increase in T's gross income and AGI to $110,000 will also trigger a decrease in T's medical expense deduction to $1,750 ($10,000 less $8,250 floor); Osborne v. Commissioner, 1995–353 T.C. Memo., aff'd on another issue, 114 F.3d 1188 (6th Cir. 1997).

2. A pays some qualifying medical expenses incurred by others. Subject to the § 213(b) floor, can A deduct the amounts paid in the current year on behalf of:

(a) A's mother, M? A provides over half of M's support because M's only source of income is a (taxable) annual pension of $24,000.

Section 213(a) allows a deduction for medical expenses paid for the medical care of the taxpayer's "dependents." M would be A's "qualifying relative" under § 152(d)(1) (and hence A's dependent under § 152(a)), except that M's gross income ($24,000) exceeds the exemption amount ($2,000); see § 152(d)(1)(B). So, even though A provides over half of M's support, A does not get a dependency exemption for M. However, in determining dependency for the purpose of the medical-expense deduction, § 213(a) tells us to disregard the gross-income test of § 152(d)(1)(B). Thus, A can get a deduction for M's medical expenses.

(b) A's late husband, D, who died last year? A remarried in the current year.

Section 213(a) allows a deduction for medical expenses paid for the medical care of the taxpayer's "spouse." According to the regulations, this means that the parties must have been married to each other either at the time the spouse received the medical care or at the time that the expenses were paid; Treas. Reg. § 1.213-1(e)(3).   Here D was A's spouse at the time the expenses were incurred, and A can deduct the expenses. It is immaterial that the A had remarried by the time A paid the medical expenses. (The special rule of § 213(c), pertaining to medical expenses paid after death, does not apply here because the expenses were not paid by D's estate.)

(c) A's 12-year old son, S? A is divorced, and S is a dependent of A's former husband, X, with whom S resides and from whom S receives a majority of his support.

Yes. Because X is the custodial parent and S receives over half his support from his parents, the default rule of § 152(e) allocates S's dependency exemption to X. However, a child of divorced parents is treated as the dependent of both parents for purposes of the medical-expense deduction; § 213(d)(5). So, A can claim a deduction for S's medical expenses.

3. Do expenditures for the following items qualify for deduction under § 213?

(a) Contact lenses.

Deductible; Treas. Reg. § 1.213–1(e)(1)(iii) (eyeglasses); Rev. Rul. 74–429, 1974–2 C.B. 83 (contact lenses). The cost of insuring the contact lenses is also deductible; id.

(b) Non-prescription nicotine gum or patches designed to help the taxpayer stop smoking.

No deduction. Although the cost of participation in a smoking-cessation program and of *prescription* drugs used to alleviate the effects of nicotine withdrawal would be deductible, non-prescription medications (other than non-prescription insulin) are not deductible; § 213(b); Rev. Rul. 99–28, 1999–1 C.B. 1269.

(c) A wig for a taxpayer whose hair loss was caused by treatment for disease.

Where the purchase of a wig is unrelated to some particular disease, it is generally not deductible; Rev. Rul. 55–261, 1955–1 C.B. 307. But hair loss caused by a disease (or its treatment) can have a marked effect on one's mental health. Rev. Rul. 62–189, 1962–2 C.B. 88, allowed a deduction for the cost of a wig where a physician had advised that the wig was essential for the patient's mental health. So, deductible, at least if the wig is recommended by the doctor.

(d) A weight-loss program.

The cost of a weight-loss program undertaken to promote "general health" is not deductible; Rev.Rul. 79–151, 1979–1 C.B. 116. But Rev. Rul. 2002–19, 2002–1 C.B. 778, allows a deduction where the program is prescribed by a physician for treatment of a particular illness, such as hypertension or diabetes. The ruling also holds that obesity can be a disease in its own right, and that a taxpayer who paid fees to join and attend meetings of a weight-reduction program could deduct those costs as medical expenses. However, no deduction was allowed for the costs of purchasing reduced-calorie diet foods from the program.

(e) Aspirin (taken on the recommendation of a physician).

Not deductible, as it is a non-prescription drug; § 213(b); Rev. Rul. 2003–58, 2003–1 C.B. 959.

(f) Non-prescription insulin and blood-sugar-test kits.

Both deductible. Insulin is the one non-prescription drug that qualifies for the medical-expense deduction; § 213(b). Medical equipment, supplies and diagnostic devices are deductible even though they may be purchased without a prescription. So, a diabetic's purchase of a blood-sugar-test kit would be deductible; Rev. Rul. 2003–58, 2003–1 C.B. 959.

(g) Teeth whitening.

Section 213(d)(9) says that the term "medical care" does not include cosmetic surgery or "similar procedures," unless necessary to ameliorate a deformity arising from a congenital abnormality, personal injury, or disfiguring disease. Teeth whitening does not treat a disease or promote the proper function of the body, but is done for the purpose of improving the patient's appearance. The discoloration is not a deformity and is not caused by a disfiguring disease or treatment. The cost of teeth whitening is therefore not deductible as a medical expense; Rev. Rul. 2003–57, 2003–1 C.B. 959.

(h) The cost of a prescribed drug that was ordered by the taxpayer from a Canadian on-line pharmacy.

Probably no deduction. Most prescription drugs cannot legally be imported by individuals, and no deduction is allowed for the cost of illegal drugs; Treas. Reg. § 1.213–1(e)(2) (term "medicine and drugs" includes only those that are "legally procured"); Rev. Rul. 97–9, 1997–1 C.B. 77 (purchase of controlled substance in violation of federal law; held, not deductible even though purchased on the recommendation of a physician in a state whose laws permit such purchase and use).

(i) A one-month stay at an alcoholism rehabilitation center.

The costs of alcoholism rehabilitation (including the cost of meals and lodging furnished as a necessary incident to the treatment) are deductible; Rev. Rul. 73–325, 1973–2 C.B. 75. See also Rev. Rul. 72–226, 1972–1 C.B. 96 (deduction allowed for cost of maintaining dependent for several months in a therapeutic center for drug addiction); Rev. Rul. 63–273, 1963–2 C.B. 112 (cost of transportation to Alcoholics Anonymous meetings deductible).

(j) Birth-control pills.

Deductible, if purchased under a prescription provided by the patient's physician; Rev. Rul. 73–200, 1973–1 C.B. 140. The costs of vasectomies and legal abortions are deductible, as both procedures affect a structure or function of the body and so constitute medical care under § 213(d)(1)(A); Rev. Rul. 73–201, 1973–1 C.B. 140.

(k) Installing railings and support bars in the bathroom of a wheelchair-bound person.

Section 213(a) generally limits the medical deduction to "expenses," and the cost of installing hardware in a bathroom is likely a capital expenditure (i.e., an expenditure having a useful life that extends substantially beyond the close of the taxable year in which made). Nevertheless, the regulations and caselaw acknowledge that an outlay which otherwise qualifies as a medical expense is not disallowed merely because it is a capital expenditure; Treas. Reg. § 1.213–1(e)(1)(iii); Ferris v. Commissioner, 582 F.2d 1112 (7th Cir. 1978) (part of the cost of installing swimming pool deductible by taxpayer who suffered degenerative disease and whose physician had recommended the pool for health reasons). *Ferris* allowed a deduction to the extent that the expenditure exceeded the increase in the value of the house.

Rev. Rul. 87–106, 1987–2 C.B. 67, provides a non-exhaustive list of expenditures that usually do not increase the value of the residence and therefore should be fully deductible. Included are the costs of modifications to a bathroom by the installation of railings, support bars and the like. So, the full cost of the modifications probably qualifies as medical expense.

(l) Transportation to a tertiary-care hospital located 250 miles from the taxpayer's home.

The cost of transportation primarily for and essential to the rendition of medical care qualifies as medical care; § 213(d)(1)(B); Treas. Reg. § 1.213–1(e)(1)(iv). Of course, even if a physician recommends medical care, a patient who travels for personal reasons to another locality (such as a resort area) to obtain treatment cannot deduct the cost of the transportation; id.

If, as appears to be the case here, the taxpayer had non-personal reasons for seeking treatment at the tertiary-care center, the transportation expenses should be deductible. In computing automobile expenses, the taxpayer can either use actual expenses or the standard mileage rate applicable to medical expenses.

(m) Meals and lodging while receiving out-patient treatment at the tertiary-care center.

The cost of lodging (but not meals) is deductible because the medical care is being provided by a physician in a licensed hospital; § 213(d)(2). It doesn't matter that the patient has not been admitted to the hospital but is being treated on an out-patient basis. No deduction is allowed where the lodging is "lavish or extravagant" or where there is a significant element of personal pleasure, recreation or vacation in the travel; id. Lodging costs of up to $50 per day can be taken into account; id.

Of course, the cost of an in-patient hospital stay (including meals and lodging) qualifies as medical expense if the patient is there to obtain qualifying medical care; Treas. Reg.§ 1.213–1(e)(1)(v).

(n) Meals and lodging paid on behalf of a family member who accompanies the taxpayer to the tertiary-care center.

The committee reports accompanying the enactment of the statutory lodging rule of § 213(d) say that the provision allows a deduction for the lodging cost of a person accompanying the patient whenever that person's transportation expense is deductible as medical expense. So, if the other person accompanies the patient because the patient is unable to travel alone, the other person's transportation and lodging costs are deductible. Lodging cost can be taken into account only up to a maximum of $50 per day each for the patient and the other person; § 213(d)(2)(last sentence).

(o) Medical insurance.

Medical-insurance premiums qualify as a cost of medical care under § 213(d)(1)(B). If the policy covers amounts other than for medical care (such as compensation for the loss of a limb or a guaranteed daily payment while the insured is hospitalized, the deduction is disallowed unless (1) the charge for the medical insurance is separately stated; (2) the taxpayer does not treat the rest of the premium as a cost of medical insurance; and (3) the medical-insurance amount is not unreasonably large in relation to the total policy premiums; § 213(d)(6).

Medical-insurance premiums paid before age 65 for coverage beginning at age 65 can be deducted within the limits prescribed by § 213(d)(7).

(p) Long-term care insurance.

Premiums for "eligible long-term care insurance" are treated as a cost of medical care under § 213(d)(1)(C).

(q) Treatment by a chiropractor.

Deductible. Medical expenses include not only payments for services to physicians, surgeons and dentists, but optometrists, chiropractors, osteopaths, psychiatrists, psychologists, and Christian Science practitioners; Rev. Rul. 63–91, 1963–1 C.B. 5; cf. Rev. Rul. 72–593, 1972–2 C.B. 180 (payments to acupuncturists deductible).

Although Treas. Reg. § 1.213–1(e)(1)(ii) says that amounts expended for illegal treatments are not deductible, Rev. Rul. 63–91 holds that the treatment is not rendered illegal just because the practitioner does not have the license required by state law to perform the medical services. So, even if the chiropractor is unlicensed, payments to the chiropractor for medical care are deductible.

(r) The 1.45–percent Medicare tax on an employee's salary.

Not deductible by the employee. (The employer's share may be deductible as a business expense.) The tax is imposed on the employee by § 3101(b), and § 275(a)(1)(A) specifically disallows deductions for taxes imposed under § 3101. When there is a conflict between § 213 and § 275, the latter prevails; § 261 ("no deduction shall in any case be allowed in respect of the items specified in this part" (IX), which includes § 275).

(s) Medicare Part D insurance (covering prescription-drug benefits).

Begun in 2006, Medicare Part D is a voluntary insurance program covering prescription drugs for seniors. The insurance premiums are treated as costs of medical care under § 213(d)(1)(D) and so can be deductible.

4. T has a serious heart condition. Upon the recommendation of his physician, T installed an elevator in his home so that he would not have to climb stairs. Installation of the elevator cost $15,000. The value of T's home immediately before the installation was $200,000. Immediately after the installation, the value of the home was $205,000.

(a) To what extent, if any, does the cost of the elevator qualify as a medical expense?

The cost of installing an elevator is a capital expenditure (i.e., an expenditure whose useful life extends substantially beyond the close of the taxable year). Although § 213(a) generally limits the medical deduction to "expenses," an outlay such as this one that otherwise qualifies as a medical expense is not disallowed merely because it is a capital expenditure; Treas. Reg. § 1.213–1(e)(1)(iii); Ferris v. Commissioner, 582 F.2d 1112 (7th Cir. 1978) (part of the cost of installing swimming pool deductible by taxpayer who suffered degenerative disease and whose physician had recommended the pool for health reasons).

Where the capital expenditure increases the value of the residence to which it is attached, the deduction is limited to the amount by which the cost of the improvement exceeds the increase in value of the residence; Treas. Reg. § 1.213–1(e)(1)(iii). Here the $15,000 expenditure increased the value of the residence by $5,000, so only $10,000 is treated as a medical expense.

(b) T's adjusted gross income for the year is $100,000. How much of the $15,000 cost should T include in his adjusted basis for the home? (For simplicity, assume that T paid no other medical expenses for the year.)

T could deduct only $2,500 of the elevator's cost ($10,000 medical expense less $7,500 floor); § 213(a). T's basis in the elevator is the excess of its $15,000 cost over the $2,500 deducted. Therefore, T's adjusted basis for the residence is increased by $12,500.

5. In year 1, S paid $10,000 of medical expenses. S's adjusted gross income for the year was $100,000 and her itemized deductions other than medical expenses totaled $15,000. In year 2, S received partial reimbursement for the expenses from her insurer. S pays the premiums on the medical-insurance policy from her after-tax income. How much should S include in gross income in year 2 if the amount of the reimbursement was:

(a) $2,000?

Section 104(a)(3) excludes insurance reimbursements from gross income, except to the extent of deductions allowed under § 213 for a prior taxable year. In this case, S's year–1 medical-expense deduction would be limited to $2,500 ($10,000 less $7,500 floor); § 213(a). The entire $2,000 reimbursement received in year 2 would therefore be includable in S's gross income. This year–2 inclusion just "makes up" for the "excess" deduction she got in year 1. If she had received the reimbursement in year 1, S's year–1 deduction would have been only $500 ($8,000 unreimbursed expense less $7,500 floor). Because she deducted $2,500 in year 1, she must restore $2,000 to income when the reimbursement is received in year 2.

(b) $6,000?

Of the $6,000 reimbursement, only $2,500 was deducted in year 1, and so only $2,500 must be included in gross income in year 2; § 104(a) ("not in excess of amounts allowed" under § 213).

6. D died in December of last year. In the mo.
death, D incurred unreimbursed medical expense of $25,
paid the expense from D's estate early this year. Can tl.
the medical expense under § 213? Explain.

Only an individual is entitled to a medical-expense deductioι
because the payment must cover the cost of medical care for the *tax*
taxpayer's spouse or dependents, and entities other than individuals dι
medical care and don't have spouses or dependents. So, the estate canι
the payments on its income-tax return. (The medical expense cannot be ι
as a deduction in respect of a decedent because medical expense is not onι
deductions enumerated in § 691(b).) The estate could, however, deduι
expense as a claim against the estate for federal estate-tax purposes; § 2053(a

At first glance, it appears that D cannot deduct the expense on his finι
return because the expenses were not paid by D before death, which closed D's lasι
taxable year. However, under the special rule of § 213(c)(1), an estate can elect to
treat medical expenses paid by it within the year following the decedent's death
as paid by the decedent when incurred. So, in this case, the estate can elect to
treat the $25,000 paid by it as having been paid by D, who is deemed to have paid
the expense when incurred last year. If the estate makes the election, then the
expense can be taken into account in determining the medical-expense deduction
on D's final return.

What does the estate give up by making this election? It must waive its right
to deduct the expense as a claim against the estate for federal estate-tax purposes;
§ 213(c)(2). Whether the estate should waive the estate-tax deduction depends
upon whether the estate will owe estate tax. Only very large estates owe federal
estate tax because of the estate-tax exclusion ($2,000,000 and increasing to
$3,500,000 in 2009) and the unlimited deduction for transfers to a surviving
spouse (the marital deduction). In those cases, the estate should waive the estate-
tax deduction if D could benefit from the income-tax deduction. But if the estate
does owe federal estate tax, it should deduct the medical expense under the estate
tax because the first dollar taxed under the estate tax is taxed at a 45% rate, and
the maximum marginal income-tax rate is only 35%. In that case, the estate-tax
deduction is more valuable than the income-tax deduction.

Chapter 34

CHARITABLE CONTRIBUTIONS

Code: § 170(a), (b), (c), (d)(1), (e)(1), (f)(2), (3), (6) & (8), (i), (j) & (*l*). Note § 1011(b). Review §§ 1221(a)(3); 1231(b)(1)(C); 1245(a) & (b)(1).

Regulations: §§ 1.170A–1(a), (b), (c)(1), (g), (h)(1), (2) & (3); 1.170A–4(b)(3); 1.170A–13(f)(8)(i).

1. **In the current year, T, an individual, made the following cash payments. How much of each payment is deductible as a charitable contribution? (Ignore the percentage limits of § 170(b). Assume that T can substantiate the contributions in the manner required by the Code and regulations.)**

(a) $15,000 paid to Y University as tuition for T's niece, N. N comes from an impecunious, single-parent home, and her immediate family is not able to assist her financially.

No deduction. Although the university is an organization described in § 170(c)(2), T is not making a contribution to the university. This case should be analyzed as though T gave the money to N, and N paid her own tuition. T cannot deduct a contribution to N because N is an individual and not an organization described in § 170(c). And, of course, N cannot deduct the payment as a charitable contribution because she is receiving a quid pro quo for the $15,000—the right to attend classes at the school.

(b) $5,000 to T's church for the saying of masses for T's late mother and father.

T can deduct the $5,000. The church is an organization described in § 170(c)(2). The issue is whether the saying of masses is a quid pro quo for the contribution. The saying of masses is an "intangible religious benefit"—i.e., a religious benefit provided by a religious organization and which is generally not sold in a commercial transaction outside the donative context; see § 170(f)(8)(B). As such, it is not considered to be a quid pro quo that precludes a deduction.

(c) $1,000 to the American Red Cross to be used for tsunami relief in Indonesia.

The American Red Cross is a § 170(c)(2) organization. The issue is whether a gift to be used outside the United States qualifies for deduction. It does. Section 170(c)(2)(A) requires that the charitable organization generally "be created or organized in the United States," which the American Red Cross is. It does not matter that the contribution is used by the organization in its work overseas. T can deduct the $1,000.

(d) $500 to the Unity Party, which, in the next presidential election, expects to nominate a ticket consisting of a member of one of the major political parties for president and a member of the other major party for vice president.

No deduction. The Unity Party cannot be a § 170(c)(2) organization because it participates in political campaigns on behalf of candidates for public office.

(e) $1,000 to the Veterans of Foreign Wars.

T can deduct the $1,000. The VFW is an organization described in § 170(c)(3).

(f) $20,000 to State University. Donors of $5,000 or more are entitled to priority seating at the school's home football games, nearly all of which sell out. (The actual cost of tickets is extra.)

Here T receives a benefit on account of the contribution—the right to purchase tickets for priority seating at the school's football games. Generally speaking, a charitable donor who receives a quid pro quo for a contribution can deduct only the excess of the amount paid over the value of the goods or services received in return; Treas. Reg. § 1.170A–1(h)(2)(i). Code § 170(*l*) was enacted to deal with the treatment of contributions that entitle the contributor to privileges at a school's athletic events. Under that provision, only 80 percent of the amount that qualifies the donor for ticket privileges is deductible. Since in this case, a donor need give only $5,000 to get the ticket priority, 80 percent of that amount is deductible. The $15,000 balance of the contribution does not involve any quid pro quo because it does not engender ticket privileges. Therefore, T can deduct $19,000 (80% of the first $5,000, plus $15,000).

(g) $2,500,000 to University Law School to endow the "T Family Chair in Federal Tax Law."

T can deduct the entire gift. Although perpetuating the family name by endowing a chair at the law school provides some "benefit" to the donor, the benefit is too nebulous and difficult to quantify, so the entire $2,500,000 is deductible.

(h) $500 for a ticket to the University Medical School "Have A Heart" Gala, which raises money for the school's heart-research program. The gala includes a dinner and dance, the reasonable cost of which would be $100 per ticket.

T can deduct $400, the excess of the ticket cost over the benefit received; see Rev. Rul. 67–246, 1967–2 C.B. 104, Ex. 8.

(i) $100 to the local public-radio station. In return for the contribution, T received a coffee mug emblazoned with the station's logo and call letters.

A charitable contribution generally must be reduced by the value of any goods or services received in return; Treas. Reg. § 1.170–1(h)(1). However, items of inconsequential or insubstantial value can be disregarded; Treas. Reg. § 1.170A–13(f)(8)(i)(A). Where the donor makes a contribution of $44.50 or more (in 2007) and receives in exchange token items (such as bookmarks, calendars, key chains, mugs, posters, tee shirts, etc.), the charitable deduction need not be reduced by the value of such items; Rev. Proc. 90–12, 1990–1 C.B. 471. (The figures from Rev. Proc. 90–12 are adjusted annually for inflation, most recently by Rev. Proc. 2006–53, 2006–2 C.B. 996.)

2. D, an individual, has today made the following gifts to an organization qualifying under § 170(c) and described in § 170(b)(1)(A). In each of the following cases, determine the amount deductible by D. Ignore the effect of the percentage limits of § 170(b). D can substantiate the amount of each contribution.

(a) Shares of X Corporation stock, which D had purchased two years ago for $40,000. The stock was worth $100,000 at the time of the gift.

Although D does not recognize gain upon the contribution of appreciated property to the charitable organization, D gets a deduction for the $100,000 value of the stock. (Subject to the exceptions of § 170(e), discussed below, gifts of property are generally taken into account at their fair market value; Treas. Reg. § 170A–1(c)(1).) From a policy standpoint, this result makes little sense, as it gives D a deduction for the appreciation on which D has never been (and never will be) taxed.

(b) Same as (a), except that D purchased the stock eight months ago.

Section 170(e)(1) generally requires that the amount of a charitable contribution be reduced by the amount of gain that would not have been long-term capital gain if the property had been sold for its fair market value. Here, a sale of the stock at the time of the gift would have resulted in a short-term capital gain because the stock (a capital asset) did not have a holding period of more than one year; § 1222(1). So, D's erstwhile $100,000 deduction must be reduced by the

$60,000 of potential short-term capital gain, and D's deduction is limited to $40,000—the basis of the stock.

(c) Same as (a), except that the stock was worth only $30,000 on the date of the gift.

D's deduction is $30,000, the fair market value of the stock; Treas. Reg. § 170A–1(c)(1). In this case, the rule giving a deduction for the value (rather than the basis) of the stock hurts D. The pain can be avoided by D's selling the stock, recognizing the $10,000 capital loss, and giving the $30,000 sales proceeds to the charity.

(d) A business computer that D had purchased several years ago for $5,000 and on which D had properly deducted $3,000 of depreciation. The equipment was worth $10,000 at the time of the gift. The donee, a university, planned to install the computer in a faculty office.

The computer is § 1245 property because it is depreciable personal (i.e., moveable) property; § 1245(a)(3). Does the contribution of the computer require D to recognize the § 1245 gain? Recall that § 1245(a)(1)(last sentence) says that on a disposition of § 1245 property the § 1245 gain must be recognized "notwithstanding any other provision of this subtitle." However, § 1245(b)(1) excepts transfers by gift from the "strong-arm" recognition rule, and D is making a gift to charity. So, D does not recognize gain on the transfer.

Section 170(e) comes into play, however, to require D to decrease his deduction by the amount of gain that would not have been long-term capital gain if the computer had been sold for its fair market value. A sale of the computer for its $10,000 value would result in some ordinary § 1245 gain. D's recomputed basis is $5,000 ($2,000 adjusted basis plus $3,000 of depreciation adjustments reflected in that adjusted basis); § 1245(a)(2). Since the $5,000 recomputed basis is less than the $10,000 amount realized on the hypothetical sale of the computer, the § 1245 gain would be $3,000 (the excess of the $5,000 recomputed basis over the $2,000 adjusted basis). The $5,000 balance of the gain would be § 1231 gain (gain from the sale of a § 1231 asset—§ 1231(a)(3)(A)(i)), the character of which as ordinary or capital would depend upon the outcome of the § 1231 hotchpot; but to avoid that inquiry, § 170(e)(1) treats § 1231 assets as capital assets, so the $5,000 balance of the gain would be characterized as long-term capital gain. Thus, a sale of the computer would have produced $3,000 of ordinary income and $5,000 of long-term capital gain. D must reduce the charitable deduction from $10,000 (fair market value) to $7,000 ($10,000 value less $3,000 ordinary-income potential).

(e) Same as (d), except that the university is going to sell the computer to raise money for student scholarships.

Now the university is going to use the computer to raise money, which is a use unrelated to the university's educational function constituting the basis of its exemption from tax under § 501; see Treas. Reg. § 1.170A–4(b)(3). Therefore, § 170(e)(1)(B)(i) requires D to reduce the charitable deduction even by the amount of gain that would have been long-term capital gain if the computer had been sold for its fair market value. As discussed above, a sale of the computer for its $10,000 value would have resulted in the recognition of $3,000 of ordinary income and $5,000 of long-term capital gain. The deduction is therefore limited to $2,000 ($10,000 value less $3,000 reduction under (e)(1)(A) and $5,000 reduction under (e)(1)(B)(i)).

(f) A portrait, painted by D. (D therefore had a zero basis.) The painting had a value of $100,000.

D gets no deduction. The painting is not a capital asset because of § 1221(a)(3)(A)(artistic composition held by the taxpayer whose personal efforts created the property). Neither is it a § 1231 asset because (1) it is not of a character subject to the allowance for depreciation, and (2) § 1231(b)(1)(C) specifically excludes it from the category of § 1231 assets. A sale of the painting by D would therefore produce ordinary gain for want of a capital (or § 1231) asset. In determining D's deduction, we must reduce the fair market value of the painting ($100,000) by the amount of ordinary gain that would have been recognized on a sale ($100,000), which leaves D without a deduction.

(g) A portrait, painted by D's mother, M. M, whose basis in the painting was zero, had given the painting to D several years ago when it was worth $20,000. D gave the painting to the charity when it was worth $100,000.

No deduction. When M gave the painting to D, D assumed M's zero basis under § 1015(a). The painting is not a capital (or § 1231) asset in D's hands because D's basis is determined by reference to the basis of the painting in the hands of its creator (M); see §§ 1221(a)(3)(C); 1231(b)(1)(C). If D sold the painting for $100,000, D would recognize $100,000 of ordinary gain. D's contribution must therefore be reduced to zero ($100,000 value of the painting less $100,000 of ordinary income recognizable if painting were sold); see § 170(e)(1)(B)(i).

(h) Same as (g), except that D had acquired the painting (then worth $20,000) by bequest at M's death.

D can deduct the $100,000 value of the painting. D's basis is determined under § 1014(a), which provides generally that the basis of property acquired from a decedent is its fair market value on the date of the decedent's death. The painting is a capital asset in D's hands because D's basis is not determined by reference to M's. (This assumes that D is not an art dealer, in which case the painting might not be a capital asset because of § 1221(a)(1).) If the painting is a capital asset, its sale would produce long-term capital gain, and § 170(e)(1)(A) would not limit the charitable deduction. (Even if D's actual holding period is not more than one year, a sale of the painting would have produced long-term capital gain because of § 1223(9).)

(i) A portrait painted by D. D had sold the painting in a bona fide sale for $1,000. Twenty years later, D saw the painting in a collection and repurchased it for $20,000. After the painting had appreciated in value to $30,000, D gave it to the § 170 organization.

D is still the taxpayer whose efforts created the property, so it appears that the painting is not a capital asset. In that case, § 170(e) effectively limits D's deduction to his basis, which would be $20,000. This is not an entirely satisfactory result, as D was compensated for his personal services in painting the portrait when he sold it for $1,000. The appreciation from $20,000 to $30,000 appears to be capital appreciation rather than being attributable to D's personal efforts. Under these circumstances, it is not apparent why any appreciation of the property in D's hands should be treated differently than the case in which property not created by D appreciated in his hands. Perhaps allowing the deduction for the appreciation would invite subterfuge—D might feign a sale and repurchase of the painting. Regardless of whether the application of § 170(e) serves its apparent purpose here, the Code seemingly limits D's deduction to his basis in the painting.

(j) One day of D's professional services, for which a client would have paid D $1,000.

D cannot deduct the value of his services; Treas. Reg. § 1.170A–1(g). D's tax benefit comes from not including in income the compensation he could have earned by working for the charity instead of a paying client.

(k) $1,000 cash, which D earned in one day performing services for professional clients.

D can deduct the $1,000 contribution. We saw in the last problem that one can perform free work for a charity and pay no tax on the value of that work. Section 170 allows the same end result when one works for a charity indirectly by pursuing one's regular employment and giving the charity the proceeds. D includes the $1,000 cash compensation in gross income. Since D neither consumes nor saves the $1,000 but gives it to charity, D should get a $1,000 deduction.

(l) Same as (j), except that D also incurred $200 of out-of-pocket expenses in performing the services.

Unreimbursed out-of-pocket expenses are deductible even though made incident to rendering gratuitous services to a charity; Treas. Reg. § 1.170A–1(g).

So, for example, deductions are allowed for the cost of a uniform (not suitable for general wear) that is required to be worn in performing donated services, transportation expenses incurred in performing donated services, and meals and lodging while away from home in the course of performing donated services (but notice the no-smile rule of § 170(j)); id. Automobile expenses can be deducted at a standard mileage rate of 14 cents per mile (the Code does not provide for inflation adjustments for this figure); § 170(i). Parking fees and tolls are also deductible; Rev. Proc. 70–12. 1970–1 C.B. 438.

(m) $1,000 worth of books received free of charge from publishers, who hoped that D, a professional book reviewer, would publish reviews of the books. D had not included the value of the books in income when received.

Although the deduction is allowable, the value of the books apparently must be included in D's gross income when he gives them to charity. At one time, the Service asserted that a book reviewer's acceptance of free books was sufficient exercise of dominion and control to require the value of the books to be included in gross income; Rev. Rul. 70–330, 1970–1 C.B. 14. That ruling was superseded by Rev. Rul. 70–498, 1970–2 C.B., in which a book reviewer gave the books to charity in the year received and claimed a charitable deduction for their value. The ruling holds that the reviewer must include the value of the books in gross income, but strongly implies that mere *acceptance* of books for review (or other free samples) is not a sufficient exercise of dominion and control to make the recipient taxable. In Haverly v. United States, 513 F.2d 224 (7th Cir. 1975), a school principal received sample texts that he donated to the school library and for which he claimed a charitable deduction. The Seventh Circuit required the principal to include the value of the books in gross income; it noted that the taxpayer exercised "complete dominion" over the books by his "unequivocal act of taking a charitable deduction for donation of the property"; 513 F. 2d at 227. Although some of the texts had been received by the principal in 1967, the court held the value of the books includable in his 1968 income since that was the year in which he donated them. So, D gets a $1,000 charitable deduction but must include the $1,000 value of the books in gross income. (This presupposes that a sale of the books by D would produce long-term capital gain.)

(n) A remainder interest in a trust created by D to pay the income to D's child, C, for life, remainder to the charitable organization. The trust corpus consisted of a well-diversified portfolio of publicly traded securities. A bank served as trustee. Based upon C's life expectancy, the actuarial present value of the remainder interest in the trust was $40,000.

No deduction is allowed for a remainder interest in a trust unless the trust is a charitable remainder annuity trust (CRAT), a charitable remainder unitrust (CRUT) or a pooled income fund (PIF); § 170(f)(2)(A).

A CRAT is a trust from which a sum certain is to be paid annually to one or more persons for life (or for a term of years) with remainder to a qualified charity. Distributions (other than the annuity payments) cannot be made to any non-charitable beneficiary; § 664(d)(1).

A CRUT is a trust from which a fixed percentage of the FMV of the trust's assets (determined annually) is to be paid to one or more persons for life (or for a term of years) with remainder to a qualified charity. Distributions (other than the unitrust amount) cannot be made to any private beneficiary; § 664(d)(2).

A PIF is a trust that is created and operated by a public charitable organization (i.e., one described in § 170(b)(1)(A)(i)—(vi)). The PIF pools the contributions of various donors, each of whom contributes an irrevocable remainder interest in the property to the charity. The grantor retains an income interest for the life of one or more non-charitable beneficiaries. Each beneficiary receives income determined by the rate of return earned by the trust as a whole; § 642(c)(5).

The charitable remainder trust in our problem does not fit into any of these categories, and D cannot deduct the value of the remainder interest.

The purpose of these rules is to prevent donors from obtaining deductions for charitable remainder gifts in circumstances where a trustee might be able to manipulate the trust investments or administration to favor the interests of the private beneficiary at the expense of the charitable remainder beneficiary.

(o) Same as (n), except that the trust corpus consisted of D's vacation home.

Again, D cannot deduct the value of the charitable remainder because the gift is in trust and the trust is not a CRAT, CRUT or PIF.

(p) Same as (n), except that D gave C a legal life estate in D's vacation home, with remainder to a qualifying charity.

In the case of a contribution (not in trust) of a partial interest in property, a deduction is generally allowable only to the extent that a deduction would be allowable if the contribution were in trust; § 170(f)(3)(A). However, there is an exception for a remainder interest in a "personal residence" or farm; § 170(f)(3)(B)(i). The vacation home is a personal residence, and the gift of the remainder is deductible.

Why the exception for a legal life estate in a personal residence or farm? Congress thought such arrangements were less susceptible to the charitable-remainder beneficiary being deprived of its interest.

(q) A check for $1,000, mailed by D on December 31, year 1. The check was received and cashed by the charity on January 4 of the following year.

The charitable deduction is usually allowed for the year in which "payment" is made; § 170(a). The delivery or mailing of a check that clears in due course is treated as a contribution on the date of delivery or mailing; Treas. Reg. § 1.170A-1(b). So, D can take the deduction in year 1.

(r) D's promissory note in the amount of $10,000, payable in two years and bearing annual market-rate interest. The note was delivered to the charity on December 31 of the current year.

D's note represents a mere promise to pay at some future time and is not a "payment" for purposes of § 170(a). D can deduct any principal payments on the note in the year paid; Rev. Rul. 68–174, 1968–1 C.B. 81. D can also deduct any interest payments as a charitable deduction in the year paid; id. The interest payments are not deductible as interest because (1) the note is probably not enforceable (because not supported by consideration) and (2) even if the note is enforceable the interest is "personal interest" and therefore disallowed by § 163(h)(1).

What if the charity discounts the note at a bank before it is paid by D? In that case D can deduct the principal payments to the bank as charitable contributions. (Any interest accrued when the charity discounted the note to the bank should also qualify as a charitable contribution.) Interest accruing after the bank obtained the note would not be deductible as a charitable contribution. Even if the bank was a holder in due course, which would make the note enforceable against D, interest accruing after the transfer of the note to the bank would not be deductible as interest, as it would constitute personal interest under § 163(h).

(s) Same as (a), except that the stock was delivered in satisfaction of D's legally enforceable pledge of $100,000. D made the pledge last year. (Would your answer differ if D were an accrual-method taxpayer?)

$100,000 deductible this year. D gets no deduction until the pledge is satisfied because § 170(a) allows a deduction only for "payment" of the charitable contribution. Even an accrual-method taxpayer cannot deduct a pledge. (But see § 170(b)(2) (where board of accrual-method corporation authorizes contribution during year and corporation pays the contribution within two and half months after the close of the year, corporation can elect to take deduction for that year).)

3. S transferred corporate stock (valued at $100,000) to a charity described in § 170(b)(1)(A) for $50,000. S's adjusted basis in the stock was $40,000. What result to S?

S had made a bargain sale to the charity. She must make a ratable allocation of the property's basis between the "sale" and "gift" portions of the transaction; § 1011(b). S has sold an undivided half-interest ($50 sales price/$100 value) in the property for $50 and made a gift of the other half-interest. S must apportion 50% of the property's $40 AB to the sale, which means that S realizes gain of $30 on the sale portion of the transaction ($50 amount realized less $20 adjusted basis). D has made a charitable contribution of $50 (i.e., of the half-interest transferred by gift).

4. In the current year, D has adjusted gross income of $100,000. How much can D deduct in the current year in each of the following alternative cases? What happens to any amount not deductible in the current year? Assume in each case that the contribution is D's only contribution for the year.

(a) $60,000 cash to Private University.

This problem raises the issue of the percentage limitations on charitable contributions under § 170(b). For individuals, the percentage limits are based upon the taxpayer's "contribution base"; § 170(b)(1)(A). The contribution base is defined as adjusted gross income computed without regard to any available net-operating-loss-carryback deduction; § 170(b)(1)(F). (Taking an NOL carryback into account would necessitate making retroactive changes in the contribution base. All of the problems assume that the taxpayer has no NOL carryback.) The application of the percentage limits on the deduction depends upon (1) the nature of the donee, (2) the type of property given and (3) (sometimes) whether the gift is outright or in trust. D's contribution base is $100,000 (AGI).

In this case, Private University is a qualifying donee under § 170(c)(2). Because the donee is an educational organization described in § 170(b)(1)(A)(ii), the contribution limit is 50 percent of the contribution base, or $50,000 (50% of $100,000 contribution base); § 170(b)(1). The $10,000 not deductible in the contribution year is carried over to the following year, when it will again be treated as a contribution to a 50–percent charity, and so on for up to five years; § 170(d)(1)(A).

(b) $60,000 worth of stock to Private University. D purchased the stock several years ago for $10,000.

Gifts of "capital gain property" are less favored than gifts of cash. Capital gain property means any capital asset which, if sold for its fair market value at the time of the contribution, would produce long-term capital gain; § 170(b)(1)C)(iv). (For this purpose, § 1231 assets are treated as capital assets, so as to avoid § 1231 hotchpot computations in the analysis; id.) Gifts of capital gain property to charities described in § 170(b)(1)(A) (such as Private University) are limited to 30 percent of the contribution base; § 170(b)(1)(C)(i). Why are gifts of capital gain property so limited? Recall that the donor is getting a deduction for unrealized appreciation on which he has never been, and never will be, taxed.

If D were to sell the stock, the sale would result in long-term capital gain, so the stock is capital gain property within the meaning of § 170(b)(1)(C). Although the gift is to a § 170(b)(1)(A) charity, D's deduction is limited to $30,000 (30% of the $100,000 contribution base) in the current year. The other $30,000 can be carried forward for up to 5 years, but always retains its character as a gift of capital gain property that will be subject to the limit of § 170(b)(1)(C); § 170(b)(1)(C)(ii).

(c) Same as (b), except that D purchased the stock several years ago for $59,000.

Again this is a gift of capital gain property, which usually means that D's contribution limit is 30 percent of the contribution base with the balance of the contribution being carried over until the following year. However, D can elect to have § 170(e)(1) apply to his contributions of capital gain property for the year; § 170(b)(1)(C)(iii). Normally, § 170(e)(1)(A) reduces the deduction just by the amount of gain that would have not have been long-term capital gain if the property were sold (see problem 2(d), above). If D makes the election, however, the contribution will be reduced by even that part of the gain that would have been long-term capital gain—i.e., D can deduct only his basis. But the deductible portion will be subject to the 50–percent rather than the 30–percent limit; § 170(b)(1)(C)(iii). Thus D can choose to deduct (1) $50,000 (50% of his $100,000 contribution base) in the current year and carry $9,000 of deduction forward to the next year or (2) $30,000 (30% of his $100,000 contribution base) in the current year and carry over $30,000 to future years. By making the election, D would permanently give up $1,000 of deduction but would get a $50,000 (rather than a $30,000) deduction currently. D might find that to be a worthwhile trade-off.

(d) Same as (a), except that D donated the money to the D Family Foundation, a non-operating private foundation. (Generally speaking, a private foundation is an exempt organization that is privately rather than publicly supported. A non-operating private foundation is one that uses its income for the making of grants rather than the active conduct of charitable activities, such as, e.g., operating a museum. Non-operating foundations are organizations described in § 170(c), but deductions to such organizations are limited by § 170(b)(1)(B) & (D).)

Up to this point we have considered charitable donees described in § 170(b)(1)(A), such as religious and educational institutions, governments, most public charities, organizations that support public charities and certain private foundations (viz., operating private foundations that use substantially all of their income in the active conduct of charitable activities). The remaining, less-favored charities for which contributions are deductible include veterans' organizations, fraternal societies, nonprofit cemeteries, and certain non-operating private foundations. These are qualifying charities under § 170(c), but deductions to such charities are more limited than are those to charities described in § 170(b)(1)(A).

As a non-operating private foundation, the D Family Foundation falls into this less-favored category of charitable organizations. Under § 170(b)(1)(B), deductions to these less-favored charities are limited to 30 percent of the donor's contribution base. So, in the contribution year D can deduct only $30,000 (30% of $100,000 contribution base) of the contribution to the D Family Foundation. The $30,000 balance of the contribution can be carried forward for five years but always retains its character as a contribution to a 30–percent charity; see § 170(b)(1)(B).

(e) Same as (b), except that D donated the stock to the D Family Foundation, a non-operating private foundation.

The deduction for a donation of capital gain property (i.e., property the sale of which would result in long-term capital gain—§ 170(b)(1)(C)(iv)) to a private non-operating foundation is generally limited to 20 percent of the donor's contribution base; § 170(b)(1)(D). Here D's deduction is limited to $20,000 (20% of $100,000 contribution base). The $40,000 balance of the contribution would be carried forward for up to five years but always retains its character as 20–percent contribution property (i.e., even in a future year it will be deductible only to the extent of 20 percent of D's contribution base); § 170(b)(1)(D)(ii).

Chapter 35

STATE AND LOCAL TAXES

Code: §§ 164(a), (b)(1), (2), (5)(A), (B), (C) & (H), (c), (d) & (f); 275(a)(1). Review §§ 62(a); 162(a); 212.

Regulations: §§ 1.164–1(a); 1.164–3(c); 1.164–4(a); 1.62–1T(d).

1. **T, a cash-method taxpayer, paid the following taxes this year. Determine which of the tax payments are deductible and whether they are deductible in computing adjusted gross income or as itemized deductions.**

(a) State income tax;

Deductible; § 164(a)(3). The deduction is an itemized deduction because it is not listed in § 62(a). Although the income tax may be at least partly attributable to business income, it is not deductible as an above-the-line deduction because it is not "directly connected" with the conduct of business; Temp. Treas. Reg. § 1.62–1T(d).

(b) State and local property tax on T's home;

Deductible as a itemized deduction; § 164(a)(1).

(c) State and local property tax on T's business building;

Allowable as a deduction under §§ 162(a) and 164(a)(2). T takes the deduction in computing adjusted gross income; § 62(a)(1).

(d) State general sales tax;

Not deductible, unless T makes an election to deduct sales tax in lieu of state income tax under § 164(a)(5)(A). Because most taxpayers will not want to keep track of their sales-tax payments, the Treasury has promulgated (pursuant to § 164(b)(5)(H)) tables for use in estimating the amount of sales tax paid based upon the taxpayer's state of residency, total available income and number of dependents.

In addition to the amount determined under the table, taxpayers can deduct the amount of sales tax paid on "big ticket" items such as motor vehicles, boats, homes and home-building materials; id.; Notice 2005–31, I.R.B. 2005–14. T should make the election if she has paid more sales tax than state income tax during the year. The deduction is an itemized deduction.

As this is being written, the optional sales-tax deduction is scheduled to expire at the end of 2007. An extension is probable.

(e) State general sales tax that covers all retail sales other than groceries and prescription medicines;

Again, sales taxes can be deducted only if the taxpayer so elects under § 164(b)(5)(A). If the election is made, only "general sales taxes" are deductible; § 164(b)(5)(A) & (B). A general sales tax is "a tax imposed at one rate with respect to the sale at retail of a broad range of classes of items"; § 164(b)(5)(B). Does a sales tax that does not apply to groceries and prescription drugs qualify as a general sales tax? Yes; the tax is general even though it does not apply to some or all of the costs of food, clothing, medical supplies and motor vehicles; § 164(b)(5)(C). (Some states exempt such items from their general sales taxes to reduce the regressivity of the levies.) So, T can deduct the sales tax as an itemized deduction if she so elects.

(f) Local-option sales tax (imposed in addition to the state general sales tax);

Amounts paid under a local-option sales tax are deductible if the taxpayer has elected to deduct sales taxes in lieu of state income taxes; Notice 2005–31, I.R.B. 2005–14.

(g) Employee's share of Social Security and Medicare taxes;

Not deductible; § 275(a)(1)(A).

(h) Employer's share of Social Security and Medicare taxes;

If the employee was employed in T's business (as opposed to, say, a nanny or housekeeper), T can deduct the employer's share of the taxes as a business expense under §§ 164(a)(second sentence) and 162(a). The deduction is allowable above the line; § 62(a)(1).

(i) Federal self-employment tax;

T can deduct one-half the tax; § 164(f)(1). An employer who incurs Social Security and Medicare taxes in carrying on business can deduct its share of the taxes as a business expense (see the preceding problem). Since a self-employed person in effect pays both the employer's and employee's share of the tax, a deduction is allowed for one-half (the "employer's share") of the tax. Section 164(f)(2) treats the tax as being attributable to business (and not the business of being an employee), so it can be deducted above the line under § 62(a)(1).

(j) Sales tax on business automobile;

If T elects to deduct sales tax in lieu of income tax, the sales tax could be deducted. If T does not make the election, the sales tax must be treated as part of the cost of the automobile; § 164(a)(last sentence). Since the car is depreciable, the sales tax is included in the basis for depreciation purposes.

(k) State severance taxes imposed upon oil production in which T has a royalty interest;

The severance tax would be deductible under §§ 164(a)(second sentence) and 212(1). The deduction would be above the line because of § 62(a)(4).

(l) Automobile registration fee based upon value of personal automobile;

The fee would be deductible as a personal property tax; § 164(a)(2). It is an itemized deduction.

(m) Automobile registration fee based upon a combination of the value and weight of the automobile;

A personal property tax means an annual ad valorem tax on personal property; § 164(b)(1). An ad valorem tax refers to one levied "substantially in proportion to the value of the personal property"; Treas. Reg. § 1.164–3(c)(1). Where the fee is based in part upon the value and in part upon the weight of the automobile, only the portion of the tax determined in accordance with the automobile's value qualifies as a personal property tax; id. For example, suppose the registration fee is $200, the automobile weighs 3,000 pounds, and the weight is taxed at 40 cents per hundredweight. The ad valorem tax would be $188 ($200 less 3,000 lbs. x $.40/100 lbs.).

Incidentally, the portion of the fee that represents a tax on the value of the automobile is a personal property tax even though in form it appears to be imposed upon the privilege of operating a motor vehicle on the state's highway; Treas. Reg. § 1.164–3(c)(3).

(n) Special real-property-tax assessment to pay for the installation of sidewalks adjacent to T's home.

Even though the special assessment may provide an incidental benefit to the public welfare, T cannot deduct the cost because the sidewalk tends to increase the value of the home; § 164(c)(1); Treas. Reg. § 1.164–4(a). Query: What if installation of the sidewalk *decreases* the value of T's home because of the sidewalk's unaesthetic appearance?

(o) Special real-property-tax assessment to pay for the repair of sidewalks adjacent to T's home.

Now the tax is deductible because it is "properly allocable to maintenance"; § 164(c)(1).

(p) Estimated property taxes paid in escrow to T's mortgagee, so that the account would contain sufficient cash to pay the taxes when they came due.

T can deduct the taxes only when they are actually paid by the mortgagee to the taxing authority; payment to the mortgagee is not sufficient; Rev. Rul. 78–103, 1978–1 C.B. 58.

2. S sells his home to P on October 9, 2008. The state's 2008 real-property tax year runs from July 1, 2008 through June 30, 2009. One-half of the taxes for the 2008 tax year are payable on September 30, 2009 and one-half on March 31, 2010. S and P are both calendar-year, cash-method taxpayers. P pays the 2008 taxes ($3,650) when due. To what extent are the taxes deductible by S? By P?

Although the tax will be paid by P on September 30, 2009 and March 31, 2010, S owned the property through October 8, 2008 (100 days into the 2008 tax year). Thus, in an economic sense, $1,000 (100/365 x $3,650) of the tax liability is S's, and at the closing the amount paid to S probably will be reduced by that accrued tax liability. But if S, who uses the cash method, does not actually pay the tax, how can she claim the deduction? And what keeps P, who does pay the tax, from claiming a deduction for the full amount he actually pays, even though that amount exceeds his economic share of the tax? The answer lies in § 164(d)(1), which requires that the deduction be allocated between the seller and buyer according to the proportion of the real-property tax year that each owned the property. As applicable to our problem, § 164(d)(2) adds that S "shall be treated as having *paid*, on the date of the sale, so much of the tax as" is imposed upon her under § 164(d)(1) (emphasis added). So, S deducts $1,000 in 2008, the year her share of the taxes are deemed paid. P deducts $1,325 (1/2 of [$3,650 – $1,000]) in 2009 and a like amount in 2010.

Chapter 36

CASUALTY LOSSES TO PERSONAL-USE PROPERTY

Code: § 165(a), (b), (c)(3), (e) & (h). Review §§ 1222(4); 1231(a)(4)(C); 1033(a)(2).

Regulations: §§ 1.165–7; 1.165–8.

Cases: White v. Commissioner, 48 T. C. 430 (1967);
Chamales v. Commissioner, 79 T.C.M. 1428 (2000).

1. **Which of the following calamities constitutes a casualty loss?**

(a) H accidentally slammed a car door on his wife's (W's) hand. W's diamond wedding ring absorbed the full impact of the blow, which broke the flanges holding the diamond in place. The excruciating pain caused W to shake her hand vigorously, and, as a result of the shaking, the diamond setting flew out of her wedding ring and was lost in the crushed-gravel driveway.

The issue is whether the accident constitutes an "other casualty" within the meaning of § 165(c)(3). Where a series of specific terms is followed in a statutory provision by a more general term, the latter takes its content from the former. (This rule of construction is called the principle of *ejusdem generis*, which means of the same kind, class or nature.) So, the question becomes whether the events in the problem are of the same kind, class or nature as fires, storms and shipwrecks. Although the accident was hardly cataclysmic, fires, storms and shipwrecks are not always cataclysmic either. Like fires, storms and shipwrecks, the accident was sudden, unexpected and violent. The regulations acknowledge that an automobile accident caused by the taxpayer's own negligence is an "other casualty" (Treas. Reg. § 1.165–7(a)(3)), and many such accidents involve only slight damage. For these reasons, a deduction was allowed on similar facts in White v. Commissioner, 48 T. C. 430 (1967). So, H and W can treat the loss as a casualty loss.

One might worry whether the holding in *White* might lead to claims of casualty losses for relatively trivial accidents. Keep in mind, however, that today the $100 per casualty and 10–percent-of-AGI floor on the casualty-loss deduction prevent trivial losses from being allowed.

(b) C and D are husband and wife. D was suffering from arthritis. To relief the arthritic pain, she took off her wedding ring, wrapped it in a tissue, and put it on a stand beside her bed. C, not realizing that the tissue contained the ring, flushed the tissue down the toilet. Despite the taxpayers' diligent efforts, the ring was never recovered.

No casualty. The events in this case were unexpected and unusual but lacked the suddenness and violence with which fires, storms and shipwrecks (and even automobile accidents) strike. Keenan v. Bowers, 91 F. Supp. 771 (E.D.S.C. 1950), which denies a deduction on similar facts, contains a useful discussion of the principle of *ejusdem generis*.

(c) N's neighbor, S, a well-known celebrity, committed a notorious murder in his house, which is located next door to N's. After the murder and ensuing trial, thousands of sightseers regularly descended upon N's neighborhood to catch a glimpse of the murder scene. Tour buses even began making the neighborhood a regular part of their rounds. Although N's property suffered no physical damage, N's realtor estimates that the notoriety of the neighborhood and the invasive crowds have caused a large drop in the value of N's home.

The issue is whether N's loss was caused by an "other casualty" within the meaning of § 165(c)(3). The homicide was a sudden, unexpected and unusual event, but the damage to N's property value was not caused by the murder itself; it was caused by the hordes of people who descended upon the neighborhood over a period of several months, and damage occurring in that way does not seem to qualify as a casualty. The murder was a violent act, but the violence was not directed toward, and did not damage N's property. Moreover, most courts that have confronted the issue say that only *physical* damage to the taxpayer's property will be treated as a casualty. See, e.g., Chamales v. Commissioner, 79 T.C.M. 1428 (involving a claimed casualty loss stemming from the O.J. Simpson case). So, N probably cannot deduct the loss in her property's value.

(d) While on vacation, T was involved in an automobile accident that was caused by his negligence. T, who had no insurance, paid to have the other party's car repaired and also paid to have his own car repaired.

The damage to T's car constitutes a casualty loss even though caused by T's faulty driving; Treas. Reg. § 1.165–7(a)(3). But T cannot deduct as a casualty loss the amount paid for damage to the other driver's car because the other car was not property belonging to T; see Tarsey v. Commissioner, 56 T.C. 553 (1971); cf. Dosher

v. United States, 730 F.2d 375 (5th Cir. 1984) (no casualty-loss deduction for amounts paid to owner of house damaged by taxpayer's negligent driving).

(e) Same as (d), except that T had both liability and collision insurance but declined to make a claim on his insurer because he thought it would drastically increase his insurance premiums.

Section 165(h)(4) disallows a deduction because T did not file an insurance claim with respect to the loss.

2. In each of the following alternative cases, determine the amount and character of T's casualty loss or gain. Ignore the effect of the $100 and 10–percent floors of § 165(h)(1) & (2).

(a) T's oriental rug (held several years for personal use) was completely destroyed by fire. The rug had an adjusted basis of $2,000 and a value of $5,000. T received no insurance proceeds.

Although T's economic loss is $5,000, his casualty loss is limited to his $2,000 basis for the rug; § 165(b). He doesn't get to deduct the loss of the unrealized appreciation on which he has never been taxed. The loss would be an ordinary loss because, even though the rug is a capital asset (§ 1221(a)), it is not disposed of by means of a sale or exchange; see § 1222(4).

(b) Same as (a), except that T received $5,000 of insurance proceeds.

Now T realizes a gain of $3,000 ($5,000 amount realized less $2,000 adjusted basis). Unless T makes an election under § 1033 and replaces the rug with similar property within the prescribed time period, T must recognize the gain. The gain is a personal casualty gain—a recognized gain from an involuntary conversion described in § 165(c)(3). If T has no personal casualty loss for the year, the gain is characterized as a long-term capital gain because the personal casualty gains exceed the personal casualty losses; see § 165(h)(2)(B).

(c) Same as (a), except that the rug had an adjusted basis of $5,000 and a value of $2,000.

T's casualty loss is limited to the $2,000 value of the rug immediately before its destruction; Treas. Reg. § 1.165–7(b)(1). If T were allowed a deduction for his adjusted basis, he would be getting a deduction for a decline in value that occurred during his personal use of the property, which should be regarded as personal living expense. If T had sold the rug for its $2,000 value immediately before the fire, his $3,000 loss would have been disallowed under § 165(c). He shouldn't be able to deduct a loss on account of the fire that he couldn't have deducted if he had sold the property.

(d) Same as (c), except that instead of a rug, the destroyed asset (which T had held for several years) was a depreciable asset used in T's business.

If T had sold the asset just before its destruction, he would have realized and recognized a loss of $3,000. Because the loss would have been sustained in business, it would have been allowable under § 165(a) & (c)(1). Therefore, Treas. Reg. § 1.165–7(b)(last sentence) allows a deduction for the full adjusted basis when the property is lost to casualty. The result differs from that in (c) because there the decline in value from $5,000 to $2,000 represented personal living expense, which should not be deductible. Also, since the loss here is a business loss, the $100 and 10–percent-of-AGI floors on the deduction do not apply. The destroyed asset was a § 1231 asset, which would be assigned to the firepot of § 1231(a)(4)(C) for characterization. If this is T's only firepot transaction for the year, the firepot loss ($5,000) exceeds the firepot gain (zero), and § 1231 does not characterize the loss. The loss is therefore an ordinary loss because (1) the asset was not a capital asset, and (2) it was not disposed of by way of a sale or exchange; see § 1222(4).

(e) T's (uninsured) vacation home was damaged by a hurricane. Immediately before the casualty, the home was worth $600,000; immediately after it was worth $200,000. T's basis for the home is $300,000.

The amount of the casualty loss is the lesser of: (1) the difference between the value of the property immediately before the casualty and the value of the property immediately after, or (2) the adjusted basis of the property; Treas. Reg. § 1.165–7(b). In this case, the decline in value of the property was $400,000 ($600,000 value before less $200,000 value after). That is more than the $300,000 adjusted basis, so T's casualty loss is limited to $300,000. T must reduce his adjusted basis to zero ($300,000 adjusted basis less $300,000 casualty loss); see § 1016(a)(1).

The regulations say that the values of the property immediately before and immediately after the casualty must "generally be ascertained by competent appraisal"; Treas. Reg. § 1.165–7(b)(2)(i). However, the loss in value can also be determined by the cost of repairs necessary to restore the property to its condition immediately before the casualty; see Treas. Reg. § 1.165–7(b)(2)(ii).

(f) Same as (e), except that, immediately after the hurricane, the home was worth $400,000.

Now the decline in value is $200,000 and the adjusted basis $300,000, so T's casualty loss is $200,000. T must reduce his adjusted basis to $100,000 ($300,000 adjusted basis less $200,000 casualty loss).

3. V suffered a $50,000 loss when her vacation home (adjusted basis $150,000) was damaged by a hurricane. She also received $10,000 of insurance proceeds when her diamond bracelet (adjusted basis $5,000) was stolen. V did not replace the bracelet. Apart from these transactions, V's gross and adjusted gross income is $100,000. What tax result to V?

V has a realized and recognized gain of $5,000 ($10,000 amount realized less $5,000 adjusted basis) from the insurance recovery on the bracelet. (Since V did not replace the bracelet, the non-recognition rule of § 1033 would not apply.) V has also sustained a casualty loss of $50,000, which is allowable under § 165(a) & (c)(3), but § 165(h)(1) limits the allowable loss to $49,900. The $5,000 gain is a "personal casualty gain," and the $49,900 a "personal casualty loss"; § 165(h)(3). Since the personal casualty loss exceeds the personal casualty gain, the loss is first offset against the gain, which leaves a balance of $44,900 ($49,900 less $5,000); § 165(h)(2)(A)(i). The net figure is allowed as a deduction only to the extent it exceeds 10 percent of AGI. V's gross income and AGI is $100,000 before taking into account the casualty gain, which must be included in gross income. The casualty gain increases gross income to $105,000. Although personal casualty losses are usually itemized deductions, § 165(h)(4)(A) allows the casualty loss to be taken into account in computing AGI to the extent that the casualty loss does not exceed the gain. V's AGI is therefore $100,000 ($105,000 gross income less $5,000 of casualty loss to the extent of the casualty gain). The net personal casualty loss is allowable (as an itemized deduction) to the extent of $34,900 ($44,900 less 10% of $100,000 AGI). The character of the loss is ordinary because, although the vacation home is a capital asset, the loss did not result from a sale or exchange; see § 1222(4).

4. How would your answer in 3 differ if V's gain on the theft of the bracelet was $50,000 and her loss on the vacation home was $5,000?

The recognized gain on the theft of the bracelet increases V's gross income to $150,000. Under § 165(h)(1), the $5,000 casualty loss is allowable only to the extent it exceeds $100, which leaves a loss of $4,900. The loss is deductible in full and allowable above the line because it doesn't exceed the casualty gain; § 165(h)(2) & (4)(A). V's AGI is thus $145,100 ($150,000 gross income less $4,900 casualty-loss deduction). Since the personal casualty gain exceeds the personal loss, both the gain and the loss are treated as arising from the sale or exchange of capital assets. V therefore has a long-term capital gain of $50,000 and a long-term capital loss of $4,900.

5. R's personal bookkeeper embezzled $750,000 from R's bank account last year. R just discovered the theft this year. In which year should R take the deduction?

An embezzlement loss is treated as a theft loss and so can be deductible under § 165(c)(3); Treas. Reg. § 1.165–8(d). A theft loss is treated as sustained in the year in which the taxpayer discovers the loss; § 165(e); Treas. Reg. § 1.165–8(a)(2). That rule prevents the Commissioner from denying a deduction on the ground that the loss was sustained in an earlier year (perhaps a year on which the statute of limitations had run).

Chapter 37

EDUCATION DEDUCTIONS AND CREDITS

Code: §§ 25A(a), (b), (c), (d), (f)(1) & (g)(3); 222.

Regulations: §§ 1.25A–2(a) & (d); 1.25A–4(b) & (c); 1.25A–5(a), (b)(1) & (3), (c)(1), (3) & (4), Exs. 1 & 2.

In working the problems, use the dollar figures set forth in the Code and ignore the effect of inflation adjustments.

1. Compare the Hope Scholarship Credit with the Lifetime Learning Credit:

(a) Ignoring inflation adjustments, what is the maximum allowable Hope Credit? The Lifetime Learning Credit?

The maximum Hope Credit is the sum of the amounts determined under § 25A(b)(1)(A) & (B). The (A) amount is 100 percent of the first $1,000 of the eligible expenses. To determine the (B) amount, we first find the "applicable limit," which is defined in § 25A(b)(4) to be twice the dollar amount in (b)(1)(A) ($1,000). So, the applicable limit is $2,000. The (B) amount is thus 50 percent of $1,000 ($2,000 applicable limit less $1,000), or $500. The maximum Hope Credit for each eligible student is the sum of the (A) and (B) amounts, or $1,500. (The reason for determining the maximum credit in such a circuitous fashion is that the dollar amount specified in § 25A(b)(1)(A) was phased in at a lower figure and is adjusted annually for inflation; the formula was designed to produce the correct result as the dollar figure changes.)

The maximum annual Lifetime Learning Credit is $2,000 (20 percent of $10,000); § 25A(c)(1).

Notice, however, that the Hope Credit is computed on a per-student basis, while the Lifetime Learning Credit is computed on a per-taxpayer basis. Thus, a parent with two children who are in their first two years of college could claim up to $3,000 in Hope Credits. But the Lifetime Learning Credit is capped at $2,000 regardless of how many of the taxpayer's dependents are receiving tuition assistance from the parent.

(b) For how many years can one use the Hope Credit? The Lifetime Learning Credit?

The Hope Credit is allowed for only two years and can be allowed for only the first two years of post-secondary education; § 25A(b)(2)(A). Thus, a student who begins her first year of college in the fall of year 1 and finishes her second year in the spring of year 3 can use the Hope Credit only for years 1 and 2. There is no limit on the number of years that one can use the Lifetime Learning Credit, which is available for all years of post-secondary education, as well as courses to acquire or improve job skills; Treas. Reg. § 1.25A–4(c)(1).

(c) Must the student be seeking a degree to use the Hope Credit? The Lifetime Learning Credit?

To be eligible for a Hope Credit, the student must be enrolled in a program leading toward a postsecondary degree or other recognized postsecondary educational credential; Treas. Reg. § 1.25A–3(d)(1)(i). A student is eligible for the Lifetime Learning Credit regardless of whether the student is pursuing a degree or other recognized credential; Treas. Reg. § 1.25A–4(c).

(d) Must the student be a full-time student to use the Hope Credit? The Lifetime Learning Credit?

To be eligible for the Hope Credit, the student must be enrolled at least half time for at least one academic period beginning during the year; Treas. Reg. § 1.25A–3(d)(1)(ii). Enrollment in a single course will suffice for the Lifetime Learning Credit; see e.g., Treas. Reg. § 1.25A–4(c)(2), Ex. 1.

(e) May a graduate student (who has never before claimed an education credit) use the Hope Credit? The Lifetime Learning Credit?

Not the Hope Credit, which is available for only the first two years of college; § 25A(a)(2)(C). A graduate can claim the Lifetime Learning Credit, as there is no limit to the number of years that a Lifetime Learning Credit may be claimed; Treas. Reg. § 1.25A–4(b).

(f) Is one who has been convicted of a felony drug offense eligible for the Hope Credit? The Lifetime Learning Credit?

Such a student would not be eligible for the Hope Credit; § 25A(b)(2)(D). There is no such restriction on the Lifetime Learning Credit.

2. Which of the following constitute "qualified tuition and related expenses" that are eligible for the credits?

(a) Tuition paid by the student to the educational institution;

Tuition qualifies; § 25A(f)(1)(A).

(b) Laboratory fees required for enrollment in the basic chemistry course;

Mandatory academic fees generally qualify; see Treas. Reg. § 1.25A–2(d)(2).

(c) Required books for courses in which the student is enrolled;

Books, even though required, do not qualify, unless the cost of the books *must* be paid to the school; see Treas. Reg. § 1.25A–2(d)(6), Ex. 2. If the books *can* be purchased elsewhere, the cost does not qualify, even if the books are in fact purchased from the school.

(d) Mandatory student-activity fee, which the school uses to defray the costs of student-run organizations;

The fee can be included in qualified tuition and related expenses if it must be paid for enrollment; Treas. Reg. § 1.25A–2(d)(2)(iii).

(e) Room and board;

The cost of room and board does not qualify even if the cost must be paid to the school as a condition of attendance; Treas. Reg. § 1.25A–2(d)(3). If the school's fees include both qualified tuition and related expenses and also personal expenses such as board and room, the school must determine what portion of the fee qualifies; Treas. Reg. § 1.25A–2(d)(4).

(f) Mandatory student health fee.

No. Same as room and board; Treas. Reg. § 1.25A–2(d)(3).

3. Q pays her tuition with a Pell Grant, R pays her tuition with the proceeds of a loan, S pays his tuition with a scholarship, and T's grandparents pay his tuition directly to the school. (T is not a claimed dependent for the year.)

(a) Do the sums paid from those sources count toward the student's qualified tuition and related expenses?

In determining the amount of the credit, qualified tuition and related expenses must be reduced by the amount of any tax-free educational assistance allocable to the period; § 25A(g)(2); Treas. Reg. § 1.25A–5(c). Tax-free educational assistance includes Pell Grants (which are excludable from income as scholarships under § 117 if the grant proceeds are used for qualified education expenses), and scholarships; see Treas. Reg. § 1.25A–5(c)(1). Tuition paid from loan proceeds qualifies for the credit, as the loan proceeds are not *excluded* from income—loan proceeds are *not* income—and the loan (generally) must be repaid from after-tax income. So, neither Q's nor S's tuition payment qualifies, but R's does.

T presents a special case. The grandparents are not eligible for the credit because T is not their dependent; see § 25A(f)(1). However, the grandparents' payment is treated as though they gave the money to T, and T paid his own tuition; Treas. Reg. § 1.25A–5(b)(1). The tuition payment may therefore qualify T for the credit.

(b) Would your answer differ if S instead used the scholarship money to pay room and board and paid the tuition from his own funds?

If the scholarship money were used to pay room and board, it would not be a "qualified scholarship" under § 117(b) and it would have to be included in S's gross income. However, S could then claim an educational credit for the tuition payment. That might be a decent tradeoff, as the greater income may not generate as much tax as the credit would save.

To avoid tracing, the regulations say that, if a scholarship can be used for both qualified tuition and other purposes (such as room and board), the student can, in effect, treat it as used for other purposes by including the scholarship in income; Treas. Reg. § 1.25A–5(c)(3).

4. A is a freshman at State College, where he pays $6,000 of tuition from earnings from part-time and summer work.

(a) Is A better off claiming the Hope Scholarship or Lifetime Learning Credit?

A's maximum Hope Credit is $1,500; see problem 1(a), above. His maximum Lifetime Learning Credit is $1,200 (20% of $6,000); see § 25A(c)(1). A is better off claiming the Hope Credit.

(b) Would your answer differ if A paid tuition of $10,000?

Yes. The maximum Hope Credit would still be $1,500, but the maximum Lifetime Learning Credit would be $2,000 (20% of $10,000).

5. B is a dependent of her parents, who pay $20,000 of college tuition for her in the current year. (Ignore the phaseout rules of § 25A(d).)

(a) What is the maximum educational credit allowable on account of the tuition payment?

The Lifetime Learning Credit would be $2,000 (20% of $10,000); § 25(c)(1)(A). Even if B is in her first two years of college, the Lifetime Learning Credit is better than the Hope Credit, which cannot exceed $1,500; see problem 1(a), above.

(b) Who is entitled to the credit?

Since the tuition was paid by B's parents and B is a dependent of her parents, her parents are entitled to the credit; see § 25A(c)(1)("paid by the taxpayer") & (f)(1)(A)(iii)("dependent"); see, e.g., Treas Reg. § 1.25A–4(a)(4), Ex. 1.

(c) Same as (b), except that $5,000 of the tuition had been paid by B.

Since B is a dependent of her parents, the tuition paid by B is treated as paid by her parents; § 25A(g)(3); Treas. Reg. § 1.25A–5(a).

(d) What result in (a) if the tuition had been paid by B's grandmother?

B's grandmother is not eligible for the credit because B is not her dependent; see § 25A(f)(1). However, the grandmother's payment is treated as though she gave the money to B, and B paid her own tuition; Treas. Reg. § 1.25A–5(b)(1). But since B is a dependent of her parents, any tuition paid by her is imputed to her parents; § 25A(g)(3). So, B's parents are treated as having paid the tuition.

6. What is the maximum deduction under § 222 for qualified tuition and related expenses?

$4,000; § 222(b)(2)(B). The deduction is scheduled to expire after 2007, but an extension is likely.

7. S, a dependent of his parents, is a freshman in college. S's parents pay for his tuition at the college. S is a full-time student. S's parents file a joint return. Should the parents claim the Hope Scholarship Credit, the Lifetime Learning Credit or the educational expense deduction of § 222 if the parents' modified AGI (under both §§ 25A(d)(3) and 222(b)(2)(C)) is $80,000, and they pay tuition of:

(a) $3,000?

The parents' MAGI is small enough that we need not be concerned with the phaseout of the benefits of the credit and the deduction. (The phaseout of the credit begins at MAGI of $80,000 and the phaseout of the deduction at $130,000 for joint filers. The Hope Credit would be $1,500; § 25A(b)(1). The Lifetime Learning Credit would be $600 (20% of $3,000). The deduction would be $4,000 (§ 22(b)(2)(B)), which in the parents' probable 25–percent tax bracket (see Appendix B) would save them $1,000 in tax. They get the greatest amount of savings from the Hope Credit and so should claim that.

(b) $10,000?

The Hope Credit still saves them $1,500 and the deduction still saves them $1,000. But now the Lifetime Learning Credit saves them $2,000 (20% of $10,000). They should take the Lifetime Learning Credit.

8. Would your answers in 8 differ if the parents' MAGI is:

(a) $90,000?

At $90,000, the parents' income is in the phaseout range for the credits but not for the deduction; cf. § 25A(d)(2) with § 222(b)(2)(B). Section 25A(d)(2) reduces the credit by one-half: ([$90,000 – $80,000]/$20,000 = $10,000/$20,000 = 1/2). If the tuition payment was $3,000, the maximum Hope Credit would be $750, and the maximum Lifetime Learning Credit would be $300. The deduction would still save them $1,000 in tax, so they should take the deduction.

If the tuition were $10,000, the Hope Credit would be limited to $750 (after the phaseout), the Lifetime Learning Credit would be $1,000 (after the phaseout), and the deduction would still save them $1,000. Although it appears that they would be indifferent between the Lifetime Credit and the deduction, the deduction is taken in computing adjusted gross income (see § 62(a)(18)), and they may benefit from having a lower AGI because of its effect on other deductions, such as the medical-expense deduction of § 213. If that is the case, they will prefer the deduction.

(b) $100,000?

At $100,000 of MAGI, the credits are fully phased out; see § 25A(d)(2). The deduction still saves them $1,000, so they will definitely prefer the deduction regardless of whether the tuition is $6,000 or $10,000.

Chapter 38

INTEREST INCOME AND DEDUCTIONS

A. DEDUCTIBLE AND NON-DEDUCTIBLE INTEREST

Code: §§ 61(a)(4); 103(a) & (c); 163(a), (d) & (h); 221; 161; 261; 265(a)(2). Review §§ 62; 67; 71; 215; 280A(d)(1) & (2); 469; 104(a)(2).

Regulations: §§ 1.163–8T; 1.163–9T; 1.163–10T(b).

1. **T, an individual, borrows money (an unsecured loan) that is allocable to the following (alternative) expenditures. Determine in each case whether (and to what extent) the interest is deductible.**

(a) A personal automobile.

Not deductible. Although § 163(a) states broadly that "all interest" is allowable as a deduction, § 163(h)(1) disallows the deduction for "personal interest," which is defined as any interest other than that described in the six categories of § 163(h)(2). Interest on an automobile loan does not fall within the exceptions and is therefore disallowed as personal interest.

(b) An addition to T's principal residence.

Not deductible. This is also personal interest, but if the loan were secured by the residence, it could be deductible as qualified residence interest, discussed below.

(c) New York Stock Exchange securities.

The interest is investment interest—i.e., interest properly allocable to "property held for investment"; § 163(d)(1)(A). (Property held for investment includes securities—i.e., property producing interest and dividends; see §§ 163(d)(5)(A); 469(e)(1)A)(i)(I).) Although investment interest is excluded from the definition of personal interest by § 163(h)(2)(B), it is allowable only to the extent of the taxpayer's net investment income for the year, with any disallowed portion being carried forward as investment interest to the following year;

491

§ 163(d)(1) & (2). So, the deductibility of the interest in the current year depends upon the amount of T's net investment income.

(d) State of Iowa bonds.

The interest on the bonds is excluded from income by § 103(a), and § 265(a)(2) disallows a deduction for interest on indebtedness incurred to purchase or carry tax-exempt bonds. So, no deduction.

(e) A business (sole proprietorship) in which T materially participates.

Business interest is not personal interest because of § 163(h)(2)(A), and the interest is therefore deductible in computing adjusted gross income; §§ 163(a); 62(a)(1).

(f) A limited partnership interest.

Generally speaking, an interest as a limited partner in a limited partnership is not treated as an interest with respect to which the taxpayer materially participates (§ 469(h)(2)), which means, as to T, the interest probably is a passive activity; § 469(c)(1). Interest allocable to a passive activity is neither personal interest (§ 163(h)(2)(C)) nor investment interest; § 163(d)(3)(B)(ii). The interest is taken into account in offsetting income from passive activities under § 469; see Treas. Reg. § 1.163–8T(a)(4)(ii),Ex. (1). If passive-activity deductions exceed passive-activity income, the result is a passive-activity loss (§ 469(d)(1)), which is disallowed; § 469(a)(1). The disallowed loss is carried forward and treated as a passive-activity deduction in the following year; § 469(b). (Passive losses are discussed in Chapter 45.)

(g) Law school tuition.

Indebtedness incurred to pay college tuition is a "qualified education loan" (§ 221(d)(1) & (2)) if it was incurred on behalf of the taxpayer or the taxpayer's spouse or dependent. Although the cost of education is usually considered to be a personal cost, interest on education loans is not treated as personal interest; § 163(h)(2)((F). If the indebtedness is a qualified education loan, T can deduct up to $2,500 of the interest as an above-the-line deduction; §§ 221(a), (b)(1); 62(a)(17). This assumes that T's modified adjusted gross income is not so high as to result in a reduction (or loss) of the deduction under § 221(b)(2).

(h) A vacation home.

Since the loan is unsecured, the interest is personal interest and not deductible; § 163(h)(1). However, as discussed below, the interest might be deductible as qualified residence interest if the loan was secured by the vacation home (or the taxpayer's principal residence).

(i) A federal income tax deficiency attributable to T's underreported business income.

The interest on indebtedness incurred to pay income taxes is non-deductible personal interest; Treas. Reg. § 1.163–9T(b)(2)(i)(A). This is true even if the deficiency relates to business income; Treas. Reg. § 1.163–9T(b)(2)(ii); Robinson v. Commissioner, 119 T.C. 44 (2002).

2. How would your answers in 1 change if the loan is secured by a mortgage on T's (previously unencumbered) principal residence?

If the indebtedness is secured by T's principal residence, the interest may be allowable as "qualified residence interest," which is excluded from the personal-interest category by § 163(h)(2)(D). Qualified residence interest is interest on "acquisition indebtedness" or "home-equity indebtedness"; § 163(h)(3)(A). Acquisition indebtedness is indebtedness "incurred in acquiring, constructing, or substantially improving a qualified residence" and secured by the residence; § 163(h)(3)(B)(i). Home-equity indebtedness is indebtedness other than acquisition indebtedness and secured by a qualified residence. A qualified residence is the taxpayer's principal residence and one other residence designated by the taxpayer as a qualified residence for the taxable year; § 163(h)(4)(A). The maximum amount of indebtedness treated as acquisition indebtedness is $1,000,000; § 163(h)(3)(B)(ii); the maximum amount of home-equity indebtedness is $100,000; § 163(h)(3)(C)(ii).

The indebtedness incurred to finance the addition to T's principal residence is acquisition indebtedness (up to the $1,000,000 limit), and the interest is deductible as qualified residence interest, an itemized deduction. Indebtedness incurred to finance the automobile, the New York Stock Exchange securities, the limited-partnership interest, the tuition and the tax deficiency would qualify as home-equity indebtedness up to the $100,000 limit, and the interest would be deductible as qualified residence interest. If the interest is classified as qualified residence interest, the investment-interest limit of § 163(d) does not apply; see § 163(d)(3)(B)(i). Nor is qualified residence interest treated as a passive-activity deduction subject to § 469; § 469(j)(7); Treas. Reg. § 1.163–8T(m)(3). If the indebtedness incurred to pay tuition is treated as home-equity indebtedness, the interest is qualified residence interest and its deductibility would not be limited by § 221; for example, the $2,500 annual limit would not apply, nor would the phaseout of the deduction for higher-income taxpayers.

Indebtedness incurred to purchase the vacation home would also be home-equity indebtedness because it is secured by T's principal residence rather than the vacation home. The maximum amount treated as home-equity indebtedness is $100,000. However, the limit on acquisition indebtedness is $1,000,000, and so T may be better off securing the loan with the vacation home, which would qualify the debt as acquisition indebtedness. (The term qualified residence includes a designated second home; § 163(h)(4)(A)(i)(II).)

Interest on indebtedness incurred to purchase or carry the State of Iowa bonds remains non-deductible because of § 265(a)(2), which overrides the allowance rule of § 163(a); see §§ 161; 261; Treas. Reg. § 1.163–8T(m)(2)(i); 1.163–10T(b).

The business interest is deductible without regard to whether it is also qualified residence interest.

3. Five years ago, S purchased a personal residence for $400,000. To finance the purchase, she used the proceeds of a five-year, interest-only loan (a loan that requires the borrower to pay only interest rather than retiring any of the principal before the loan matures) in the amount of $250,000. The loan was secured by the residence. At the beginning of this year (when the principal of the loan remained $250,000), S refinanced the loan (still secured by the residence) and increased the principal to $450,000. (The value of the residence had increased to $600,000.) S spent $25,000 of the additional borrowing on improvements to the home and spent the balance on personal consumption. S paid $45,000 in interest on the refinanced loan this year. To what extent is the interest deductible by S?

The original $250,000 loan was acquisition indebtedness, and the refinanced debt remains acquisition indebtedness up to the $250,000 balance of the original loan; § 163(h)(3)(B)(i). Of the additional $200,000 borrowed at the refinancing, the $25,000 devoted to improving the home is acquisition indebtedness. Another $100,000 qualifies as home-equity indebtedness. (The value of the residence exceeds the acquisition debt by $325,000, so T is comfortably within the limit of § 163(h)(3)(C)(i).) The interest on $375,000 ($275,000 acquisition debt plus $100,000 of home-equity debt) of the indebtedness is qualified residence interest, so T can deduct interest of $37,500 ($375,000/$450,000 of $45,000).

4. Is § 265(a)(2) consistent with the purpose of § 103(a)?

Section 103(a) exempts from tax interest received on state and local government bonds (often referred to as "municipal bonds"). Its purpose is to lower the borrowing costs of state and local governments. To see why it has that effect, consider an investor in the 35–percent bracket: She would be indifferent between a taxable bond yielding 10–percent interest and a comparably risky state bond yielding 6.5 percent because, after a 35–percent tax, the taxable bond yields only 6.5 percent. So, state governments can sell their bonds at lower interest rates because of the tax exemption for the interest.

If, however, the state cannot meet its borrowing needs by selling its bonds to investors in the top tax bracket, it must pay higher interest rates to attract investors in lower tax brackets. For example, suppose it must raise the interest rate to 7 percent in order to entice investors in the (hypothetical) 30–percent bracket. The higher interest rate results in a windfall to the 35–percent-bracket investor, who would have been willing to purchase the bond even if it paid only 6.5–percent interest. A 7–percent bond saves the state only $30 of interest on each $1,000 bond (i.e., the difference in cost between the 10–percent interest it would have to pay on a taxable bond and the 7 percent it pays on the exempt bond). Yet, the exemption from tax costs the federal government $35 on each 7–percent, $1,000 bond sold to an investor in the 35–percent bracket (i.e., 35 percent of the $100 of interest that would be earned if the bond were taxable). So, the § 103 exclusion is an inefficient way to aid the states, in that it costs the federal government more than the state governments save. It is as if the federal government mails the state a check for $35, but by the time the check arrives in the state capital the amount has shrunk to $30. Section 265(a)(2) exacerbates this inefficiency by excluding from the municipal-bond market people who are in a high tax bracket but who would have to borrow in order to buy the state's bonds.

Apologists for § 265 contend that it disallows a deduction for an interest payment that would make no economic sense apart from the tax law. That is, an investor in the 35–percent bracket might borrow at, say 8–percent interest in order to purchase a state bond yielding 7–percent interest. In a non-tax world, no rationale person would borrow at 8 percent to invest in a 7–percent bond that had no real prospect of appreciating sufficiently to make up the difference. But, of course, in a non-tax world (or a tax world without § 103), no one would buy a state bond yielding 7 percent when a comparably risky corporate bond pays 10 percent. That is, § 103(a) is intended to encourage a certain type of "uneconomic" transaction in order to aid state governments. To the extent that § 265 makes the subsidy less efficient by excluding high-bracket borrowers from buying municipal bonds, it undermines the function of § 103.

5. B borrows $20,000 for the purchase of a automobile (to be used for personal use) and pledges corporate stock as collateral for the loan. B has ample investment income. Is the interest deductible?

No. Debt is allocated to expenditures in accordance with the *use* of the debt proceeds. Except in the case of qualified residence interest, interest is allocated in accordance with the allocation of the debt. The interest in the problem is personal interest because the borrowed funds were used in making a personal expenditure. The character of the interest is not changed just because investment property was used as collateral for the loan; see Treas. Reg. § 1.163–8T(c)(1).

6. R borrowed $100,000 on margin from his stockbroker and invested the loan proceeds in publicly traded stocks and bonds. In the current year, T received dividends of $4,000 and interest income of $2,500. He paid a $5,000 fee for stock-market investment advice and spent $1,200 on commissions on approximately 30 stock trades. He had no net recognized capital gains or losses for the year. R paid margin interest for the year of $10,000. R's adjusted gross income is $200,000. Except for the items mentioned above, R's only itemized deductions (totaling $40,000) were for qualified residence interest, charitable contributions and state income and property taxes.

(a) How much of the margin interest can R deduct in the current year?

Stocks and bonds are investment property, and the interest is investment interest; § 163(d)(5)(A) & (d)(3)(A). (R's 30 trades are not sufficient to constitute a *business* of trading in securities so as to make the interest fully deductible as business interest; see Estate of Yeager v. Commissioner, 889 F.2d 29 (2d Cir. 1989) (average of 1,200 sales or purchases a year not sufficient).) Investment interest is not personal interest (see § 163(h)(2)(B)), but it is allowable only to the extent of the taxpayer's net investment income; § 163(d)(1). Net investment income is the excess of investment income over investment expenses; § 163(d)(4)(A).

Investment income includes gross income from property held for investment, which, in this case, would include both the dividend and interest income. However, "qualified" dividend income is included in investment income only if the taxpayer elects to treat the income as investment income and waives the benefit of the maximum 15–percent tax rate that applies to qualified dividends; §§ 163(d)(4)(B); 1(h)(11)(D)(i). Let's first assume that R elects to treat the dividends as investment income. Then R's investment income is $6,500 ($4,000 of dividends plus $2,500 of interest).

Investment expenses are the allowable deductions (other than for interest) that are directly connected with the production of investment income; § 163(d)(4)(C). The commissions are not expenses; commissions paid on purchases are added to the security's basis and those paid on sales reduce the amount realized; Treas. Reg. § 1.263(a)–2(e). The investment advisory fee is an investment expense, but is it taken into account only to the extent that it is otherwise allowable. It is a miscellaneous itemized deduction (defined in § 67(b)) and deductible only to the extent that all such deductions exceed 2 percent of adjusted gross income; § 67(a). R's other itemized deductions (for qualified residence interest, charitable contributions and state income and property taxes) are not *miscellaneous* itemized deductions; see § 67(b)(1), (2) & (4). The miscellaneous itemized deduction is allowable only to the extent of $1,000 ($5,000 miscellaneous itemized deduction less $4,000 AGI floor), and R's investment expense is therefore $1,000.

Net investment income is $5,500 ($6,500 investment income less $1,000 investment expense). The $10,000 of investment interest is deductible in the current year to the extent of $5,500. It is an itemized deduction, though not a miscellaneous itemized deduction; see § 67(b)(1). In summary, R includes the dividends and interest income in gross income and deducts $1,000 as a miscellaneous itemized deduction and $5,500 as a (non-miscellaneous) itemized deduction for investment interest.

When dividends were taxed at ordinary-income rates, they were treated as investment income. But since they are today taxed at a maximum rate of 15 percent, dividends generally are not treated as investment income; if they were, one could use dividends taxed at 15 percent to increase the investment-interest deduction that reduces ordinary income taxable at rates of up to 35 percent. Today a taxpayer can count the dividends as investment income only if she waives the benefit of the 15–percent tax rate; §§ 163(d)(4); 1(h)(11)(D). (Likewise, the net capital gain arising from the sale or exchange of investment property is not treated as investment income unless the taxpayer waives the benefit of the 15–percent tax rate with respect to such gain; §§ 164(d)(4)(B)(iii) & 1(h)(2).)

Although we assumed above that R elected to treat the dividends as investment income, that might not be a wise choice. R may prefer to pay tax on the dividends at 15 percent and carry over the additional $4,000 of investment interest that would be disallowed if the dividends do not count as investment income. After all, R may have plenty of investment income next year, so postponing the investment-interest deduction may be a small price to pay for a significant reduction in tax on the dividends.

If R does not elect to treat the dividends as investment income, net investment income is $1,500 ($2,500 of investment income less $1,000 investment expense), and the investment interest is allowable in the current year only to that extent, with $8,500 carried over to the following year.

(b) What happens to any interest not deductible in the current year?

Under § 163(d)(2), it is carried over to the following year, where it retains its character as investment interest and will be allowable only to the extent of net investment income, with any excess carried to the following year, etc.

(c) How would your answer in (a) change if R's adjusted gross income was $100,000?

If R's AGI was $100,000, the allowable miscellaneous itemized deduction would be $3,000 ($5,000 of miscellaneous itemized deductions less $2,000 AGI floor). If R elected to treat the dividends as investment income, the net investment income would be $3,500 ($6,500 investment income less $3,000 investment expense), and $3,500 of the investment interest would be deductible, with the other $6,500 carried over. If R did not treat the dividends as investment income, net investment income would be zero ($2,500 of investment income less $3,000 investment expense). None of the investment interest would be allowable in the current year; all of it would carry over to the following year.

7. H and W were divorced last year. The divorce decree requires that, for the next five years (that is, until their daughter, D, attains age 18), H make the mortgage payments on a residence owned by W and H as tenants-in-common and in which W and D reside. H's obligation is to terminate in the event of W's death. When D attains age 18, the property is to be sold and the proceeds divided equally between H and W. H and W are jointly liable on the mortgage liability, which was incurred when H and W purchased the residence. In the current year H pays $5,000 on the indebtedness ($2,000 of interest and $3,000 of principal). To what extent can H deduct the $5,000?

Of the $5,000 paid, $2,500 is treated as an indirect payment to W because it was paid in discharge of her legal obligation; see Old Colony Trust Co. v. Commissioner, 279 U.S. 716 (1929) (employer's payment of taxpayer's income-tax liability treated as payment to taxpayer because payment discharged his legal obligation). That portion of the payment must be analyzed under § 71. Since H's obligation terminates at W's death, the $2,500 should qualify as alimony under § 71(b) and Temp. Treas. Reg. § 1.71–1T(b), A–6. The $2,500 is deductible by H and includable in W's gross income; §§ 215; 71(a). (W can deduct her $1,000 share of the mortgage interest as qualified residence interest—i.e., the transaction is treated as if H paid W $2,500 cash and W used the money to pay her half of the mortgage payments.)

As to the $2,500 that H paid on his own behalf, the $1,500 paid on the mortgage principal is not deductible. The issue is whether the $1,000 of interest paid is non-deductible personal interest or deductible qualified residence interest. That in turn depends upon whether the mortgage debt is acquisition indebtedness. The liability was incurred in acquiring the residence, but is the residence a "qualified residence" as to H? A qualified residence includes the taxpayer's principal residence, which this is not, but also includes one other residence designated by the taxpayer and "which is used by the taxpayer as a residence (within the meaning of section 280A(d)(1))"; § 163(h)(4)(A)(i)(II). Section 280A(d)(1) says that a taxpayer uses a house as a residence if he uses it for "personal purposes" for more than 14 days during the year. Although H himself presumably has not used the property in the current year, H is credited with personal use whenever the property is used by (1) another person who has an interest in the house or (2) a member of H's family. Thus, use by W and D counts as personal use by H: W because she owns a half-interest in the property and D because she is a member of H's family under § 267(c)(4). (W is not a member of H's family because she is no longer his spouse.) If H designates the residence as a qualified residence, he can deduct the $1,000 of interest that he paid on his own behalf. In that case, H can deduct $2,500 of alimony in computing AGI (because of § 62(a)(10)) and $1,000 of qualified residence interest as an itemized deduction.

8. P suffered serious physical injuries in an automobile accident. In compensation, the tortfeasor agreed to pay P $200,000 at the rate of $10,000 a year for twenty years, plus 10% (market-rate) interest on the unpaid principal balance.

(a) Must P include the annual interest in gross income?

Yes. Explicit interest received on a personal-injury award is includable as interest income; it's not considered compensation for the personal injury; see, e.g., Kovacs v. Commissioner, 100 T.C. 124 (1993), aff'd, 25 F.3d 1048 (6th Cir. 1994).

(b) If you were P's attorney, how would you recommend that the settlement be structured?

Section 104(a)(2) excludes amounts received as "periodic payments," so you would want to structure the settlement as an annuity, in which the interest portion is implicit rather than explicitly stated. For example, a 20–year annual annuity of $23,492 has a present value of $200,000 (when discounted at 10 percent). (You will find problems on the present value of an annuity in Chapter 47.) If the settlement were structured in that way, each payment would be fully excludable under § 104(a)(2). Under the annuity arrangement, P will be left with more after taxes since the implicit interest portion of the payment is not taxed. Although the payor may lose a deduction for the interest, that may not matter if payment of the settlement amount is itself deductible by the payor.

9. B has a balance of $5,000 in her checking account. She borrows (without security) $15,000 from the bank and places the loan proceeds in her checking account. B intends to pay both personal and business expenses from the account. Which expenses will be treated as paid with the borrowed funds?

Because cash is fungible, the regulations necessarily lay down arbitrary rules for determining what funds are being dispersed when the taxpayer commingles borrowed and personal funds. Generally speaking, the borrowed amounts are treated as being expended before unborrowed amounts that were in the account when the borrowed funds were deposited; Treas. Reg. § 1.163–8T(c)(4)(ii). Since B will want the indebtedness allocated to business, the business expenses should be paid before any other expenditure is made from the account. (The expenditure is generally treated as made at the time the check is written; checks written on the same day may be treated as written in whatever order the taxpayer chooses; id.) However, the taxpayer can treat any expenditure made from the account within 15 days after the loan proceeds are deposited as made from the loan proceeds; Treas. Reg. § 1.163–8T(c)(4)(iii). So, if the business expenses are paid in the first 15 days, the order in which the expenditures are made does not matter. The best practice is to segregate loan proceeds in a separate account, so as to avoid the question of which funds are being expended.

10. Suppose (in 9) that $10,000 of the borrowed funds is properly allocable to business and $5,000 to personal expenditures. B repays $7,500 of the loan. What portion of the $7,500 balance is allocable to business?

Here, too, arbitrary rules are needed to determine which portion of a multi-purpose loan is being repaid. The regulations treat the least desirable portions of the loan as being repaid first; see Treas. Reg. § 1.163–8T(d)(1). S is deemed to have repaid the $5,000 personal portion of the loan and $2,500 of the business portion, leaving $7,500 of the business loan outstanding.

B. INTEREST-FREE LOANS

Code: § 7872.

1. P has $100,000 earning interest in the bank. At the midpoint of year 1, P directs the bank to begin paying the interest on the account to her adult child, C, and the bank does so. P reserves the right to revoke the assignment at any time, and she revokes it at the midpoint of year 2. Before P revokes the assignment, the bank pays C $5,500 of interest in each of years 1 and 2. What result to P and C?

This is a straightforward assignment-of-income problem. P gets taxed on the interest income because she owns the investment that earned the income. P is then treated as having made a gift of the money to C, who excludes the gift from income under § 102(a). Before the enactment of § 7872, however, P could shift the taxability of the interest to C by making an interest-free loan to her. If P lent C the $100,000 without interest, P would have no interest income, and C would be taxable on the earnings generated by the $100,000. Today § 7872 thwarts this mischief, as illustrated by the next problem.

2. At the midpoint of year 1, P lends her adult child, C, $100,000. The loan does not bear interest. C delivers to P her promissory note, which is payable on demand. C invests the money and earns interest of $5,500 in each of years 1 and 2. C repays the loan at the midpoint of year 2. The applicable federal rate is 10 percent. What results to P and C?

This is a "below-market loan" because it is a demand loan on which no interest is payable; see § 7872(e)(1). It is also a "gift loan," as P's forgoing of interest is in the nature of a gift; see § 7872(f)(3). Section 7872 applies to any below-market loan that is a gift loan; § 7872(c)(1). The forgone interest is treated as transferred from P to C (as a gift) and then retransferred from C to P as interest; see § 7872(a)(1). The transfers are treated as occurring on the last day of the year; § 7872(a)(2).

Since the loan is an interest-free, demand loan, the forgone interest is the amount of interest that would have been payable if the loan accrued interest at the applicable federal rate, compounded semiannually, and were payable on the last day of the year; § 7872(e)(2) & (f)(2)(B). Since we are told that the applicable federal rate is 10 percent, P is deemed to have transferred $5,000 (10% x $100,000 x 1/2) to C as a gift on December 31, year 1, and C is deemed have paid P the $5,000 as interest on that day. C could exclude the gift from income and would be entitled to deduct $5,000 as investment interest to the extent that she has net investment income; see § 163(d)(1). (Of course, the $5,500 of interest that C received is investment income.). P must include the $5,000 in gross income for year 1. A similar transfer and retransfer occurs in year 2, with similar results for both parties.

3. Same as 2, except that C earned interest of $4,000 in each year.

In the case of a gift loan, § 7872(d)(1)(A) generally limits the amount deemed to be retransferred from the borrower to the lender to the amount of the borrower's net investment income for the year. If the interest earned were C's only investment income (and C incurred no investment expenses other than interest), only $4,000 would be treated as interest income to P and as investment interest to C in each year.

Section 7872(d)(1)(E) incorporates the definition of "net investment income" found in § 163(d). Recall that today dividends are not treated as investment income under § 163(d) unless the taxpayer waives the application of the capital-gains tax rates to the dividends; see §§ 163(d)(4); 1(h)(11)(D). Does not this create a loophole in § 7872? Suppose, for example, that C invested the $100,000 in stock that paid $4,000 of dividends in year 1. Under the default rule of § 163(d)(4), the dividends are not investment income. If C had no other investment income, she would be deemed to have retransferred no interest to P, P would have no interest income, and the parties would achieve the income-shifting that § 7872 was intended to thwart. Notice, however, that the retransfer is not limited to the amount of net investment income if the parties have tax-avoidance as one of their principal purposes; § 7872(d)(1)(B). Perhaps the Service would invoke the tax-avoidance exception in the dividend case.

4. Same as 2, except that the loan was a one-year term loan.

The result would be the same as in 2. Although some term loans are treated differently than demand loans, a term loan that is a gift loan is treated in the same manner as a gift loan that is payable on demand; see 7872(a).

5. Same as 2, except that P is a corporation (with a large amount of accumulated earnings) and C is a shareholder of the corporation.

Now the transfer from P to C is treated as a dividend instead of a gift. So, on December 31, year 1, C is treated as receiving a $5,000 dividend and paying $5,000 of investment interest to P. C has $5,500 of investment income (the interest earned on the investment—remember the dividend is not treated as investment income unless C waives the application of the capital-gains tax rates) and a deduction for $5,000 of investment interest (assuming that C's *net* investment income is at least $5,000). P has $5,000 of interest income; it cannot deduct the dividend paid.

Chapter 39

ALIMONY, PROPERTY SETTLEMENTS
AND RELATED ISSUES

Code: §§ 71(a)–(f); 215; 62(a)(10); 1041; 152(e) 1223(2); 1245(b)(1); 453B(g).

Regulations: §§ 1.71–1T; 1.1.1041–1T.

Cases: Okerson v. Commissioner, 123 T.C. 258 (2004);
Kean v. Commissioner, 407 F.3d 186 (3d Cir. 2005);
Young v. Commissioner, 240 F.3d 369 (4th Cir. 2001).

Ruling: Rev. Rul. 2002–22, 2002–1 C.B. 849.

1. H recently moved out of the family home that he shared with his wife, W, and their 13–year old child, C. H and W are considering divorce, though neither has commenced legal action nor even consulted with an attorney about the matter. At the beginning of each month, H transfers $5,000 to W, just as he did when the parties lived together. W uses the money to pay the costs of maintaining the household and providing for C and herself. If H and W file separate returns, how should they treat the monthly payments?

The payments are not includable in W's income nor deductible by H. The deduction/inclusion treatment applies only if the payments are alimony within the meaning of § 71(b)(1); §§ 71(a); 215(a). In order to be alimony under § 71(b), the payments must be received under a divorce or separation instrument; § 71(b)(1)(A). Since there is no decree of divorce or separate maintenance or decree for support, the payments would be alimony only if made under a written separation agreement (§ 71(b)(2)), and here there does not appear to be any such agreement. Voluntary payments do not qualify as alimony. If the parties want future payments to be taxable to W and deductible by H, they will need to formalize their support arrangement with a written agreement.

2. A and B have obtained a divorce. The decree requires A to pay B $3,000 monthly for 10 years. If B dies within the ten-year period, A is to pay $2,000 a month to their adult child, C, for the remainder of the ten-year period. The decree specifically provides that all payments be deductible by A and includable in B's income. How should A and B treat the payments on their tax returns?

Only $1,000 of each payment qualifies as "alimony" under § 71(b). The other $2,000 does not satisfy the termination-at-death rule of § 71(b)(2)(D) because, even though the payments to B terminate at B's death, A is then required to make substitute payments to C. It makes no difference that the decree says the payments are to be deductible by A and includable in B's income; see Okerson v. Commissioner, 123 T.C. 258 (2004). The deduction/inclusion treatment applies only if the payments are alimony under § 71(b), and in this case $2,000 of each payment is not alimony. A can deduct $1,000 of each payment and B must include $1,000 of each payment in income.

3. A dissolution decree requires C to pay the following amounts to C's former husband, D. Which of the payments are deductible by C and includable in D's gross income?

(a) Spousal support of $10,000 a month (terminable at D's death);

Assuming that the decree does not designate the payments as being non-deductible (see § 71(b)(1)(B)), the spousal support meets all the requirements of § 71(b) and so is alimony in the tax sense. The $10,000 is includable in D's gross income and deductible by C in computing adjusted gross income; §§ 71(a); 215(a); 62(a)(10).

(b) Child support of $5,000 a month for the couple's two children.

The child support is not includable in D's income nor deductible by C; § 71(c)(1).

4. Would your answer to 3 differ if the child support was "bundled" into a $15,000 "family-support allowance" (terminable at D's death)?

When a divorce court awards a "family-support allowance," the judge determines the appropriate level of support for both the ex-spouse and the children and combines those amounts into a single figure, which is then adjusted for the increased tax that the ex-spouse will have to pay on the child-support portion of the package. The purpose of bundling child and spousal support into a single, undifferentiated payment is to obtain deduction/inclusion treatment for the entire payment and thereby reduce the spouses' aggregate tax burden.

The issue in the bundled-support cases is whether the termination-at-death requirement is violated. The payor-spouse has a state-law obligation to continue to support the children after the payee-spouse's death, and those support payments could be viewed as a substitute for the child-support portion of the family-support allowance. Although the courts are divided on the application of the termination-at-death rule in this context, several recent cases have held that the existence of a general state-law obligation to the children after the death of the payee-spouse does not violate § 71(b)(1)(D); e.g., Kean v. Commissioner, 407 F.3d 186 (3d Cir. 2005). (If the bundled-support approach works, it is just a matter of time before every state offers the family-support option, thus rendering child-support payments deductible for the well-advised.)

One non-tax problem posed by these arrangements is that the payor-spouse will probably have to go to court to have the support order modified whenever there is a change of circumstance, such as a child attaining majority. However, that may be a small price to pay to obtain a tax deduction for the child support.

5. **Suppose the following tax rates apply to unmarried taxpayers:**

If taxable income is:	The tax is:
Not over $30,000	10 percent of taxable income.
Over $30,000 but not over $60,000	$3,000 plus 20 percent of the excess.
Over $60,000	$9,000 plus 30 percent of the excess.

(a) **A and B are negotiating a divorce settlement. Apart from the effect of any alimony payments, A has annual income of $100,000 and B has annual income of $20,000. Suppose that the parties agree that A will pay $30,000 annually, and the payment is not alimony. How much will each party have left after tax?**

	A	B	Total
Income	$100,000	$20,000	$120,000
Paid to B	(30,000)	30,000	-------
Tax	(21,000)	(2,000)	(23,000)
Left after tax	$49,000	$48,000	$97,000

(b) Same as (a), except that A will pay B $40,000, and the payment is alimony.

	A	B	Total
Income	$100,000	$20,000	$120,000
Paid to B	(40,000)	40,000	------
Tax	(9,000)	(9,000)	(18,000)
Left after tax	$51,000	$51,000	$102,000

(c) Which arrangement is preferable?

Obviously, the arrangement in (b) is preferable, as it leaves both parties better off than would the arrangement in (a). Payors of alimony are usually in a higher tax bracket than their payees. In such cases, the parties are usually better off structuring support payments as alimony within the meaning of § 71(b)(1). As this problem shows, the payor can afford to pay more if the payments are deductible, and the higher payments can more than offset the recipient's tax on those payments.

6. A divorce decree requires I to pay the premiums on a term life-insurance policy on her life. The policy is owned by her ex-husband, J. I's obligation terminates at J's death. Are the premium payments deductible by I?

Apparently so. In order to qualify as alimony, the payment must be made in cash, but it is not necessary that the ex-spouse *receive* cash; see § 71(b)(1). A payment to the insurer can be a payment made "on behalf of" the former spouse. Some cases held that such premium payments were not alimony under the pre-1985 version of § 71 because the former spouse got "no benefit" from the payments if the insured did not die during the year; e.g., Brodersen v. Commissioner, 57 T.C. 412 (1971). However, Treas. Reg. § 1.71–1T, A–6, says that premiums paid for insurance on the payor's life qualify as payments on behalf of the former spouse if the former spouse owns the policy. So, I can deduct the premium payments, and J must include the amount of the premiums in gross income.

7. As part of a divorce property settlement, M transferred to M's former spouse, N, the items of property listed below. In each case, determine the consequences of the transfer to M and N.

(a) Greenacre, which had a value of $100,000 and in which M had an adjusted basis of $20,000.

M recognizes no gain on the transfer because of § 1041(a). That provision was enacted to overturn United States v. Davis, 370 U.S. 65 (1962), which required the recognition of gain in divorce property settlements.

N is treated as acquiring the property by gift (§ 1041(b)(1)), and so the value of the property is excluded from N's gross income under § 102(a). Although N is treated as acquiring the property by gift, the basis of the property is determined by § 1041(b)(2) rather than § 1015; see § 1015(e). N assumes M's $20,000 adjusted basis for the property. In calculating the property's holding period, N can include ("tack on") the period during which the property was held by M because N's basis is determined by reference to M's; § 1223(2).

(b) Blueacre, which had a value of $20,000 and in which M had an adjusted basis of $100,000.

M recognizes no loss on the transfer; § 1041(a). N has no income and assumes M's $100,000 basis for the property; § 1041(b)(2). As noted above, the transferee's basis is not determined under § 1015; that is important in this case because § 1041(b)(2) does not contain the lower-of-basis-or-value rule of § 1015(a). If N sells Blueacre for $20,000, N realizes and recognizes a loss of $80,000. (If 1015(a)'s lower-of-basis-or-value rule applied, N's adjusted basis for determining loss would be the $20,000 value of the property on the date of transfer, and N would not realize loss on the sale.) N's holding period for the property includes the period during which the property was held by M.

(c) A claim for $5,000 of unpaid rent due from the lessee of Greenacre.

The issue here is whether the $5,000 should be taxed to M under the assignment-of-income doctrine since the income accrued while M was still the owner of the property. Income that accrues while the property was held by a cash-method transferor is generally taxed to the transferor even if the money is collected by the transferee. Although the Service once took the position that the assignment-of-income doctrine overrides § 1041(a), Rev. Rul. 2002–22, 2002–1 C.B. 849, concludes that § 1041(a)'s non-recognition rule trumps the assignment-of-income doctrine. Thus N assumes M's zero basis for the claim and has $5,000 of income when the claim is collected.

(d) An installment obligation arising from M's sale of a capital asset. M had been reporting the gain under the installment method of § 453. M's adjusted basis in the obligation was $40,000. It had a value (and face amount) of $200,000.

The holder of an installment obligation who transfers it by gift must recognize gain to the extent the value of the obligation exceeds its adjusted basis; § 453B(a). However, § 453B(g) excepts transfers covered by § 1041. Therefore, M recognizes no gain on the transfer, N assumes M's $40,000 adjusted basis for the obligation, and, as payments are received, N continues reporting the gain in the same manner as M would have.

(e) Business equipment (§ 1245 property) with an adjusted basis of $20,000 and a value of $50,000. M had originally purchased the equipment for $100,000 and had properly deducted $80,000 of depreciation with respect thereto.

If M had sold the equipment for its $50,000 value, the $30,000 gain would be ordinary gain under § 1245. Section 1245(a)(1) generally requires that § 1245 gain be recognized "notwithstanding any other provision * * *." Recall, however, that § 1041 treats N as acquiring the property by gift, and § 1245(b)(1) makes the recapture rule inapplicable to a transfer of property by gift. (Technically, § 1041(a)(2) says the property is considered to be *acquired* by gift and 1245(b)(1) excepts *dispositions* by gift. But the exception surely applies here, maybe on the theory that the transferor of property *acquired* by the transferee by gift must necessarily have *disposed of* the property by gift.) So, M recognizes no gain, and N acquires the property with an adjusted basis of $20,000. The equipment remains § 1245 property in the hands of N even if N does not use it in profit-seeking activity because it "has been" § 1245 property (in the hands of M); see § 1245(a)(3). N's recomputed basis includes the depreciation taken by M because N assumes M's adjusted basis in which those adjustments are reflected. Therefore, N's recomputed basis is $100,000 ($20,000 adjusted basis plus $80,000 of M's depreciation reflected in that adjusted basis); § 1245(a)(2)(A).

(f) M's $100,000 promissory note, which was payable (without interest) in 4 years.

The giving of the promissory note has no tax consequences to M. As to N, however, there is a question as to the basis of the note. Section 1041(b)(2) says that N assumes M's basis "in the case of any transfer of property" to which § 1041(a) applies. Is the giving of a note a *transfer of property*? Although the note is property in N's hands, it was not in M's hands. The "property" comes into being only when the debtor-creditor relationship is created by the transfer to N, and so it is a little awkward to speak of N's assuming M's adjusted basis in this situation—M really does not have a basis for the note because it is not property in M's hands. In other contexts, the Commissioner usually insists that one has a zero basis in one's own note, though sometimes the courts have disagreed and assigned the note a basis equal to its face amount; see Peracchi v. Commissioner, 143 F.3d 487 (9th Cir. 1998) (shareholder transferred his note to controlled corporation as a contribution to capital; *held*, shareholder could increase his stock basis by the face amount of the note). If M had transferred $100,000 cash to N, the receipt would not have been taxable to N (assuming that it wasn't alimony), and there's no good reason to tax N just because the receipt of the cash is delayed by 5 years. N should therefore get a $100,000 basis in the note so that N has no income when the $100,000 is collected. That is the right answer, though getting there through § 1041(b) is problematic.

A second issue is whether interest should be imputed on the deferred payment since explicit is not provided for. It is well-established that interest is not imputed in § 1041 transfers; e.g., Treas. Reg. §§ 1.483–1(c)(3)(i); 1.1274–1(b)(3)(iii).

8. M (in 7) failed to pay the $100,000 due on the promissory note that was due after 4 years. N sued M and obtained a judgment for the $100,000. M satisfied the judgment in the fifth year after the decree by transferring to N Purpleacre, which had a value of $100,000 and in which M had an adjusted basis of $30,000. What result to the parties?

The issue is whether M's $70,000 gain realized on the transfer of Purpleacre is recognized. That depends upon whether 1041 applies. Section 1041(a)(2) provides for non-recognition on a transfer to a former spouse, but only if the transfer is "incident to the divorce." Since the transfer did not occur within one year of the divorce, the transfer is considered to be incident to the divorce only if the transfer was "related to the cessation of the marriage"; Temp. Treas. Reg. 1.1041–1T(b), Q & A 6. Q & A 7 says that in order to meet the latter requirement, the transfer must be "pursuant to" the decree and must occur within 6 years of the decree. Any transfer not meeting those two conditions is presumed not to be related to the cessation of the marriage.

Although the transfer was made within 6 years of the decree, one can strongly argue that the transfer was not made "pursuant to" the decree but to the judgment that N had obtained against M. (There was nothing in the decree that required the transfer of Purpleacre.) So, the transfer is presumed not to be related to the cessation of the marriage. Yet, this is merely a presumption that can be rebutted "by showing that the transfer was made to effect the division of property owned by the former spouses at the time of the cessation of the marriage"; Temp. Treas. Reg. 1.1041-1T(b) Q & A 7. Here M's liability arose from the property division required by the divorce.

Of course, N would contend that the transfer of the building was not made to her in her capacity as M's former spouse but because she was M's judgment creditor. (N has an important stake in the controversy: If M's gain is not recognized, N must assume M's basis for the property under 1041(b).) It does seem unfair that N gets stuck with M's low basis, but, of course, N did not have to accept the property in satisfaction of the judgment; she could have insisted that M sell the property and pay her cash.

Although this is a close case, the presumption is probably overcome, and the transfer would be considered to be related to the cessation of the marriage; for a similar case, see Young v. Commissioner, 240 F.3d 369 (2001), in which the court, over a strong dissent, held the transferee assumed the transferor's basis in the property because the transfer was related to the cessation of the marriage and hence incident to the divorce. Thus, M probably qualifies for 1041 non-recognition and N assumes M's $30,000 adjusted basis.

9. Re-examine problem 4 in Chapter 12.

See the solution in Chapter 12.

10. Re-examine problems 7 and 8 in Chapter 18.

See the solutions in Chapter 18.

11. Re-examine problems 7, 8 and 9 in Chapter 22.

See the solutions in Chapter 22.

12. Examine problems 5, 6 and 7 in Chapter 40.

See the solutions in Chapter 40.

Chapter 40

PERSONAL AND DEPENDENCY
EXEMPTIONS AND FILING STATUS

A. PERSONAL AND DEPENDENCY EXEMPTIONS

Code: §§ 151(a), (b), (c) & (d); 152.   Note §§ 24(c)(1); 213(d)(5); 21(e)(5); 32(c)(3)(A).

Regulations: §§ 1.151–1(b); 1.152–1(a) & (b); 1.152–3; 1.152–4(b); Temp Treas. Reg. § 1.152–4T.

1. T furnishes over half the support of the following persons. For whom is T entitled to a dependency exemption? (Ignore the effect of inflation adjustments.)

(a) T's son, A, who is 23 years old and attends medical school at State University in University City. For the past two years, A has resided alone in University City, approximately 120 miles from T's home. A's gross income for the year is $4,500.

In order to be T's dependent, A must be either T's "qualifying child" or "qualifying relative"; § 152(a). A qualifying child means one who (1) bears a § 152(c)(2) relationship to the taxpayer; (2) shares the same principal place of abode as the taxpayer for more than half the year; (3) meets the age requirements of § 152(c)(3); and (4) has not provided over half of his own support for the year; § 152(c)(1). A meets all of these requirements except the second one: He has not had the same principal place of abode as T for the year. Therefore, A cannot be T's qualifying child.

The question then becomes whether A can be T's qualifying relative. To be a qualifying relative, one must (1) bear a § 152(d)(2) relationship to the taxpayer; (2) not have gross income in excess of the exemption amount ($2,000 before inflation adjustments—§ 151(d)(1)); (3) have received over half of her support from the taxpayer; and (4) not be the qualifying child of the taxpayer or of any other person; § 151(d)(1). A meets all of these requirements except for the gross-income

511

requirement; his gross income exceeds the $2,000 exemption amount. Therefore A cannot be T's qualifying relative. If A had had gross income of $2,000 or less, A would have been T's qualifying relative, and T would have been entitled to a dependency exemption for him.

(b) T's 19–year–old step-daughter, B, who resides with T. B attends a local college half time. B has gross income of $4,500.

First consider whether B can be T's qualifying child under § 152(c)(1). B bears the proper relationship (§ 152(c)(1)(A)) to T because she is T's child, as the term "child" includes a stepdaughter; § 152(f)(1)(A)(i). B also satisfies the principal-place-of-abode and support tests; see § 152(c)(1)(B) & (D). Does B satisfy the age requirement of § 152(c)(1)(C) and (c)(3)? B is over age 19, but that's permitted if she is under age 24 and a "student"; see § 152(c)(3)(A)(ii). However, the term student means one who is a "full-time" student for a part of at least 5 months during the year; § 152(f)(2). Since B is only a part-time student, she does not satisfy the age requirement and cannot be T's qualifying child.

Can B be T's qualifying relative? No, because she has too much gross income; see § 152(d)(1)(B). T cannot claim B as a dependent.

(c) T's 15–year–old adopted daughter, C, who resides with her father (T's former spouse). The parties' divorce decree is silent as to the allocation of the dependency exemption for C. C had gross income of $1,500.

Although the term "child" includes an adopted child (§ 152(f)(1)(B)), C cannot be T's qualified child because C's principal place of abode is not with T but with C's father; see § 152(c)(1)(B). Can C be T's qualifying relative? No, because of § 152(d)(1)(D); C would be a qualifying child of her father with whom she resides, and therefore she cannot be T's qualifying relative. T is not allowed a dependency exemption for C.

(d) D, age 13, who resides with T as a foster child.

The term child includes a foster child if placed with the taxpayer by an authorized placement agency or by court order; § 152(f)(1)(A)(ii) & (C). D meets all of the requirements to be T's qualified child under § 152(c)(1), and T is allowed a dependency exemption for D.

(e) T's domestic partner J, who has resided with T for several years. J's only income ($1,500) was from a part-time job.

J is T's qualified relative because they share a principal place of abode, and J is a member of T's household; see § 152(d)(2)(H). (This assumes that § 152(f)(3) does not apply—i.e., that the *relationship* between J and T does not violate local law.) Thus, the relationship test is satisfied, as are the other tests of § 152(d)(1). T can therefore claim J as a dependent.

(f) K, age 16, who is the child of T's domestic partner, J (in (e)), and who resides with T and J. K has no gross income.

K cannot be T's qualified child because they do not have one of the relationships specified in § 152(c)(2). K does bear a § 152(d)(2)(H) relationship to T, but K still cannot be T's qualifying relative because of § 152(d)(1)(D), as K is J's qualifying child.

2. N, age 20, resides with his aunt, A, and her husband, U, while N attends college as a full-time student. U furnishes over 50 percent of N's support. N's only income is $4,500 earned from a part-time job. He pays no rent, though he contributes to the household by helping with laundry, cooking, yard work, and minor repairs. S and U file a joint return. Does B qualify as their dependent?

Is N the qualified child of A? N bears the proper relationship to A (a descendant of A's brother or sister); § 152(c)(2)(B). N shares A's principal place of abode, meets the age requirements (because N is under age 24 and a full-time student), and does not furnish more than half of his own support. So, N is a qualified child of A. Although U furnishes over half of N's support and they have a § 152(d)(2)(H) relationship, N cannot be U's qualified relative because (1) N has too much gross income and (2) N is the qualified child of A; see § 152(d)(1)(B) & (D). A, rather than U, gets the dependency exemption, but that doesn't matter here where A and U are filing a joint return.

3. R's 90–year-old grandmother, G, resides with R's sister, S. R contributes 40, S 40, and G 20 percent of G's support. All of G's contribution comes from her savings. G's only income is interest of $1,800 on her bank savings account.

G bears to R and S one of the relationships specified by § 152(d)(2)(C) (ancestor of the taxpayer's father or mother), G does not have gross income in excess of the exemption amount, and G is not the qualifying child of another. G could therefore be the qualifying relative of either R or S if either furnished over half of G's support; see § 152(d)(1). They could overcome that obstacle by executing a multiple-support agreement under § 152(d)(3). Under a multiple-support agreement, either can be treated as furnishing over half of G's support. The conditions of § 152(d)(3) are met because (1) no one furnished over half of G's support, (2) over half of G's support came from people (R and S) who could have claimed G as a dependent but for the support requirement, and (3) both R and S furnished over 10% of G's support. Thus, R and S can agree who will claim G as a dependent for the year by filing the declaration required by § 152(d)(3)(D).

4. D (age 12) and her single mother, M, share a home with M's parents, GM and GF. Although M contributes to the cost of the household from her $25,000 per year salary, GM and GF, who file a joint return, pay most of the family's living expenses. Who is entitled to the dependency exemption for D?

D meets the requirements to be the qualifying child of both M and her grandparents. When a person "may be and is" claimed as a qualifying child by two or more taxpayers, the person is treated as the qualifying child of her parent; § 152(c)(4)(i). So, if both M and the grandparents claim D as a dependent, she will be treated as the dependent of M. However, the statute's "may be and is" language would permit M to waive the exemption in favor of the grandparents, which she might want to do if the exemption would be more valuable to them than it would be to her.

5. M has physical custody of her 13-year-old son, S, who resides with her. M has waived her right to the dependency exemption for S so that it can be claimed by S's father (S's former husband), F (see § 152(e)(1) & (2)). Under these circumstances, determine whether M or F is entitled to:

(a) The child tax credit of § 24;

When a custodial parent releases her claim to the dependency exemption under § 152(e), she gives up more than just the exemption. The custodial parent's waiver results in the child being treated as the qualifying child of the non-custodial parent. The application of other Code provisions depends upon who can treat the child as a qualifying child. The child tax credit of § 24 is one example. It affords a $1,000 credit to a taxpayer who has a qualifying child under the age of 17; § 24(a) & (c). Thus, M's waiver of the personal exemption also costs her the child tax credit for S, which can be claimed by F.

(b) The medical-expense deduction of § 213 for medical expenses paid on behalf of S;

A taxpayer may deduct medical expenses paid on behalf of her "dependent." When M makes a waiver for the year under § 152(e), S is not treated as a dependent of M for that year. However, § 213(d)(5) treats the child of divorced parents as a dependent of both parents for purposes of the medical-expense deduction. So, subject to the 7.5–percent-of-AGI floor, S can deduct medical expenses paid on behalf of S.

(c) The dependent-care credit of § 21 for child-care expenses paid by M so that she could work;

Section 21 allows a partial credit for amounts expended for the care of a "qualifying individual"—as pertinent here, a "dependent" under age 13—in order to enable the taxpayer to be gainfully employed. As noted above, S is not M's dependent because she has waived her right to the exemption. However, § 21(e)(5) provides that a child is treated as the qualifying individual of the custodial parent even though the custodial parent has waived her right to the exemption under § 152(e).

(d) Count S as a qualifying child for the purpose of the earned income credit of § 32.

The earned income credit is a refundable credit intended to supplement the incomes of low-income working people. Larger credits are available to those with one or more "qualifying children"; § 32(c)(1)(A)(i), (b)(1) & (2). For this purpose a qualifying child has the same meaning as in § 152(c), except § 152(e) does not apply; § 32(c)(3)(A). So, M can count S as a qualified child for the purpose of the earned income credit even though she has waived her right to the exemption.

6. In November of year 1, H moved out of the house that he had occupied with his wife, W, and their two young children, ages 3 and 6, and moved into an apartment. The children continued to reside in the house with W. In December, W filed for divorce, but the parties were still married at the end of year 1. H and W are filing separate returns for year 1, even though H's income is considerably higher than W's. Who is entitled to the dependency exemptions for the two children for year 1?

The children appear to be qualifying children of both H and W under § 152(c)(1). If both parents claim the exemptions for the children, the conflict is resolved by § 152(c)(4)(B)(i): If the parents do not file a joint return together, the children are the qualifying children of the parent with whom they resided for the longest period during the year. In this case, they resided with W all year and with H only until November. So, they are the qualifying children of W for the year, and she gets the dependency exemptions.

7. Would your answer in 6 differ if H had moved out of the home in January, year 2 (after residing there with W and the children throughout year 1)?

Now the children reside with both parents for all of year 1. In that case, they are treated as the qualifying children of the parent with the higher adjusted gross income; see § 152(c)(4)(B)(ii). H gets the exemptions.

8. K, age 17, resides with her parents, who furnish all of her support. She earns $4,500 at a part-time job. Is K entitled to a personal exemption on her return?

No. A person with respect to whom a personal exemption is allowable to another is not entitled to a personal exemption. The mechanism for achieving that result is § 151(d)(2), which treats the dependent's exemption amount (the amount for which a deduction is usually allowed—§ 151(b)) as being zero. K is the qualifying child of her parents, who are entitled to a dependency exemption for K.

Although § 151(d)(2) applies whenever a dependency exemption is "allowable" (rather than "allowed") to another, the Service sometimes treats as a non-dependent a person who *could* be claimed as a dependent by another but who was not in fact claimed as a dependent; see Treas. Reg. § 1.25A–1(f)(1) & (2). Therefore, K might be able to claim her own exemption if her parents do not in fact claim her as a dependent.

9. L, a single person (not a surviving spouse or head of household), has adjusted gross income of $140,000. L is entitled to three personal and dependency exemptions. How much can L deduct for the exemptions if the year is 2009? 2010?

The benefit of the personal and dependency exemptions are reduced (phased out) as the taxpayer's income increases. The phaseout is at the rate of 2 percentage points for each $2,500 (or fraction thereof) by which the taxpayer's AGI exceeds the "threshold amount"; § 151(d)(3). For a single person (not a surviving spouse or head of household), the threshold amount is $100,000; § 151(d)(3)(C)(iii). L's AGI exceeds the $100,000 threshold amount by $40,000. Dividing $40,000 by $2,500, we get 16 increments, and the otherwise allowable exemptions ($6,000 here) must be reduced by 2 percent for each of the 16 increments, or 32 percent. The reduction would be $1,920 (32% of $6,000), except that the phaseout itself is being phased out. In 2009, only 1/3 of the reduction is taken into account; § 151(d)(3)(E); in 2010, the phase out terminates; § 151(d)(3)(F).

In 2009, the reduction is $640 (1/3 of $1,920), leaving a deduction of $5,360. In 2010, the full $6,000 will be deductible.

B. FILING STATUS AND RELATED ISSUES

Code: §§ 6012(a)(1) & (b)(1); 6013(a), (c) & (d); 2. Note §§ 1(a), (b) & (c) (Appendix B); 7701(a)(38); 7703(a)(1).

In working these problems, ignore the effect of inflation adjustments.

1. T has taxable income of $100,000. Use the tax-rate schedules in Appendix B to determine T's tax before credits if T's filing status is:

(a) Married filing jointly with T's spouse. (The $100,000 of taxable income is their combined income.)

$20,205.50 ($17,167.50, plus 28% of [$100,000 – $89,150]); § 1(a).

(b) Surviving spouse (defined in § 2(a)).

$20,205.50 (same as (a)). A surviving spouse uses the rates for married filing jointly; see § 1(a).

(c) Head of household (defined in § 2(b)).

$22,248 ($15,640, plus 28% of [$100,000 – $76,400]); § 1(b).

(d) Single (not a head of household or surviving spouse).

$23,835 ($10,815, plus 28% of [$100,000 – $53,500]); § 1(c).

Notice that the married couple filing a joint return and the surviving spouse pay the least tax, the head of household pays more, and the single person who is neither a surviving spouse nor a head of household pays the most.

2. Does the taxpayer's filing status determine the treatment of items other than the computation of tax liability?

Yes. Filing status often is taken into account in determining the amount by which deductions or credits are reduced at higher-income levels. For example, the phaseouts of the personal exemptions, the deduction and credits for qualified tuition and related expenses, the deduction for interest paid on student loans, and the deduction for contributions to traditional IRAs all depend at least in part upon the taxpayer's filing status; §§ 151(d)(3)(C); 222(b)(2)(B); 221(b)(2)(B); 219(g)(3)(B). The taxpayer's eligibility to make a contribution to a Roth IRA is also dependent upon filing status; see § 408A(c)(3). One's filing status also determines whether one must file a return, as illustrated by the next problem.

3. Each of the following taxpayers has gross income of $7,000. Determine which of them must file a federal income-tax return:

(a) S, a 25–year-old single person (not a surviving spouse or head of household);

Generally speaking, a single person (who is neither a surviving spouse nor a head of household) must file a return if the person has gross income in excess of $5,000—the sum of the exemption amount ($2,000 under § 151(d)(1)) and the basic standard deduction ($3,000 under § 63(c)(5)); § 6012(a)(1)(A)(i). S must file a return because she has gross income of $7,000.

(b) H, a 25–year-old head of household (within the meaning of § 2(b));

As a head of household, H must file if her gross income exceeds $6,400, which is the sum of her standard deduction ($4,400) and personal exemption ($2,000); see § 6012(a)(1)(A)(ii). H must file because her gross income exceeds $6,400.

(c) P, a 60–year-old surviving spouse (within the meaning of § 2(a));

As a surviving spouse, P must file if her gross income exceeds $8,000, which is the sum of her standard deduction ($6,000) and personal exemption ($2,000); see § 6012(a)(1)(A)(iii). Since P's gross income is only $7,000, she is not required to file.

(d) W, a 70–year old widow who is a head of household (because she maintains a household in which she resides with (only) her 12–year old grandchild).

Since W has attained age 65, the $6,400 filing threshold for a head of household is increased by the amount of the additional standard deduction to which W is entitled under § 63(f)(1)(A) & (3), or $750 in this case; § 6012(a)(1)(B). So, W faces a filing threshold of $7,150. Since her gross income is only $7,000, she need not file.

4. H and W have been married for ten years and have a child, age 6. Last December H moved out of the family home and filed for divorce, though, of course, no decree had been entered by the end of the year. What is the parties' filing status for last year?

The parties are still husband and wife at the close of the year, so they can either file a joint return or file separate returns; see §§ 7703(a); 6013(d)(1)(A). The parties to a joint return are jointly and severally liable for the tax; § 6013(d)(3). If they file separate returns, alimony is taxed to the recipient and deductible by the payor under §§ 71 and 215. Since there has been no divorce decree, the payments are considered to be alimony only if they are based upon a written separation agreement or a decree for support; § 71(b)(1)(A) & (2).

5. What result in 4 if the parties had entered into a written separation agreement that required H to make payments to W for her support?

Same as 4. The parties are considered married until there is a decree of divorce or separate maintenance; § 6013(d)(2).

6. On June 30 of the current year, a decree of divorce was entered (in 4). W was awarded custody of the child. W waived her right to the dependency exemption for the child. What is the filing status of H? Of W?

The parties are not married on the last day of the year, so H must file as a single person under § 1(c). H is not a head of household because the child does not reside with him; see § 2(b)(1)(A). W may qualify as a head of household, as the child is a qualifying child with respect to her and the child resides with her. In order to qualify, however, W must furnish over half the cost of maintaining the household; § 2(b)(1)(last sentence).

7. W died on August 15, 2007, survived by her husband, H, and a 10–year old son, S. Can H file a joint return on behalf of the couple for 2007?

W's last taxable year ends on the date of her death; Treas. Reg. § 1.451–1(b)(1). Although spouses generally cannot file jointly if they have different taxable years, joint filing is permitted when the spouses' taxable years begin on the same day and end on different days only because of the death of one spouse; see § 6013(a)(2). As a general rule, only the decedent's executor or administrator can execute a joint return on behalf of the decedent; § 6013(a)(3). In this case, however, H can execute a joint return on behalf of W and him if (1) no return had been made by W (W died before the end of the year), and (2) no executor or administrator had been appointed for W before the due date of the return; see id. The joint return will include H's income and deductions for all of 2007 and W's income and deductions for the period from January 1 through August 15, 2007.

If H files a joint return for the couple, and an executor or administrator is appointed for W after the due date of the return, the executor or administrator may disaffirm the joint return by filing a separate return for W within one year of the due date of the original return; § 6013(a)(3). If H's executor disaffirms the joint return, H will have to file a separate return under § 1(d) because he is considered married for 2007 under § 7703(a)(1).

If an executor or administrator had been appointed before the due date of the return, H, acting alone, could not file a joint return for 2007; see § 6013(a)(3). The executor could either assent to the filing of a joint return or file a separate return for W. If H has filed a joint return before the executor is appointed, he would have to file an amended return, unless the executor assents to the joint return.

8. What is H's filing status for 2008 if H and S continue to reside in a household furnished by H?

Assuming he does not remarry during the year, H would qualify in 2008 (and 2009) as a "surviving spouse" under § 2(a) because his wife died within one of the two preceding taxable years and H maintains as his home a household which constitutes the principal place of abode of his qualifying child, S. H can therefore use the rate schedule in § 1(a).

9. What is H's filing status for 2010 if H and S continue to reside in a household furnished by H?

If in 2010 H continues to maintain a home as a household for S, he can qualify as a "head of household" under § 2(b) and use the rate schedule of § 1(b).

Chapter 41

PERSONAL TAX CREDITS

A. THE CHILD TAX CREDIT

Code: §§ 24(a), (b) & (c); 152(c).

1. S, an unmarried, single parent, has two children, A and B, who reside with her. A is age 14. B is age 19 and a full-time college student. Both are dependents of S. What is the amount of S's child tax credit if S's modified adjusted gross income (as defined in § 24(b)(1)) is:

(a) $50,000?

S can take the credit only for a qualifying child under age 17. Thus, A is the only child who qualifies. (The term qualifying child is defined in § 152(c); A meets the requirements of that provision.) Although the credit is reduced for higher-income taxpayers, S is below the phaseout threshold for single persons—$75,000; § 24(b)(2). S gets a credit of $1,000; § 24(a).

(b) $80,000?

Now S is above the $75,000 phaseout threshold, so A must reduce the credit by $50 for each $1,000 by which her modified AGI exceeds $75,000. Here her MAGI exceeds the threshold by $5,000 ($80,000 – $75,000), and S must reduce her credit by $250 ($5,000/ $1,000 x $50), leaving her a credit of $750 ($1,000 – $250).

(c) $100,000?

S's MAGI exceeds the $75,000 threshold amount by $25,000. Her credit must be reduced by $1,250 ([$25,000/$1,000] x $50); § 24(b)(1). The reduction exceeds the amount of the credit, but the credit cannot be reduced below zero; id. S therefore gets no child tax credit for the year.

2. Would your answers in 1 differ if S was divorced and had waived her right to the dependency exemption for A so that the exemption can be claimed by A's father under § 152(e)?

Yes. In order to qualify for the child tax credit, the taxpayer must have a "qualifying child"; § 24(a). The term qualifying child has the same meaning as it does in the dependency-exemption provision, § 152(c). Although it appears that A would be S's qualified child under § 152(c), S has waived her right to the dependency exemption under § 152(e). Therefore, A is treated as the qualifying child of the non-custodial parent; see § 152(e)(1)(B), and S cannot claim the child tax credit for A.

This problem illustrates some of the stakes involved in divorce negotiations. The allocation of the dependency exemptions for the parties' children also determines which parent gets the child tax credit and also the Hope and Lifetime Learning Credits of § 25A.

B. THE CREDIT FOR HOUSEHOLD AND DEPENDENT CARE SERVICES

Code: § 21(a), (b), (c), (d) & (e). Note § 129.

Regulations: Prop. Treas. Reg §§ 1.21–1; 1.21–2; 1.21–4.

1. M, a single parent, is employed full time. M makes the following alternative expenditures for the care of her child, C, while M works. Which of the expenditures qualify as "employment-related expenses" under § 21?

(a) C is 3 years old. M sends C to nursery school. The nursery school provides meals and some educational services.

Section 21 allows a credit against tax for a portion of the taxpayer's "employment-related expenses"; § 21(a). Employment-related expenses include expenses for (1) household services and (2) expenses for the care of a "qualifying individual"; § 21(b)(2)(A). C is a qualifying individual because C is under age 13 and a dependent of M; § 21(b)(1)(A). Expenses for nursery school for a child below the level of kindergarten may be employment-related expenses; Prop. Treas. Reg. § 1.21–1(d)(5). Although the expenses are incurred for services provided outside M's home, that is permissible in the case of a dependent under age 13; § 21(b)(2)(B). Expenditures qualify as employment-related only if they are incurred to enable the taxpayer to be gainfully employed (§ 21(b)(2)(A)), which appears to be the case here. Although amounts paid for food and education generally are not considered to be for the care of a qualifying individual (Prop. Treas. Reg. § 1.21–1(d)(1)), here the providing of meals and education seems to be incidental to, and inseparable from, the care of the child, and therefore the entire expense should be deemed to be for care; see Prop. Treas. Reg. § 1.21–1(d)(12), Ex.

1 (lunches and snacks provided by pre-school incidental to child care and their cost can be included as employment-related expenses). The cost of C's nursery school qualifies as employment-related expense.

(b) C is 9 years old. Instead of taking C to day care, M sends her for a week to a summer day camp specializing in soccer.

The cost of the day camp should qualify as employment-related expense without allocation of part of the cost for soccer instruction; see Prop. Treas. Reg. § 1.21–1(d)(7) & (12), Ex. 4 (cost of day camp specializing in computers qualifies as employment-related expense).

(c) Would your answer in (b) differ if the soccer camp were an overnight camp?

The expenses of an overnight camp do not qualify; § 21(b)(2) (last sentence), which overrules Zoltan v. Commissioner, 79 T.C. 490 (1982) (allowing a deduction for summer camp that was "virtually as inexpensive as" alternative forms of day care.

(d) C is 9 years old. M pays her mother $5,000 a year to keep C after school and during days when school is not in session.

Payments to (some) relatives qualify, provided that the taxpayer (or her spouse) is not entitled to a dependency exemption for the relative; § 21(e)(6)(A). In this case, however, the mother has too much gross income to be M's dependent; see § 152(d)(1)(B). So, the amount paid the mother qualifies.

(e) Same as (d), except that M's 18–year-old daughter, D, keeps C. D is not M's dependent.

The payments to D do not qualify because D is M's child and has not attained age 19; § 21(e)(6)(B). In the case of payments to a child under age 19, it makes no difference that the child is not a dependent.

(f) Same as (d), except C is age 13.

The payments do not qualify because C is not a qualifying individual; see § 21(b)(1)(A) ("who has not attained age 13"). Of course, if C were physically or mentally incapable of caring for herself, the payments would qualify because of § 21(b)(1)(B).

(g) Same as (a). M is divorced and her former husband is entitled to the dependency exemption for C because M waived her right to the exemption under § 152(e)(2).

Even though M has waived her right to the dependency exemption for C, § 21(e)(5) makes C the qualifying child of the custodial parent, M, instead of the non-custodial parent. The expenses qualify.

2. N, who works full time, employs a nanny to care for her two children, ages 3 and 14. The nanny cooks meals and cleans the apartment in which N and the children reside. Do the amounts paid the nanny qualify as employment-related expenses?

Expenses for household services qualify if the services are provided in connection with the care of a qualifying individual; Prop. Treas. Reg. § 1.21–1(d)(3). The nanny performs household services in caring for the children, but must the expense be allocated between the children since one (the 14–year old) is not a qualifying individual? No, allocation is not required; see Prop. Treas. Reg. § 1.21–1(d)(12), Ex. 3.

3. A and B, husband and wife, provide a home for A's aged father, F, who is incapable of self-care. They pay a housekeeper to watch over F while they are at work. F is not their dependent because his income exceeds the limit of § 152(d)(1)(B). Do amounts paid the housekeeper qualify as employment-related expenses?

Yes. Even though F must be the dependent of A and B in order for his dependent-care expenses to qualify, the determination of whether F is their dependent is made without regard to the gross-income test of § 152(d)(1)(B); see § 21(b)(1)(B).

4. Same as 3, except that instead of caring for F in their home, A and B contribute to the cost of F's care at a nursing home for the last three months of the year. The rest of the year F resided with A and B. Do the amounts paid the nursing home qualify?

No. Expenses paid for out-of-home care do not qualify (except for a dependent under age 13) unless the qualifying individual regularly spends at least eight hours a day in the taxpayers' household; § 21(b)(2)(B)(ii).

5. M and F, husband and wife, file a joint return. They have two children, ages 3 and 6. In each of the following cases, determine the amount of their dependent-care credit.

(a) M is employed full time at a salary of $30,000 a year. F is self-employed and his income for the current year is $4,000. They paid a dependent-care center (which complies with all applicable laws) $5,000

to care for the children to enable them to work. The AGI on their joint return (see § 21(e)(2)) is $34,000.

Both of the children are qualifying individuals, so up to $6,000 of employment-related expenses can potentially be taken into account; § 21(c)(2). (The amount cannot, of course, exceed the $5,000 that they actually paid.) Furthermore, under the earned-income limit of § 21(d)(1), the expenses taken into account cannot exceed the earned income of the lesser-earning spouse—here $4,000. So the couple has $4,000 of qualifying employment-related expenses.

The credit is the product of the "applicable percentage" and the employment-related expenses. The applicable percentage is 35 percent, reduced by 1 percentage point for each $2,000 (or fraction thereof) by which the taxpayers' AGI exceeds $15,000. Here the couple's $34,000 AGI exceeds $15,000 by $19,000. Dividing $19,000 by $2,000 yields 8.5, which must be rounded up to 9. The applicable percentage is therefore 26 percent (35% less 9%). The credit is $1,040 (26% of $4,000).

(b) Same as (a), except that M was reimbursed for $3,000 of the child-care expense through her employer's cafeteria plan.

The couple can exclude the reimbursement from income under § 129(a), but they must reduce the § 21(c) ceiling on employment-related expenses by the amount of the reimbursement; § 21(c) (last sentence). Here the limit is reduced to $3,000 ($6,000 less $3,000). The $3,000 figure is less than the earned income of F, the lesser-earning spouse, so the credit is $780 (26% of $3,000).

(c) Same as (a), except that H earned $10,000 (and the couple's AGI was $40,000), and they paid the dependent-care center $7,000.

The § 21(c) limit ($6,000) is less than the earned income of the lesser-earning spouse ($10,000), so the credit is the applicable percentage of $6,000. The reduction in the applicable percentage is 13 percentage points ([$40,000 − $15,000]/$2,000) (remember to round up), and the applicable percentage is 22 percent (35% less 13%). The credit is therefore $1,320.

(d) M is employed full time at a salary of $30,000 a year. F is a full-time student throughout the year and has no earned income. The couple's AGI is $30,000. They pay the dependent-care center $5,000 to care for the children while M works and F attends school.

Now F, the lesser-earning spouse, has no actual earned income and is not *gainfully employed*. However, § 21(d)(2) treats a full-time student as being gainfully employed and having earned income of $500 ($250 if there is only one qualifying individual) for each month he was a student. Since F was a full-time student for 12 months, we pretend that he had earned income of $6,000 ($500/month x 12 months). That is more than the $5,000 of employment-related expenses that the couple paid, so we take $5,000 of the employment-related expenses into account.

The applicable percentage is 35 percent less 1 percentage point for each $2,000 by which their $30,000 AGI exceeds $15,000; § 21(a)(2). The reduction is 8 percent ([$30,000 − $15,000]/$2,000) (rounded up), the applicable percentage is 27 percent (35% − 8%), and the credit is $1,350 (27% of $5,000).

(e) Same as (d), except that both M and F are full-time students. Although they have investment income (and AGI) of $15,000, they have no actual earned income.

Now neither spouse is *actually* gainfully employed nor has *actual* earned income. The relief for full-time students does not help them because that applies to only one spouse for any one month; see § 21(d)(2) (last sentence). As a result, the other spouse will not have earned income or be gainfully employed for that month. In other words, at no time will *both* spouses be gainfully employed, and so their dependent-care expenses are not employment-related expenses.

C. THE EARNED-INCOME CREDIT

Code: § 32(a), (b), (c)(1) & (3) & (i). Note §§ 32(k); 152(c) & (e).

Ignore the effect of inflation adjustments in working the following problems.

1. A is the single parent of her 15–year old child who resides with her. (The child does not furnish over half her own support.) What is the amount of A's earned-income credit for 2007 if she has earned income of:

(a) $10,000?

A is a "qualifying individual" under § 32(c)(1)(A)(i) because her child is a "qualifying child" under § 152(c). A's earned income is below the "phaseout amount" (§ 32(b)(2)(A)), so her earned-income credit is the product of the "credit percentage" and the "earned income amount"; § 32(a)(2). Since A has one qualifying child, her credit percentage is 34 percent (§ 32(b)(1)(A)) and her earned-income amount is $6,330. A's credit is therefore $2,152 (34% of $6,330).

(b) $20,000?

Now A's earned income of $20,000 exceeds the "phaseout amount" at which A begins to lose a portion of the credit. Since A has one qualifying child, the phaseout percentage is 15.98 percent (§ 32(b)(1)(A)), and the phaseout begins at $11,610 (§ 32(b)(2)(A)). A's earned income exceeds the phaseout amount by $8,390 ($20,000 earned income less $11,610 phaseout amount). Her credit is reduced by

$1,341 (15.98 % of $8,390), leaving an allowable credit of $811 ($2,152 less $1,341). That's the equivalent of an additional 13–percent tax on the last $10,000 of income.

A's credit would be reduced to zero when her earned income reaches $25,077—i.e., 15.98 % of (25,077 − $11,610) = $2,152.

2. A (in 1) has earned income of $10,000 in 2007. She marries B, who has earned income of $10,000 and has a 12–year-old child who resides with him. How does their marriage affect the amount of their aggregate earned-income credits?

Before they marry, A and B would each be entitled to a credit of $2,152 (see problem 1(a)), or total credits of $4,304. After they marry, they have two qualifying children, so their credit percentage is 40 percent and their earned income amount is $8,890. Their credit before phaseout is therefore $3,556. The phaseout is $1,135—21.06 % of the excess of their combined earned incomes ($20,000) over the phaseout amount ($14,610); see § 32(b)(2)(B). Their credit is $2,421 ($3,556 − $1,135). So when A and B marry, their earned-income credit is reduced by $1,883—a stiff marriage penalty indeed.

3. What result in problem 1(b) if A also received $2,500 of dividend income during the year?

A's credit would be disallowed because she has "disqualified income" (the dividends) of more than $2,200; see § 32(i)(1) & (2)(A). So, the credit does not encourage saving.

4. What result in problem (1)(b) if the Service had disallowed A's earned income credit for 2005 and had determined that her claim of the credit was due to reckless disregard of the rules (but not due to fraud)?

Maybe in part because of its complexity, the EITC has been an invitation to tax fraud. A taxpayer who wrongly claims the credit because of recklessness or intentional disregard of rules and regulations cannot claim the credit again for two years; § 32(k)(1)(A) & (B)(ii). One who fraudulently claims the credit cannot get any further credit for ten years; § 32(k)(1)(A) & (B)(i). A taxpayer who has been denied the credit for the two-year or ten-year period cannot claim it again, even after the period expires, until the Service has received evidence that the taxpayer qualifies for the credit; § 32(k)(2). In our problem case, A recklessly disregarded the rules in 2005, and therefore she is disallowed the credit for 2006 and 2007. Whether she will be allowed the credit in future years depends upon her compliance with § 32(k)(2).

5. S is a single law student with no children. S's earned income for 2007 is $10,000. Is S eligible for the earned-income credit if he is:

(a) Age 23?

No, because an "eligible individual" who does not have a qualifying child must have attained age 25 (but not attained 65); § 32(c)(1)(A)(ii)(II).

(b) Age 26?

S could qualify for the credit if his principal place of abode is in the United States and he is not the dependent of another; see § 32(c)(1)(A)(ii). (S would not be disqualified under § 32(c)(1)(B) because he is too old to be the qualifying child of another; see § 152(c)(1)(C) & (c)(3).)

D. EDUCATION CREDITS

See Chapter 37.

Section J

TIMING OF INCOME AND DEDUCTIONS

Chapter 42

"ANNUAL" vs. "TRANSACTIONAL" ACCOUNTING

A. NET OPERATING LOSSES

Code: § 172(a), (b)(1)(A), (2) & (3), (c), (d)(1), (2), (3) & (4).

1. Explain the rationale for the net operating loss (NOL) deduction.

The idea underlying the NOL rules of § 172 is that deductions in excess of gross income in a particular year should be allowed to offset the taxpayer's income in years preceding or following the loss year. In effect, § 172 is an acknowledgment that the computation of income on an annual basis is somewhat arbitrary and does not necessarily measure long-run income accurately. Suppose, e.g., that the tax rate is a flat 40 percent. Taxpayer A has income of $100,000 in year 1 and a loss of $50,000 in year 2. B has income of $25,000 in each year. If the statute provided no relief for A, A would pay $40,000 in tax and B $20,000, even though over the two years their total incomes were identical. Section 172 provides relief in this situation by allowing the loss in one year to be carried backward or forward to offset income in preceding or succeeding years.

2. Explain the difference between the NOL and the NOL deduction.

The NOL is the excess of deductions over gross income for the loss year; § 172(c). The NOL deduction is allowed in the year(s) to which the NOL is carried back or forward from the loss year; § 172(a). If, for example, in 2008 T has a $50,000 NOL (i.e., $50,000 of deductions in excess of gross income), the NOL can be carried back to the two preceding years and forward for as many as twenty years; § 172(b)(1). The NOL would generally first be carried to 2006, where T would be entitled to a NOL deduction to offset that year's taxable income, with any amount of the carryback not used in that year carried to 2007, and then to 2009, etc., until the NOL carryover is exhausted.

3. L Corp. has a net operating loss (NOL) of $250,000 in year 3. Apart from the effect of the NOL deduction, it has taxable income of $100,000 for year 1, 50,000 for year 2, and $120,000 for year 4. How does the year–3 NOL affect L's taxable income for years 1, 2 and 4?

The NOL for the loss year (year 3) is a NOL carryback to the two years preceding the loss year and a NOL carryover to each of the twenty years following the loss year; § 172(b)(1)(A). The NOL is first carried to the earliest of the years to which it may be carried—year 1 in this case; § 172(b)(2). In year 1, the NOL deduction offsets the $100,000 of taxable income, and L is entitled to an immediate refund of the tax it paid for year 1. The amount of the NOL that is carried to each of the other years is the excess of the NOL over the sum of the taxable income for each of the prior years to which the loss was carried; id. So, $150,000 ($250,000 loss less $100,000 taxable income offset for year 1) of the NOL can be carried forward to year 2, where it reduces year–2 taxable income to zero and entitles L to a refund of the year–2 tax. That leaves $100,000 ($250,000 loss less $150,000 of taxable income offset in years 1 and 2) of the NOL to carry to year 4, where it reduces year 4 taxable income to $20,000.

4. M, an individual sole proprietor, has $100,000 of business gross income, $40,000 of non-business gross income, $150,000 of business deductions, $30,000 of non-business deductions (other than her personal exemption), and a $2,000 personal exemption. Determine M's NOL for the year.

M's NOL is the excess of allowable deductions over gross income. M's deductions ($182,000) exceed her gross income ($140,000) by $42,000. That is not the amount of M's NOL, however, as the NOL must be computed with the modifications prescribed by § 172(d). Section 172(d)(3) requires that the personal-exemption deduction be disregarded. The modification of § 172(d)(4) does not apply because non-business deductions do not exceed non-business income. So, disregarding the personal-exemption deduction, M's deductions exceed her gross income by $40,000. That is her NOL.

5. Same as 4, except that M had $30,000 of non-business gross income and $40,000 of non-business deductions (other than the personal exemption).

Now M's deductions ($192,000) exceed her gross income ($130,000) by $62,000. The personal exemption is not allowable in computing the NOL; § 172(d)(3). The non-business deductions (other than the personal exemption) ($40,000) are allowable only to the extent of the non-business income ($30,000). So, M's deductions for NOL purposes total $180,000 ($150,000 business deductions, plus $30,000 non-business deductions); her gross income is $130,000; and her NOL is $50,000.

6. Late in the current year, J, an individual who uses the cash method, seeks your advice. J anticipates that her business expenses will considerably exceed her business gross income for the year. J expects to have $20,000 of non-business ordinary income (from dividends and interest) and has paid $30,000 of non-business expenses. J could pay another $10,000 of non-business expenses before the end of the year. Would you advise J to do so, or should she wait until next year to pay the remaining non-business expenses?

J should wait until the following year to pay the remaining non-business expenses. It appears that J will have a NOL for this year because her business expenses exceed her business gross income. The payment of any additional non-business expenses will not reduce this year's tax because J is going to have a loss this year even without any additional deductions. Nor will payment of additional non-business expenses increase the NOL. J has already paid non-business expenses in an amount exceeding her expected non-business income for the year, and, in computing the NOL, non-business deductions in excess of non-business income are disregarded; § 172(d)(4). So the possible tax benefit of any additional payment of non-business expenses will be wasted. If J pays the expenses next year, the deduction may produce a tax benefit.

7. Individual A, a self-employed person, has gross income and deductions as follows:

Gross income	
Ordinary business income	$200,000
Dividends	5,000
Alimony	10,000
Capital gain on sale of investment property	10,000
Deductions	
Business deductions	$250,000
Capital loss on sale of investment property	30,000
State income taxes	15,000
Interest	20,000
Personal exemption	2,000

Both the capital gain and the capital loss are long-term. The interest was paid on indebtedness incurred by A to purchase her principal residence. A's standard deduction would be $3,000.

Determine A's taxable income and NOL for the year.

A has gross income of $225,000 (the sum of the business income, dividends, alimony and capital gain). A's above-the-line deductions comprise the $250,000 of business deductions and $13,000 of capital loss (losses to the extent of gains, plus $3,000) for a total of $263,000. A's AGI is negative $38,000 ($225,000 gross income less $263,000 of above-the-line deductions). Itemized deductions and the personal exemption total $37,000 ($15,000 of state income taxes, plus $20,000 of qualified residence interest, plus $2,000 personal exemption). Taxable income is therefore negative $75,000.

The NOL is the excess of deductions over gross income, but it must be computed with the modifications required by § 172(d); § 172(c). Since A is a non-corporate taxpayer, the capital losses are deductible only to the extent of capital gains; § 172(d)(2)(A). So, the $3,000 of capital loss deducted against ordinary income must be added back to taxable income. No personal-exemption deduction is allowed; § 172(d)(3). The $2,000 personal exemption must accordingly be added back to taxable income. Finally, A's non-business deductions are allowable only to the extent of her non-business income; § 172(d)(4). In determining the non-business deductions, the personal exemption is disregarded; § 172(d)(4)(B). A thus has non-business deductions of $45,000 ($10,000 capital loss, plus $15,000 state income tax, plus $20,000 interest). Non-business income is $25,000 ($5,000 of dividends, plus $10,000 of alimony, plus $10,000 capital gain). The $20,000 excess of non-business deductions over non-business income must be added back to taxable income in computing the NOL. The NOL is $50,000:

Taxable income		($75,000)
Add:		
Capital loss	$ 3,000	
Exemption	2,000	
Non-business deductions	20,000	
		25,000
Net operating loss		($50,000)

Although computation of the capital-loss carryover is not called for by the problem, you may be interested in knowing that A is also entitled to a $20,000 long-term-capital-loss carryover under § 1212(b). Since both the capital gain and the capital loss are long-term, A has a net long-term capital loss of $20,000 ($30,000 LTCL less $10,000 LTCG); § 1222(8). There are no short-term transactions. (No make-believe capital gain is created under § 1212(b)(2)(A) because "adjusted taxable income" (defined in § 1212(b)(2)(B)) is less than zero.) The LTCL carryover is $20,000 ($20,000 NLTCL less zero NSTCG).

B. THE TAX-BENEFIT RULE

Code: § 111.

Regulation: § 1.111–1(a).

Cases: Continental Illinois Nat'l Bank and Trust Co. v. Commissioner, 69 T.C. 357 (1977) (Acq.);
Hillsboro Nat'l Bank v. Commissioner, 460 U.S. 370 (1983).

1. In year 1, T, a single person, would have been entitled to a $3,000 standard deduction, but because T had $15,000 of itemized deductions T elected to itemize. Included in the $15,000 of itemized deductions was $5,000 of state income tax that had been withheld from T's salary. In year 2, T filed a state income-tax return for year 1 and received a $2,000 refund. T's year–1 taxable income was $50,000. Must T include the $2,000 refund in gross income?

Yes, T must include the reimbursement in gross income. T deducted the $2,000 (as part of the $5,000 of state income tax) in year 1, but recovered it in year 2. T therefore obtained the benefit of a deduction for an expense whose burden T ultimately did not bear. We don't require T to disgorge the deduction by amending her year–1 return, but she must include the $2,000 in year–2 income to "make up" for the "excess" deduction in year 1. This is an application of the inclusionary tax-benefit rule, which requires the taxpayer to include in income the recovery of an amount deducted in a prior year. The rationale for the rule has been explained thusly:

> Income tax liability must be determined for annual periods on the basis of facts as they existed in each period. When recovery or some other event which is inconsistent with what has been done in the past occurs, adjustment must be made in reporting income for the year in which the change occurs.

Estate of Block v. Commissioner, 39 B.T.A. 338, 341 (1939), aff'd sub nom., Union Trust Co. v. Commissioner, 111 F.2d 60 (7th Cir.). The tax-benefit rule originated in the courts, though § 111 implicitly approves the rule.

Requiring T to include the $2,000 in year–2 income puts T in roughly the same tax position she would have been in if her employer had withheld only the amount of state income tax that T actually owed ($3,000), in which case her year–1 deduction would have been $2,000 smaller, but she would not have the "make-up" inclusion in year–2 gross income.

What if T was in a higher tax bracket in year 2 than in year 1? The year–2 inclusion would cost the taxpayer more in tax than the year–1 deduction saved. Nevertheless, it is clear that the recovery is taxed at the rates applicable to the year of recovery rather than those for the year in which the deduction was taken; see Alice Phelan Sullivan Corp. v. United States, 381 F.2d 399 (Ct. Cl. 1967).

2. Same as 1, except that in year 1 T had total itemized deductions of only $4,000, of which $3,000 was state income tax withheld from T's salary. Must the $2,000 refund for year 1 be included in T's year–2 gross income?

T must include only $1,000 in gross income. Although T deducted $3,000 of state income tax in year 1, only $1,000 of that deduction produced a tax benefit. That is, if T had paid $1,000 less in state tax, her itemized deductions would have been only $3,000, and she would have taken the $3,000 standard deduction. So, only that incremental $1,000 lowered T's year–1 taxable income, and only that amount is includable in year–2 gross income. This is an aspect of the exclusionary tax-benefit rule. That is, even though an amount is tentatively includable under the inclusionary tax-benefit rule, the amount is finally includable in gross income only if its deduction in the earlier year reduced the amount of tax owed in that year; see § 111(a) & (b)(4).

3. In year 1, D donated a building with a value of $100,000 to University City for use as a government building and properly deducted the $100,000 as a charitable contribution under § 170. In year 2, the City decided that it could not afford to maintain the building and, though it had no legal obligation to do so, re-conveyed the building, then valued at $90,000, to D. D had ample income to offset the $100,000 deduction. Must D include some amount in gross income in year 2? If so, how much?

D must include either $90,000 (the value of the property when recovered) or $100,000 (the amount for which a deduction was taken) in gross income in year 2. This is an application of the tax-benefit rule. D deducted the $100,000 contribution in year 1. If the charity had returned the property in year 1, surely no charitable deduction would have been allowed for that year. The return of the building is fundamentally inconsistent with the taking of a charitable deduction.

As to how much should be included in income, the Commissioner conceded in Rosen v. Commissioner, 71 T.C. 226 (1978), that only the value of the property at the time it was returned should be included. In view of the Commissioner's concession, Judge Raum, writing for the Tax Court, "did not consider the possible contention that proper application of the tax benefit rule would require a complete reversal of the deduction in the earlier year by including in income of the later year the full amount previously deducted upon complete restoration of the identical property which gave rise to the deduction"; id. at 234, n. 16.

D might contend that the tax-benefit rule has no application where the return of the property was a gift, and, since the City had no legal obligation to return the property, it made a gift to him. A similar contention was rejected in *Rosen*, the court noting that "the purpose of the reconveyances was a desire by the donees to reverse the original gift transactions, and that the reconveyances without consideration would not have been made to petitioners were it not for the fact that they were the original donors of the property"; id. at 233.

4. How would your answer in (3) change if, because of the § 170(b) limits on the charitable-contribution deduction, D had been able to deduct only $30,000 of the contribution in year 1 (and carried over the balance to year 2)?

D should include in year 2 only the $30,000 that was deducted with tax benefit in year 1; Rev. Rul. 54–566, 1954–2 C.B. 96 (returned charitable contribution includable in income to the extent previously taken as a deduction). No deduction is allowable in year 2 or any future year on account of the year–1 contribution.

5. In year 1, L lent $100,000 to B, who was not related to L. In year 2, before repaying any of the principal of the indebtedness, B obtained a discharge in bankruptcy, and L treated the $100,000 as a worthless non-business bad debt (i.e., as a short-term capital loss under § 166(d)). (This was L's only capital-gain or capital-loss transaction in year 2.) In year 3, B inherited some money and, though B had no legal obligation to do so, repaid $40,000 of the indebtedness. Must L include the $40,000 in gross income if, because of the limits on the deductibility of capital losses imposed by § 1211(b), L had been able to deduct only $3,000 of the loss (in year 2) by the time the repayment occurred? (L had positive taxable income in year 2.)

First, let's think about L's tax situation in year 2. Since L had no other capital gains or losses in that year, he deducted $3,000 of capital loss against ordinary income (§ 1211(b)) and carried over $97,000 of short-term capital loss to year 3—i.e., since L had no long-term transactions, the short-term-capital-loss carryover is equal to the net short-term capital loss, which is the excess of the short-term capital loss ($100,000) over the short-term capital gain ($3,000 because of § 1212(b)(2)(A)).

Two issues arise in year 3: (1) Is there a sufficient nexus between the bad-debt deduction and the subsequent repayment to invoke the tax-benefit rule? (2) If the recovery is includable in income, how much should be included?

As to the first issue, L can argue that the debt ceased to exist when it was discharged in bankruptcy, and that B's voluntary payment was a gift. As noted above, however, the gift exclusion does not apply where no payment would have been made to L but for the fact that L was the creditor whose debt was discharged; e.g., Rosen v. Commissioner, 71 T.C. 226, 233 (1978); see also, e.g., Bear Mill Mfg. Co. v. Commissioner, 15 T.C. 703 (1950) (voluntary payment received from shareholder of discharged debtor treated as payment on debt). So, L has a partial recovery of the discharged debt.

The $40,000 should be excluded under the exclusionary tax-benefit rule. L would recompute his year–2 taxable income and capital-loss carryover as if he had only $60,000 of capital loss in that year. Assuming that L had no other capital losses for year 2, his year–2 capital-loss deduction remains $3,000, and his capital-loss carryover to year 3 would be $57,000 ($60,000 – $3,000).

6. In year 1, L lent $100,000 to B Corp. In year 2, before repaying any of the principal of the indebtedness, B Corp. filed a petition under Chapter 11 of the Bankruptcy Act. In the bankruptcy proceeding, L received 1,000 shares of B Corp. stock in satisfaction of the indebtedness. The stock had a value of $1,000, and L deducted $99,000 as a loss with full tax benefit. Several years later, the B Corp. stock had appreciated in value to $120,000, at which point L gave the shares to State University and properly claimed a $120,000 charitable deduction for the gift. Does L have gross income in the year of the gift as a result of these events?

No. The exchange of the indebtedness for the stock closed out the debtor-creditor transaction. It is as if L received $1,000 cash and invested the cash in B Corp. stock. So, the appreciation in the value of the stock cannot be related back to the indebtedness, and the tax-benefit rule does not apply; Continental Illinois Nat'l Bank & Trust Co. v. Commissioner, 69 T.C. 357 (Acq.).

7. P purchased a building (held for investment) for $100,000, properly deducted $30,000 of straight-line depreciation, and then sold the building for $120,000. P did not have sufficient income to absorb the $30,000 of depreciation deductions and therefore got no tax benefit from the deductions. What result to P on the sale?

When P sells the property for a $50,000 gain ($120,000 amount realized less $70,000 adjusted basis), the entire gain is taxable, even though $30,000 of the gain just "makes up" for depreciation deductions for which P obtained no tax benefit. The exclusionary tax-benefit rule generally does not apply to depreciation. Section 1016(a)(2) requires that the taxpayer reduce the basis of the property by the amount of depreciation "allowed * * * and * * * resulting * * * in a reduction for any taxable year of the taxpayer's taxes * * * but not less than the amount allowable * * *." P's only relief for the depreciation deduction that is wasted in a loss year is the net-operating-loss deduction of § 172.

8. Would your answer in 7 differ if P had mistakenly deducted $40,000 of depreciation instead of the $30,000 that was properly allowable?

Yes, where the amount of depreciation allowed (i.e., actually allowed as a deduction) exceeds the amount allowable (i.e., the amount that *should* have been deducted under the statute), the allowed depreciation reduces adjusted basis only to the extent that it resulted in a reduction of the taxpayer's taxes. P's "extra" $10,000 of depreciation did not reduce his taxes, and so that amount does not reduce his basis. As pointed out above, however, the basis is always reduced by the amount of depreciation properly allowable ($30,000 in this case) regardless of whether the deduction reduced the taxpayer's tax. So, the answer here is the same as in 7: P recognizes $50,000 of gain.

9. In year 1, T was injured in an automobile accident caused by the negligence of N. T paid $15,000 of medical expenses in year 1, of which only $10,000 was deductible (because of the 7.5–percent floor of § 213(a)). In year 2, T received a settlement from N that included reimbursement for the $15,000 of year–1 medical expenses. T had positive taxable income in year 1. Must T include the $15,000 reimbursement in gross income for year 2?

T must include only the $10,000 which was actually deducted in year 1. This is the rule of § 104(a), which requires inclusion of medical-expense recoveries but only to the extent of amounts not exceeding "deductions allowed under § 213" for a prior year. Only $10,000 was allowed in year 1, and only that amount is includable in year 2. The year–2 inclusion just makes up for the year–1 deduction for an expense that, in the actual working out of events, T did not bear.

10. Would your answer in 9 differ if, because of very large itemized deductions, T had not had sufficient year–1 income to absorb the $10,000 medical-expense deduction?

The issue in this case is whether the exclusionary tax-benefit rule overrides the explicit inclusionary rule of § 104(a). It should. There's no reason to tax the recovery unless its receipt in the earlier year produced a tax benefit, which in this case it did not.

C. SECTION 1341

Code: § 1341(a).

Regulation: § 1.1341–1(b)(2), (c), (d)(2)(iii), (d)(4)(ii), (h).

Case: Van Cleave v. United States, 718 F.2d 193 (6th Cir. 1983).

1. In year 1, B, a beneficiary of a trust, received a cash distribution of $50,000 from the trust and included that amount in gross income. In year 2, the trustee discovered a miscalculation in the amount to which B was entitled in year 1 and commenced an action to recover the $20,000 excess distribution. B restored the $20,000 to the trust in year 3. Is B entitled to use § 1341 in the calculation of her year–3 tax liability?

Yes. B included the income in gross income in year 1 because it appeared that she had an unrestricted right to the item, B is entitled to deduct the repayment in year 3 because it was established after the close of year 1 that B did not have an unrestricted right to the funds, and the repayment exceeds $3,000; § 1341(a)(1)–(3); Prince v. United States, 610 F.2d 350 (5th Cir. 1980).

2. In year 1, E embezzled $750,000 from his employer. E's defalcation was discovered in year 3, he promptly filed an amended return for year 1, including the $750,000 in gross income, and he repaid $100,000 to the employer later that year. Can E invoke § 1341 in calculating his year–3 tax liability?

No. The repayment entitles E to a deduction for a loss in a transaction entered into for profit under § 165(a) and (c)(2); Rev. Rul. 65–254, 1965–2 C.B. 50. (The loss is not treated as a business loss, so it cannot contribute to a net operating loss because, in computing the NOL, non-business deductions are allowable only to the extent of non-business income.) E cannot use § 1341 because an embezzler does not have "*any* right to the funds, much less 'an unrestricted right' to them"; McKinney v. United States, 574 F.2d 1240, 1243 (5th Cir. 1978).

3. In year 1, S sold some stock in a closely held corporation and reported a long-term capital gain of $100,000 on the sale (S's only capital-gain or -loss transaction for year 1). In year 3, P, the purchaser of the stock, brought an action against S for negligent misrepresentation in the sale. Although continuing to deny any wrongdoing, S settled the suit in year 4 by refunding to P $40,000 of the purchase price. Under Arrowsmith v. Commissioner, 344 U.S. 6 (1952), the $40,000 payment must be treated as a capital loss in year 4. S has no capital gains in year 4.

(a) May S use § 1341 to compute his year–4 tax liability?

Yes; Rev. Rul. 78–25, 1978–1 C.B. 270.   S meets the requirements of § 1341(a)(1)–(3). (Section 1341(a)(3) is satisfied, though S can deduct only $3,000 of the loss in year 4 because of the limits on capital losses imposed by § 1211(b); eligibility for relief under § 1341 is determined without regard to § 1211; Treas. Reg. § 1.1341–1(c).)

(b) Assume that at all times the tax rate is 15 percent for capital gains and 40 percent for ordinary income.   How much tax does S save in year 4 by using § 1341?

If the deduction is taken for year 4, the year–4 tax would be reduced by $1,200, as $3,000 of the capital loss could be applied to offset ordinary income taxable at 40 percent; see § 1211(b). If the $40,000 loss had occurred in year 1, the entire $40,000 would be allowable, as the loss would have been less than the capital gain. Therefore, the $40,000 is excluded from year–1 income in computing the reduction in tax for year 1; Treas. Reg. § 1.1341–1(d)(2)(iii). The exclusion reduces the amount of the capital gain taxable at a 15–percent rate, which reduces year–1 tax by $6,000. (The exclusion would reduce year–1 AGI and increase year–4 AGI. Those changes might affect the amount of other deductions; if so, those changes must be taken into account in computing the tax; Treas. Reg. § 1.1341–1(d)(4)(ii). In this problem, however, let's assume that no other deductions are affected by the recomputations.) So, the § 1341 computation saves S $4,800 in tax.

S cannot, of course, carry the year–4 capital loss forward under § 1212(b) because he has been given the benefit of that loss in the recomputation for year 1; Treas. Reg. § 1.1341–1(b)(2).

(c) Suppose that S also paid $10,000 in legal fees in resisting P's claim.   Does § 1341 apply to that payment?

The fees probably are deductible only as a capital loss under Arrowsmith v. Commissioner, 334 U.S. 6 (1952) (discussed in Chapter 30) since legal fees paid in connection with the sale of the stock would reduce the amount realized on the sale and hence reduce the capital gain. However, § 1341 does not apply to the fees; Treas. Reg. § 1341–1(h).

4. E, an executive of X, has an employment contract that requires E to repay to X any amounts of compensation that the Commissioner determines to be "unreasonable" and hence non-deductible by X under § 162(a). In year 3, E is required under this provision to repay to X $40,000 of the compensation received in year 1. Apart from any effect of the repayment, E's taxable income is $120,000 for year 1 and $90,000 for year 3. The (hypothetical) tax rates applicable to both years provide that the tax is 20% on the first $100,000 of taxable income and 30% on income exceeding $100,000. What result to E under § 1341?

This problem is based upon Van Cleave v. United States, 718 F.2d 193 (6th Cir. 1983). In *Van Cleave*, the Government argued that § 1341 did not apply because the taxpayer "had more than an *appearance* of an unrestricted right to the excess compensation" and the right became restricted only when the Service audited the corporation's return; 718 F.2d at 196–97. The Sixth Circuit rejected that argument and held § 1341 applicable even though the restriction on the taxpayer's right to the income did not arise until a subsequent year. So, E can invoke § 1341.

Without the year–3 deduction, the year–3 tax would be $18,000. If we assume that excluding the $40,000 in year 1 would reduce taxable income in that year to $80,000, the savings would be $10,000 ($26,000 less $16,000). Therefore, E's tax liability for year 3 is $8,000 ($18,000 less $10,000).

Chapter 43

AN INTRODUCTION TO
TAX ACCOUNTING

A. INTRODUCTION

Code: §§ 446(a), (b), (c) & (d). Note § 6001.

Regulation: §1.446–1(a), (b), (c)(1)(i) & (ii)(A).

Case: Thor Power Tool Co. v. Commissioner, 439 U.S. 522 (1979).

1. What is a method of accounting?

The taxpayer's method of accounting determines *when* an item of income or deduction is taken into account. Section 446(a) prescribes generally that taxable income be computed under the method of accounting used by the taxpayer in keeping his books. In many instances, however, the tax law specifies the treatment of particular items in a manner that differs from the way in which the taxpayer's books reflect such items (e.g., depreciation, prepaid income and expense, the installment method of § 453, etc.), and so departures from book income are common.

The taxpayer must maintain adequate "accounting records" to enable him to file a correct return; Treas. Reg. § 1.446–1(a)(4). Accounting records include the taxpayer's regular books of account and such other records and data as necessary to support the entries on the books and return; id. The accounting records also include a reconciliation of any differences between the taxpayer's books and return; id.

The principal overall methods of accounting are the cash method and an accrual method; § 446(c). But the term method of accounting includes not only these overall methods but also the accounting treatment of any item, such as depreciation, net operating losses, etc.; Treas. Reg. § 1.446–1(a)(1).

The taxpayer's methods of accounting must be used consistently from year to year. Once adopted, a method of accounting generally cannot be changed without the Commissioner's assent; § 446(e). As a condition to permitting the change, the Commissioner may require transitional adjustments to prevent the omission or double-counting of items of income or deduction; see § 481(a).

Keep in mind that no method of accounting is acceptable unless, *in the opinion of the Commissioner*, it clearly reflects income; Treas. Reg. § 1.446–1(a)(2), (b)(1), (c)(1)(ii)(C); Thor Power Tool Co. v. Commissioner, 439 U.S. 522, 531–32 (1979). When a taxpayer's accounting method is challenged, the issue is not whether the method reflects income clearly but whether the Commissioner's insistence upon a different method was an abuse of discretion.

2. What is *your* method of accounting?

You may be wondering what your method of accounting is, especially since you probably do not maintain a formal set of books. The regulations should put you at ease: If your sole source of income is wages, you need not keep formal books in order to have a method of accounting, as tax returns or other records may be sufficient to establish the use of a method of accounting; Treas. Reg. § 1.446–1(b)(2).

A taxpayer filing her first return may adopt any permissible method of accounting (Treas. Reg. § 1.446–1(e)(1)), but most of us adopted the cash method without even realizing that we were doing so. That's why wage-earners almost invariably use the cash method.

One who operates a separate and distinct business may adopt any permissible method of accounting when reporting income from the business for the first time; Treas. Reg. § 1.446–1(e)(2). So, even one using the cash method could use an accrual method for a new business; see Treas. Reg. § 1.446–1(c)(1)(iv)(b).

3. Describe in general terms when income is includable and deductions allowable under the cash method.

Under the cash method, a taxpayer usually includes items in income when actually or constructively received in the form of cash or property; Treas. Reg. §§ 1.446–1(c)(1)(i); 1.451–1(a). (Constructive receipt occurs whenever income is credited to the taxpayer's account, set apart for her, or otherwise made available so that she could draw upon it at any time, provided that the taxpayer's control of the receipt is not subject to any substantial limitations or restrictions; Treas. Reg. § 1.451–2(a).)

A cash-method taxpayer generally deducts expenses when paid; Treas. Reg. §§ 1.446–1(c)(1); 1.461–1(a)(1). Of course, even a cash-method taxpayer generally cannot deduct capital expenditures in the year made; Treas. Reg.

§§ 1.446–1(a)(4)(ii); 1.461–1(a)(1). Some deductions (e.g., depreciation) are allowable even though they do not involve any current expenditure of cash; id.

4. Describe in general terms when income is includable and deductions allowable under an accrual method.

Under an accrual method, the taxpayer generally takes income into account when all the events have occurred that fix the taxpayer's right to the income and when the amount of the income can be ascertained with reasonable accuracy (the "all-events" test); Treas. Reg. §§ 1.446–1(c)(1)(ii); 1.451–1(a).

Accrual-method taxpayers take deductions when (1) all the events have occurred that fix the fact of liability, (2) the amount of the liability can be ascertained with reasonable accuracy, and (3) economic performance has occurred with respect to the liability; Treas. Reg. §§ 1.446–1(c)(1)(ii); 1.461–1(a)(2).

Suppose, for example, that December 31, year 1, falls in the middle of an employee's pay period, so that on December 31 the employer owes its employee $1,000 for services that the employee performed before the end of the year. The $1,000 is paid at the end of the pay period in January, year 2. Both the employee and the employer use the calendar year as their taxable year and use an accrual method of accounting. The employee must include the $1,000 in income for year 1 because by the end of the year the employee had performed the services that fixed her right to income and the amount of the income can be ascertained with reasonable accuracy. The employer, for whom the $1,000 is a business expense, takes the deduction in year 1 because by December 31 the employee's performance of services has fixed the employer's liability, the amount of the liability is determinable with reasonable accuracy, and economic performance (the employee's performing services for the employer—see § 461(h)(2)(A)(i)) has occurred.

Notice that the statute speaks of "the" cash method and "an" accrual method. That signifies that there may be more than one acceptable method for computing income under the accrual method; see, e.g., Treas. Reg. § 1.446–1(c)(1)(ii)(C).

5. Can a taxpayer use the cash method for one business and an accrual method for another?

Yes; if the taxpayer keeps a separate and complete set of books for each business, she may use the cash method in one business (e.g., a personal-service business) and an accrual method in the other (e.g., a shop that sells merchandise) § 446(d); Treas. Reg. § 1.446–1(d)(1).

Indeed, even where an accrual method is used in accounting for purchases and sales of inventory, the cash method can be used for other items in the same business; Treas. Reg. § 1.446–1(c)(1)(iv). Of course, a taxpayer must use the same method of accounting for items of income and deduction. For example, a cash-method taxpayer cannot report gross income using the cash method while using the accrual method for deductions; Treas. Reg. § 1.446–1(c)(1)(iv)(a).

As this answer suggests, accounting methods are attributes of activities, not of taxpayers; yet it is permissible (and common) to refer to "cash-method taxpayers" or "accrual-method taxpayers" so long as one remembers that a taxpayer can adopt different accounting methods for different businesses. A reference to a "cash-method taxpayer" or an "accrual-method taxpayer" should be understood as referring to a taxpayer who uses that method in accounting for the items under discussion.

6. Explain generally when use of the accrual method is required.

As discussed above, a taxpayer starting a new business is generally free to adopt either the cash method or an accrual method, if the taxpayer's books are kept in the same way; § 446. For our purposes, the most important exception to this rule applies whenever the production, purchase or sale of merchandise is an income-producing factor. In such cases, inventory must be accounted for, and an accrual method generally must be used for purchases and sales of the inventory; Treas. Reg. § 1.446–1(c)(2)(i).

Section 448 denies the use of the cash method to most C corporations with gross receipts of more than $5 million per year, and § 447 requires use of the accrual method by C corporations engaged in farming if their annual gross receipts are over $1 million ($25 million in the case of a "family corporation"). Those provisions are beyond our scope.

7. For tax purposes, T Corporation uses a method of accounting that is acceptable in the preparation of its financial statements under generally accepted accounting principles. Does it follow that the method is acceptable for tax purposes?

No. Although the regulations provide that a method of accounting that comports with generally accepted accounting principles will ordinarily be regarded as clearly reflecting income (Treas. Reg. § 1.446–1(a)(2)), the Supreme Court has rejected the notion that generally accepted accounting principles presumptively reflect income clearly; see Thor Power Tool Co. v. Commissioner, 439 U.S. 522, 540–44 (1979). The Court stressed the "vastly different" objectives of tax and financial accounting:

> The primary goal of financial accounting is to provide useful information to management, shareholders, creditors, and others properly interested; the major responsibility of the accountant is to protect these parties from being misled. The primary goal of the income tax system, in contrast, is the equitable collection of revenue; the major responsibility of the Internal Revenue Service is to protect the public fisc. Consistently with its goals and responsibilities, financial accounting has

as its foundation the principle of conservatism, with its corollary that "possible errors in measurement [should] be in the direction of understatement rather than overstatement of net income and net assets." In view of the Treasury's markedly different goals and responsibilities, understatement of income is not destined to be its guiding light. Given this diversity, even contrariety, of objectives, any presumptive equivalency between tax and financial accounting would be unacceptable.

Id. at 542–43. So, the Commissioner has broad power to reject a method of accounting as not clearly reflecting income even when that method bears the imprimatur of generally accepted accounting principles. Remember: No method of accounting is acceptable unless, *in the opinion of the Commissioner*, it clearly reflects income. When the Commissioner challenges a taxpayer's accounting method, the issue is not whether the method reflects income clearly but whether the Commissioner's rejection of the method was an abuse of discretion.

Incidentally, neither is the Commissioner bound by accounting rules imposed by regulatory agencies; e.g., Old Colony R.R. Co. v. Commissioner, 284 U.S. 552, 562 (1932).

B. THE CASH METHOD OF ACCOUNTING

Code: §§ 451(a); 461(a), (g); 409A.

Regulations: §§ 1.446–1(c)(1)(i); 1.451–1(a); 1.451–2; 1.461–1(a); 1.83–3(e); 1.263(a)–4(d)(3) & (f)(1).

1. In year 1, L performed legal services for C and billed C for $1,000, which will be deductible as a business expense by C. Both C and L are calendar-year, cash-method taxpayers. In each of the following cases, determine when C is entitled to a deduction and when L has gross income.

(a) C pays L in cash in year 2.

L has income, and C a deduction, in year 2 when cash is received and paid; Treas. Reg. §§ 1.451–1(a); 1.461–1(a)(1). Although income can be received in the form of property, and C's enforceable promise to pay is property (in the property-law sense), C's promise to pay is not "property" for tax purposes so as to make L taxable in year 1; see Treas. Reg. § 1.83–3(e) ("unfunded and unsecured promise to pay money or property in the future" not "property" for purposes of § 83). To treat C's promise as property would effectively abolish the distinction between the cash and accrual methods in this context.

(b) C gives L a check for the $1,000 on December 31, year 1. L deposits the check on January 4, year 2. The check clears C's bank in due course.

L has year–1 income and C a year–1 deduction. The check is considered payment when received; see Kahler v. Commissioner, 18 T.C. 31 (1952) (check includable in year received even though received after 5 p.m. on December 31st). The mailing of a check is considered payment if the check clears the payor's bank in due course; see, e.g., Estate of Witt v. Fahs, 160 F.Supp. 521 (S.D. Fla. 1956).

(c) Same as (b), except that C died on January 1, year 2. (Although C's estate could have challenged the bank's payment of the check, it did not.)

L still has year–1 income, and C the year–1 deduction, because the check cleared in due course; see, e.g., Commissioner v. Bradley, 56 F.2d 728 (6th Cir. 1932).

(d) Same as (b), except that C asked L to hold the check until January because C was short of funds, and L agreed. In January, L deposited the check and it cleared C's bank in due course.

L has income (and C a deduction) only in year 2; see Fischer v. Commissioner, 14 T.C. 792 (1950). In effect, the oral agreement restricting the deposit of the check causes it to be treated as if it were a non-negotiable promissory note.

(e) C mails the check to L on December 31; L receives it on January 4. L promptly deposits the check and it clears in due course.

C gets a year–1 deduction, as mailing the check is treated as payment under the above authorities. L has income in year 2, when the check is received; see, e.g., Davis v. Commissioner, 37 T.C.M. 42 (1978). If a taxpayer receives in January a check that could have been picked up in person in the preceding year, the Commissioner treats the check as constructively received in the preceding year; see, e.g., Rev. Rul. 68–126, 1968–1 C.B. 194 (retirement check mailed and received in 1968 but included on 1967 form W–2 includable in 1967 income because retiree could have picked up check from employer on December 31, 1967); Rev. Rul. 73–99, 1973–1 C.B. 412 (employee constructively received income represented by check that he could have picked up from employer on last day of the year). The constructive-receipt theory was rejected in *Davis* because the taxpayer had no notice that the funds were available. It is unlikely that the constructive-receipt doctrine would apply to the facts in the problem.

(f) In year 2 C gives L a $1,000 promissory note, payable (with market rate interest) $500 in year 3 and $500 in year 4. Soon after receiving the note, L sells ("discounts") it to a bank for $950, plus accrued interest. C makes the required note payments (to the bank) as scheduled.

A promissory note is generally not considered to be the equivalent of cash unless it is easily negotiable and freely transferable, as the note in this case appears to be. The value of the note is includable in L's income when received in year 2; Rev. Rul. 76–135, 1976–1 C.B. 114. (The amount includable is $950, unless the value of the note changed between the time it was received by L and sold to the bank).

C's giving of the note is not a payment. C can deduct $500 in each of years 3 and 4; id.

(g) Late in year 1, C charges the payment to L on a VISA credit card. C pays the charge in year 2, and L collects payment from L's processing bank in year 2.

L has year–1 income and C a year–1 deduction. The credit-card payment is treated as if C borrowed the money from the card issuer and paid the money to L. C gets a year–1 deduction, even though C does not pay the charge-card bill until year 2; Rev. Rul. 78–38, 1978–1 C.B. 68.

(h) L performs the services without charge in exchange for the free use of C's vacation condominium for a week in year 2. The fair rental value of a week's stay at the condominium is $1,000.

Even though L uses the cash method, the fair rental value of the condominium stay must be included in gross income when received in year 2; see Treas. Reg. §§ 1.446–1(c)(1)(i) (cash-method taxpayer can receive income in the form of cash, property or services); 1.61–2(d)(1) (services paid for in exchange for other services). C should be treated as though the condominium was rented out for $1,000 and C paid L's $1,000 fee. C therefore has $1,000 of year–2 gross income, unless § 280A(g) applies (i.e., if C rented the condominium for fewer than 15 days during the year). If C must include the $1,000 in income, C would also have a year–2 deduction of $1,000.

2. F, a farmer, offers to sell grain to D, with delivery to be made in December but payment to be deferred until the following January. Although D tells F that he would be willing to make payment in December, the parties enter into a sales agreement calling for December delivery and January payment. Is F in constructive receipt of the sales price in December?

No. The parties are free to make their own contract, and the date specified in the agreement is controlling; Schniers v. Commissioner, 69 T.C. 511 (1977); Amend v. Commissioner, 13 T.C. 178 (1949). So, F is not in constructive receipt even though D would have been willing to enter into a contract calling for December payment. Although this rule undoubtedly encourages tax avoidance, a rule based on speculation about what the parties would have been *willing* to do seems unworkable; see Rev. Rul. 60–31, 1960–1 C.B. 174, 178.

3. C, a cash-method taxpayer, makes the following payments of business expenses on December 31, year 1. Determine in each case whether the payment is deductible in year 1.

(a) Interest (covering the period from January 1, year 2 through December 31, year 2).

The interest is not deductible until year 2; § 461(g).

(b) Rent on the business premises covering the same period as in (a).

Prepaid rent generally must be capitalized and amortized over the period covered; Treas. Reg. § 1.263(a)–4(d)(3)(i) & (ii), Ex. 2. However, under the "12–month rule," an immediate deduction is allowed for an amount paid for a right that does not extend beyond the end of the taxable year following the taxable year in which the payment is made; Treas. Reg. § 1.263(a)–4(f)(1)(ii). So, the payment is deductible in year 1.

4. T is an employee of corporation X. In addition to salary, T is entitled to additional compensation from X for each year. The amount of the additional compensation is credited to a bookkeeping reserve on X's books. It is to be paid upon the earlier of (1) the termination of T's employment or (2) T's becoming totally incapacitated. If T dies before receiving payment, the balance in the account is to be paid to T's estate. Must T, a cash-method taxpayer, include the deferred compensation in gross income as earned?

This problem is loosely based upon Rev. Rul. 60–31, 1960–1 C.B. 174, Situation (1), which holds that the taxpayer is not in constructive receipt of the deferred compensation. The reference to a bookkeeping reserve means that the firm is tracking T's entitlement on its books; it has *not* set aside any money to pay T; this is therefore an unfunded deferred-compensation plan, under which T has only a contractual right to payment. Although the deferred compensation is substantially vested—T's entitlement to the additional compensation is not conditioned upon T's performance of future services—X's mere unfunded and unsecured promise to pay is not considered "property" in the § 83 sense; Treas. Reg. § 1.83–3(e).

The only remaining question is whether the enactment in 2004 of § 409A changes the result. It does not. Section 409A makes the deferred compensation payable under a nonqualified deferred compensation plan immediately taxable, unless the deferred-compensation plan complies with (1) the distribution requirements of § 409A(a)(2), (2) the prohibition on acceleration of benefits of § 409A(a)(3), and (3) the rules regarding elections to defer the income of § 409A(a)(4). The distribution requirement is satisfied because distributions cannot be made earlier than T's separation from service, disability, or death. (This assumes that the plan's definition of "totally incapacitated" complies with the definition of disabled in § 409A(2)(C).) The plan does not permit the acceleration of the payment of the deferred compensation. Nor does the plan permit any further deferral beyond that required under the original employment contract, which should satisfy § 409A(a)(4)(B)(ii), at least if the deferred-compensation provision was not retroactive.

5. Same as 4, except that T can elect on or before December 31 to have the following year's additional compensation paid to him or deferred until the earlier of his retirement, disability or death.

This arrangement satisfies the requirements of § 409A(a)(4)(B)(i) because the election must be made before the close of the year preceding the service year. The income is deferred.

6. Same as 4, except that each year X transferred the deferred compensation earned in that year to a trust located in the United States. T will be entitled to the trust assets at the earlier of his retirement, disability or death (in which case, the trust assets become the property of his estate). Until the occurrence of one of those "triggering" events, the trust assets remain subject to the claims of X's general creditors.

For tax purposes, X's promise to pay deferred compensation is still "unfunded," as the trust assets are subject to the claims of X's general creditors. (This type of trust is called a "rabbi trust" because the first favorable ruling involved the deferred compensation of a rabbi.)

7. Same as 6, except that the plan provides that the trust assets will become restricted to the provision of benefits to T if X's financial health deteriorates in specified ways.

That provision would make T immediately taxable under § 83 because of § 409A(b)(2).

8. Same as 6, except that the trust was located in the Bahamas. (T's services for X are performed in the United States.)

When the trust assets are located offshore, the assets are treated as property for purposes of § 83, even though the assets remain subject to the claims of X's general creditors; § 409A(b)(1). Since T's rights are substantially vested, T is taxable on the value of the assets added to the trust each year.

C. THE ACCRUAL METHOD OF ACCOUNTING

Code: §§ 451(a); 461(a), (f) & (h); 267(a)(2), (b)(2), (c)(2) & (4)

Regulations: §§ 1.446–1(c)(1)(ii); 1.451–1(a); 1.461–1(a)(2); 1.461–2(a)(3) & (4), Ex. (2); 1.461–2(c)(1); 1.461–4(d) & (e); 1.263(a)–4(d)(3), (f)(1), (6) & (8), Ex. 10.

Cases: Schlude v. Commissioner, 372 U.S. 128 (1963); North American Oil Consol. v. Burnet, 286 U.S. 417 (1932).

Rulings: Rev. Proc. 2004–34, 2004–1 C.B. 991; Rev. Rul. 96–51, 1996–2 C.B. 36.

1. Describe the all-events test.

The all-events test is the method by which an accrual-method taxpayer determines *when* items of income are includable in gross income and items of deduction are allowable. With respect to income, the taxpayer generally takes income into account when all the events have occurred that fix the taxpayer's right to the income and when the amount of the income can be ascertained with reasonable accuracy (the "all-events" test); Treas. Reg. §§ 1.446–1(c)(1)(ii); 1.451–1(a). Deductions are taken when (1) all the events have occurred that fix the fact of liability, (2) the amount of the liability can be ascertained with reasonable accuracy, and (3) economic performance has occurred with respect to the liability; Treas. Reg. §§ 1.446–1(c)(1)(ii); 1.461–1(a)(2).

2. L practices law as a solo practitioner. In year 1, L performs $1,000 of legal services for C, who can deduct the cost of the services as a business expense. L bills C in year 1, and C pays L in year 2. Both L and C use the accrual method. What results to L and C?

By the end of year 1, all of the events have occurred that fix L's right to payment—i.e., L has performed the legal services. The amount of the income is ascertainable with reasonable accuracy—the $1,000 amount billed to C. L must therefore include the $1,000 in gross income in year 1. L obtains a tax-cost basis for the $1,000 account receivable, so that L has no further income when the receivable is collected in year 2.

By the end of year 1, all of the events have occurred that fix C's liability (L's performing the legal services), and the amount of the liability is determinable with reasonable accuracy. Whenever the liability arises from another person's performing services *for* the taxpayer, economic performance occurs when the services are furnished; § 461(h)(2)(A)(i). Here economic performance occurs in year 1 when L performs the services, and the all-events test is satisfied in year 1. Therefore, C is allowed a year–1 deduction for the $1,000.

3. L (in 2) leases her law office from R at a rental of $4,000 a month. The lease term runs from October 1, year 1, through September 30, year 2. On October 1, year 1, L pays the rent for the entire lease year. What results to L and R, who also uses the accrual method?

As an accrual method taxpayer, L cannot deduct the rent until the all-events test is satisfied. The all-events test cannot be satisfied before economic performance occurs; § 461(h)(1). When the taxpayer's liability arises out of another person's providing property to the taxpayer, economic performance occurs only as the property is provided; § 461(h)(2)(A)(ii). In particular, where the liability arises out of the use of property, as in this case, economic performance occurs ratably over the period of time the taxpayer is entitled to the use of the property; Treas. Reg. § 1.461–4(d)(3)(i). Thus, in year 1 economic performance has occurred only with respect to the months of October, November and December. L can therefore deduct in year 1 only $12,000 of the rental payment. The remaining $36,000 is deductible in year 2 when economic performance occurs for the other 9 months.

Apart from the economic-performance requirement, prepaid expenses generally must be capitalized; Treas. Reg. § 1.263(a)–4(d)(3)(i). However, there is an exception for a payment covering a period of not more than 12 months following the taxable year in which the payment is made; Treas. Reg. § 1.263(a)–4(f)(1). Although it appears that L's rental payment falls within the 12–month rule, no amount is deductible by an accrual-method taxpayer until the economic performance test is satisfied, and here the test is satisfied in year 1 only for the last 3 months of the year; see Treas. Reg. § 1.263(a)–4(f)(6) & (8), Ex. 10.

R, the recipient of the rental payment, must include the $48,000 in gross income when received. Section 451(a) requires income to be included in gross income of the year in which received, unless under the taxpayer's method of accounting the income is includable in a different year. So, the issue becomes whether R can defer the rental income under his accrual method of accounting. R can argue that at the end of year 1 he has not "earned" the portion of the rent attributable to year 2—that all the events that fix his right to the year–2 portion of the rent do not occur until year 2 as R furnishes the premises to L. However, the Commissioner has long (and generally successfully) contended that prepaid income is taxable to an accrual-method taxpayer in the year received; e.g., Schlude v. Commissioner, 372 U.S. 128 (1963) (advance payment for services taxable in year received rather than in year when services were performed). Yet, R is not without hope, as the Supreme Court has never said in so many words that the Commissioner's discretion extends to prohibiting deferral of prepaid income in every case. For example, in Artnell Co. v. Commissioner, 400 F.2d 981 (7th Cir. 1968), the taxpayer was allowed to defer income from selling season tickets to baseball games because the dates of performance were fixed. The dates of the performance are fixed in this case also. And financial-accounting principles would *require* deferral of the income. Yet, the thrust of *Schlude* and other cases suggest that R's chances of prevailing are not high; see, e.g., RCA Corp. v. United States,

664 F.2d 881 (2d Cir. 1981) (deferral not allowed; court noted the "vastly different objectives" of tax and financial accounting).

Rev. Proc. 2004–34, 2004–1 C.B. 991, permits limited deferral by accrual-method taxpayers of income from advance payments, but the ruling generally does not apply to rental income.

4. L (in 2) also paid $12,000 of interest on a business loan. The interest was paid on November 1, year 1, and covered the 12–month period ending on October 31, year 2. What result to L?

Here again, the all-events test cannot be satisfied with respect to the entire liability in year 1 because economic performance has not occurred. In the case of a liability for interest, economic performance occurs as the interest cost economically accrues; Treas. Reg. § 1.461–4(e). Thus, economic performance has occurred in year 1 only with respect to the interest for the last two months of year 1, and only that portion of the interest is deductible in year 1. The remainder of the interest is deductible in year 2, when economic performance with respect to that portion of the interest liability accrues. (Section 461(g) does not apply here because it applies only to cash-method taxpayers.)

5. In June, year 1, L (in 2) also paid a $1,000 fee to the State Supreme Court to renew her license to practice for the period July 1, year 1, through June 30, year 2. When is the payment allowable?

L's payment is a prepaid expense, which generally must be capitalized; see Treas. Reg. § 1.263(a)–4(d)(3). However, the 12–month rule applies because the payment provides a right that does not extend beyond 12 months after the first date on which L realizes the right attributable to the payment (July 1, year 1); Treas. Reg. § 1.263(a)–4(f)(1) & (8), Ex. 5. So, the entire $1,000 is allowable in year 1.

6. S is in the business of offering dancing lessons in a studio that she owns. A customer can purchase lessons at the lowest cost per lesson by paying in advance for a 2–year contract under which the customer pays $1,000 for 100 hours of instruction over the 2–year period beginning on the date the contract is signed. The customer can schedule the lessons at any time during the contract term, but the payment is not refundable. On October 1, year 1, C enters into a 2–year contract and pays S the $1,000 fee. In the financial statements that S furnishes to her bank lender, she recognizes as income $125 in year 1, $500 in year 2, and $375 in year 3. For income-tax purposes, S wishes to defer the income to the extent permitted. For what years (and in what amounts) must S include the $1,000 in gross income?

This problem is similar to that confronting the Court in Schlude v. Commissioner, 372 U.S. 128 (1963), in which the taxpayer attempted to defer income from advance payments for services to be rendered, in part, in future years. The Commissioner, exercising his discretion to require use of a method of accounting that clearly reflects income, refused to permit deferral. The Court held that the Commissioner had not abused his discretion in requiring that the income be taxed when the advance payments were received.

In Rev. Proc. 2004–34, however, the Service authorized deferral for some advance payments where the taxpayer deferred recognition of the income in its financial statement or earned the payment in a subsequent year. The procedure applies to advance payments for services (among other things), and S is deferring recognition of the income in her financial statements. Under the procedure, S includes $125 in income for year 1 (the same amount that she recognized on her financial statements). The $875 balance of the income must be included in gross income for year 2, even though S defers a portion of that until year 3 for financial-statement purposes.

7. In January, year 1, P commenced an action against D to determine title to a tract of land of which both P and D claimed ownership. While the litigation was pending, D, who was in possession of the land, continued to collect the rent from the lessee of the land. In January, year 2, the court entered judgment for P and ordered D to pay P money damages in the amount of the year–1 rents collected by D. D paid the amount of the judgment in year 3. Both P and D use the accrual method. Who is taxable on the year–1 rents?

Although P is ultimately adjudicated the owner of the property, P is not required to include the income in year 1 because all of the events had not occurred in year 1 to fix her right to the income; that right was established only by the judgment in year 2. D must include the year–1 rents in gross income because he received the rental payments under a *claim of right*:

> If a taxpayer receives earnings under a claim of right and without restriction as to its disposition, he has received income which he is required to return [i.e., include in gross income] even though it may still be claimed that he is not entitled to retain the money, and even though he may still be adjudged liable to restore its equivalent.

North American Oil Consol. v. Burnet, 286 U.S. 417, 424 (1932). The claim-of-right doctrine applies regardless of whether the taxpayer uses the cash or accrual method; id. at 423–24. So, D includes the rents in year–1 income.

P must include in income the amount of the year–1 rents when the judgment becomes final in year 2. D, however, can deduct the amount paid to P only when actually paid, as that is when economic performance occurs; see Treas. Reg. § 1.461–4(g)(7). D can also invoke § 1341 in computing his tax for year 3. Section 1341 is discussed in Chapter 42.

8. **T contests $20,000 of a $100,000 bill received from C, who provided services to T's business in year 1. (The cost of the services would be deductible by T as a business expense.) In year 2, T pays C the undisputed portion of the bill ($80,000). The dispute is settled in year 3 by T's paying C $5,000 of the claimed $20,000 balance. T uses the accrual method of accounting.**

(a) What results to T?

Under the all-events test, T can deduct the undisputed portion of the bill in year 1. Although the all-events test requires that the amount of the liability be ascertainable with reasonable accuracy, the fact that the exact amount cannot be determined does not prevent T from taking into account the $80,000 that *can* be determined with reasonable accuracy; see Treas. Reg. § 1.461–1(a)(2)(ii). (The economic-performance requirement is satisfied in year 1 because C rendered the services in that year; see § 461(h)(2)(A)(i).) Under the accrual method, T's year–2 payment is irrelevant. T can deduct an additional $5,000 in year 3 when the dispute is settled and that remaining portion of the liability becomes ascertainable with reasonable accuracy.

(b) Suppose instead that T had paid the disputed $20,000 into escrow in year 2 under an agreement between T, C and the escrow agent that the funds would be held until the dispute was resolved and then disbursed in accordance with the settlement. The dispute was settled in year 3, and the escrowee disbursed $5,000 to C and the remaining $15,000 to T.

Section 461(f) allows T a deduction for the additional $20,000 in year 2 because: (1) T contests the asserted liability; (2) T transfers money to satisfy the liability and the transfer places the money beyond T's control; see Treas. Reg. § 1.461–2(c)(1)(i); (3) the contest continues after T makes the transfer in year 2; and (4) but for the contest, a deduction would have been allowable to T for year 1 under the all-events test (after application of the economic-performance requirement). Subject to the exclusionary tax-benefit rule (discussed in Chapter 42), T must include the $15,000 refund in gross income for year 3; Treas. Reg. § 1.461–2(a)(3) & (4), Ex. (2).

9. **A and B, husband and wife, respectively own 40 percent and 20 percent of the stock of X Corporation. B has also lent money to the corporation. For year 1, interest of $20,000 accrued on the loan, but X did not pay the interest until year 2. X uses the accrual method and B the cash method. What results to X and B?**

Section 267(a)(2) postpones an accrual-method payor's deduction for items paid to a related person who uses the cash method until the year in which the item is includable in the payee's income. A and B are members of a family, so the stock owned by A is treated as being constructively owned by B, which makes B the owner of 60 percent of the stock; see § 267(c)(2) & (4). The transaction between B and X is covered by § 267(a)(2) because B owns (actually and constructively) more than 50 percent in value of the X stock; see § 267(b)(2). As a cash-method taxpayer, B includes the interest payment in gross income when it is received in year 2. Although X's interest payment satisfies the all-events test in year 1, § 267(a)(2) requires it to postpone its deduction until year 2 when the payment is includable in B's income.

D. INVENTORIES

Code: § 471(a).

Regulations: §§ 1.61–3(a); 1.471–1.

1. **A started a retail widget business in year 1. In year 1, A purchased 3 widgets at $1 and sold 2 for $3 each. In year 2, she purchased 4 units at $2 and sold 3 at $4. Assume (contrary to fact) that A can deduct the purchase of widgets as a business expense. Determine A's income from the sale of widgets for :**

(a) Year 1.

Gross income	$6
Expenses	3
Net income	$3

(b) Year 2.

Gross income	$12
Expenses	8
Net income	$ 4

Total net income over the two years is $7.

Both years' income is understated because the cost of all the inventory was charged to expense, even though there were units still on hand at the close of each year. The cost of the units in ending inventory represents a cost of earning income in a future year, and the deduction for those items should be deferred until they are sold. That's why Treas. Reg. § 1.471–1 requires the use of inventories whenever the production, purchase or sale of merchandise is an income-producing factor.

2. **Same as 1, except that A uses the first-in-first-out (FIFO) method of inventory accounting.**

The cost of goods sold during the year must be offset against the sales revenue to arrive at the gross income from sales. Rather than trying to specifically identify which items of inventory were sold during the year, most firms adopt a "convention" or mandatory presumption as to the flow of goods out of inventory. Under the FIFO convention, the first items acquired for inventory are considered to be the first sold. The cost of those items are charged to cost of goods sold, and the ending inventory comprises the last items of inventory acquired.

The cost of goods sold is determined as follows:

Cost of Goods Sold = Beginning Inventory + Inventory Purchases – Ending Inventory.

The sum of the Beginning Inventory and Inventory Purchases is sometimes shown as "Goods Available for Sale."

For year 1, the cost of goods sold is:

Beginning Inventory	none
Inventory Purchases	$3
Goods Available for Sale	$3
Less: Ending Inventory	1 (1 unit at a cost of $1)
Cost of Goods Sold	$2

Gross income from sales is $4 ($6 of sales revenue less $2 of cost of goods sold).

For year 2, the cost of goods sold is:

Beginning Inventory	$1
Inventory Purchases	8
Goods Available for Sale	$9
Less: Ending Inventory	4 (2 units at a cost of $2 each)
Cost of Goods Sold	$5

Gross income from sales is $7 ($12 sales revenue less $5 cost of goods sold). Over the 2–year period, gross income from sales is $11.

3. Same as 1, except that A uses the last-in-first-out (LIFO) method of inventory accounting.

Under the LIFO convention, we assume that the last items acquired for inventory were the first items sold, which means that the first items acquired remain in ending inventory. For year 1, the cost of goods sold is:

Beginning Inventory	none
Inventory Purchases	$3
Goods Available for Sale	$3
Less: Ending Inventory	1 (1 unit at a cost of $1)
Cost of Goods Sold	$2

Gross income from sales is $4 ($6 of sales revenue less $2 of cost of goods sold).

For year 2, the cost of goods sold is:

Beginning Inventory	$1
Inventory Purchases	8
Goods Available for Sale	$9
Less: Ending Inventory	3 (1 unit at a cost of $1 and 1 unit at a cost of $2)
Cost of Goods Sold	$6

Gross income from sales is $6 ($12 sales revenue less $6 cost of goods sold). Over the 2–year period, gross income from sales is $10.

4. Why does LIFO result in lower gross income when prices are rising?

LIFO results in lower gross income when prices are rising because the inventory items charged to cost of goods sold are the items that were purchased most recently and whose cost is therefore higher. The earlier-purchased (lower-cost) items remain in ending inventory.

5. What is the "LIFO conformity requirement"?

The LIFO conformity requirement is found in § 472(c). It requires that a taxpayer who uses LIFO for tax purposes must also use LIFO for book purposes. The concern was that taxpayers would use LIFO for tax purposes for the tax savings but report to shareholders and creditors using FIFO, which would produce higher net income. It is debatable whether the LIFO conformity requirement serves any useful purpose. Taxpayers can, for example, use the rapid depreciation permitted by § 168 for tax purposes, while using a more-restrained approach for book purposes. There are many other instances of differences in the tax and book treatment of items of income and deduction. It is puzzling why Congress singled out LIFO inventory accounting for insistence on book-tax conformity.

6. What is the policy justification for permitting the use of LIFO for tax purposes?

The rationale is that LIFO tends to reduce "imaginary" gains attributable to inflation. Using the facts in problem 1 for illustration, we note that one unit purchased in year 1 for $1 is sold in year 2 for $4, but in year 2 it costs the taxpayer $2 to replace that unit. So, the argument goes, the taxpayer really only has $2 of profit ($4 sales price less $2 replacement cost) rather than $3 ($4 sales price less $1 cost) of profit from the sale of the unit in year 2. Of course, other taxpayers (e.g., a person who earns interest on a bank savings account) must include the inflation component of their income in gross income. It is hard to see why sellers of inventory should be treated differently.

7. Why must a taxpayer who maintains inventories account for purchases and sales under the accrual method?

Treas. Reg. § 1.446–1(c)(2)(i) requires that an accrual method be used for purchases and sales of the inventory. This requirement is a relic of the pre-computer era, when use of the cash method for purchases and sales could lead to discrepancies in matching sales revenue against the cost of goods sold. Suppose, for example, that an item of merchandise has been shipped but payment has not yet been received at year's end. The item will not show up in a physical count of ending inventory and hence its cost would be included in cost of goods sold, even though the sales proceeds (if reported under the cash method) were not reflected in sales revenue for the year. To prevent such discrepancies, the taxpayer is required to accrue the sales revenue in the year the merchandise is sold.

Section K

CONGRESSIONAL EFFORTS TO COMBAT TAX SHELTERS

Chapter 44

THE AT-RISK RULES

Code: §§ 465(a)(1) & (2); (b)(1), (2), (5) & (6); (c)(1) & (3)(A), (d), (e); 49(a)(1)(D)(iv) & (v).

Regulation: Prop. Treas. Reg. §§ 1.465–12(a) & (b); 1.465–39(b).

1. **In year 1, T, an individual, purchases equipment for use in an activity to which the at-risk rules apply. T pays $200,000 cash and finances the $800,000 balance of the purchase price with a non-recourse bank loan secured by the equipment.**

(a) **What is T's basis for the equipment immediately after the purchase?**

T's unadjusted basis is $1,000,000; § 1012. Under Crane v. Commissioner, 334 U.S. 1 (1947), and its progeny, the basis includes the portion of the investment financed by non-recourse debt.

(b) **To what extent is T at risk immediately after the purchase?**

T is at risk to the extent of $200,000 (the amount of money contributed to the activity); § 465(b)(1)(A). The borrowed funds are not risk because T is not personally liable for repayment of the funds and has not pledged non-activity property as security for the loan; § 465(b)(1)(A) & (2).

(c) **In year 1, T's gross income from the activity is $100,000. Apart from the effect of § 465, T could deduct depreciation of $200,000 and interest of $80,000. How much can T deduct after applying § 465? Ignore § 469.**

T sustains a loss of $180,000 ($100,000 gross income less $280,000 of deductions allocable to the activity); § 465(d). Since T's loss is less than the $200,000 aggregate amount with respect to which T is at risk at the close of the year, the loss is allowable; see § 465(a)(1).

(d) How do these events affect T's amount at risk?

The regulations provide that the § 465(d) losses which are allowed as deductions for the year reduce the taxpayer's amount at risk at the close of the *immediately succeeding* year; Prop. Treas. Reg. § 1.465–39(b). That is because the disallowance of losses is based upon the amount with respect to which the taxpayer is at risk at the end of the year. We therefore cannot reduce T's amount at risk for the allowable year–1 loss until after the close of year 1. The next occasion on which the amount at risk will be significant is the end of year 2, and so that is when the adjustment for the year–1 loss is made.

At the end of year 2, T's amount at risk must be reduced by the amount of loss allowable for year 1, which, assuming no other changes in the amount at risk, leaves T with an at-risk amount of $20,000 ($200,000 initial amount at risk less $180,000 loss); § 465(b)(5).

(e) In year 2, gross income is again $100,000, depreciation is $320,000, interest is $80,000, and T pays $100,000 on the loan principal. How much can T deduct for year 2?

The $100,000 payment on the principal of the loan increases T's amount at risk to $120,000 at the end of year 2. T's § 465(d) loss for year 2 is $300,000 ($400,000 deductions less $100,000 gross income). The loss is allowable only to the extent of T's $120,000 at risk; § 465(a). The $180,000 portion of the loss disallowed in year 2 is carried over to year 3, where it is treated as a deduction attributable to the activity in year 3; § 465(a)(2). If we assume that there are no other changes to T's amount at risk, T's amount at risk at the end of year 3 will be zero ($120,000 at risk at the end of year 2, less $120,000 loss allowed in year 2); § 465(b)(5).

(f) In year 3, T sells the property. The purchaser pays T $100,000 cash and takes the property subject to the remaining $700,000 of indebtedness. Before the sale, the activity generated operating gross income of $100,000, depreciation of $100,000 and interest expense of $70,000.

(i) What is T's realized gain or loss on the sale?

T's adjusted basis at the time of sale is $380,000 ($1,000,000 cost less $620,000 of depreciation for years 1–3). The realized gain on the sale is $420,000 ($800,000 amount realized less $380,000 adjusted basis).

(ii) How much can T deduct under § 465 in year 3?

In year 3, T has income from the activity of $520,000 ($100,000 operating gross income, plus $420,000 gain on the sale). Income from an activity includes the gain recognized on the disposition of the activity; the character of the gain as ordinary or capital is irrelevant for this purpose; Prop. Treas. Reg. § 1.465–12 (a) & (b). T's deductions attributable to the activity total $350,000 ($170,000 of current deductions, plus $180,000 carried over from year 2). Since the income exceeds the deductions, T has no loss from the activity for the year, and the deductions are fully allowable.

2. In year 1, S, an individual, purchases for $40,000 cash equipment for use in an activity to which the at-risk rules apply. The purchase was made from S's personal funds. For years 1–6, S's cash income from the property equals her cash expenses with respect to the property, and she properly deducts a total of $40,000 of depreciation. In year 7, S's cash gross income from the property again equals her cash expenses, but S borrows $10,000 on a non-recourse note (secured by the equipment) and withdraws the $10,000 from the activity. What result to S?

Ignoring for the moment the $10,000 withdrawal, the $40,000 of deductions in excess of the gross income from the property have reduced S's amount at risk to zero at the end of year 7. The cash withdrawal reduces S's amount at risk to negative $10,000. Whenever the at-risk amount is negative at the end of the year, § 465(e)(1) includes in gross income for the year an amount equal to the negative at-risk figure. So, S must include $10,000 in gross income for year 7. The $10,000 is treated as a deduction allocable to the activity in the following year; § 465(e)(2). Thus, it could be deducted in year 8 to the extent that S is at risk by the end of year 8.

3. P, an individual, purchases a building for $1,000,000, paying $100,000 cash down from his personal funds and executing a non-recourse note (secured by the building) to the seller for the $900,000 balance of the purchase price.

(a) To what extent is P at risk immediately after the purchase?

P is not considered to be at risk for the $900,000 borrowed on the non-recourse note because P is not personally liable for repayment of the loan; see § 465(b)(2). Although the borrowing occurred with respect to P's activity of holding real property, the indebtedness is not qualified non-recourse financing because the seller of the property is not a "qualified person"; see §§ 465(b)(6)(B)(ii) & (C); 49(a)(1)(D)(iv)(II). P's amount at risk is limited to the $100,000 down payment.

(b) Would your answer in (a) differ if the $900,000 non-recourse loan had been made by a bank?

Yes, because the bank would be a "qualified person" (a "person which is actively and regularly engaged in the business of lending money"); § 49(a)(1)(D)(iv). (This assumes that P and the bank are not related parties under § 465(b)(3)(C); see § 49(a)(1)(D)(iv)(I) & (v).) The indebtedness would therefore be qualified non-recourse financing, and P would be considered at risk on the $900,000, as well as her $100,000 down payment; see § 465(b)(6).

Chapter 45

THE PASSIVE-LOSS RULES

Code: §§ 469(a), (b), (c)(1), (2), (4) & (7), (d)(1), (e)(1) & (3), (g)(1) & (2), (h)(1), (2), (3) & (5), (i)(1), (2), (3) & (6), (j)(8), (*l*)(3).

Regulations: § 1.469–2(f)(6); 1.469–1T(f)(2)(A); 1.469–2T(6)(i); 1.469–5T.

1. Which of the following are passive activities with respect to the taxpayer?

(a) A is a limited partner in a limited partnership that is producing a movie.

Generally speaking, an interest as a limited partner is not one in which the taxpayer materially participates; § 469(h)(2). Since A is not a material participant, the activity is a passive activity; § 469(c)(1)(B).

(b) B is a member of a limited-liability company that is engaged in the restaurant business; B is strictly an investor and plays no role in the management or operation of the restaurant.

B is not a material participant; work done by B in his capacity as an investor is not treated as participation unless B is directly involved in the day-to-day management or operation of the restaurant; Temp. Treas. Reg. § 1.469–5T(f)(2)(ii)(B). The activity is passive; § 469(c)(1)(B).

(c) C owns an apartment building. Although C practices law nearly full time, he actively manages the apartment building.

Rental activity is a passive activity; § 469(c)(2).

2. Trailerhouse Records, Inc., is an S corporation engaged in the business of recording and producing music for local artists. Several shareholders participate in the firm's business, though all of them earn most of their income from other activities. In each of the following *alternative* cases, determine whether the shareholder is a material participant in the firm?

(a) A devotes 600 hours per year to the business.

Participation of more than 500 hours is material; Temp. Treas. Reg. § 1.469–5T(a)(1). A is thus a material participant.

How does one prove the extent of her participation? Temp. Treas. Reg. § 1.469–5T(e)(4) says that the taxpayer can use "any reasonable means," including "the identification of services performed over a period of time and the approximate number of hours spent performing such services during such period, based upon appointment books, calendars, or narrative summaries." Contemporaneous daily time reports are not required.

(b) B devotes 250 hours per year to the business; no shareholder or employee devotes more time to the business.

B qualifies as a material participant because she devotes more than 100 hours to the activity and B's participation is not less than that of any other shareholder or employee; Temp. Treas. Reg. § 1.469–5T(a)(3).

(c) C devotes 90 hours per year to the business; the business has no employees, and no other shareholder participates in the business.

C is a material participant because her participation constitutes substantially all of the participation in the activity; see Temp. Treas. Reg. § 1.469–5T(a)(2).

(d) D devotes 400 hours per year to the business; D's spouse, S, devoted 200 hours a year to the business.

D (and S) are both material participants. In determining whether the taxpayer materially participates, the participation of the taxpayer's spouse is treated as participation by the taxpayer; § 469(h)(5). D is therefore credited with more than 500 hours of participation, which makes D a material participant; Treas. Reg. § 1.469–5T(a)(1).

(e) E devoted 600 hours per year to the business until her retirement 3 years ago.

E is a material participant because E is retired and was a material participant for at least 5 of the preceding 10 years; see Temp. Treas. Reg. § 1.469–5T(a)(5).

(f) Same as (e), except that E retired 6 years go.

Now E does not qualify, as she was a material participant for only 4 of the preceding 10 years; see Temp. Treas. Reg. § 1.469–5T(a)(5).

3. In year 1, T, a full-time lawyer, had $40 (000 omitted throughout) of loss passed through to him from a limited partnership in which T is a limited partner; $20 of dividend income; $12 of income passed through from an S corporation that is engaged in a business in which T does not materially participate; and $20 of loss from an apartment building that T owns. All of the losses would be deductible but for the application of § 469.

(a) What result to T in year 1?

T is not a material participant with respect to the limited-partnership interest; see § 469(h)(2). Neither is he a material participant in the S corporation's business; § 469(h)(1). Both of those activities are passive because of T's lack of material participation; § 469(c)(1). The operation of the apartment building constitutes "rental activity" (because the payments received are principally for the use of tangible property—§ 469(j)(8)), and rental activity is always passive (unless one is a real-estate professional, which T is not); § 469(c)(2). So, the income or loss from the limited partnership, the S corporation, and the apartment building is passive income or loss. The dividend income is not treated as income from a passive activity; § 469(e)(1). (The items of investment income and expense excluded from the passive basket by § 469(e) are often referred to as "portfolio income.")

T has passive income of $12 (from the S corporation) and passive losses of $60 ($40 from the limited partnership and $20 from the apartment building). T's passive-activity loss (PAL) is $48 ($60 of passive losses less $12 of passive income); § 469(d)(1). The $48 net loss is disallowed; § 469(a)(1). The disallowed loss is apportioned between the limited-partnership interest and the rental interest in proportion to the amount of losses from those two activities; Temp. Treas. Reg. § 1.469–1T(f)(2)(A). Since $40 of the total $60 of passive loss is attributable to the partnership interest, $32 ($40/$60 x $48) of the disallowed loss is allocated to that interest and $16 ($20/$60 x $48) is allocated to the rental interest. T carries these disallowed losses forward year 2, where each will be treated as a passive-activity deduction allocable to the activity; § 469(b). So, T begins year 2 with a passive-activity deduction of $32 with respect to the partnership interest and $16 with respect to the rental interest.

(b) In year 2 (before taking account of the deductions from § 469(b)), T had $20 of loss passed through from the limited partnership, $30 of dividend income, $18 of income from the S corporation, and $10 of loss from the apartment building. What result?

T has passive-activity deductions carried over from year 1 of $32 with respect to the limited partnership (which increases the loss from that activity to $52) and $16 with respect to the rental activity (which increases the loss from that activity to $26). For year 2, T has total passive losses of $78 and passive income (from the S corporation) of $18, for a PAL of $60; see § 469(d)(1). The $60 PAL is disallowed under § 469(a)(1). It is allocated $40 ($52/$78 x $60) to the partnership interest and $20 ($26/$78 x $60) to the rental interest; Temp. Treas. Reg. § 1.469–1T(f)(2)(A). T carries these disallowed losses forward to year 3, where each will be treated as a passive-activity deduction allocable to the activity; § 469(b). So, T starts year 3 with a passive-activity deduction of $40 with respect to the partnership interest and $20 with respect to the rental interest.

4. T owns an asset used in an activity to which § 465 applies. The activity produces a loss of $250 for the year. At the end of the year, T was at risk with respect to the activity only to the extent of $100. The activity is also a passive activity. T has no passive income. To what extent is the loss deductible?

Section 465 limits the loss to the $100 for which T is at risk at the end of the year. The passive-activity deduction is limited to the $100 not disallowed by § 465; Temp. Treas. Reg. § 1.469–2T(6)(i). That is, § 465 does its work first, and then § 469 comes into play to further limit any loss allowable after the application of § 465. Since the activity was a passive one, none of the $100 is allowable as a deduction in the current year. The disallowed deductions carry over to the following year—$150 under § 465(a)(2) and $100 under § 469(b).

5. B owned an apartment building that produced a passive loss of $100 for the year. B also owned an office building that he leased to his wholly owned C corporation, in which B was employed full-time. That rental produced income of $60 for the year. To what extent is the $100 loss deductible?

If, in accordance with the usual rule of § 469(c)(2), we treat the two rental activities as passive, B has a net passive-activity deduction from the apartment building of $100, net passive-activity income from the office building of $60, a passive activity loss of $40, and only $40 of B's loss on the apartment building would be disallowed. If, on the other hand, the rental income from the office building is not considered to be passive, the passive-activity loss would be $100, and none of the loss on the apartment building would be deductible.

Section 469(*l*)(3) authorizes the Treasury to issue regulations necessary to carry out the provisions of § 469, including regulations "requiring the net income * * * from a limited partnership or *other passive activity* to be treated as *not from a passive activity* * * *" (emphasis added). Using that authority, the Treasury promulgated Treas. Reg. § 1.469–2(f)(6), which provides that rental income is treated as non-passive if the rental property is used in a business in which the taxpayer materially participates (the "self-rental rule").

As a full-time employee, B materially participates in the C corporation's business, and under the regulation the rental income derived from the corporation is treated as non-passive. Accordingly, B has $100 of passive loss and no passive income. The $100 passive-activity loss is not allowable in the current year, but can be carried forward to the following year.

The validity of the self-rental rule has been litigated fervently, but the taxpayers have been rebuffed in every court of appeals to consider the issue. The latest is Beecher v. Commissioner, 481 F.3d 717 (9th Cir. 2007).

6. P purchased an apartment building for $500, properly deducted $200 of depreciation, and then sold it. At the time of the sale, P had $100 of suspended passive losses attributable to the property. (P just broke even in the year of the sale.) The rental of the apartment building is P's only passive activity. What result to P if she sells the property for:

(a) $350?

P's rental activity is a passive activity; § 469(c)(2). P's adjusted basis for the property is $300 ($500 unadjusted basis less $200 depreciation). She realizes and recognizes a gain of $50 on the sale ($350 amount realized less $300 adjusted basis). The gain is passive-activity gross income. For the year of sale, P has total passive loss with respect to the rental activity of $50 ($100 of passive-activity deduction, less $50 of passive-activity gain on sale). Since P has disposed of the property in a fully taxable transaction, P can deduct her $50 loss from the activity for the year because the loss is not considered to be a loss from a passive activity; § 469(g)(1)(A).

Assume that the gain on the sale of the building is a long-term capital gain (which is taxed at lower rates than apply to ordinary income). P reports $50 of capital gain and $100 of ordinary loss. (This assumes that the deductions attributable to the rental of the apartment building were ordinary deductions, which they almost certainly would be on these facts.)

(b) $250?

P realizes and recognizes a loss of $50 on the sale ($300 adjusted basis less $250 amount realized). The loss is allowable under § 165(a) and (c)(1), subject to possible disallowance under § 469. For the year of sale, P has total passive-activity deductions with respect to the rental activity of $150 ($100 of suspended deductions, plus $50 loss on sale). The loss is deductible in the year of sale because the property was disposed of in a fully taxable transaction; § 469(g)(1)(A).

7. D owned an apartment building with an adjusted basis of $300. D died when the building was worth $360. At the time of D's death, D had $100 of suspended passive losses with respect to the property. (The transferee of property acquired from a decedent generally obtains a basis equal to the fair market value of the property at the date of the decedent's death—see 1014(a).) What result to D?

When an interest in a passive activity is transferred by reason of the death of the taxpayer, the suspended passive loss can be deducted to the extent that it exceeds the difference between the basis of the property in the hands of the transferee and the taxpayer's adjusted basis immediately before death; § 469(g)(2). Here, the transferee obtains a basis of $360 under § 1014(a). D's adjusted basis immediately before death was $300. In other words, the transferee's basis is being stepped-up by $60 as a result of D's death. D's suspended passive loss ($100) can be deducted to the extent that it exceeds the step-up in basis. D can therefore deduct $40 ($100 suspended loss less $60 basis step-up) on D's final return. The other $60 of loss cannot be deducted at any time.

The idea here is that the loss is a real economic loss only to the extent that the property ("activity") actually declined in value. Only the real economic loss should be deductible. If the property had been worth only $250 at D's death, all of the suspended loss would have been deductible on D's final return; if the property had been worth $450, none of the loss would have been deductible.

8. B spends 1500 hours a year working as partner in a real-estate brokerage firm. That is more than half the time B devotes to performing personal services. B also owns an apartment building which produced a $100,000 loss in the current year. All of the loss would be deductible but for the application of § 469. B materially participates in the operation of the apartment building. Can B use the loss to offset her considerable income from her brokerage and investment activities?

Yes. Under § 469(c)(7)(A) the rental activities of real-estate professionals are not automatically classified as passive activities. To qualify, the taxpayer must devote more than one-half of her personal services (and more than 750 hours) to "real property trades or businesses" in which the taxpayer materially participates; § 469(c)(7)(B). (Services by an employee do not count unless the employee is a 5–percent owner of the business (§ 469(c)(7)(D)(ii)); hence the significance of B's being a partner.) Real property trades or businesses include, among others, real-property development, construction, rental, management, leasing or brokerage. B satisfies these requirements since more than half her personal services are performed in her brokerage business and she devotes more than 750 hours to that business. Section 469(c)(7)(A) trumps § 469(c)(2), which automatically classifies rental activity as passive, but B must materially participate in the operation of the apartment building in order for that activity to be non-passive; see § 469(c)(1). B does so here, which means that the rental activity is non-passive, and she can use the loss from that activity to offset her other income.

9. A, a single person who practices law nearly full-time, owns and manages an apartment building. A handles all leasing, hires contractors to make necessary repairs and does the bookkeeping for the project. In the current year, A has a loss of $45,000 from the rental of the building, all of which would be allowable but for § 469. A's adjusted gross income is $110,000. A has no other passive deductions or passive income. How much of the loss can A deduct?

Although rental activities are usually treated as passive, § 469(i)(1) treats as non-passive a loss attributable to rental real-estate activities in which the taxpayer *actively* participated. The active-participation standard is less rigorous than that for material participation. The active-participation requirement "can be satisfied without regular, continuous, and substantial involvement in operations, so long as the taxpayer participates, e.g., in the making of management decisions or arranging for others to provide services (such as repairs), in a significant and *bona fide* sense"; S. Rep. No. 99–313, 99th cong., 2d Sess. 737.

A clearly satisfies the active-participation standard here and, within the limits of § 469(i)(2), A's loss is treated as non-passive. Subsection (i)(2) generally limits the amount of loss re-classified as non-passive to $25,000. However the $25,000 figure is reduced by 50 percent of the amount by which the taxpayer's adjusted gross income exceeds $100,000. In this case, A's AGI exceeds $100,000 by $10,000, and the maximum deduction is therefore reduced by $5,000 (50% of $10,000) to $20,000 ($25,000 less $5,000). A can therefore deduct $20,000 of the loss as non-passive. The $25,000 balance is disallowed as a passive-activity loss. It can be carried forward to the following year under § 469(b).

Chapter 46

THE ALTERNATIVE MINIMUM TAX

Code: §§ 55(a), (b)(1)(A) & (2), (c)(1), (d)(1); 56(a)(1)(A) & (6), (b)(1) & (3), (e)(1) & (2); 57(a)(5).

1. On their joint return, H and W report taxable income of $75,000, computed as follows:

Salaries		$120,000
Less: Alimony paid		(20,000)
Adjusted gross income		$100,000
Less:		
State and local taxes	$5,000	
Charitable contribution	3,000	
Medical expenses	5,000	
Mortgage interest	4,000	
Miscellaneous itemized deductions	2,000	
Personal exemptions	6,000	
Total deductions		25,000
Taxable income		$75,000

They also received $10,000 interest on "specified private-activity bonds" (defined in § 57(a)(5)(C)). Upon exercise of an incentive stock option, W paid $10,000 for stock of her employer that had a value of $50,000. The mortgage interest was paid on a home-equity loan the proceeds of which were used to make a down payment on an airplane for recreational use. The charitable contribution represents a gift of stock with an adjusted basis of $1,000 and a value of $3,000. The total amount of medical expenses was $12,500. They are entitled to no credits against tax.

Determine the couple's alternative minimum taxable income (AMTI).

Section 55(b)(2) defines AMTI as taxable income with the adjustments provided in §§ 56 and 58 and increased by the items of tax preference described in § 57.

In computing AMTI, the state and local taxes are not allowable; § 56(b)(1)(A).

The charitable deduction is allowable in full. A previous version of the AMT limited the charitable deduction to the adjusted basis of the donated property; that provision was repealed, thanks largely to lobbying by universities and other charities.

For regular-tax purposes, medical expenses are allowable to the extent that they exceed 7.5 percent of adjusted gross income; § 213(a). So here the couple could deduct the amount by which their $12,500 of medical expenses exceeded 7.5 percent of their $100,000 AGI, or $5,000 ($12,500 less $7,500). In computing AMTI, they are allowed medical expenses only to the extent the expenses exceed 10 percent of AGI; § 56(b)(1)(B). So, their deduction is limited to $2,500 ($12,500 expenses less $10,000 AGI floor).

The mortgage loan is home-equity indebtedness, and the interest paid on the loan is qualified residence interest and deductible for regular-tax purposes. For AMT purposes, however, a deduction is allowed only for "qualified housing interest"; § 56(b)(1)(C)(i). Qualified housing interest is limited to interest paid on indebtedness incurred in acquiring, constructing or substantially improving the taxpayer's principal residence or a vacation home; § 56(e). The term does not include home-equity indebtedness the proceeds of which are devoted to a purpose other than home improvement. So the mortgage interest is not deductible in computing AMTI.

Miscellaneous itemized deductions are completely disallowed in computing AMTI (§ 56(b)(1)(A)(i)), as are the personal-exemption deductions; § 56(b)(1)(E).

Although excludable in computing regular-tax liability, interest on "specified private-activity bonds" must be included in AMTI; § 57(a)(5).

For regular-tax purposes, an employee's exercise of an incentive stock option does not result in income to the employee; see § 421. But § 421 does not apply for AMT purposes (§ 56(b)(3)), and so W must include in AMTI the $40,000 excess of the value of the stock on the date of exercise over the amount she paid upon exercise.

After making these adjustments to the couple's taxable income for regular-tax purposes, we determine the couple's AMTI to be $144,500:

Regular-tax TI		$75,000
Add:		
State taxes	$5,000	
Medical expenses	2,500	
Interest	4,000	
MID	2,000	
Exemptions	6,000	
Bond interest	10,000	
ISO income	40,000	
Total		69,500
AMTI		$144,500

2. A, a single person (not a surviving spouse), owes $16,000 of regular tax. Assume that the exemption amount for singles is $45,000. Compute A's alternative minimum tax (AMT) if her AMTI is:

(a) $112,500;

The tax base for the AMT is the "taxable excess" of AMTI over the "exemption amount"; § 55(b)(1)(A)(i) & (ii). The AMT tax rates are applied to that taxable excess to determine the "tentative minimum tax." The AMT is the excess of the tentative minimum tax over the regular tax for the year; § 55(a).

In this case, the exemption amount (§ 55(d)(1)) is *given* as $45,000. (Because Congress frequently tinkers with the exemption amount, the use of a given figure saves confusion. In any event, we are more interested in the concept than in the precise dollar amount.) The exemption is phased out whenever the taxpayer's AMTI exceeds a specified figure; § 55(d)(3). The phaseout is not an issue in this problem because for a single person the phaseout begins at $112,500 of AMTI, and so A is entitled to the entire exemption amount.

A's taxable excess is $67,500 ($112,500 AMTI less $45,000 exemption amount). A's tentative AMT is $17,550 (26% of $67,500 taxable excess); see § 55(b)(1)(A). A's minimum tax is $1,550 ($17,550 tentative minimum tax less $16,000 regular tax).

(b) $212,500.

Now A is in the phaseout range for the AMT exemption; see § 55(d)(3). A must reduce the exemption by 25 percent of the $100,000 by which her AMTI exceeds $112,500. The reduction is $25,000 (25% of $100,000), leaving A an exemption of $20,000 ($45,000 less $25,000). A's taxable excess is $192,500 ($212,500 AMTI less $20,000 exemption). Her tentative minimum tax is $50,400, which is the sum of $45,500 (26% of $175,000) and $4,900 (28% of the $17,500 by which the taxable excess exceeds $175,000); see § 55(b)(1)(i). A's minimum tax is $34,400 ($50,400 tentative minimum tax less $16,000 regular tax); see § 55(a).

3. What is A's marginal tax rate in problem 2(b)?

The marginal rate of tax is the rate that would apply if the taxpayer had one additional dollar of income. If A had $1 more income, her exemption would be reduced by $.25, so her taxable excess would increase by $1.25. The nominal tax rate applied to that $1.25 is 28 percent (§ 55(b)(1)(A)(i)(II)), which would increase A's minimum tax by $.35 (28% of $1.25). The marginal rate is 35% ($.35/1.00).

4. In January, C paid $100,000 for a business machine (5–year property) for use in business (a sole proprietorship). For regular-tax purposes, her depreciation deduction for the equipment is $20,000, leaving her with an adjusted basis of $80,000 at the end of the year.

(a) How much deprecation is allowable in computing AMTI?

For AMT purposes, depreciation generally must be computed using the 150–percent declining-balance method; § 56(a)(1)(A)(ii). (The straight-line method is used for depreciable real property and property depreciated under the straight-line method under § 168; id.)

C's deprecation for AMT purposes is $15,000. The straight-line rate for 5–year property is 20 percent. The 150–percent declining-balance percentage is 30 percent (150% of 20%). A full year's depreciation would be $30,000. After applying the half-year convention, the deduction is $15,000 (1/2 of $30,000).

(b) At the end of the year, what is C's adjusted basis for the machine for purposes of the AMT?

The use of different depreciation methods for regular tax and AMT purposes results in an asset's having different bases for purposes of the two taxes. Under the AMT, C's adjusted basis is $85,000 ($100,000 unadjusted basis less $15,000 of depreciation). If the asset is sold, the amount of gain or loss will differ under the two taxes.

5. R received a state income-tax refund that was fully includable in gross income for regular-tax purposes. How should the refund be treated in computing AMTI?

Since state taxes are not deductible under the AMT (§ 56(b)(1)(A)(ii)), a refund of such taxes is excludable from AMTI; see § 56(b)(1)(D).

6. The AMT was originally conceived as a tax on a few hundred wealthy taxpayers who used tax preferences extensively. In 2005, the President's Advisory Panel on Federal Tax Reform estimated that, unless Congress provides relief, 52 million taxpayers may be liable for the AMT by 2015. What features of the AMT (or the regular tax) are turning the AMT into a mass tax?

The AMT disallows deductions for personal exemptions, the standard deduction, and state and local taxes—all of which are important to many middle-income taxpayers. The AMT rates and exemption amounts are not indexed for inflation, which results in more AMT liability for taxpayers whose incomes have increased because of inflation. The most important factor, however, has been the reduction of regular-tax rates, which diminished regular-tax liability and thus resulted in the minimum tax exceeding the regular tax in many more cases. In other words, some of the regular-tax rate cuts were recovered by increased minimum taxes on the very people whose rates were cut.

Section L

OTHER TOPICS

Chapter 47

PRESENT AND FUTURE VALUE

In working the problems in this chapter, use the tables in Appendix A and ignore the effect of taxes (!).

A. FUTURE VALUE

1. R invests $10,000 today at a rate of return of 9 percent. How much should R expect to have after ten years?

Using Table I in Appendix A, we see that the future value of $1 invested for 10 years at 9% is $2.36736. The future value of $10,000 is $23,673.60 ($10,000 x 2.36736).

2. I plans to invest $1,000 in a 6–year certificate of deposit. What will the investment cumulate to if I invests with:

(a) Bank A, which offers interest of 12 percent annually on such CDs?

$1,973.82 ($1,000 x 1.97382).

(b) Bank B, which offers 12 percent compounded semi-annually?

$2,012.20. When we are given a nominal annual interest rate and told that the interest will be compounded m times each year, we can find the appropriate future-value factor in Table I by dividing the nominal rate by m and multiplying by m the number of years during which the fund will be invested. Here, we use the factor for $r = 6\%$ (12%/year x 1/2 year) and $n = 12$ periods (6 years x 2 periods/year). The factor is 2.01220. Multiplying the factor by $1,000 gives us $2,012.20.

(c) Bank C, which offers 12 percent compounded quarterly?

$2032.79. The factor for $r = 3\%$, $n = 24$ periods is 2.03279. Multiplying the factor by $1,000 gives us $2,032.79.

3. What is the effective annual interest rate offered by each bank in 2? (Use the first year's interest to determine the effective annual rate.)

The effective annual rate means the equivalent rate of interest compounded on an annual basis.

Since it compounds interest only on an annual basis, Bank A's effective annual interest rate is 12%.

Bank B compounds semi-annually, which means that after the first year, the $1,000 investment cumulates to $1,123.60 ($1,000 x 1.12360). Thus after 1 year, I has earned interest of $123.60, which puts him in the same position as if he had earned 12.36% ($123.60 interest/$1,000 principal) interest compounded annually. Thus, the effective annual rate is 12.36%.

Bank C compounds quarterly, which means that after 1 year the $1,000 would cumulate to $1,125.51 ($1,000 x 1.12551). The $1,000 has earned $125.51 interest, for an effective annual rate of 12.55% ($125.51 interest/$1,000 principal).

This problem illustrates why, in comparing interest rates, one must always consider the frequency of compounding. The more frequently the interest is compounded, the higher the effective annual rate.

4. T anticipates that on account of a certain transaction he will owe approximately $15,000 in taxes after ten years. If T can earn an after-tax rate of return of 10% annually, how much should T set aside today in order to have $15,000 for the tax payment after ten years?

$5,783.15. Let X equal the amount to be invested today. We know that X x K (n = 10 years, r = 10%) = $15,000. K ($n$ = 10 years, r = 10%) is 2.59374. Therefore, X = $15,000/2.59374 = $5,783.15.

5. At what approximate rate of (after-tax) return must B invest her money if she wishes to double her investment in ten years?

7 percent. To determine the rate of return, go across the 10–period row in Table I until you find a factor approximately equal to 2. That is at 7 percent, where the factor is 1.96715. If she invests, say, $1,000, for 10 years at 7 percent, the fund will grow to $1,967.15.

6. J has $10,000 of cash to invest today. If J wants to increase that amount to $15,000 over six years, what approximate rate of return must J earn on the investment?

7 percent. We know that $10,000 x K ($r$ = X, n = 6) = $15,000, from which we can infer that K = $15,000/$10,000 = 1.5000. If we go across the 6–period row in

Table I, we see that K is approximately equal to 1.5000 at 7 percent, where the factor is 1.50073.

7. G is going to invest $10,000 at an after-tax rate of return of 6 percent. For approximately how long must the fund be invested to cumulate to $19,000?

Eleven years. We know that $10,000 x K ($r$ = 6%, n = X) = $19,000, from which we can infer that K (r = 6%, n = X) = $19,000/$10,000 = 1.9000. Now we go down the 6–percent column until we find the value of the factor approaches 1.9000, which is at 11 years, where the factor is 1.89830.

B. FUTURE VALUE OF AN ANNUITY

1. A is going to set aside $10,000 at the end of each of the next 20 years. A can earn an after-tax return of 8 percent. What will be the balance in the fund after 20 years?

This involves the calculation of the future value of an annuity. The factor for (n = 20, r = 8%) is found in Table III to be 45.76196. The expected value of the fund after 20 years is $457,619.60 ($10,000 x 45.76196).

2. B will invest $5,000 on January 1, year 1, and a like sum on each subsequent January 1 through January 1, year 10. After B's last contribution, the fund will remain invested through January 1, year 15. If B earns an after-tax return of 8 percent at all times, what will be the balance in the fund on January 1, year 15?

After the tenth contribution to the fund on January 1, year 10, the balance in the fund will be $72,432.80 ($5,000 x 14.48656). The future value of that sum after five years of compounding at 8 percent is $106,427.69 ($72,432.80 x 1.46933).

3. D is planning to start a savings fund for her child, C, who turns 11 years old today. Beginning on C's 12th birthday, D will invest $1,000 a year in the fund, which earns a return of 12 percent at all times. D will make the final contribution when C attains age 21. What will be the balance in the fund when C attains 21?

When D makes the tenth contribution to the fund on D's 21st birthday, the fund balance will be $17,548.74 ($1,000 x 17.54874).

4. Suppose instead that D made the first contribution on C's 11th birthday and the tenth (and final) contribution on C's 20th birthday. What would be the balance in the fund on C's 21st birthday?

This problem involves an annuity in advance, in which the contribution is made on the first rather than the last day of the year. Table III provides factors for an annuity in arrears. However, its factors can be converted to value an annuity in advance. Notice, for example, that we could use the factor for an 11–year annuity in arrears (as if D was going to make an eleventh payment on C's 21st birthday), but then subtract 1.00000 from the factor (because that 11th payment will not really be made). Using this approach, the factor for the 10–year annuity in advance would be (K [$n = 11$, $r = 12\%$] minus 1.00000), or K = (20.65458 − 1.00000) = 19.65458. The value of the fund on C's 21st birthday would be $19,654.58 ($1,000 x 19.65458).

Alternatively, we could find the value of a 10–year annuity in arrears on C's 20th birthday and then calculate the amount to which that figure would cumulate after one more year of compounding. Using that approach, we determine that the value of the fund on C's 20th birthday is $17,548.74 ($1,000 x 17.54874). By the end of the following year, when C turns 21, the fund will be $19,654.59 ($17,548.74 x 1.1200).

5. The terms of E's $100,000 student loan require repayment in a single payment due ten years after E's graduation. E graduates on June 1, year 1. In addition to paying the interest each year, E plans to invest a fixed amount on the anniversary of her graduation for each of the next ten years, which sum will then be used to pay the student loan when it matures on June 1, year 11. E thinks she can earn a 10 percent after-tax return on her investments. How much must E invest on each anniversary of her graduation in order to repay the loan in timely fashion?

Here we know the future value of the annual payments, the rate of return and the number of periods, but we don't know the amount of the annual payment. The constant, K ($n = 10$, $r = 10\%$), is 15.93742. If we let X = the annual contribution, we know K x X = $100,000, from which we can infer that X = $100,000/K = $100,000/15.93742 = $6,274.54. So, E must set aside $6,274.54 annually to fund the repayment of the loan after ten years.

6. Same as 5, except that E will make the first contribution to the fund on her graduation day and the final contribution on June 1, year 10 (one year before the principal is due). Determine the amount of E's annual contribution.

Now the problem requires us to determine the contribution required for an annuity in advance. As in problem 4, we can determine the factor for a 10–year annuity in advance by subtracting 1.00000 from the factor for an 11–year annuity in arrears. The annuity-in-arrears factor is 18.53117 (Table III), so the factor for the 10–year annuity in advance is 17.53117. The required annual contribution is $5,704.13 ($100,000/17.53117).

7. **F would like to be able to purchase a new car in three years. F estimates that the car will cost $25,000. How much must F set aside at the end of each month in order to accumulate sufficient funds for the purchase after three years? F thinks he can earn 12% interest (compounded monthly) on the investment.**

F is going to make 36 monthly contributions, and the interest rate is 1 percent a month. The factor for the future value of an annuity ($n = 36$, $r = 1\%$) is 43.07688, and the amount of each contribution is given by $25,000/43.07688$, which is $580.36 a month.

C. PRESENT VALUE

1. **If A can earn 7 percent annual interest on a comparably risky investment, how much should A be willing to pay for a $1,000 zero-coupon bond due in ten years? (The purchaser of a zero-coupon bond does not receive periodic interest payments but instead receives a single payment at maturity. The bond is purchased at a discount from its face amount (i.e., the amount payable at maturity) for an amount equal to the present value of the future payment.)**

In most instances, the purchaser of a bond obtains two financial rights: (1) the right to periodic interest payments; and (2) the right to the principal payment at the bond's maturity. The value of a bond is simply the sum of the present values of those rights discounted at the discount rate for investments involving a comparable degree of risk. In the case of the zero-coupon bond, however, the bondholder is not entitled to periodic interest payments but to only the face amount of the bond at maturity. Since investors can earn 7 percent on comparably risky investments, we use Table II to discount the $1,000 future payment at that rate, which gives us a present value of $508.35 ($1,000 x .50835).

2. **B sells property for $500,000, payable (without interest) after five years. What is the equivalent cash selling price for the property if B can earn 8 percent on comparably risky investments?**

In essence, B is making a 5–year loan to the purchaser. If B can earn 8 percent by making a comparably risky loan, B would be indifferent between the immediate receipt of an amount equal to the present value of $500,000 discounted for 5 years at 8 percent and the receipt of $500,000 after 5 years. So, the equivalent cash sales price is $340,290 (.68058 x $500,000).

3. **Same as 2, except that the expected return on comparably risky investments is 8% compounded quarterly.**

Recall that when the interest (or the expected return) is going to be compounded m times a year, we determine the appropriate factor by multiplying the number of years, and dividing the interest (discount) rate, by m. So, here we want to determine the present value of $500,000 discounted for 20 periods at 2 percent. From Table II, we see that the factor is .67297, and the present value is therefore $336,485.

4. Explain why your answer in 3 is less than in 2.

The expected rate of return (discount rate) is higher in 3 than in 2 because of compounding. At a higher expected rate of return, the present value of the right to the future $500,000 cash payment decreases. If B can earn 8 percent compounded quarterly by lending his money to an equally credit-worthy borrower, why should he accept any lower rate of return from the purchaser? When interest rates increase, the value of a dollar in hand increases (and the value of a dollar to be received in the future decreases) because the dollar in hand can then earn a higher rate of return. The value of the right to a future payment therefore decreases.

5. A seller of property offers it at $100,000, payable immediately, or $130,000 payable (without interest) after 5 years. C wishes to purchase the property. If C can earn a return of 5 percent on comparable investments, which payment method would she prefer?

The present value of $130,000 discounted for 5 years at 5 percent is $101,859 ($130,000 x .78353). That means that C would have to set aside that amount at 5 percent to accumulate the $130,000 after 5 years. It is therefore cheaper for C to pay the $100,000 today.

D. PRESENT VALUE OF AN ANNUITY

1. In settlement of a suit for personal injury, P is entitled to receive $100,000 at the end of each of the next 20 years. If the appropriate discount rate is 9 percent, what is the present value of P's right?

This problem requires to determine the present value of an annuity. Using Table IV, we see that the factor for a 20–year annuity at 9 percent is 9.12855. The present value of P's entitlement is therefore $912,855 (9.12855 x $100,000).

2. R intends to make a partial gift to a charitable organization specified in § 170(c)(2). R transfers $100,000 cash to the charity in exchange for an annuity of $8,137.27 payable at the end of each of the next ten years. To what extent has R made a charitable contribution? Assume that the annuity is valued using a discount rate of 10 percent.

The amount of the charitable contribution is the excess of the amount of cash transferred by R over the value of the annuity to be received. The present value of a 10–year annuity discounted at 10 percent is $50,000 (6.14457 x $8,137.27). The charitable gift is thus $50,000 ($100,000 cash transferred less $50,000 value of annuity).

3. On January 1, year 1, S sold a farm for $600,000, payable $100,000 down and $100,000 on January 1 of each of the following 5 years. The contract made no provision for interest on th e deferred payments. Comparably risky credits earn interest at the rate of 6%. What is the equivalent cash selling price of the farm on January 1, year 1?

This stream of six $100,000 payments represents an annuity in advance—i.e., an annuity where the first payment is made at the *beginning* of the first period. Table IV gives the factors for an annuity in arrears, where the first payment is made at the *end* of the first period. However, we can derive the factor for an annuity in advance from Table IV by adding 1.00000 (representing the first payment to be received) to the factor for an annuity of 5 years (payable at the end of each of years 1 through 5). The factor for an annuity in arrears ($n = 5$, $r = 6\%$) is 4.21236. Adding 1.00000 to that figure gives us 5.21236, and the present value of the right to the six $100,000 payments is $521,236. That is the equivalent cash sales price of the farm.

4. T is to receive property rentals of $1,000 a month for a 12–month lease. Each month's rent is due at the beginning of the month, and the appropriate discount rate is 12% compounded monthly. What is the present value of the lease payments at the inception of the lease?

The rentals represent a 12–payment monthly annuity in advance. The factor for an n-period annuity in advance is determined by adding 1.00000 to the annuity-in-arrears factor for $(n - 1)$ periods. Here, the factor for an *11*–period annuity in arrears ($r = 1\%$) is 10.36763, from which we can deduce that the factor for the *12*–period annuity in advance is 11.36763. The present value of the lease payments is thus $11,367.63.

5. A $1,000 bond (the "old bond") with a remaining term of 6 years bears interest at 6% payable semiannually. If a new bond of comparable riskiness yields 8% compounded semi-annually, at what price will the old bond sell?

The purchaser of the bond acquires two separate financial rights: (1) the right to the semi-annual interest payments of $30 (6% x $1,000 x 1/2); and (2) the right to the return of the $1,000 bond principal at maturity—in this case, after six years. The value of the bond is the sum of the present values of these two rights to future cash payments. In valuing the bond, we must discount the future cash flows using current market rates on comparably risky instruments, as that is the rate an investor can earn today. Since the amount of interest to be paid on the bond is fixed by contract, the market adjusts the interest rate by re-valuing the bond when interest rates change.

To evaluate the stream of semi-annual interest payments of $30 each, we turn to Table IV. With $n = 12$ (i.e., 6 years x 2 payments/year) and $r = 4\%$ (8%/2), the factor for the present value of an annuity is 9.38507. The present value of the right to the interest payments is therefore $281.55 ($30 × 9.38507).

To determine the present value of the right to the $1,000 principal payment, we return to Table II. The present-value factor ($n = 12$ and $r = 4\%$) is .62460, and the present value of the right to receive the principal payment is therefore $624.60 ($1,000 x .6246).

The value of the bond is therefore $906.15, the sum of the present values of the rights to the interest and principal payments.

6. U, who can earn 10% annually on his investments at all times, expects to accumulate $998,474 in his Roth IRA by the time of his 65th birthday. He wants to withdraw the balance in the account in 25 equal annual installments beginning when he attains age 65. How much can U withdraw in each year?

In this case, we know the present value of the fund on U's 65th birthday ($998,474). We want to know the amount that U can withdraw annually. U wants to withdraw an installment on his 65th birthday and another installment each year thereafter for 24 years. This is another annuity in advance, and the factor can be determined by adding 1.00000 (representing the withdrawal on his 65th birthday) to the factor for a 24–payment annuity in arrears (representing the payments at age 66 and after). The 24–payment arrearage factor (at $r = 10\%$) is 8.98474, and the factor for the 25–payment annuity in advance is therefore 9.98474. Let X equal the amount of the annual payment. Then, X x 9.98474 = $998,474, which implies that X = $998,474/9.98474 = $100,000. So, U can withdraw $100,000 each year through his 89th birthday.

7. On January 1, year 1, H borrows $120,000 from a bank at 10–percent annual interest for the purpose of purchasing a home. The loan must be amortized (repaid) in equal annual installments at the end of each of the next twenty years. Each payment will be credited first to interest and then to principal.

(a) What is the amount of each annual payment?

H issues a promissory note to the bank in exchange for $120,000 cash. In this arm's length transaction, the note has a present value of $120,000. Let X equal the amount of the payment. We know that X x K ($n = 20$, $r = 10\%$) = $120,000 and K = 8.51356 (Table IV), from which we can infer that X = $120,000/8.51356 = $14,095.16.

(b) How is the first payment apportioned between interest and principal?

At the end of the first year, when the first payment is due, the amount of accrued interest is $12,000 (10% of $120,000). The payment will be allocated $12,000 to interest and $2,095.16 to principal, thus reducing the principal balance to 117,904.84.

8. The tiny island country of Bikinia is offering a new issue of its bonds that will pay $240 a year annual interest in perpetuity but with no return of principal (ever). I, an investor, thinks that she can earn 12 percent annually on comparably risky securities. What price should I be willing to pay for one of the Bikinia bonds?

The bond is a perpetuity—i.e., a bond on which only interest is paid. The holder is entitled to a stream of annuity payments stretching into the indefinite future. The value of the payments is given by dividing the annual payment by the appropriate discount rate. In this case, the bond is worth $2,000 ($240/.12).

Notice that the purchaser of the bond will receive income of $240 a year on an investment of $2,000, for a yield of 12 percent ($240/$2,000), which is the expected rate of return.

Chapter 48

PRACTICE EXAMINATION QUESTIONS

---

1. (2 hours) *Basic Facts*: Theresa (T) (who is in the 35% tax bracket) owns a building (ignore the land) that she purchased several years ago at a price of $500 (000 omitted throughout). She has properly deducted $100 of straight-line depreciation (through the date of disposition of the property in the current year) and her adjusted basis is $400. During her ownership of the property, T has not sustained any loss with respect to the property (i.e., the gross income from the property has been sufficient to cover her out-of-pocket and depreciation expenses). Assume that, except where otherwise stated, (1) the property was worth $600 when it was disposed of by T; (2) the disposition of the building is T's only disposition of property for the year; (3) all parties are unrelated; and (4) all sales are bona fide.

Explain fully the tax consequences to T (and only T), including the tax rate applicable to any recognized gain, in each of the following *alternative* transactions.

(a) The building is in downtown University City and is held for use in T's business. T sells the building for $600 cash and pays a brokerage commission of $40 on the sale.

T's amount realized is $560 ($600 selling price less $40 brokerage commission), and her realized gain is $160 ($560 amount realized less $400 adjusted basis); § 1001(a). The gain is recognized; § 1001(c). Since the building is depreciable and used in business, it is not a capital asset (see § 1221(a)(2)), but it is a 1231 asset (see § 1231(b)(1)). It is also 1250 property (depreciable real property—1250(c)), but 1250 does not recapture any part of the gain because only straight-line depreciation was used and therefore there is no "additional depreciation" within the meaning of § 1250(b)(1). The gain is a § 1231 gain (arising from the sale of a § 1231 asset—§ 1231(a)(3)(A)(i)), and since it is T's only § 1231 gain for the year, the § 1231 gain ($160) exceeds the § 1231 loss (zero), and the gain is characterized as a long-term capital gain; § 1231(a)(1).

The "unrecaptured § 1250 gain," though a long-term capital gain, is subject to tax at a 25–percent rate; § 1(h)(1)(D). The unrecaptured § 1250 gain is the *additional* amount that would be treated as ordinary income if § 1250 recaptured *all* depreciation rather than just the excess of accelerated depreciation over straight-line; § 1(h)(6)(A)(i). In this case, T has deducted $100 of straight-line depreciation, and that would have been recaptured if § 1250 recaptured *all* depreciation, so that is the amount of the unrecaptured § 1250 gain, which is subject to tax at 25 percent. The remaining $60 of gain is part of the adjusted net capital gain and taxable at a maximum rate of 15 percent. (Notice that, at least if we ignore the effect of inflation, the $60 is the "economic" gain on the transaction—the excess of the $560 amount realized over the $500 cost of the property—while the $100 of unrecaptured § 1250 gain is a "make-up" gain that restores to income the depreciation deductions in excess of the building's decline in value.)

(b) The building (held for investment) is located in University City and held for rent. T receives $600 cash for the property when the City, through exercise of its power of eminent domain, condemns the building to build a parking ramp. T promptly reinvests $550 of the condemnation proceeds in an oceanside condominium (also to be held as investment rental property). The condominium is located in Puerto Vallarta, Mexico.

On the condemnation, T realizes gain of $200 ($600 amount realized less $400 adjusted basis). This is an involuntary conversion of the building into money, and T can elect to limit the recognition of gain under § 1033(a)(2)(A). T replaced the building by purchasing replacement property within the time required (3 years following the year in which the property was involuntarily converted, since the building was held for use in investment and was condemned—§ 1033(g)(4)).

In order to qualify for § 1033 non-recognition, the replacement property must usually be "similar or related in service or use" to the property involuntarily converted. In the case of investment real property that is condemned, however, property of "like kind" may be treated as satisfying the "similar" test; § 1033(g)(1). Unfortunately, the like-kind test is not helpful to T here because real property located outside of the United States is not considered to be of like kind with real property located within the country; § 1031(h)(1) So, the Mexican property would not be of like kind with T's University City property.

Nevertheless, the properties may qualify under the similar-use test because both are real property and both are held for rental. Where the taxpayer is an investor, the test is applied by considering the similarity in the uses to which the converted and replacement properties have been put by the taxpayer. If the taxpayer is a lessor, as here, the test focuses on whether the properties are of similar service to the taxpayer, the nature of the business risks connected with the properties, and what management services the lessor furnishes to tenants. Here both buildings are held for investment, and even though the buildings have different end uses, both are held by T as rental properties. Assuming that the level of services that T provided the tenants was similar and that the nature of T's business risks in the two properties were similar, the properties should satisfy the satisfy the similar-use test, so that T can limit the recognition of gain.

If T elects § 1033 non-recognition, the $200 realized gain is recognized only to the extent of $50 (the amount by which the $600 amount realized on the involuntary conversion exceeds the $550 cost of the replacement property); § 1033(a)(2)(A)). The University City building was a capital asset (investment property), so the $50 of recognized gain qualifies as a 1231 gain (gain from condemnation of a long-term capital asset held in connection with investment); § 1231(a)(3)(A)(ii)(II). Since the § 1231 gain ($50) exceeds the § 1231 loss (zero), the gain will be a long-term capital gain; § 1231(a). As in (a), the gain will be taxed at the 25–percent rate as unrecaptured § 1250 gain (i.e., make-up gain).

T's adjusted basis for the condominium is $400 ($550 cost less $150 of unrecognized gain); § 1033(b)(2). The holding period for the condo includes the period during which T held the University City building; § 1223(1).

(c) T exchanges the building (held for investment) for an apartment building (to be used in business). The apartment building is worth $450, and T also receives a vintage Mercedes worth $150 to equalize the exchange. (The automobile had a basis of $60 in the hands of the other party to the exchange.)

T's amount realized is $600 ($450 value of new building plus $150 value of car). Her realized gain is $200 ($600 amount realized less $400 adjusted basis). The exchange qualifies as a like-kind exchange (real property for real property) under § 1031. (It doesn't matter that one building was held for investment and the other for business; Treas. Reg. § 1.1031(a)–1(a)(1).) Section 1031(a) does not apply because the exchange is not solely for property of like kind, but § 1031(b) permits non-recognition except to the extent of the $150 boot (i.e., the value of the car) received. The building is a capital asset (investment property), it was exchanged, and the gain is therefore a long-term capital gain; § 1222(3). The $150 gain consists of $100 of unrecaptured § 1250 gain (taxable at 25 percent) and $50 of economic gain (taxable as adjusted net capital gain at 15 percent).

T's basis for the two assets received is $550 ($400 AB of old building, plus $150 gain recognized); § 1031(d). In allocating the total basis between the two assets, T must allocate to the car an amount equal to its value ($150), leaving $400 to allocate to the new building; id. T can tack on to her holding period for the new building the period during which she held the old because her basis for the new building is determined by reference to her adjusted basis for the old, and the old building was a capital asset; 1223(1). Her holding period for the car begins with its acquisition because it gets a fair-market-value basis.

The other party's basis for the car is legally irrelevant.

(d) T transferred the building (held for investment) to Y Corp. in exchange for $500 cash and $100 worth of Microsoft stock. Half of the stock of Y Corp. is owned by T's son-in-law, (S) and half by her daughter, D.

T's amount realized is $600 ($500 cash plus $100 value of stock). T's realized and recognized gain is $200 ($600 amount realized less $400 adjusted basis). The building is a capital asset (because held for investment). The gain is therefore a long-term capital gain unless § 1239 makes it ordinary.

Whether § 1239 applies depends upon whether Y is a "controlled entity" with respect to T (i.e., whether T owns more than 50% in value of the Y stock); § 1239(b)(1) & (c)(1)(A). T is not a shareholder of Y, but § 1239(c)(2) requires that share ownership be determined under the attribution rules of § 267(c). Under § 267(c)(2), T is treated as owning any shares owned by her "family," a term defined in § 267(c)(4) to include T's lineal descendant (D) but not her son-in-law, S. Although D is treated as owning S's shares (because S is D's spouse and S is therefore a member of D's family under 267(c)(4)), shares owned constructively by D under the family-attribution rule of § 267(c)(2) cannot be re-attributed to T under the family-attribution rule because of § 267(c)(5). So, T constructively owns exactly (not *more than*) 50% of the value of the Y stock and Y is not a controlled entity with respect to T. The gain is therefore long-term capital gain, $100 of which is taxable at 25 percent (the unrecaptured § 1250 gain) and $100 at 15 percent (the adjusted net capital gain).

T obtains a tax-cost basis of $100 for the Microsoft stock (the amount at which it was includable in T's amount realized).

(e) The building was held for use in business. When T purchased the building, she paid $100 cash down and borrowed the $400 balance of the purchase price from a bank on a non-recourse note secured by the building. Although T made all interest payments on time, T paid only $20 on the note principal. This year, when the value of the building was $350 and its adjusted basis $400, T surrendered the property to the lender. T was hopelessly insolvent at that time.

Because T is not personally liable, the entire amount of the encumbrance is includable in T's amount realized, even though it exceeds the value of the building; Treas. Reg. § 1.1001–2(a)(1) & (4)(i), & (c), Ex. (7). T's amount realized is therefore $380, and T realizes and recognizes loss of $20 ($400 adjusted basis less $380 amount realized). The loss is allowable under § 165(a) & (c)(1) as a business loss. (The value of the building is legally irrelevant, as is the fact that T is insolvent.) The building is a § 1231 asset (real property used in business—§ 1231(b)(1)), and the loss is a § 1231 loss (§ 1231(a)(3)(B)). Since this is T's only transaction for the year, the loss is ordinary; § 1231(a)(2).

(f) The building, which T held for investment, had an adjusted basis of $400 and was encumbered with a $500 mortgage that secured a loan on which T was personally liable. (The liability was incurred when T borrowed part of the purchase price for the building.) When the value of the building was $380, T surrendered it to the lender. Although T was not insolvent, the lender discharged T from further liability.

Because T is personally liable, the transaction must be bifurcated into a "sale" of the building to the lender for an amount equal to its value, and a discharge of indebtedness to the extent that the discharged debt exceeds the value of the building; Treas. Reg. § 1.1001–2(c), Ex. (8). T's amount realized on the sale of the building to the lender is thus $380 (the value of the building), and T realizes a loss of $20 ($400 adjusted basis less $380 amount realized). The loss is recognized and allowable (subject to the limits on the deductibility of capital losses) under § 165(a) & (c)(2). The building was a capital asset in T's hands, and the transfer to the mortgagee is a "sale or exchange," so the loss is a long-term capital loss. Section 1211(b) limits the deductibility of capital losses to the extent of capital gains, though, if the losses exceed the gains, up to $3,000 can be used to offset ordinary income. Any portion of the loss that is not deductible in the current year can be carried forward indefinitely under § 1212(b).

T also realizes debt-discharge income of $120 ($500 debt discharged less $380 value of building surrendered). That amount is taxable to T as ordinary-income.

2. (1 hour, 20 minutes) **Discuss the income-tax results to P of the following transactions. (Ignore the effect of inflation adjustments and §§ 68 and 151(d)(3). Computation of the tax is not required.)**

P holds a half-time appointment as a professor on the faculty of State University, where he serves on the botany faculty. He is also employed as chief research scientist by Superplant, Inc., a firm that attempts to develop exotic hybrid plants.

P's salary from the University is $120,000 ($10,000 a month). P is very concerned that R, his principal post-doctoral research assistant at the University, may leave her post because the University has skimped on her salary. He has therefore requested the University to pay his salary for the month of December to R, and the University has agreed to do so.

Superplant pays P a salary of $250,000 for the current year. It also has a non-statutory stock-option plan. Five years ago, when Superplant stock was selling at $10,000 a share, the firm granted P a non-statutory option to purchase one of its shares for $20,000. P exercised the option today, when the share has a value of $50,000. There are no restrictions on the share.

Because some of P's work at Superplant exposes him to hazardous chemicals, P must wear protective clothing in the Superplant lab. He spent $6,000 on such clothing during the current year. P also spent $1,000 commuting between his office at the University and his laboratory at Superplant (a distance of 15 miles).

This year P began receiving annual payments of $10,000 under a single-premium annuity contract that his father had purchased for him ten years ago at a cost of $121,000. The annuity payments were to commence when P attained age 60, which he did this year, and continue until P's death.

P owns his home (Greenacre), which is valued at $400,000. Although P long ago retired the mortgage on Greenacre, he re-mortgaged it this year for $250,000 and applied the loan proceeds toward the purchase of a vacation home in Florida. During the year, he paid $25,000 of interest on the loan. He also paid $4,000 of property taxes on Greenacre and $6,000 of property taxes on the Florida vacation home.

P is divorced and pays alimony to his former wife, W, in the amount of $50,000 a year for the duration of W's life. In addition, if W survives P, the payments to W continue and must be made from P's estate. The divorce decree also requires that P pay the property taxes on the home in which W resides (the former marital home of P and W, which is now owned by W). P paid $5,000 of such taxes in the current year.

P also made two gifts to charities qualifying under § 170(c)(2): $10,000 worth of X stock that he purchased six months ago for $8,000, and $20,000 worth of Y stock that he inherited from his father five years ago when its value was $5,000.

P's $370,000 of salary paid by his two employers must be included in gross income; § 61(a)(1). Even if the University pays P's December salary to R, P must include that $10,000 in gross income under Lucas v. Earl (income from performance of personal services taxed to the person who earns it).

P may, however, be able to deduct the $10,000 as a business expense under § 162(a) (an employee is in business). Unfortunately, however, the deduction would be an itemized deduction (because an employee's unreimbursed business expenses are not deductible in computing AGI; (§ 62(a)(1)). Moreover, the deduction would be a miscellaneous itemized deduction (67(b)), and such deductions are allowable only to the extent that, in the aggregate, they exceed 2 percent of AGI; § 67(a).

P's exercise of the non-statutory option is taxable under § 83(a), as the share is substantially vested. P must include in income the excess of the $50,000 value of the share over the $20,000 paid for it. So, P has $30,000 of compensation income from the exercise of the stock option. P obtains a basis of $50,000 for the stock ($20,000 actual cost plus $30,000 tax cost); § 1012.

The $6,000 cost of the protective clothing should be allowable as an employee-business expense under § 162(a). Although clothing costs are generally non-deductible personal living expenses (see § 262), a deduction is permitted where the clothing is not suitable for wear (and is not worn) outside of the workplace. The protective gear is not suitable for general-purpose wear, and its cost is deductible. But because P is an employee, the deduction is an itemized deduction and also a miscellaneous itemized deduction, which, as discussed above, is limited in its deductibility.

The $1,000 cost of commuting between the two places of work should be allowable under § 162(a) as an employee business expense (i.e., as a miscellaneous itemized deduction).

Fifty percent of the $10,000 annuity payment, or $5,000 must be included in gross income. Under § 72(b), P can exclude from income a portion of the annuity payment represented by the product of the amount received and the exclusion ratio; see § 72(b)(1). The exclusion ratio is determined by dividing the investment in the contract by the expected return under the contract; id. The investment in the contract is the aggregate amount of consideration (premiums) paid for the contract; § 72(c)(1). (It makes no difference here that P's father rather than P furnished the consideration for the contract. The father's purchase of the contract was a gift and excludable from P's income by § 102(a).) The expected return is the product of the annual annuity payment ($10,000) and the expected-return multiple based, in the case of a life annuity such as this, on the annuitant's life expectancy; § 72(c)(3)(A). The Service has promulgated Table V in Treas. Reg. § 1.72–9 for determining the expected-return multiple. For a 60–year old, the multiple is 24.2, and the expected return is therefore $242,000 (24.2 x $10,000). The exclusion ratio is thus 50 percent ($121,100/$242,000). P can exclude $5,000 (50% of $10,000) and must include $5,000 in gross income.

The interest paid on the mortgage covering Greenacre appears to be personal interest and hence non-deductible, unless it is "qualified residence interest"; § 163(h)(1) & (2). Qualified residence interest is interest paid on acquisition indebtedness or home-equity indebtedness with respect to a qualified residence; § 163(h)(3). Greenacre is a qualified residence because it is P's principal residence; § 163(h)(4)(A)(i)(I). (The vacation home could also be a qualified residence because P uses the home as a residence, even though it's not P's principal residence; § 163(h)(4)(A)(i)(II).) The indebtedness does not qualify as acquisition indebtedness because the mortgage does not secure the home *acquired*, as required by § 163(h)(2)(B)(i)(II). The indebtedness is home-equity indebtedness because the loan is secured by a qualified residence (Greenacre), and the amount of the indebtedness ($250,000) does not exceed the value of Greenacre ($400,000) less any acquisition indebtedness encumbering Greenacre (zero); see § 163(h)(3)(C)(i). However, the maximum amount treated as home-equity indebtedness is $100,000;

§ 163(h)(3)(C)(ii). So, only $10,000 ($25,000 x [$100,000/$250,000]) of the interest is deductible by P. (The interest deduction is allowed by § 163(a)). It is an itemized deduction (but not a miscellaneous itemized deduction—§ 67(b)(1)).

The $10,000 total property-tax payments on Greenacre and the Florida home are allowable under § 164(a)(1). These are itemized deductions, but not miscellaneous itemized deductions—§ 67(b)(2).

The $50,000 of cash alimony is deductible by P as an above-the-line deduction; §§ 215; 62(a)(10). The payments terminate at W's death, as required by § 71(b)(1)(D). (It does not matter that the payments continue beyond the payor's death, as is the case here.) The other aspects of the alimony definition in § 71(b) appear to be satisfied, so P gets the $50,000 deduction.

The property taxes that P pays on W's home are not deductible by P as property taxes because P does not own the property. However, the $5,000 could be deductible as alimony (a cash payment made "on behalf of" W—§ 71(b)(1)(A)), if P's obligation to pay the taxes ceases at W's death (§ 71(b)(1)(D))—a fact that is (deliberately) not provided here. So, if the property-tax payments cease at W's death, P can deduct the payments. If the payments do not cease at W's death, P cannot deduct them.

P recognizes no gain on the transfer of the stock to the charities. P is entitled to a charitable deduction for the gifts under § 170. In general, the amount of the deduction for contributed property is the fair market value of the property; Treas. Reg. § 1.170A–1(c)(1). But the deduction for the X stock must be reduced by the amount of gain that would not be long-term capital gain if the stock were sold for its fair market value; § 170(e)(1)(A). A sale of the X stock would result in $2,000 of gain, but the gain would be short-term capital gain because P has not held the stock for more than one year; see § 1222(1). The deduction is therefore limited to $8,000 ($10,000 value less $2,000 potential short-term capital gain). P can deduct the $20,000 value of the Y stock. (His basis for the stock is $5,000, as the stock is property acquired from a decedent and the basis of such property is generally its value at the decedent's death; § 1014(a) & (b)(1). But the basis of the stock is irrelevant here, as its sale would have produced long-term capital gain.) P's total charitable deduction is $28,000. (P is comfortably within the 30–percent and 50–percent limits of § 170(b)(1)(A) & (C).) The charitable deduction is an itemized deduction, but not a miscellaneous itemized deduction; see § 67(b)(4).

To summarize, P's gross income is $405,000 ($370,000 salary, plus $30,000 from exercise of the option, plus $5,000 of the annuity payment).

P's adjusted gross income is $350,000 ($405,000 gross income less $55,000 alimony). This assumes that P's obligation to pay W's property taxes ceases at W's death and therefore is deductible as alimony. If the obligation extends beyond W's death, then the property taxes could not be deducted, and P's AGI would be $355,000.

Next we compute P's itemized deductions. We begin with the $17,000 of miscellaneous itemized deductions ($10,000 of salary expense, $6,000 of clothing expense, and $1,000 of transportation expense). The miscellaneous itemized deductions are allowable only to the extent that they exceed 2 percent of AGI, or $7,000 (2% of $350,000). So, the allowable portion of the miscellaneous itemized deductions is $10,000 ($17,000 less $7,000).

To this $10,000, we add the $10,000 of interest expense, $10,000 of property taxes on P's two homes, and $28,000 in charitable contributions for total itemized deductions of $48,000 (ignoring § 68 per instructions). Since total itemized deductions exceed P's standard deduction ($3,000 under § 63(c)(2)(C)), P will itemize.

P's personal exemption is $2,000 (ignoring § 151(d)(3) per instructions).

P's taxable income is $300,000 ($350,000 AGI less $48,000 of itemized deductions and the $2,000 personal exemption).

Although a tax computation is not required, notice that for minimum-tax purposes the $10,000 of miscellaneous itemized deductions, $10,000 of property taxes and $2,000 exemption would be disallowed; § 56(b)(1)(A) & (E). So, P's alternative minimum taxable income would be $322,000.

3. (1 hour) Renowned sketch artist Avare Artiste (A) resides in New York City, where his studio is located. In November of this year, he spent a week in University City (for which he received a handsome stipend), where he gave a series of lectures and demonstrations of his technique in State University's Department of Art.

On the last night of his visit, he and his wife dined at University City's most-prominent local eatery, the Bistro Café Restaurant, where they ran up a $200 bill. The restaurant is owned by Betty Bistro (B), who also serves as the principal chef. At the conclusion of the couple's meal, B approached their table, introduced herself, gushed that she had long admired A's work, and requested his autograph. In response, A sketched B's portrait on the back of a napkin and signed it: "For Betty Bistro, with thanks for your superb cuisine and warm hospitality. Avare Artiste 11/25/XX." B thanked A profusely and tore up the unpaid dinner check.

The next day B learned that similar sketches signed by A typically sell for $300.

(a) Describe fully the tax results of these events to A and B.

A is a self-employed person, who is (temporarily) traveling away from his "tax" home (New York City, where his principal place of business is located) while he is serving as a paid lecturer in University City. Because he is in business-travel status, his traveling expenses (including airfare, lodging and meal expenses) are (generally) allowable as expenses incurred in carrying on business under § 162(a). These are above-the-line deductions under § 62(a)(1) (expenses incurred in trade or business, but not in the trade or business of being an employee; (cf. § 62(a)(2)).

He is accompanied by his wife, but her travel, meals and lodging expenses are not deductible; § 274(m)(3). (There is no indication that her presence served a bona fide business purpose.) As to the lodging costs, however, A should be allowed to deduct the "single equivalent" rate for lodging (i.e., A should be allowed to deduct the amount that he would have had to pay even if he had not been accompanied by his wife, and if her staying in the room did not increase the cost over what A would have had to pay in her absence, then the full lodging cost should be deductible).

As to meal expenses, only 50% of A's share is deductible because of 274(n)(1).

The most challenging issue is the treatment of A's meal at the Bistro Café Restaurant, where A and his wife ran up a $200 bill. What are we to make of the "transaction" between A and B? On the one hand, A appears to have made a gift of the sketch to B and B a gift of the meal to A. Because there was no bargained-for exchange, can we say that the parties have made mutual gifts (tax-free under § 102(a))? Not necessarily, since the tax definition of a gift differs from the common-law definition. Whether A's transfer of the sketch to B is a gift depends, under *Duberstein*, upon the transferor's intention, as objectively inferred by the factfinder. In *Duberstein*, the Court said that a gift in the tax sense proceeds from disinterested generosity and is not motivated by the anticipation of economic benefit to the transferor. Duberstein was held to be taxable on the value of the automobile that he received, even though its receipt did not involve a bargained-for exchange.

When A drew the sketch, did he intend (expect?) that B would "comp" the meal? (For what it's worth, avare is the French adjective for "cheap." It is said that Picasso was notorious for paying for lunch by drawing a sketch for his restauranteur host.) Had A done this before? Did he have reason to believe that the result of his "generosity" would be B's tearing up the check? By making the gift-versus-compensation issue one of fact, *Duberstein* makes it difficult to predict the outcome here. If the factfinder determines that A's transfer of the sketch proceeded from the anticipation of economic benefit (a free meal), the value of the sketch would be includable in B's gross income. (The *Duberstein* case shows that the finding of the trial court will generally be difficult to overturn on appeal.)

Section 102(c), which makes the gift exclusion inapplicable to transfers to employees, does not apply here because B is not A's employee.

If the transfer is not a gift, B has received substantially vested "property" (the sketch) in connection with the performance of services (preparing and serving the meal), and she will be taxable on the excess of the value of the sketch ($300) over the amount that she paid for it (zero, since the cost of preparing the meal is included in her cost of goods sold and business expenses); § 83(a). She obtains a tax-cost basis of $300 in the sketch under § 1012. This analysis also affects A's side of the transaction because the transferor's business expense is the amount includable in the transferee's income ($300); § 83(h). And this is true even though the amount includable in the transferee's income exceeds the stipulated value of the services ($200, plus tip in this case). Of course, § 274(n)(1) would still limit A's deduction to 50 percent of his share of the meal's cost.

If the transfer of the sketch to B was not a gift, A must recognize gain on the transfer in an amount equal to the excess of the value of the property ($300) over its adjusted basis (zero, because A does not get basis credit for the value of his services that went into making the sketch). The sketch was not a capital asset in A's hands because his personal efforts created the property; § 1221(a)(3). So, the $300 gain would be ordinary.

Assuming that the meal was paid for (by the transfer of the sketch) a secondary issue is whether the cost of the meal at the Bistro Café Restaurant was "lavish and extravagant," for § 162(a) does not allow deductions for such costs. However, the menu price of the meal does not seem unreasonable—$200 for two persons hardly seems lavish by today's standards—but under the above analysis A is treated as having paid $300. Still, even that amount may not be lavish and extravagant.

So, it appears that either (1) B receives an excludable gift of the sketch and A receives a free meal and deducts nothing, or (2) B receives $300 of compensation and A recognizes $300 of ordinary income and deducts half of his share of the cost of the meal.

(b) What further tax consequences to B if B had the sketch covered with glass, framed, and hung in a prominent place in the restaurant for her customers to admire?

If B's receipt of the sketch is compensation, the transaction is treated as if A paid B $300 and B purchased the sketch for that amount. Is the cost of the sketch allowable to B as a business expense under § 162? Although B devotes the sketch to business use (hanging it in the restaurant), its cost would not be deductible as a business expense because the outlay is a capital expenditure (its economically useful life extends substantially beyond the end of the taxable year). Nor is it depreciable; the encased print is not subject to wear and tear and has no limited and ascertainable useful life. So, there are no tax consequences to devoting the painting to the business, even if the sketch was received as compensation. (If B received the sketch as a gift, she would assume A's zero basis under § 1015(a) and would have nothing to deduct anyway.)

(c) What are the tax consequences to B if she donated the sketch (then worth $400) to the State University Museum of Art?

Whether B can get a charitable deduction under § 170 depends upon whether A's transfer of the sketch to B was a gift or taxable compensation. If the transfer was a gift, then B assumes A's zero basis for the sketch (under § 1015(a)), and the sketch is not a capital asset in B's hands because her basis would be determined by reference to the basis of the sketch in the hands of A, who created it; § 1221(a)(3)(C). Although a taxpayer usually can deduct the value of property donated to an organization such as the art museum (which is a qualified recipient under § 170(c)(1) & (2)), § 170(e)(1)(A) reduces the deduction by the amount of gain that would not have been long-term capital gain if the property had been sold for its fair market value. A sale of the sketch at its $400 fair market value would have resulted in $400 of ordinary income because the sketch is not a capital asset, as discussed above. So, no charitable deduction would be allowed.

If the sketch was received as compensation, however, B would obtain a cost basis for the sketch, and it would be a capital asset in B's hands (it wouldn't fall within any of the exclusions of § 1221(a)). A charitable deduction would therefore be allowed for $400 if B's holding period for the sketch was more than one year. If B's holding period were not more than one year, B's deduction would be limited to $300 (because a sale of the sketch for its $400 value would have produced a short-term capital gain of $100, and the charitable deduction must be reduced by that amount); see § 170(e)(1)(A).

Appendix A

PRESENT AND FUTURE VALUE TABLES

Table I

Future Value of $1.00

$f = p \ (1 + r)^n$, where r = interest rate; n = number of compounding periods; p = $1.00.

Periods = n	1%	2%	3%	4%	5%	6%	7%	8%	9%	10%	12%	15%
1	1.01000	1.02000	1.03000	1.04000	1.05000	1.06000	1.07000	1.08000	1.09000	1.10000	1.12000	1.15000
2	1.02010	1.04040	1.06090	1.08160	1.10250	1.12360	1.14490	1.16640	1.18810	1.21000	1.25440	1.32250
3	1.03030	1.06121	1.09273	1.12486	1.15763	1.19102	1.22504	1.25971	1.29503	1.33100	1.40493	1.52087
4	1.04060	1.08243	1.12551	1.16986	1.21551	1.26248	1.31080	1.36049	1.41158	1.46410	1.57352	1.74901
5	1.05101	1.10408	1.15927	1.21665	1.27628	1.33823	1.40255	1.46933	1.53862	1.61051	1.76234	2.01136
6	1.06152	1.12616	1.19405	1.26532	1.34010	1.41852	1.50073	1.58687	1.67710	1.77156	1.97382	2.31306
7	1.07214	1.14869	1.22987	1.31593	1.40710	1.50363	1.60578	1.71382	1.82804	1.94872	2.21068	2.66002
8	1.08286	1.17166	1.26677	1.36857	1.47746	1.59385	1.71819	1.85093	1.99256	2.14359	2.47596	3.05902
9	1.09369	1.19509	1.30477	1.42331	1.55133	1.68948	1.83846	1.99900	2.17189	2.35795	2.77308	3.51788
10	1.10462	1.21899	1.34392	1.48024	1.62889	1.79085	1.96715	2.15892	2.36736	2.59374	3.10585	4.04556
11	1.11567	1.24337	1.38423	1.53945	1.71034	1.89830	2.10485	2.33164	2.58043	2.85312	3.47855	4.65239
12	1.12683	1.26824	1.42576	1.60103	1.79586	2.01220	2.25219	2.51817	2.81266	3.13843	3.89598	5.35025
13	1.13809	1.29361	1.46853	1.66507	1.88565	2.13293	2.40985	2.71962	3.06580	3.45227	4.36349	6.15279
14	1.14947	1.31948	1.51259	1.73168	1.97993	2.26090	2.57853	2.93719	3.34173	3.79750	4.88711	7.07571
15	1.16097	1.34587	1.55797	1.80094	2.07893	2.39656	2.75903	3.17217	3.64248	4.17725	5.47357	8.13706
16	1.17258	1.37279	1.60471	1.87298	2.18287	2.54035	2.95216	3.42594	3.97031	4.59497	6.13039	9.35762
17	1.18430	1.40024	1.65285	1.94790	2.29202	2.69277	3.15882	3.70002	4.32763	5.05447	6.86604	10.76126
18	1.19615	1.42825	1.70243	2.02582	2.40662	2.85434	3.37993	3.99602	4.71712	5.55992	7.68997	12.37545
19	1.20811	1.45681	1.75351	2.10685	2.52695	3.02560	3.61653	4.31570	5.14166	6.11591	8.61276	14.23177
20	1.22019	1.48595	1.80611	2.19112	2.65330	3.20714	3.86968	4.66096	5.60441	6.72750	9.64629	16.36654
22	1.24472	1.54598	1.91610	2.36992	2.92526	3.60354	4.43040	5.43654	6.65860	8.14027	12.10031	21.64475
24	1.26973	1.60844	2.03279	2.56330	3.22510	4.04893	5.07237	6.34118	7.91108	9.84973	15.17863	28.62518
26	1.29526	1.67342	2.15659	2.77247	3.55567	4.54938	5.80735	7.39635	9.39916	11.91818	19.04007	37.85680
28	1.32129	1.74102	2.28793	2.99870	3.92013	5.11169	6.64884	8.62711	11.16714	14.42099	23.88387	50.06561
30	1.34785	1.81136	2.42726	3.24340	4.32194	5.74349	7.61226	10.06266	13.26768	17.44940	29.95992	66.21177
32	1.37494	1.88454	2.57508	3.50806	4.76494	6.45339	8.71527	11.73708	15.76333	21.11378	37.58173	87.56507
34	1.40258	1.96068	2.73191	3.79432	5.25335	7.25103	9.97811	13.69013	18.72841	25.54767	47.14252	115.8048
36	1.43077	2.03989	2.89828	4.10393	5.79182	8.14725	11.42394	15.96817	22.25123	30.91268	59.13557	153.1519
38	1.45953	2.12230	3.07478	4.43881	6.38548	9.15425	13.07927	18.62528	26.43668	37.40434	74.17966	202.5433
40	1.48886	2.20804	3.26204	4.80102	7.03999	10.28572	14.97446	21.72452	31.40942	45.25926	93.05097	267.8635
50	1.64463	2.69159	4.38391	7.10668	11.46740	18.42015	29.45703	46.90102	74.35752	117.3909	289.0022	1,083.66
100	2.70481	7.24465	19.21863	50.50495	131.5013	339.3021	867.7163	2,199.76	5,529.04	13,780.6	83,522.3	117×10^4

603

Table II

Present Value of $1.00

$p = f/(1 + r)^n$, where r = discount (interest) rate; n = number of periods until payment; f = $1.00.

Periods = n	1%	2%	3%	4%	5%	6%	7%	8%	9%	10%	12%	15%
1	.99010	.98039	.97087	.96154	.95238	.94340	.93458	.92593	.91743	.90909	.89286	.86957
2	.98030	.96117	.94260	.92456	.90703	.89000	.87344	.85734	.84168	.82645	.79719	.75614
3	.97059	.94232	.91514	.88900	.86384	.83962	.81630	.79383	.77218	.75131	.71178	.65752
4	.96098	.92385	.88849	.85480	.82270	.79209	.76290	.73503	.70843	.68301	.63552	.57175
5	.95147	.90573	.86261	.82193	.78353	.74726	.71299	.68058	.64993	.62092	.56743	.49718
6	.94205	.88797	.83748	.79031	.74622	.70496	.66634	.63017	.59627	.56447	.50663	.43233
7	.93272	.87056	.81309	.75992	.71068	.66506	.62275	.58349	.54703	.51316	.45235	.37594
8	.92348	.85349	.78941	.73069	.67684	.62741	.58201	.54027	.50187	.46651	.40388	.32690
9	.91434	.83676	.76642	.70259	.64461	.59190	.54393	.50025	.46043	.42410	.36061	.28426
10	.90529	.82035	.74409	.67556	.61391	.55839	.50835	.46319	.42241	.38554	.32197	.24718
11	.89632	.80426	.72242	.64958	.58468	.52679	.47509	.42888	.38753	.35049	.28748	.21494
12	.88745	.78849	.70138	.62460	.55684	.49697	.44401	.39711	.35553	.31863	.25668	.18691
13	.87866	.77303	.68095	.60057	.53032	.46884	.41496	.36770	.32618	.28966	.22917	.16253
14	.86996	.75788	.66112	.57748	.50507	.44230	.38782	.34046	.29925	.26333	.20462	.14133
15	.86135	.74301	.64186	.55526	.48102	.41727	.36245	.31524	.27454	.23939	.18270	.12289
16	.85282	.72845	.62317	.53391	.45811	.39365	.33873	.29189	.25187	.21763	.16312	.10686
17	.84438	.71416	.60502	.51337	.43630	.37136	.31657	.27027	.23107	.19784	.14564	.09293
18	.83602	.70016	.58739	.49363	.41552	.35034	.29586	.25025	.21199	.17986	.13004	.08081
19	.82774	.68643	.57029	.47464	.39573	.33051	.27651	.23171	.19449	.16351	.11611	.07027
20	.81954	.67297	.55368	.45639	.37689	.31180	.25842	.21455	.17843	.14864	.10367	.06110
22	.80340	.64684	.52189	.42196	.34185	.27751	.22571	.18394	.15018	.12285	.08264	.04620
24	.78757	.62172	.49193	.39012	.31007	.24698	.19715	.15770	.12640	.10153	.06588	.03493
26	.77205	.59758	.46369	.36069	.28124	.21981	.17220	.13520	.10639	.08391	.05252	.02642
28	.75684	.57437	.43708	.33348	.25509	.19563	.15040	.11591	.08955	.06934	.04187	.01997
30	.74192	.55207	.41199	.30832	.23138	.17411	.13137	.09938	.07537	.05731	.03338	.01510
32	.72730	.53063	.38834	.28506	.20987	.15496	.11474	.08520	.06344	.04736	.02661	.01142
34	.71297	.51003	.36604	.26355	.19035	.13791	.10022	.07305	.05339	.03914	.02121	.00864
36	.69892	.49022	.34503	.24367	.17266	.12274	.08754	.06262	.04494	.03235	.01691	.00653
38	.68515	.47119	.32523	.22529	.15661	.10924	.07646	.05369	.03783	.02673	.01348	.00494
40	.67165	.45289	.30656	.20829	.14205	.09722	.06678	.04603	.03184	.02209	.01075	.00373
50	.60804	.37153	.22811	.14071	.08720	.05429	.03395	.02132	.01345	.00852	.00346	.00092
100	.36971	.13803	.05203	.01980	.00760	.00295	.00115	.00045	.00018	.00007	.00001	.00000

Table III

Future Value of Annuity of $1.00 in Arrears

$$F = [\,(1 + r)^n - 1\,]/r, \text{ where } r = \text{interest rate}; \quad n = \text{number of payments.}$$

No. of Payments = n	1%	2%	3%	4%	5%	6%	7%	8%	9%	10%	12%	15%
1	1.00000	1.00000	1.00000	1.00000	1.00000	1.00000	1.00000	1.00000	1.00000	1.00000	1.00000	1.00000
2	2.01000	2.02000	2.03000	2.04000	2.05000	2.06000	2.07000	2.08000	2.09000	2.10000	2.12000	2.15000
3	3.03010	3.06040	3.09090	3.12160	3.15250	3.18360	3.21490	3.24640	3.27810	3.31000	3.37440	3.47250
4	4.06040	4.12161	4.18363	4.24646	4.31013	4.37462	4.43994	4.50611	4.57313	4.64100	4.77933	4.99338
5	5.10101	5.20404	5.30914	5.41632	5.52563	5.63709	5.75074	5.86660	5.98471	6.10510	6.35285	6.74238
6	6.15202	6.30812	6.46841	6.63298	6.80191	6.97532	7.15329	7.33593	7.52333	7.71561	8.11519	8.75374
7	7.21354	7.43428	7.66246	7.89829	8.14201	8.39384	8.65402	8.92280	9.20043	9.48717	10.08901	11.06680
8	8.28567	8.58297	8.89234	9.21423	9.54911	9.89747	10.25980	10.63663	11.02847	11.43589	12.29969	13.72682
9	9.36853	9.75463	10.15911	10.58280	11.02656	11.49132	11.97799	12.48756	13.02104	13.57948	14.77566	16.78584
10	10.46221	10.94972	11.46388	12.00611	12.57789	13.18079	13.81645	14.48656	15.19293	15.93742	17.54874	20.30372
11	11.56683	12.16872	12.80780	13.48635	14.20679	14.97164	15.78360	16.64549	17.56029	18.53117	20.65458	24.34928
12	12.68250	13.41209	14.19203	15.02581	15.91713	16.86994	17.88845	18.97713	20.14072	21.38428	24.13313	29.00167
13	13.80933	14.68033	15.61779	16.62684	17.71298	18.88214	20.14064	21.49530	22.95338	24.52271	28.02911	34.35192
14	14.94742	15.97394	17.08632	18.29191	19.59863	21.01507	22.55049	24.21492	26.01919	27.97498	32.39260	40.50471
15	16.09690	17.29342	18.59891	20.02359	21.57856	23.27597	25.12902	27.15211	29.36092	31.77248	37.27971	47.58041
16	17.25786	18.63929	20.15688	21.82453	23.65749	25.67253	27.88805	30.32428	33.00340	35.94973	42.75328	55.71747
17	18.43044	20.01207	21.76159	23.69751	25.84037	28.21288	30.84022	33.75023	36.97370	40.54470	48.88367	65.07509
18	19.61475	21.41231	23.41444	25.64541	28.13238	30.90565	33.99903	37.45024	41.30134	45.59917	55.74971	75.83636
19	20.81090	22.84056	25.11687	27.67123	30.53900	33.75999	37.37896	41.44626	46.01846	51.15909	63.43968	88.21181
20.	22.01900	24.29737	26.87037	29.77808	33.06595	36.78559	40.99549	45.76196	51.16012	57.27500	72.05244	102.4436
22	24.47159	27.29898	30.53678	34.24797	38.50521	43.39229	49.00574	55.45676	62.87334	71.40275	92.50258	137.6316
24	26.97346	30.42186	34.42647	39.08260	44.50200	50.81558	58.17667	66.76476	76.78981	88.49733	118.1552	184.1678
26	29.52563	33.67091	38.55304	44.31174	51.11345	59.15638	68.67647	79.95442	93.32398	109.1818	150.3339	245.7120
28	32.12910	37.05121	42.93092	49.96758	58.40258	68.52811	80.69769	95.33883	112.9682	134.2099	190.6989	327.1041
30	34.78489	40.56808	47.57542	56.08494	66.43885	79.05819	94.46079	113.2832	136.3075	164.4940	241.3327	434.7451
32	37.49407	44.22703	52.50276	62.70147	75.29883	90.88978	110.2182	134.2135	164.0370	201.1378	304.8477	577.1005
34	40.25770	48.03380	57.73018	69.85791	85.06696	104.1838	128.2588	158.6267	196.9823	245.4767	384.5210	765.3654
36	43.07688	51.99437	63.27594	77.59831	95.83632	119.1209	148.9135	187.1021	236.1247	299.1268	484.4631	1,014.35
38	45.95272	56.11494	69.15945	85.97034	107.7095	135.9042	172.5610	220.3159	282.6298	364.0434	609.8305	1,343.62
40	48.88637	60.40198	75.40126	95.02552	120.7998	154.7620	199.6351	259.0565	337.8824	442.5926	767.0914	1,779.09
50	64.46318	84.57940	112.7969	152.6671	209.3480	290.3359	406.5289	573.7702	815.0836	1,163.91	2,400.02	7,217.72
100	170.4814	312.2323	607.2877	1,237.62	2,610.03	5,638.37	12,381.7	27,484.5	61,422.7	137,796	696,011	783×10^4

Table IV

Present Value of Annuity of $1.00 in Arrears

$P = (1 - 1/[1 + r]^n)/r$, where r = discount (interest) rate; n = number of payments.

No. of Payments = n	1%	2%	3%	4%	5%	6%	7%	8%	9%	10%	12%	15%
1	.99010	.98039	.97087	.96154	.95238	.94340	.93458	.92593	.91743	.90909	.89286	.86957
2	1.97040	1.94156	1.91347	1.88609	1.85941	1.83339	1.80802	1.78326	1.75911	1.73554	1.69005	1.62571
3	2.94099	2.88388	2.82861	2.77509	2.72325	2.67301	2.62432	2.57710	2.53129	2.48685	2.40183	2.28323
4	3.90197	3.80773	3.71710	3.62990	3.54595	3.46511	3.38721	3.31213	3.23972	3.16987	3.03735	2.85498
5	4.85343	4.71346	4.57971	4.45182	4.32948	4.21236	4.10020	3.99271	3.88965	3.79079	3.60478	3.35216
6	5.79548	5.60143	5.41719	5.24214	5.07569	4.91732	4.76654	4.62288	4.48592	4.35526	4.11141	3.78448
7	6.72819	6.47199	6.23028	6.00205	5.78637	5.58238	5.38929	5.20637	5.03295	4.86842	4.56376	4.16042
8	7.65168	7.32548	7.01969	6.73274	6.46321	6.20979	5.97130	5.74664	5.53482	5.33493	4.96764	4.48732
9	8.56602	8.16224	7.78611	7.43533	7.10782	6.80169	6.51523	6.24689	5.99525	5.75902	5.32825	4.77158
10	9.47130	8.98259	8.53020	8.11090	7.72173	7.36009	7.02358	6.71008	6.41766	6.14457	5.65022	5.01877
11	10.36763	9.78685	9.25262	8.76048	8.30641	7.88687	7.49867	7.13896	6.80519	6.49506	5.93770	5.23371
12	11.25508	10.57534	9.95400	9.38507	8.86325	8.38384	7.94269	7.53608	7.16073	6.81369	6.19437	5.42062
13	12.13374	11.34837	10.63496	9.98565	9.39357	8.85268	8.35765	7.90378	7.48690	7.10336	6.42355	5.58315
14	13.00370	12.10625	11.29607	10.56312	9.89864	9.29498	8.74547	8.24424	7.78615	7.36669	6.62817	5.72448
15	13.86505	12.84926	11.93794	11.11839	10.37966	9.71225	9.10791	8.55948	8.06069	7.60608	6.81086	5.84737
16	14.71787	13.57771	12.56110	11.65230	10.83777	10.10590	9.44665	8.85137	8.31256	7.82371	6.97399	5.95423
17	15.56225	14.29187	13.16612	12.16567	11.27407	10.47726	9.76322	9.12164	8.54363	8.02155	7.11963	6.04716
18	16.39827	14.99203	13.75351	12.65930	11.68959	10.82760	10.05909	9.37189	8.75563	8.20141	7.24967	6.12797
19	17.22601	15.67846	14.32380	13.13394	12.08532	11.15812	10.33560	9.60360	8.95011	8.36492	7.36578	6.19823
20	18.04555	16.35143	14.87747	13.59033	12.46221	11.46992	10.59401	9.81815	9.12855	8.51356	7.46944	6.25933
22	19.66038	17.65805	15.93692	14.45112	13.16300	12.04158	11.06124	10.20074	9.44243	8.77154	7.64465	6.35866
24	21.24339	18.91393	16.93554	15.24696	13.79864	12.55036	11.46933	10.52876	9.70661	8.98474	7.78432	6.43377
26	22.79520	20.12104	17.87684	15.98277	14.37519	13.00317	11.82578	10.80998	9.92897	9.16095	7.89566	6.49056
28	24.31644	21.28127	18.76411	16.66306	14.89813	13.40616	12.13711	11.05108	10.11613	9.30657	7.98442	6.53351
30	25.80771	22.39646	19.60044	17.29203	15.37245	13.76483	12.40904	11.25778	10.27365	9.42691	8.05518	6.56598
32	27.26959	23.46833	20.38877	17.87355	15.80268	14.08404	12.64656	11.43500	10.40624	9.52638	8.11159	6.59053
34	28.70267	24.49859	21.13184	18.41120	16.19290	14.36814	12.85401	11.58693	10.51784	9.60857	8.15656	6.60910
36	30.10751	25.48884	21.83225	18.90828	16.54685	14.62099	13.03521	11.71719	10.61176	9.67651	8.19241	6.62314
38	31.48466	26.44064	22.49246	19.36786	16.86789	14.84602	13.19347	11.82887	10.69082	9.73265	8.22099	6.63375
40	32.83469	27.35548	23.11477	19.79277	17.15909	15.04630	13.33171	11.92461	10.75736	9.77905	8.24378	6.64178
50	39.19612	31.42361	25.72976	21.48218	18.25593	15.76186	13.80075	12.23348	10.96168	9.91481	8.30450	6.66051
100	63.02888	43.09835	31.59891	24.50500	19.84791	16.61755	14.26925	12.49432	11.10910	9.99927	8.33323	6.66666

Appendix B

STATUTORY TAX RATES
FOR 2005-2010

Section 1(i), adopted in 2001 and most recently amended in 2004, creates a ten-percent bracket for individual taxpayers and reduces the 28–percent, 31–percent, 36–percent, and 39.6–percent rates for individuals, trusts, and estates. Section 1(f)(8), also adopted in 2001 and most recently amended in 2004, changes the maximum amount of taxable income in the 15–percent bracket for married taxpayers filing jointly. Section 1(a) through 1(e) as it would read for 2005 through 2010 after application of the adjustments of § 1(i) and § 1(f) appear below. (These measures are scheduled to expire after 2010.) Note that the dollar amounts of § 1(a) through 1(e) are adjusted for inflation; these adjustments are not incorporated in this presentation.

§ 1. Tax imposed

(a) **Married individuals filing joint returns and surviving spouses.**—There is hereby imposed on the taxable income of—

(1) every married individual (as defined in section 7703) who makes a single return jointly with his spouse under section 6013, and

(2) every surviving spouse (as defined in section 2(a)), a tax determined in accordance with the following table:

If taxable income is	The tax is:
Not over $14,000	10% of taxable income.
Over $14,000 but not over $44,200	$1,400, plus 15% of the excess over $14,000.
Over $44,200 but not over $89,150	$5,930, plus 25% of the excess over $44,200.
Over $89,150 but not over $140,000	$17,167.50, plus 28% of the excess over $89,150.
Over $140,000 but not over $250,000	$31,405.50, plus 33% of the excess over $140,000.
Over $250,000	$67,705.50, plus 35% of the excess over $250,000.

(b) **Heads of households.**—There is hereby imposed on the taxable income of every head of a household (as defined in section 2(b)) a tax determined in accordance with the following table:

If taxable income is:	The tax is:
Not over $10,000	10% of taxable income.
Over $10,000 but not over $29,600	$1,000, plus 15% of the excess over $10,000.
Over $29,600 but not over $76,400	$3,940, plus 25% of the excess over $29,600.
Over $76,400 but not over $127,500	$15,640, plus 28% of the excess over $76,400.
Over $127,500 but not over $250,000	$29,948, plus 33% of the excess over $127,500.
Over $250,000........................	$70,373, plus 35% of the excess over $250,000.

(c) Unmarried individuals (other than surviving spouses and heads of households).—There is hereby imposed on the taxable income of every individual (other than a surviving spouse as defined in section 2(a) or the head of a household as defined in section 2(b)) who is not a married individual (as defined in section 7703) a tax determined in accordance with the following table:

If taxable income is:	The tax is:
Not over $7,000	10% of taxable income.
Over $7,000 but not over $22,100	$700, plus 15% of the excess over $7,000.
Over $22,100 but not over $53,500	$2,965, plus 25% of the excess over $22,100.
Over $53,500 but not over $115,000	$10,815, plus 28% of the excess over $53,500.
Over $115,000 but not over $250,000	$28,035, plus 33% of the excess over $115,000.
Over $250,000........................	$72,585, plus 35% of the excess over $250,000.

(d) Married individuals filing separate returns.—There is hereby imposed on the taxable income of every married individual (as defined in section 7703) who does not make a single return joint with his spouse under section 6013, a tax determined in accordance with the following table:

If taxable income is:	The tax is:
Not over $7,000	10% of taxable income.
Over $7,000 but not over $22,100	$700, plus 15% of the excess over $7,000.
Over $22,100 but not over $44,575	$2,965, plus 25% of the excess over $22,100.
Over $44,575 but not over $70,000	$8,583.75, plus 28% of the excess over $44,575.
Over $70,000 but not over $125,000	$15,702.75, plus 33% of the excess over $70,000.
Over $125,000........................	$33,852.75, plus 35% of the excess over $125,000.

Index

References are to pages
